Mike Meyers' Certification

Passport ★

CompTIA

A+®

Sixth Edition

Certification

Exams 220-901 & 220-902

MIKE MEYERS' CERTIFICATION
Passport ★

CompTIA
A+®

Sixth Edition

Certification
Exams 220-901 & 220-902

MIKE MEYERS
TRAVIS A. EVERETT
SCOTT JERNIGAN

New York   Chicago   San Francisco
Athens   London   Madrid   Mexico City
Milan   New Delhi   Singapore   Sydney   Toronto

Library of Congress Cataloging-in-Publication Data

Names: Meyers, Mike, 1961- author. | Everett, Travis A., author. | Jernigan, Scott, author.
Title: Mike Meyers' CompTIA A+ certification passport, (exams 220-901 & 220-902) / Mike Meyers, Travis A. Everett, Scott Jernigan.
Other titles: CompTIA A+ certification passport, (exams 220-901 & 220-902) | Exams 220-901 & 220-902
Description: Sixth edition. | New York : McGraw-Hill Education, 2017. | Series: Mike Meyers' certification passport | Earlier edition covers Exams 220-801 & 220-802.
Identifiers: LCCN 2016027906 (print) | LCCN 2016029606 (ebook) | ISBN 9781259589607 (set : alk. paper) | ISBN 1259589609 (set : alk. paper) | ISBN 9781259588938 (book : alk. paper) | ISBN 1259588939 (book : alk. paper) | ISBN 9781259588945 (CD) | ISBN 1259588947 (CD) | ISBN 9781259588921 ()
Subjects: LCSH: Microcomputers—Maintenance and repair—Examinations—Study guides. | Computing Technology Industry Association—Examinations—Study guides. | Computer technicians—Certification.
Classification: LCC TK7887 .M4577 2017 (print) | LCC TK7887 (ebook) | DDC 004.165—dc23
LC record available at https://lccn.loc.gov/2016027906

McGraw-Hill Education books are available at special quantity discounts to use as premiums and sales promotions, or for use in corporate training programs. To contact a representative, please visit the Contact Us pages at www.mhprofessional.com.

Mike Meyers' CompTIA A+® Certification Passport, Sixth Edition (Exams 220-901 & 220-902)

1 2 3 4 5 6 7 8 9 DOC 21 20 19 18 17 16

ISBN: Book p/n 978-1-25-958893-8 and CD p/n 978-1-25-958894-5
of set 978-1-25-958960-7

MHID: Book p/n 1-25-958893-9 and CD p/n 1-25-958894-7
of set 1-25-958960-9

Sponsoring Editor Amy Stonebraker	**Technical Editor** Christopher Crayton	**Production Supervisor** James Kussow
Editorial Supervisor Janet Walden	**Copy Editor** Bart Reed	**Composition** Cenveo Publisher Services
Project Manager Vastavikta Sharma, Cenveo® Publisher Services	**Proofreader** Richard Camp **Indexer** Karin Arrigoni	**Illustration** Cenveo Publisher Services **Art Director, Cover** Jeff Weeks
Acquisitions Coordinator Claire Yee		

We dedicate this book to our students, past, present, and future.
You're why we do what we do!

About the Authors

Mike Meyers, lovingly called the "AlphaGeek" by those who know him, is the industry's leading authority on CompTIA A+ certification. He is the president and co-founder of Total Seminars, LLC, a provider of computer and network repair seminars, books, videos, and courseware for thousands of organizations throughout the world. Mike has been involved in the computer and network repair industry since 1977 as a technician, instructor, author, consultant, and speaker.

Author of numerous popular PC books and videos, including the bestselling *CompTIA A+ Certification All-in-One Exam Guide,* Mike is also the series editor for the highly successful *Mike Meyers' Certification Passport* series, the *Mike Meyers' Computer Skills* series, and the *Mike Meyers' Guide To* series, all published by McGraw-Hill.

As well as writing, Mike has personally taught (and continues to teach) thousands of students, including U.S. senators, U.S. Supreme Court justices, members of the United Nations, every branch of the U.S. Armed Forces, most branches of the U.S. Department of Justice, and hundreds of corporate clients, academic students at every level, prisoners, and pensioners.

E-mail: michaelm@totalsem.com
Facebook: Mike Meyers (Houston, TX)
Twitter/Skype/Most IMs: desweds
Web Forums: www.totalsem.com/forums

Travis A. Everett is a software developer, writer, editor and designer. He has held editorial, technical, design, and advisory roles at three literary publications, including editor-in-chief of *Harbinger* (Texas Tech University), founding technical editor of *Barely South Review* (Old Dominion University), and founder/editor-in-chief of *escarp*. Before co-authoring this book, Travis contributed writing, technical editing, and copy editing to the *CompTIA A+ All-in-One Certification Exam Guide* and the *CompTIA Network+ All-in-One Certification Exam Guide* (both by Mike Meyers). He also holds a Master of Fine Arts in creative writing from ODU, where he was a Perry Morgan Fellow.

About the Editor-in-Chief

Scott Jernigan wields a mighty red pen as editor-in-chief for Total Seminars. With a Master of Arts degree in medieval history, Scott feels as much at home in the musty archives of London as he does in the warm computer glow of Total Seminars' Houston headquarters. After fleeing a purely academic life, he dove headfirst into IT, working as an instructor, editor, and writer. Scott has written, edited, and contributed to dozens of books on computer literacy, hardware, operating systems, networking, and certification. His latest book (aside from the one in your hands) is *Computer Literacy: Your Ticket to IC³ Certification*. Scott co-authored the best-selling *CompTIA A+ Certification All-in-One Exam Guide,* the *Mike Meyers' A+ Guide to Managing and Troubleshooting PCs,* and the *CompTIA Strata IT Fundamentals All-in-One Exam Guide* (all with Mike Meyers). He has taught computer classes all over the United States, including stints at the United Nations in New York and the FBI Academy in Quantico, Virginia.

About the Technical Editor

Chris Crayton, MCSE, is an author, technical consultant, and trainer. He has worked as a computer technology and networking instructor, information security director, network administrator, network engineer, and PC specialist. Chris has authored several print and online books on PC repair, CompTIA A+, CompTIA Security+, and Microsoft Windows. He has also served as technical editor and content contributor on numerous technical titles for several of the leading publishing companies. He holds numerous industry certifications, has been recognized with many professional teaching awards, and has served as a state-level SkillsUSA competition judge.

About Total Seminars

Total Seminars provides certification training services to thousands of schools, corporations, and government agencies. Total Seminars produces the #1 selling CompTIA A+ and best-selling CompTIA Network+ certification books, and develops training materials such as the Total Tester for superior exam preparation. You can find Total Seminars on the Web at www.totalsem.com.

Contents at a Glance

Contents

Acknowledgments

As with every book, a lot of work from a lot of people went into making this happen.

Our acquisitions editor, Amy Stonebraker, kept us on track with kind words and pointy sticks. Always a pleasure working with you!

Our acquisitions coordinator, Claire Yee, did an outstanding job acquiring and coordinating . . . with gentle yet insistent reminders for us to get stuff to her on a timely basis. Fun project and we look forward to the next one!

Michael Smyer provided great photographs for the book, and Ford Pierson added his incredible illustrations. Thanks guys!

Bart Reed did great work as our copy editor. He transformed every awkward stumble of language into a grammatical gem.

Our technical editor, Chris Crayton, took what some would describe as gleeful delight in pointing out every technical error he found. But since he helped us fix every error, too, we won't hold it against him. Thanks, once again, for your technical expertise.

The layout team at Cenveo Publisher Services did a remarkable job, putting the prose and pictures into printable form, that you get to enjoy now!

Finally, thanks to our proofreader, Richard Camp, for catching every last error. There's no error too big or small—he'll find them all. Thank you.

Great work, team!

CompTIA.

Becoming a CompTIA Certified IT Professional Is Easy

It's also the best way to reach greater professional opportunities and rewards.

Why Get CompTIA Certified?

Growing Demand

Labor estimates predict some technology fields will experience growth of more than 20 percent by the year 2020. (Source: CompTIA 9th Annual Information Security Trends study: 500 U.S. IT and Business Executives Responsible for Security.) CompTIA certification qualifies the skills required to join this workforce.

Higher Salaries

IT professionals with certifications on their resume command better jobs, earn higher salaries, and have more doors open to new multi-industry opportunities.

Verified Strengths

Ninety-one percent of hiring managers indicate CompTIA certifications are valuable in validating IT expertise, making certification the best way to demonstrate your competency and knowledge to employers. (Source: CompTIA Employer Perceptions of IT Training and Certification.)

Universal Skills

CompTIA certifications are vendor neutral—which means that certified professionals can proficiently work with an extensive variety of hardware and software found in most organizations.

Learn

Learn more about what the exam covers by reviewing the following:

- Exam objectives for key study points.

- Sample questions for a general overview of what to expect on the exam and examples of question format.

- Visit online forums, like LinkedIn, to see what other IT professionals say about CompTIA exams.

Certify

Purchase a voucher at a Pearson VUE testing center or at CompTIAstore.com.

- Register for your exam at a Pearson VUE testing center.

- Visit pearsonvue.com/CompTIA to find the closest testing center to you.

- Schedule the exam online. You will be required to enter your voucher number or provide payment information at registration.

- Take your certification exam.

Work

Congratulations on your CompTIA certification!

- Make sure to add your certification to your resume.

- Check out the CompTIA Certification Roadmap to plan your next career move.

Learn More: Certification.CompTIA.org/aplus

CompTIA Disclaimer

CAQC Disclaimer

The logo of the CompTIA Approved Quality Curriculum (CAQC) program and the status of this or other training material as "Approved" under the CompTIA Approved Quality Curriculum program signifies that, in CompTIA's opinion, such training material covers the content of CompTIA's related certification exam.

The contents of this training material were created for the CompTIA A+ exams covering CompTIA certification objectives that were current as of the date of publication.

CompTIA has not reviewed or approved the accuracy of the contents of this training material and specifically disclaims any warranties of merchantability or fitness for a particular purpose. CompTIA makes no guarantee concerning the success of persons using any such "Approved" or other training material in order to prepare for any CompTIA certification exam.

Check-In

May I See Your Passport?

What do you mean you don't have a passport? Why, it's sitting right in your hands, even as you read! This book is your passport to a very special place. You're about to begin a journey, my friend—a journey toward certification! It's magical, isn't it? You don't need a ticket, you don't need a suitcase—just snuggle up and read this passport, because it's all you need to get there. Are you ready? Let's go!

Your Travel Agent: Mike Meyers

Hello! I'm Mike Meyers, president of Total Seminars and author of a number of popular certification books. On any given day, you'll find me replacing a hard drive, setting up a website, or writing code. I love every aspect of this book you hold in your hands. It's part of a powerful book series called the *Mike Meyers' Certification Passports*. Every book in this series combines easy readability with a condensed format—in other words, it's the kind of book I always wanted when I went for my certifications. Putting a huge amount of information in an accessible format is an enormous challenge, but I think we have achieved our goal and I am confident you'll agree.

I designed this series to do one thing and only one thing—to get you the information you need to achieve your certification. You won't find any fluff in here. We packed every page with nothing but the real nitty-gritty of the CompTIA A+ certification exams. Every page has 100 percent pure concentrate of certification knowledge! But we didn't forget to make the book readable, so I hope you enjoy the casual, friendly style.

My personal e-mail address is michaelm@totalsem.com. Please feel free to contact me directly if you have any questions, complaints, or compliments.

Your Destination: CompTIA A+ Certification

This book is your passport to CompTIA A+ certification, the vendor-neutral industry standard certification for PC hardware technicians, the folks who build and fix PCs. To get CompTIA A+ certified, you need to pass two exams, 220-901 and 220-902. Past CompTIA A+ exams used friendly names like "Essentials" and "Practical Application," but these terms don't apply anymore.

The 220-901 exam concentrates on four areas: Hardware, Networking, Mobile Devices, and Hardware and Network Troubleshooting. This exam focuses on your understanding of the terminology and hardware technology used in each of the four subject areas.

The 220-902 exam works the same way, covering Windows Operating Systems, Other Operating Systems & Technologies, Security, Software Troubleshooting, and Operational Procedures. The 902 exam is very Windows focused—installing, updating, maintaining, troubleshooting, and more. The other operating systems covered—Mac OS X, Linux, iOS, Android, and Windows Phone/Mobile—get more of a big picture view. Security and troubleshooting—Windows and applications—make up half the exam questions.

Both of the exams are extremely practical, with little or no interest in theory. When you take the exams, you will see four types of questions: multiple choice, fill in the blank, picture matching, and simulation.

The following is an example of a multiple-choice question you will see on the exams:

An impact printer is printing blank pages. Which item should you check first?

> A. Printer drivers
>
> B. Platen
>
> C. Print head
>
> D. Ribbon

The correct answer is D, the ribbon. You can make an argument for any of the others, but common sense (and skill as a PC technician) tells you to check the simplest possibility first. You might also see multiple-response questions, essentially multiple choice with more than one answer.

Fill-in-the-blank questions work a lot like the multiple-choice questions, but instead of being provided with possible answers, you will need to type the answer into an empty box. For example:

> An impact printer is printing blank pages. To troubleshoot this problem, first check the _____.

To answer the question, you would type "ribbon."

Picture-matching questions involve dragging and dropping a picture onto the relevant text. For example, you might see the words "Inkjet" and "Laser," and then two printer diagrams next to them. You would need to drag the inkjet printer diagram onto the word "Inkjet," then drag the other diagram onto the word "Laser."

Simulation questions ask you to re-create a real process used by techs when working on PCs. You might be asked to copy a file or change a setting in Control Panel, but instead of picking a multiple choice answer, your screen will look like a Windows desktop and you will follow the provided instructions, just like you were using the real thing.

Always read the questions very carefully, especially when dealing with fill-in-the-blank and simulation questions. Remember to look for the *best* answer, not just the right answer.

CompTIA A+ certification can be your ticket to a career in IT or simply an excellent step in your certification pathway. This book is your passport to success on the CompTIA A+ certification exams.

Your Guides: Mike Meyers and Travis Everett

You get a pair of tour guides for this book—both me and Travis Everett. I've written numerous computer certification books—including the best-selling *All-in-One CompTIA A+ Certification Exam Guide* and the *All-in-One Comp-TIA Network+ Certification Exam Guide*. More to the point, I've been working on PCs and teaching others how to make and fix them for a very long time, and I love it! When I'm not lecturing or writing about PCs, I'm working on PCs or spanking Travis in *Counter-Strike: Global Offensive*—on the PC, naturally!

It was all fun and games when Travis first got his hands on his stepdad's computer in 1991 (except that time he deleted the OS…), but he got hooked on computer-aided creativity when he started designing and developing websites in the late 1990s. In his spare time, Travis contributes code and documentation to open-source software projects; develops and administrates an old MUD (the text-based ancestors of modern MMOs); reads all he can; drops his expensive smartphone too often; buys more books than he has time to read; and edits *escarp*. Oh, and he smacks Mike mightily in *Counter-Strike: GO,* despite claims to the contrary.

Why the Travel Theme?

The steps to gaining a certification parallel closely the steps to planning and taking a trip. All the elements are the same: preparation, an itinerary, a route—even mishaps along the way. Let me show you how it all works.

This book is divided into 22 chapters. Each chapter begins with an itinerary that provides the objectives covered in each chapter as well as an ETA to give you an idea of the time involved learning the skills in that chapter. Each chapter is broken down by objectives, either those officially stated by the certifying body or our expert take on the best way to approach the topics. Windows troubleshooting appears in several CompTIA A+ competencies, for example, but the topic works best in book form when covered in a single chapter. Also, each chapter contains a number of helpful items to call out points of interest:

Exam Tip

Points out critical topics you're likely to see on the actual exam.

Travel Assistance

Shows you additional sources, such as books and websites, to give you more information.

Local Lingo

Describes special terms, in detail and in a way you can easily understand.

Travel Advisory

Warns you of common pitfalls, misconceptions, and downright physical peril!

The end of the chapter gives you two handy tools. The checkpoint reviews each objective covered in the chapter with a handy synopsis—a great way to review quickly. Plus, you'll find end-of-chapter questions to test your newly acquired skills.

CHECKPOINT

But the fun doesn't stop there! After you've read the book, pull out the CD and take advantage of the free practice questions! Use the full practice exam to hone your skills and keep the book handy to check answers.

When you're acing the practice questions, you're ready to take the exam.

Go get certified!

The End of the Trail

The IT industry changes and grows constantly, and so should you. Finishing one certification is just a step in an ongoing process of gaining more and more certifications to match your constantly changing and growing skills. Read the Career Flight Path at the end of the book to see where this certification fits into your personal certification goals. Remember, in the IT business, if you're not moving forward, you are way behind!

Good luck on your certification! Stay in touch.

Mike Meyers, Series Editor
Mike Meyers' Certification Passport

The Art of
the Tech

ETA	NEWBIE	SOME EXPERIENCE	EXPERT
	3 hours	1.5 hours	1 hour

When a mission-critical computer goes down, regardless of the industry, people get upset. Workers can't work, so they feel guilty. Employers can't get product out on time, so they feel anxious. Supervisors blame employees for fouling things up, or at least the employees fear such blame, even if they did not break the machine.

Into this charged atmosphere comes the tech, ready to fix the computer and move on to the next challenge. To accomplish this task, the tech requires three things. First, a good tech must know the broken machine inside and out, how it's *supposed* to work when it's working properly. Second, the tech has to calm the workers and supervisors and ask the right questions to gain relevant information about the problem. Finally, the tech must troubleshoot the problem and fix the machine.

This chapter starts with an overview of how computers work and then dives into dealing with customers, including how to get them to tell you what you need to know. The chapter wraps up with a proven troubleshooting methodology to help you find a problem's source and guide you to the quickest fix.

Objective 1.01   How Computers Work

Computers work through a three-stage process: *input*, *processing*, and *output* (see Figure 1.1). Input requires specific devices, such as the keyboard, mouse, or touch screen, that enable you to tell the computer to do something, such as open a program or display a word that you just typed. The *operating*

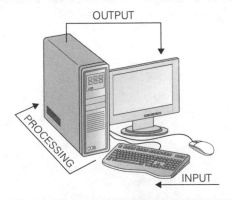

FIGURE 1.1   Input, processing, and output—the computing process

system (OS) provides the interface and the tools so that the microprocessor and other chips can process your request. The image on the monitor or sound from the speakers effectively tells you that the computer interpreted your command and has spit out the result.

Making this process work requires the complex interaction of many components, including multiple pieces of hardware and layers of software. As a tech, you need to understand the components and how they work together so that when something doesn't work properly, you can track down the source and fix it. A look at a modern program reveals that even a relatively simple-seeming action or change on the screen requires many things to happen within the computer.

Modern games such as *Team Fortress 2* can take up many gigabytes of space on a hard drive. They simply won't fit into the *random access memory (RAM)* in most computers, so developers have found ways to minimize RAM usage.

Team Fortress 2 is a multiplayer online first-person shooter (FPS) that offers a distinctly comedic, cartoonish twist on the genre, and also demonstrates how older game genres have been influenced by developments in mobile and massively multiplayer online (MMO) gaming. *Team Fortress 2* has a functioning economy, for example, that enables you to trade both useful and cosmetic items for virtual currency—although the more common scenario is spending real money to get these virtual possessions.

Players in *Team Fortress 2* compete on maps developed by both the official developers and community members. Each of these maps specifies a virtual environment the players can compete in, defining its shape, boundaries, appearance, sounds, where players will start, and more. It wouldn't make much sense to load up all these maps when you open the game, so when players connect to a new game server, or the server changes to a new map, the server notifies each connected game program to load the appropriate data into RAM (see Figure 1.2).

The game sends a signal to the OS that it needs a specific map loaded into RAM. The OS sends a signal to the *central processing unit (CPU)* that it needs data stored on the hard drive plus information stored on the *Team Fortress 2* servers. The CPU then sends the commands to the hard drive controller so it can grab the desired stored data and send it to RAM, while at the same time sending a command to the *network interface card (NIC)* to download the updated information (see Figure 1.3).

The hard drive controller tells the hard drive to cough up the data—megabytes' worth—and then sends that data through the motherboard to the memory controller, which puts it into RAM and communicates with the CPU when it's finished. The network card and network operating system

FIGURE 1.2 *Team Fortress 2* loading Dustbowl map

communicate with the *Team Fortress 2* servers and download the necessary updated information. As the game application on each player's system loads the map, it integrates this updated information from the server about how and where to display other players, which of the map's objectives are complete, and more. The CPU then uses the application and OS to process the new information, sending video data to the video card and sound data to the sound card, again through the motherboard (see Figure 1.4).

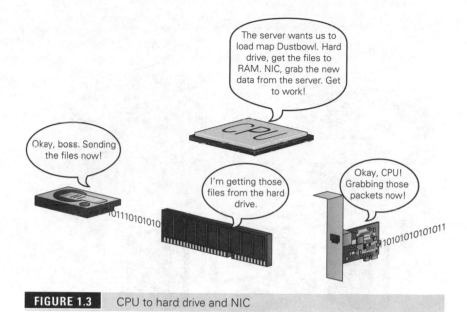

FIGURE 1.3 CPU to hard drive and NIC

The video card processor—called the *graphics processing unit (GPU)*—puts the incoming data into its RAM, processes the data, and then sends out commands to the monitor to update the screen. The sound card processor likewise processes the data and sends out commands to the speakers to play a new sound (see Figure 1.5).

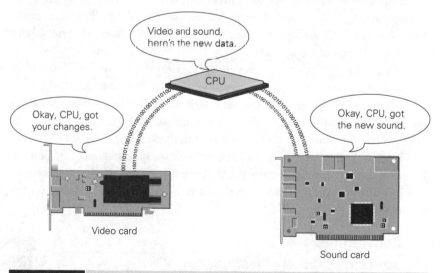

FIGURE 1.4 CPU to video card and sound card

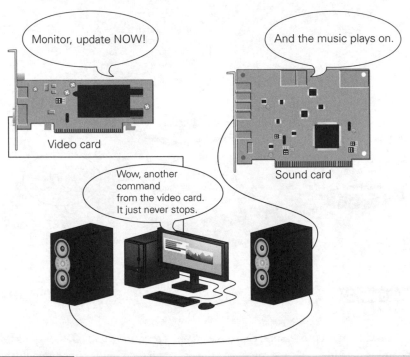

For all of this to work, the computer must have electricity. Both the alternating current (AC) going into the power supply from the wall socket and the direct current (DC) going from the power supply to the computer must have the proper voltage and amperage.

Once the game is ready, the player can spawn into the action. Here's what happens when the player presses the keyboard's w key to make the character take its first step forward: the keyboard controller reads the grid of the keyboard and, on discovering the input, sends the information to the CPU through the wires of the motherboard (see Figure 1.6). The CPU understands the keyboard controller because, when the computer was first booted, it loaded a small program into RAM from the system basic input/output services (BIOS) stored in the system read-only memory (ROM) chip on the motherboard.

Local Lingo

Most techs today refer to the *S* in BIOS as "system" (that is, basic input/output system). System or services, either term works fine.

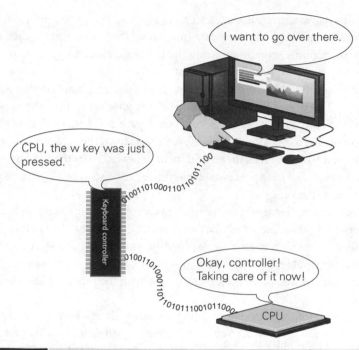

FIGURE 1.6   Keyboard to CPU

The CPU and the application determine what should happen in the game, and on discovering that the character is now moving, they trigger a series of actions. Because *Team Fortress 2* is a network application, the OS has to send information through the NIC and onto the Internet to update the server on what actions the player is taking (see Figure 1.7). That way, the other characters in the game world can receive updates from the server that enable them

FIGURE 1.7   Computer to *Team Fortress 2* servers

to see this player move forward a step. Meanwhile, the game application and hardware components are furiously integrating the current map, data about the player's actions, and updates from the server quickly enough to maintain a steady stream of audio and visual output.

What does the player see and hear with all these electrons zipping all over the place? The player sees his or her team charging off to find the opposing team as the match clock begins ticking (see Figure 1.8) and, soon enough, the audio-visual chaos of cartoonish combat streams from the screen and speakers (see Figure 1.9). Many megabytes of data have flowed from the hard drive and across the Internet, were processed by multiple processors, and were sent to the monitor and speakers.

Good techs understand the components involved in inputting, processing, and outputting data, including data storage devices such as hard drives. That's because, if something doesn't work properly, a good tech can start answering the ultimate troubleshooting question—What can it be?—accurately. If your screen freezes or the sound goes "wonky," where in the process could the problem be?

As you go into any troubleshooting scenario, always keep the computing process in mind. This helps you sort through possibilities quickly and accurately. If you know all the stages, you won't miss a simple step—such as figuring out that a user can't print because the cleaning service accidentally turned off the print server the night before—and you won't waste time reinstalling printer drivers when the real issue was a stalled print job in the print queue.

FIGURE 1.8   Blue team's first steps

FIGURE 1.9   Close encounter with a rocket

Travel Assistance

This book outlines the processes involved with each facet of computing in the appropriate chapter. Chapter 18, for example, details networking processes. Chapter 22 covers the essentials of printing processes.

Objective 1.02 # Dealing with Customers

When you work with users, managers, and owners who are frustrated and upset because a computer or network is down and they can't work, your job takes on the roles of detective and psychologist rolled into one. Such charged situations call for a tech to interact with customers respectfully, effectively, and professionally.

Respectful Personal Interaction

You will encounter all sorts of people as a tech. Emotions will run from anger, to fear, to frustration. You'll find bluster, smiles, patience, impatience, and much more. Treat the customer with respect. That means dealing graciously with cultural differences. Always use the appropriate title, personal or professional. Don't call that nice but upset woman "Sue" when you should call her "Dr. Rampy." If a title happens to be in a language you don't speak, figure out how to say it before arriving on the scene. That's what Google is for! Be culturally sensitive.

Maintain a positive attitude when dealing with a difficult customer or situation. Project confidence that you can solve the problem efficiently and get the user back to work. Don't argue with the customer or get defensive if he or she somehow projects a computer problem as somehow your fault. It happens!

Finally, take a customer's problem seriously, because it *is* serious to him or her, even if it's easily solvable by a great tech like you. Avoid dismissing the problem and don't judge. Fix it, smile, and wish the customer a happy day.

Effective Communication

Effective communication in "computerese" requires active listening to get to the heart of the problem, which in turn calls for the proper use of language. You know and speak tech. Chances are that your customer doesn't. Getting through this language barrier is essential for solving problems.

Actively listening means focusing your attention on the customer's words. They might not make sense at first, so take notes. The customer might say something like, "I was working away, but a clock started ticking inside the CPU, then my screen went blue and I can't get the computer to start at all." Oy! Don't interrupt the customer. Let him or her tell you the story. Because you wrote it down, you can break the non-technical language into something that potentially makes sense.

Clarify customer statements. Ask open-ended questions, such as "What other strange or unusual things about the computer have you noticed recently?" A "nothing, really," from the customer has a wildly different meaning than an "I burned my hand on the CPU a couple of days ago." Open-ended questions help narrow the scope of the problem.

Also, *restate the issue or question to verify your understanding*, but use proper, simple language. Avoid jargon and acronyms. Definitely skip the silly computer guy slang, like calling a Windows PC "the *comp*" or a motherboard a "mobo." That stuff just makes customers defensive. Once you think you understand both the scope and nature of the problem, go back to your notes and you might find a good explanation.

Many users call the case or system unit a CPU. A ticking sound inside a case often points to a dying hard drive. A blue screen is a classic sign of a non-maskable interrupt (NMI), better known as the Blue Screen of Death in Windows (see Figure 1.10). The user's hard drive might have just died. If the user

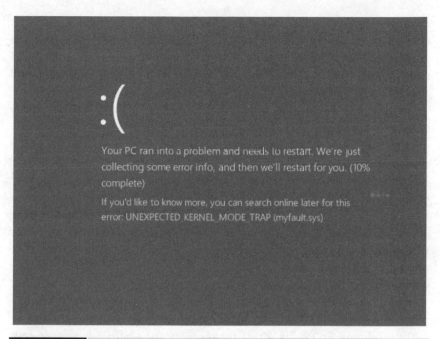

FIGURE 1.10   The Blue Screen of Death (BSoD) in Windows 10

has burned his hand on the case, that could point to an overheating issue that caused the problem—and potentially a lot more than just a dying drive.

Practice effective communication. The best techs know both technology and how to talk with users.

Professionalism

Professionalism as a tech has a lot of meanings, from maintaining personal hygiene to managing time efficiently. Wear crisp clothes. Bathe. Comb your hair. Avoid garlic and onion pizza right before taking an on-site call. All that should be obvious, so let's look at five other aspects of professionalism: promptness, avoiding distractions, confidentiality, expectations management, and finishing the job right.

Be on time, whether making a phone call or arriving at a job site. If you run late, you almost always have enough time to contact the customer before missing a deadline. We live in the future: call, text, or alert your dispatcher to help the customer. This is more than common courtesy; it's an essential skill for the professional tech.

Avoid distractions that take your focus away from the user and his or her computer problem. Don't take a personal call when interacting with a customer.

Don't text or tweet or respond to messages on other social media sites. Don't chat with a favorite coworker who walks by about the next baseball game you two should attend. Interact with the customer, not the co-worker. Any kind of personal interruption that doesn't deal directly with fixing the computer will only irritate the customer.

You have a lot of power as a tech at someone else's computer. You can readily access files, history, downloads, and more. Don't do it! *You need to deal appropriately with customers' confidential and private materials.* This includes files on the computer, items on a physical desktop, and even pages sitting in a printer tray.

Expectations management means to give a customer as accurate a guess as to how long it will take you to fix the computer problem. Plus, it means communicating when you will finish more quickly or when things seem to be taking longer than first predicted. Also, many times with a computer issue, you can fix the problem and avoid a similar problem in the future in several ways. These options boil down to money. If applicable, offer different repair/replacement options and let the customer decide which route to take.

At the completion of work, *provide proper documentation* of the services provided. Describe the problem, including the time and day you started work, and the solution. *Follow up* with a customer/user at a later date to verify satisfaction. This can be a simple follow-up, usually just a phone call, to confirm that the customer is happy with your work.

After you finish a job (or even during one in progress), refrain from sharing any "funny" stories about the customer or the activities around you. Certainly share professional and technical details with coworkers and any personal issues with your supervisor, but definitely *do not disclose experiences via social media outlets* such as Facebook and Instagram. Someone knows someone without fail, and your words will come back to haunt you.

Objective 1.03 **Troubleshooting Methodology**

Following a sound troubleshooting methodology helps you figure out and fix problems quickly. But because troubleshooting is as much an art as a science, no detailed step-by-step list of things to try in a particular order will suffice. You need flexibility in real-world troubleshooting, but following are some general steps.

First, you need to secure the proper tools for the job. Second, you should back up everything important before you start doing repair work. And third, analyze, test, and complete your troubleshooting. The CompTIA A+ 902 exam objectives offer a very good model (which you should memorize for the exam!).

Tech Toolkit

A tech toolkit should include a few basic tools and some spare parts for testing. The basic technician toolkit consists of a Phillips-head screwdriver and not much else—seriously—but a dozen or so tools and tool variations round out a fully functional toolkit. Most kits have several different-sized Phillips-head screwdrivers, plus several star-headed Torx wrenches, nut drivers, tweezers, a little grabber tool, and various opening tools (see Figure 1.11). An extension magnet can help you reach and grab any stray screws or other metal parts. If you'll be working with a lot of networking equipment, cable testers and loop-back plugs can make your job easier. You might also carry a flashlight, a magnifying glass, and an antistatic wrist strap.

Always carry several *field replaceable units (FRUs)*—a fancy way to say *spare parts*—when going to a job site or workstation. Having several known-good components on hand lets you swap out a potentially bad piece of hardware to test whether that's the problem. I generally carry a couple of RAM sticks (DDR2, DDR3, and DDR4), a PCIe video card, a NIC, and a 500-watt power supply.

Backup

In many troubleshooting situations, you should back up critical files before making changes to a system. This is partly a maintenance issue. If you're in

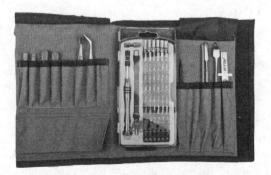

FIGURE 1.11   Typical technician toolkit

charge of a set of devices for your company, for example, make sure they're set up to back up critical files automatically on a regular basis.

Travel Assistance

It's so important to protect critical data with backups that this book goes into detail on relevant tools and practices for both modern desktop and mobile device operating systems. On the desktop side, Chapter 15 covers recent Windows versions, while Chapter 17 looks at OS X and Linux. Chapter 11 looks at backing up critical data on devices running mobile operating systems such as Android, iOS, and Windows Phone/Mobile.

If you run into a partially functional device for which you might have to reinstall the OS but can access the hard drive or other storage media, you should definitely back up essential data. Back up e-mail, favorites, personal documents, and any data not stored on a regularly backed-up server.

Exam Tip

The CompTIA A+ certification exams assume that techs should *always* back up systems before working on them, even though that's not how it works in the real world.

Because you can always boot to a recovery environment (such as System Recovery Options in Windows 7) or an OS installed on a bootable optical disc or flash drive, you should never lose essential data, barring anything short of a full-blown hard drive death.

Travel Advisory

Dead hard drives retain their data, so you can recover it—if you're willing to pay a lot of money. Having a good backup in place makes a lot more economic sense.

Troubleshooting Theory

An effective *troubleshooting theory* follows a set of steps to diagnose and fix computing devices. Troubleshooting theory includes talking to users to determine how and when the problem took place, determining a cause, testing, verifying, and documenting. CompTIA defines a six-step trouble-shooting theory:

1. Identify the problem.
2. Establish a theory of probable cause (question the obvious).
3. Test the theory to determine cause.
4. Establish a plan of action to resolve the problem and implement the solution.
5. Verify full system functionality and, if applicable, implement preventative measures.
6. Document findings, actions, and outcomes.

In the initial troubleshooting step, *identify the problem* by talking to the user. Get the user to show you what does not work. Question the user and identify user changes to the computing device. Always back up before making any changes.

Next, analyze the issue and come up with a theory as to what is wrong—a *theory of probable cause*. Fall back on your knowledge of the *computing process* to localize the issue based on the symptoms. In many situations, you'll need to access other resources to root out the most probable cause of the problem. If necessary, you should conduct external or internal research based on the symptoms.

Google the problem. Ask other techs onsite if they've run into similar issues. Observe your surroundings for anything that might have led to the problem.

Once you've decided on a theory that makes sense, *test the theory* to see if it fixes the problem. If your theory doesn't pan out, on the other hand, come up with a new theory and test it. (In CompTIA speak, if the theory is not confirmed, you need to reestablish a new theory.) If you verify and the fix lies within your skill set, excellent.

At this point, you need to check in with management to make certain you have permission to make the necessary changes. Always consider corporate policies, procedures, and impacts before implementing changes. Having the boss walk in frowning while you're elbows-deep in a machine with the question "Who gave you permission?" can make for a bad day!

If you don't have the skills—or the permissions—to fix the issue, you need to *escalate* the problem. Call your boss or a senior tech.

Once the problem is solved through either your careful work or escalation, you need to *verify* full system functionality to make sure the user is happy. Then, if applicable, *implement preventative measures.* Educate the user on various behaviors, such as clicking suspicious links or eating cookies over the keyboard.

For the final step in the troubleshooting theory and process, *document* your findings, actions, and outcomes. This documentation might be highly formalized in some organizations, or it might just be a few notes you jot down for your own use—but you must document!

Documenting problems helps you track the troubleshooting history of a computing device over time, enabling you to make longer-term determinations about retiring it or changing out more parts. If you and your fellow techs fix a specific problem with Mary's laptop several times, for example, you might decide to swap out her whole system rather than fix it a fourth time.

Documenting helps fellow techs if they have to follow up on a task you didn't finish or troubleshoot a machine you've worked on previously. The reverse is also true. If you get a call about Frank's computer, for example, and check the records to find other service calls on his computer, you might find that the fix for a particular problem is already documented. This is especially true for user-generated problems. Having documentation of what you did also means you don't have to rely on your memory when your coworker asks what you did to fix the weird problem with Jane's computer a year ago!

Documenting also comes into play when you or a user has an accident onsite. If your colleague Joe drops a monitor on his foot and breaks both the monitor and his foot, for example, you need to fill out an *incident report,* just as you would with any kind of accident: electrical, chemical, or physical. This report should detail what happened and where it happened. This helps your supervisors take the appropriate actions quickly and efficiently.

CHECKPOINT

✔**Objective 1.01: How Computers Work**   Computers work in a three-stage process: input, processing, and output. Almost every process requires the complex interaction of many devices, including multiple pieces of hardware and layers of software. Good techs understand each process to facilitate troubleshooting.

✔**Objective 1.02: Dealing with Customers**   A tech's job takes on the role of psychologist as well as detective when users get into the mix. Treat the customer with respect. Deal graciously with cultural differences and use appropriate titles. Remain positive. Asking the right questions—and avoiding the wrong ones—helps elicit answers for your troubleshooting. Avoid accusatory questions and focus on open-ended ones. Practice professionalism. Good hygiene is a must. Be on time and manage expectations. Document your work and follow up with customers to ensure satisfaction with your work.

✔**Objective 1.03: Troubleshooting Methodology**   You need to have the right tools to accomplish your job. At the least, carry a Phillips-head screwdriver; also carry some FRUs for part swapping. Back up critical files before making changes to a computer. Analyze, test, and complete your troubleshooting. Use the CompTIA troubleshooting theory to help resolve issues: identify the problem, establish a theory of probable cause, test the theory to determine the cause, establish a plan of action, verify full system functionality, and document your findings.

REVIEW QUESTIONS

1. While you are troubleshooting a fairly routine printing problem, the customer explains in great detail precisely what he was trying to do, what happened when he tried to print, and what he had attempted as a fix for the problem. At what point should you interrupt him?

   A. After he describes the first problem

   B. As soon as you understand the problem

   C. As soon as you have a solution

   D. Never

2. What are the first two steps (in order) of the CompTIA troubleshooting theory?

   A. Establish a theory of probable cause; test the theory to determine the cause.

   B. Document findings, actions, and outcomes; verify full system functionality.

   C. Identify the problem; establish a theory of probable cause.

   D. Test the theory to determine the cause; identify the problem.

3. While manning the help desk, you get a call from Sharon in accounting. She's lost a file that she knows she saved to her hard drive. Which of the following statements would direct Sharon to open her Documents folder in the most efficient and professional manner?

   A. Sharon, check Documents.

   B. Sharon, a lot of programs save files to a default folder—often to a folder called Documents. Let's look there first. Click the Start button and move the mouse until the cursor hovers over Documents. Click the left mouse button and tell me what you see when Documents opens.

   C. Probably just defaulted to Docs. Why don't you open Excel or whatever program you used to make the file, and then open a document and point it to Documents?

   D. Look Sharon, I know you're a clueless noob when it comes to computers, but how could somebody lose a file? Just open up Documents and look there for the file.

4. What tool must be in every technician's toolkit?

   A. Pliers

   B. Hammer

   C. Straight-slot screwdriver

   D. Phillips-head screwdriver

5. When is it appropriate to yell at a customer?

   A. When he screws up the second time

   B. When he interrupts your troubleshooting

   C. When he screws up the fifth time

   D. Never

6. Al in marketing calls in for tech support, complaining that he has a dead computer. What is a good first question or questions to begin troubleshooting the problem?

   A. Did the computer ever work?

   B. When did the computer last work?

   C. When you say "dead," what do you mean? What happens when you press the power button?

   D. What did you do?

7. While manning the help desk, you get a call from Bryce in sales complaining that he can't print, and every time he clicks the network shared drive, his computer stops. He says he thinks it's his "hard driver." What would be a good follow-up question or statement?

   A. Bryce, you're an idiot. Don't touch anything. I'll be there in five minutes.

   B. Okay, let's take this one step at a time. You seem to have two problems, one with printing and the second with the network shared drive, right?

   C. First, it's not a hard *driver,* but a hard *drive.* It doesn't have anything to do with the network share or printing, so that's just not right.

   D. When could you last print?

8. When troubleshooting a software problem on Phoebe's computer and listening to her describe the problem, you get a text from your boss. What would be an acceptable action for you to take?

   A. Excuse yourself, walk out of the cube, and use a cell phone to call your boss.

   B. Pick up Phoebe's phone and dial your boss's number.

   C. Wait until Phoebe finishes her description and then ask to use her phone to call your boss.

   D. Wait until Phoebe finishes her description and run through any simple fixes; then explain that you need to call your boss on your cell phone.

9. You've just installed new printer drivers into Roland's computer for the big networked laser printer and verified that everything works. Using the CompTIA troubleshooting theory, how should you complete the repair?

   A. Document that you installed new printer drivers.

   B. Tell Roland to print a test page.

   C. Print a test page and go to the printer to verify the results. Assuming everything works, you're done.

   D. Print a test page and go to the printer to verify the results. Document that you installed new printer drivers successfully.

10. What's an FRU?

    A. Foreign replacement unit—a cheaper part to replace an expensive, American-made part

    B. Field replaceable unit—a known-good computer part to swap in or out in the troubleshooting process

    C. Free repair unit—a gimmick used by some companies to provide free tech support for the first-time customer

    D. Short for FRU Linux, a Linux distribution

REVIEW ANSWERS

1. **D**   Don't interrupt the customer when he or she is explaining the problem!

2. **C**   Always begin by identifying the problem and establishing a theory of probable cause.

3. **B**   The better explanation tells about the probable location of the file—in this case, in Documents—and does so without slang or jargon. It also doesn't assume knowledge on the part of the user. Finally, never call a user a "clueless noob"!

4. **D**   The minimum tool every computer tech needs is a Phillips-head screwdriver.

5. **D**   Never yell at customers.

6. **C**   It's always a good idea to ask follow-up questions that clarify the situation. Both A and B are questions you'll ask during the questioning of the user, but C is the better first question.

7. **B**   Taking a non-accusatory approach with a question or questions to help clarify the problems is a good initial follow-up. Answer D would come up probably as a second or third question.

8. **D**   This is a tough one, but because the user is in the midst of explanation, you shouldn't interrupt her. You should use your own cell phone, not the user's equipment, if at all possible.

9. **A**   Always document your findings, actions, and outcomes.

10. **B**   An FRU is a field replaceable unit.

Ports and Connectors

	NEWBIE	SOME EXPERIENCE	EXPERT
ETA	2.5 hours	1.5 hours	1 hour

Mastering the craft of the computer tech requires that you learn a lot of details about what sometimes seem to be thousands of individual parts, connections, and settings. Good techs don't go around saying, "Just plug that *doohickey* into the *whatchamacallit*," and you shouldn't either. These things have names, after all.

Fortunately, it's much simpler than it seems! Computer makers use only a few types of connectors for most devices, so once you learn one type of connector, you'll know how to use it on any type of system. Every cable has a *connector* at the end that plugs into a corresponding *port* on a computer. Connectors carry data and sometimes power between devices attached to the computer. Ports are the *interfaces,* the "doorways" used to connect devices to the system. Connectors and ports can be either male or female, defined as having pins or sockets, respectively.

This chapter describes *integrated I/O devices*—the major connectors, plugs, and sockets that you'll find on a typical computer—and spells out many of the acronyms and abbreviations used by techs. The CompTIA A+ certification exams expect you to recognize a particular part simply by seeing what type of connector attaches to that part, so pay attention, folks!

Objective 2.01

Standard Single-Function Ports

Most computers sport at least a few single-function ports for connecting peripherals, such as monitors (including TVs and projectors), audio devices, keyboards, and mice, and for plugging into a wired network. With only a couple of exceptions, these standard ports support only a single type of device.

The Keyboard Port

Keyboards come in a variety of styles, from the plain-Jane, rectangular typewriter substitute, to the exotically curved, multifunction gadget that's bristling with special function *hotkeys* and equipped with ports of its own. Regardless of their appearance, however, all keyboards enable you to do one thing: enter commands into your computer. While most modern wired keyboards use USB, this hasn't always been the case.

Some computers offer the legacy purple 6-pin mini-DIN port (commonly called a *PS/2 port*). The mini-DIN port is keyed so you can insert the keyboard connector only one way.

> ### Exam Tip
> The CompTIA A+ objectives refer to the mini-DIN port as a miniDin-6 connector.

The Mouse Port

Like keyboards, mice come in an array of sizes and shapes, and they have used a couple of connectors to attach to the computer (see Figure 2.1). Modern wired mice use USB; earlier mice plug into a green mini-DIN port. All mice enable you to manipulate the operating system (OS) and applications.

Aside from color, the green mouse port appears identical to the purple PS/2 keyboard port, but they're not interchangeable. You can plug a PS/2 mouse connector into a PS/2 keyboard port, and vice versa, but they won't work. Some systems ignore this rule by providing a combo port, often half purple and half green (you'll need to trust me on the colors in Figure 2.1).

Video Ports

Monitors and projectors connect to a computer using one of four single-function video ports: VGA, DVI, DisplayPort, or HDMI. (Some use the Thunderbolt multifunction port that we'll look at a little later.)

VGA

The oldest of the video connectors, *Video Graphics Array (VGA)*, uses a 15-pin, three-row D-subminiature connector with several names: DB-15, DE-15, and

FIGURE 2.1   Six-pin mini-DIN (PS/2) connectors; keyboard (left), mouse (center), combined (right)

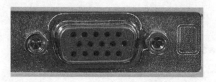

FIGURE 2.2   A female 15-pin D-sub connector

HD-15 (see Figure 2.2). VGA handles analog signals, meaning that it sends video information to the monitor as a modulated frequency wave.

Exam Tip

CompTIA's current objectives drop the hyphens; don't be surprised if you see these on the exam as HD15, DB15, or DE15.

DVI

Many monitors and projectors use a *Digital Visual Interface (DVI)* connector that plugs into a DVI port on a computer. DVI offers three connectors that look very much alike: DVI-D is for digital, DVI-A is for analog, and DVI-A/D or DVI-I (interchangeable) accepts either DVI-D or DVI-A (see Figure 2.3). DVI-D and DVI-A are keyed differently and are not interchangeable.

Travel Assistance

Digital connections such as DVI-D and all the video connections discussed later in this chapter send video information to a monitor as a series of ones and zeroes.

DVI-I and DVI-D also support a configuration called Dual-Link DVI, which supports higher resolutions and features a similar connector that simply

FIGURE 2.3   DVI-I connector

has extra pins. This clever arrangement allows a regular Single-Link DVI display to be driven by a Dual-Link connection. (Chapter 9 covers monitors and projectors in more detail.)

DisplayPort

DisplayPort features a compact 20-pin connector that is slightly larger than a USB port, as well as a smaller Mini DisplayPort connector that is less than a centimeter wide (see Figure 2.4).

DisplayPort supports the transmission of resolutions of up to 2560×1600 and refresh rates of up to 120 Hz (though not at the same time). When coupled with supporting monitors, up to four displays can be driven simultaneously by a single port. DisplayPort is optionally capable of encryption and the transmission of audio.

HDMI

High Definition Multimedia Interface (HDMI) was designed for home theater use, so its compact digital interface (see Figure 2.5) handles both the

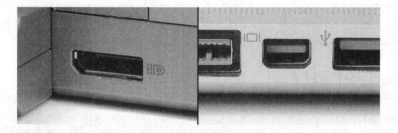

FIGURE 2.4 DisplayPort and Mini DisplayPort connectors

FIGURE 2.5 HDMI connector

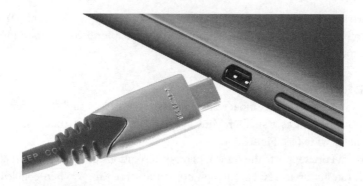

FIGURE 2.6 Micro HDMI port

high-definition video signal and multichannel digital audio streams. The desire to interconnect computers with home theater components has made HDMI pretty common on monitors, motherboards, and video cards. Some portable computers and mobile devices even use smaller versions of HDMI called Mini HDMI and Micro HDMI. Figure 2.6 shows a Micro HDMI port on an ASUS tablet.

Audio Ports

Most dedicated audio ports take the form of the popular 3.5-mm mini-audio connectors commonly seen on the iPhone and other mobile devices. A computer typically has at least three color-coded sound ports: a green speaker output port, a pink microphone input port, and a blue auxiliary input port; better cards will have more (see Figure 2.7). Note the differing shades of gray and use your imagination!

Travel Advisory

Some sound cards have audio ports that are all the same color. If you run into one of those, you can try to figure out what the obscure symbols mean or get the information from a user manual or the manufacturer's website.

As the quality of the audio system increases, you'll find features such as a greater number of audio channels, separate outputs for different audio channels, and digital audio outputs such as the *Sony/Philips Digital Interface (S/PDIF)*.

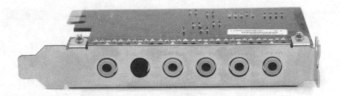

FIGURE 2.7 Sound card 3.5-mm mini-audio connectors

FIGURE 2.8 S/PDIF connectors: electrical (left) and optical (right)

S/PDIF ports come in two flavors: electrical and optical (see Figure 2.8). The electrical port usually uses an RCA connector on a coaxial cable; the optical port uses a fiber connector.

Multimedia Ports

The convergence of television and audio systems with the computer has many newer computers sporting various multimedia connectors. Some of these connectors, such as the *RG-6 coaxial* connector, have been around for a long time. The RG-6 connector sits on the video card or a dedicated TV tuner card and enables your computer to receive video and audio signals from a cable company or antenna. *Component* video connects with three RCA connectors (see Figure 2.9) that split the video signal into its components, using one cable for brightness, and two for color information.

Other older connectors include *S-Video*—for sending video content from the computer to the TV—and *composite* connectors—for connecting left- and

FIGURE 2.9   Component connectors

FIGURE 2.10   Video card with multimedia ports

right-channel audio and a single video source. Figure 2.10 shows a video card with many multimedia connectors. The latest media-center PCs, designed to fit into living room décor rather than office space, come with HDMI ports for connecting the computer to a high-definition television (HDTV).

MIDI/Joystick Ports

Very old motherboards and sound cards have an integrated female DB-15 port for connecting joysticks or other game controllers. These ports also support Musical Instrument Digital Interface (MIDI) devices, such as a music

MIDI/joystick port

synthesizer keyboard, although you need a special breakout box to make the MIDI connection. Unlike DB-15 video connectors, MIDI/joystick connectors have pins arrayed in two rows, with eight on the top and seven on the bottom, as shown in Figure 2.11.

Modem Ports

Dial-up modem ports look identical to traditional wired telephone jacks and use two-wire *RJ-11* telephone cables and connectors (see Figure 2.12). The locking clips on the male RJ-11 connectors secure the cable into the port. Most modems also have an output port for a telephone.

RJ-11 connectors on a modem

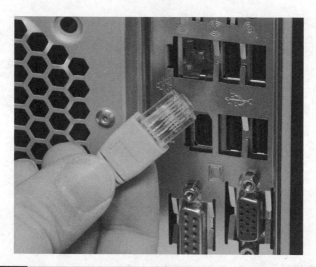

FIGURE 2.13 An RJ-45 connecter and port

Network Interface Ports

Network interfaces come in several varieties. Most network interface cards (NICs) and motherboards have an eight-wire *RJ-45* port (see Figure 2.13). RJ-45 connectors look like wide RJ-11 telephone connectors and plug into the female RJ-45 ports in the same manner that RJ-11 telephone cables plug into a modem.

> ### Local Lingo
> **NIC** A network interface card enables a computer to connect to a network. Techs call them NICs, even when the network adapter is built into a motherboard and thus is distinctly lacking in "card-ness."

High-end NICs have two fiber connections (in/out) of one variety or another. The most common fiber connectors are ST, SC, and LC (see Figure 2.14). Other fiber connectors that you might see are FDDI, MT-RJ, and FC.

> ### Exam Tip
> Very old NICs might have a bayonet-style coax connector called a BNC connector, used for 10Base2 or Thinnet networking. You won't see these on working systems, but you might on the exams!

FIGURE 2.14 ST (left), SC (center), and LC (right) fiber connectors

eSATA Ports

Some motherboards sport one or two eSATA ports (see Figure 2.15), enabling you to connect external mass storage devices such as an optical drive or backup hard drive. You'll learn more about eSATA (and its internal brother, SATA) in Chapter 8.

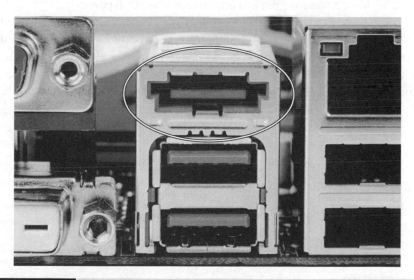

FIGURE 2.15 eSATA port

Objective 2.02

Modern Multifunction Ports

Modern computers use one or more multifunction ports to connect a host of useful peripherals. All newer machines have *universal serial bus (USB)* ports, and some have additional ports such as *IEEE 1394 (FireWire)* and *Thunderbolt.*

> **Local Lingo**
>
> **IEEE**   IEEE stands for the *Institute of Electrical and Electronics Engineers,* the international organization that creates standards for electrical things, such as ports, cables, and connectors.

USB

Many current devices, such as keyboards, mice, joysticks, microphones, scanners, printers, modems, tablets, digital cameras, lap warmers, cup heaters, personal fans, lamps, personal cube-based missile launchers, and more, connect via USB. Most computing devices offer one or more USB ports.

You can add extra USB ports to a system using either a USB expansion card or a USB hub (see Figure 2.16). USB hubs come in powered and bus-powered varieties. Powered USB devices have their own power plug, whereas bus-powered USB devices do not and instead draw their power from the USB bus. Too many bus-powered devices on a bus-powered hub can cause problems, so it's best to use powered hubs in such situations.

FIGURE 2.16   Typical USB hub

Travel Assistance

For more information about USB, visit www.usb.org.

USB devices are *hot-swappable*, which means that you can connect or disconnect them at any time without powering down your computer. USB technology lets you use hubs to connect up to 127 devices to a single host controller on your computer.

Travel Advisory

For the purposes of the CompTIA A+ certification exams, you need to know that you can connect 127 devices to a single USB port. But for real-life, on-the-job situations, it's a bad idea to hit this maximum. Some applications reserve bandwidth, and you could wind up with quite a mess. Too much of a good thing isn't good!

At this point there have been several generations of USB standard, along with a number of connector types; let's start with the standards. Instead of just throwing all of these numbers at you and hoping they stick, Table 2.1 provides a quick reference to help you sort it all out.

USB offers many connector types that are interchangeable among the many versions, for the most part. Whether a PC has a USB 1.1 or 2.0 port, for

TABLE 2.1   USB Standards

Name	Standard	Maximum Speed	Cable Length
Low-Speed USB	USB 1.1	1.5 Mbps	3 meters
Full-Speed USB	USB 1.1	12 Mbps	3 meters
Hi-Speed USB	USB 2.0	480 Mbps	5 meters
SuperSpeed USB	USB 3.0, recently renamed USB 3.1 Gen 1	5 Gbps	3 meters*
SuperSpeed USB 10 Gbps SuperSpeed+ USB	USB 3.1 Gen 2	10 Gbps	3 meters*

* USB 3.*x* doesn't specify a limit, but interference can make longer cables slower. I try to keep my cables under 2 meters, and avoid going over 3 meters.

TABLE 2.2	USB Connection Types	
Connector	**Plug Type**	**Plugs Into...**
Type A	Keyed	Computers
USB 3.1 Standard-A	Keyed	Computers
Type B	Keyed	Larger peripherals
USB 3.1 Standard-B	Keyed	Larger peripherals
Mini-B	Keyed	Smaller peripherals
Micro-B	Keyed	Tiny peripherals
USB 3.1 Micro-B	Keyed	Tiny peripherals
USB Type-C	Reversible	Computers and peripherals

example, you can plug a Type-A connector into it. (Type A is the ubiquitous rectangular connector type we've used for more than a decade that has three orientations: up, down, and then the way that plugs in.) USB 3.x uses separate and clearly marked ports and connectors and isn't as readily backward compatible as previous versions. The USB 3.0 standard suggests that the ports should be colored blue to differentiate them from earlier versions. The latter ports are usually black. You can still plug older USB devices into a USB 3.0 port, but they will run at the slower speeds.

Table 2.2 lists the common USB connectors and their purposes. Note that "keyed" means the plug fits into the socket in only one direction. Figure 2.17 displays many varieties of USB connectors.

Finally, it's good to be aware that plenty of companies have made "USB" cables with one of the standardized USB connectors on one end, and a proprietary or nonstandard connector just for their devices on the other. A good example of this is the Apple Lightning connector in Figure 2.18.

FIGURE 2.17   Many USB connector types

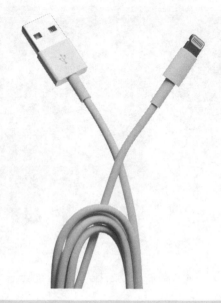

FIGURE 2.18   Apple Lightning connector on a USB cable

FireWire

The original specification for FireWire—*1394a*—calls for data transfers of up to 400 Mbps. The current generation of FireWire—*1394b*—is capable of speeds up to 800 Mbps. FireWire devices can use bus mastering, which enables devices such as video cameras, external hard drives, backup storage devices, and other hardware to communicate directly.

You can daisy chain up to 63 FireWire devices together, although at some point the devices will need their own power supplies. One cool feature of Fire-Wire chains is that you can use a device somewhere down the chain even if one or more devices in between the port and device are powered down.

The 6-pin standard FireWire 400 ports are slightly taller than USB ports and rounded on one end. The connector plugs are, of course, shaped to fit, as shown in Figure 2.19. Some devices, such as digital camcorders, use a 4-pin mini-FireWire connector, similar to the mini-USB connector, although they are certainly not interchangeable (see Figure 2.20). FireWire 800 devices use a square 9-pin connector (see Figure 2.21). You can get adapters and two-headed cables to connect a FireWire 400 device into a FireWire 800 port.

FIGURE 2.19 FireWire 400 (IEEE 1394a) port and connector

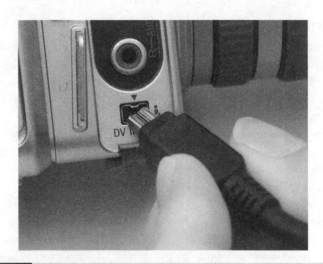

FIGURE 2.20 Mini-FireWire port and connector

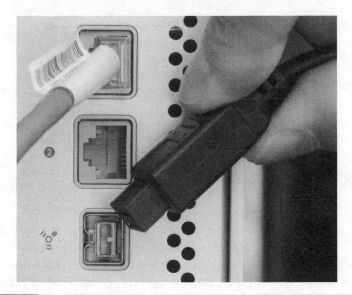

FIGURE 2.21   FireWire 800 (IEEE 1394b) port and connector

Travel Assistance

For more information regarding FireWire and the IEEE 1394
standard, visit www.ieee.org.

Thunderbolt

Intel developed the *Thunderbolt* interface to connect peripherals via PCIe and
DisplayPort simultaneously, combining their capacity. Consult Table 2.3 for the
basics on each version of the Thunderbolt standard.

TABLE 2.3   Thunderbolt Standards

Standard	Connector	Maximum Speed	Cable Length
Thunderbolt 1	Mini DisplayPort (MDP)	10 Gbps	3 m (copper) / 60 m (fiber)
Thunderbolt 2	Mini DisplayPort (MDP)	20 Gbps	3 m (copper) / 60 m (fiber)
Thunderbolt 3	USB Type-C	40 Gbps	3 m (copper) / 60 m (fiber)

FIGURE 2.22 Thunderbolt 2 port

Thunderbolt can use copper or fiber cabling, though the optical cables are still pretty rare. The copper cables can run up to 3 meters (whether a single cable, or chained). Optical runs can extend much, much farther—up to 60 meters—but optical cables of that length are several hundred dollars, and you'll need another way to power the device. Thunderbolt 3 can use a regular USB 3.0 cable at reduced performance.

The only way to tell the difference between a standard DisplayPort and a Thunderbolt 1 or 2 port (see Figure 2.22) is that the latter has a little lightning bolt symbol next to it—and you'll need the same trick to tell a Thunderbolt 3 port apart from a regular USB Type-C port.

 # Objective 2.03 Adapters and Converters

Adapters and converters enable you to connect devices in interesting ways. You can use a cable with DVI on one end and HDMI on the other end, for example, to plug into a DVI port on the video card and the HDMI socket on the monitor. These devices fall into two broad categories based on the problems they solve: connecting one type of video cable or port to another, and connecting almost anything to USB.

For Video

Adapters and converters for video take two primary forms: relatively small devices that fit at one end of a cable, converting it to the desired interface, and cables with built-in converters that have different connectors on each end.

FIGURE 2.23 DVI-to-HDMI cable

The former are more flexible, but the latter are easier to use. Here are the ones CompTIA wants you to know:

- DVI to HDMI (see Figure 2.23)
- DVI to VGA (see Figure 2.24)
- Thunderbolt to DVI
- HDMI to VGA

There are a few things to watch out for with these. Because HDMI can carry audio but DVI and VGA can't, some converters just drop the audio, while others have an audio port. Also, remember that DVI has multiple connector types; pay careful attention to what you need and what you're getting.

FIGURE 2.24 DVI-to-VGA adapter

For USB

USB offers converters to support many devices, such as legacy I/O ports or plugging old keyboards into new systems. Here are the ones CompTIA wants you to know:

- PS/2 to USB
- USB A to USB B
- USB to Bluetooth
- USB Optical Drive
- USB-to-RJ-45 dongle, also called USB to Ethernet
- USB-to-Wi-Fi dongle

We've already introduced all of these except for Bluetooth, optical drives, and Wi-Fi. If you aren't familiar with them, refer to Chapter 8 for optical drives, Chapter 9 for Bluetooth, and Chapter 19 for Wi-Fi.

CHECKPOINT

✔**Objective 2.01: Standard Single-Function Ports** While most modern wired mice and keyboards connect to the motherboard via USB, much older ones use a dedicated 6-pin mini-DIN (PS/2) connector. Make sure you remember that the 15-pin, three-row D-subminiature port is for video, whereas the 15-pin, two-row D-subminiature port is for MIDI devices or joysticks. Know the remaining video ports—VGA, DVI, DisplayPort, and HDMI—as well as the audio ports: 3.5-mm mini-audio and S/PDIF. Finally, know the difference between the RJ-11 connectors for modems and the RJ-45 connectors for NICs. Most modern motherboards sport one or two eSATA ports, enabling you to connect external mass storage devices such as an optical drive or backup hard drive.

✔**Objective 2.02: Modern Multifunction Ports** USB enables you to hot-swap devices and daisy-chain up to 127 devices to a single USB port. The Type-A connector goes into the USB port; the Type-B, or mini connector, goes into the USB device. The new, smaller Type-C connector is the same at each end, and is designed to eventually replace the other connector types. USB (aka normal USB 1.1) is capable of throughput speeds up to 12 Mbps, whereas Hi-Speed USB is good for up to 480 Mbps. SuperSpeed USB (USB 3.0, renamed USB 3.1 Gen 1) devices run at up to 5 Gbps, and SuperSpeed USB 10 Gbps (USB 3.1 Gen 2) runs at up to 10 Gbps.

IEEE 1394 is also known as FireWire. The 1394a version is capable of speeds up to 400 Mbps, and 1394b runs at up to 800 Mbps. Either version of IEEE 1394 enables you to connect up to 63 devices to a single IEEE 1394 port.

Thunderbolt combines the capacity of PCIe and DisplayPort (and Thunderbolt 3 adds USB 3.0 into the mix) to connect peripherals at very high speeds: 10 Gbps for Thunderbolt 1, 20 Gbps for Thunderbolt 2, and 40 Gbps for Thunderbolt 3. Thunderbolt can run up to 3 meters on copper cable, and up to 60 meters on expensive fiber optic cable. Thunderbolt 1 and 2 use the Mini DisplayPort connector, whereas Thunderbolt 3 uses the USB Type-C connector. Thunderbolt-enabled MDP and USB Type-C ports have a lightning bolt symbol next to them.

✔**Objective 2.03: Adapters and Converters**   Adapters and converters for video enable you to connect different systems together. You should know four options at least:

- DVI to HDMI
- DVI to VGA
- Thunderbolt to DVI
- HDMI to VGA

USB enables many devices to use converters to connect to systems. With these types of adapters and converters, you should know six:

- PS/2 to USB
- USB A to USB B
- USB to Bluetooth
- USB Optical Drive
- USB-to-RJ-45 dongle/Ethernet
- USB-to-Wi-Fi dongle

REVIEW QUESTIONS

1. Which of these connectors can you use to connect a keyboard to a computer? (Select all that apply.)
   A. Mini-DIN
   B. HDMI
   C. S/PDIF
   D. USB

2. Which DVI connector can accept either digital or analog signals?
   A. DVI-D
   B. DVI-A
   C. DVI-I
   D. DVI-X

3. Which of the following ports can be found on network cards?
   A. HDMI
   B. Thunderbolt
   C. RJ-45
   D. USB

4. Which port(s) can accept a USB 3.0 cable with a Type-B plug?
   A. USB 1.1 Type-B
   B. USB 2.0 Type-B
   C. USB 3.0 Type-B
   D. All of the above

5. What kind of connector does Thunderbolt 3 use?
   A. Lightning
   B. USB Type-C
   C. Thunderbolt
   D. Mini DisplayPort

6. In theory, how many USB devices can you connect to a single host controller?
   A. 1
   B. 2
   C. 63
   D. 127

7. Which connector provides high quality video *and* audio?
    A. HDMI
    B. S/PDIF
    C. S-Video
    D. VGA

8. To what does a Type-A USB connector connect?
    A. To a USB port on the computer
    B. To a USB device
    C. To a PS/2 on the back of your computer
    D. To a USB modem

9. What is the top data-transfer speed possible under the USB 3.0 standard?
    A. 50 megabits per second
    B. 480 megabits per second
    C. 400 megabytes per second
    D. 5 gigabits per second

10. How many devices can you daisy-chain on a single FireWire connection?
    A. 63
    B. 65
    C. 127
    D. 1023

REVIEW ANSWERS

1. **A D**   Keyboards can use a mini-DIN or USB connector.

2. **C**   DVI-I (or interchangeable) can connect with either DVI-D or DVI-A and accept either digital or analog signals.

3. **C**   Most network cards have RJ-45 ports.

4. **C**   Only USB 3.0 Type-B ports can accept the larger USB 3.0 Type-B connector.

5. **B**   Thunderbolt 3 makes use of the USB Type-C connector.

6. **D**   You can, in theory, connect 127 USB devices to a single host controller.

7. **A**   The HDMI connector can handle high-definition video and multiple digital audio signals.

8. **A** The Type-A connector on a USB cable connects to a USB port on a computer. USB devices have a Type-B port.

9. **D** The USB 3.0 SuperSpeed standard enables data transfers of up to 5 gigabits per second.

10. **A** You can daisy-chain up to 63 devices on a single FireWire port.

Maintenance and Safety Precautions

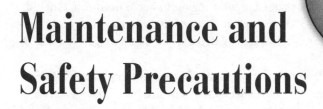

	NEWBIE	SOME EXPERIENCE	EXPERT
ETA	3 hours	2 hours	1 hour

There's more to keeping a computer running smoothly than launching an occasional chkdsk or deleting some temporary Internet files. Computers are machines, and all machines need regular maintenance. This doesn't include changing the oil every 3000 miles, but it does include cleaning and dusting, among other things. Yes, *dusting!* Being a tech doesn't get you out of housework!

Don't be fooled by the benign appearance of a typical computer, monitor, or printer. Underneath that unassuming exterior lurk dozens of voltage-carrying wires and circuits. Any one of these can reach out and bite an unwary tech.

Finally, all computers and components have a finite service life. Where do old monitors, batteries, and toner cartridges go to die?

This chapter covers the important cleaning and maintenance routines that you should follow to keep your system in optimal running condition. These routines take you into the very guts of your computer, so to prevent damage to your computer and to you, it's vital that you use the appropriate tools and follow proper safety precautions. This chapter wraps up with a discussion on how to dispose of dead or obsolete equipment properly.

Objective 3.01   Cleaning and Maintenance Procedures

To prolong the life of your computer, you must inspect and clean it regularly. Inspecting your system alerts you to any dangerous or damaging conditions that exist, such as rust and corrosion, damaged connectors, damaged and improperly installed components, frayed cables, loose connections, and heat damage. Cleaning your computer rids it of the dirt, dust, and grime that build up from normal use. This does more than simply maintain a neat appearance; it helps you prevent two of the most damaging conditions: overheating and electrostatic discharge (ESD).

Local Lingo

ESD   ESD is a quick electrical charge that occurs when two objects with different electrical potentials come into contact with each other. For more on this subject, see the section "Electrostatic Discharge Precautions and Procedures," later in this chapter.

Your cleaning routine should include the computer and monitor case, the monitor screen, the keyboard and mouse, and any printer, switch, scanner, or other device connected to the system. Don't forget the inside of the case: the motherboard, adapter cards, drives, and power supply.

Following is a look at the safest cleaning compounds and tools you can use to keep your computer looking and running its best, plus steps for properly cleaning and maintaining your system, monitor, and peripherals.

Exam Tip
Regular cleaning of the computer will prolong the life of your components, help to prevent ESD, and help to prevent overheating.

Liquid Cleaning Compounds

You can safely use several kinds of liquid cleaners on the computer, from plain water to specially formulated commercial compounds.

Clean or Soapy Water

Many cleaning chores require nothing more than a cloth dampened with some clean water. Common tap water is usually fine, but some local water is heavy with minerals and may leave a residue. If this is the case in your area, use filtered or distilled water instead.

If water alone cannot do the job, use a mild soap solution. Dish soap is best, but make certain that you dilute it thoroughly.

Denatured Alcohol

Use denatured alcohol to clean electrical contacts and components such as the drive heads on removable media drives. Make certain, however, that you never use alcohol on mechanisms such as motors or rubber drive belts. The alcohol dissolves the lubricants in motor bearings, and rubber belts may stretch or become brittle when exposed to alcohol.

Local Lingo
Denatured alcohol   Denatured alcohol is alcohol with stuff added to make it poisonous if consumed. That way, manufacturers can sell it to anyone rather than only to people old enough to drink alcohol. Standard rubbing alcohol, mineral spirits, or isopropyl alcohol with a high percentage of alcohol (think 95 percent) work well for computer components.

Glass Cleaner

Glass cleaners such as Windex are usually safe to use on most metal and plastic surfaces on computers. Ironically, they're not always recommended for use on a computer's glass surfaces, such as the monitor screen. Some monitor screens have special coatings that can be damaged by commercial glass cleaners. In particular, you should never use glass cleaner on older liquid crystal display (LCD) screens. You will melt the screens! Instead, use either clean water or a vinegar and water solution. For modern LCD screens, check the user's manual or the manufacturer's website for best practices. Each company has different recommendations for its LCDs.

Vinegar and Water Solution

A solution of one part vinegar to four parts water is great for removing dirt, grime, and fingerprints from surfaces such as your monitor screen, LCD screen, or scanner bed. Use plain white vinegar, not the fancier balsamic or red wine vinegar. Save those for your salads!

Commercial Computer Cleaning Solutions

If you want to save yourself the trouble of custom-brewing your own cleaning solution, try commercial products from 3M and Belkin. These come in spray form and as premoistened towelettes (minus the lemon scent). These work just fine, although it's debatable if they work any better than homemade solutions. Still, if you don't want to lug a jug of white vinegar from job to job, commercial cleaners are a good alternative.

As a general rule, remember to read the labels of any commercial cleaning product before applying it to your computer. If you have any doubts about its safety, contact the manufacturer before using it.

Cleaning Tools

Along with your trusty Phillips-head screwdriver and multimeter, a complete toolkit should contain the following cleaning tools: canned air, lint-free cloths, a small soft-bristled brush and swabs, and a non-static vacuum. Some techs recommend used fabric softening sheets from your dryer to pick up dust, but avoid using the scratchy ones on LCD screens.

Canned Air

Use canned air to loosen dirt and dust from delicate components. Canned air comes in a couple of forms: the liquid propellant kind and the kind that uses small cartridges of compressed CO_2. You can find both at computer stores, office supply stores, camera shops, and big-box stores that sell electronics.

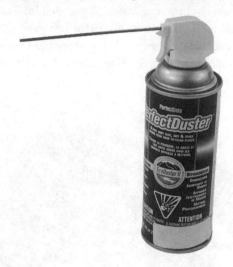

Follow three rules when using canned air:

- Never breathe this stuff in. It's not *that* kind of air, and inhaling it can, quite literally, kill you!
- With regard to the liquid propellant type of canned air, always keep the can upright. Tilting or turning the can upside down causes the liquid inside to come squirting out. This liquid can cause frostbite to the tech and irreparable damage to any computer components that it touches.
- Don't shake canned air cans. They don't need to be shaken to work, and you run a small but real risk of the can exploding in your hand.

Lint-Free Cloths

Lint-free cloths such as the type used for cleaning eyeglasses or cameras work well for general computer cleaning. These cloths are better than plain paper towels because they don't leave residue and won't scratch plastic surfaces.

Travel Advisory

Make sure you never use "dry dusting" cleaning products in or on your computer. Products such as the Swiffer Sweeper use statically charged cloths to collect the dust. Static electricity and computers don't mix!

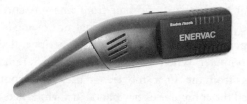

| **FIGURE 3.1** | A non-static vacuum |

Brushes and Swabs

Try using soft-bristled brushes and lint-free swabs to clean dust and dirt from hard-to-reach areas and to wipe grime from electrical contacts.

Some technicians use rubber pencil erasers to clean contacts, but I don't recommend this practice because some erasers contain acids that can leave a residue or destroy your contacts. Plus, they may rub the metal coating completely off the contacts—a bad thing.

Non-static Vacuums

Small, hand-held vacuums designed specifically for use on electronics (shown in Figure 3.1) suck up dirt and dust loosened by a brush or canned air. Note that you should definitely *not* use a common household vacuum cleaner. These create static electricity and can toast your computer! Some computer vacuums can also act as blowers. Some stand-alone blower products go by names such as "electric dusters." They can be used as alternatives to canned air and do not create condensation or contain harmful liquid propellants.

Cleaning the Outside of the Computer, Monitor, and Peripherals

For regular cleaning, wipe down the exterior of your computer, monitor, and peripherals with a lint-free cloth dampened, not soaked, with clean water. Take care not to drip water or anything else onto or into your computer's components.

If you're dealing with a buildup of grime, use a mild soap solution. For harder cleaning chores, such as ink, crayon, and tape adhesive, try using a vinegar and water solution, denatured alcohol diluted with water, or commercial cleaners.

Travel Assistance
Chapter 22 covers printer-specific cleaning and maintenance.

Use canned air to blast dust and hair from air vents and other openings. This helps keep the hot air flowing out and cool air flowing in to maintain the appropriate temperature inside the computer or peripheral. This will extend the life of your computer. When you're using canned air, remember the words of Corporal Hicks from the *Aliens* movie, and use "short, controlled bursts." If you haven't dusted the computer or peripheral in a while, take it outside before spraying. Otherwise, you'll spread dust everywhere.

Travel Advisory
Read the label on any commercial cleaning solution before using it on your computer. If you have any doubts, contact the manufacturer before using it.

You can use one or more of these solutions to clean your system and the majority of your peripherals safely and effectively. Because they get the majority of the grime, mice, keyboards, and monitor screens warrant a little more discussion.

Mice

An optical mouse has no moving parts to clean, but it does have an optical sensor behind a recessed lens. It's important that you keep this lens clean for optimal tracking. A lint-free swab dipped in denatured alcohol diluted with water does a good job.

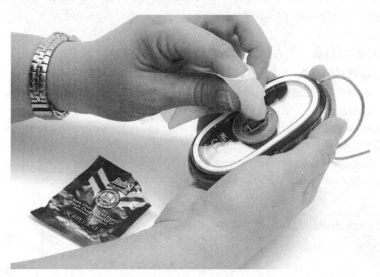

Keyboards

Out of any component, the keyboard tends to accumulate the most grunge. Use canned air and a soft-bristled brush to lift out dirt, crumbs, hair, and other unmentionables from between the keys. Wipe down the exterior thoroughly with a dampened lint-free cloth. If necessary, use soapy water or one of the other cleaning solutions to remove stickier messes, but make sure that you disconnect the keyboard from the computer first. Be careful to avoid dripping cleaning liquids onto or into your keyboard. As a general rule, let your keyboard air-dry for 48 hours before plugging it back into the computer.

Monitor Screens

Monitor screens sometimes take a little extra effort to get clean and streak-free. The vinegar and water solution works quite well on both CRT and LCD monitors, as do commercial cleaners (on CRTs, but not LCDs). Make certain that you never spray cleaners directly onto the screen; always put the cleaner onto a lint-free cloth first. Dripping fluid into a monitor is a bad thing.

Cleaning Contacts, Connectors, Motherboard, and Components

Once you've got the exterior of your computer and components in tip-top shape, it's time to do the same for your computer's contacts, connectors, motherboard, and components. Before you go tugging on cables and removing the cover of your computer, read the "Electrostatic Discharge Precautions and Procedures" and "Safety and Environmental Issues" sections of this chapter to protect you and your system from electrical hazard.

Contacts and Connectors

Start by unplugging and inspecting the cables from the back of the computer. Look for signs of dirt, rust, or corrosion on the contact pins or sockets. Believe it or not, the main culprit in dirty contacts is you! Your skin contains natural oils, and touching the contacts while handling components leaves behind a small amount of oily residue. Given time, this residue leads to dirt and dust buildup, corrosion, and electrical interference.

The best way to protect your electrical components from becoming dirty is to avoid touching the contact pins, connectors, and sockets. If you must touch the contacts or pins, clean them immediately afterward with a lint-free swab dipped in denatured alcohol.

If you see signs of dirt on the contacts, use a lint-free swab dipped in denatured alcohol to loosen and remove it. You can also use a soft-bristled brush. If you see signs of rust or corrosion, you should replace the cable or component.

Motherboards and Components

Next, remove the case cover to clean accumulated dust, dirt, and hair off the motherboard and adapter cards. Use canned air to loosen the dust and dirt from the delicate electrical components, and use a non-static vacuum to suck it up. Pay particular attention to the case air vents and the power supply intake and exhaust vents. Note also that dust tends to collect inside the central processing unit (CPU) heat sink.

Thoroughly clean any fans you can touch. The fans draw cool air into the computer or push hot air away from components, protecting your computer from overheating. Heat kills electrical components, so it's important to do this right. Don't open the power supply to clean the fan inside! Use the tiny straw that comes with canned air to blow out as much dust as possible.

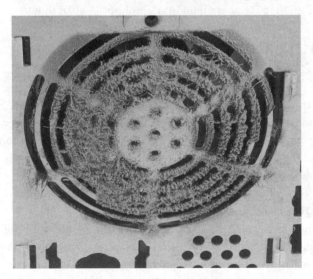

After you've cleaned out the dust and dirt, check to make sure that the adapter cards and drive cables are properly seated. Follow all of the precautions listed in Objective 3.03 to prevent ESD damage while working inside the case. When you've finished your inspection and maintenance, replace the cover on the computer and reattach the cables. Plug in the computer power cable as the last step.

Turn on the computer and listen. If you placed the fans and plugged in the cables properly, the computer should sound right and boot nicely. If all does not go well, shut down the computer, unplug the cables, open the case, and start with a visual inspection to determine what is not properly connected.

Objective 3.02 Component Protection and Storage

Computers need electricity to work, as you know, but that same juice can kill a computer or its data if it doesn't flow correctly. This section discusses the causes of power disturbances and covers steps and tools you can use to protect working equipment. Components not currently in use also run risks, so this section wraps up with a bit about properly storing computer components.

Power Problems

Your computer needs power to run properly, but various factors can turn what should be a steady stream of electricity from the wall socket into either a trickle or a fire hose. It's important that you know how to protect your computing environment from electrical power sags and power losses, power spikes, lightning strikes, and electromagnetic interference. Let's start with a look at the causes of these power problems.

A *brownout* occurs when the supply of electricity drops dramatically but does not go out completely. During a brownout, you'll notice lights flickering or growing dim. When the power rises back up to its original level, your computer might not be able to handle the drastic change, and damage may occur.

Blackouts occur when power goes out completely. The danger of a blackout is twofold. First, you may have data loss or corruption when the power goes out. Second, the power surge when the electricity comes back on may damage your system's electronics.

Power spikes or *power surges* occur when the voltage on your power line rises suddenly to above-normal levels. Power spikes are extremely dangerous and can destroy computers, monitors, and any other component plugged into the affected power line.

Exam Tip
You need to know the differences among surges, brownouts, and blackouts. Plus, keep in mind the devices that help in each situation: surge suppressors and battery backups such as a UPS.

Lightning storms are an underrated hazard. Using a computer or even leaving it plugged in during a lightning storm is asking for trouble. Keep in mind that no accessory can completely protect your system from the damage caused by a lightning strike.

All electrical equipment puts out a certain amount of electrical noise caused by the signal running through wires, cables, and circuits. *Electromagnetic interference (EMI)* occurs when two signals get too close together and the noise of one is picked up by the other. In computers and networking, this can cause problems such as wavy screens or slow or corrupted data transfers. Long cable runs tend to pick up EMI, especially if a power cable is running alongside a data cable.

Local Lingo

EMI   Electromagnetic interference occurs when two signals in close proximity interfere with each other.

Saving Your Computer from Electrical Problems

Many products help protect a computer from power problems, such as a UPS and a surge protector. You can also prevent certain problems by optimizing the computing space.

Uninterruptible Power Supplies

An *uninterruptible power supply (UPS)* protects your computer from brownouts and blackouts. A UPS has built-in batteries that supply power to your system when the electricity traveling through the power line drops below a certain level. Most UPS devices have an integrated alarm that tells you when your computer is running on battery power. Many techs call a UPS a *battery backup*. Note that a UPS does not provide unlimited power so you can keep working while the city lights are out! A UPS gives you a short window of opportunity to save your data and shut down the system properly.

Local Lingo

Battery backup   An uninterruptible power supply is sometimes called a *battery backup*.

UPSs come in two main varieties: *standby power systems (SPSs)* and *online UPSs*. Both of these protect your system in the event of a brownout or blackout, but they work differently and provide different levels of protection. A subvariety of UPS that you might encounter is called a *line-interactive UPS*.

Standby Power Systems

An SPS actively monitors the electricity traveling through the power line and begins supplying power as soon as the unit detects a sag. It takes a split second for the SPS to come online, however, and therein lies the main disadvantage. The brief lapse of time can result in data loss or damage before the SPS has kicked in.

Online UPS

An online UPS, in contrast, acts as a power source to the system, using the electricity from the alternating current (AC) outlet simply to recharge its internal batteries. If an electrical brownout or blackout occurs, your computer doesn't even flinch! Of course, as mentioned earlier, you don't have a tremendous amount of time to work, but you certainly have a safe window in which to save your work and shut down properly before the UPS runs out of juice.

As an added bonus, most online UPS boxes act as power conditioners— that is, they regulate the flow of electricity to your computer to even out any fluctuations your power line might experience. An online UPS costs more than an SPS, but in the long run its benefits justify the expense.

Travel Advisory

Don't plug a laser printer into a UPS. Laser printers draw massive amounts of electricity and may interfere with the function of the UPS and prevent you from shutting down safely.

Line-Interactive UPS

A line-interactive UPS is similar to a standby UPS but has special electronic inverter/converter circuitry that can handle moderate AC sags and surges without the need to switch to battery power. This allows for faster response to a power loss than a standby UPS. Due to the circuitry that adapts to undervoltage and overvoltage conditions, a line-interactive UPS may draw more or less electrical current for a device than is normally needed. As a result, when using a line-interactive UPS, be aware of the impact an increase in current consumption might have on any fuses or circuit breakers in the electric supply.

Surge Suppressors

Surge suppressors help to absorb power surges so that your computer does not feel their effects. They come as either separate modules or are integrated into the UPS. Good surge suppressors come with long-term or lifetime guarantees against damage to your computer. Avoid purchasing or using cheap surge suppressors. These are usually little more than power strips and provide virtually no protection against power surges or spikes.

Exam Tip

The 902 exam calls power surges, brownouts, and blackouts *environmental impacts.* Using an appropriate surge suppressor or battery backup *applies the appropriate controls* to counter those impacts.

Unplug Your Computer

Even if you have any or all of the layers of protection mentioned so far, the only sure protection against severe threats such as lightning is to shut down and unplug your computer and peripherals. Leave no stone unturned: make sure that you unplug even your modem, because lightning can travel up the telephone line to give your system a shock. (I've seen it happen, folks!)

> **Exam Tip**
>
> Remember that in the event of an electrical storm, the only way to protect a system is to unplug it completely, plus unplug all peripherals with external power cords.

EMI Noise Filters

EMI can be controlled by using cables with a Mylar coating and through the use of special EMI noise filters. Noise filters can be purchased as stand-alone products or are sometimes integrated into a UPS. You can also minimize EMI by moving data cables away from power cables and by shortening the cables you use.

Power fluctuations can wreak havoc on an unprotected system, and not just in the obvious ways. Surges and sags can damage power supplies and components and cause file corruption. The cost of a good UPS or surge suppressor is nothing compared to the cost in time and money caused by lost components or corrupted files that you may have to endure if you don't use either one.

Storing Components for Future Use

If you plan on storing computer components for future use, you need to protect them from ESD, corrosion, and other damage.

Storage Environment

Even when your computer is not in use, heat, moisture, and dirt are still hazards. Heat causes plastics to fade and become brittle, moisture encourages rust and corrosion, and dirt is, well, *dirty.* For these reasons, components and peripherals should be stored indoors in a climate-controlled environment.

Electrical Precautions

Take precautions to prevent electrical damage when storing computers and components. Always store computer equipment away from high-voltage devices, and never store batteries of any kind for long periods of time. Old batteries leak or corrode, so if you are not planning on reusing them during their recommended lifetime, recycle them and purchase new ones as needed.

The safest way to store your components for future use and to protect them from ESD is to put them in antistatic bags (discussed in the section "Electrostatic

Discharge Precautions and Procedures"). For the ultimate in component safety, store the components in their manufacturers' original boxes and packaging. That should be encouraging news to the packrats among you!

Exam Tip
The safest way to store components for future use is in their original packaging or in antistatic bags.

Moisture

Moisture and computers don't mix. You must control moisture to keep rust and corrosion at bay and to ensure that your components are still functional when you return them to service. *Silica-gel* packets are available from electronics stores and shipping supply companies. Place one or more small packets inside your component's antistatic bags and inside your computer case. Heed the manufacturers' warnings when using this stuff! It is poisonous, so don't eat it, and don't get any in your eyes.

Objective 3.03

Electrostatic Discharge Precautions and Procedures

ESD is one of the main enemies of your computer. To maintain your computer and prolong the life of components, you need to learn about the effects of ESD and how to protect your computer from those effects.

A prime example of ESD is the small shock you receive when you walk across a carpeted floor and then touch a metal doorknob. *Zap!* The small discharge doesn't cause any lasting damage to your body, but such a seemingly harmless shock will destroy computer components. In fact, even discharges well below the level that you can feel can damage or destroy computer components.

Types of ESD

The types of ESDs that affect computers can be placed into three broad categories: catastrophic damage, hidden damage, and gradual degradation.

Catastrophic ESD Damage

Catastrophic ESD causes a computer component to fail immediately. When catastrophic ESD occurs, it will be obvious to you, because, in all likelihood, you will be the one who caused it! Picture the scenario described a couple paragraphs ago with you walking across a carpeted floor. This time, instead of the doorknob, picture a RAID (redundant array of independent [or inexpensive] disks) controller, video card, or hard drive full of vital data. Are you concerned yet?

Hidden ESD Damage

Dust buildup on computer components causes *hidden ESD* damage. Over time, this buildup creates a small electrical charge. This charge is not enough to cause obvious damage, and in most cases you will not even be aware that a problem exists until a component begins to behave erratically. By that point, it is extremely difficult or impossible to pinpoint the original source of the problem. Hidden ESD is a good reason to clean your computer regularly.

ESD Degradation

ESD degradation occurs when the effects of ESD are cumulative. This is caused by situations in which low levels of ESD occur repeatedly. Damage caused by ESD degradation is not immediately apparent in full force; instead, the effects gradually get more and more noticeable. Like hidden ESD, degradation will cause your components to behave erratically, and it can make the original problem hard to recognize.

> **Exam Tip**
>
> Make sure you understand what ESD is, how it can damage your computer, and what you can do to protect against it.

Common ESD Protection Devices

ESD protection devices help to ensure a longer and more productive life for your computer components. These devices include antistatic wrist and ankle straps, antistatic mats, antistatic floor mats, and antistatic bags. Antistatic devices make your body's electrical potential the same as the electrical potential of your computer or component.

One of the most important steps you can take to prevent the effects of ESD is to ground yourself before you handle computer components. Do this *self-grounding* by touching a metal surface such as the exterior of the power supply before touching any of your system components.

Antistatic Wrist and Ankle Straps

Antistatic wrist and ankle straps, fondly called "nerd bracelets" by many techs, keep you at the same relative electrical ground level as the computer components on which you're working. Antistatic straps wrap around your wrist or ankle with an elastic strap attached to a long grounding wire. On some models, the grounding wire attaches to a metal clip that you attach to a metal device to ground yourself. Figure 3.2 shows an antistatic wrist strap grounded to a computer chassis. Others have a prong that you plug into the ground wire of an electrical wall outlet.

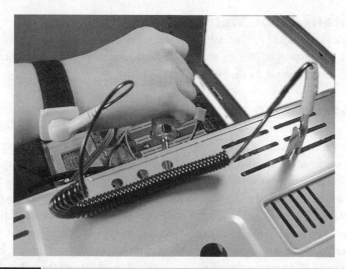

FIGURE 3.2   An antistatic wrist strap grounded to a computer

By the way, don't forget to remove your antistatic strap before walking away from your work area! Or, if you forget frequently, try to leave a camcorder running so you'll have something funny to show at your next family reunion.

Antistatic Mats

Portable antistatic mats provide a work surface that dissipates ESD. They look like large place mats or those baby-changing mats that come with diaper bags. They are distinguished by a small metal clip that you can attach to an antistatic strap to ground out ESD. In addition to helping prevent ESD, these mats help keep your work area organized by giving you a place to put your tools and components while you work.

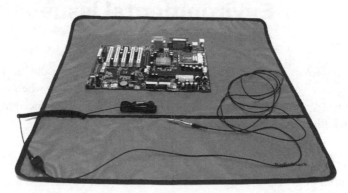

Antistatic Floor Mats

Antistatic floor mats are basically the same as portable antistatic mats, except much larger. Instead of placing them on top of your work area, you place them on the floor and stand on them while you work.

Antistatic Bags

Antistatic bags have a special coating or contain small filaments that help dissipate any static charge. Always store adapter cards and drives in antistatic bags when they're not in use and when transporting them—even if you're just going down the hall or across the room. Antistatic bags dissipate charge most effectively when they're closed, so it's a good idea to fold the end over and tape it down with an antistatic sticker if possible. Do not place components on top of antistatic bags, as charge is directed from the inside of the bag to the outside. Note that regular plastic or paper bags will *not* protect your components. In fact, plastic baggies conduct static electricity rather than preventing it, so don't use them!

Travel Advisory

Special antistatic sprays dissipate static charges built up in your clothing. Commonly used to prevent unsightly static "cling," they are also good to use before you start working on computers. Some folks also use these sprays to try to protect their work areas from the effects of ESD, but this is not an effective or recommended procedure. Never use these sprays directly on your components!

 **Objective 3.04**   # Safety and Environmental Issues

Certain factors increase the risk of injury, both to the computer and to the tech. Some factors can be controlled, such as what you wear when working on computers, and some can't, such as the weather. You simply need to know and avoid other issues to stay safe.

Tech-Controlled Factors

Take control of the computing environment to minimize the risk of damage to you or to any computers around you. You make all the difference when it comes to what you wear and how orderly or disorderly the computer space is kept. Plus, you need to use the proper tool for the job at hand and, if anything goes wrong, report it properly.

What to Wear

What you wear, including your hairdo (I'm serious!), affects both the risk of electrostatic discharge and electrical shorts. Different fabrics have different electrical potentials. Wear natural-fiber clothing, such as cotton or linen, when working on computers. Don't wear silk, though, because it picks up static electricity. Definitely avoid synthetic fabrics. They have a tendency to *produce* static electricity. If you needed an excuse to give the double-knit polyester leisure suit to charity, now you have one! Finally, wear rubber-soled shoes rather than leather-soled shoes.

Keep your hair short or pulled back away from the computer. I've seen techs with long hair shock a computer by brushing it with their hair. That's never fun!

Rings, bracelets, necklaces, watches, and other metal adornments can short out devices if touched on the wrong part of a computer. They can also scratch (or be scratched) by scraping against the computer's surfaces. Remove jewelry and watches before working on or inside of a computer. Just remember to put your wedding ring back on before you head home to the spouse!

Control Those Cords!

A disorderly computing environment invites problems, so successful techs keep it neat. People place computers or peripherals in crazy places: on rickety desks, cardboard boxes, and other places where they could easily fall (see Figure 3.3). Arrange your computer and peripherals safely on the floor or on a sturdy desk. Tape or cover cords (using cable raceways or trays) running along the ground to avoid people tripping on them or accidentally ripping a computer off a desk—two very not-funny options. If you see a potential hazard at a work site—even one that's not yours—report it or fix it. You're the expert, so take charge!

Use the Right Tool for the Job

Whenever possible, use the tool designed to do the job at hand. This might seem obvious to most of you, but don't use a knife when you need a screwdriver. Don't use a screwdriver designed for large heads on small-head screws. Using the wrong tool for a job can cost you, both in time and equipment. Bleeding all over a motherboard you just sliced into would just add insult to injury, so avoid it!

FIGURE 3.3   Don't do this!

Heavy Devices

It seems that everything we use—computers, printers, monitors—comes to us in heavy boxes. Remember never to lift with your back; lift with your legs, and always use a hand truck if available. You are never paid enough to risk your own health.

Also pay attention to weight limitations when wall-mounting monitors. Even relatively light LCD monitors require a mounting arm strong enough to support them.

Incident Reports

When accidents happen—and they will—at the workplace, always provide an *incident report* that details the accident, conditions that contributed to the accident, and, if you know, the cost to replace the equipment damaged. A small company might accept a verbal report; larger companies most likely prefer a formal, written report. Be sure always to follow company procedures concerning incident reporting.

Environmental Factors

Proper environmental controls help secure servers and workstations from the environmental impact of excessive heat, dust, and humidity. Such *environmental controls* include air conditioning, proper ventilation, air filtration, and monitors for temperature and humidity. A CompTIA A+ technician maintains an awareness of temperature, humidity level, and ventilation so that he or she can tell very quickly when proper levels or settings are out of whack.

Dust and debris aren't good for any electronic components. Equipment closets filled with racks of servers need proper airflow to keep things cool and to control dusty air. Make sure that the room is ventilated and air-conditioned and that the air filters are changed regularly. This provides protection from airborne particles as well as heat and humidity.

Exam Tip

Ensuring proper protection from airborne particles encompasses devices and people. Put your electronics into the right enclosures with good air filters. Give your people good masks or air-filtering devices to keep those precious lungs safe.

Good techs keep up with weather conditions. Believe it or not, the temperature and humidity level *outside* can dramatically affect the risk of ESD *inside*. If the weather is cold and dry, the potential for a computer-killing zap is greatly increased. Take extra precautions to prevent ESD when the weather calls for it.

High-Voltage Equipment

The capacitors in computer power supplies and laser printers carry very high voltages that can cause severe injury if you touch them. Fortunately, manufacturers mark high-voltage equipment with a bright yellow warning sticker, making it easy to identify. Watch for these labels and heed them!

Further, any time you work with a piece of high-voltage equipment, make sure the device is unplugged and that you have *removed* your antistatic wrist strap.

Power Supplies

In the old days, the conventional thinking was that you should leave the system plugged in while working inside it to ensure electrical grounding. The opposite is true for modern computers, because modern motherboards always have a small amount of voltage running any time the system is plugged in, even if it's not running. Therefore, you should completely unplug the system before servicing or you'll likely toast something!

Unplugging power supplies does not make them safe enough to work on. The capacitors inside can hold a dangerous charge even when the unit is unplugged, making them extremely risky to open. As the label says, "No serviceable components inside." With that in mind, the safest method of repairing power supplies is not to repair them at all. It's better to dispose of them properly (as discussed in the "Special Disposal Procedures and Environmental Protection Guidelines" section of this chapter) and install a brand-new power supply.

Travel Advisory

As electricians will tell you, it's amperage (the amount of electricity) that's dangerous, not voltage. Power supplies have relatively low voltages, but high amperage. It's not worth the risk for you to attempt to service a power supply.

Fires

Thankfully, the risk of fire occurring inside your computer is relatively low. If, however, you do experience a computer fire, or any electrical fire for that matter, never try to extinguish it with water. This can cause the electrical current to travel up and straight into you! Instead, use a fire extinguisher certified for fighting electrical fires. These are type C and type ABC fire extinguishers.

Exam Tip

Make sure you know that you need to use a type C or type ABC fire extinguisher to put out a fire in a computer.

 Objective 3.05

Special Disposal Procedures and Environmental Protection Guidelines

Many computer components, such as batteries, CRTs, chemical solvents, and toner kits, contain harmful ingredients. Don't throw these items in the garbage, as this is wasteful and possibly illegal. Recycle, recycle, recycle! If you can't recycle an item, dispose of it properly. We all share the same planet.

Different cities and counties have different requirements for safe disposal of materials such as computer components. Always check with the appropriate authorities before tossing that old Pentium on the curb! Proper compliance to local government regulations is essential. Visit your city's official website for more information.

Exam Tip
Make sure you know the proper disposal procedures for each of the following items prior to taking the exam. Check the material safety data sheet (MSDS) documentation for handling and disposal of any electronic equipment.

Batteries

Batteries often contain lithium, mercury, nickel-cadmium, and other hazardous materials. If they are thrown in the garbage and carried off to a landfill, they will contaminate the water and soil. Take batteries to a recycling center or send them back to the manufacturer. Most batteries have disposal instructions printed on them. Familiarize yourself with these instructions and follow them.

CRTs

Many CRT monitors contain lead and mercury. Both materials are poisonous, so CRTs must be disposed of properly to avoid contamination. To dispose of nonfunctional CRTs, send them to a commercial recycler or contact your city's hazardous waste management department. They will give you the proper procedure for disposing of them.

Toner and Inkjet Cartridges

You have a couple of options when dealing with depleted toner and inkjet cartridges. You can refill them yourself, which saves on environmental wear, but this can wreak havoc on your printer if it is not done properly. You can also search the Web to see if commercial toner recyclers service your area. Alternatively, many toner cartridge manufacturers have a recycling program. Check with your vendor and see if this is an option for you.

Travel Assistance

Most cities in the United States have one or more *environmental services centers* that you can use to recycle electronic components. For your city, try a Google (or other search engine) search on the term "environmental services" and you'll almost certainly find a convenient place for e-waste disposal. Use these centers to comply with local governmental regulations on disposal.

Chemical Solvents and Cans

Chemical solvents or canned products for computer use (such as canned air mentioned earlier) contain harmful chemicals that should not be loosed in the environment. Instead, dispose of these through your city's hazardous waste program.

Material Safety Data Sheet

All batteries, chemicals, and other hazardous materials come with a *material safety data sheet (MSDS)* that documents any safety warnings about the product, safe methods of transportation, and safe disposal requirements. If you have any doubts or questions about how to handle or dispose of chemicals or compounds, check the MSDS. If an item comes without an MSDS, you can obtain one from the manufacturer, or you can locate one on the Internet.

Travel Assistance

For more information about MSDSs, or to search for an MSDS, visit www.msdssearch.com.

CHECKPOINT

✔**Objective 3.01: Cleaning and Maintenance Procedures** You should regularly inspect and clean your computer and peripherals. Plain water or a solution of mild soap and water does a great job of cleaning most computer surfaces. Canned air, non-static vacuums, and soft-bristled brushes help maintain a clean system. Electrical contacts get dirty from the oily residue from your fingers, so you should exercise care when handling components. Denatured alcohol is the best solution to use for cleaning drive heads and contacts. Keep fans and vents clean and dust free to protect a computer from overheating.

✔**Objective 3.02: Component Protection and Storage** A UPS battery backup protects your system against power sags, brownouts, and blackouts. A surge suppressor protects your system from power surges. Noise filters help prevent electromagnetic interference. In the event of a lightning storm, make sure you completely unplug the computer and any peripherals with external power cords. When storing components for future use, make sure to store them in a cool, dry place in antistatic bags or in their original packaging.

✔**Objective 3.03: Electrostatic Discharge Precautions and Procedures** To help protect your system from the effects of ESD, always use an antistatic wrist strap or ankle strap while working on the system, unless you're working around high-voltage devices such as power supplies and laser printers. Antistatic mats, floor mats, and sprays can also protect your work area from ESD.

✔**Objective 3.04: Safety and Environmental Issues** Wear natural-fiber clothing and rubber-soled shoes when working on computers. Keep your hair pulled back and remove excess jewelry. Keep the computing environment neat, but if accidents happen, file an incident report. The capacitors in power supplies and laser printers carry very high voltages that can cause severe bodily injuries. Don't touch them! Monitor temperature and humidity levels and make sure computing devices have the proper ventilation. Protect devices and people from airborne particles with proper enclosures and air filters/masks.

✔**Objective 3.05: Special Disposal Procedures and Environmental Protection Guidelines** Batteries contain nasty chemicals, CRTs contain lead and mercury, and even innocuous-seeming toner cartridges contain environmentally unfriendly chemicals. Always be sure to recycle batteries, monitors, and toner cartridges, or have them picked up as hazardous waste. Consult the MSDS documentation for every device and comply with local governmental regulations for disposal.

REVIEW QUESTIONS

1. Steve in accounting was rearranging his cubicle and knocked his new monitor off the side of the desk, breaking the frame and cracking the screen. As the tech on site, what should you do?

   A. Clean up and quietly replace the monitor so Steve can get back towork.

   B. Prepare an incident report to send to your supervisor.

   C. Prepare an accident report to send to your supervisor.

   D. Start yelling at Steve so everyone knows it wasn't your fault.

2. After wiping down your keyboard with a mild cleaning solution, what should you do?

   A. Use canned air to dry it out.

   B. Use antistatic spray to give it a protective coating.

   C. Use a pencil eraser to clean the contact pins.

   D. Let it air-dry for 48 hours.

3. Which of the following products will do the best job of completely removing the dust from your computer? (Select two.)

   A. Lint-free cloths

   B. Canned air

   C. Non-static vacuums

   D. Paint brushes

4. What type of fire extinguisher should you use to put out a computer fire?

   A. Type A

   B. Type B

   C. Type C

   D. Type D

5. When should you always remove your antistatic wrist strap?
   A. When working around high-voltage devices such as power supplies and laser printers.
   B. When cleaning your computer.
   C. When changing a toner cartridge in your printer.
   D. You should never remove your antistatic wrist strap.

6. If you use an antistatic wrist strap with a prong, where do you attach the prong?
   A. To the grounding wire of a wall outlet
   B. In the slot of a wall outlet
   C. In a special hole that is incorporated into every computer case
   D. Into the back of the power supply

7. If you do not receive an MSDS with a product, where can you obtain one? (Select two.)
   A. The Internet
   B. The outside of the box the product came in
   C. The manufacturer
   D. Any good technical book

8. Which of the following should you avoid using on LCD displays?
   A. Distilled water
   B. Commercial glass cleaners
   C. Mild soap solution
   D. Vinegar and water solution

9. What should the conditions be like in the area where you store computer components? (Select two.)
   A. Cool
   B. Warm
   C. Humid
   D. Dry

10. What weather conditions are most likely to be associated with ESD? (Select two.)
   A. When it is cold
   B. When it is dry
   C. When it is hot
   D. When it is humid

11. How can you completely protect your computer in the event of a lightning storm?

    A. With a UPS

    B. With a suppressor

    C. By unplugging the computer and all of its components

    D. By turning off the computer

REVIEW ANSWERS

1. **B** Although it might be fun to yell at Steve, it's best to prepare an incident report for your supervisor.

2. **D** Let the keyboard air-dry for 48 hours before plugging it back into the computer.

3. **B C** Canned air loosens dirt and dust. Non-static vacuums remove the dust from your system.

4. **C** You would use a type C fire extinguisher to put out a computer or other electrical fire. If a choice on the exam is type ABC, that type of fire extinguisher can also be used.

5. **A** You should always remove your antistatic wrist strap when working around laser printers and power supplies. The wrist strap provides a connection from the computer to your body, and wearing a wrist strap while working on either of these components could cause your body to absorb extremely high electrical charges, which could harm or kill you.

6. **A** If you are using an antistatic wrist strap with a prong, the prong should be attached in the wire ground of a wall outlet. The wire ground is the round hole—*never* place the prong in one of the slots because they contain electricity.

7. **A C** If you do not receive an MSDS with a product, you can obtain one from the manufacturer or you can find one on the Internet. Technical books won't have MSDS information, and you won't find it on the outside of the box.

8. **B** Commercial glass cleaners such as Windex will melt LCD display screens. Use plain or mildly soapy water or a vinegar and water solution to clean LCDs.

9. **A D** The area where you store computer components should be kept cool and dry. Computer components do not like extreme heat, and condensation could cause corrosion.

10. **A B** ESD is most likely to occur when it is cold and dry.

11. **C** The only way to protect your system completely in the event of an electrical storm is to unplug it and all of its components. Simply turning off the machine or using a suppressor will not fully protect your system.

Motherboards, Power Supplies, and Cases

	NEWBIE	SOME EXPERIENCE	EXPERT
ETA	5 hours	3 hours	2 hours

Certain core components live at the heart of all personal computers. The *motherboard* is the framework on which every other component builds; the *power supply* provides direct current (DC) to feed the hungry motherboard and components; the *case* or *system unit* holds it all together. Every good tech needs to understand these building blocks and their common variants.

 **Objective 4.01** # Motherboards

Every device in your computer connects directly or indirectly to the motherboard. The motherboard, in essence, defines the type of computer you have.

Local Lingo
System boards, mobos   Many techs call motherboards *system boards* or *mobos*.

Manufacturers decide three things when creating a new motherboard. First, they select the set of chips—appropriately called the *chipset*—that supports everything that plugs into the motherboard. Second, they select a *form factor* that defines the size and shape, among other things. Finally, manufacturers decide which connectors to include for internal and external devices.

This section looks at the chipsets, form factors, and connections available on motherboards. It wraps up with notes on installation and troubleshooting.

Chipsets

The chipset determines what type of processor the motherboard accepts and which internal and external devices it supports. For older systems, the chipset determines how much and what kind of random access memory (RAM) a system can accept. The system *read-only memory (ROM)* chip provides part of the *basic input-output system (BIOS)* for the chipset, but only a bare-bones, generic level of support. The chipset still needs drivers (loaded from a CD or downloaded from the manufacturer's website) to support the rest of its capabilities. Three companies make the vast majority of computer chipsets: Intel, NVIDIA, and AMD.

Travel Assistance

Chapter 7 covers the system BIOS—both traditional and more recent UEFI variations—and the system ROM chip in detail.

Travel Advisory

Like most devices, motherboards ship with dated drivers. Smart techs download updated drivers from the manufacturer's website.

In today's marketplace, chipsets come in three distinct configurations: traditional, modern, and post-modern.

Traditional Chipsets

The oldest configuration of the chipset consists of two chips: the northbridge and the southbridge (see Figure 4.1). The *northbridge* connects the CPU to the fastest devices. The northbridge is connected to the *southbridge*, which, in turn, connects to lower-speed devices. Intel likes to call the northbridge the Memory Controller Hub (MCH) and the southbridge the I/O Controller Hub (ICH), but different vendors use different terms for the chips.

The northbridge helps the CPU work with RAM and the video card. The northbridge does a lot of work, so it has its own heatsink and fan assembly (see Figure 4.2).

Travel Assistance

Chapter 5 covers CPUs in detail.

The southbridge handles some expansion devices and data storage drives. Most southbridge chips don't need more than a heatsink for cooling. This makes the southbridge a great place to read the chipset's manufacturer (see Figure 4.3).

Some motherboard manufacturers add a third chip called the *super I/O chip* (see Figure 4.4) to handle older legacy devices that were once the southbridge's job. The super I/O chip isn't part of the chipset, but they do collaborate.

Northbridge

Southbridge

FIGURE 4.1 Northbridge and southbridge

Northbridge with heatsink and fan

FIGURE 4.2 Heatsink and fan on a northbridge

FIGURE 4.3 An Intel Corporation southbridge chip on a motherboard

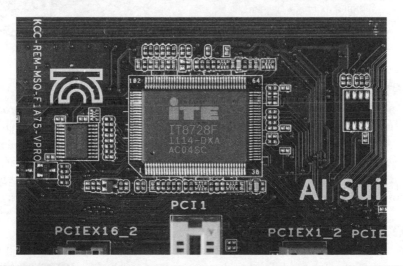

FIGURE 4.4 Super I/O chip on an ASUS motherboard

Modern Chipsets

When processor makers moved the memory controller onto the CPU, the northbridge no longer had to communicate with the RAM. This changed its duties to communicating with the video card(s) and the southbridge. AMD adopted this configuration in 2003, and Intel switched in 2008. In the process, Intel further refined its terminology, calling the northbridge simply the *I/O Hub (IOH)*, since the memory controller was no longer located on the chip; Intel refers to the southbridge as the *Legacy I/O Controller Hub.*

Post-Modern Chipsets

Current CPUs incorporate both the memory controller and the video interface, eliminating the need for a northbridge chip altogether. As you should expect by now, Intel has another new name for the lonely southbridge: the *Platform Controller Hub (PCH)*; AMD calls it the *Fusion Controller Hub (FCH).*

Exam Tip

For some reason, CompTIA doesn't follow chipset development closely. Be sure you can identify and explain the function of various chipsets on both older and more current motherboards. Know the differences between the norhtbridge and southbridge chipsets. Also, look for split terms: North Bridge and South Bridge.

Motherboard Form Factors

Most motherboards come in two form factors, ATX or ITX, though you'll probably see proprietary form factors as well. Each form factor has a few varieties.

A form factor defines the motherboard's size, orientation, location of built-in sockets and expansion slots, and so on. Form factors are not interchangeable, and they determine the type of power supply and case a computer can use; ATX motherboards fit into ATX cases, and ITX motherboards fit into ITX cases.

ATX

In 1995, Intel introduced the ATX motherboard form factor (see Figure 4.5) to replace the aging AT form factor originally developed by IBM. The ATX form factor rearranged expansion slots, CPU, and RAM for easier access and enhanced performance, and to prevent long expansion cards from colliding with the CPU (a common problem in AT systems).

RAM

CPU

Power

I/O ports

Expansion slots

FIGURE 4.5   ATX motherboard

ATX motherboards collect ports for built-in peripherals at an I/O panel on the back of the case. A sheet metal *I/O shield* with cutouts and labels for the ports typically covers any unused space.

There have been several revisions of the ATX standards over the years. The more notable changes are new power connectors for modern, power-hungry motherboards, and updated recommendations for power supply fans and airflow.

Two ATX variations are *microATX* and *FlexATX* (though FlexATX is long gone). These share the power connectors and basic layout with ATX but are scaled for much smaller cases. Full-size ATX motherboards will not fit into microATX or FlexATX cases, though most full-size cases support the smaller motherboards.

ITX

VIA Technologies created the standard for the current leader in *small form factor (SFF)* motherboards: ITX. Although the full-size ITX design flopped, VIA created smaller form factors that fared better: Mini-ITX, Nano-ITX, and Pico-ITX.

Mini-ITX is the largest and the most popular, and at a miniscule 6.7 inches square, it competes with the much larger microATX (see Figure 4.6). For comparison, microATX motherboards are 9.6 inches square.

If you think that's small, *Nano-ITX* at 4.7 inches square and *Pico-ITX* at 3.8 by 2.8 inches are even smaller. These tiny motherboard form factors are commonly used for embedded systems and specialized devices such as routers.

> ### Exam Tip
>
> Motherboard form factors you'll see on the 901 exam include ATX, microATX, Mini-ITX, and ITX.

FIGURE 4.6   Mini-ITX

Proprietary Form Factors

Several major computer makers, including Dell and Sony, make *proprietary* motherboards just for their own cases, enabling them to create systems that stand out from the generic ones and push you to get services and upgrades from authorized dealers. One feature you'll see in proprietary systems is a special *riser card* (see Figure 4.7), also called a *daughterboard*—part of a motherboard separate from the main one, but connected by a cable of some sort. The other feature is unique power connections. Proprietary motherboards drive techs crazy because replacement parts tend to cost more and are not readily available.

Motherboard Connections

Motherboards come with connectors for literally dozens of devices—from the core components of CPU and memory, to sophisticated high-speed networking. You've already seen the most common integrated I/O ports in Chapter 2, which covered keyboard, mouse, video, audio, multimedia, MIDI/joystick, modem, network, eSATA, USB, FireWire, and Thunderbolt ports. Four of the next five chapters of this book cover the rest—CPU, RAM, data storage, and expansion slots—so there's no reason to go through these in detail here.

FIGURE 4.7   Riser card on an older motherboard

When you recommend upgrades, you must address one question: Can the hardware do what your client wants? If your client wants to play the latest games, you need to evaluate the system and determine its capability. Can it handle a better CPU? How much RAM does the processor or chipset support? Narrow it down; then inform your client of the options, costs, and benefits.

Travel Advisory

Protect the motherboard from electrostatic discharge (ESD) by wearing an ESD wrist strap properly affixed to the case or power supply.

Installing a Motherboard

Let's walk through replacing a motherboard—it's not as hard as it sounds. You'll probably have to swap the existing I/O shield with one that came with the new motherboard to get started. Second, adjust the standouts on the case to align all of them with the motherboard's mounting holes. Third, angle the motherboard into the I/O shield (see Figure 4.8) and screw it down snugly. Assuming the CPU and RAM are already installed, you're ready to plug in the power

FIGURE 4.8   Installing a motherboard (note spare I/O shield)

connectors, storage devices, expansion cards, any fans that need to connect to the motherboard, and the front panel connections for the case. The next section of this chapter covers power supply connections, and later chapters will cover storage and expansion, so let's take a moment to discuss fans and the front panel connections.

Motherboard Fan Connections

Most motherboards support one or more case fans that plug directly into three- or four-wire standouts (see Figure 4.9). These provide 12-volt power and enable the motherboard to monitor the fans, so you'll get a warning if one stops spinning and a chance to shut down your system before it overheats. Use the motherboard connectors if you can.

Front Panel Connections

The last step is connecting the light-emitting diodes (LEDs), buttons, and front-mounted ports on the front of the case to the motherboard. The case usually provides wires for the following: soft power switch, reset button, internal speaker, hard drive activity LED, power LED, front- or top-mount USB ports, and audio ports.

These wires have matching pin connections to the motherboard. Although you can refer to the motherboard manual to determine their location, a quick inspection of the motherboard will usually suffice for an experienced tech (see Figure 4.10).

FIGURE 4.9   Two three-wire fan standouts

Wire connections labeled on the motherboard

The motherboard manual also tells you which wire goes where, but a few tips might help:

- The lights are LEDs, so they have a positive and negative side. If they don't work one way, turn the connector around.
- When in doubt, guess. Incorrect installation results only in the device not working; it won't damage the computer.
- With the exception of the soft power switch on an ATX system, you do not need any of these wires for the computer to run! Feel free to ignore them on your own system, but connect them for your clients.

Troubleshooting Motherboards

Motherboards can go bad over time because of external factors such power spikes and sags, electrostatic discharge, and excessive heat—or the damage might happen in an instant. A motherboard can be faulty right out of the box, too, so if you run into a new system that you have trouble getting to work, you can add the new motherboard to the list as a possible culprit. In Chapter 7 we'll look at how you can use the BIOS/UEFI interface to troubleshoot motherboard issues, so let's focus on what's left: rule out other components involved, and err on the side of replacing the motherboard.

Many of the classic signs of a *catastrophic failure,* such as smoke, pops, and burning smells, can point to either the power supply or the motherboard. Refer to the "Troubleshooting Power Supplies" section, later in this chapter; recognize these symptoms and, in a scenario where you experience any of them, check the power supply first. You don't want to connect shiny replacements up to a bad power supply. Once you know the power supply itself is good, the main scenarios you'll have to deal with are systems that won't start, devices that won't work, and intermittent instability or failures.

Exam Tip

It isn't a given, but sometimes capacitors—devices that smooth power by storing and releasing energy—will bulge when they fail, which the 901 exam calls *distended capacitors.* They're a clearly visible sign of a failed motherboard.

When the system won't start, a good place to start is to check all the power and data connectors, especially if the system has been serviced recently. If you have a good reason to suspect a specific component, try replacing it with one you know works. If not, disconnect everything but the motherboard's power connectors, the CPU, and the heatsink fan; then start the system, and listen for a successful POST beep code (see Chapter 7 if you need more info on the POST process.) If it works, add components back one by one until the system fails to start.

Travel Assistance

POST cards, discussed in Chapter 7, can help with the troubleshooting process.

When the system fails after you've added a component, or you're in some other situation where one or more specific components don't work, you can swap devices and connectors to narrow the culprit down to the motherboard, power supply, or a component. Try different connectors on the motherboard and power supply, disconnect all other devices on the same cable from the power supply, and try replacing the component with a known-good one.

Intermittent failures can be a real pain to diagnose, and a good rule of thumb is that when you suspect a motherboard has gone or is going bad, replace it. A computer must have a rock-solid foundation, and a buggy motherboard is simply not acceptable. That said, refer to the power-supply troubleshooting section, and be alert to the possibility that an intermittent failure could mean the power supply can't quite meet the power needs under heavier loads, such as intense gaming or video rendering.

Objective 4.02   Power Supplies

The computer's power supply (see Figure 4.11) converts high-voltage AC power into lower-voltage DC power for your motherboard and devices. Its internal fan also helps cool the components and drives. When connected to a properly grounded outlet, the power supply also provides grounding for all the other equipment inside the case.

In the United States, standard AC comes in somewhere between 110 and 120 volts, often written as ~115 VAC. Most of the rest of the world uses 220–240 VAC, so many power supplies offer a little *dual-voltage* switch on the back that enables you to use them anywhere. Power supplies that can handle different voltages are called *switched-mode power supplies* (though the "switch" in this case refers to the internal components and not the little switch on the back).

Exam Tip

The power connector for the AC plug on the back of a power supply is called an *IEC 60320 connector*. Also, look for the acronym *PSU*, for *power supply unit*, on the CompTIA A+ exams.

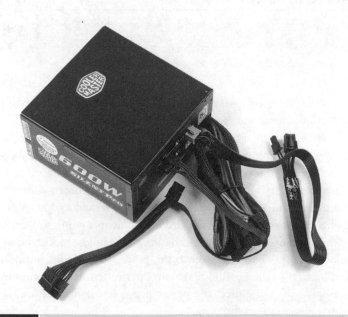

FIGURE 4.11   Power supply

Power supplies come in various form factors that determine the physical size, shape, and connectors. Power supplies also vary in output, efficiency, the number of 12V *rails* used, and how much power each rail can supply. While a *single-rail* power supply is usually enough for an average computer, high-end systems may need a *multi-rail* (or, as CompTIA says, *dual-rail*) power supply. In practice, avoid running too many devices off one rail in a multi-rail power supply.

Local Lingo

Multi-rail A power supply configuration where the current is split into multiple pathways, each with a maximum capacity and its own Over Current Protection circuitry. CompTIA calls two-rail versions of this technology *dual-rail* power supplies.

Power Supply Form Factors

ATX is by far the most popular PSU form factor available. Full-size ATX cases use ATX power supplies. Smaller cases that house smaller form-factor motherboards such as microATX and Mini-ITX may use smaller form-factor PSUs. Note that many manufacturers have created proprietary power supplies that come in all sorts of shapes and sizes (such as the one shown in Figure 4.12). They might not conform to the ATX power standards, and using one in a regular system can damage the motherboard and components.

FIGURE 4.12 Proprietary power supply

Power Supply Connectors

Power supplies offer many connectors; let's break them down into those for devices inside the system, and those for the motherboard itself. The device connectors you're most likely to see are *serial ATA (SATA)*, *Molex*, and *mini* (see Figure 4.13). Better power supplies have a dedicated six- or eight-wire *PCIe* connector for PCI Express video cards (see Figure 4.14).

Exam Tip	

The 901 objectives use the term *PCIe 6/8-pin* to refer to the six- and eight-wire connectors for PCIe video cards.

Power supplies connect to the motherboard with up to four connectors: the 20- or 24-pin (wire) *P1* connector, the primary power circuit; a four-wire *P4* secondary power connector, which typically supplies power to the CPU; and a six-wire auxiliary connector (referred to as an *AUX* connector) that very few motherboards use (see Figure 4.15).

Exam Tip 	

The 5-volt orange wire on the P1 connector is called *power good* and is used in the initial boot sequence. See Chapter 7 for the boot sequence.

Many modern ATX motherboards use an 8-pin CPU power connector, variously referred to as EPS12V, EATX12V, and ATX12V 2×4. Half of this connector will be pin-compatible with the P4 power connector; the other half may be under a protective cap.

FIGURE 4.13   Mini, Molex, and SATA power connectors

FIGURE 4.14   PCIe power connector

FIGURE 4.15   P1, P4, and AUX connectors (left to right)

Check the motherboard installation manual for recommendations on whether and when to use the full 8 pins. For backward compatibility, some power supplies have a version of this connector that can split into two 4-pin sets, one of which is the P4 connector. Although they look similar, the 8 pin CPU power connector is not compatible with the 8-pin PCIe power connector. Table 4.1 lists the common connectors of the *ATX12V* power supplies—the current standard—with their voltages and uses.

Exam Tip

The 901 objectives refer to the secondary motherboard power connector as a *4/8-pin 12V* connector.

Travel Assistance

Power connectors are keyed so you can't easily plug them in backward, but some older designs can be forced. Reversing the power on a device will fry it. Don't force a power connector.

TABLE 4.1	Power Connectors and Voltages	
Connector	**Voltages**	**Common Use**
Molex	5 V, 12 V	Legacy storage and optical drives; some PCIe video cards and motherboards
Mini	5 V, 12 V	Floppy drives
SATA	5 V, 12 V	SATA drives
PCIe	12 V	PCIe video cards
P1 (20-wire)	3.3 V, 5 V, 12 V	Primary power for older ATX motherboards
P1 (24-wire)	3.3 V, 5 V, 12 V	Primary power for current ATX motherboards
P4 and 8-pin CPU power connector	12 V	Secondary power for current ATX motherboards
AUX	3.3 V, 5 V, 12 V	Auxiliary power for motherboards

Output: Wattage and Harmonics

Power supplies provide a certain *wattage* that the motherboard, drives, and fans draw on to run. That's the desired output. Power supplies also produce *harmonics,* the hum you hear when the power supply runs, that can cause problems if not controlled.

Local Lingo

Wattage   Wattage is the amount of amperage flowing at a specific voltage, usually written as $W = VA$.

A computer requires sufficient wattage to run properly. Every device in the system also requires a certain wattage to function. For example, a typical magnetic hard drive draws 15 watts of power when accessed (SSDs use less), whereas a quad-core Intel i7-4790K CPU draws a whopping 151 watts at peak usage—with average usage around 70 watts. The total combined wattage needs of all devices is the minimum you need the power supply to provide.

If the power supply can't produce the wattage needed by a system, that computer won't work properly. Because most devices in the system require maximum wattage when starting, the typical outcome of insufficient wattage is a paperweight that looks like a computer. The only fixes for this situation are to

FIGURE 4.16   Power supply secured in case

remove the device or get a power supply with more wattage. Today's systems require 500+ watt power supplies to function.

Good computer power supplies come with *active power factor correction (active PFC)*, extra circuitry that smoothes power taken from the power company to eliminate harmonics. Older and poorer power supplies without this circuitry should be avoided.

Most active PFC power supplies are *auto-switching*, meaning they can detect the voltage coming from the wall and adjust accordingly. You can use an auto-switching power supply anywhere in the world, from the ~115 VAC in New York City to the ~230 in Hong Kong. This is especially important with portable computers!

Installation Notes

Before you connect the power supply, you'll need to mount it inside the case with four standard case screws (see Figure 4.16). The only exceptions are some small or proprietary cases.

Troubleshooting Power Supplies

When power supplies die suddenly, the computer will not start and the fan in the power supply will not turn. In this case, verify that electricity is getting to the power supply before you do anything else.

Assuming that the system has electricity, the best way to verify that a power supply is working or not working is to check the voltages coming out of the power supply with a multimeter (see Figure 4.17).

FIGURE 4.17   Testing one of the 5-volt DC connections

The voltages supplied by most computer power supplies can safely vary by as much as ±10 percent of their stated values. This means that the 12-volt line can vary from roughly 10.5 to 12.9 volts without exceeding the tolerance of the computer's various systems. The 5.0- and 3.3-volt lines offer similar tolerances.

If the power supply provides no power, throw it into the recycling bin and get a new one. Do *not* open a power supply and try to service it yourself, because it contains dangerous high-voltage capacitors.

Power supplies that die suddenly are often accompanied by telltale signs. You might see smoke, or get a whiff of a burning electronics smell. You might hear a loud noise. You'll definitely get a dead system.

Power supplies require some load, like being connected to a motherboard, before they'll start. If you don't have a motherboard handy, you can use a dedicated PSU tester (see Figure 4.18). Many companies make these devices.

FIGURE 4.18   Power supply tester

Look for one that supports both 20- and 24-pin motherboard connectors plus the other connectors on your motherboard.

When power supplies die slowly, bad things happen to the computer intermittently. The computer locks up every once in a while, perhaps with a *proprietary crash screen* such as the Blue Screen of Death (BSoD) in Windows or the spinning *pinwheel of death* in Mac OS X. Or it takes two tries before it boots up in the morning. You might get intermittent device failure. Because a BSoD or pinwheel can have many causes, tracing a lockup to the power supply is tough. The key is the word *intermittent*. If you run into phantom problems, switch out the power supply to see if that makes a difference. Every tech should have a known-good power supply as a *field replaceable unit (FRU)*.

If you press the power button on a fresh build and the fans and indicator lights flip on but nothing else happens, you forgot to connect the 4/8-pin secondary power connector to the motherboard. Oops! Power down, plug it in, and then power up the system (and hope no one noticed).

Many devices use an AC adapter (see Figure 4.19) rather than an internal power supply. Even though it sits outside a device, it converts AC current to DC just like a power supply. Just because you can plug an AC adapter from your friend's laptop into your laptop does not mean you should; unlike power supplies, AC adapters are rarely interchangeable.

Make sure three things match before you plug an AC adapter into a device: voltage, amperage, and polarity. If the voltage or amperage output is too low, the device won't run. If the polarity is reversed or the voltage is too high, you may damage or destroy the device.

FIGURE 4.19   AC adapter

Objective 4.03 Cases

Cases come in many sizes, such as slimline, desktop, mini-tower, mid-tower, tower, and cube. Slimline and desktop models generally sit beneath the monitor. The various tower cases usually occupy floor space next to the desk. The mini-tower and mid-tower cases are the most popular choices. Make sure you get a case that will fit your motherboard—many microATX cases are too small for a regular ATX motherboard. Cube cases generally require a specific motherboard, so be prepared to buy both at once. A quick test fit before you buy saves a return trip.

Exam Tip

The six case sizes listed here apply only to consumer or workstation computers. Server computers come in several different varieties, such as huge dual-PSU behemoths and rack-mounted systems too slim to fit a normal expansion card. Chapter 9 covers other custom form factors, such as home theater PCs and thin clients.

The typical case has four screws on the back, two of which you remove with a Phillips-head screwdriver. This releases the side panel and enables access to the interior of the case. Panels slide into a slot, so they should fit snugly.

Vendors such as Alienware offer many colors and exotic body styles. More important, these cases are outfitted with details such as additional cooling fans or liquid cooling systems, high-output power supplies, cable management systems, roomier interiors, screwless body panels that require no tools to remove, and front-mounted monitors and controls for system performance.

CHECKPOINT

✔**Objective 4.01: Motherboards** All motherboards have a chipset. Traditional chipsets are composed of two chips: a northbridge and a southbridge. The northbridge communicates with the fastest devices—namely, the RAM and the video card—and the southbridge communicates with slower devices such as the lower-throughput expansion busses, I/O ports, and integrated peripherals. In many recent system architectures, the CPU communicates with RAM directly, instead of relying on the northbridge—and in the latest architectures, the northbridge has been eliminated since the CPU possesses all of its functionality. The ATX form factor—including full-size and microATX—dominates the market. Mini-ITX is also quite popular today. Motherboards support literally dozens of device types through integrated I/O and expansion slots. Installation is a matter of placing standouts properly and screwing down the motherboard. Troubleshooting is tough, though, because of all the variables in the computer, but the fix for a bad motherboard is simple: replace it.

✔**Objective 4.02: Power Supplies**   The PSU converts AC power into the DC power your motherboard and drives need. Its internal fan helps cool the system and components. ATX power supplies plug into all ATX form-factor motherboards. You'll see many varieties of connectors on power supplies—Molex, mini, SATA, PCIe, 20-pin, 24-pin, P4 (or ATX12V 2×4), and AUX—for drives, video cards, and motherboards. Power supplies are rated in wattage, such as 400 watt or 1 kilowatt; plus, better PSUs employ active PFC to stop harmonics. Single-rail power supplies are enough to meet the needs of an average system, whereas dual-rail and multi-rail power supplies are designed for power-hungry systems. Power supplies die either suddenly or slowly over time. With the latter, the clue is intermittent problems. Don't try to fix a dead or dying power supply; replace it.

✔**Objective 4.02: Cases**   Computer cases come in six basic sizes: slimline, desktop, mini-tower, mid-tower, tower, and cube. Make sure you get a case that will fit your motherboard—microATX and Mini-ITX cases are not designed for a regular ATX motherboard. Cube cases generally require a specific motherboard, so be prepared to buy both pieces at once.

REVIEW QUESTIONS

1. What part of the computer is the framework on which everything is built?
   A. I/O busses
   B. Expansion slots
   C. CPU
   D. Motherboard

2. Which of the following motherboards are you most likely to see in modern systems? (Select two.)

   A. AT

   B. ATX

   C. Baby ATX

   D. MicroATX

3. If you have a computer with an ATX motherboard and case and you decide you would like to upgrade the motherboard, can you replace it with an ITX motherboard?

   A. No

   B. Yes, if you reset the jumpers

   C. Yes, if you add more screw holes

   D. Yes, if you remove the integrated ports

4. If you have a computer with a full-size ATX motherboard and case and you decide you would like to upgrade the motherboard, can you replace it with a microATX motherboard? (Select the best answer.)

   A. No

   B. Yes, if you reset the jumpers

   C. Yes, if you add more screw holes

   D. Most likely, if you move the standouts

5. What types of connectors attach the ATX power supply to a modern ATX motherboard? (Select two.)

   A. 24-pin

   B. PDC

   C. 4/8-pin 12V

   D. P9

6. Which part of the chipset traditionally helps the CPU work with the RAM and video card?

   A. SATA controller

   B. Northbridge

   C. Southbridge

   D. RAID controller

7. Mario bought a PCI Express video card. What type of connector might he need to plug into the card? (Select two.)
   A. Molex
   B. 24-pin
   C. 4/8-pin 12V
   D. PCIe 6/8-pin

8. Which motherboard type uses a riser card?
   A. ATX
   B. ITX
   C. MicroATX
   D. Proprietary

9. Molex connectors supply electricity to which devices? (Select two.)
   A. Newer hard drives and optical drives
   B. Older hard drives and optical drives
   C. Fans
   D. Thumb drives

10. A client notices the 115/230 switch on the back of a power supply you're installing and asks, "What's the switch used for?" Which of the following is the correct response?
    A. Powering computers in countries that run at a higher standard voltage than that used in the United States
    B. Powering computers in countries that run at a lower standard voltage than that used in the United States
    C. Powering server computers that need double the normal voltage
    D. Overclocking

11. In what circumstance should you open a power supply?
    A. You open a power supply for routine cleaning.
    B. If the computer suddenly won't start up, you can check and replace the fuse inside the power supply.
    C. If you see a flash of light or see smoke coming out, you should open the power supply.
    D. Never open a power supply. It's not safe.

12. Which voltages does a power supply provide through a Molex connector?
    A. 3.3 V, 5 V
    B. 5 V, 12 V
    C. 3.3 V, 12 V
    D. 115 V, 230 V

13. After installing an additional drive into a working computer, the computer won't power up at all—no lights, no spinning drives, nothing. What's most likely the problem?
    A. Dead hard drive
    B. Dead power supply
    C. Insufficient DC wattage provided by the power supply
    D. Insufficient AC wattage provided by the electrical outlet

14. ATX PSUs can be used with which form factors?
    A. ATX
    B. Pico-ITX
    C. Mini-ITX
    D. Nano-ITX

15. What feature do you find on better power supplies that eliminates harmonics?
    A. Active PFC
    B. Active scan
    C. Passive PFC
    D. Passive scan

REVIEW ANSWERS

1. **D** The motherboard can be considered the cornerstone of the computer. All your system devices are either directly or indirectly attached to the motherboard, making it the most important part of your system.

2. **B D** You'll find primarily ATX and microATX motherboards in modern systems. AT motherboards are old, and baby ATX motherboards don't exist.

3. **A** You cannot replace an ATX motherboard with an ITX motherboard using the same case. ATX motherboards go into ATX cases, and ITX motherboards go into ITX cases.

4. **D** Most full-size ATX cases support microATX motherboards.

5. **A C** Modern ATX motherboards use a 24-pin connector for primary power and 4/8 12V for secondary power.

6. **B** The northbridge helps the CPU work with the RAM and video card.

7. **A D** Some PCIe video cards use a Molex connector, although most require a PCIe connector.

8. **D** These days you're most likely to find a riser card on proprietary motherboards.

9. **B C** Molex connectors can supply power for fans and older hard drives and optical drives.

10. **A** When powering up computers in countries that use ~230 VAC, you simply flip the switch from ~115 to ~230.

11. **D** Don't open that power supply, because the capacitors can bite. Hard.

12. **B** Molex connectors provide 5 V and 12 V.

13. **C** If a power supply does not have enough DC wattage to power up the computer, you'll get a completely inert computer.

14. **A** ATX PSUs can be used with the ATX form factor.

15. **A** Active power factor correction (PFC) helps smooth out those nasty harmonics.

CPUs

ETA

	NEWBIE	SOME EXPERIENCE	EXPERT
	3 hours	2 hours	1 hour

The microprocessor, or as most techs call it, the *central processing unit (CPU)*, is what enables a computer to compute. Everything else on the computer can be considered part of the CPU's life-support system. So what does the CPU do? Move numbers. Amazingly fast. Today's CPUs add, subtract, multiply, divide, and move billions of numbers a second. Despite advancements in artificial intelligence, the CPU is more like a super-powerful calculator than some sort of machine brain on the verge of declaring, "I think, therefore I am."

These calculations drive everything your computer does: displaying your operating system (OS) desktop, processing print jobs, grabbing web pages, and doing everything else that you ask it to do. Of all the whiz-bang pieces of engineering that go into a computer, the CPU is by far the most impressive. The CPU has gone through many evolutions since its introduction decades ago, but even the most advanced CPUs still operate in much the same manner as the old Intel 8088 that powered the first IBM PC.

Today's desktop CPU market is dominated by two vendors, as shown in Table 5.1: Intel and Advanced Micro Devices (AMD). Intel's CPU offerings include the Pentium, Celeron, Atom, Core, Core 2, Core i5, Core i7, Xeon, and Itanium processor lines. AMD gives us the Sempron, Turion, Athlon 64, Athlon II, Phenom, Phenom II, FX, and A product families, and the server-oriented Opteron processors.

Travel Advisory

Over the years, other companies have tried to get into the CPU business, but the only other big player in CPUs is ARM, a British company that designs the CPUs used in many mobile devices, such as the Apple iPad.

TABLE 5.1	Current Intel and AMD Product Lines and Names	
Market	**Intel**	**AMD**
Mainstream and enthusiast desktop	Core i7/i5/i3	A-Series, FX
Budget desktop	Pentium, Celeron	Sempron, Athlon
Portable/mobile	Core i7/i5/i3 (mobile), Core M, Atom	A-Series
Server	Xeon	Opteron

The CompTIA A+ certification exams focus on what you need to know about CPUs to service business computers: enough about the internal components and what they do to make informed decisions and recommendations, how to install a CPU and its cooling system, and how to troubleshoot CPUs.

 **CPU Technology**

Modern CPUs are composed of multiple distinct components, and the variations among them can give you pause when you look at the price. Why is one Intel processor so much more expensive than another? How do you compare AMD and Intel CPUs? This section looks at components shared by all CPUs and variations in computing processes, and then it finishes with a discussion of technological innovations.

Inside the CPU

Ancient CPUs operated much like simple calculators, but modern CPUs have dedicated circuitry (see Figure 5.1) to process amazingly complex things. You can't fix any of this stuff, but it's good to know how processors work, because the knowledge enables you to see differences between CPUs.

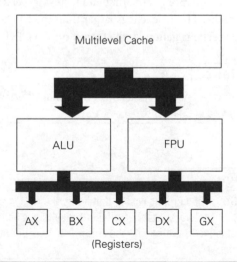

FIGURE 5.1   Inside the CPU

Arithmetic Logic Unit

The *arithmetic logic unit (ALU)* is the primary processing component of the CPU. The ALU takes data from the CPU registers, processes it, and copies it back into the registers before moving on to the next batch of data.

Registers

Registers are memory circuits inside the CPU that hold data before and after processing. In essence, the registers are the ALU's workbenches. Early CPUs in PCs used 16-bit or 32-bit, general-purpose registers; modern CPUs use 64-bit, general-purpose registers.

Floating-Point Unit

The *floating-point unit (FPU)* handles complex calculations for applications that require them, such as graphics programs and 3-D games. The modern FPU is integrated with the CPU. Ancient, pre-Pentium CPUs relied on a separate FPU chip, sometimes called the *math coprocessor,* to handle FPU mathematics.

Cache Memory

Modern CPUs have two sets of ultra-fast *static RAM (SRAM)* memory built in, called *cache.* Normal system RAM is called *dynamic RAM (DRAM),* because it can hold data for only a very short duration before it needs to be *refreshed—* ensuring a 1 stays a 1 rather than draining to become a 0. (It's all just binary, after all!) SRAM is much faster than DRAM because it never needs refreshing. The *Level 1 (L1)* cache memory is the first and fastest. *Level 2 (L2)* cache memory is the second cache. The L2 cache is larger than the L1 cache and is usually slower. *Level 3 (L3)* cache is generally the largest on the CPU.

Travel Assistance

The dominant DRAM technology these days, *synchronous DRAM (SDRAM),* is discussed in Chapter 6.

Local Lingo

Package and die   The ceramic casing that holds the CPU is called the *package.* The silicon wafer that has all the transistors is called the *die.* Components incorporated into the silicon, such as L2 cache memory, are *on-die.*

Multicore cache configuration

Cache design is critical in multicore processors. Each core has its own L1 cache. In some configurations, the L2 cache is shared by all cores; in other configurations, each core also has its own L2 cache and an L3 cache is shared among cores (see Figure 5.2).

Since SRAM is so much faster, why don't computers use it for system RAM instead of SDRAM? The answer is simple: cost. SRAM is roughly 10 times more expensive than SDRAM.

Address Space

The number of wires on the address bus defines the maximum RAM a CPU can theoretically address. This is called the *address space*. With a 32-bit address bus, for example, the most memory the CPU can address is 2^{32}, or 4,294,967,296 bytes (4GB). Modern CPUs with larger address busses can support substantially more than 4GB of RAM; see "64-Bit Processors," later in this chapter, for more.

Concepts

You can use a few concepts and terms to help judge quickly which make and model fits your client's needs. Specifically, the pipeline, clock speed, and clock multipliers indicate the caliber of the CPU.

Pipeline

The discrete steps the CPU follows to process commands is its *pipeline*. Think of a pipeline in terms of doing laundry, which follows an ordered series of steps: wash, dry, iron, and hang up. You don't have to wait until the first load of laundry is done to start the second—you just have to wait for the washer. This is the basic concept behind pipelining: multiple instructions are in flight at once in a pipelined processor.

Early CPUs with a single pipeline could only process a single stream of commands at a time. When the CPU was working on a complex mathematical command, for example, the FPU might have been working hard while the ALU sat idle. Multiple pipelines enable the CPU to break down the instructions into separate streams to process simultaneously; current CPUs use many pipelines to process more commands at once (see Figure 5.3).

Don't confuse pipelining with simultaneous multithreading or multicore processing. Although pipelined processors can process multiple instructions at once, they can handle instructions originating from only a single stream, or *thread,* at a time. We'll look at the special circuitry needed to process multiple threads at once later in this chapter.

Clock Speed

The CPU clock speed, or *frequency,* tells you how many calculation cycles a CPU can theoretically execute per second. One calculation cycle per second is equal to 1 hertz (Hz), but nobody measures clock cycles in hertz. Instead, we use millions or billions of calculation cycles per second, respectively called megahertz (MHz) or gigahertz (GHz)—see Figure 5.4.

Two things determine clock speed: the maximum speed of the CPU itself and what the motherboard can handle. The CPU speed is determined by the manufacturer and set at the factory. The *system crystal*—a quartz crystal circuit that oscillates at a fixed frequency when fed current—sets the motherboard's clock speed.

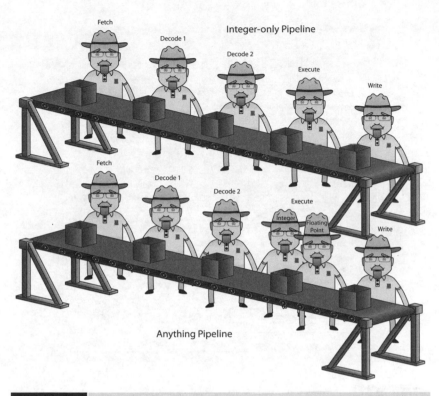

Integer-only Pipeline

Anything Pipeline

FIGURE 5.3 Multiple pipelines

Multipliers

Modern CPUs run at a multiple of the system clock speed. The system bus on my 3.4-GHz Core i7 system runs at 100 MHz, so the clock multiplier goes up to ×35 at full load to support the maximum speed. Early CPUs ran at the speed of the bus, but engineers realized the CPU was the only thing working much of the time; if they could speed up just the CPU, they could speed up the whole process. Note the CPU multiplier listed in Figure 5.4.

Old motherboards used jumpers to set the system bus speed and clock multiplier, but today's CPUs report to the motherboard via *CPUID (CPU identifier)* so the system bus speed and multiplier can be set automatically. Many motherboards offer manual configuration for tweaking systems; see the "Overclocking" section, later in this chapter, for more detail.

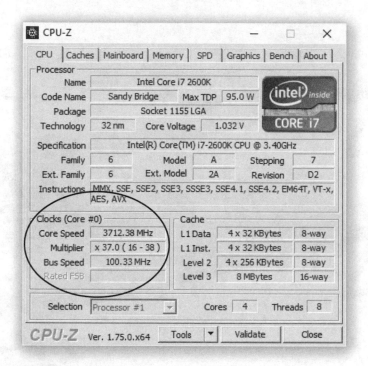

CPU Packages

All current CPUs come in a square package called a *pin grid array (PGA)*, like that shown in Figure 5.5, but variations exist within and among manufacturers. Collectively, Intel and AMD have used close to 100 variations of the PGA package over the years for hundreds of different CPU models with names such as staggered-PGA, micro-PGA, ball grid array (or BGA, which uses tiny balls instead of pins), and land grid array (which uses flat pads instead of pins).

Many varieties of the PGA CPU are based on the number of pins sticking out of the CPU. These CPUs snap into special matching sockets on the motherboard.

To make CPU insertion and removal easier, these *zero insertion force (ZIF) sockets* hold the CPU in place with a small arm on the side of the socket (see Figure 5.6) or a cage that fits over it. ZIF sockets are easily identified by their squarish shape. Most modern Intel sockets have official names such as

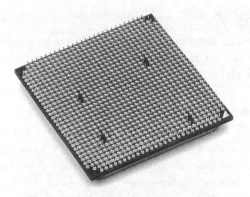

FIGURE 5.5   Typical PGA CPU

"Socket T," but they are usually referred to by names such as "Socket LGA 775" that reflect the number of pins it accepts. AMD's latest sockets go by names such as "Socket AM3" and are generally not referred to by the number of pins on the CPU or in the socket.

FIGURE 5.6   ZIF socket (arm up)

Variations

Several innovations have created a great divide between high-end CPUs and all the rest. Technology innovations include Hyper-Threading, 64-bit processors, multicore CPUs, and mobile CPU varieties.

Hyper-Threading

CPUs can handle multiple *processes*—opening a file, playing an MP3, and so on—nearly simultaneously by switching rapidly back and forth between *threads,* the subunits that make up a process. Many processes have only one thread, but some processes have many threads.

Hyper-Threading Technology is Intel's implementation of *simultaneous multithreading,* which executes multiple threads simultaneously on a single processor core to increase performance. A multithreaded processor looks like more than one CPU to the OS, but it's limited by having just one set of CPU resources.

64-Bit Processors

The address and general-purpose registers in a 64-bit CPU are typically 64 bits wide and can access tons more memory than a 32-bit CPU. Whereas 32-bit CPUs can only allocate 4 GB of RAM to a process, 64-bit CPUs already support hundreds of terabytes of RAM even though they're using just a fraction of what they can theoretically support. In practical terms, this greatly enhances the performance of programs such as video editors that work with huge files. Most new CPUs are 64 bit, and 64-bit CPUs are even increasingly common in smartphones.

> ### Local Lingo
>
> **x64**   You'll also see 64-bit processors referred to by a poorly conceived marketing term: *x64*. This was meant to echo the *x86* used to describe traditional processors, but 64-bit CPUs are still x86 processors! Therefore, you may also see *x86-64* in use.

Multicore CPUs

CPU clock speeds hit a practical limit of roughly 4 GHz around the years 2002–2003, motivating the CPU makers to combine multiple CPUs onto the same physical processor die, creating *multicore* CPUs. Unlike Hyper-Threading, where a single processor core shares execution resources among threads, a true dual-core CPU has two discrete processor cores, each possessing its own resources.

The first batch of multicore processors combined two CPU cores onto one chip, creating a *dual-core* architecture, but today's CPUs often have four or more (see Figure 5.7).

Exam Tip

Intel i_series CPUs differ internally in very specific ways. The Core i3 CPUs have two cores; the Core i5 and i7 CPUs have four cores. Core i5 processors don't support Hyper-Threading. AMD CPUs are all over the map, so expect Intel-specific questions on the 901 exam.

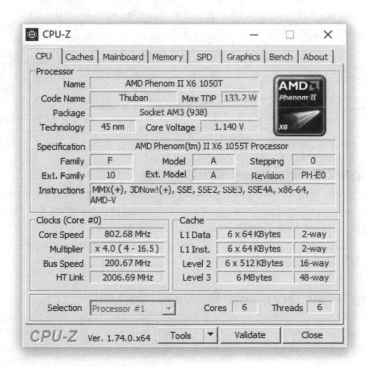

FIGURE 5.7 CPU-Z showing an AMD Phenom II with six cores

Mobile CPUs

The inside of a laptop is a cramped, hot environment, where no self-respecting CPU should ever need to operate. Since the mid-1980s, CPU manufacturers have endeavored to make specialized versions of their processors for laptops. These are called *mobile processors*.

CPUs made by Intel and AMD are often available in a mobile version that uses less power than an equivalent desktop model. This enables the laptop's battery to last longer, and makes it easier to keep the CPU and laptop running cool. Modern CPUs also use *throttling* to reduce processing cycles and lower clock speeds when temperatures climb or the system is idle.

Virtualization Support

Intel and AMD have built-in support for *virtualization*, a process that enables you to run one or more virtual computers on a single hardware computer. Early virtualization worked entirely through software. Programmers had to write a ton of code to enable a CPU designed to run one OS at a time to run more than one OS, but hardware-based virtualization enables the CPU to take on most of this burden.

Travel Assistance

If you need extra info, Chapter 14 looks at virtualization in detail.

Integrated Memory Controller

An *integrated memory controller (IMC),* located inside the CPU instead of on the motherboard, optimizes the flow of information into and out from the CPU. An IMC enables faster control over items such as the large L3 cache shared among multiple cores, but it also means the CPU you choose has an effect on what RAM you can use.

Integrated Graphics Processing Unit

Computers traditionally have a discrete special-purpose microprocessor designed for video processing, known as a *graphics processing unit (GPU)*. Because graphics processors handle some tasks more efficiently than a standard

CPU, integrating a GPU into the CPU enhances the overall performance of the computer and reduces its energy use, size, and cost.

Intel and AMD design their integrated GPUs a little differently. The *Intel HD Graphics* integrated into many Core i3/i5/i7 processors, for example, has the CPU cores and the GPU core sharing the "last level cache," which is either L2 or L3, depending on the processor. With the AMD *accelerated processing unit (APU)*, such as the AMD Fusion, the GPU has access to all levels of cache on the CPU.

Security

Modern processors use the *NX bit*, which CompTIA calls the *disable execute bit*, to protect sections of memory, helping the OS defend its critical files from attacks. Unfortunately, everyone uses a different name: Microsoft calls it Data Execution Prevention (DEP), Intel calls it XD bit (eXecute Disable), AMD uses Enhanced Virus Protection, and ARM uses XN (eXecute Never).

Exam Tip

Things you need to know about CPUs, both as a tech making a recommendation and for the CompTIA A+ 901 exam, include the following:

- Hyper-Threading
- Multicore CPUs
- Virtualization support
- 32-bit vs. 64-bit architecture
- Integrated GPU
- Disable execute bit

Recommending a CPU

For a workstation that works primarily with documents, e-mail, and the Web, *any* modern processor will do; save your clients some money and recommend a lower-end CPU. High-end processors earn their keep in 3-D modeling programs, high-end photograph and video editing, and 3-D games. Consider how long the client expects these computers to keep up with the evolving requirements of relevant software, and whether that software is designed to make full use of multicore processors.

Objective 5.02 Installing CPUs

For all the complexity inside CPUs, they're actually pretty easy to install, especially if you plan ahead to avoid a few issues. This section first looks at some common compatibility issues you'll need to navigate to know what CPUs work, then turns to the process of installing the CPU and cooling system, and ends with a look at overclocking.

Compatibility Issues

Since no processors work in all motherboards, you should check the motherboard's documentation (or its manufacturer's website) for a chart listing the CPUs it supports. Because Intel and AMD CPUs are not pin-compatible, motherboards made since the mid-1990s support *either* Intel CPUs *or* AMD CPUs—not both. The type of CPU socket that the motherboard uses (such as PGA) determines which model of Intel or AMD CPU you can install. Many motherboards accept more than one model of CPU. Likewise, some CPU models can fit more than one socket.

Tables 5.2 and 5.3 list the sockets and processors you'll find on the CompTIA A+ 901 exam, with the exceptions noted.

Travel Advisory

Tables 5.2 and 5.3 leave out many older or less mainstream products, so neither contain a complete list of what's in the field.

Exam Tip

Because the CompTIA A+ exam has had pin-related questions in the past, I've included the pins for the AMD sockets. Intel socket names are the number of pins associated with those sockets.

TABLE 5.2	Intel-based Sockets and Processors
Socket	**CPU**
LGA 775	Pentium 4, Celeron, Pentium 4 Extreme Edition, Core 2 Duo, Core 2 Quad, Xeon, and many others
LGA 1155[1]	Core i3/i5/i7, Pentium, Celeron, Xeon
LGA 1156[2]	Core i3/i5/i7, Pentium, Celeron, Xeon
LGA 1366[3]	Core i7, Xeon, Celeron
LGA 2011[4]	Core i7, Core i7 Extreme Edition, Xeon
LGA 1150[5]	Core i3/i5/i7, Pentium, Celeron, Xeon
LGA 1151[6]	Core i3/i5/i7, Pentium, Celeron, Xeon

[1] Socket LGA 1155 CPUs are based on Sandy Bridge or Ivy Bridge architecture.
[2] Socket LGA 1156 CPUs are based on the pre–Sandy Bridge architecture.
[3] The very first Core i7 processors used LGA 1366.
[4] Intel uses LGA 2011 for several generations of Core i7 and Core i7 Extreme Edition CPUs. Socket 2011 does not support integrated graphics. Plus, the retail version does not come with an OEM fan and heatsink assembly. You need to buy that separately.
[5] Socket 1150 CPUs are based on the Haswell or Broadwell architecture.
[6] Socket 1151 CPUs are based on the Skylake architecture. (Skylake is not listed in the 901 exam objectives at the time of this writing.)

TABLE 5.3	AMD-based Sockets and Processors	
Socket	**Pins**	**CPU**
AM3[1]	941	Phenom II, Athlon II, Sempron, Opteron
AM3+	942	FX
FM1	905	A-Series[2]
FM2	904	A-Series
FM2+	906	A-Series
G34[3]	1974	Opteron
G32[3]	1207	Opteron

[1] Though the names of some Socket AM3 processors match those of CPUs designed for earlier sockets, they're *not* the same CPUs. They are specific to AM3 because they support different types of RAM (see Chapter 6). Just to make things even crazier, though, AM3 CPUs work just fine in earlier Socket AM2/2+ motherboards.
[2] The A-series features integrated GPUs and other chips.
[3] You won't find the Opteron sockets on the 901 exam.

CPU Physical Installation

First, power down the computer and unplug the power cable. Put the computer case on your antistatic mat, if you have one, somewhere with enough room and light to work. Next, remove the cover from the case.

If you plan to upgrade the CPU, strap on your nerd bracelet to ground yourself, skip to "Installing the Cooling System" for steps on removing the heatsink and fan assembly, and then return here. If the motherboard isn't already installed in the case, it's easier to proceed with it on an antistatic mat. Different socket designs have different steps for CPU installation, so be sure to read the documentation for the exact procedure, but the steps should follow this general pattern:

1. Lift the CPU release lever arm (see Figure 5.8).

2. Locate the orientation mark, usually an arrow or raised dot, on the corner of the CPU and socket. Double-check the orientation by looking at the pin configuration—the CPU and socket should be oriented so any corners with missing pins align (see Figure 5.9).

FIGURE 5.8   Lifting the arm

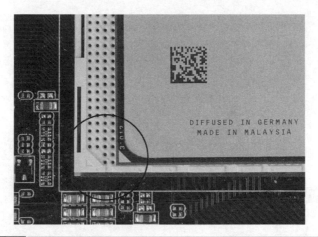

DIFFUSED IN GERMANY
MADE IN MALAYSIA

FIGURE 5.9   CPU orientation marks

3. Take the CPU by its edges, position it over the socket, and gently set it in place. If the pins and socket holes are oriented correctly, the CPU should drop right in without any force (*zero* insertion force—get it?). If the CPU doesn't fit easily into the socket, check the orientation and try again. A seated CPU package should sit flush on the socket mount with no pins showing.

4. Lower and lock the release lever into place.

If you install CPUs on a motherboard designed for multiple microprocessors, you should install them in the proper order. A single CPU goes into the socket for CPU 0, for example. Add a second CPU and you'd put it in the socket for CPU 1. Note that this applies only to motherboards that support multiple physical CPUs—what's called *symmetric multiprocessing*—not multiple-core single CPUs.

Now we can install the cooling system.

Installing the Cooling System

CPUs have no moving parts (that you can see with the naked eye), but they generate considerable heat. Excessive heat causes system instability, lockups, and dead CPUs. CPU packages are made from high-tech thermal plastics and ceramics that dissipate heat, but they still can't provide enough relief without help. This help comes in the form of *active cooling* via *heatsink and fan assemblies* (see Figure 5.10) and *liquid cooling systems*.

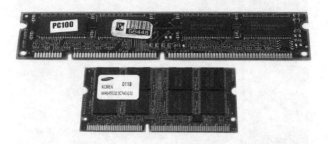

| FIGURE 5.10 | Retail heatsink and fan assembly |

Exam Tip

Some systems get by on *fanless* or *passive cooling*. Smartphones and tablets are the passively cooled devices you're most likely familiar with. Passive CPU heatsinks may still rely on other fans to create good airflow in the case.

Unlike the CPU socket, heatsink and fan assemblies take more force than you'd expect to mount properly! A small flathead screwdriver will help.

Heatsink and fan assemblies for PGA-packaged CPUs usually come as a unit; if not, attach the fan to the heatsink before installing both onto the CPU. Again, different CPUs, socket designs, and heatsinks require different installation procedures, so be sure to read the documentation. The general steps for installation are as follows:

1. If your CPU has thermal paste pre-applied, remove and discard the protective tape. If not, apply a very thin film of thermal paste to the raised center of the CPU package (see Figure 5.11).

2. Align the heatsink and fan's mounting bracket hardware with the mounting notches on the CPU socket.

3. With Intel stock fans, push the mounting pins in until they click in place. It's easy with the motherboard outside the case. Support the motherboard with one hand and push with the other so the motherboard does not flex.

4. For AMD fans, attach the mounting bracket to one side of the CPU socket.

FIGURE 5.11   Applying thermal compound

5. Rotate the built-in locking lever on the opposite side to secure the assembly (see Figure 5.12).

6. Finally, plug the fan's power cable into the appropriate socket or header on the motherboard. Check your motherboard documentation for information.

FIGURE 5.12   Secure the assembly with the locking lever

Installing a Liquid Cooling System

The essential installation steps for modern liquid cooling systems are similar:

1. Follow the manufacturer's instructions to attach the hoses from the coolant reservoir tank to the CPU cooling element and the heat exchanger unit. Confirm that all hoses are secure and crimped properly.

2. Fill the coolant reservoir with the recommended amount of distilled water.

3. Apply a small amount of thermal compound to the CPU.

4. If your liquid cooling system uses a separate CPU temperature sensor on the cooling element, attach it to the appropriate slot or groove and secure it with the supplied metal tape. Mount the cooling element to the CPU with the attached bracket and secure it in place with the tension screw (see Figure 5.13). Be careful not to overtighten the screw. You're ready to go!

Overclocking

Some motherboards enable you to adjust CPU settings manually by changing a UEFI BIOS setting, or using other software. Many enthusiasts practice *overclocking*: deliberately changing these settings to enhance performance. A successful overclock usually takes two adjustments: increasing the system's bus speed, and increasing CPU voltage a little to provide stability. Always do only one thing at a time, document your change, and then reboot.

FIGURE 5.13   Cooling element mounted on CPU

FIGURE 5.14 Using the clear CMOS jumper

In addition to the slight risk of overheating, unstable CPU settings can make the UEFI/BIOS settings unreachable. Most motherboards have a button or jumper setting called *CMOS clear* (see Figure 5.14) that resets UEFI/BIOS to default settings. Before you try overclocking, find CMOS clear and know how to use it.

Objective 5.03 Troubleshooting CPUs

CPUs are robust beasts that rarely have problems once installed. You're most likely to encounter problems with installation, although heat issues can manifest over time.

Installation Problems

Look (and listen) for these signs of installation problems:

- It's normal for CPU fan speed to fluctuate, but if it doesn't spin for more than 5 seconds or so, turn the system off and make sure the fan is plugged in correctly.
- If the fan spins but the computer doesn't boot, confirm the speed and voltage settings.
- If you hear a loud alarm a few minutes after booting, the system is overheating. Turn it off immediately and check for good CPU/heatsink contact and confirm the fan is functioning properly.
- If the system does not boot and the fan does not spin, confirm the CPU is seated properly and that no other components or cables have been unseated or disturbed.

Heat Issues

Excessive heat can seriously damage your CPU and other components inside your computer. The fan on the CPU pushes hot air away from the CPU and into the case, while fans in the case and power supply draw cool air in and force hot air out. Cables can impede this flow from the start (see Figure 5.15), or it could degrade over time as fans age and dust, dirt, and hair build up in fans, vents, filters, and heatsinks.

The warning signs include spontaneous reboots, especially on warm days with limited air conditioning; occasional alarms from the tinny internal speaker; lockups; and excessively loud fans. The fixes are easy: once you confirm new components work, secure cables out of the airflow; check fans and replace as necessary; remove dust and hair anywhere they collect.

Travel Assistance

Good fans make a world of difference to the user. No one wants a computer that sounds like a helicopter! I always install the largest, quietest fans a case accommodates. Bigger fans move more air at lower (quieter) speeds. Check out the "quiet fans" at one of my favorite online retailers, DIRECTRON (www.directron.com). I recommend Papst, but all the top brands listed (Zalman, Cooler Master, Antec, and Panaflo) produce excellent products.

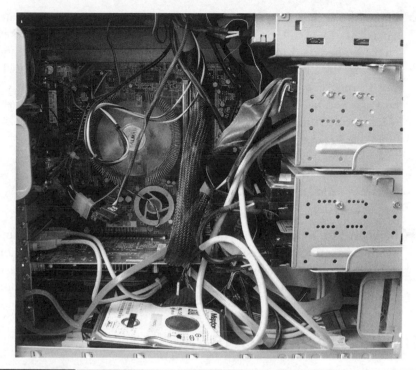

FIGURE 5.15   Messy cables

CHECKPOINT

✔**Objective 5.01: CPU Technology**   CPUs are composed of multiple distinct components; the ALU, registers, and FPU support processing; the L1, L2, and L3 cache leverage SRAM for quick data access. Modern CPUs use multiple processing pipelines and run at a clock speed that is some multiple of the system bus speed. Every current processor comes in some form of PGA package. Advances in CPUs include Hyper-Threading; 64-bit processing; multicore processors; cool, energy-sipping mobile processors; virtualization support; integrated memory controllers; integrated GPUs; and security features (disable execute bit) to protect the OS from malware.

✔**Objective 5.02: Installing CPUs**   Motherboards are made to accommodate a narrow range of CPU types. The CPU must be compatible with the socket on the motherboard. Installing a CPU is simple, but you must be careful not to damage the CPU pins or package. Proper cooling is absolutely essential. Use thermal compound between the CPU and the cooling element or heat sink and fan assembly. You can deliberately run the CPU faster than recommended through overclocking.

For the 901 exam, keep in mind the Intel and AMD socket types:

- **Intel**   775, 1150, 1155, 1156, 1366, and 2011
- **AMD**   AM3, AM3+, FM1, FM2, and FM2+

✔**Objective 5.03: Troubleshooting CPUs**   Installation errors and heat buildup over time are the two biggest problem areas for CPUs. Look and listen for erratic fan noise, silent fans, or alarms. Crashes and lockups on warm days are also good clues. To fix the problem, check your installation; replace your fans; and clean your fans, vents, and heatsink.

REVIEW QUESTIONS

1. Which component inside the CPU holds data before and after processing?
   A. ALU
   B. FPU
   C. Pipeline
   D. Registers

2. Which component inside the CPU is the primary processing component?
   A. ALU
   B. FPU
   C. Pipeline
   D. Registers

3. What type of memory is an L1 cache?
   A. DRAM
   B. ROM
   C. SRAM
   D. VRAM

4. Which component sets the clock speed of the motherboard?

    A. Cache

    B. CPU

    C. System crystal

    D. ZIF crystal

5. What form factor do modern CPUs use?

    A. EGA

    B. SVGA

    C. PGA

    D. VGA

6. What function enables motherboards to set up BIOS for CPUs automatically?

    A. BIOS

    B. CPUID

    C. CPUNow!

    D. Processor ID

7. What technology enables a single-core CPU to appear as two CPUs?

    A. Dual-core

    B. Hyper-Threading

    C. Multicore

    D. Z-core

8. The Intel Core i7 is an example of what sort of processor? (Select two.)

    A. Multicore

    B. Hyper-Threading

    C. BGA

    D. SEC

9. Which of the following must you do to install a CPU successfully?

    A. Align the orientation marks on the CPU with the marks on the socket.

    B. Push hard to seat the CPU properly.

    C. Lift the socket arm to lock the CPU into place.

    D. Plug in the power cable.

10. Intentionally increasing the clock speed of a CPU beyond the manufacturer's recommendation is called _____.

    A. CMOS clear

    B. Overclocking

    C. SpeedStep

    D. Underclocking

11. John installed a new CPU. When he boots the system, it comes up for a few seconds and then shuts down. What could be the problem?

    A. John forgot to plug in the fan, and the CPU is overheating.

    B. John installed an AMD CPU in an Intel motherboard.

    C. John installed an Intel CPU in an AMD motherboard.

    D. John failed to raise the arm on the socket to lock down the CPU.

12. What should be placed between the processor and the heatsink or cooling element?

    A. Thermal compound/paste

    B. Fan

    C. Denatured alcohol

    D. Power supply

13. What is a CPU heatsink without a fan called?

    A. Integrated GPU

    B. Active

    C. Passive

    D. DEP

14. Which of the following is a valid Intel CPU socket type?

    A. FM2+

    B. L3

    C. LGA 1150

    D. AM3+

15. What do modern processors use to protect sections of memory, helping the OS defend its critical files from attacks?

    A. Thermal paste

    B. Disable execute bit

    C. Virtualization support buffer

    D. Active heatsink

REVIEW ANSWERS

1. **D** The registers hold data before and after processing.

2. **A** The arithmetic logic unit (ALU) handles the primary processing duties.

3. **C** The L1 cache uses SRAM.

4. **C** The system crystal sets the motherboard clock speed.

5. **C** Modern CPUs use the pin grid array (PGA) form factor.

6. **B** The motherboard scans the CPUID to set up BIOS automatically.

7. **B** Hyper-Threading makes a single CPU appear to be a dual-core CPU.

8. **A B** The Intel Core i7 is a multicore CPU with Hyper-Threading Technology.

9. **A** To install a CPU, align the orientation marks on the CPU with the marks on the socket.

10. **B** Although you might need to use the CMOS clear jumper in case it fails, *overclocking* is the term for cranking up your CPU speed.

11. **A** Starting and closing down at boot is a classic sign of overheating. Plug in that fan!

12. **A** Thermal compound/paste should be applied to the processor before installing the heatsink or cooling element.

13. **C** Some systems get by on *fanless* or *passive cooling.* Passive CPU heatsinks may still rely on other fans to create good airflow in the case.

14. **C** Intel CPU socket types you need to know for the exam include LGA 775, 1155, 1156, 1366, 1150, and 2011.

15. **B** Modern processors use the *NX bit,* which CompTIA calls the *disable execute bit,* to protect sections of memory, helping the OS defend its critical files from attacks.

RAM

ETA	NEWBIE	SOME EXPERIENCE	EXPERT
	1.5 hours	1 hour	45 minutes

Computer users are curious people, and before long one of them is going to ask you, the learned tech, "Where are programs stored as they run?" Without hesitation, you might answer, "In system RAM, of course!" If you're like most techs, you might continue to talk about how random access memory (RAM) works until her eyes glaze over and she asks you to go away.

Many computer users falsely believe that programs run directly off of the hard drive. This is rarely the case, because even the fastest hard drive can't keep up with the slowest CPU. Instead, programs must be copied to a super-fast medium that can supply the CPU with the data it needs to run an application at a speed it can use: this is the function of RAM. Launching an application loads the necessary files from the hard drive into RAM, where the CPU can access the data to run the program.

Travel Assistance

Technically you can use a hard drive or flash drive as *virtual memory* to expand available RAM—a process we'll look at in Chapter 12—but these devices are not nearly as fast as RAM, and it isn't quite the same as running a program from where it is stored on a hard drive.

In this chapter, you'll learn how to identify types of RAM, how to handle RAM safely, how to install RAM correctly, what to look for when you suspect a RAM error, and what steps you can take to correct RAM errors.

Objective 6.01   RAM Overview

RAM was once a precious commodity, and even a small upgrade cost hundreds of dollars. These days, adding more RAM is often the best upgrade for a sluggish system. This doesn't mean that you can just grab any type of RAM; you've got to match the motherboard with the right type of RAM, running at the right speed. Manufacturers have produced RAM in many physical form factors (sometimes called *packages*) and technologies over the years. This section looks at several types of RAM, including those covered on the 901 exam.

RAM Form Factors

Manufacturers originally installed RAM directly onto the motherboard, but this took up too much room and made upgrading difficult. The next step was to put RAM memory chips onto special removable circuit boards, called RAM *sticks,* that fit into sockets on the motherboard. There's only one form factor you'll see in modern systems, but if you go spelunking in dusty old cases or printers, you may see single inline memory modules (SIMMs).

Dual inline memory modules (DIMMs) are the sticks you'll see these days, including a popular variant used in compact systems such as laptops and all-in-one desktops: *small outline DIMM (SO-DIMM).* DIMMs have 184, 240, or 288 pins; are 64-bits wide; and have a capacity of up to 32 GB at this writing. Figure 6.1 shows 184-pin and 240-pin DIMMs. Modern DIMMs have a *serial presence detect (SPD)* chip that identifies a DIMM's capacity, speed, and *latency*—the latter being a measurement of how long the RAM takes to respond to the memory controller.

SO-DIMM modules come in 72-pin, 144-pin, 200-pin, 204-pin, and 260-pin configurations. Generally, you can find SO-DIMMs with capacities comparable to those of their full-sized counterparts.

> ### Exam Tip
> You should know the most common memory module sizes: 168-, 184-, 240-, and 288-pin DIMMs, and 200-, 204 , and 260-pin SO-DIMMs. Note also that you see the latter written with or without the hyphen.

FIGURE 6.1   184-pin (top) and 240-pin DIMMs

There's one big exception to the DIMM form factor's dominance: on-board memory. More and more manufacturers are returning to the old ways of soldering RAM directly to the motherboard, especially in tightly integrated devices. You obviously won't have to swap out sticks in one of these; in fact, you generally cannot upgrade the memory at all.

RAM Packaging

RAM manufacturers produce an amazing variety of RAM packages. You'll find sticks that offer the same capacity, for example, but vary in number or location of memory chips. One stick, for example, might have four chips on the front and four on the back (a double-sided stick), another might have eight chips on the front only (a single-sided stick). A third one might be single-sided with only four chips, and a fourth, double-sided with 16 chips!

The rule on memory packaging is *never mix packages* if you can help it. It can lead to system instability in enough cases that a prudent tech picks uniform RAM sticks.

Exam Tip

Some techs say they've mixed RAM packages for years without problem, but mixing packages can cause *RAM compatibility* problems that you might see on the 901 exam and in the field.

Memory Channels

Current motherboards use multichannel memory configurations to increase memory performance. With a 64-bit data bus, DIMMs deliver 64 bits of data at a time. That's pretty logical! This is a *single memory channel*. Memory controllers can be designed to use two channels simultaneously, a *dual-channel* configuration. As you'd expect, *triple-channel* and *quad-channel* configurations use three and four channels, respectively.

In dual-channel mode, the memory controller's 128-bit-wide data path uses two DIMMs per bank. In triple-channel mode, the 192-bits data path requires three DIMMs per bank. On multichannel systems, the DIMM slots for a given bank are typically the same color. Use identical RAM sticks to populate a bank for multichannel memory modes. Always check the motherboard book for details.

Motherboards that support a multichannel mode can also run in the lower-channel modes, but you'll get the best performance using the highest mode the motherboard supports.

RAM Types

RAM comes in two forms: static RAM (SRAM) and dynamic RAM (DRAM). As you saw in Chapter 5, SRAM is faster than DRAM because it never needs to be refreshed. SRAM, however, is so expensive that it's reserved for special purposes, such as L1, L2, and L3 system cache memory. DRAM is used for system memory and needs to be refreshed every few nanoseconds (ns). During this time it is inaccessible to the CPU. This interval is called a *wait state*. Faster RAM has a shorter wait state. The paragraphs that follow describe the various types of DRAM you'll need to know for the 901 exam.

DDR SDRAM

Older motherboards support *double data rate (DDR) SDRAM,* usually referred to as simply *DDR*. Before we dive into the DDR part, it helps to know about its ancestor, *synchronous dynamic RAM (SDRAM)*. SDRAM ran at the speed of the system bus to improve performance by *synchronously* delivering data in high-speed bursts just as the system needed it.

DDR performs data operations on both the rising and falling edge of the clock signal, effectively doubling operations—note how the DDR Speed Rating column in Table 6.1 doubles the clock speed. DDR comes in these packages: 184-pin DIMM, 200-pin SO-DIMM, and 172-pin MicroDIMM.

TABLE 6.1	DDR Speeds	
Clock Speed	**DDR Speed Rating**	**PC Speed Rating**
100 MHz	DDR200	PC1600
133 MHz	DDR266	PC2100
166 MHz	DDR333	PC2700
200 MHz	DDR400	PC3200
217 MHz	DDR433	PC3500
233 MHz	DDR466	PC3700
250 MHz	DDR500	PC4000
275 MHz	DDR550	PC4400
300 MHz	DDR600	PC4800

Travel Advisory

The *PC####* that often follows the name of a DDR stick—such as *DDR 333 (PC2700)*—refers to the data throughput possible with that particular stick. A DDR 333 stick, therefore, has a bandwidth of 2.7 GB per second (GBps). PC2 refers to DDR2, and PC3 refers to DDR3.

DDR2

Improvements in DDR2's electrical characteristics enable it to run faster than DDR while using less power. The big speed increase from DDR2 comes by clock-doubling the input/output circuits on the chips instead of speeding up the memory itself. Speeding up the input/output and adding special buffers (sort of like a cache) makes DDR2 run much faster than regular DDR.

DDR2 comes in two packages: 240-pin DIMM and 200-pin SO-DIMM. DDR2 modules and systems are not compatible with DDR memory. You'll find motherboards running both single-channel and dual-channel DDR2. Table 6.2 shows common DDR2 speeds.

DDR3

DDR3 boasts higher speeds, more efficient architecture, and around 30 percent lower power consumption than DDR2. DDR3 uses these packages: 240-pin DIMM (slotted differently than 240-pin DDR2) and 204-pin SO-DIMM; neither will fit into a DDR2 socket.

DDR3 doubles the size of the prefetch buffers, giving its bandwidth a huge boost when reading contiguous data. Table 6.3 lists common DDR3 speeds. Many DDR3 systems support dual- and triple-channel memory configurations.

TABLE 6.2	DDR2 Speeds		
Core RAM Clock Speed	**DDR I/O Speed**	**DDR2 Speed Rating**	**PC Speed Rating**
100 MHz	200 MHz	DDR2-400	PC2-3200
133 MHz	266 MHz	DDR2-533	PC2-4200
166 MHz	333 MHz	DDR2-667	PC2-5300
200 MHz	400 MHz	DDR2-800	PC2-6400
250 MHz	500 MHz	DDR2-1000	PC2-8000

TABLE 6.3	DDR3 Speeds		
Core RAM Clock Speed	**DDR I/O Speed**	**DDR3 Speed Rating**	**PC Speed Rating**
100 MHz	400 MHz	DDR3-800	PC3-6400
133 MHz	533 MHz	DDR3-1066	PC3-8500
166 MHz	667 MHz	DDR3-1333	PC3-10667
200 MHz	800 MHz	DDR3-1600	PC3-12800
233 MHz	933 MHz	DDR3-1866	PC3-14900
266 MHz	1066 MHz	DDR3-2133	PC3-17000

> **Exam Tip**
>
> You should be familiar with the various RAM speeds.

To familiarize yourself with the many RAM standards and specifications for both desktops and laptops, visit www.crucial.com. Pay special attention to descriptions such as Module Size, Package, and Features. Be sure to check out the Crucial's memory compatibility tools while you're there.

> **Local Lingo**
>
> **DDR4**   DDR4 offers lower voltages and faster data rates than DDR3. Released in 2014 to support the (then latest) Intel Haswell chipset, subsequent chipsets also support it. AMD has been slow to adopt DDR4, but has some chipsets in the works. You'll inevitably need to work with DDR4 in the future if you haven't already, but you won't see it on the 901 exam.

RAM Features

Over the years, RAM features come and go. Some of these developments become essential and live on in all RAM, whereas others are created to meet special needs and disappear when no longer needed. Here are a few RAM features CompTIA wants you to know for the 901 exam.

Error-Checking RAM: Parity and ECC

High-end, mission-critical systems often use special *parity* or *error-correcting code (ECC)* RAM. These types of RAM use special circuitry to detect and, in some cases, correct errors in data. The older parity RAM used a dedicated parity chip mounted on the RAM stick that added an extra bit—the parity bit—to each byte of data. Parity checking protected early desktop computers from early DRAM's relatively high failure rate, but today's DRAM is so dependable that few computers still support parity.

ECC RAM contains circuitry that not only detects errors, but corrects them on the fly without interrupting system processes. ECC RAM is common on performance-enhanced workstations and servers.

Note that the computer's motherboard and basic input/output system (BIOS) must be designed to support either parity or ECC RAM; this support can usually be disabled in the UEFI/BIOS setup utility to use regular RAM.

Registered and Buffered Memory

Registered or *buffered RAM* has a small register (or buffer) between the DIMM and the memory controller that compensates for electrical problems that crop up in systems with many memory modules (that is, servers). Motherboards will use one or the other—not both.

Exam Tip

Look for questions contrasting *parity* with *non-parity*, *ECC* with *non-ECC*, and *buffered* with *unbuffered* RAM.

 **Objective 6.02**

Handling and Installing RAM

Proper RAM handling and installation procedures prevent damage to your system. In this section, you will learn the proper way to handle RAM, how to install it, and how to confirm the installation.

Handling RAM

RAM is extremely sensitive to ESD, so take precautions while transporting, handling, and installing it. Always store RAM in antistatic bags or sleeves when it's not installed on a computer, and keep it labeled with the type, size, and speed so that you can identify it later. Don't take a RAM stick out of its bag before you actually need to install it. Handle RAM by the edges, and avoid touching the contacts or circuits.

Installing RAM Modules

First, power down the computer and unplug it from the AC outlet. DIMM sticks fit into their sockets vertically. You'll note on the motherboard that the guide notches on the sockets match up to the notches on the RAM (refer back to Figure 6.1) to prevent you from inserting it the wrong way. Make sure that the RAM retention clips at either end of the socket are pushed completely outward.

Hold the RAM stick by the edges, position it above the RAM socket, and press it straight down into the slot with gentle pressure (see Figure 6.2). When the RAM is fully inserted, the retention clips will rotate into the retention notches on each end of the stick. Snap the clips firmly into place, and you're done.

Barring ESD, not a lot can go wrong. The main thing to look for is improper seating. If the retention clip doesn't engage fully, your RAM stick isn't inserted completely. Double-check the positioning, and insert the RAM again. If it doesn't go in easily, it's not in the right position.

FIGURE 6.2   Properly seating a DIMM module

To remove a DIMM, push the retention clips on the socket outward. These clips act as levers to eject the stick partially so that you can then pull it all the way out.

Confirm RAM Installation

Once you've installed the RAM, confirm that the computer recognizes it by booting up and checking the RAM count message or by looking in the UEFI/ BIOS setup utility (see Figure 6.3). Modern systems automatically detect the RAM size and configure the system accordingly. You rarely need to reconfigure these RAM settings. You can also verify the amount of installed RAM from within the operating system (OS)—in any version of Windows, simultaneously press the WINDOWS LOGO and PAUSE keys to bring up the System Properties applet.

FIGURE 6.3   Confirm RAM installation by checking total memory in UEFI BIOS Utility

Objective 6.03 Troubleshooting RAM Errors

When you encounter a "RAM" error, first determine if RAM is indeed at fault. If it is, you can pinpoint the cause and take corrective measures. The following sections list symptoms of false and genuine RAM errors, causes of errors, and how to correct them.

False Memory Errors

Several errors that mimic RAM errors are page faults, exception errors, the dreaded Blue Screen of Death (Windows) or spinning pinwheel of death (Mac OS X), a system slowdown or freeze, and the ever-popular spontaneous reboot. These are often tied to other factors, such as a badly fragmented hard disk, an overtaxed CPU, or faulty applications and drivers. Overheating caused by dust and dirt accumulating inside the computer case or a failed cooling fan is also a common culprit. Finally, a dying power supply can cause any or all of these random types of errors.

If you see a parity or ECC error, write down the memory address and wait for it to turn up again. If it's a *real parity error,* it'll be at the same address—if you have parity or ECC memory, that is; *phantom parity errors* may turn up on a system without any installed.

Common Symptoms of RAM Errors

The majority of genuine memory errors happen after you've made a change to your system's hardware and restart the system, at which time it goes through the *power-on self test (POST)* routine. Common startup errors include the following:

- System won't boot, accompanied by a loud, continuously repeating beep.
- System boots, but the display screen is blank.
- System boots, misreports RAM size.
- System boots, reports memory or address error.
- Continuous reboots after new RAM is installed.

Once you've found a genuine RAM error, you can determine the cause and take corrective measures.

Common Causes of RAM Errors

Genuine RAM-related system errors generally have one of three causes: a RAM installation error, RAM stick incompatibility, or a faulty RAM component.

Improper installation can mean you didn't fully seat or snap a RAM stick into its socket, or that some factor such as dirt, dust, or corrosion on the RAM contact pins or socket is preventing a good connection. Remove and inspect the RAM and socket for dirt or corrosion; clean as necessary. Then reinstall the RAM and test the system again.

If you install RAM of differing speeds or configurations (that is, single-sided vs. double-sided), RAM compatibility issues can create system instability. Some motherboards handle these differences; others have all kinds of problems (such as frequent crashes, system lockups, or unexpected shutdowns). If you mix different modules within a RAM channel (slots of the same color), it'll run at the lowest speed. This is easy enough to test. Pull out any non-identical sticks and see if the problems go away. If so, replace the removed sticks with matching RAM.

Faulty RAM is less common. Sometimes it comes out of the factory that way, but it's more likely that the RAM was damaged (perhaps by ESD) during transport, storage, or installation.

To test for bad RAM, replace it with known-good RAM and see if the error stops or recurs. You can also use the included Windows Memory Diagnostics tool to check your system for hardware memory errors.

CHECKPOINT

✔**Objective 6.01: RAM Overview** DRAM requires periodic refreshing, unlike SRAM, but it costs substantially less. SRAM is used mainly for the L1, L2, and L3 cache. SDRAM runs at the speed of the data bus and moves data in synchronized high-speed bursts. Current systems sport DDR2 or DDR3 RAM using differently keyed 240-pin DIMMs, though the DDR4 rollout is underway. To increase throughput, memory may be organized in multichannel configurations (dual-channel, triple-channel, quad-channel). The two most common styles of error-checking RAM are parity and ECC. Consumer machines usually run unbuffered RAM, though servers may use registered or buffered RAM to guard against power fluctuations.

✔**Objective 6.02: Handling and Installing RAM** RAM is very sensitive to ESD, so always keep it in an antistatic bag or package until you're ready to install it. Make certain that you orient the RAM sticks properly using the motherboard socket's guide notches, and be sure to lock the RAM into place. Following installation, confirm the RAM count during bootup.

✔**Objective 6.03: Troubleshooting RAM Errors** Many errors can mimic RAM errors. Genuine RAM errors are caused by improper RAM installation and faulty or damaged RAM. Confirm the RAM is properly seated and banked. With parity or ECC errors, write down the location and wait for them to recur. If you suspect faulty or damaged RAM, swap it out with known-good RAM of the same type and speed.

REVIEW QUESTIONS

1. Which type of RAM never needs periodic refreshing?
    A. SRAM
    B. DRAM
    C. SDRAM
    D. DDR SDRAM

2. How many pins does a stick of DDR3 RAM for the desktop use?
    A. 108 pins
    B. 186 pins
    C. 205 pins
    D. 240 pins

3. Which type of RAM is used mainly for cache memory?
    A. SRAM
    B. DRAM
    C. SDRAM
    D. DDR SDRAM

4. What is stored in RAM?
    A. Currently running programs.
    B. Programs that aren't running.
    C. Nothing is stored in RAM.
    D. Hardware information.

5. What is the purpose of buffered RAM?

    A. Improve RAM response times

    B. Improve RAM throughput

    C. Improve performance on low-RAM systems

    D. Improve resistance to electrical problems in high-RAM systems

6. What were parity chips used for?

    A. Error checking for RAM

    B. To increase the speed of RAM

    C. To increase the capacity of RAM

    D. To speed up Windows

7. How many bits wide is the data path of triple-channel RAM?

    A. 33.33

    B. 64

    C. 128

    D. 192

8. How many pins does a DDR2 SO-DIMM module have?

    A. 168

    B. 184

    C. 200

    D. 240

9. What's a simple way to test for faulty RAM that applies to all versions of Windows?

    A. Open all programs to see if the system will lock up.

    B. Watch the startup screen for memory error reports.

    C. Swap out the suspect RAM module with a known-good module and see if the problem goes away.

    D. RAM doesn't go bad, so this is not a legitimate question.

10. What feature of modern memory modules enables motherboards to support memory at the proper speed and latency?

    A. Virtual memory

    B. Spinning pinwheel

    C. Triple-channel

    D. SPD

REVIEW ANSWERS

1. **A** SRAM requires no refreshing and, therefore, incurs no CPU wait states.

2. **D** DDR3 DIMMs use 240 pins.

3. **A** SRAM is used mainly for cache memory because it's extremely expensive, but it doesn't need to be refreshed.

4. **A** Currently running programs are stored in RAM. When you start a program, part of the program is taken from the hard drive and placed into RAM to make access speeds quicker.

5. **D** Buffered RAM protects against electrical problems on systems with many RAM modules.

6. **A** Parity chips were used to check RAM for errors.

7. **D** The data path of triple-channel RAM is 192 (3×64) bits wide.

8. **C** DDR2 SO-DIMM modules have 200 pins.

9. **C** The best way to check for faulty RAM is to swap out for a known-good stick. Windows comes with a memory tester.

10. **D** The serial presence detect (SPD) chip on memory modules enables proper motherboard support for the RAM.

BIOS

	NEWBIE	SOME EXPERIENCE	EXPERT
ETA	2 hours	1.5 hours	1 hour

After you press the power button, your computer goes through ordered steps called the *boot process*. The vital components that drive the boot process are the system ROM, the system *basic input/output system (BIOS)*, and the *complementary metal-oxide semiconductor (CMOS)* memory chip and setup utility. The system ROM—for *read-only memory*—is the special memory chip that stores the BIOS programs. System BIOS is hundreds of tiny programs that tell your computer everything from what time it is to what *kind* of computer it is. The CMOS memory chip and the setup utility enable you to configure important aspects of your computer, such as the boot device sequence.

> **Local Lingo**
>
> **BIOS**   The term BIOS correctly refers to the traditional BIOS, but since the release of UEFI it has become a common catch-all term for traditional BIOS and UEFI *support software*.
>
> **UEFI BIOS**   Unified Extensible Firmware Interface (UEFI), covered later in the chapter, is the newest form of BIOS. You may see it (correctly) referred to as UEFI, but many resources use UEFI BIOS.
>
> **CMOS Setup Utility**   This book refers to the configuration utility for both traditional BIOS and UEFI BIOS as the *CMOS setup utility/program*, the *system setup utility/program*, or the *UEFI/BIOS setup utility*.

With only slight variations, BIOS and CMOS work the same on practically any computer. You will enter CMOS often as a tech, and the CompTIA A+ certification exams expect you to demonstrate an understanding of the system ROM, system BIOS, and CMOS setup utility functions.

Objective 7.01   Boot Process and POST

The three main stages of the boot process are power-on, *power-on self test (POST)*, and loading the operating system (OS).

Power-on/CPU Wakes

You start the process by powering the system on, sending current to the motherboard and drives. The power supply tells the system to wake up by charging a special *power good* wire on the CPU. The CPU then communicates with the system ROM chip and starts the BIOS programs.

POST

A computer literally rediscovers itself every time it powers up via the POST process. During POST, the system BIOS asks all essential hardware components to identify themselves. The devices—the keyboard, mouse, drives, RAM, display adapter, and so on—run internal diagnostic routines and report back to the BIOS. If a device reports an error to the BIOS, the BIOS alerts the user with special POST *error codes.*

Beep Codes

Beep codes vary by BIOS manufacturer, but some are common. A single chirp at bootup signals all is well. A long, repeating beep signals a problem with RAM. A series of beeps—one long and three short—usually points to a problem with the video card.

Numeric and Text Codes

Numeric error codes are somewhat standardized into certain code *ranges.* For instance, an error code in the range 100–199 indicates a motherboard error, and an error code in the 200–299 range indicates a RAM error.

Text errors tend to be direct statements, such as "Keyboard failure," that display on your monitor and may require input to continue.

POST Cards

POST cards aren't how you send snail-mail holiday greetings. Some hardware problems keep the system from communicating POST errors, but a *POST card* (see Figure 7.1) plugs into an expansion slot and displays which device the system is currently testing.

Exam Tip
A POST card can reveal how dead a system that won't boot is. If you see POST readings on the card, you'll know at least the CPU, RAM, and BIOS work and can check other settings or devices.

Loading the OS

During POST, the BIOS also locates the first bootable device in its boot device sequence. Usually this is a hard drive containing an OS, but it could also be a

FIGURE 7.1   POST card error code readout

USB device or optical drive. Once the POST process succeeds, the BIOS passes control to the OS. The process differs by OS, but one or more vital system files load into memory to start the ball rolling. From here, the OS loads its core files, drivers, and services into RAM.

Objective 7.02   System ROM

The system ROM chip stores the system BIOS routines and CMOS setup utility. System ROM is often distinctively labeled with the BIOS maker's name, but can also appear as a tiny chip near the southbridge (see Figure 7.2).

There's a big difference between system ROM chips and RAM: RAM is called *volatile* because it stores data only while the computer is powered. System ROM is *non-volatile* and retains data even when the system is not powered. Except for replacing the CMOS battery (described in the next section) if it dies, system ROM requires no specific maintenance.

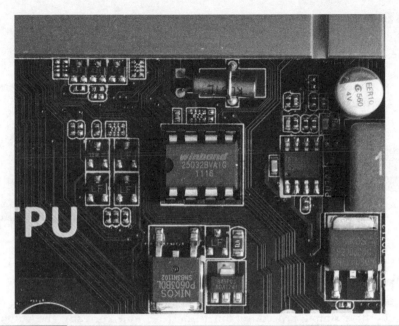

FIGURE 7.2   System ROM chip (center, labeled *winbond*)

Objective 7.03   System BIOS and CMOS Setup Utility

You interact with the BIOS through the CMOS setup utility. Motherboard manufacturers buy BIOS from third-party BIOS makers such as American Megatrends (AMI) and Phoenix Technologies (which produces BIOS under both the *Phoenix* and *Award* brands). In practice, this means BIOS software is all pretty similar.

System BIOS

System BIOS uses routines called *services* to initialize and support the many devices that make up a modern computer. Unlike most software, BIOS routines rarely change. BIOS makers update only to fix bugs and support new technology.

UEFI

The current BIOS is the *Unified Extensible Firmware Interface (UEFI)*. Here are the essentials:

- UEFI is often associated with graphical system setup utilities, whereas traditional BIOS is associated with text-mode utilities—even on the 901 exam. However, this isn't a given. You can find graphical BIOS utilities and text-mode UEFI utilities.
- UEFI supports booting to drives larger than 2.2 TB.
- Unlike with BIOS, the UEFI setup utility can be opened from within the OS.
- UEFI supports a security feature (discussed later in the chapter) called Secure Boot.

Updating the System BIOS

Techs refer to *firmware upgrades*, or updating system BIOS, as *flashing the BIOS*. It's a simple procedure, but it must be done correctly and without interruption: an interrupted BIOS flash usually renders the motherboard useless. Before flashing your BIOS, back up your important documents and update any system repair media. Make certain the process isn't disturbed once you start.

Exam Tip
The CompTIA A+ 901 exam refers to flashing the BIOS as a *firmware upgrade*.

Some motherboards come with a Windows-based utility that will go to the Web, download an updated BIOS, and enable you to flash the BIOS from within Windows. When it works, it's sweet. Otherwise, BIOS makers provide flashing utilities on their websites.

CMOS Setup Utility

The CMOS setup utility stored in the system ROM enables you to configure important system BIOS settings stored in the CMOS chip, which is built into the southbridge on most computers. These settings include CPU setup, boot

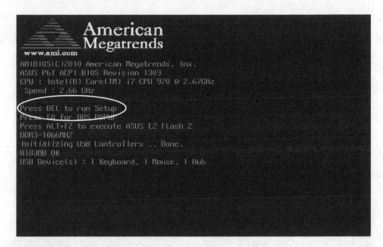

FIGURE 7.3   Each BIOS maker provides instructions for entering CMOS at bootup.

device sequence, power management, and a number of others, as described here. Every motherboard has a CMOS battery that enables it to retain CMOS settings when disconnected from external power.

Entering the CMOS Setup Utility

With a traditional BIOS, you can't enter the CMOS setup utility from within the OS; you must do it early in the boot process. Methods differ by maker, but instructions for entering CMOS usually appear on your monitor during bootup (see Figure 7.3). Watch the messages carefully or check your motherboard documentation on what to press.

Navigating the CMOS Setup Utility

Mouse-friendly graphical setup utilities are increasingly common, but if you find yourself in a text-mode utility, you'll navigate with the keyboard. Both interface styles typically open to a screen with information about your system, components, and settings (see Figure 7.4); this interface provides a good overview of your CPU, RAM, hard drives, and optical drives. Navigation instructions may vary but should be prominently displayed. Usually the ARROW keys move the cursor and the ENTER key makes selections. If you get stuck, press the F1 key to bring up a Help menu.

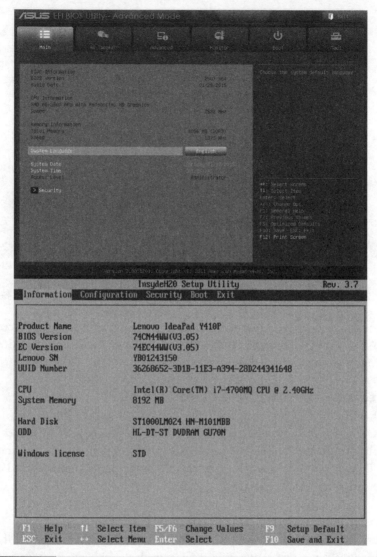

FIGURE 7.4 System information screen in graphical (top) and text-mode (bottom) setup utilities

Even though Figure 7.4 shows you can't count on tab names being the same on different utilities, there are still many common settings and organizational patterns that will help you find your way. Before we dive in, there are two more navigation features to keep in mind:

- **Save & Exit Setup** To avoid accidents, *only* use this option when you intend to make a change, and you're absolutely certain what the effect will be. Typically, selecting this option brings up a confirmation prompt such as "Are you sure you want to make these changes? Y/N."
- **Exit Without Saving** Exit Without Saving discards your changes. Choosing this option brings up another "Are you sure? Y/N" confirmation prompt. Press Y to take your leave of CMOS setup without doing any damage.

Travel Advisory

There's enough variety in how tabs, menus, and options are labeled in different setup utilities that you'll inevitably find yourself hunting for what you need. Common keywords in *italics* throughout this section will guide you through most of the time, but keep an open mind.

System Status In addition to information about your system, the setup utility often reports important *fan speeds, clock speeds, bus speeds, temperatures,* and *voltages,* which enables you to evaluate and *monitor* the *health* and *performance* of your *system* and *hardware.* You'll probably find related settings to *control* variable-speed fans and sound alarms or shut down when a fan fails or the system reaches a given temperature. These *built-in diagnostics* are often—but not always—grouped on a single tab (see Figure 7.5).

Components and Features Many of the *components,* ports, *peripherals,* and features your motherboard supports have *configuration* settings (see Figure 7.6) in the setup utility, though they're rarely all in one place. These options range from basic—such as setting the system date and time—to the intimidatingly *advanced.* Common options enable, disable, or change the mode for *chipset* features such as SATA, USB, wireless networking, integrated video, and more. Some components, such as the CPU, may have a sub-menu with an array of additional low-level features; for the exam, know that one of these toggles virtualization support, which enables the CPU-assisted virtualization feature we looked at in Chapter 5.

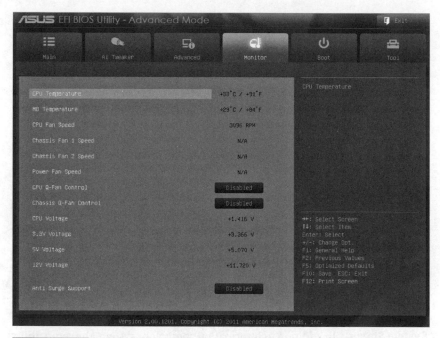

Version 2.00.1201. Copyright (C) 2011 American Megatrends, Inc.

FIGURE 7.5 Monitor tab in graphical setup utility

Exam Tip

Remember that there are CMOS settings for many components and peripherals; some day you'll be fed up with troubleshooting a feature that doesn't work properly or at all, only to find it's disabled or set to an incorrect mode in the system setup utility.

Security CompTIA wants you to know about several *security* options you might find in the setup utility, whether collected on a single tab (see Figure 7.7) or scattered about other menus:

- **Set Password** When a user CMOS password is set, the system won't boot without the correct password. A supervisor CMOS password restricts access to the CMOS utility itself.

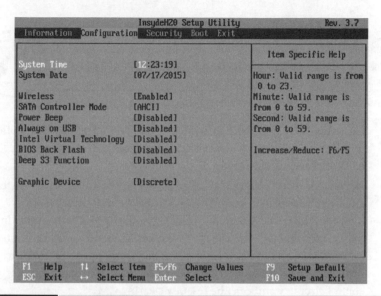

FIGURE 7.6 Configuration tab in text-mode setup utility

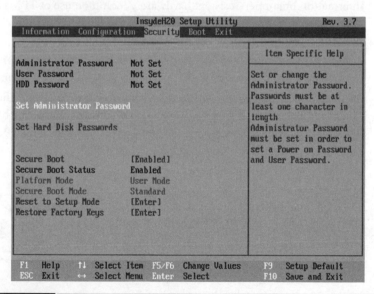

FIGURE 7.7 Security tab in text-mode setup utility

Exam Tip

Remember that CMOS settings—including passwords—can be wiped via the CMOS clear jumper or button, or by removing and replacing the CMOS battery.

- **Intrusion Detection/Notification** Most new systems have an option in CMOS that reports when the side of the case is opened, alerting techs to potential tampering.
- **DriveLock** *DriveLock* (also called *HDD/SSD Password*) uses master and user passwords to control access to a system's hard drive. In high-security mode, both passwords can grant access to the drive. In max security mode, only the user password grants access. The master password can be used to reset the user password, but all data on the protected drive will be lost. The passwords are stored in the hard drive's control circuitry and can't be reset by clearing CMOS.
- **Trusted Platform Module** The *Trusted Platform Module (TPM)* acts as a secure cryptoprocessor: a hardware platform for accelerating cryptographic functions and securely storing the associated information in tamper-resistant hardware. A common use of TPMs is accelerating and securing hard drive encryption, such as the BitLocker Drive Encryption feature of Microsoft Windows.
- **LoJack** If your computer is stolen, *LoJack* enables you to track its location, install a key logger, or even remotely shut down the system.
- **Secure Boot** Protects the system from some low-level malware and other exploits by refusing to load driver or OS software that hasn't been properly signed by a trusted party. Secure Boot requires an Intel CPU, a UEFI BIOS, and an operating system designed for it.

Exam Tip

Be familiar with TPM, LoJack, and Secure Boot security settings for the 901 exam.

Boot The *boot* (see Figure 7.8) or *startup* options hold one of the most-changed settings in the setup utility: the *boot device sequence*. This setting decides which devices your system will attempt to boot from and in what order. Other options you're likely to find here dictate whether the system boots

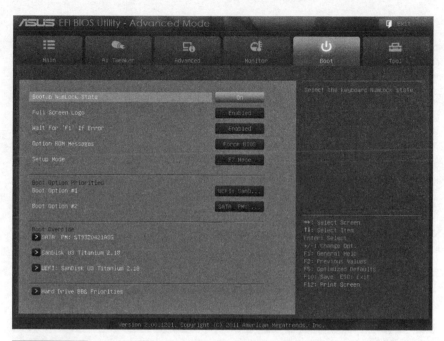

FIGURE 7.8   Boot tab in graphical setup utility

from USB devices or network locations, displays detailed POST information, displays the key combination to reach the setup utility, and so on.

Travel Advisory

The boot device sequence is the first place to check if you have a computer that attempts to boot to an incorrect device or gives an *invalid boot device* error. If you have a USB thumb drive inserted and this CMOS setting has removable devices ahead of hard drives in the boot order, the computer will dutifully try to boot from the thumb drive.

Overclocking   The intrepid *tweakers* who tempt fate and *overclock* their systems will become very familiar with the setup utility's overclocking options (see Figure 7.9). On systems not designed for overclocking, these may be absent or minimal, whereas systems designed for tweaking may have both automatic overclocking features and a dizzying array of sub-menus for adjusting *voltages, multipliers, clock speeds, bus speeds,* and *timings* for the *CPU, RAM,* and sometimes more.

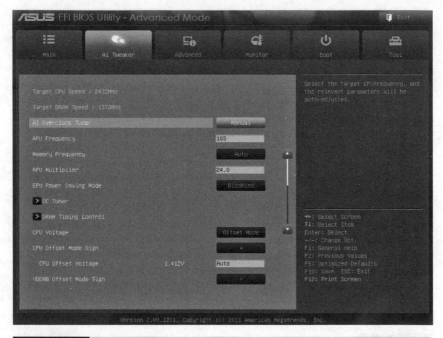

| **FIGURE 7.9** | Ai Tweaker tab |

Other Settings Outside of these well-tread options, there are a few more you're likely to run into, often with mobile-specific or legacy options:

- **Power Management** These settings work in concert (sometimes in conflict) with the Windows power management settings to control how and when devices turn off and back on to conserve power.

Travel Assistance

For more information on power management, check out Chapter 10.

- **PCI/PnP** Plug and Play (PnP) is how devices automatically work when you snap them into your computer. Peripheral Component Interconnect (PCI) is a type of slot used for cards. Odds are very good you'll never deal with this screen.

FIGURE 7.10   CMOS battery

Replacing the CMOS Battery

CMOS batteries fail gradually. If you notice your system clock running slow, or
if you're consistently prompted to enter the date and time when you boot the
PC, it's time to replace the CMOS battery. Replacing the CMOS battery (see
Figure 7.10) is simple: slide the old one out of the bracket and slip a new one
with matching voltage in its place.

CHECKPOINT

✔**Objective 7.01: Boot Process and POST**   After the CPU powers up, the
system BIOS loads and runs the POST to test built-in and common devices.
The POST sounds a beep code or displays numeric or text error messages
in the event of hardware failure. POST cards let you interpret POST error
codes and troubleshoot a dead system. At the end of the POST, the operating
system loads.

✔**Objective 7.02: System ROM**   The system ROM chip stores the system BIOS programs and CMOS setup utility. System ROM maintains data even while the computer is turned off through the use of a CMOS battery.

✔**Objective 7.03: System BIOS and CMOS Setup Utility**   The system BIOS or UEFI includes hundreds of small programs that establish communication between your hardware and the OS. System BIOS can be updated (*flashed*) to fix bugs or support new technologies. The CMOS setup utility enables you to modify settings for built-in and common devices such as hard drives. You usually access CMOS by pressing one or more keys during boot, though UEFI systems can access it from within the OS. Only save CMOS changes if you are certain of the effect. The CMOS setup utility also includes settings and features for securing your system, such as Secure Boot, intrusion detection, DriveLock, LoJack, and the Trusted Platform Module.

REVIEW QUESTIONS

1. Which of the following can you configure in the CMOS? (Select three.)
   A. Boot device order
   B. System time
   C. Hard drive
   D. Video resolution

2. When should you update your system BIOS?
   A. When you upgrade your OS
   B. Every time you boot your computer
   C. Every time you defragment your computer
   D. To support new technologies or fix known bugs

3. What should you do before making any changes to your CMOS settings?
   A. Reboot your computer.
   B. Know exactly what the changes will do.
   C. Remove all the cables from your system.
   D. Replace the BIOS.

4. What do you need to do if the clock on your system starts losing time?
   A. Replace your BIOS.
   B. Replace the CMOS battery.
   C. Replace your hard drive.
   D. Reinstall Windows.

5. If a user password has been set in CMOS, what will happen?

    A. An unauthorized person will be unable to enter the CMOS settings program.

    B. The user must enter the correct password to boot the system.

    C. Nothing will happen.

    D. Only certain settings in the CMOS will be available to unauthorized users.

6. If you've set and forgotten a supervisor password for your CMOS, how can you get into the CMOS settings program in many systems? (Select two.)

    A. Reboot the computer and press F1.

    B. Set a jumper on your motherboard to clear the password.

    C. Reinstall Windows.

    D. Remove and reinstall the CMOS battery.

7. At startup, where does your computer receive its first set of instructions?

    A. Operating system

    B. RAM BIOS

    C. ROM BIOS

    D. CMOS

8. How can you access a hard drive if DriveLock is enabled and set to max security mode, but you have forgotten or lost the user password?

    A. Reinstall Windows; your data will be unaffected.

    B. Without the user password, you can never access the hard drive again; your hard drive is permanently useless.

    C. Use a jumper to clear the password; your data will be unaffected.

    D. Use the master password to reset the user password; your data will be destroyed.

9. Which Windows feature uses a Trusted Platform Module (TPM)?

    A. Windows Update

    B. Windows Easy Transfer

    C. BitLocker Drive Encryption

    D. Windows Defender

10. Tim believes someone has been tampering with his components. What feature might alert him that his computer case has been opened?

   A. LoJack

   B. Secure Boot

   C. Virtualization support

   D. Intrusion detection/notification

REVIEW ANSWERS

1. **A B C** Boot device order, system time, and your hard drive are all configurable in the CMOS settings program.

2. **D** System BIOS should be updated only when a new BIOS version will fix a problem or to add new technologies.

3. **B** Before making any changes in the CMOS, you should know exactly what they will do.

4. **B** If the clock on your system starts losing time, this is a good indication that you need to change the CMOS battery.

5. **B** If a user password is set in the CMOS, the computer won't fully boot until the correct password is entered by the user.

6. **B D** If you've set and forgotten a supervisor password in the CMOS, you can still enter the CMOS by setting a jumper on the motherboard to clear the password or by removing and reinstalling the CMOS battery.

7. **C** At startup, your computer receives its first set of instructions from the system BIOS, also called ROM BIOS. There's no such thing as RAM BIOS, a fact you should remember for the exam.

8. **D** The best course of action would be to use the master password to reset the user password, although your data would be lost.

9. **C** Windows BitLocker Drive Encryption uses a Trusted Platform Module (TPM).

10. **D** Most newer systems have an intrusion detection/notification option in CMOS that reports when the case has been opened, alerting techs to potential tampering.

Data Storage

	NEWBIE	SOME EXPERIENCE	EXPERT
ETA	6 hours	4 hours	2 hours

Data storage devices hold the operating systems, programs, and data that drive modern computers and mobile devices. Some of this data is priceless, so techs must know how to protect it. This chapter looks at data storage technologies and interfaces, as well as how to install them, configure and optimize them, and maintain and troubleshoot them.

Objective 8.01 Data Storage Technologies

Data storage devices read and write data to a physical storage medium, and despite the many varied storage devices, there are only a few low-level methods you need to know: magnetic, optical, and flash.

Magnetic

Devices that encode and decode data on magnetic media have had a long run as the dominant long-term digital data storage technology, but the writing is on the wall. Now that floppy drives have been retired from the 220-901 exam, the last magnetic media types standing are hard disk drives and tape drives.

Hard Disk Drives

Traditional *hard disk drives (HDDs)* store data magnetically on spinning platters, using a fast-moving actuator arm with read/write heads (see Figure 8.1). The important properties are physical size, storage capacity, spindle speed, cache size, and interface.

Most modern HDDs are *2.5* or *3.5* inches wide and have storage capacities measured in *gigabytes (GB)* or *terabytes (TB)*. As you'd expect, size relates to capacity: 2.5-inch drives presently top out around 2 TB, whereas 3.5-inch drives exceed 8 TB. Drives with higher spindle speed seek faster but consume more power and generate more heat and noise; Table 8.1 shows common HDD spindle speeds with typical use. Cache size, measured in *megabytes (MB)*, affects the drive's sustained throughput. We'll look at interfaces later in the chapter.

Travel Assistance

Although rare, you can find 1.8-inch drives in the wild; we'll discuss them in Chapter 11.

Tape Drives

Whereas the read/write head in an HDD can quickly seek to data at any location on its spinning platters, tape drives read and write data sequentially on long spools of flimsy ribbon encased in a protective cartridge (see Figure 8.2).

TABLE 8.1   Typical HDD Spindle Speeds

Spindle Speed	Typical Purpose
5400 rpm	Standard for portable computers
7200 rpm	Standard for desktop computers
10,000 rpm	Enthusiast and server computers

FIGURE 8.2   Backup tapes

This makes seek times slow. Tape's saving grace is a relatively low cost; 1.5-
and 2.5-TB tapes currently cost a fraction of the price of similarly sized
HDDs, making tape a good storage option for large-scale backup and archival
applications.

Optical

Compact disc (CD), *digital versatile disc (DVD)*, and *Blu-ray Disc (BD)* drives
use lasers to read (and sometimes write) data on shiny *optical discs*. Riding
the popularity of these formats for delivering music, movies, video games, and
software, writable versions of all three technologies have been used to back up
and archive data. The capacity and speed of optical media have not kept pace
with other technologies, and its popularity is fading.

Local Lingo

burn   Another term for writing to an optical disc is *burning*, so write-
capable optical drives are called *burners*.

Optical Media Formats

Optical media comes in three main styles: read-only, write-once, and rewritable. Current optical *combo drives* read and write to many optical media types,
though you should always check compatibility, especially with older drives.
Here's a list of common optical standards:

- CD-ROM
- CD-R
- CD-RW
- DVD-ROM
- DVD-Video
- DVD-R

- DVD-R DL
- DVD-RW
- DVD-RW DL
- DVD+R
- DVD+R DL
- DVD+RW

- DVD+RW DL
- DVD-RAM
- BD-ROM
- BD-R
- BD-RE

> **Travel Advisory**
>
> Manufacturers label DVD drives that read and write multiple DVD types as *DVD±RW*, but there's no ± media, just – and +.

The endings indicate style: *ROM* is read-only; *R* is write-once; *RW* and *RE* discs are rewritable. DVD-Video, also a DVD-ROM movie, is the iconic *DVD*. Blu-ray Discs, also used for movies, support high-definition resolutions and more features on a single disc. DVD-RAM is just different—an RW type in a special cartridge. *DL* is *dual-layer*, but expect CompTIA to abbreviate single-layer and dual-layer DVD as *SL DVD* and *DL DVD*.

> **Local Lingo**
>
> **ISO 9660**   Optical discs use a unique *Compact Disc File System (CDFS)*, more accurately called the *ISO 9660 file system.* The International Organization for Standardization (ISO) provides standards for many technologies.

Optical Media Capacity

CDs come in 650-MB or 700-MB capacity, and Table 8.2 shows DVD and Blu-ray Disc capacities.

Optical Speeds

Though relatively slow, newer optical drives are much faster than the first 150-KBps CD-ROM drive. Modern drives list up to three speeds (in order: read, rewrite, and write) per media using a "number times" format such as 40×. It's simple math: to find throughput in KBps, expand 40× and multiply (40 × 150 = 6000). A CD-RW will list all three speeds in a format such as 48×32×52×.

TABLE 8.2	Common DVD/Blu-ray Disc Capacities in DVD-Industry Gigabytes	
	Single Layer	**Dual Layer**
Single-sided DVD	4.7 GB	8.5 GB
Double-sided DVD	9.4 GB	17.1 GB
Blu-ray Disc	25 GB	50 GB
Mini Blu-ray Disc	7.8 GB	15.6 GB

DVD drives read, write, and rewrite DVDs nine times faster than 150 KBps, so a 1× DVD drive and disc have a throughput of 1.32 MBps. They read and write CDs even faster, so they often list an extra set of CD speeds.

A 1× Blu-ray drive has a speed of 4.5 MBps; Blu-ray Disc burners can write to BD-R media at speeds up to 54 MBps (12×), rewrite BD-RE discs at speeds up to 9 MBps (2×), and read BD-ROM discs as fast as 36 MBps (8×). Blu-ray Disc burners can also burn to CD and DVD media and often list three sets of speeds.

Flash

Flash memory is displacing many other data storage technologies. You need to know about three flash memory families: solid-state drives, USB thumb drives, and memory cards. *Solid-state drives (SSDs)* are basically a flash-media hard drive; *USB thumb drives* contain a standard USB connection; and *memory card* is a generic term for a number of different tiny cards that are used in cameras, tablets, and other devices. Both of these types can show up as drives in modern operating systems, but they have different jobs. USB thumb drives have replaced virtually all other rewritable removable media as the way people transfer files or keep copies of important programs.

Solid-State Drive

SSD, which uses flash memory chips to store data, is running the HDD out of town. SSDs weigh less, have no moving parts, seek faster, have higher throughput, consume less power, produce less heat, have better shock resistance, and last longer than HDDs. For a time HDDs retained a price and capacity advantage, but as SSDs catch up in capacity, the only advantage left is cost.

Most consumer SSDs use a 2.5-inch hard drive format, though the adaptability of flash means you can find SSD cards and sticks that fit a few interfaces. Back when SSDs were much more limited in space, flash memory was mixed with a traditional magnetic HDD to make the *hybrid hard drive (HHD)*. These realized some SSDs advantages at higher capacity and lower cost, but current HHDs are a lukewarm choice.

Travel Advisory

Confused by all of the *xx*D acronyms yet? *Hard drive* and *hard disk* were traditionally synonyms, but in this book, aside from the term "hybrid hard drive," we use *hard drive* as an umbrella term including HDD, SSD, and HHD.

USB Thumb Drives

The *USB flash memory drive* (see Figure 8.3)—also known as the *USB thumb drive, jump drive,* or *flash drive*—has effectively replaced floppy disks and optical media for easy file transfers and portability. As of this writing you can pick up one of these tiny drives—the smallest are a bit larger than an adult thumbnail—with more storage than any optical disc for about 25 cents a gigabyte.

Flash Cards

Many small devices such as digital cameras and smartphones store data on flash memory cards. Memory cards come in a number of incompatible formats, such as *CompactFlash (CF)* and *Extreme Digital (xD) Picture Card*. The most popular format is *Secure Digital (SD)* and its smaller siblings, shown in Figure 8.4, *miniSD* and *microSD*. Most devices support a single format, though some smaller cards fit into a converter that itself fits a larger slot.

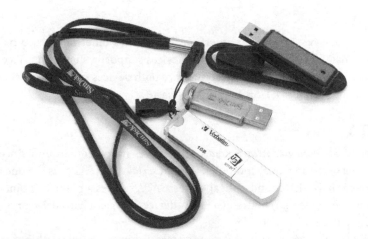

FIGURE 8.3   USB thumb drives

FIGURE 8.4   Assortment of SD memory cards

Exam Tip

SD cards evolved out of MultiMediaCard (MMC). The embedded version of MMC, *eMMC,* is common in mobile devices, but beyond knowing it's there for the 901 exam, there's not much a tech can do.

Objective 8.02   Data Storage Interfaces

Storage devices have a data interface that enables other devices to read or write data. It's critical to make sure devices support a shared interface, but it's also important to use the fastest interface both devices support. A fast external SSD connected to a USB 1.1 port is a waste.

SATA

Advanced Technologies Attachment (ATA) drives have been around since the beginning of the personal computer, though *serial ATA (SATA)* is the one used for current hard drives and optical drives. SATA creates a point-to-point connection (see Figure 8.5) between a SATA device, such as a hard drive or optical drive, and the SATA controller.

A SATA device's stream of data traverses a thin seven-wire cable that can reach up to a meter; speeds depend on which version of the SATA standard is

FIGURE 8.5   SATA power and data connectors

in use. The versions—1.0 (1.5 Gbps), 2.0 (3 Gbps), and 3.0 (6 Gbps)—have a maximum throughput of 150 MBps, 300 MBps, and 600 MBps, respectively; the 901 objectives refer to these as *SATA1, SATA2,* and *SATA3.*

External SATA (eSATA) extends the SATA bus to external devices at the same speed as the internal SATA bus. The connector (see Figure 8.6) is similar to internal SATA but is keyed differently; it supports cables up to 2 meters outside the case and is *hot-swappable.*

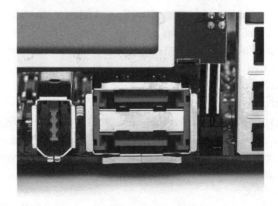

FIGURE 8.6   eSATA connectors (in center of photo)

> ### Local Lingo
> **hot-swappable**   A hot-swappable drive will be recognized even if it is connected, swapped, or replaced while the system is running.

Protecting Data with RAID

A *redundant array of independent (or inexpensive) disks (RAID)* uses multiple hard drives to increase performance and protect data. Motherboards with built-in RAID controllers may have a BIOS/UEFI setting to enable or disable RAID (see Figure 8.7). Of many RAID *levels,* CompTIA expects you to know 0, 1, 5, and 10:

> ### Local Lingo
> **array**   A RAID *array* collects two or more hard drives.

- **RAID 0: Disk striping**   Disk striping requires at least two drives. It increases performance by splitting work over multiple drives, and does not provide redundancy to data. If any drive fails, all data is lost.
- **RAID 1: Disk mirroring/duplexing**   RAID 1 arrays require at least two hard drives, although they also work with any even number of drives. RAID 1, which *mirrors* data across multiple drives, provides safety at the cost of storage space (since data is duplicated).
- **RAID 5: Disk striping with distributed parity**   RAID 5 distributes data and parity information evenly across all drives. This is the fastest way to provide data redundancy. RAID 5 arrays effectively use one drive's worth of space for parity, requiring a minimum of three drives. In RAID 5, three 2-TB drives provide a capacity of 4 TB, while four 2-TB drives provide a capacity of 6 GB.
- **RAID 10: Stripe of mirrored pairs**   RAID 10 takes two mirrored pairs of drives and stripes them together. This creates an array with excellent speed and redundancy, though it takes four drives as a minimum. RAID 10 is not one of the original RAID levels, but is fairly common today.

Settings for RAID in a UEFI BIOS

Travel Advisory

RAID 0 and 1 can be combined. Mirroring two striped-drive pairs results in *RAID 0+1*. Striping two mirrored-drive pairs produces *RAID 1+0*, or *RAID 10*. Arrays combining single RAID types are called *multiple RAID solutions* or *nested RAID*.

Windows 8 and later include a tool in Disk Management called Storage Spaces that enables you to create a number of RAID array varieties via software. We'll cover Storage Spaces a little later in this chapter.

Local Lingo

JBOD *JBOD* stands for Just a Bunch of Disks (or Drives). It's a storage system with multiple independent disks, rather than RAID-organized disks. It provides no redundancy and no performance increase.

FIGURE 8.8 External hard drive enclosure

Multifunction Interfaces

A number of storage devices connect using multifunction ports and slots such as USB, Thunderbolt, and PCIe.

- **USB**   While USB thumb drives are obvious, you'll also find *external* optical drives and hard drives (that is, a hard drive with an *external enclosure,* as in Figure 8.8) that rely on the ubiquity of USB ports.
- **Thunderbolt**   Though still rare, Thunderbolt's blazing speeds make it a good way to connect external drives. You'll find it primarily on higher-end Mac OS X computers.
- **PCIe**   Technically any storage drive can connect through PCIe via a SATA, USB, or Thunderbolt card. Flash memory's speed and adaptability have led to the important one: PCIe SSDs.

Card Readers

Computers need a *card reader* to access flash card data directly. A number of inexpensive USB card readers are available (see Figure 8.9), and some computers have built-in readers.

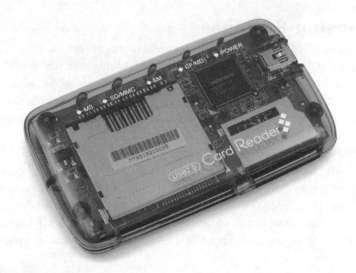

FIGURE 8.9 USB card reader

Other Interfaces

Some interfaces not listed in CompTIA's objectives are often used in devices they do list; you should know them.

- Flash media is so adaptable and efficient that portable-friendly SSDs have been developed for the *M.2* slot—which is turning up on recent portable computers and many desktop motherboards—and a miniaturized version of SATA called *mSATA*.

- Some interfaces used in enterprise-grade storage rarely show up on consumer-grade equipment; tape drives have been relegated to such environments, so most use these interfaces: *small computer system interface (SCSI)*, *serial-attached SCSI (SAS)*, and *Fibre Channel (FC)*.

 **Objective 8.03** Installing Storage Devices

Installing drives is fairly simple if you take the time to make sure you've got the right drive for your system, configure it properly, and run a few tests to confirm it works.

Choosing Storage

Picking a drive is the hard part these days, and there's not always a right answer. Therefore, make a list of questions to answer and qualities you need. Understand the capacity needed, how portable the data needs to be, what sort of system(s) it's going in, what interfaces are common to these systems, the speeds they support, whether you should use RAID for speed or redundancy, how many ports the system has free, and so on.

Obviously, 250 GB is smaller than 2 TB, but a 250-GB SSD will perform much better than a 2-TB HDD, and it's plenty of space for many devices. A 5400-rpm drive is more efficient and quiet than a 7200-rpm drive, but has a slower seek time; an SSD would be even more quiet and efficient and have an even lower seek time, but at a higher price. A drive with a 2-MB cache won't support the sustained throughput of a busy system as well as a drive with a 16-MB cache.

Installing SATA Drives

There used to be a few catches when installing SATA drives; these days, just connect the power, plug in the controller cable (see Figure 8.10), and wait for

FIGURE 8.10 Properly connected SATA cables

the OS to automatically detect the drive. The keyed SATA data and power connectors make it impossible to install either incorrectly.

Since motherboards come with many SATA connectors, how does the system find the right hard drive to boot up to? That's where the BIOS/UEFI settings come into play. By default, boot order and drive letter priority follow SATA controller ID: SATA 0 is C:, SATA 1 is D:, and so on.

> **Travel Advisory**
>
> BIOS/UEFI setup utilities enable you to change boot order easily, which is great for multi-OS computers.

Installing Optical Drives

Most optical drives connect via internal SATA or an external port. The hitch is the bundled software: burners need applications to enable burning features, while DVD and Blu-ray drives (see Figure 8.11) need software to play movies. If you only plan to use your Blu-ray drive for storage, requirements are

FIGURE 8.11   Blu-ray Disc drive

minimal; the requirements to watch Blu-ray movies in HD resolution (720p, 1080i, or 1080p) are a little more:

- **Processor**   At least a Pentium 4, Pentium D, or dual- or multicore processor; or an AMD Athlon 64 X2 or Phenom multicore processor
- **System memory**   At least 2 GB of RAM for Windows Vista/7/8
- **Video**   A DVI or HDMI video card and drivers compliant with High-Bandwidth Digital Content Protection (HDCP)

Installing Removable Storage

Removable storage devices self-install when connected to an external port. In the case of external drives, this port is usually USB, Thunderbolt, or eSATA. Flash thumb drives use a USB port, and flash memory cards typically use a built-in memory card reader or a reader plugged into a USB slot. Memory cards either slide into a slot with enough surface exposed to remove them, or they may slip all the way into a slot with a spring to eject the card when you press again; don't force them.

Objective 8.04 Configuring and Optimizing Storage Devices

After installing a hard drive, you need to prepare it for data. After creating any desired RAID arrays, *partitioning* establishes the framework upon which your file system is built, and *formatting* creates the file system.

Implementing RAID

RAID is implemented in hardware or software. Software is used if price trumps performance; hardware is used if speed wins out. Software RAID doesn't use special controllers—but you do need "smart" software. The most common software RAID comes with some Windows editions. On the desktop, Disk Management (see Figure 8.12) configures drives for RAID 0 and RAID 1; Windows Server adds RAID 5. Storage Spaces handles multiple levels of RAID.

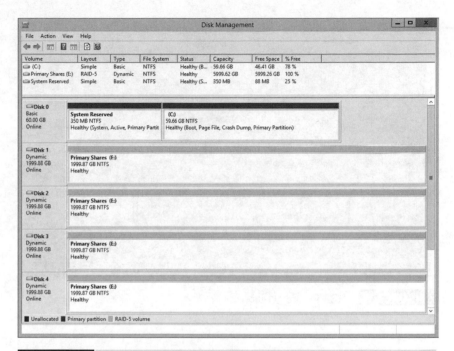

Volume	Layout	Type	File System	Status	Capacity	Free Space	% Free
(C:)	Simple	Basic	NTFS	Healthy (B...	59.66 GB	46.41 GB	78 %
Primary Shares (E:)	RAID-5	Dynamic	NTFS	Healthy	5999.62 GB	5999.26 GB	100 %
System Reserved	Simple	Basic	NTFS	Healthy (S...	350 MB	88 MB	25 %

Disk 0
Basic
60.00 GB
Online

System Reserved
350 MB NTFS
Healthy (System, Active, Primary Partit

(C:)
59.66 GB NTFS
Healthy (Boot, Page File, Crash Dump, Primary Partition)

Disk 1
Dynamic
1999.88 GB
Online

Primary Shares (F:)
1999.87 GB NTFS
Healthy

Disk 2
Dynamic
1999.88 GB
Online

Primary Shares (E:)
1999.87 GB NTFS
Healthy

Disk 3
Dynamic
1999.88 GB
Online

Primary Shares (E:)
1999.87 GB NTFS
Healthy

Disk 4
Dynamic
1999.88 GB
Online

Primary Shares (E:)
1999.87 GB NTFS
Healthy

■ Unallocated ■ Primary partition ▨ RAID-5 volume

FIGURE 8.12 Disk Management in Windows Server

Software RAID means the OS is in charge of RAID functions. It works for small RAID solutions but can overwork and your OS easily; hardware RAID is the answer. Hardware RAID has an *intelligent* controller handling RAID functions (see Figure 8.13).

FIGURE 8.13 Serial ATA RAID controller

```
        Intel(R) Rapid Storage Technology - Option ROM - 14.5.0.2241
             Copyright (C) Intel Corporation. All rights reserved.
        ════════════════[ CREATE VOLUME MENU ]════════════════

                        Name:  Storage
                  RAID Level:  RAID10(RAID0+1)
                       Disks:  Select Disks
                  Strip Size:  64KB
                   Capactiy:   4000  GB
                        Sync:  N/A
                               Create Volume



        ══════════════════════[ Help ]══════════════════════




            RAID 10: Mirrors data and stripes the mirror.






        [↑↓]Change   [TAB]-Next  [ESC]-Previous Menu  [ENTER]-Select
```

FIGURE 8.14   RAID configuration utility

Hardware RAID is invisible to the OS (the OS only sees the combined drive). RAID systems may be configured from CMOS, or have a special configuration utility in flash ROM that you access after CMOS but before the OS loads. Figure 8.14 shows typical firmware for configuring hardware RAID. Hardware RAID, which has features such as *hot-swapping* to support easy upgrades and repairs, wins the day.

Partitioning

Windows supports the older *master boot record (MBR)* partitioning scheme, its own proprietary *dynamic storage partitioning* scheme, and the newer *GUID partition table (GPT)*. Microsoft calls an MBR-partitioned or GPT-partitioned drive a *basic disk* and a dynamic-storage-partitioned drive a *dynamic disk*. Windows doesn't mind if you mix schemes on different drives.

Local Lingo

GUID   A *globally unique identifier (GUID)* is a number with an almost-impossible chance of duplication that's used to uniquely identify different objects.

Basic Disks

MBR basic disk partitioning creates two tiny data structures in a drive's *boot sector* (the first sector): the MBR and a *partition table*. The MBR is just a tiny bit of code that takes control of the boot process from the system basic input/output system (BIOS). When the computer boots to a hard drive, the BIOS automatically checks the boot sector for MBR code. The MBR has one job: check the partition table for a partition with a valid OS (see Figure 8.15).

Travel Advisory
Only one MBR and one partition table exist per basic disk.

MBR basic disk partition tables support up to four partitions. The partition table supports two types: primary and extended partitions. *Primary partitions* support bootable operating systems; *extended partitions* don't. A single basic MBR disk supports up to four primary partitions, or three primary partitions and one extended partition. The partition table stores a binary *active* setting for each primary partition on the drive; at boot, the MBR uses it to determine which primary partition to boot to.

Each partition needs a unique identifier to distinguish it. Microsoft operating systems traditionally assign a drive letter from C: to Z:. Extended partitions do not get drive letters. After you create an extended partition, you must create logical drives within that extended partition. A logical drive traditionally gets a drive letter from D: to Z:.

Note that when you create partitions and logical drives in Windows, the OS prompts you to create *volumes*. Further, it creates logical drives automatically after you exceed four volumes on a single drive.

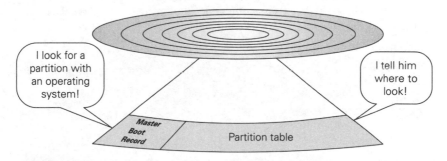

| **FIGURE 8.15** | Functions of the MBR and partition table |

With the exception of the partition that stores boot files for Windows (always C:), primary partitions and logical drives can be assigned a drive letter or mounted as a folder on an existing primary partition. A *volume mount point* (or simply mount point) is the folder on one volume that points to another volume or partition. The mounted volume functions like a folder, but files stored in it are written to the mounted volume.

Local Lingo

GPT partitioning   MBR-partitioned disks have tangible limits such as a capacity no larger than 2.2 TB and no more than four partitions. The GUID partition table (GPT) partitioning scheme effectively overcomes these limits. GPT drives are basic drives, though you need a UEFI motherboard and a UEFI-compatible OS to boot to one.

Dynamic Disks

Windows' proprietary *dynamic storage partitioning*, better known as *dynamic disks*, use the term *volume* to describe dynamic-disk partitions. There is no dynamic-disk equivalent to primary and extended partitions. A volume is still technically a partition, but it can do things a regular partition can't, such as spanning. A *spanned volume* encompasses more than one drive (up to 32 drives in a single volume). Dynamic disks also support RAID 0, 1, and 5, though support differs among various Windows editions and versions (see Table 8.3).

TABLE 8.3	Dynamic Disk Compatibility		
Volume	Windows Vista (Business/Ultimate/ Enterprise)	Windows 7/8/8.1 (Professional/Ultimate/ Enterprise)	Windows Server
Simple	X	X	X
Spanned	X	X	X
Striped	X	X	X
Mirrored		X	X
RAID 5			X

How to Partition Using Disk Management

Disk Management is the go-to tool for adding drives or adding arrays to a Windows system, as well as for modifying them. Follow these steps to create a new partition:

1. To access Disk Management, open the Control Panel and then open Administrative Tools. Double-click Computer Management.

2. Expand the Storage branch in the left pane to access the storage management tools, and then click Disk Management.

3. Right-click an unallocated section of the disk, and then select New Simple Volume to start the New Simple Volume Wizard (see Figure 8.16). Follow prompts from the wizard to specify partition size, assign a drive letter or path (*mounting* the partition to a folder), and format the partition with a file system.

Exam Tip

The CompTIA A+ 902 exam objectives mention "splitting" partitions, but there's no "split" option. To turn one partition into two, remove the existing partition and create two new ones, or shrink the existing partition and add a new one in the unallocated space. If you see it on the exam, know that this is what CompTIA means.

FIGURE 8.16   The New Simple Volume Wizard in Windows Disk Management

Disk Management can also extend and shrink volumes in current versions of Windows without using dynamic disks; CompTIA calls this *extending partitions* and, oddly, *shrink partitions*. You can shrink a volume with available free space (though you can't shrink it by the whole amount, based on the location of unmovable sectors such as the MBR), and you can expand volumes with unallocated space on the drive.

To shrink a volume, right-click it and select Shrink Volume. Disk Management calculates how much it can shrink and lets you choose up to that amount. Extending volumes is equally straightforward; right-click and select Extend Volume.

Disk Initialization

Every hard drive in a Windows system has special information placed on it through *disk initialization* (CompTIA calls this *initializing* the disk). This data identifies what system the drive belongs to, and what its role is—such as whether it is part of a software RAID array or a spanned volume.

New drives must be initialized before use. When you install an extra hard drive and start Disk Management, it notices the new drive and starts the Hard Drive Initialization Wizard. If you don't let it run, the drive will show as unknown (see Figure 8.17).

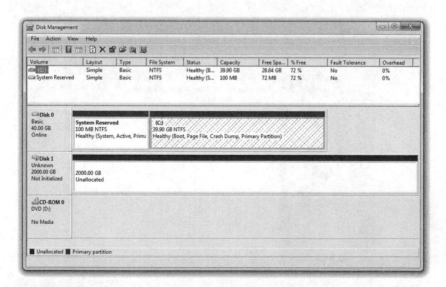

FIGURE 8.17   Unknown drive in Disk Management

To start, right-click a disk and select Initialize. You will get the option to select MBR or GPT partitioning. Disk Management shows the *drive status* of every initialized mass storage device in your system, making it handy for troubleshooting. Hopefully you'll see each drive listed as *Healthy*. You're familiar with statuses *Unallocated* and *Active*, but here are a few more:

- **Foreign drive** Shown when you move a dynamic disk to another system.
- **Formatting** Shown while you're formatting a drive.
- **Failed** The disk is damaged or corrupt; you've probably lost some data.
- **Online** The disk is healthy and communicating properly with the computer.
- **Offline** The disk is either corrupt or having communication problems.

A newly installed drive is set as a basic disk; there's nothing wrong with basic disks, though you miss out on some handy features.

Formatting

Formatting adds a *file system* to the drive—like a big spreadsheet that tracks what piece of data is stored where. Current Windows versions support four file systems: FAT/FAT16, FAT32, NTFS, and exFAT/FAT64. Each has its own merits and limitations.

FAT

Formatting a drive with FAT creates a 16-bit *file allocation table (FAT)*—the big spreadsheet. FAT's strength is ubiquitous support, but it has considerable limitations: no support for disk partitions larger than 2.1 GB, and no local file-level security. The reason to keep FAT (also called *FAT16*) around is compatibility with older systems.

FAT32

FAT32 supports partitions up to 2 terabytes (TB) and is more efficient than FAT16—but it too lacks local file security.

NTFS

Older versions of Windows ran well enough on FAT and FAT32, but you need *New Technology File System (NTFS)* to get the most out of modern versions. It supports partitions up to 16 TB, built-in compression and encryption, disk quotas, expanding dynamic partitions on the fly, and local file security.

Exam Tip

By default, NTFS supports partitions of up to 16 TB minus 4 KB, but MBR-partitioned drives are still limited to 2.2 TB. Use GPT if you can.

NTFS uses an enhanced file allocation table, the *master file table (MFT)*, to track the file and folder locations. NTFS partitions keep a backup copy of the most critical MFT parts in the middle of the disk, reducing the chance a serious drive error will wipe out both the MFT and the partial MFT copy.

Compression and Encryption   NTFS can compress individual files and folders to save space at the expense of slower data access; it can also encrypt files and folders to make them unreadable without a key. Microsoft calls the encryption utility in NTFS the *encrypting file system (EFS)*, but it's simply an aspect of NTFS, not a standalone file system. We'll take a closer look at EFS in Chapter 13.

Disk Quotas   NTFS enables administrators to set *disk quotas* that limit drive space use per user. To set quotas, log in as Administrator, right-click the hard drive, and select Properties. In the Local Disk Properties dialog box, select the Quota tab (see Figure 8.18) and make changes. Disk quotas on multiuser systems prevent individual users from monopolizing storage space.

FAT64

As thumb drive capacities grow, the FAT32 file system has proven inadequate. It won't work on drives over 2 TB, and it limits individual files to 4 GB. Microsoft wisely developed a replacement called *exFAT* or *FAT64* that supports files and partitions up to 128 petabytes (PB). Like FAT32, exFAT still lacks NTFS features such as permissions, compression, and encryption.

Travel Advisory

The current implementation of exFAT limits partition size to 2 TB. Current hardware limits the maximum partition size to 2 PB. The theoretical maximum is some amazing figure, like 64 zettabytes (ZB). Here are the definitions of some big number terms. A *petabyte* is 2^{50} bytes, an *exabyte* is 2^{60} bytes, and a *zettabyte* is 2^{70} bytes. For comparison, a terabyte is 2^{40} bytes. Remember your binary: each superscript number doubles the overall number, so 2^{41} = 2 TB, 2^{42} = 4 TB, and so on.

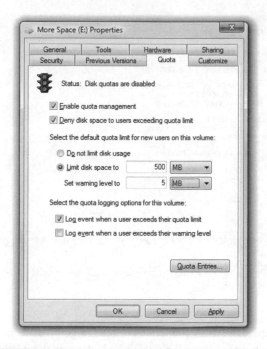

FIGURE 8.18 Hard drive quotas

File Systems in Mac OS X and Linux

Mac OS X uses the *Hierarchical File System Plus (HFS+)* by default, although the latest versions can read and write to FAT32 and exFAT; it also has read-only NTFS support.

Most Linux distributions use the *Fourth Extended File System (ext4)* by default. Ext4 supports volumes up to 1 exabyte (EB), with file sizes up to 16 TB, and is backward compatible with predecessors ext2 and ext3. Just know ext4's maximum volume and file size and that these are Linux file systems.

Linux file system capabilities exceed those of Mac OS X; it can read and write to NTFS, FAT32, exFAT, HFS+, ext2, ext3, and ext4.

How to Format a Partition

You can format partitions from the command line using the **format** command, and graphically through Computer or the Disk Management console.

Using format The syntax for **format** is

```
format drive [/v:label]
```

```
Administrator: C:\Windows\system32\cmd.exe

C:\>format f: /fs:ntfs
The type of the file system is RAW.
The new file system is NTFS.

WARNING, ALL DATA ON NON-REMOVABLE DISK
DRIVE F: WILL BE LOST!
Proceed with Format (Y/N)? y
Verifying 2047M
Volume label (ENTER for none)?
Creating file system structures.
Format complete.
    2096482 KB total disk space.
    2083612 KB are available.

C:\>_
```

FIGURE 8.19   Using the **format** command from a Windows command-line window

To format a hard drive with the letter D:, open a command-line window and type **format d:**. It warns that all data will be lost; press the Y key to proceed or press N to cancel (see Figure 8.19). The label switch is optional but useful to give the drive a user-friendly name. Windows also offers the switch **/fs:** *file system* to specify whether to format with FAT or NTFS.

Using Computer   All Windows versions enable you to right-click a partition or volume in Computer or Windows Explorer/File Explorer and choose Format from the drop-down menu to open a Format dialog box (see Figure 8.20).

Using Disk Management   Access the Disk Management console as described earlier and right-click an unformatted partition. Select Format from the pop-up menu to open the Format dialog box (shown in Figure 8.21). Type a volume label (optional), select a file system from the drop-down menu, and specify any other options. Then click OK.

Travel Advisory

If a drive was previously formatted, you can select *quick format* to save time. This just replaces the file table with a blank one. A *full format* checks the drive clusters for read/write integrity.

Using Computer to format a flash drive volume

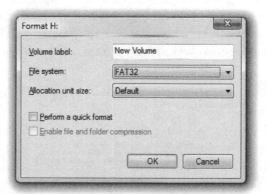

Windows Vista Disk Management Format dialog box

Storage Spaces

Starting with Windows 8, you can group one or more physical drives of any size into a *storage pool. Storage Spaces* is like a RAID management tool, but magic. To start, search and run **storage spaces**. The opening screen, shown in Figure 8.22, gives you one option, so click *Create a new pool and storage space*.

Storage Spaces will show you available installed and formatted physical drives, and give you a warning that proceeding will erase them (see Figure 8.23). Select the drives to include in the pool and click the Create pool button.

Once you've created a pool, you need to select what Microsoft calls the *resiliency mechanism,* which provides one or more layers of redundancy, so you can lose a hard drive or two without data loss. Sounds a lot like RAID, right? Figure 8.24 shows the Create a storage space window with a *Two-way mirror* storage layout. Here's where things get cool; Storage Spaces offers three storage space types:

- *Simple spaces* are pooled storage, like JBOD, with drives of any capacity joined as a single virtual drive with no resiliency.

- *Mirror spaces* keep more than one copy of data, like a RAID mirror array, so you can lose one or more drives without data loss. The number of drives in the array determines your mirror options. A two-way mirror requires at least two drives; a three-way mirror requires five or more. Mirror spaces work like RAID 1 or RAID 10.

- *Parity spaces* add another layer of resiliency similar to RAID 5. In two-way mirroring, 10 GB capacity requires installing 20 GB of storage; with parity spaces, 10 GB capacity only requires installing 15 GB of storage. A three-drive parity space can recover from one lost drive; a seven-drive parity space can recover from two lost drives.

FIGURE 8.22   Storage Spaces opening window

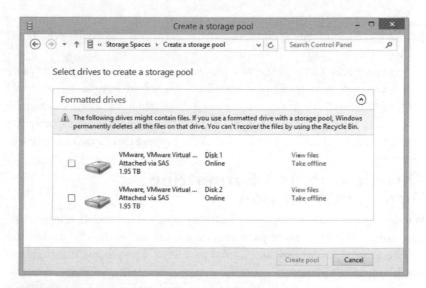

FIGURE 8.23   Formatted drives revealed

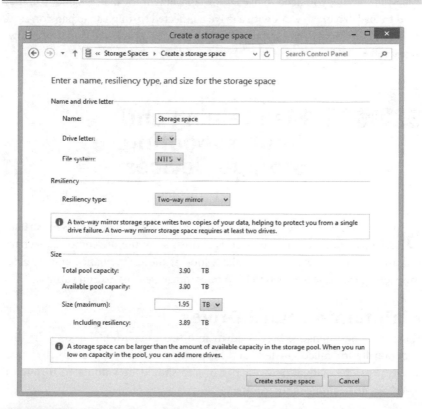

FIGURE 8.24   Ready to create the storage space

When a disk fails, Storage Spaces sends a warning through the Windows Action Center. You can open Storage Spaces to reveal and replace the failed drive.

Storage Spaces can also use *thin provisioning* to create a space with more stated capacity than is actually installed. You might have a storage pool composed of two 2-TB drives and one 3-TB drive, laid out as a two-way mirror. Rather than limit your capacity to 3 TB, you can assign whatever capacity you want for now, such as 12 TB, and add disks to support that capacity as needed.

Partitioning and Formatting During Installation

Windows has a partitioning and formatting tool for the installation process. You can create one or more partitions on a blank drive, delete partitions on a drive already partitioned, and format partitions. The process is straightforward; just read the screen.

There are two potential limitations. First, the installer tool will not delete a dynamic volume; you need to use Disk Management for that. Second, you may need to load drivers to work with a drive connected through an expansion card. If so, click the Load driver option in the installation process to signal Windows that you have drivers.

Objective 8.05

Maintaining and Troubleshooting Storage Devices

Storage devices run the gamut from simple to complicated; HDDs in particular, with platters rotating thousands of times a minute, are complex mechanical and electrical devices. Let's take a look at the maintenance and troubleshooting knowledge we need to keep our storage devices up and running.

Maintaining Hard Drives

Hard drive maintenance breaks down into two categories: checking the disk occasionally for failed clusters, and keeping data organized for quick access. Some steps are manual, but others can and should be automated through a *scheduled disk maintenance* routine.

Error Checking

Some individual clusters on hard drives inevitably go bad, and we use *drive-checking utilities* to find and flag bad clusters so the system can avoid them. Many techs use the names of two older Microsoft tools—*ScanDisk* and *chkdsk* (pronounced "check disk")—though it's called *Error checking* in current versions of Windows.

Travel Advisory

Windows Vista and Windows 7 called it Error-checking, with a hyphen. It's the same tool with or without the hyphen. Thanks, Microsoft!

Most drive-checking tools also try to find and fix other problems, such as files with invalid names, clusters with no filenames associated (*lost chains*), and lost links between parent and child folders.

To access Error checking, open Computer, Windows Explorer, or File Explorer, right-click the drive you want to check, and choose Properties to open the drive's Properties dialog box. Select the Tools tab and click the Check or Check now button (see Figure 8.25) to display the Check Disk

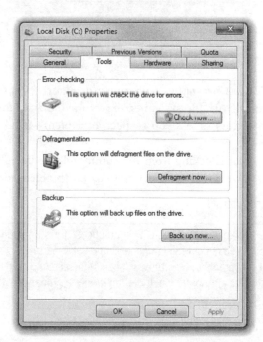

FIGURE 8.25   The Tools tab in the Local Disk Properties dialog box in Windows 7

FIGURE 8.26   Check Disk Local Disk dialog box options

dialog box, which has two options, as shown in Figure 8.26. Check the box next to Automatically fix file system errors, but avoid Scan for and attempt recovery of bad sectors unless you suspect a problem—it takes a while on bigger hard drives.

You can run Error checking from the command line using the **chkdsk /f** command. The **/f** switch tells the program to fix any problems discovered.

Exam Tip

The CompTIA 902 objectives mention "best practices" for scheduled check disks, which implies you might run Error checking weekly via Task Scheduler/Scheduled Tasks. In practice, the utility will balk and *schedule* chkdsk to run automatically on reboot if you try to run it on the primary drive while the OS files are in use.

Defragmentation

Fragmented clusters can increase drive-access times, so it's a good idea to defragment (or *defrag*) your HDDs as regular maintenance. SSDs don't fragment like HDDs, so don't defragment them manually; let Windows handle the task.

You access the defrag tool, called Disk Defragmenter, the same way you access Error checking—right-click a drive in Computer, Windows Explorer, or File Explorer, and choose Properties—except you click the Optimize or Defragment Now button on the Tools tab to open the Disk Defragmenter (see Figure 8.27).

Windows schedules defrag to run at night automatically. You need to do nothing manually any more.

> ## Exam Tip
>
> Best practice for scheduled defragmentation is to just let Windows follow its default automatic defrag schedule; leave the computer on but in sleep mode on Wednesday nights.

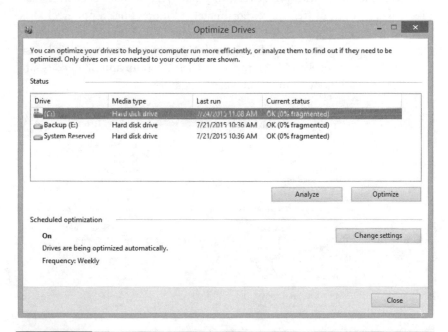

FIGURE 8.27   Optimize Drives, the defragmentation tool in Windows 8.1

Disk Cleanup

The average hard drive fills up with various junk files such as the following:

- **Files in the Recycle Bin**   When you delete a file, it's actually placed in the Recycle Bin (see Figure 8.28) in case you change your mind and want to recover the file.

- **Temporary Internet files**   Windows keeps copies of files from websites you visit so it can load faster on your next visit. You can see these files by opening the Internet Options applet in the Control Panel, clicking Settings, and then clicking the View files button (see Figure 8.29).

- **Downloaded program files**   They rarely add up to much, but your system keeps a copy of applets it downloads. View them in the Internet Options applet.

- **Temporary files**   Many applications create temporary files that are supposed to be deleted when the application is closed, but sometimes they aren't. The location varies by Windows version, but they always reside in a folder called Temp.

Drives tend to fill with junk over time, and Windows can become erratic if its drives run out of free space. Fortunately, Windows has a powerful Disk Cleanup tool (see Figure 8.30). You can access Disk Cleanup in Windows Vista/7 by choosing Start | All Programs | Accessories | System Tools | Disk Cleanup. In Windows 8 and later, just type **Disk Cleanup** and press ENTER to load the tool. Run it once a month to keep junk at bay.

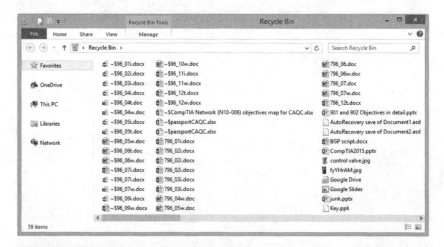

FIGURE 8.28   Mike's Recycle Bin

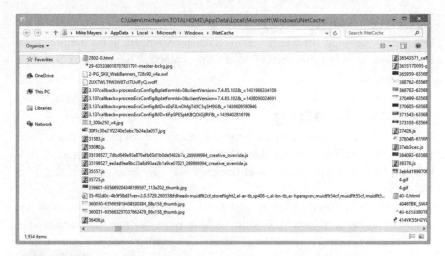

FIGURE 8.29   Lots of temporary Internet files

FIGURE 8.30   Disk Cleanup dialog box

Maintaining Flash Media

Other than keeping the media clean, flash media needs little maintenance. Don't run it through the wash or touch the contacts. There's no fix if it dies; just replace it.

Troubleshooting

This section looks at some of the more common problems that occur with storage drives and how to fix them. Issues fall into several categories: installation, data corruption, dying hard drives, RAID problems, and optical discs and drives.

If you have to troubleshoot many data storage problems, there are tools you can keep on hand to make life easier. A USB universal memory card reader, external combination optical drive, and a spare hard drive enclosure can enable you to run diagnostic tests on systems, media, and drives quickly. When clients bring in dead computers, for example, you can pop their hard drive out and slip it into one of the slots in a hard drive dock (see Figure 8.31)—connected via eSATA or USB—and start chkdsk in seconds.

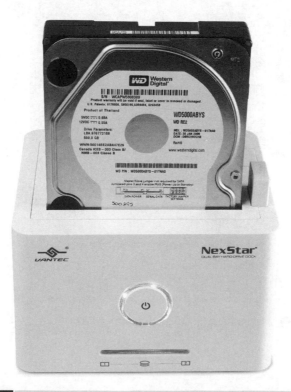

| FIGURE 8.31 | Hard drive dock |

Troubleshooting Installation Errors

It takes a few steps to get an installed drive to hold data: connectivity, BIOS/UEFI settings, partitioning, and formatting. For drives in a RAID array, consult the upcoming RAID troubleshooting section. If you make a mistake at any point during any of these steps, the drive won't work; but if you make an error, you can walk back through each step to check for problems.

Connectivity   To state the obvious, connectivity errors mean something isn't plugged in right. These virtually always show up at boot time. Here are some classics:

- Hard drive error
- No fixed disks present
- HDD controller failure
- No boot device available
- Drive not found

You can usually conquer connectivity errors by carefully inspecting the entire data and power connection system to find the silly mistake. If you get a controller failure with an expansion card, remove and reseat it; the controllers are prone to static buildup. Cables can go bad, but this is rare unless it is obviously ripped or pinched. The BIOS/UEFI autodetect function will not find a drive until everything is installed correctly, making the setup utility a good place to confirm the installation.

BIOS/UEFI Settings   Modern systems rarely get firmware errors, but make sure the controller is enabled and confirm the motherboard and BIOS support the drive you're installing. If they don't, check and see if there's a BIOS update that adds support. Confirm the boot order, too. Here are some other errors that can point to firmware problems:

- CMOS configuration mismatch
- No boot device available
- Drive not found
- Missing OS or OS not found

If Autodetect fails to see the drive, grab a screwdriver and go look for a connectivity issue inside the system. This is also the one time where your hard drive's S.M.A.R.T. (Self-Monitoring, Analysis, and Reporting Technology) functions may help. Unplug the drive and add it to a dock or working system.

Go to the hard drive manufacturer's website and download its diagnostic tool and run it. If you get a failure, the drive is dead; be really happy you back up your data all the time.

Partitioning   Partitioning errors are often a matter of forgetting to do it, or accidentally setting the wrong size. You'll recognize the former when you open Computer, Windows Explorer, or File Explorer after installing a drive; if you forgot to partition, the drive won't show up. If you made the partition too small, it will become painfully obvious as you start adding files. The fix is to redo it. If you've already added files, don't forget to back them up first.

Formatting   Failing to format leaves the drive unable to hold data, and accessing it in Windows triggers an "is not accessible" error; at a C:\ prompt you'll see an "Invalid media" error. Format the drive unless you're certain it already is. Corrupted files can also create the "Invalid media" error. See the upcoming "Troubleshooting Data Corruption" section for a fix.

Formatting is usually boring, but sometimes the drive makes "bad sounds" and spews errors (see Figure 8.32).

Allocation unit is the Windows term for a cluster, so the drive is trying to fix a bad cluster it found. For years I told techs that a few (610) of these errors doesn't mean much since every drive comes with a few bad spots. This is no longer true: modern drives hide a significant reserve of sectors used to replace bad sectors automatically. If a new drive triggers a lot of these, it needs replacing. Get the manufacturer's diagnostic to be sure; bad clusters are reported by S.M.A.R.T.

Mental Reinstall   Focus on the common thread—you just installed a drive! Installation errors don't show up on a system that has run fine for weeks, so do a "mental reinstall." Does the drive show up in the setup utility? No? Recheck data and power cables. If it does show up, did you remember to partition and format it? Did it need to be set to active? These are common-sense questions that come to mind as you march through your mental reinstall.

```
A:\>format C:/s

WARNING:  ALL DATA ON NON-REMOVABLE DISK
DRIVE C:  WILL BE LOST!
Proceed with Format  (Y/N)?y

Formatting 30709.65M

Trying to recover lost allocation unit 37,925
```

FIGURE 8.32   The "Trying to recover lost allocation unit" error

Troubleshooting Data Corruption

Hard drives occasionally get corrupted data in individual sectors. Power surges, accidental shutdowns, corrupted installation media, and viruses, along with hundreds of other problems, can cause this corruption. In most cases these show up (see Figure 8.33) while Windows is running.

You might see these Windows errors:

- The following file is missing or corrupt
- The download location information is damaged
- Unable to load file

If core boot files become corrupted, you may see text errors at boot, such as the following:

- Error loading operating system
- BOOTMGR is missing

On older programs, a command prompt may open with errors such as this:

```
Sector not found reading drive C: Abort, Retry, Fail?
```

The first fix for any of these is to run the Error checking utility. It will go through, mark bad clusters, and hopefully move your data to good clusters.

This app can't run on your PC
To find a version for your PC, check with the software publisher.

Close

FIGURE 8.33 A corrupted data error

If the errors persist after you run Error checking, the drive may have bad sectors. Most drives have built-in error correction code (ECC) to check for bad sectors and mark them in the drive's internal error map (don't confuse this error map with a FAT); if the ECC finds a bad sector, you'll find a corrupted data error as the computer tries to read the bad sector. Drive-checking utilities fix this most of the time.

Troubleshooting Dying Hard Drives

Physical problems are rare but devastating, and there's little you or any service tech can do. Fortunately, magnetic hard drives are designed to take much punishment without failing. Physical problems manifest in two ways: either the drive works but makes a lot of noise, or the drive seems to disappear. Windows will give error messages on read/write failures; only dying drives cause these.

HDDs make noise—the hum of spinning platters and occasional light noise as the read/write heads work are normal. If your drive begins to make any of these, back up critical data and replace it:

- Continuous high-pitched squeal
- Series of clacks or clicks, a short pause, and then another series of clacks or clicks
- Continuous grinding or rumbling

Travel Advisory

Solid-state drives don't make noise; they don't have mechanical parts that will fail. The only thing to worry about with SSDs is age. SSDs have a limit to the number of times they can be erased and rewritten. That limit is high enough that in common usage they'll last many years.

Chapter 15 covers backup tools bundled with Windows. You'll know when a drive just disappears; if it's the drive that contains your OS, the system will lock up. You might get a crash screen, such as a Blue Screen of Death (BSoD) in Windows, or a pinwheel of death in Mac OS X. When you try to restart, you'll get a failure-to-boot error:

```
No Boot Device Present
```

If it's a secondary drive, it will just stop showing up in Computer, Windows Explorer, or File Explorer. Fire up the system setup utility to check whether it sees the drive. If it does, the drive doesn't have a physical problem. If it fails, shut off the system and remove the data cable, but leave the power cable attached. Restart the system and listen to the drive. If it spins up, it is probably good; look for mundane problems such as a loose connector. If the drive doesn't spin, try another power connector. If it still doesn't spin up, the onboard electronics might be toast and the drive dead.

Travel Advisory

Most hard drives have multiyear warranties. Check with the manufacturer and ask for a return material authorization (RMA) if the hard drive is still under warranty. You may get a free replacement (often one newer and larger); it never hurts to check.

Troubleshooting RAID

Drive problems in a RAID array are mostly identical to those on individual drives, but there are a few errors unique to RAID that you should know.

Drives Not Recognized   If you're using hardware RAID and the configuration firmware doesn't recognize a drive, confirm the drives are powered and properly connected.

RAID Stops Working   When a drive in a RAID array fails, several things can happen depending on the type of array and the RAID controller. With RAID 0, the effect is dramatic. Many enthusiasts use RAID 0 to make their OS drive faster. When such a rig (with no redundancy) loses a drive, you'll most likely get a critical stop error (a BSoD or pinwheel of death). On reboot, the computer will fail to boot or you'll get a message that the OS can't be found.

Other RAID levels shouldn't do anything extraordinary when a drive fails. On reboot the RAID controller (if hardware) or Windows (if you've used the built-in tools) will squeal and tell you a drive has failed. Often, a failing drive will slow to a crawl, and that *slow performance* is your clue to check Device Manager or the RAID controller firmware. Some drive failures cause the computer to crash, but others won't show up until you get error messages at reboot. Regardless, replace the failed drive and let the RAID rebuild itself.

RAID Not Found   The 901 objectives use the term "RAID not found," which isn't so much an error message as several circumstances that cause an existing RAID array not to appear, and these vary greatly by the make and model of hardware RAID or (heaven forbid) software RAID.

A properly functioning hardware RAID array always shows up in the configuration utility. If you enter the configuration utility only to find an existing array gone, you probably have dead drives or faulty controllers to replace.

Troubleshooting Optical Drives and Discs

Optical drives are extremely reliable. The single biggest problem in a new installation is the connection, but your next guess should be that the drive has not been properly installed in some way. Double-check the connections, and check whether the BIOS (see Figure 8.34) or system setup utility can see the optical drive. If the BIOS detects it, Windows should too; look for it in Computer, Windows Explorer, File Explorer, and Device Manager.

If the drive won't read a CD-R or CD-RW disc, first try a commercial CD-ROM disc that is in good condition; CD-R and CD-RW discs sometimes have compatibility issues with CD-ROM drives. The same goes for a DVD-RW or any other writable DVD in your DVD drive. As mentioned, DVD drives

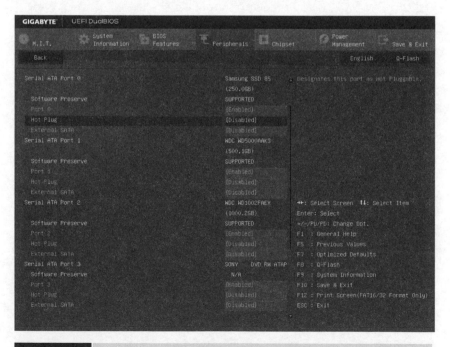

FIGURE 8.34   System setup utility recognizing DVD drive on SATA port 3

have issues with media incompatibility. Also, no optical drive will read badly scratched discs. Also, try the disk in a known-good drive.

Optical drives are not cleaned much, but the discs are; most can be cleaned with just a damp, soft cloth. Always wipe from the center of the optical disc to the edge—never clean an optical-media disc using a circular motion.

If the drive still does not see a disc and you know the disc works elsewhere, try cleaning the drive. Modern optical drives may have built-in cleaning mechanisms; if not, use a commercial cleaning kit.

The final problem with optical drives—stuck discs—is not actually the fault of the drives. I can't tell you the number of times I've pulled an optical drive out of a system to replace it, only to discover that I or my customer left an essential disc inside the now-powerless drive. Luckily, most optical drives have a small hole in the front, usually just below the drive opening, into which you can insert a wire—an unbent paper clip is the standard tool for this purpose—and push on an internal release lever that will eject the disc.

CHECKPOINT

✔**Objective 8.01: Data Storage Technologies**   Magnetic hard drives have high capacity and lower cost, but are losing ground to solid-state drives; tape drives, which store data sequentially on magnetic tapes, fit into a backup and archival niche.

Optical discs have read-only, write-once, and rewritable styles. The typical CD holds 650 MB; the lowest-capacity DVD holds 4.7 GB; a dual-layer Blu-ray Disc can hold 50 GB. Optical is being displaced by faster, higher-capacity, high-convenience flash media.

Solid-state drives, which share a form factor with HDDs, are taking over the hard drive market; the hybrid hard drive, which combines SSD and HDD technologies, has become a lukewarm choice. Flash thumb drives and cards are cheap, compact, and easy to use. Secure Digital (SD), including miniSD and microSD, are the reigning card formats.

✔**Objective 8.02: Data Storage Interfaces**   Current internal drives primarily use SATA and connect at 150 MBps, 300 MBps, and 600 MBps, depending on SATA version. They also use the SATA power connector. RAID, or redundant array of independent (or inexpensive) disks, leverages multiple drives to increase performance, make data more durable, or both. External drives and flash media use interfaces such as USB, Thunderbolt, and eSATA, or a card reader. SSDs may also be built on a PCIe card, or take advantage of formats such as M.2 and mSATA.

✔**Objective 8.03: Installing Storage Devices** Storage devices are easy enough to install; just plug in the data and power connectors. You may need to visit the system setup utility to enable a given interface or modify the boot order. Optical drives may require installing software for writing discs or playing movies. Picking the right storage is harder and requires plotting out requirements.

✔**Objective 8.04: Configuring and Optimizing Storage Devices** After physically installing a drive, configure any desired RAID arrays before preparing the drives for use. Partitioning and formatting establish the framework upon which your file system is built. Formatting creates the file system. Use NTFS whenever possible. You can use Disk Management to do both partitioning and formatting. Software RAID can also be implemented through the flexible Storage Spaces utility in Windows.

✔**Objective 8.05: Maintaining and Troubleshooting Storage Devices** Apart from HDDs, most storage devices require little maintenance beyond basic cleaning. Hard drives require regular error checking and removal of unneeded files; HDDs in particular also need regular defragmentation. Installation errors can be resolved by mentally retracing the install process to check all connections, set up utility options, and confirm the drive was properly partitioned and formatted. Be alert for the sound of a dying HDD, and replace it swiftly. Most RAID errors come down to controller or drive failure; replace the dead or dying components. Most optical drive issues are fixed by confirming the installation and cleaning the optical discs and drive.

REVIEW QUESTIONS

1. Which is the most likely application of a modern tape drive?
   A. Storing your digital music collection
   B. Archiving old project files
   C. Listening to sweet tunes
   D. Simple file transfers

2. What is the minimum capacity of a single-sided Blu-ray Disc?
   A. 650 MB
   B. 4.7 GB
   C. 25 GB
   D. 50 GB

3. What is the maximum data cable length for an internal SATA drive?
   A. 18 inches
   B. 36 inches
   C. 1 meter
   D. 2 meters

4. A CD-RW has a speed rating of 48×32×52×. What do the three numbers refer to, in order?
   A. Write, rewrite, read
   B. Read, write, rewrite
   C. Rewrite, read, write
   D. Write, read, rewrite

5. What type of video card must you have to watch Blu-ray Discs on your computer?
   A. AGP
   B. HDCP-compliant
   C. HDMI-compliant
   D. ISA

6. What partitioning method creates an MBR?
   A. Dynamic storage
   B. Master boot record
   C. Volume boot record
   D. Dynamic volume

7. What must a partition be to be bootable?
   A. Basic disk, active
   B. Dynamic disk, active
   C. Primary partition, active
   D. Extended partition, active

8. When do you format extended partitions?

   A. Immediately after you create them.

   B. After you create a primary partition.

   C. After you create a dynamic partition.

   D. You don't format extended partitions; you create logical drives in the extended partition and then format those.

9. Which of these are types of Storage Space? (Select two.)

   A. Mirror spaces

   B. Striping spaces

   C. Trading spaces

   D. Parity spaces

10. Eileen has been called in to look at a client's machine and discovers that the computer has a second hard drive, but it doesn't have a drive letter. Instead, to access that drive she clicks a drive icon that says "My Stuff." What kind of partition is the "My Stuff" drive?

   A. Basic disk

   B. Extended partition

   C. Mounted volume

   D. Primary partition

11. What advantage does FAT have over FAT32?

   A. Larger partition size

   B. Better security

   C. Better compression

   D. None

12. Which format offers local file security?

   A. FAT

   B. FAT32

   C. NTFS

   D. NTFS32

13. What is the minimum number of drives required for disk striping with parity?

   A. One

   B. Two

   C. Three

   D. Four

14. What tool enables you to create a RAID 0 array in some editions of Windows?

    A. Disk Management

    B. Storage Spaces

    C. RAID Management

    D. SCSI configuration utility

15. What tool scans and corrects hard drive problems?

    A. Disk Management

    B. Disk Defragmenter

    C. Error checking

    D. File Checker

REVIEW ANSWERS

1. **B** Tape drives are best suited to an archiving project.

2. **C** A single-layer Blu-ray Disc holds 25 GB of data.

3. **C** SATA cables can be up to 1 meter long.

4. **A** If a CD-RW has a speed rating of 48×32×52×, the three numbers refer, in order, to the write, rewrite, and read speeds.

5. **B** To watch Blu-ray Discs on your computer, your video card must be HDCP-compliant.

6. **B** A master boot record partitioning method creates an MBR.

7. **C** You need a primary, active partition to be bootable.

8. **D** Format the logical drives in an extended partition.

9. **A D** Mirror spaces add the most redundancy; parity spaces compromise to add redundancy while requiring less installed capacity.

10. **C** "My Stuff" is a mounted volume.

11. **D** FAT32 blows FAT out of the water.

12. **C** NTFS supports local file security.

13. **C** You need at least three drives to support a RAID 5 array.

14. **A** Disk Management is the tool for creating a software striped (RAID 0) array.

15. **C** Error checking is the official name (Windows 8/10) for the tool that scans and fixes hard drive problems. (Windows Vista/7 add a hyphen, so Error-checking.)

Peripherals and Specialty Computers

	NEWBIE	SOME EXPERIENCE	EXPERT
ETA	4 hours	3 hours	1.5 hours

Now that you know ports, processing, and storage, it's time to learn the final step in the computing process—input/output (I/O)—and put it all together. Most I/O devices plug into ports on the motherboard, or to expansion cards that you add and configure. This chapter looks at input devices, expansion cards, and output devices, then discusses building a custom computer.

 **Objective 9.01 Input Devices**

Input devices enable you to interact with a computer by typing, clicking, speaking, and touching. Modern operating systems support common devices out of the box, but specialty input devices need drivers and configuration. Let's look at input devices you're likely to see in the field and on the 901 exam.

Keyboards

The keyboard has been the primary computer input device since the original IBM PC several decades ago. Today's keyboards are wired (USB, PS/2) or wireless (Bluetooth, radio frequency [RF]). Each OS comes with support for standard QWERTY keyboards, but extra features like fancy controls (see Figure 9.1) require drivers. You can adjust settings such as how fast keys repeat in the Keyboard Control Panel applet (Windows) or System Preferences (OS X). Linux supports these options, but the menu name and location differ among distros.

> **Travel Advisory**
>
> The eternal struggle with keyboards is keeping them clean; educate users who need a replacement not to eat or drink over it!

| **FIGURE 9.1** | Fancy multimedia keyboard |

Pointing Devices

Pointing devices enable us to instruct the computer to perform an action at some spot on the screen. Most computers have a mouse attached (same connection options as keyboards) with two buttons and a scroll wheel (see Figure 9.2). Modern *optical mice* use light-emitting diodes (LEDs) or lasers to track and translate movement to the screen.

A touchpad (see Figure 9.3) uses finger movements to scroll, control the cursor, and issue other commands. Most of these are on portable computers,

FIGURE 9.2 Basic mouse

FIGURE 9.3 Wacom touchpad

but you can find standalone USB or Bluetooth touchpads. We'll revisit portable-computer touchpads in Chapter 10.

> **Travel Advisory**
>
> The Windows 8 Start screen is designed like a tablet or smartphone interface, where you use your fingers to get around. If you lack a touchscreen, use a touchpad or scroll wheel to navigate the interface.

Imaging Tools

Four peripherals capture and digitize visual information: scanners, digital cameras and camcorders, and webcams. Most modern imaging devices connect via USB.

Scanners

Scanners make digital copies of existing paper photos, documents, drawings, and other items. Some can copy directly from a photographic negative or slide, providing images of stunning visual quality (if the original was decent).

These days, traditional *flatbed* consumer-grade scanners are usually combined with a printer to make a multifunction device, which we'll discuss in Chapter 22. You can also find scan-only devices for various purposes. A camera-based *document* or *book scanner* combines a digital camera with some hardware for positioning it squarely above a book or document, and sheet-fed document scanners can be found in desktop or travel-friendly formats for scanning full-sized documents, receipts, business cards, and so on.

Digital Cameras and Camcorders

Not that I have anything against your smartphone and selfie stick, but a dedicated digital camera (see Figure 9.4) or camcorder (see Figure 9.5) can offer higher quality, features tuned to the task at hand, and more room for creativity.

They typically store data on flash memory cards or internal hard drives, but may also have Wi-Fi for quick sharing. Windows and Mac OS X both have programs for basic photo and video organization, editing, and sharing, though professional image- and video-editing software can unlock your creativity (for a price).

FIGURE 9.4 Typical dedicated digital camera

FIGURE 9.5 Typical camcorder

Web Cameras

Unlike regular cameras, where higher quality is better, *webcams* tend to have modest, bandwidth-friendly resolutions. They often include a microphone, but you can also use a standalone mic or headset.

Windows' own webcam drivers are limited, so always install drivers supplied with a camera before you plug it in. Individual programs use webcams differently, but generally you:

- Tell the program you want to use a webcam.
- Choose whether the program can turn it on automatically.
- Configure the image quality.
- Confirm a test session works.

If you have problems, go through general I/O troubleshooting first; if that doesn't work, close other programs that might be using the webcam.

Audio Devices

The computer is a great platform for recording and editing sound and music. The most common option is plugging a *microphone* (see Figure 9.6) into a microphone jack or a USB port to record your voice, make phone and video calls, coordinate with teammates in online games, and control a computer with voice commands. Musicians, however, need special hardware.

FIGURE 9.6   A standard microphone

FIGURE 9.7 A MIDI keyboard

Most *Musical Instrument Digital Interface (MIDI)* devices, also known as *MIDI controllers,* look like standard music keyboards (see Figure 9.7). Others use a grid or row of square buttons—the best ones even light up! Some include knobs, sliders, and buttons for controlling digital audio workstation software; each program should include options and instructions for configuring the MIDI device, but you can often just plug it in a USB port and start playing.

Exam Tip
The CompTIA A+ objectives describe MIDI-enabled devices as both input and output devices.

Game Controllers

You can control most modern computer games with a mouse and keyboard, but some also support joysticks, gamepads, and steering wheels. Modern controllers connect via USB, and you'll need to install drivers for complex ones. *Joysticks* (see Figure 9.8) mimic the iconic aircraft control stick; *gamepads* (see Figure 9.9) resemble gaming console controllers; *steering wheels* may come with pedals and shifters.

You'll need to configure your controller to get the most out of it. In Windows Vista, open the Game Controllers applet. In Windows 7 and later, open the Devices and Printers applet. Right-click the controller and select *Game controller settings.* Select your device from the list of controllers and

FIGURE 9.8   A joystick

click Properties. Depending on your controller, you'll be able to configure the buttons, sticks, triggers, pedals, and more (see Figure 9.10). You can calibrate any analog controls so they accurately register your movements. You can even adjust the amount of vibration used by the controller's *force feedback* (if available).

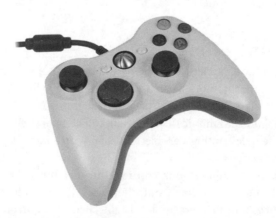

FIGURE 9.9   A gamepad

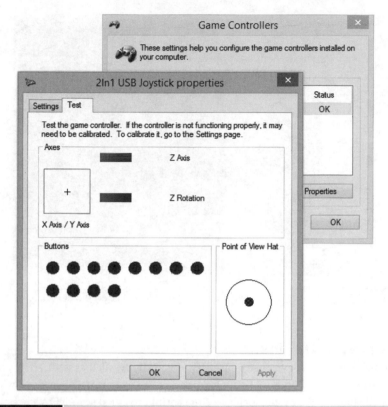

FIGURE 9.10   Game controller properties

Travel Advisory

You also need to enable and configure your controller within the game.

Specialty Input Devices

You should be aware of several other types of I/O device: biometric devices; motion sensors; smart card readers; bar code readers; touchscreens; graphics tablets; and keyboard, video, mouse (KVM) switches. Let's look at these specialized devices.

FIGURE 9.11 Microsoft fingerprint scanner integrated with a keyboard

Biometric Devices

Biometric security devices scan aspects of your body, such as your retina, iris, face, or fingerprint, and use this information as a key to restrict access to whatever the biometric device (such as a fingerprint or retinal scanner) secures.

For example, if you press your finger against the Microsoft fingerprint scanner (see Figure 9.11) when a program or website asks for credentials, it will verify your fingerprint before supplying the program or website with your stored user name and password. After installing one, you follow a scanning process to register with the device, and configure what it should do when it recognizes you.

Motion Sensors

Motion sensors watch for (and sometimes interpret) movement in their field of vision. Cameras (think surveillance here) can use motion sensors to trigger recording, for example. The Microsoft Kinect recognizes user movements and uses them to control games and programs. If an app is selected onscreen and you push your hand forward and pull it back (like pressing a big button), the app will load.

Smart Card Readers

Some businesses use a smart card system that requires employees to display proper credentials to obtain the correct level of access to company resources.

FIGURE 9.12   Smart card reader

A *smart card reader* could be a small device built into a laptop computer, or a panel next to a secure door (see Figure 9.12) that scans chip-embedded *ID badges* or other devices.

Bar Code Readers

Bar code readers read standard Universal Product Code (UPC) bar codes (see Figure 9.13) to track inventory and update inventory databases. Newer readers use USB, but you may see older ports in the wild. Configuration is rare, but confirm the reader works with your database and *point-of-sale (PoS)* software.

FIGURE 9.13   Typical UPC read by bar code readers

Touchscreens

A *touchscreen* is a monitor with a sensing device that tracks finger or stylus contact to interact with the OS. Touchscreens are either built into a device or in a standalone touchscreen monitor; think of the latter as a monitor with a built-in mouse. Most touchscreens are in the portable and mobile devices we'll look at in Chapters 10 and 11, but they also turn up in information kiosks, PoS systems, and all-in-one desktop computers.

Exam Tip

The CompTIA A+ objectives refer to touchscreens as both input and output devices.

Graphics Tablets

A *graphics tablet* or *digitizer* (also known as a *pen tablet*) enables users to paint and draw with a computer (see Figure 9.14). Its special surface transforms (or digitizes) the analog movement and pressure of its *stylus* (pen) into digital information that tablet-aware art software can translate into virtual brush or pen strokes (see Figure 9.15).

Travel Advisory

Some digitizers are designed for handwriting, technical drawings, writing complex characters, or even as a mouse replacement.

FIGURE 9.14 A type of digitizer known as the Wacom pen tablet

FIGURE 9.15   Drawing with a digitizer

Install drivers before you connect the device to a USB port; then use its configuration utility to adjust pressure sensitivity, configure buttons, and set the screen area it uses. You may also have to calibrate it by tapping a series of marks onscreen to make sure your movements map to this screen area as you expect.

KVM Switches

A *keyboard, video, mouse (KVM) switch* enables a single mouse, keyboard, and monitor to control multiple computers (though some KVMs reverse this). KVMs are useful in data centers with many rack-mounted servers and limited space. Once you connect a keyboard, mouse, and monitor to the KVM and connect the KVM to the desired computers, you can use keyboard hotkeys (such as pressing the SCROLL LOCK key twice) to toggle between computers connected to the KVM.

Objective 9.02   # Expansion Cards

Expansion cards add functions to the system; video cards, for example, install and configure an essential output signal: video. Expansion card slots connect, via the expansion bus, to the central processing unit (CPU) and chipset.

FIGURE 9.16 PCI expansion bus slots

You may find older motherboards with the Peripheral Component Interconnect (PCI) general-purpose internal expansion bus, but modern motherboards come with its successor: PCI Express (PCIe).

PCI

Intel introduced the PCI bus architecture (see Figure 9.16) in the early 1990s and released it into the public domain to attract manufacturers. PCI was wider (32 bits), faster (33 MHz), and more flexible than any previous expansion bus, and its self-configuration feature led to the Plug and Play (PnP) standard. The exceptional technology and lack of a price tag led manufacturers to quickly replace earlier busses with PCI.

PCI-X

PCI-X, which has been eclipsed by newer technologies, enhanced PCI with a 64-bit bus (see Figure 9.17) while still accepting regular PCI cards. The PCI-X 2.0 standard features four speed grades (measured in MHz): PCI-X 66, PCI-X 133, PCI-X 266, and PCI-X 533.

FIGURE 9.17 PCI-X slot

Mini-PCI

Mini-PCI (see Figure 9.18) was designed to use low power and to lie flat—both good features for a laptop expansion slot. You may find mini-PCI on older portable computers, though not on modern ones.

PCI Express

PCI Express (PCIe) is the latest, fastest, and most popular expansion bus in use today. PCI Express is still PCI, but it uses a point-to-point serial connection instead of PCI's shared parallel communication. The serial interface reduces transfer overhead and supports higher speeds without causing interference to other parts. A PCIe device's direct (point-to-point) connection to the northbridge means it does not wait for other devices.

A PCIe *lane* uses a wire each to send and receive, and runs at 2.5 Gbps. Better yet, each connection can use 1, 2, 4, 8, 12, 16, or 32 lanes for up to 160 Gbps bandwidth. The *encoding scheme*—how the data is split and reassembled—limits the effective data rate a little, but full-duplex data throughput can go up to 12.8 GBps on a ×32 connection.

> ### Local Lingo
>
> **Mini PCIe** A lot of laptop computers offer an internal PCIe expansion slot called PCI Express Mini Card, usually just stated as Mini PCIe. It works like any PCIe expansion slot, though it's not compatible with full-sized cards.

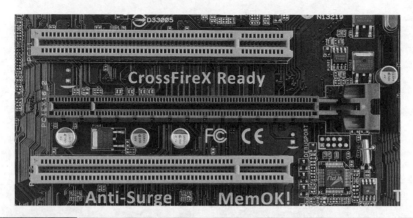

FIGURE 9.19 PCIe ×16 slot (middle) with PCI slots

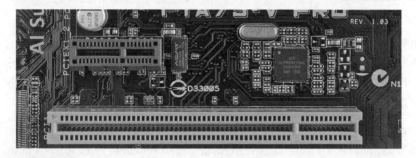

FIGURE 9.20 PCIe ×1 slot (top)

The most common PCIe slot is the 16-lane (×16) version most video cards use (see Figure 9.19), while ×1 (see Figure 9.20) and ×4 are the most common general-purpose PCIe slots. The first PCIe motherboards used a single PCIe ×16 slot and several standard PCI slots.

Travel Advisory

Pronounce lanes as "by" rather than "ex." So "by 1" and "by 8" are the correct pronunciations of *×1* and *×8*.

Installing Expansion Cards

Successful expansion card installation has four steps. First, confirm the card works with your motherboard and OS. Second, insert the card in an expansion slot properly. Third, provide proper drivers for the specific OS. Finally, verify the card functions properly before you walk away.

> ### Exam Tip
>
> The 901 exam may ask about common cards (sound, video, and networking), legacy cards (modems), and special-purpose cards (cellular, riser, TV tuner, and video capture). The 901 exam might even ask how to install a USB, FireWire, Thunderbolt, or storage card. You install all of them using the same four steps: knowledge, physical installation, device drivers and other software, and verification.

Step 1: Knowledge

Learn about the device you plan to install. Microsoft used to maintain the *Windows Compatibility Center* for this information, but they removed it in late 2015. You can check compatibility on the manufacturer's website, though most people just check the device's box (see Figure 9.21). Windows-certified devices proudly display that they work with Windows.

Step 2: Physical Installation

For installation to succeed, you must avoid damaging the card, the motherboard, or both; know how to handle a card, avoid electrostatic discharge (ESD), and remove all power from the system. Insert the card firmly and completely into an available expansion slot.

Ideally, a card should always be either in a computer or in an antistatic bag. When inserting or removing a card, hold the card only by its edges without touching the contacts or any components on the board (see Figure 9.22).

Use an antistatic wrist strap properly attached to the system as noted in Chapter 3. If you don't have one, at least touch the power supply after you

FIGURE 9.21   Compatible with Windows 7 logo on a box

FIGURE 9.22   Where to handle a card

remove the expansion card from its antistatic bag to put you, the card, and the computer at the same electrical potential and minimize the ESD risk.

Modern systems have a trickle of voltage to the motherboard any time the computer is plugged into a power outlet. As noted in Chapter 4: *Always unplug the computer before inserting an expansion card! Failure to do so can destroy the card, the motherboard, or both.*

Never insert or remove a card at an extreme angle; this can damage it. A slight angle is acceptable and even necessary to remove a card. Always secure (and ground) the card to the case with a connection screw (see Figure 9.23) to keep the card from coming loose and shorting out on other cards.

Step 3: Device Drivers and Other Software

Installing device drivers is fairly straightforward. If you're upgrading, unload the current drivers first. Next, install the *correct* drivers. If you have a problem, uninstall the new drivers or roll back to a stable one.

Check the manufacturer's website for the best possible driver. The included drivers may work fine, but there's often a newer, better driver on the website. To know if they are newer, check the disc. Often the version is printed on the optical media itself; if not, load the disc and poke around.

FIGURE 9.23 Always screw down all cards.

Many driver discs have an Autorun screen or Readme file (see Figure 9.24) that advertises the version.

Not all driver makers use the Windows Certification program. When Windows runs into such a driver, it brings up a scary-looking screen (see Figure 9.25) that says you're about to install an unsigned driver. The fact that a company refuses to use the Windows Certification doesn't mean that its drivers are bad—it simply means that they haven't gone through Microsoft's exhaustive quality-assurance certification procedure.

If I run into this, I check the driver's version to make sure it's not outdated, and then I just take my chances. I've yet to encounter a problem with an unsigned driver that I haven't also seen with Windows-certified drivers.

Travel Advisory

Starting with 64-bit versions of Windows Vista, Microsoft requires signed drivers to provide the most stable platform possible. You simply cannot install unsigned drivers without clunky workarounds. If you upgrade a legacy system, make sure signed drivers exist for its hardware before upgrading.

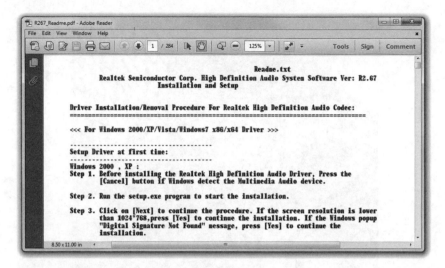

FIGURE 9.24 Part of a Readme file showing the driver version

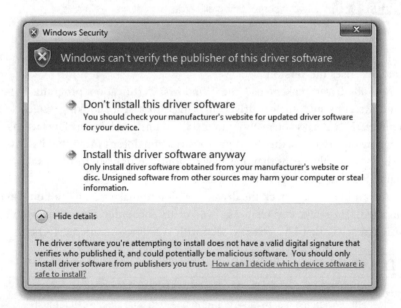

FIGURE 9.25 Unsigned driver warning

FIGURE 9.26 Driver rollback feature

If you install drivers and your system becomes unstable, roll back to the drivers that worked: open the Device Manager, access the properties for the device you want to adjust, and click the Roll Back Driver button on the Driver tab (see Figure 9.26).

Some devices—notably video cards—have additional support software. These include configuration utilities that live in the Control Panel or notification area. Support software used to be a separate installation from the drivers, but most manufacturers now bundle them in one executable.

Step 4: Verify

Finally, inspect the results of the installation and verify the device works properly. Immediately after installing, open Device Manager and confirm Windows sees the device (see Figure 9.27). Assuming Device Manager shows the device with no errors, put the device through the paces. If you installed a printer, print something; if you installed a scanner, scan something. If it works, you're done!

FIGURE 9.27   Device Manager shows the device working properly

Troubleshooting Expansion Cards

A properly installed expansion card rarely makes trouble—it's the botched installations that produce headaches. Chances are you'll have to troubleshoot an expansion card install someday, usually one you botched yourself.

The first sign of an improperly installed card is usually whatever it's supposed to do and it doesn't do it. When this happens, your primary troubleshooting process—after checking in with Device Manager—is a reinstall.

Device Manager should be your first troubleshooting stop in Windows, because it gives you many clues if something has gone wrong. Occasionally, Device Manager may not even show the new device. If that happens, confirm you inserted the device properly and, if needed, that the device has power. Run the Add Hardware Wizard and see if Windows recognizes the device.

If the Device Manager doesn't recognize the device at this point, you have one of two problems: either the device is physically damaged and needs replacing, or something is disabled in the UEFI/BIOS settings. More commonly, device problems manifest themselves in Device Manager via error icons:

FIGURE 9.28 The "!" symbol in Device Manager, indicating a problem with the selected device

- A black exclamation point (!) on a triangle indicates a device is missing (see Figure 9.28), Windows does not recognize it, or there's a driver problem. A device causing this error may still work.

- A black downward-pointing arrow on a white field indicates a disabled (manually turned off or damaged) device. A disabled device will not work.

The "!" symbol is both more common and easier to fix. Double-check the device's connections, then try reinstalling the driver with the Update Driver button. To get to the Update Driver button, right-click the device in the Device Manager and select Properties. In the Properties dialog box, select the Driver tab. On the Driver tab, click the Update Driver button to launch the Hardware Update Wizard (see Figure 9.29).

If you get a downward-pointing arrow or a red "X" icon, confirm the device isn't disabled. Right-click the device and select Enable. If that doesn't work (it rarely does), try rolling back the driver (if you updated it) or uninstalling it. Shut the system down and make triple-sure you have the card physically installed.

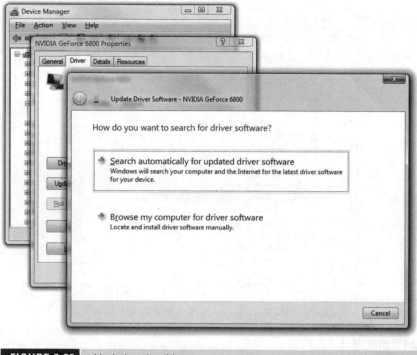

FIGURE 9.29 Updating the driver

Confirm you have the latest driver and redo the entire driver installation procedure. If none of these work, return the card—it's almost certainly bad.

Objective 9.03 Output Devices

Output devices enable you to see or hear feedback from the computer. When you provide input, the computer processes it and provides output. There are three main categories: sound, video, and hard copy. Chapter 22 looks at printers in detail, so this section concentrates on sound and video.

Klipsch 2.1 speaker set

Sound

Sound output is generated by the sound card and speakers. Most computers use sound cards built into the motherboard, but these often have an audible hum or buzz of interference from the rest of the motherboard (which headphones can exacerbate). In any case, speakers affect customer satisfaction much more than the sound card or built-in sound circuits. Spend a little extra money to get decent speakers. If you can fit only a 2.1 set, go for a subwoofer and nice satellites (see Figure 9.30).

Local Lingo

2.1, 5.1, 7.1 The numbers used to describe speaker sets define the number of satellite speakers and a subwoofer. A 2.1 system, for example, means two satellites and a subwoofer. A 5.1 set, in contrast, has two front satellites, two rear satellites (for surround sound), a center channel speaker, and a subwoofer.

Install a sound card like you would any expansion card. Plug things into the correct ports, and they should work fine. If you don't see errors but get no sound, check the Sound applet (see Figure 9.31) in the Control Panel to confirm the correct devices are ready, connected, set to default, and that the playback indicator shows activity on the correct device.

Sound applet

Video

The video card and monitor have a similar relationship to the sound card and speakers. The video card processes commands from the CPU and OS and tells the monitor to update what it shows. Let's look at video cards first and then the LCD monitors and projectors used as displays.

Exam Tip

The 901 objectives list plasma and OLED as monitor types. *Plasma* screens are horrid monitors because stationary interface elements cause *burn-in* that leaves permanent shadows behind. High cost has limited *organic light-emitting diode (OLED)* screens to mobile devices and TVs, so we look at OLED in Chapter 11. That said, the earliest OLED monitors are rolling out in early 2016; expect to see them as prices fall.

FIGURE 9.32 Monitor and display adapter properties

Video Cards

For the CompTIA A+ certification exams, treat a video card (or *graphics card*) like any expansion card. It goes into a PCIe slot; you install drivers and use Device Manager to confirm it works. Then, you configure the video card (or *display adapter*) in the Display Control Panel applet or with included software (see Figure 9.32).

A good, well-configured video card is so critical for some uses that we should dig deeper. Its main parts are video RAM and a video processor. Ages ago video data was stored on memory just like the motherboard's RAM, but modern video cards often use better RAM. The video processor takes information from the video RAM and shoots it out to the monitor. Early video processors were little more than an intermediary between the CPU and video RAM, but powerful modern video cards need fans to cool their video processors (see Figure 9.33).

Among techs, video card discussions revolve around the *graphics processing unit (GPU)* and RAM used. The two major GPU makers, NVIDIA and AMD, develop and sell new GPUs to card manufacturers. Let's break down a typical

FIGURE 9.33 Video card with a cooling fan

card name: XFX Radeon HD7970 3GB 384-bit GDDR5 PCI Express 3.0. XFX is the card's manufacturer; Radeon HD7970 is the (AMD-branded) GPU; 3GB 384-bit GDDR5 describes the dedicated video RAM and the connection between the video RAM and GPU; and PCI Express 3.0 describes the expansion slot it uses.

Low-end graphics processors are enough to write letters or run a web browser, but high-end graphics processors support intensive uses such as beautiful 3-D games, graphics rendering (3-D, animation, video), and even certain kinds of data processing (scientific research, for example) that GPUs are well suited for. Don't be shocked if someone who knows zilch about the latest games needs a system with one or more high-end GPUs—don't skimp on their hardware, and don't assume they need a GPU tailored to gaming.

Drivers   Manufacturers constantly tweak video drivers to make them work better with Windows as well as with popular games and applications. By the time you install a video card, the bundled drivers are inevitably outdated. Skip the bundled drivers and hit the manufacturer's website to download the latest non-beta drivers.

DirectX and Video Cards   In *ye olde days,* many applications communicated directly with the computer's hardware and, as a result, their bugs could crash your computer. Microsoft tried letting Windows smoothly control the hardware, but programmers balked because Windows added *overhead* to the

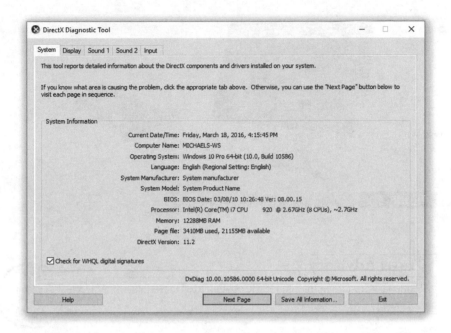

FIGURE 9.34 The DirectX Diagnostic Tool

video process that hurt performance; demanding programs, such as games, needed direct hardware access.

This need to bypass Windows led Microsoft to create *DirectX*. Programmers use a given DirectX *application programming interface (API)* to directly control specific hardware. Because Microsoft's goal was to create a stable environment for running 3-D applications and games within Windows, DirectX includes many APIs (with names like Direct3D) that support direct access to audio and graphics hardware.

Because specific cards and applications support different DirectX versions, you'll eventually need the DirectX Diagnostic Tool (see Figure 9.34) to confirm a specific DirectX version is installed and working. To access it, use the Start Search bar in the Start menu: type **dxdiag** and press ENTER.

LCD Monitors

Unlike earlier *cathode-ray tube (CRT)* monitors, the *liquid-crystal displays (LCDs)* that dominate today are thin, light, energy-efficient, virtually flicker free, and don't emit potentially harmful radiation. LCD panels are used for both standalone (see Figure 9.35) and built-in displays.

Travel Advisory

Remember from Chapter 3 that CRTs contain toxic materials; recycle old CRTs properly.

A color LCD is composed of tiny liquid-crystal *sub-pixels* arranged in rows and columns between polarizing filters. A translucent sheet above the sub-pixels is colored red, green, or blue. Each tiny distinct group of three sub-pixels—one red, one green, and one blue—form a physical pixel (see Figure 9.36).

Sub-pixel   Pixel

FIGURE 9.36   LCD pixels

LCD Resolution   Common resolutions for early monitors—640 × 480, 800 × 600, and 1024 × 768—match a 4:3 *aspect ratio*. You can find some 4:3 monitors today, but the vast majority use 16:9 or 16:10 and are generically called *wide-screen monitors*. Three common wide-screen resolutions are 1366 × 768, 1600 × 900, and 1920 × 1080.

LCD monitors are sharpest at their *native resolution,* such as 1920×1080, because the pixels are fixed; you can't run one at a higher resolution, and a lower-than-native resolution severely degrades image quality. Always set an LCD at native resolution to avoid a fuzzy display.

> **Travel Advisory**
>
> LCD panels of the same physical size may have different native resolutions.

LCD Technologies   Most LCD panels today use an *active matrix* technology called *thin film transistor (TFT)* to create a responsive, color-saturated display, and most of these TFT displays in turn use *twisted nematic (TN)* technology to produce a decent, cheap display; panels that require better color fidelity use *In-Plane Switching (IPS)* technology.

LCD Components   The main LCD components are the LCD panel, backlight(s), and inverters. The LCD panel creates the image, and inverters power the backlights that illuminate the image. Figure 9.37 shows a typical internal component layout.

LCDs traditionally use *cold cathode fluorescent lamp (CCFL)* backlights, but manufacturers currently use several types of *light-emitting diode (LED)* for backlighting, either directly illuminating pixels from behind or flooding the panel from the edges of the bezel. The former produces outstanding contrast and color, for a price. The cheaper edge-lit types function similar to CCFL-style displays, with contrast and colors to match. LCD monitors with LED backlighting are marketed as *LED monitors*.

Contrast Ratio   A good *contrast ratio*—the difference between the darkest and lightest spots that the monitor can display—is 450:1, although a quick trip to a computer store will reveal LCDs with lower levels (250:1) and higher levels (1000:1). The advertised *dynamic contrast ratio,* which measures the difference between a full-on and full-off screen, is much less useful; use the true contrast ratio.

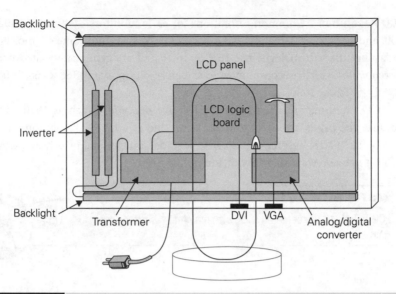

FIGURE 9.37   LCD internals

Response Rate   An LCD panel's *response rate* measures how fast all of the sub-pixels go from pure black to pure white and back. Manufacturers measure LCD response rate in milliseconds (ms), and lower is better. A low-end screen with a 20+ ms response rate may look fine, but you'll see ghosting with movies and fast-paced games; single-digit response rates minimize this.

Refresh Rate   The *refresh rate* of an LCD monitor measures how often a screen can completely update. People experience an image updating more than 24 times a second—the frame rate used in movie theaters—as full-motion, so industry-standard 60-Hz monitors, at 2.5 times faster, are fine for most purposes. Monitors and TVs with higher refresh rates display fast-moving images in sports and video games with fewer artifacts, but keep in mind that the ideal refresh rate usually matches the content's frame rate.

Comparing LCDs   Size and native resolution, of course, should take top consideration. The panel technology (TN vs. IPS) and backlight (CCFL vs. LED) impact both overall quality and price. Because monitors are the primary visual component and have long useful lives, these decisions matter. Most modern monitors have acceptable brightness, response rate, refresh rate, and contrast ratio, but keep them in mind for the exam.

Add-on Filters   Anti-glare filters correct some overly reflective screens. Privacy filters limit the viewing angle to shield the screen from prying eyes.

Projectors

Projectors shoot an image out the front, ideally onto a screen positioned at the proper distance. Front-view projectors (see Figure 9.38) connected to computers running Microsoft PowerPoint have been the cornerstone of almost every meeting since the Clinton administration. The qualities that matter most are brightness (measured in lumens) and throw (expressed in image size at a given distance from the screen).

A *lumen* is the amount of light emitted by a light source from a certain angle that is perceived by the human eye. The greater the lumen rating, the brighter the projector will be, and larger rooms need brighter projectors.

A projector's *throw* is the size of the image at a certain distance from the screen. All projectors have a recommended minimum and maximum throw distance. For instance, a projector with a 16:9 image-aspect ratio needs to be 11 to 12 feet away from the screen to create a 100-inch diagonal image.

Projector lamps work hard to generate a tremendous amount of light, and a lot of heat in the process, so projectors come with a fan to keep the lamp from overheating. Replacement lamps are costly.

Common Features

Regardless of the technology used, you can usually adjust a display's image. All displays have an On/Off button or switch, but additional settings can have

FIGURE 9.38   Front-view projector (photo courtesy of Dell, Inc.)

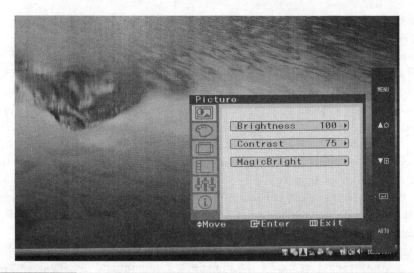

FIGURE 9.39   Typical menu controls

dedicated buttons or live in an onboard menu system (see Figure 9.39). These vary widely, but you should be able to adjust the brightness and contrast, the size and position of the viewable area, and color qualities such as hue and saturation. Make sure the user understands how to adjust these.

Travel Assistance

Connectors are also a major common feature—refer back to our discussion of video connectors in Chapter 2 and make sure you remember the various analog and digital connectors in use.

Display Settings

Beyond directly adjusting the display itself, the Display applet in Control Panel enables you to adjust monitor resolution, refresh rate, driver information, color depth, and more. The specifics differ by operating system, although the options are fairly obvious once you know you *can* make these changes. In Windows 7, for example, click the Adjust resolution link on Display and then click the arrow in the Resolution drop-down (see Figure 9.40). Manually slide the marker to change resolution.

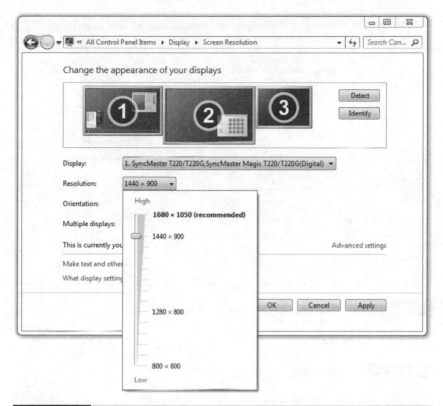

FIGURE 9.40   Screen Resolution options in Windows 7 Display applet

Similar options are in the Display applet in Windows 8.1 (see Figure 9.41). Windows displays only resolutions that your video card/monitor combination can accept, but use the *recommended* value, which matches your monitor's *native resolution*. For those with trouble seeing small screen elements, Windows supports rescaling them to a larger size (though some applications don't handle this well). Table 9.1 shows some common resolutions.

The color quality, also called *color depth,* is how many colors the screen can display. Unless you have an older video card or a significant video speed issue, set your color depth to the highest supported value.

Another option you may see is multiple monitors or *multiple displays* (which CompTIA calls *dual displays*). Most systems can use two (or more) monitors

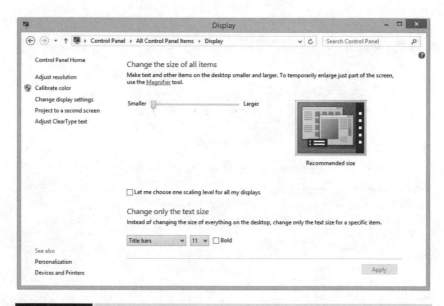

FIGURE 9.41 Display applet in Windows 8.1

TABLE 9.1 Typical Display Modes

Video Mode	Resolution	Aspect Ratio	Typical Device
SVGA	800 × 600	4:3	Small monitors
HDTV 720p	1280 × 720	16:9	Lowest resolution that can be called HDTV
SXGA	1280 × 1024	5:4	Native resolution for many desktop LCD monitors
WXGA	1366 × 768	16:9	Widescreen laptops
WSXGA	1440 × 900	16:10	Widescreen laptops
SXGA+	1400 × 1050	4:3	Laptop monitors and high-end projectors
UXGA	1600 × 1200	4:3	Larger CRT monitors
HDTV 1080p	1920 × 1080	16:9	Full HDTV resolution
WUXGA	1920 × 1200	16:10	For 24"+ widescreen monitors
QWXGA	2048 × 1152	16:9	For smaller, fine monitors
WQXGA	2560 × 1600	16:10	For 27"+ widescreen monitors
WQUXGA	3840 × 2400	16:10	For smaller, fine monitors
4K UHD	3840 × 2160	16:9	High-end monitors

FIGURE 9.42   Scott hard at work with two monitors

like two halves of one large monitor, or to duplicate what's happening on the first. Multiple monitors are handy if you need lots of screen space but don't want to buy a really large, expensive monitor (see Figure 9.42).

Each video card supports one or more monitors, so the first step is to confirm you have one or more video cards that, combined, can support the monitors you need. From here, it's easy. Just plug in the monitors and Windows should detect them. Windows will show each monitor in the Display applet (see Figure 9.43). Select the appropriate option to extend or duplicate your desktop on the new monitor.

> ### Exam Tip
>
> The 902 objectives include troubleshooting *multiple monitor misalignment/ orientation*, which means that the image displayed on your multiple monitors doesn't match their physical arrangement or orientation. The Display applet in Figure 9.43 enables you to change display orientation and arrangement.

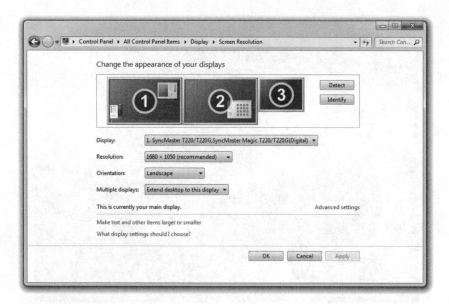

FIGURE 9.43 Enabling multiple monitors

If you need more advanced settings, click the cleverly labeled Advanced or Advanced Settings button. The title of this dialog box reflects the monitor and video card (see Figure 9.44).

Troubleshooting Video

Video problems fall into several categories: video cards, drivers, monitors, OS settings, and application settings (though the 902 exam is surprisingly uninterested in the last two). Each can degrade screen output, so techs need to recognize common video and display issues and know how to fix them. Let's take a look.

Troubleshooting Video Cards/Drivers

Video cards rarely go bad, so bad or incompatible drivers and incorrect settings cause most problems. Confirm you have the correct driver installed. Incompatible drivers can cause a Blue Screen of Death (BSoD) when Windows starts to load. A suddenly corrupted driver usually doesn't manifest until you reboot, when Windows will go into SVGA mode, blank the monitor, lock up, or display a garbled screen with incorrect color patterns or a very distorted image.

FIGURE 9.44 Advanced video settings for Samsung SyncMaster T220 monitor running on ATI Radeon 5700 Series video card

These distortions can include oversized images and icons, or a 3-D image with distorted geometry.

Regardless, reboot into Safe Mode in Windows Vista or 7 and roll back or uninstall the driver. In Windows 8 or later, you'll need to boot to the recovery media to get to the Windows Recovery Environment (WinRE). Keep in mind that more advanced video cards may have driver programs installed under Programs and Features; check there first before you try removing a driver with Device Manager. Download the latest driver and reinstall.

> **Exam Tip**
>
> The CompTIA A+ 902 objectives suggest buggy drivers can force Windows into VGA mode (640 × 480). This was once true, but current versions will use SVGA (800 × 600). Be prepared for "VGA mode" to be the only correct-ish answer.

Video cards are durable, but the fan and RAM can still fail. Lucky for you, both tend to show the same symptom—bizarre distortions followed by a screen lockup. Usually Windows keeps running; you may see your mouse pointer moving around and windows refreshing as the screen melts into a huge mess. Bad drivers can also cause this, so first try Safe Mode—if this clears the problem up, the video card isn't bad.

Excessive heat can create some interesting effects. An overheating computer might shut down, which you'll recognize because it will come back up only to shut down again as soon as you push it hard. Sometimes the screen will get bizarre artifacts or distortions. Check your case fans and make sure the video card has enough clearance for good airflow. You might need to blow out (outdoors!) the dust filters, vents, heatsinks, and fans.

Troubleshooting LCDs

An LCD panel's pixels can have a few problems: a pixel that never lights up is a *dead pixel,* a pixel that is stuck on pure white is a lit pixel, and a pixel stuck on a certain color is a stuck pixel. You can't repair bad pixels; replace the panel. Even on a brand-new monitor, LCD warranties specify how many pixels must go bad before the manufacturer will replace it.

- If your LCD monitor cracks, it is not repairable and must be replaced.
- A flickering LCD usually points to a cheap panel with too much light bleed from the backlight, or a dying CCFL backlight. LED backlights don't flicker. Replace the backlight if necessary.
- A dim image, especially on only half of the screen, points to a dead or dying backlight in a multi-backlight system. Replace as necessary.
- If the LCD goes dark but you can still barely see the image under bright lights, you lost either the backlight or the inverter. In many cases, especially with super-thin panels, you'll replace the entire panel and backlight as a unit. On the other hand, an inverter can be on a separate replaceable circuit board.
- If your LCD makes a distinct hissing noise, an inverter is about to fail and can be replaced.

Don't open an LCD to work on the inside. The inverter can bite you in several ways. First, its high-voltage electrical circuit can shock you. Worse, the inverter both retains a charge after you unplug it and gets hot enough to burn you. Finally, ESD can irreparably damage the inverter. You can buy replacement LCD parts, but just leave it up to people who can do it faster, cheaper, and safer. Find a specialty LCD repair company.

 **Custom PC Configurations**

Now it's time to bring all of this component knowledge together. Let's look at eight types of custom PCs and their typical components and configurations:

- **Standard thick client**   These systems meet the recommended requirements for running Windows (or selected OS) and standard desktop applications, such as office productivity and networking applications.

- **Thin client**   Thin clients are low-power computers with network connectivity that run or access an OS and applications housed on a server, leveraging the server's power. A thin client runs basic applications—to do e-mail and access the Web—and meets minimum OS requirements.

- **Virtualization workstation**   Essentially the opposite of a classic thin client; runs multiple operating systems at once through virtual machines. Correspondingly, it needs maximum RAM and a multicore CPU.

- **Audio/video editing workstation**   These media workstations require specialized audio and video cards; a large, fast hard drive; multiple monitors; maximum RAM; and a very fast multicore CPU.

- **Graphic/CAD/CAM design workstation**   This mouthful refers to a computer built around specialized computer-aided design (CAD) software, such as AutoCAD, for designing and modeling physical objects. Such a machine needs a powerful multicore processor, high-end video equipment, and maximum RAM.

- **Gaming computer**   Similar in needs to a graphics workstation, though the video card should use a high-end game-oriented GPU rather than a workstation GPU. It also needs a powerful multicore processor, high-definition sound card, and high-end cooling.

- **Home server PC**   A home server today has several roles, such as central file storage, print server, and streaming media machine. As such, a home server PC needs processing power, robust networking, and fast redundant storage. CompTIA specifically lists the following requirements:
  - Media streaming
  - File sharing
  - Print sharing
  - Gigabit network interface card (NIC)
  - RAID array

Local Lingo

Media center   Although the 901 competencies don't list specific software, most home servers use media center software, such as Kodi (see Figure 9.45) or Plex.

- **Home theater PC**   The home theater PC (HTPC) differs most from the standard thick client. Many look like a piece of stereo equipment; CompTIA calls these cases the *HTPC compact form factor* (see Figure 9.46).

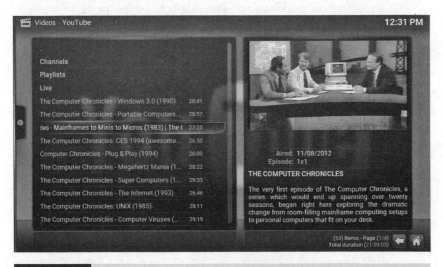

FIGURE 9.45   Kodi

| FIGURE 9.46 | HTPC |

HTPCs often include a TV tuner to display and record standard cable or broadcast television signals, and surround-sound audio—usually with four satellites, a center speaker, and a subwoofer (5.1 audio). Finally, the HTPC connects to a big monitor via a High Definition Multimedia Interface (HDMI) cable that carries both audio and high-definition video.

Two devices that enable you to watch video streamed over the Internet are undermining the HTPC's usefulness. A *smart TV* is a television with network capabilities—both hardware and software—so you can plug it in and hit the Web. A *set-top box*, such as a Roku 3 (see Figure 9.47), adds the same features to a dumb TV. Streaming movies from Netflix or Amazon has never been easier.

| FIGURE 9.47 | Roku 3 |

CHECKPOINT

✔**Objective 9.01: Input Devices** Input devices enable you to interact with the computer through typing, clicking, speaking, and more. Modern operating systems support common devices, such as a keyboard or mouse, straight out of the box, but specialty input devices require drivers and configuration. Other common input devices include scanners, digital cameras and camcorders, and webcams. Audio peripherals include microphones and MIDI devices. Game controllers run riot, but most common are joysticks and gamepads. Specialty input devices include biometric devices, motion sensors, smart card readers, bar code readers, and touchscreens. A graphics tablet or digitizer enables you to use a special pen to draw directly into the computer. A KVM switch enables you to connect a single keyboard, mouse, and monitor to multiple systems.

✔**Objective 9.02: Expansion Cards** PCI expansion cards come in several subtypes, such as PCI-X, Mini-PCI, PCI Express, and Mini-PCIe. A successful expansion card install has four steps: knowledge of the proper device, physical installation, device driver installation, and verification of success.

✔**Objective 9.03: Output Devices** Output devices enable you to see or hear feedback from the computer and come in three main categories: sound, video, and hard copy. Sound output requires a sound card and speakers. Video output requires a video card or display adapter and a display, such as an LCD monitor or a projector.

✔**Objective 9.04: Custom PC Configurations** CompTIA expects techs to evaluate and recommend hardware for specialized computers. These systems include thick and thin clients; virtualization, audio/video editing, and graphics/CAD/CAM workstations; gaming computers; home server PCs; and home theater PCs.

REVIEW QUESTIONS

1. Which of the following devices enables you to input a picture into a computer easily?
   A. Keyboard
   B. Mouse
   C. Printer
   D. Scanner

2. Which of the following devices enables voice and video connection over the Internet?
   A. Dedicated digital camera
   B. Printer
   C. Scanner
   D. Webcam

3. Which of the following is an example of a biometric device?
   A. Digital camera
   B. Flatbed scanner
   C. Retinal scanner
   D. Webcam

4. What device enables you to enter data directly into a computer using only your fingers?
   A. Bar code reader
   B. Flatbed scanner
   C. Touchscreen
   D. Webcam

5. How many PCIe lanes does a video card typically use?
   A. 4
   B. 8
   C. 16
   D. 32

6. Which of the following is a common use of smart card technologies?

   A. Automatically uploading digital camera images over Wi-Fi

   B. Controlling access to company resources by verifying employee credentials and access levels

   C. Minimizing power consumed by inactive internal expansion cards

   D. Enabling cellular carriers to associate your phone number with your cellular phone

7. Which of these are LCD backlight technologies? (Select two.)

   A. Cold cathode fluorescent lamp

   B. Incandescent luminance inverter

   C. Light-emitting diode

   D. Organic light-emitting diode

8. Mary wants to add a new sound card to a client's system. What should she do before inserting the card into the motherboard? (Select two.)

   A. Isolate the card.

   B. Install the drivers.

   C. Ground herself.

   D. Unplug the computer.

9. After installing an updated sound card driver, Tiffany's Windows system boots but now no sound comes out of the speakers. She has the speakers plugged in properly and powered up. What can she do to get the sound working again?

   A. Roll back the drivers.

   B. Reinstall the drivers.

   C. Reload Windows.

   D. Unsign the drivers.

10. Which of the following devices are examples of output devices? (Select two.)

    A. Keyboard

    B. Mouse

    C. Monitor

    D. Speaker

11. Why do plasma screens make poor computer displays?
    A. Their vivid colors cause eye strain.
    B. They generate so much heat that they must be turned off every few hours in order to cool.
    C. Their image quality is insufficient when viewed from just a few feet away.
    D. Static screen elements may leave a permanent burn-in shadow.

12. Akili gets a tech call about a new LCD that's "fuzzy." What might he check first?
    A. Check the resolution and set it at the native resolution.
    B. Check the refresh rate and increase the vertical refresh rate.
    C. Check the refresh rate and increase the horizontal refresh rate.
    D. Check the lamp and replace it if necessary.

13. What's a typical adjustment you can make on a monitor?
    A. Increase the brightness.
    B. Increase the inverter.
    C. Increase the lamp.
    D. Increase the response rate.

14. Which of these can you use in Windows to adjust the resolution of a monitor?
    A. Display applet
    B. Monitor applet
    C. Resolution applet
    D. Video applet

15. What type of workstation would you recommend to a client who needs to run multiple instances of operating systems at the same time?
    A. Thin client
    B. Virtualization workstation
    C. Standard thick client
    D. Audio/video editing workstation

REVIEW ANSWERS

1. **D**   You can import or input pictures easily into a computer using a scanner.

2. **D**   A webcam enables you to chat with both voice and video over the Internet.

3. **C**   A retinal scanner is an example of a biometric device.

4. **C**   A touchscreen enables direct input of data using your fingers or a stylus.

5. **C**   Video cards typically use 16 PCIe lanes.

6. **B**   Some companies use smart cards to verify employee credentials and confirm access to a given resource.

7. **A C**   CCFL and LED are backlight technologies, but OLED doesn't technically use a backlight.

8. **C D**   Mary should both ground herself to the computer and unplug it to turn off the trickle charge on the motherboard before inserting the card.

9. **A**   The quickest fix here would be to reinstall the old card and do a driver rollback.

10. **C D**   Monitors and speakers are the two most common output devices on the computer, with the printer (not an option here) being the third.

11. **D**   Static elements may cause burn-in, leaving permanent, shadowy traces of those elements on the screen.

12. **A**   A fuzzy LCD often is just running in a resolution that's not its native resolution. That's the first thing to check in such a situation.

13. **A**   All monitors have some option to increase or decrease the brightness.

14. **A**   You can use the Display applet in Windows to adjust the resolution of a monitor.

15. **B**   A virtualization workstation can run multiple instances of operating systems at the same time through virtual machines.

Portable
Computers

	NEWBIE	SOME EXPERIENCE	EXPERT
ETA	3 hours	2 hours	1 hour

Portable computing devices compromise between desktop power and the convenience of not being anchored to a desk. Classic portables usually run Windows, Mac OS X, or some flavor of Linux, but operating systems based on Linux—like Chrome OS—also exist. This chapter examines what portable computing devices are and then looks at how to extend their capabilities, manage and maintain them, upgrade and repair them, and troubleshoot them.

Travel Advisory

Many portables have keys or switches to change settings that you can also modify via OS settings, applets, and menus. This chapter focuses on what portables do differently; you can still accomplish these tasks through your OS.

Objective 10.01 Portable Computing Devices

The traditional clamshell *notebook* computer, with built-in LCD monitor, keyboard, and input device (such as a *touchpad,* for example), is also called a portable or a *laptop.* Other portables combine a computer operating system with hardware that resembles mobile devices (which run a mobile OS). Let's consider how to identify various portables.

Travel Assistance

Chapter 11 discusses mobile devices, such as smartphones and tablets.

Types of Portable Device

Let's take a look at some of the terms used to describe portable devices and put them in context. Keep in mind that these categories can be slippery; don't think of them as mutually exclusive.

Notebooks

A *desktop replacement* dwarfs the traditional clamshell notebook we just discussed (see Figure 10.1), leaving room for a massive screen, dedicated graphics,

Desktop replacement (left) next to a standard laptop (right)

a full-size keyboard, an optical drive, and plenty of hard drive space. Think power first, portability second. Expensive *gaming laptops* are a type of high-performance desktop replacement with high-quality displays, graphics cards, and customizable keyboards.

Subnotebooks

Unsurprisingly, *subnotebooks* are smaller and lighter than a regular notebook, though this distinction is becoming moot as subnotebook popularity grows. Before the category gained traction, *netbooks* (see Figure 10.2) were tiny (with displays around 10 inches), light, cheap, and had long battery life. The netbook category is dead, but the need it met is bigger than ever.

ASUS netbook sitting on a normal laptop

FIGURE 10.3   MacBook Air

Its most direct successor is the *Chromebook*. Technically, a Chromebook is any portable running Google's Linux-based Chrome OS, but most are light and inexpensive, have modest computing power and storage, and appear on the small end of the laptop spectrum. Much like a thin client, Chromebooks leverage the power of networked servers to store data and run programs over the Web.

Thin, light, and powerful, *Ultrabooks* are for those willing to pay more for performance in a small package. They use power-sipping Intel processors with integrated graphics, are thinner than 23 mm, and last at least 6 hours of HD video playback. Many copy the thin-slice aesthetic of the MacBook Air (see Figure 10.3), leave out optical drives, and use SSDs.

2-in-1s

A *2-in-1* can be roughly understood as a touchscreen portable on the spectrum from laptop-and-tablet to tablet-and-laptop. Microsoft *Tablet PCs* (see Figure 10.4) pioneered the category in 2001 with portables running a tablet-and-stylus-aware version of Windows, though you won't catch Microsoft using "Tablet PC" anymore. Modern 2-in-1 devices are a renewed attempt to capitalize on the success of mobile tablets by using convertible and hybrid form factors.

> ### Local Lingo
> **Laplet**   A hybrid device with a full desktop OS and laptop-level specs tucked away in a tablet form factor.

FIGURE 10.4   A Tablet PC

A *convertible* laptop uses one of several mechanisms to "convert" into something you use like a tablet. Some have removable screens that become standalone tablets (leaving behind any hardware built into the keyboard half), and others use innovative hinges that enable you to open the screen until it's flush with the bottom of the laptop; flip the screen to expose it when the laptop is closed; or pop the screen up from a default tablet position, revealing a keyboard.

A *hybrid* laptop/tablet has a tablet form factor that integrates with a detachable keyboard, which may double as a cover (see Figure 10.5). The line between a hybrid tablet that can attach to a keyboard and a convertible laptop with a removable tablet screen is hard to draw, so focus on what is lost when you use the tablet portion alone: if you just lose a keyboard, it's a hybrid.

FIGURE 10.5   Microsoft Surface Pro 3 with its keyboard cover

Keyboard comparison

Input Devices

Portable computers come with a variety of input devices. Most have a fully functional keyboard and a device to control the mouse pointer.

Keyboard

Laptop keyboards use the QWERTY key layout, just like regular keyboards (see Figure 10.6), but some get "creative" with the size and placement of other keys. Most use a *Function (FN) key* to enable other keys to double as media controls, hardware feature toggles, a number pad, and so on.

Pointing Devices

The most common laptop pointing device today is the *touchpad*, which is a flat, touch-sensitive pad near the keyboard (see Figure 10.7). You simply glide

Touchpad on a laptop

your finger across its surface to move the pointer, and tap the surface once or twice to single- or double-click. You can also click by using buttons at the bottom of the pad. A *multitouch* touchpad enables you to perform multifinger *gestures* such as scrolling or swiping to another screen, and Apple's game-changing *Multi-Touch trackpad* is better than a mouse in many ways.

Exam Tip

Before touchpads could detect and ignore accidental input, it was easy to "use" a touchpad with your palm while typing; some older portables have a hardware switch or FN key combination to disable the touchpad.

A growing number of portables also have *touchscreens* that enable users to fluidly perform complex actions with gestures. In some cases these are otherwise traditional laptops, but most are 2-in-1s that function as a tablet *and* laptop. We'll take a closer look at touchscreens along with mobile devices in Chapter 11.

Webcams and Microphones

Most new mobile and portable devices have some sort of front-facing video camera—a *webcam* in the case of laptops—and one or more built-in microphones. A single *microphone* is suitable for picking up the user's voice, but noise-cancellation routines use additional microphones to improve audio quality. These have all the uses we discussed in Chapter 9.

There's a catch: anyone who controls these near-ubiquitous input devices can spy on you. Many webcams include a recording indicator, but built-in microphones don't do the same; it may not matter, because some vulnerabilities enable disabling the indicator.

Display Types

Portables come in a variety of sizes and at varying costs. One major contributor to the overall cost is the LCD screen size, which typically ranges from 10.1 inches to 17.3 inches, though a few are just over 20 inches. You know all about the technology in these panels from Chapter 9; the biggest difference is that the laptop's LCD frame may contain a Wi-Fi antenna, webcam, and microphone.

Exam Tip

The major 901 objectives for laptop displays are explored in other chapters. Chapter 9 introduced you to LCD panels and looked at how to compare TN with IPS and CCFL with LED backlights. OLED laptops are just hitting shelves in early 2016. We look at OLED displays in Chapter 11 alongside the smaller mobile devices that use them.

As discussed in Chapter 9, almost all the screens you find in present-day laptops will be 16:9 or 16:10. Very old laptop screens had a 4:3 aspect ratio. Screens with a *matte* finish reduce glare but wash out in bright light unless the brightness is cranked up; those with a *high-gloss* finish have sharper contrast, richer colors, and wider viewing angles, but they pick up lots of reflection in bright light.

 ## Objective 10.02 Extending Portables

You can enhance more traditional portable computers through external ports or internal card slots, though options are limited on more compact portables such as Ultrabooks and 2-in-1s. Let's look at single-function ports and slots, networking options, portable-specific expansion slots, and general-purpose ports.

Single-Function Ports and Slots

Single-function ports work the same way on portable computers as they do on a desktop. You plug in a device to the correct port and, as long as the operating system has the proper drivers, it'll work. We've looked at these—audio, video, smart card, and flash storage cards—in previous chapters, so let's see how they manifest in portables.

Standard 3.5-mm audio-out ports are the most ubiquitous, and larger portables may also have a microphone-in port (see Figure 10.8), though built-in microphones are increasingly common. You can plug in headphones, regular

FIGURE 10.8 Standard audio ports

computer speakers, or even a nice surround sound set to play music that sounds as good as any you'll hear on a desktop system. Some portables have hardware controls or function keys that can mute or adjust volume (see Figure 10.9).

Most portables support multiple displays via one of the digital ports we looked at in Chapter 2, with a preference for smaller versions such as Mini-HDMI, Micro-HDMI, DisplayPort, and Mini DisplayPort. You might find an older or special-purpose portable with an analog VGA port. Portables may use an FN key combination (see Figure 10.10) to cycle through multiple-monitor configurations such as extending or mirroring displays.

It isn't really a port, but some portable computers—especially laptops marketed to business users—are secured with a thin, credit-card-size *smart card reader* and a smart-card-chipped ID badge. You've probably seen the chip in

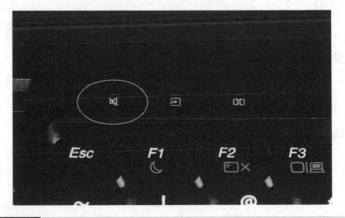

FIGURE 10.9 The mute button on a laptop

FIGURE 10.10   Laptop Function (FN) key and additional key combinations

FIGURE 10.11   Smart card

Figure 10.11 in one of its other applications: securing credit and debit cards. We'll look at using smart cards for authentication in Chapter 21.

Finally, portable computers commonly include one or more flash-memory card slots (usually one of the popular SD formats you saw in Chapter 8) to enable you to add storage or transfer files.

Networking Options

It's tough to find a portable computer without at least one network connection option. We'll look at each technology when we discuss networking in Chapters 18, 19, and 20—so for now we'll focus on what you'll find in portables. Today's portables come with 802.11, Bluetooth, or wired Ethernet connections.

Virtually all modern portables have some version (standard) of *802.11 Wi-Fi* built directly into the chipset; 802.11b and 802.11g standards are common on

FIGURE 10.12 Wireless switch

older laptops, and newer portables use 802.11n or 802.11ac. Portables are getting powerful enough to live longer lives than they used to, so don't be surprised if you find devices with built-in support for an older standard.

It's not quite as ubiquitous, but most portables also include a *Bluetooth* wireless radio; it's great for adding wireless peripherals such as mice, keyboards, and headsets, not to mention teaming up with smartphones, speakers, and a legion of other Bluetooth devices.

Hardware switches (see Figure 10.12) or special FN hotkeys enable you to toggle specific features such as wireless networking, cellular networking, GPS, and Bluetooth. They're also handy when saving battery life is more important than networking.

Larger laptops usually have an RJ-45 wired Ethernet network connection (see Figure 10.13), but hybrids, Ultrabooks, and other smaller portables often leave this out.

FIGURE 10.13 Ethernet port on a laptop

Portable-Specific Expansion Slots

For many years, the *Personal Computer Memory Card International Association (PCMCIA)* established standards for portable computer expansion cards and slots. USB's dominance has made these once-common expansion slots almost impossible to find. The last standard was called ExpressCard.

ExpressCard comes in two widths (see Figure 10.14): 34 mm and 54 mm, called *ExpressCard/34* and *ExpressCard/54*. Both are 75 mm long and 5 mm thick.

ExpressCards connect to either the Hi-Speed USB 2.0 bus or the PCI Express bus. These differ phenomenally in speed: the USB version has a miserly maximum throughput of 480 Mbps compared to the PCIe version, which roars in at 2.5 Gbps. PCMCIA announced ExpressCard 2.0 in 2009 with speeds up to 5 Gbps and support for SuperSpeed USB 3.0, but PCMCIA dissolved and shut its offices before any devices rolled out.

> **Travel Advisory**
>
> You may see ExpressCards that claim to support USB 3.0. While they technically have USB 3.0 ports, the PCIe bus they use can't reach true USB 3.0 speeds of 5 Gbps. Still, they offer an excellent update to an older laptop by adding USB ports that surpass USB 2.0 speeds by a large margin!

FIGURE 10.14   34-mm and 54-mm ExpressCards

General-Purpose Ports

Today's portable computers usually have one or more USB ports to give you the option to add more hardware. Some special-purpose laptops still provide legacy general-purpose expansion ports (PS/2, RS-232 serial ports, and so on) for installing peripheral hardware; you can also find modern ports such as Thunderbolt, eSATA, and FireWire. You're familiar with these general-purpose ports from earlier chapters, so let's look instead at how you can get by with a portable's more limited connections: docking stations and adapters.

Laptops can connect (Transformers style) with *docking stations* that provide a host of legacy and modern single- and multi-function ports (see Figure 10.15). The typical docking station uses a proprietary connection but has extra features built in, such as an optical drive or ExpressCard slot for extra enhancements. You can find docking stations for many older small laptops. A docking station makes an excellent companion to such portables.

When you don't need access to many ports at once, just use a USB adapter. We looked at these in Chapter 2, but they really shine at supplementing a compact portable such as an Ultrabook that has just one or two USB ports. I don't know about you, but I haven't spun up an optical disc in months, nor am I sure when I last opened my laptop near a wired Ethernet connection. Why lug around a large laptop stuffed with hardware you rarely use when you can get by with a USB optical drive or USB-to-RJ-45 dongle and a much smaller/lighter laptop instead?

USB adapters also shine at updating connectivity support for older devices. A USB-to-Wi-Fi dongle or a USB Bluetooth adapter can update an old laptop to 802.11ac, or add Bluetooth to a laptop that didn't come with it.

Exam Tip

The 901 exam expects you to be familiar with USB-to-RJ-45 and USB-to-Wi-Fi dongles as well as USB-to-Bluetooth, USB-to-optical-drive, and USB-to-Ethernet adapters.

FIGURE 10.15 Docking station

Objective 10.03 **Managing and Maintaining Portables**

Beyond the standard hardware, OS, and storage maintenance, managing and maintaining portables is mostly about taking care of the batteries, extending battery life through proper power management, keeping the machine clean, and avoiding excessive heat. This section examines issues specific to portables, with one caveat: for compact and hybrid portables that are built like mobile devices, you should combine the steps mentioned here with troubleshooting ideas from Chapter 11.

Batteries

Today's powerful *Lithium-Ion (Li-Ion)* batteries (see Figure 10.16) last much longer than the Nickel-Metal Hydride (Ni-MH) and Nickel-Cadmium (Ni-Cd) ones used in the 1990s. There's a tiny downside: Li-Ion batteries explode if overcharged or punctured, but they do have built-in circuitry to prevent accidental overcharging. Lithium batteries can only power systems designed to use them.

Lithium polymer (LiPo) batteries are technically a rare Li-Ion variant that places the heart of the battery—the electrolyte—into a solid polymer rather than an organic solvent, enabling the battery to take exotic shapes. In practice, the LiPo label is often applied to traditional Li-Ion electrolyte packed in polymer bags instead of a rigid case. These impostor LiPo batteries haven't replaced Li-Ion, but they are used a lot in small, compact devices such as hybrids and Ultrabooks.

FIGURE 10.16   Li-Ion battery

In any case, always store batteries partially charged (around 70 to 80 percent) in a *cool* place. Not the freezer; that's a *cold* place. Rechargeable batteries have only a limited number of charge-discharge cycles before overall battery performance is reduced, so avoid pointless discharges and never drain a battery completely unless required for *battery calibration* (using steps provided by the manufacturer). Remember the explosion part? *Never* handle a ruptured or broken battery, and protect yourself, other people, and the environment by *always* recycling old batteries properly.

Power Management

Each component in a portable needs power, so the hardware, UEFI/BIOS, and OS in modern systems cooperate—a process called *power management*—to shut down unused devices.

System Management Mode

Intel started power management with a series of features—*System Management Mode (SMM)*—that enabled the 386SX CPU to slow or stop its clock without erasing register information, and supported power-saving peripherals. To do much good, SMM needs BIOS and OS support from Intel's Advanced Power Management (APM) specification and Advanced Configuration and Power Interface (ACPI) standard.

APM and ACPI require an SMM-capable CPU, an APM/ACPI-compliant BIOS or UEFI/BIOS that enables the CPU to turn off devices, Energy Star devices that accept being shut off, and an OS programmed to turn off unused devices and slow the CPU when reasonable.

Local Lingo
Energy Star   The EPA awards Energy Star status to devices that can enter a low-power state that consumes much less power than normal.

APM/ACPI Levels

APM defines four power-usage levels; all but the first use power management:

- **Full On**   Everything at full power.
- **APM Enabled**   CPU and RAM at full power. Unused devices may shut down.
- **APM Standby**   RAM keeps data, but the CPU and other devices stop. Device configurations retained to skip reinitializing the devices.

- **APM Suspend**   All devices are shut down or at the lowest power-consumption level. Systems that use *hibernation* save RAM contents to the hard drive and restore them on a wake-up event.

ACPI, the successor to APM, handles all these levels plus a few more, such as "soft power on/off," which enables you to define the function of the power button. ACPI also supports hot-swapping. Be familiar with these ACPI global (G) and sleeping (S) system power states:

- **G0 (S0)**   Working state
- **G1**   Sleeping state mode. Further subdivided into four *S* states:
  - **S1**   CPU stops processing. Maintains power to the CPU and RAM.
  - **S2**   CPU powers down.
  - **S3**   Sleep or Standby mode. Maintains power to RAM.
  - **S4**   Hibernation mode. Saves RAM contents to the hard drive.
- **G2 (S5)**   Soft power-off. Powers off components not needed to wake up later.
- **G3**   Mechanical off. Powers off the system and devices except the real-time clock (RTC).

Configuration of APM/ACPI

You can configure APM/ACPI via power-management settings in both CMOS and the OS. Because the APM/ACPI standards are flexible, CMOS settings are all over the place (see Figures 10.17 and 10.18); the universal constant is

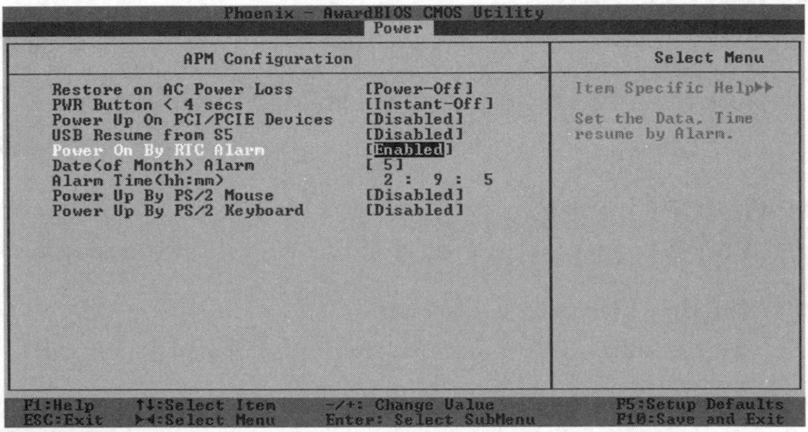

FIGURE 10.17   Setting an APM wake-up event in CMOS

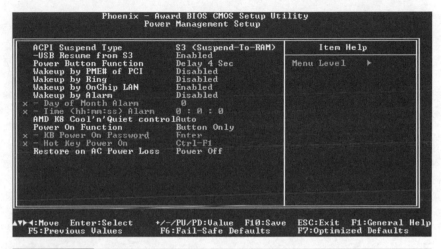

FIGURE 10.18   CMOS with ACPI setup option

the initialize power-management toggle. Additional settings may control time frames for entering Standby and Suspend modes, which events take place in each mode, which events wake the system, and what states the hardware power buttons trigger.

In Windows, APM/ACPI settings are in the Power Options Control Panel applet (also accessible via the Power icon in the notification area—if it is present). Windows *power plans*—Balanced, High performance, and Power saver—enable better control over power (see Figure 10.19). You can customize a power

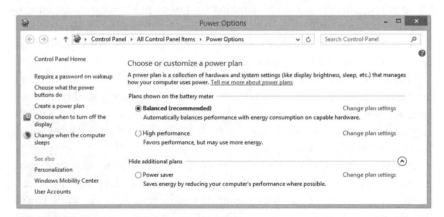

FIGURE 10.19   Windows Balanced, High performance, and Power saver power plan options

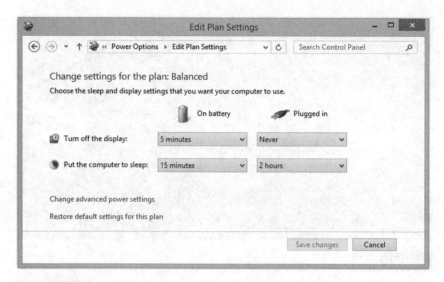

FIGURE 10.20   Customizing a laptop power plan in Windows

plan for your portable (see Figure 10.20) that will turn off the display or put the computer to sleep at different time intervals when on battery or AC power.

Hibernate mode (see Figure 10.21) takes everything in active memory and stores it on the hard drive before the system powers down, and reloads it into RAM when the system wakes.

Manual Control of Power Use

We've already discussed the low-hanging fruit of manual power management: switches, buttons, and keyboard combinations for disabling wireless devices such as Wi-Fi and Bluetooth. Beyond these, there are a few more settings that help, after which we'll look at how planning ahead can help.

Today's portables and operating systems often borrow a mobile-device feature: *airplane mode*. Beyond its intended use, airplane mode quickly disables several power-sucking components. You can also reduce the LCD backlight's brightness using an FN hotkey (see Figure 10.22) as well as disable the keyboard backlight, if you have one.

One of the best ways to conserve battery is to minimize the number of programs and hardware devices/radios you need while on battery power. Instead of throwing files on a flash drive or into Dropbox, transfer them while you're still plugged in.

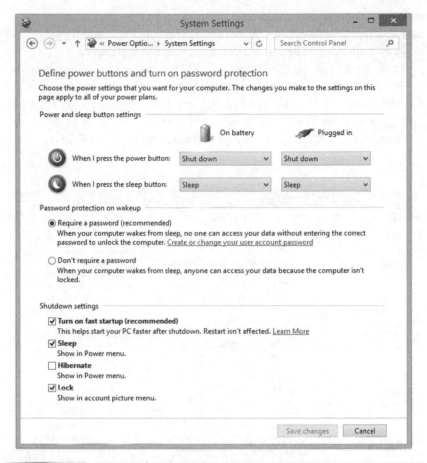

Windows 8.1 hibernation settings in the Power Options applet

Keys for adjusting screen brightness

Windows stores and synchronizes a local copy of network files you designate as *offline files*. Instead of overwriting something important if changes are made on both sides while you're away, a sync conflict will pop up.

To designate and sync a folder, right-click it and select *Always available offline* (see Figure 10.23). When you want to open the files offline, go to the Control Panel and open the Sync Center applet (see Figure 10.24). Click the *Manage offline files* link in the Tasks list to open the Offline Files dialog box (see Figure 10.25). Click the *View your offline files* button and you're in.

FIGURE 10.23 Setting up offline files

FIGURE 10.24   Sync Center applet

Exam Tip

Another option for extending battery life is to just bring a spare battery. Some smaller portable devices have range-extending external rechargers that can also help.

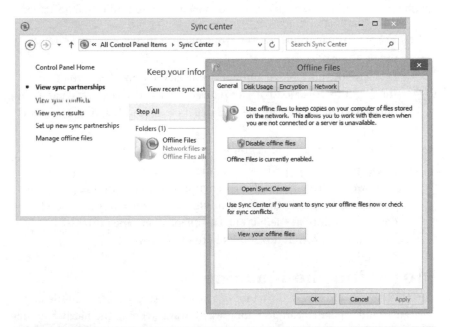

FIGURE 10.25   Offline Files dialog box

Cleaning

Portables have more chances to get dirty than desktops, so clean them regularly. Use an appropriate *screen cleaner* to remove fingerprints and dust from the fragile LCD panel. Compressed air works great for blowing out dust and crumbs from the keyboard and for keeping any ports, slots, and sockets clear. Don't use water on your keyboard—even a little inside the portable can toast a component.

Travel Assistance

Chapter 21 discusses general environmental threats such as smoke and chemicals.

Heat

Portables are a stack of electronic components crammed into a small package. Unlike desktops, they lack the air space fans need to work well, leaving them more vulnerable to overheating that can cause lockups and hardware failure. Very compact portables handle heat like mobile devices, which we'll discuss in Chapter 11; follow these guidelines to manage heat in traditional portables:

- Use power management, even while plugged in, because lower power use means less heat.
- Don't use the portable in a hot or insulated environment. Avoid running it in direct sunlight, or on well-insulated surfaces such as a pillow or blanket. Elevate the portable if possible; otherwise, use a hard, flat surface.
- Don't use a keyboard protector for extended amounts of time.
- If your portable has a fan, pay attention to it. If it runs loudly, examine the power management settings, environment, and running programs for whatever is generating or retaining heat. These fans can fail, but they stay off until needed; if one falls silent, check the portable's temperature and shut down if it's hotter than normal.

Protecting the Machine

Portable devices are exposed to a lot of risks a desktop isn't, but a little extra awareness and vigilance can go a long way toward keeping the hardware safe and avoiding lost money, data, and time.

- If a person or pet trips on the power cord, they can launch your portable to a violent end; run it carefully, especially in public.
- A good case or bag protects from damage, dust, and pet hair. For long periods, store the portable with a partially charged battery in that good case and top off as needed to avoid a full discharge; better yet, remove the battery if possible.
- When traveling, reduce the risk of theft with a case or bag that doesn't obviously hold a computer; compact portables such as Ultrabooks can hide in less obvious bags. Keep an eye on your portable; on transit, stow your bag where you can see it. A *laptop lock* (also called a *cable lock*) loops around a solid object and locks to the small security hole on the side of the laptop (see Figure 10.26). Plan for the worst—in Chapter 21 we'll look at software tracking systems that can help locate your portable if stolen, capture evidence with its sensors, and remotely wipe sensitive data.
- Before traveling, remove optical discs from drives, back up important data, and make sure your portable has a charge—you might have to turn it on to show it's not a dummy for smuggling. For international travel, remember that North America uses ~115V power outlets while most of the world uses ~230V outlets. Many portable computers have *auto-switching power supplies* that detect and adjust to the outlet's voltage; a simple plug converter works for these. Some have *fixed-input power supplies* that require a step-down or step-up *transformer*.

FIGURE 10.26 Cable lock

- Most of the storage and travel advice also applies to shipping. Beyond that, pack the portable securely in a discreet container, and verify warranty coverage. Ship with a reputable carrier using a tracking number and, if possible, delivery signature. Shipping insurance is worthwhile, but don't advertise the contents: just declare it as electronics.

Objective 10.04   Upgrading and Repairing Laptops

A competent tech can upgrade and repair traditional portable computers to a degree, but true portable techs are specialists. Simple upgrades just take a screwdriver and the ESD-avoidance techniques we've reviewed. *Repairing* portables, on the other hand, requires research, patience, organization, special tools, documentation, and a ridiculously steady hand. The growing number of form factors and the shrinking size of portable devices mean there are many exceptions to the advice given here, especially for compact portables; these devices may be trickier to take apart, and their components can be soldered on or use less-common interfaces.

Disassembly Process

Disassembling a portable is hard unless it was designed to be upgraded or serviced by casual users, and reassembly is usually harder. Here's the four-step process you should know for the exam:

- *Document and label every cable and screw location.* There are few standards, and you can easily strip or jam a screw if you use the wrong one.
- *Organize any parts you extract from the laptop.* Seriously, put a big white piece of construction paper on your work surface, lay each extracted piece out in logical fashion, and clearly mark every connection. You can also document your workspace with a webcam or smartphone camera in case something goes missing.
- *Refer to the manufacturer's resources.* As I said, there are few standards. Two models from one manufacturer can have both obvious and insidiously small differences.

- *Use the appropriate hand tools.* You can do more harm than good without proper tools, including pry bars, tiny-headed Phillips and Torx drivers, and so on. An entry-level laptop-tech toolkit, such as the one from iFixit.com in Figure 10.27, is a good start.

Now that you have the official line on the disassembly process, let's get one thing clear: many manufacturers provide their resources only to authorized repair centers, leaving you two options. You can refer your clients to a dedicated portable tech, or find repairs documented on third-party sources such

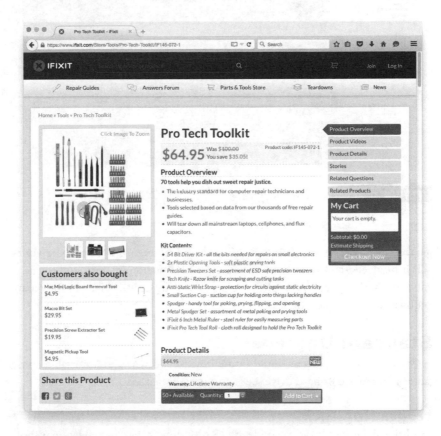

FIGURE 10.27 Bare-minimum laptop repair tools

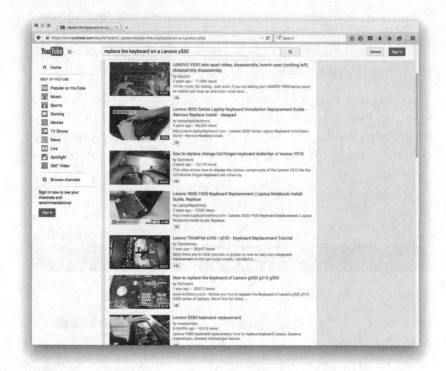

FIGURE 10.28 YouTube search result

as YouTube (see Figure 10.28) and iFixit.com (see Figure 10.29). Spare your-self a headache and refer them if you can't find documentation *and* replace-ment parts, the repair is complex, the portable is mission-critical, or the repair requires expensive new tools.

Standard Upgrades

Every CompTIA A+ tech should know how to add RAM to a portable com-puter and replace its hard drive. Let's go through the steps.

Upgrading RAM

Traditional laptops have upgradeable RAM slots; other portables may not. Remember that portable RAM has its own SO-DIMM form factors (though you may see them in some compact all-in-one desktops). Older systems may have 144-pin SDRAM SO-DIMMs or 200-pin DDR and DDR2 SO-DIMMs (see Figure 10.30). Most current systems use 204-pin DDR3 SO-DIMMs,

FIGURE 10.30 A 200-pin SO-DIMM stick (front and back)

but the first portables with 260-pin DDR4 SO-DIMMs started hitting shelves late in 2015.

Exam Tip
Memorize the SO-DIMM form factors—and the associated memory technologies—for the 901 exam.

How to Add or Replace RAM   Just like with a desktop, protect yourself and the portable by removing all power. With portables, this includes removable batteries. If it has built-in batteries, consult the manufacturer's resources to check if and how you can safely work on it.

Travel Advisory
Some portables have both built-in and removable batteries.

Once you know you can work safely, confirm what kind of RAM you need with the manufacturer's website or manual. Next, check the existing RAM configuration to confirm what you need to buy. To go from 4 GB to 8 GB, you need to know if the portable has one 4GB module or two 2GB modules.

Second, locate the RAM slots. They're often both behind a panel (see Figure 10.31) on the bottom of the portable, but sometimes they're separated.

FIGURE 10.31   Removing a RAM panel

FIGURE 10.32 Releasing the RAM

Then you press out on the retaining clips and the RAM stick pops up (see Figure 10.32). Gently remove the old stick of RAM and insert the new one by reversing the steps.

Shared Memory Some portables (and desktops) have *shared memory* that enables the video card to borrow regular system RAM, providing performance comparable to its mega-memory alternative at a much lower cost. Unfortunately, the term *shared* is a bit misleading: the video card reserves this memory, and performance can suffer if the system runs out.

Some CMOS utilities can change the amount of shared memory, while others can just toggle the setting. In both cases, more system RAM will improve overall performance when the OS and CPU get more usable RAM; the upgrade can also improve video performance if the system either shares a percentage of all RAM or lets you adjust the amount.

Upgrading Mass Storage
You can replace a hard disk drive (HDD), solid-state drive (SSD), or solid-state hybrid drive (HHD or SSHD) in a recent traditional laptop easily; it's almost certainly a 2.5-inch SATA drive. If you find an ancient laptop using PATA, look for cabling and jumper instructions in the manufacturer resources for both the

FIGURE 10.33 The 2.5-inch and 3.5-inch drives are mostly the same.

drive and laptop. Otherwise, no difference exists between 2.5-inch drives and their larger 3.5-inch brethren (see Figure 10.33).

> ### Exam Tip
>
> 1.8-inch HDDs have fallen out of favor as flash memory usurps their role in portable music players and other small portables. These days, they are quite rare. If you find one, it almost certainly will be in an older portable on the small end of the scale.

One of the best laptop upgrades is to an SSD from an HDD. It's less storage for the money, but SSDs are faster, lighter, quieter, cooler, use less power, and lack mechanical parts easily damaged by bumps, drops, and travel.

Hard drive replacement mirrors replacing RAM: find the hard drive hatch—either along one edge or on the bottom—and remove the screws (see Figure 10.34). Remove the old drive and slide the new drive into its place (see Figure 10.35). Reattach the hatch, boot the computer, and install an OS if necessary.

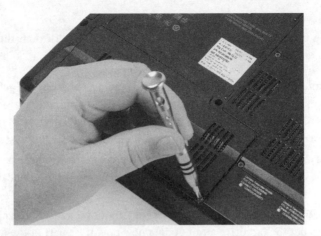

FIGURE 10.34 Removing the drive compartment hatch

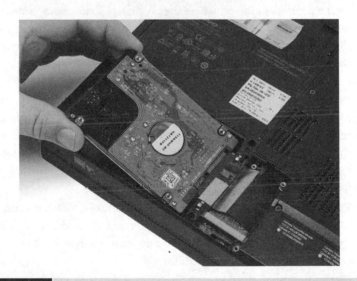

FIGURE 10.35 Inserting a replacement drive

Hardware Replacement

Because every portable differs, this section provides guidance, not concrete steps; a relatively simple repair on one device might take a full teardown on another. Beware the trend toward more integrated parts in compact systems: confirm the part is replaceable in the *exact model* you're working on.

Components

Replacing these components generally requires more work than the RAM or drive upgrades while remaining "doable."

- **Battery**   When battery life falls below an acceptable level, get a manufacturer or aftermarket replacement. This should be a simple swap (if the battery isn't built in), but if the new battery fares no better, you may have an inadequate or malfunctioning charging system.

- **Keyboard**   Removing a laptop keyboard can involve little pry bars, screws, clips, and so on. Keyboards connect via a short, delicate cable, often taped down.

- **Optical drive**   If the drive is part of a modular system, you can just pop out the old drive and pop in a new one. If it's part of the internal chassis, you're looking at a full dissection.

- **Speakers**   Replacing the internal speaker(s) can be simple or a total pain, depending on where they connect. Some are mounted on the outside of the chassis: you just pry off the cover, pull out the little speaker, disconnect the cable, and reverse the process for the replacement. If the speakers are inside the chassis, you need to dismantle the portable.

- **Frame**   A portable's components are secured by a variety of plastic, metal, and rubber parts. These too can be repaired, if you can find a replacement. Start with the device model, and use manufacturer or third-party resources to find the part number; be careful, and don't just eyeball it. A tiny part can set you back a silly sum if it's sold only in a larger assembly.

- **Expansion cards**   Some portables have true expansion slots such as Mini-PCIe (see Figure 10.36) and M.2 for add-on cards. As with RAM, remove power and avoid ESD. If you upgrade a wireless expansion card, remember to reattach the antenna.

- **CPU**   Replacing the CPU is a bit more work. Once again, start by removing all power. Next, take off the hatch to expose the CPU. There's typically an elaborate heatsink and fan assembly (see Figure 10.37) that includes both the CPU and the chipset. Unscrew the assembly and lift out the CPU. Replace it with another CPU, apply thermal paste, and reattach the assembly. Reconnect the fan power connector and you're good to go. If the laptop uses passive cooling, you may have to remove the keyboard and a heatsink to reach the CPU.

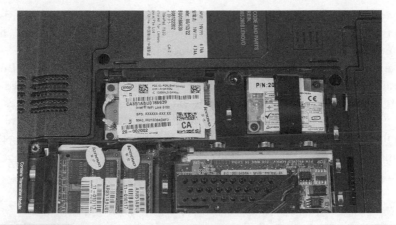

FIGURE 10.36 Mini-PCIe expansion slot on a laptop

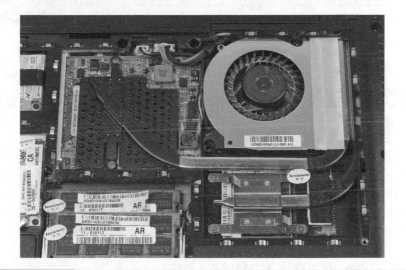

FIGURE 10.37 CPU heatsink and fan assembly exposed

Integral Parts

Some repairs go as far as stripping the portable down to the bare chassis, and I leave them to portable repair specialists. CompTIA still expects you to understand the process, so let's see how it pertains to four components: the screen, DC jack, touchpad, and system board.

You open a portable by peeling away layers down through the keyboard or up from the base; both demand systematic attention to tiny parts, screws, and connectors—the four-step disassembly process.

All of these require detaching the screen from the main chassis. Aside from finding the connection points and removing the proper screws, you need to note connection points for the display and any antennas or other devices in the frame. After you replace the bad component, it's time to carefully reassemble. If you miss a single connection as you rebuild, you'll be repeating the whole process.

> **Exam Tip**
>
> The DC jack, which is soldered to the main board, requires extra love. You'll need to strip the laptop to the bare metal, unsolder the old part, and solder the new part. CompTIA can't expect you to know how to do this stuff, but they may expect you to know if it *can* be done.

Objective 10.05 Troubleshooting Portables

For most issues, it's sufficient to combine desktop troubleshooting techniques with the processes you've learned throughout this chapter for keeping track of parts and protecting yourself and the portable. Additionally, here are some portable-specific suggestions for dealing with power, performance, and component issues.

Laptop Won't Power On

- A faulty peripheral device can keep the laptop from powering up. Remove USB, FireWire, or Thunderbolt devices.
- Find an AC power outlet that works with another device. If the portable won't start while connected to it, swap in a known-good AC adapter. If it doesn't start, find a laptop tech.

Poor Performance

- Applications and processes consuming high resources can slow performance. Each OS has a way to check for this (Task Manager in Windows, Activity Monitor in Mac OS X)—you may need to close or stop problem processes, reboot, or update an application.
- Extreme performance issues can freeze the system. If they don't self-resolve and you can't interact with the device, perform a hard reboot (usually by holding down the power button for 10 seconds; you'll lose unsaved work). If all else fails, cut power by pulling the battery.

Travel Advisory

The *mobile device* concepts of hard and soft resets are *not* equal to hard and soft reboots. If a resource suggests resetting a portable device, look for a clear resource to be certain you are performing the right operation. See Chapter 11 for more on hard and soft resets.

Battery Issues

- Defects and overcharging (if the circuits to prevent it fail) can cause a *swollen battery,* but the early signs are subtle: wobbling on flat surfaces, the screen doesn't close flush, touchpad or keyboard problems, and trouble removing or inserting the battery. Eventually, the device may obviously deform. Battery packs are designed to swell a little, but it increases the risk they'll puncture—and a punctured battery is dangerous. Don't ignore these symptoms; open the case carefully to check the battery, and very carefully deliver it to an e-waste recycling or disposal site.
- If the battery won't charge, check the AC adapter by removing the battery to run the portable on AC only and replace the adapter if it doesn't run. Otherwise, replace the battery.
- If the battery charges properly but doesn't last long, either a performance problem is drawing more power than usual or the battery has outlived its useful life. Confirm usually disabled wireless devices are off and follow the "Poor Performance" tips.

Overheating

- Be alert to any device that is hotter than usual. If the device feels dangerously hot, shut it down, remove the battery, and set it on a cool, hard surface (out of direct sunlight, with the hottest parts exposed to air if possible).
- Note which parts are hot. If the entire device is hot, likely causes are direct sunlight and a hot environment. Cool the device down and see if the trouble goes away. There's usually a distinct hot spot if a component or performance issue is the cause.
- Check a device for overheating if you see signs such as inconsistent reboots, graphical glitches, and system beeps.
- Listen for fans. Although some portables don't have any, complete silence may indicate a failed fan, and unusual noise may signal one on its way out.
- Avoid stacking predictable causes of heat, such as charging, intensive processing, large downloads, poor airflow or insulation, hot environment, and so on.
- When unexpected heat persists, check fan vents for blockages; open the device if necessary to check fans and heatsinks.

Display Problems

- If you hear the laptop booting but the screen doesn't come on, press the FN key combination to activate the screen or change display modes a few times. Check for a stuck LCD cutoff switch (usually near the hinge). If it is removable, confirm the screen is properly attached.
- A dead inverter can leave the display dim; inverters never go quietly and tend to finally fail when you plug in the AC adapter. Though less common, backlights can also die.
- If the screen won't come on or is damaged, try an external monitor port.
- If an external monitor does not display, try the FN key combination to switch display modes. If the internal display works, you can use the Windows Display applet in Control Panel or OS X System Preferences.
- Some cheap displays with LED backlights dim by turning them on and off rapidly to reduce visible light and electricity use. If noticeable, these *flickering displays* can cause headache and eyestrain. Crank up the brightness or replace the laptop.

- If screen auto-rotation is giving you fits, you can lock or unlock auto-rotation, and then manually change the screen orientation with the Display applet (also with the Settings charm, and possibly with FN key combinations).

Wireless Devices (Bluetooth, Wi-Fi, Mobile Broadband, NFC, or GPS) Don't Work or Work Intermittently

- Check the device edges for wireless radio or airplane mode switches. Try FN key combinations. Check the OS notification area and any hardware indicator LEDs.
- If the portable was serviced recently, a wireless antenna may be disconnected.
- Physically walk the portable to the wireless router or access point to rule out range issues.
- The Bluetooth pairing process requires action or configuration on both devices. Turn on the Bluetooth device, actively seek it, and try again.
- If GPS is not functioning, check privacy options, confirm GPS is enabled, and ensure location services are enabled systemwide *and* for the right programs. In Windows, try the Location Settings applet in Control Panel or the Privacy section of the Settings app; look for similar settings in System Preferences on Mac OS X or your Linux distro's equivalent.
- You'll learn about near field communication (NFC) in Chapter 11, but if your portable supports NFC and it isn't working, check for a setting to enable communication with nearby devices. In Windows, open the Proximity applet in the Control Panel (only present if you have NFC hardware!) and confirm Proximity support is enabled.

Audio Problems

- Plug in a pair of headphones or external speakers.
- If these don't work, check hardware volume controls and the notification area. Confirm both OS and program-specific output device settings.
- If they do work and the device was serviced lately, verify the speakers are connected.

- Before concluding the speakers are damaged, try the following: reboot the system, double-check audio output device settings, change and reset the default output device, and disable and re-enable the appropriate hardware device.

Input Problems

- Confirm the system otherwise runs smoothly; input devices will misbehave if the system is freezing up.
- If no keys work, a connector may be loose. Use the manufacturer's disassembly steps to locate and reseat connectors.
- If you get numbers when you expect letters, toggle the number lock (NUMLOCK) FN key.
- If keys stick, clean them out with compressed air. If you have serious goo, disconnect and remove the keyboard to clean it, and verify it's dry before reconnecting.
- A key with an out-of-place switch may look askew, feel sticky, or not register presses. You need to reseat it, but switches (and clips) can be delicate. Don't proceed until you identify the clip and how to detach and reattach it via manufacturer or third-party websites.
- An erratic touchpad might just need to be reconfigured. Try the various options in the Control Panel | Mouse applet, or the equivalent location in System Preferences. If this fails, remove the keyboard to access the touchpad sensors and clean them with compressed air.
- If a touchscreen is erratic or unresponsive, confirm it isn't registering an unintentional touch (most common when you hold the device near the screen). Use a dry microfiber cloth to clean dirt, grease, or liquids.
- The CMOS menu may have touchscreen diagnostics to quickly separate hardware and software/configuration issues.
- Reset and recalibrate the display through the Tablet PC Settings applet in Control Panel.

> **Exam Tip**
>
> A *ghost cursor* can mean a trail of ghost cursors behind the real one (due to an aging display or bad refresh rate setting), or a cursor that moves erratically or drifts steadily (also called *pointer drift*). If pointer drift persists after a reboot and good cleaning, replace the touchpad.

CHECKPOINT

✔**Objective 10.01: Portable Computing Devices** The portable device category includes the traditional clamshell laptop and a number of larger/smaller variants, such as desktop replacements, gaming laptops, Ultrabooks, and Chromebooks. Newer hybrid 2-in-1 devices use many mechanisms to combine the functions of a laptop and a tablet. Most have input devices such as keyboards, webcams, and microphones—all have some form of pointing device, typically a touchpad or touchscreen. Most use an FN key to toggle various features on and off. Current displays are CCFL- or LED-backlit LCDs, though OLEDs are poised to move in.

✔**Objective 10.02: Extending Portables** Portable devices leverage single-function ports and slots, network connections, portable-specific expansion slots, and general-purpose ports. Single-function ports support outputs such as audio and multiple monitors; business-oriented portables may include a smart card reader slot that uses smart card authentication to enhance security; flash memory card slots are also common. Wireless connectivity features include 802.11 Wi-Fi, cellular data, Bluetooth, and GPS; larger laptops also have a wired Ethernet port. Portable-specific expansion slots such as ExpressCard are getting hard to find as they're displaced by general-purpose ports such as USB, Thunderbolt, eSATA, and FireWire.

✔**Objective 10.03: Managing and Maintaining Portables** Beyond basic computer maintenance, most portable-specific work focuses on keeping the batteries in good health as well as protecting the hardware from dirt, heat damage, and other physical threats. Store batteries partially charged in a cool place, and avoid pointless discharges that shorten battery life. Li-Ion batteries are dangerous—don't handle ruptured ones, and always recycle them properly. Both automatic and manual power management are about conserving power (and reducing heat) by taking steps to minimize device use and disabling unused devices entirely. Preserve your investment by avoiding messes, carefully cleaning the device, keeping the device cool, and taking steps to avoid damage while using, transporting, shipping, storing, and traveling with it.

✔**Objective 10.04: Upgrading and Repairing Laptops** Portables have fewer standards and many tiny, fragile parts, so it's critical to methodically document and label cables and screws, organize anything you extract, refer to manufacturer resources, and use appropriate tools. Basic upgrade options are limited to replacing RAM and hard drives in more traditional laptop portable computers. Other upgrades, repairs, and replacements, which are often best left up to professionals since they vary widely in complexity, include the battery, keyboard, optical drive, speakers, frame parts, expansion cards, CPU, display, DC jack, touchpad, and system board.

✔**Objective 10.05: Troubleshooting Portables** Portable-specific trouble-shooting breaks down into power and performance issues and component problems. Power and performance issues include trouble turning the device on, poor performance, battery problems, and overheating. The main culprits for component problems are the display, wireless devices, speakers, and input components such as the keyboard, touchpad, and touchscreen.

REVIEW QUESTIONS

1. What's the first thing you should do when disassembling a laptop after removing all electricity?
   A. Document and label every cable and screw location.
   B. Organize any parts you extract from the laptop.
   C. Install a fresh battery.
   D. Call a repair shop.

2. Rick wants to upgrade the memory in his laptop. He currently has a 2GB stick of DDR3. Which of the following options would give him the best result?
   A. Replace the DDR3 RAM with DDR4.
   B. Replace the 204-pin SO-DIMM with a 260-pin SO-DIMM.
   C. Replace a 2GB 204-pin SO-DIMM with a 4GB 204-pin SO-DIMM.
   D. Replace a 2GB 204-pin SO-DIMM with a 4GB 260-pin SO-DIMM.

3. Which of the following are standard internal expansion slots in portable computers? (Select two.)
   A. M.2
   B. Mini-PCIe
   C. PCI
   D. PCIe

4. Which of the following portable computer display types use a backlight? (Select two.)

    A. LCD

    B. LED

    C. OLED

    D. Plasma

5. Which Control Panel applet enables you to change a laptop's power plan from Balanced to Power saver?

    A. Power Management.

    B. Power Options.

    C. Power Plans.

    D. There isn't one. Windows shifts power plans automatically.

6. Aldo gets a tech call from a user who complains that his laptop keyboard is broken. Every time the user starts to type, some letters work but others come out as numbers. What should Aldo do?

    A. Tell the user to send in the laptop for a replacement keyboard.

    B. Tell the user that keyboards can't be replaced and he needs a new laptop.

    C. Tell the user to press and hold the FN key and toggle the NUMLOCK key.

    D. Escalate the problem to his supervisor.

7. Which input devices might you find built into the display frame on a clamshell laptop? (Select three.)

    A. Webcam

    B. Touchpad

    C. Touchscreen

    D. Microphone

8. How do ExpressCards interface with portable computers? (Select two.)

    A. PCI

    B. Bluetooth

    C. PCIe

    D. USB 2.0

9. What is the term used to describe a power supply that can adjust to the voltage detected?

   A. Auto-tuning

   B. Auto-switching

   C. Fixed-input

   D. Step-up transformer

10. If you encounter a laptop that doesn't seem to recharge, what might be the problem? (Select the best answer.)

   A. AC adapter

   B. CPU

   C. RAM

   D. Thermal process

REVIEW ANSWERS

1. **A**   After removing the electricity (including the battery), you should document and label every cable and screw location before disassembling a laptop.

2. **C**   Laptops that use DDR3 memory have one or more 204-pin SO-DIMM slots. You can't change memory technology types on laptops any more than you can on desktops (that is, going from DDR3 to DDR4), nor can you put a 260-pin stick in a 204-pin slot.

3. **A B**   Most new laptops have an M.2 expansion slot. Older laptops have a Mini-PCIe slot.

4. **A B**   Of the four listed here, LCD with a traditional CCFL backlight (LCD) and with an LED backlight (LED) are the two types of backlit monitors you'll see on portable computers. Although CompTIA lists OLED and plasma as display types for portables, OLED doesn't use a backlight, and burn-in makes plasma a terrible computer display.

5. **B**   Use the Power Options applet to change power plans.

6. **C**   The NUMLOCK key is toggled on. It happens. Have the user toggle it off.

7. **A C D**   In addition to Wi-Fi antennas, a webcam and microphone are commonly included in the display frame. A touchscreen, if included, must also be in the frame. The touchpad, however, will be in the base of the laptop with the keyboard.

8. **C D**   ExpressCards use PCIe or USB 2.0 to interface with portable computers.

9. **B**   Power supplies that can adjust for a detected voltage are called auto-switching power supplies.

10. **A**   A laptop that doesn't recharge has a problem with either the AC adapter or the battery. The former is the logical choice for this question.

Mobile Devices

	NEWBIE	SOME EXPERIENCE	EXPERT
ETA	5 hours	4 hours	2 hours

Even though the smartphone and other mobile devices have revolutionized our work and play, it's hard to find a definition everyone agrees on. For our purposes, a *mobile device* is a small, lightweight computer running a mobile-specific operating system.

The last point is important—it's the easy way to tell a hybrid portable computer in a tablet form factor from a tablet mobile device. The typical portable computer runs a desktop OS such as Windows, Mac OS X, or some form of Linux distribution. A true mobile device runs a mobile OS such as Apple iOS, Google Android, Microsoft Windows Phone or Mobile, and so on.

This chapter explores mobile devices and operating systems, including how to configure, troubleshoot, and secure them. The CompTIA A+ exams are serious about mobile devices, so we have a lot of ground to cover.

Objective 11.01   Mobile Computing Devices

The definition in the introduction helps separate mobile devices from other categories, but you also need to be familiar with the kinds of hardware you can expect to find in mobile devices, and how that hardware is combined in common mobile device types. Tightly integrated mobile devices don't really have user-replaceable or field-replaceable hardware, and must go to specialized (and in some cases, authorized) service centers for repair.

Mobile Hardware Features

Much of the usefulness of mobile devices is driven by the many hardware features they include. This section explores the basics: screen technologies, cameras, microphones, digitizers, and GPS connectivity.

Screen Technologies

Most mobile devices use LCD or OLED displays. We saw the LCD panels in Chapter 9; less expensive devices use TN panels, and better ones use IPS. Gold-standard *organic light-emitting diode (OLED)* displays precisely apply electrical current to an organic compound, causing it to glow in a specific location. This makes OLEDs lighter and more efficient, especially since they display true black by applying no current. Cost once limited OLED to small, high-quality mobile devices, but it continues to spread as prices fall.

Cameras

Many mobile devices have distinct front-facing and rear-facing cameras that shoot stills and video. Beyond taking selfies and serving as impromptu mirrors, front cameras also enable video chat, facial recognition, and eye-tracking controls; rear-facing cameras enable shooting general-purpose stills and video, scanning documents, and more. The most recent round of camera upgrades on mobile devices, particularly on smartphones (see Figure 11.1), rival dedicated point-and-shoot cameras.

Microphones

Almost all mobile devices incorporate a microphone. Smartphones need them to make calls or video chat, of course, but you can also use them to dictate notes, issue voice commands, and record other sounds. Mobile devices commonly have more than one microphone to support noise-cancelling routines; take care to avoid blocking them.

Digitizers

A *digitizer* provides the "touch" part of a touchscreen. When your finger contacts a touchscreen, the digitizer's fine grid of sensors under the glass tracks your finger and sends the OS its location on the grid. As with modern trackpads, you can use one or more fingers to interact with most touchscreens.

FIGURE 11.1   Author's camera app on his Galaxy S6

Global Positioning System

Mobile devices can track their own location with *global positioning system (GPS)*, cellular, or Wi-Fi connections. These *location services* conveniently find nearby stores and restaurants, or determine when an Uber driver will arrive. The GPS-enabled *Waze* app (see Figure 11.2) navigates and provides real-time data on the road ahead, and the Find My iPhone app (see Figure 11.3), included with an iOS device's iCloud service, can locate a lost device.

These *geotracking* features are great…when you don't mind your mobile OS recording your location history. If you mind, turn them off (see Figure 11.4).

Travel Advisory

Because mobile devices tap into the Internet and cellular phone networks, they have identifying numbers such as MAC addresses that service providers and government agencies can use to pinpoint your location.

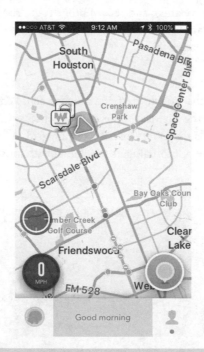

FIGURE 11.2   Waze in action

FIGURE 11.3   Find My iPhone app

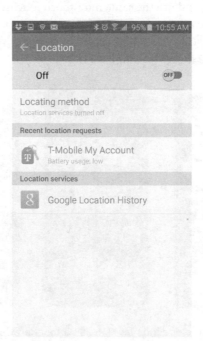

FIGURE 11.4   Turning off Location on an Android device

Device Types

The 901 objectives have a long list of mobile device types to cover, so let's look at them in groups: general-purpose devices, purpose-built devices, and wearable devices.

General-Purpose Mobile Devices

Most general-purpose mobile devices run one of three operating systems (see Figure 11.5): Apple iOS, Google Android, or Microsoft Windows Phone/10 Mobile. Only the Apple devices run iOS because Apple designs the hardware and OS for each other, but many manufacturers make Android and Windows devices.

- **Smartphone** In 2007, Apple introduced the first iPhone *smartphone* (see Figure 11.6): a small touchscreen-equipped computer with great support for backups, synchronization, and third-party apps, all piggybacking on some decades-old voice communication device called a "cell phone." Smartphones continually fold in new features as they move to the center of the trend toward ever-present connectivity and seamless data access across all our devices.

- **Tablet** *Tablets* are very similar to smartphones; they run the same OSs and apps, and use the same multitouch touchscreens. From a tech's perspective, they are like large smartphones (without the phone). Whereas a typical smartphone screen is around 5 inches, tablets run around 7 to 12 inches (see Figure 11.7).

FIGURE 11.5 Examples of the big three smartphone OSs: Android (left), iOS (center), and Windows Phone (right)

FIGURE 11.6 Early Apple iPhone

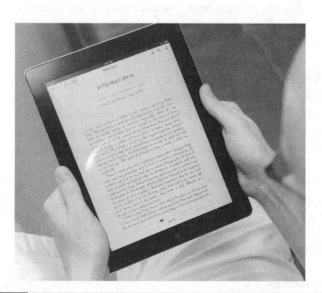

FIGURE 11.7 Typical tablet

| FIGURE 11.8 | Two popular phablets: Samsung Note 4 (left) and iPhone 6 Plus (right) |

- **Phablet**   If you're the kind of person who absolutely must have a smartphone and tablet with you at all times but find it cumbersome to carry both, you're in luck. *Phablets* straddle the line between tablets and smartphones, providing all the features of a smartphone with the expansive vistas of a huge screen (see Figure 11.8).

Purpose-Built Mobile Devices

Because purpose-built mobile devices aim to be really good at a specific task, their hardware and software can be tailored to getting it right. Unfortunately, standalone devices (such as the MP3 player) tend to get gobbled up over time as soon as smartphones do the task well enough that convenience wins.

- **E-reader**   To give the obvious definition, an *e-reader* is a tablet designed for reading electronic books (e-books). They often use eye-friendly low-power grayscale e-paper screens that enable days or weeks of reading on a charge, and a simple touch (see Figure 11.9) or button interface for obtaining, reading, and annotating e-books.

Travel Advisory

The popular Amazon Kindle and Barnes & Noble Nook e-reader lines have spawned reader apps and full-fledged tablets, but don't confuse either with a standalone e-reader.

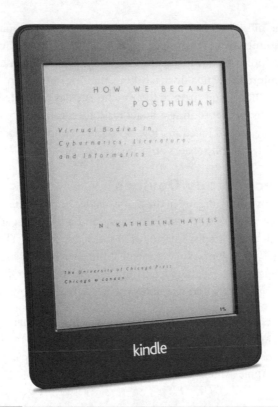

FIGURE 11.9   Kindle Paperwhite e-reader

- **Smart camera**   If you unite the interface, operating system (typically Android), networking, and apps of a smartphone with a dedicated digital camera, you get a *smart camera*. Beyond the obvious ability to edit, transfer, and post photos and video, these cameras tend to have better interfaces than those not built atop a mobile OS.

Exam Tip

The 901 objectives list a *smart camera* mobile device, but it's not crystal clear what this means. The sophistication and quality of smartphone front- and rear-facing cameras could make them smart cameras—especially given the optics on some devices marketed as "camera phones." There are also "smart camera" add-ons that connect to a smartphone to enhance its camera.

- **GPS**   The most common purpose-built GPS device is the navigational aid that mounts on a car's dash or windshield, and you can buy the equivalent for boats, airplanes, bicycles, and more—or even hand-held versions tailored to scuba diving, hiking, hunting, and so on. They have features that better suit them to their niche, such as preloaded special-purpose maps, waterproofing, impact resistance, route memory, bookmarking, stored locations, low-power use, simple replaceable batteries, other useful sensors or tools, and so on.

Wearable Technology Devices

The most important part is already in the name, but *wearable technology devices* are tiny, limited computers with novel interfaces and a featherweight OS that leverages a host device (often a smartphone) for heavy lifting. The wearable devices in the 901 objectives—smart watches, fitness monitors, and glasses/headsets—seamlessly gather data (such as how active we are) and create new interfaces that integrate data and technology with the natural flow of daily life.

- **Smart watch**   A *smart watch* minimizes the effort of smartphone tasks such as controlling music playback and checking e-mail, texts, notifications, time, and weather. Figure 11.10 shows a typical smart watch, the Apple Watch.

FIGURE 11.10   Apple Watch

- **Fitness monitor**   Common *fitness monitor* or tracker features include monitoring your steps, heart, and exercise as well as vibrating to prompt you to keep up with fitness goals. The most popular formats are fobs that clip to your body and more sophisticated fitness wristbands like my well-worn Fitbit Surge (see Figure 11.11).

- **Glasses/headsets**   Wearable *glasses* and *headsets,* which we expect to eventually overlay a useful data interface on the world and record life from our perspective, haven't made it to the mainstream yet—but it's a matter of time: *Google Glass* got close in its initial beta test, but was hamstrung by privacy objections to its ability to surreptitiously take videos and pictures; Microsoft just started shipping its futuristic HoloLens glasses to developers interested in writing apps to overlay the world with videos, apps, and games.

In any event, organizations with sensitive areas will have to deal with wearable tech policies and procedures. It's one thing to ask people to place their phones in a box outside of a secure area, but often people forget about their watches, glasses, pens, and other innocuous items cropping up with cameras, microphones, and other sensors.

FIGURE 11.11   Mike's battered Fitbit Surge

Objective 11.02

Mobile Operating Systems

Most mobile devices run either Apple iOS or Google Android. This section discusses their development and implementation models, as well as some of their major features, including how their app stores work. We'll also consider mobile-specific versions of Microsoft Windows, though these have substantially smaller market share than iOS and Android.

Travel Assistance
Tablets running a mobile OS are true "mobile" tablets—refer to Chapter 10 for more on portable computers that run a desktop OS in a tablet form factor.

Development Models

The 902 objectives include identifying how the mobile OSs differ on a number of features, including their software development model. Conveniently, you can actually make more sense of the differences between each with a little background on these software development models: closed source and open source. You may have heard these terms regarding how software is released and licensed (if not, Chapter 21 will discuss how these terms apply to licensing), but they can be applied to how any product is developed and released.

Exam Tip
The CompTIA A+ 902 exam objectives want you to compare features among the three mobile OS competitors: *Android vs. iOS vs. Windows*. The next sections explore those variations, though not in that order. Pay very close attention here.

Closed Source

Closed source describes making and selling a product while keeping the plans secret. This makes intuitive sense because these trade secrets give you a competitive edge, whereas sharing could inspire competitors to use your design or cause potential customers to make their own.

Sometimes we describe a closed-source product or technology as *proprietary* or *vendor-specific* to say it doesn't use common, open standards. The terms are related to closed source, but they aren't interchangeable. These labels imply a host of problems that come with ignoring common standards: not interoperating with other products, having rare or expensive connectors and cables, being difficult to repair, and so on.

These terms can be slippery. Later in the chapter, you'll see a device with ports and cables that technically use part of the open USB 3.0 standard, but add their own custom connector; we call this *proprietary* because the custom connector isn't interoperable.

Open Source

Think of a product as *open source* if its maker releases the instructions for making it—it doesn't have to be software (though that's usually the context). A company committed to open sourcing has to operate differently than companies using a closed-source model. Knowing that anyone could make its products, the company has to compete on price, service, support, convenience, quality, innovation, and so on.

Just releasing these instructions doesn't mean anyone else owns them; the owners or authors of the instructions for making a product specify terms for how others can use them—for example, allowing personal and educational but not commercial uses. In open-source software, these terms specify whether companies who modify the software are obliged to publish their changes, and whether they're allowed to profit from its use.

Development Models and the Mobile OS

Now let's use these models to place our mobile operating systems on a scale from open to closed. Google exercises little control over how its open-source Android OS is used and who can modify it. Because Microsoft develops its closed-source Windows Phone/Windows 10 Mobile OS and then licenses it to device makers, it knows the OS won't be modified and controls which devices get a license. Apple doesn't even license its closed-source iOS, electing instead to retain control and tailor-fit the software to its own devices.

Companies building devices that use an open-source OS such as Android don't have to share the OS developer's philosophy. If the operating system's license allows it, each of the device makers can modify the OS before installing it on their own closed-source devices—and never release those modifications. The modifications might only enable special hardware to work, but they can also install apps you don't want and can't remove, cause third-party apps to malfunction, or collect information.

Travel Advisory

Devices running "Android" with significant closed-source modifications can be so vastly different from familiar Android devices that you have to throw the rulebook out to manage them. We describe what is normal for Android devices, but none of these are rules.

Apple iOS

Apple's closed-source mobile operating system, *iOS* (see Figure 11.12), runs on the iPhone, iPad, and iPod Touch. Apple tightly controls the development of the hardware, OS, developer tools, and app deployment platform. Apple's strict development policies and controls for third-party developers contribute to its

FIGURE 11.12 iOS 9

high level of security. iOS apps are almost exclusively purchased, installed, and updated through Apple's *App Store*.

Google Android

For simplicity, think of Google Android and iOS as opposites. *Android* (see Figure 11.13) is an open-source OS, based on yet another open platform, Linux. Google writes the core Android code and occasionally releases new versions (named after a dessert or candy), at which point vendors modify it to support unique hardware features or customize the look and feel; this means "Android" differs from vendor to vendor.

You can purchase and download Android apps through various app stores, such as *Google Play* and the Amazon Appstore. Android app stores tend to be fairly open compared to the Apple's tight controls on third-party app developers, and Android makes it easier to install apps downloaded from a website.

FIGURE 11.13 Android 5 (Lollipop)

Microsoft Windows Phone

Microsoft's Windows Mobile OS once powered millions of mobile devices, but the company fell far behind Apple and Google in the early smartphone era and didn't release a modern mobile OS until 2010. *Windows Phone* (see Figure 11.14) is a closed-source OS, but Microsoft licenses it to device manufacturers for use on their devices. Microsoft asserts more control over the OS portion of its platform than its Windows Phone Store. It has developer requirements—they just aren't as strict as Apple's. There are also third-party app providers.

Travel Advisory

After the release of Windows 10 on the desktop, Microsoft slowly began rolling out Windows 10 Mobile—note the name change to *Mobile*—as the successor to Windows Phone 8.1. As with Windows 10 on the desktop, Windows 10 Mobile isn't covered (yet) on the CompTIA A+ 220-902 exam, but be aware it exists and is trickling out to new and existing devices.

FIGURE 11.14   Windows Phone 8.1

Mobile OS Features

Despite differing interfaces, flavors, and features, mobile OSs have a great deal in common. Most OS differences boil down to hardware and app support, look and feel, and philosophical differences that manifest in how the OS goes about a common task.

User Interfaces

All mobile OSs have a *graphical user interface (GUI)*, meaning you interact with elements visible on the screen. This interface is the scaffold you use to navigate to and between apps as well as access device settings. In addition to screen elements, you can also issue commands with touch *gestures,* such as *swiping* to navigate between screens and *pinching* to zoom in or out.

Most mobile devices extend the user interface to include how you move the device itself with an *accelerometer* and a *gyroscope*—one to measure movement in space and the other to detect device orientation. A common use is changing the *screen orientation* when you rotate a device from vertical to horizontal to watch videos in widescreen format.

iOS supports minimal customization of the user interface while maintaining a consistent look and feel. You can group and reposition most apps for your convenience. On Android, *launcher* apps customize the interface. Manufacturers ship devices preloaded with a launcher they make or prefer. Samsung devices use the company's TouchWiz launcher; I use Nova launcher on my Android phablet, enabling me to change icon size, animations, gestures, and more.

Screen Calibration

The 902 exam objectives mention mobile OS *screen calibration,* but it isn't clear what this means because modern mobile device screens, sensors, and input devices come precalibrated. The ability to calibrate screen features (including screen color, auto-brightness, auto-rotation, and touch-input) for troubleshooting will depend greatly on device, OS, and OS version. If these can be calibrated on your device, you'll either use the Settings app or hidden service menus to start, and then follow the calibration instructions.

You can also find apps and devices for "calibrating" some of these features, but they lack the low-level access required to calibrate your mobile device or its sensors—they just work around calibration issues (with varying success). Know that calibration (and miscalibration!) of these features is a thing (especially on older devices), and check device and OS documentation to see if this applies to your device.

FIGURE 11.15   Skype app on Windows Phone

Wi-Fi Calling

Many mobile devices use *Wi-Fi calling* to make both audio and video calls over Wi-Fi networks. Strictly speaking, this feature enables a smartphone to place a traditional phone call over Wi-Fi, but in practice it's hard to draw a clean line between this and applications such as Skype (see Figure 11.15) that can call landlines over the Internet.

Virtual Assistants

Virtual assistants such as Apple's Siri, Google Now, and Microsoft's Cortana enable you to use voice commands to get directions, search the Internet, send texts, place calls, and so on. You can also install apps that provide other virtual assistant services.

Software Development Kits

Most mobile operating systems have a *software development kit (SDK)* or application development kit that programmers can use to create custom apps or add

FIGURE 11.16 Xcode running an app written with the iOS SDK

features to existing apps. Figure 11.16 shows the development (programming) environment for the iOS SDK, *Xcode,* with the code for an iOS app open in the background window, and the same app code running in the iPhone 6s. simulator on top.

> ### Exam Tip
>
> A software development kit (SDK) is used to write apps. Don't confuse it with the *Android application package (APK),* a package file compiled from an Android app's code, which is then used to install the app on Android devices.

Emergency Capabilities

The *emergency notification* feature enables smartphones to receive broadcasts (about severe weather, missing children, and so on) from national emergency broadcast systems, such as the Emergency Alert System (EAS) in the United States. These alerts may force your phone to emit a very loud sound or vibrate incessantly to get your attention.

When you're the one in trouble, the modern *Enhanced 911 (E911)* system uses GPS and cellular networks to triangulate the location of your phone by its distance from cell towers, its transmission delay time, and other factors, in order to dispatch emergency responders.

Mobile Payment Service

The *mobile payment service* connects to your bank information and automatically transfers the funds from your bank to the merchant, enabling you to pay for goods and services with your device. Near field communication (for more, see "NFC," later in the chapter) refines the process further: just place your device on or near the special pad at the register to authorize payment.

Apple Pay supports major credit card payment terminals and point-of-sale systems, including those fielded by Visa, MasterCard, and American Express. Apple Pay on your iPhone or Apple Watch can use contactless payment terminals with NFC, and it supports in-app payments for online purchases.

Airplane Mode

Airplane mode (see Figure 11.17) is simply a hardware or software switch that turns off all cellular and wireless services, including Bluetooth. The aptly

FIGURE 11.17 Airplane mode enabled on iOS 9

named mode disables these features so passengers can comply with restrictions protecting aircraft instruments from interference, although it's also a shortcut for turning off communication functions.

Radio Firmware

Mobile devices use a wide variety of radio technologies to access cellular services, and these radios have their own firmware that occasionally needs updates. There's not much to do here, but you may end up troubleshooting a device with connection problems that just needs a radio firmware update.

Local Lingo

CDMA Code division multiple access (CDMA) is a channel access method used by various radio communication technologies.

PRL, PRI, and Baseband Updates As mobile devices travel, they frequently have to pass through areas that don't have strong signals, or into areas that the carrier does not service, and maintain connection by *roaming* on another carrier's network. Your phone's firmware gets occasional updates to its *Preferred Roaming List (PRL)*, a priority-ordered list of other carrier networks and frequencies, sent via your phone's cellular connection (called baseband updates, or over-the-air updates) or through normal OS updates.

CDMA devices may also receive *product release instruction (PRI)* updates that modify a host of complex device settings. Don't worry about specifics, here—but a device may need PRI updates if the network evolves during its life, it is moving to a new network, or it has a new owner.

Exam Tip

PRL and PRI updates are handled automatically during firmware/OS updates. They are only for CDMA networks. No one but the nerdiest of nerds will ever see these updates.

IMEI, ICCID, and IMSI There are three identifiers you need to manage mobile devices with cellular service:

- The 15-digit *International Mobile Equipment Identity (IMEI)* number uniquely identifies a mobile *Global System for Mobile Communications (GSM)* device (including 4G LTE and LTE-advanced). Carriers can use the IMEI, which is often printed inside the battery compartment, to block a device from the network.

- The *Integrated Circuit Card Identifier (ICCID)* uniquely identifies a *subscriber identity module (SIM)*. The SIM, which authenticates the subscriber to the network, can usually be moved from phone to phone with no problems.

- The *International Mobile Subscriber Identity (IMSI)* number, included on the SIM, represents the actual user associated with the SIM. This number can be used to unlock a phone or ensure a stolen phone isn't misused.

Local Lingo

LTE   Long Term Evolution (LTE) has replaced earlier access technologies and offers theoretical speeds up to 300 Mbps download and 75 Mbps upload.

You might need to inventory these numbers or use them with your *mobile device management (MDM)* software (we'll discuss managing mobile devices with an MDM later in the chapter). You can (but won't always) initially locate these through device information or configuration menus (see Figure 11.18), or through the carrier, but the MDM should store them with other information (such as the telephone number or MAC address) it needs to provision new devices.

FIGURE 11.18   Android device information, including IMEI and ICCID numbers

Exam Tip

Remember the differences between the IMEI and IMSI numbers for the CompTIA A+ 902 exam. The IMEI number represents the device. The IMSI number is tied to the user's account with the carrier and is included with the SIM.

VPN

A *virtual private network (VPN)* securely connects a remote client and the corporate infrastructure, or a branch office and the corporate office. VPNs create an encrypted tunnel through an unsecure network such as the Internet. The most popular ways use either a combination of the Layer 2 Tunneling Protocol (L2TP) and IPsec, or Secure Sockets Layer (SSL).

Using the L2TP/IPsec method, you configure a client (see Figure 11.19) to match server settings (the UDP port, usually 1701 must be open), connect to

FIGURE 11.19 Configuring a VPN

the corporate network, and then use your e-mail client or map shares as if you were actually connected onsite to the corporate infrastructure. An SSL-based VPN typically connects through a web browser via the standard SSL port (TCP 443) instead of a specially configured client, but lacks direct access to network resources.

Objective 11.03 Configuring Mobile Devices

Modern devices come preconfigured with everything but your user account and network credentials. Once you're up and running, you can add capabilities by enhancing hardware and installing productivity apps. You also need to set up network connectivity, add Bluetooth devices, configure e-mail account(s), and enable the device to synchronize with other devices. Plus, you have a lot of add-on options; let's look at how to configure them.

Enhancing Hardware

A mobile device is organized much like any other computer; most of its components attach to a primary circuit board, the *motherboard*. It's powered by a *system on a chip (SoC)* that combines a CPU (often designed by ARM), GPU, and other support logic onto a single, efficient, space-saving silicon die. Mobile devices store data on small, efficient, fast flash media such as a *solid-state drive (SSD)* or microSD card.

Mobile devices differ from other computers in that you can't upgrade them, and they lack parts the user can replace or service; if something breaks, the user has to send the device back to the manufacturer, visit a manufacturer-supported store, or take it to a specialized repair shop.

Despite this, every device still has expansion capabilities, but they vary so widely that it's hard to generalize about them. The closest you can get is the 3.5-mm audio jack (see Figure 11.20), but even though virtually every smartphone and tablet has one, you won't find them on many wearables or purpose-built devices.

Apple devices are a big part of the market, but most expansion on Apple devices is limited to proprietary cables and devices. The iPhone and iPad have historically used a single proprietary port for charging (see Figure 11.21)

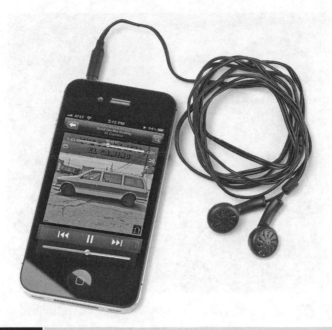

FIGURE 11.20 Earbuds plugged into a smartphone

FIGURE 11.21 USB charger connected to proprietary port

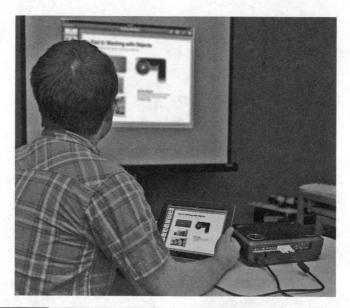

FIGURE 11.22 Apple Keynote on an iPad and a projector

and connecting to external devices. Current devices can mirror the screen to another display (see Figure 11.22) via an adapter (see Figure 11.23).

Devices that use Google Android come with a variety of connections and expansion capabilities, but the most common are USB ports for charging and

FIGURE 11.23 Apple Digital AV Adapter

FIGURE 11.24 microSD card and slot

expansion, and microSD-card slots for adding storage (see Figure 11.24). Some of these USB ports (almost always on a tablet) use a proprietary connector (see Figure 11.25). Many tablets (but rarely smartphones) also have a connector such as Mini- or Micro-HDMI (see Figure 11.26) for using an external screen or projector.

Regardless of OS, the wireless Bluetooth standard is an increasingly popular expansion option. The traditional additions are a headset, mouse, and keyboard

FIGURE 11.25 ASUS proprietary power connector

| FIGURE 11.26 | Micro-HDMI port and connector |

(see Figure 11.27), but Bluetooth-enabled wearable devices are growing in popularity.

Travel Assistance

For more on Bluetooth, see configuration instructions later in this chapter and discussion of Bluetooth technology in Chapter 19.

| FIGURE 11.27 | Small Apple keyboard paired with an iPad |

Adding Apps

Mobile devices come with vital apps installed for accessing e-mail and websites, taking notes, making entries in a calendar, listening to music, taking and viewing pictures and videos, sending messages, and making phone calls.

Beyond the essentials, you install apps through an app store. Remember the development models we looked at as you read about each OSs app ecosystem. The app stores reflect the development model, but don't assume the apps on offer will—there are closed-source apps for Android and open-source apps for Windows Phone and iOS.

iOS Apps

Apple exerts more control over the user experience than any other manufacturer by insisting all iOS app developers follow strict guidelines and limiting iOS devices to installing apps from the Apple App Store (see Figure 11.28). Apple approves apps in the App Store and refuses to distribute apps that fail to measure up.

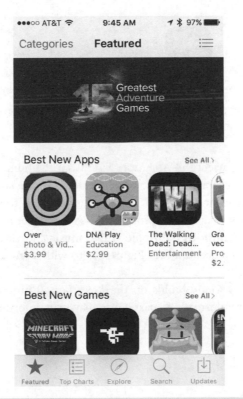

FIGURE 11.28 App Store

FIGURE 11.29 Searching for Monument Valley

To add an app, select the App Store icon from the home screen. You can select from featured or top apps, browse categories, or simply search (see Figure 11.29) for what you want. You need an account to purchase an app through the App Store; you'll be prompted to set one up or use an account you created previously through the Apple iTunes music and video store. You can create a new iCloud account (see Figure 11.30) with a few quick steps and a valid credit card.

The *iCloud Key Chain* builds on the *Key Chain* feature in Mac OS X to synchronize user information, passwords, payment information, and other

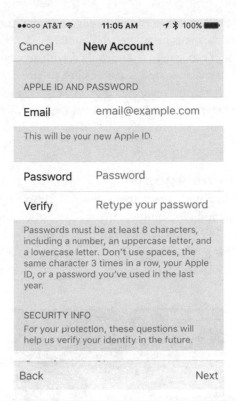

FIGURE 11.30   Creating an Apple ID for iCloud and App Store purchases

credentials (for providers such as Facebook, Amazon, and so on) with all your Apple devices, enabling you to auto-complete repetitive forms and avoid authorizing each app or site to keep copies of this information.

Android Apps

Google gives Android away, enabling manufacturers to craft versions better suited to their devices. HTC, for example, develops a custom interface called HTC Sense to change the look and feel of Android on its devices. Few Android users ever use "stock" or unmodified Android, and one manufacturer's interface can trip up users familiar with another. In addition to the Android version, the manufacturer's modifications have a version number.

The most common app source is Android's default app store, *Google Play*—but manufacturers can change this; Amazon's line of Fire devices even replace Google Play with Amazon's own app store. Many manufacturers have an additional *vendor-specific* store with apps developed for their devices. Third-party stores have apps that probably work with your device, but there's no guarantee.

Windows Phone Apps

Microsoft is a bit less strict than Apple, but still closely mirrors its control of app development and distribution. Anyone can write an app for Windows Phone or Windows 10 Mobile, but it must be accepted by the Windows Store (see Figure 11.31) for public distribution.

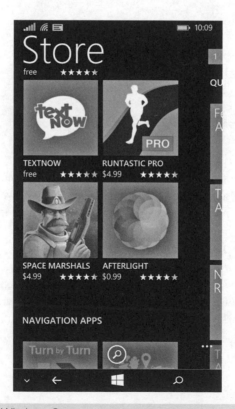

FIGURE 11.31 Windows Store

Network Connectivity

To use 802.11 Wi-Fi, you need to enable Wi-Fi and actively connect to a network. If the network uses encryption, you'll need access credentials. You can connect through the Settings app (see Figure 11.32). To join a network, tap Wi-Fi (or Networks) to view the available networks (see Figure 11.33), select one, and type the passphrase or passcode. Give the mobile device a moment to get IP and DNS information from the DHCP server, and you're on the network.

Travel Assistance

Refer to Chapter 19 if you need to brush up on 802.11 Wi-Fi.

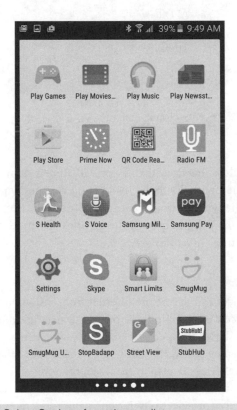

FIGURE 11.32 Select Settings from the app list.

Browsing available networks

FIGURE 11.33

On a successful connection, the device will store a network access *profile* associated with the network's SSID; if the SSID changes, your mobile device won't recognize the new network name. You'll need to delete the profile and reconnect; delete the profile through the Settings app by choosing the Wi-Fi network and selecting *Forget this network*.

Data

Many mobile devices can access the Internet from just about anywhere using cellular data services. By default, these mobile devices use *data roaming;* local providers usually have inexpensive roaming agreements, but roaming in another country can be costly. If you're going outside your cell provider's coverage area, get a travel-friendly plan or turn data roaming off.

You'll find the feature in the Settings app, where you can also turn off cellular data entirely (or selectively if your device has more than one type).

Turn off cellular data, for example, before hitting your data limit. We'll explore some security reasons to disable cellular connections while traveling later in the chapter.

E-mail

The 902 objectives want you to know about this whale of a phrase: *integrated commercial provider e-mail configuration*. iOS, Android, and Windows mobile devices have baked-in e-mail service from the OS developer. iOS devices integrate perfectly with iCloud, Apple's one-stop shop for e-mail, messaging, and online storage. Android devices assume a Gmail account, so they feature Gmail/Inbox front and center. Windows devices integrate Outlook.com e-mail. Mobile devices also support corporate and ISP e-mail. Almost every mobile device also enables you to add other e-mail providers as well, such as Yahoo! and AOL.

Apple devices go through the Settings app, then the Mail, Contacts, Calendars option (see Figure 11.34). Tap the Add Account option for the default e-mail

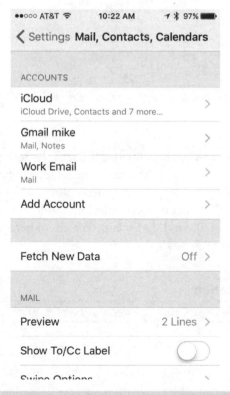

FIGURE 11.34   The Mail, Contacts, Calendars screen on the iPhone

●●○○○ AT&T 🛜   10:22 AM   ✦ ✳ 97% ▬▶

‹ Mail...   **Add Account**

☁️iCloud

E⬚ Exchange

Google™

YAHOO!

Aol.

O✉ Outlook.com

Other

FIGURE 11.35 The default e-mail types on the iPhone

options (see Figure 11.35). For a Microsoft Exchange Server e-mail account, tap the appropriate option and enter the e-mail address, domain, user name, password, and description. Apple's suggested options skip POP3 and IMAP4; to find them, click the Other option on the initial Add Account screen. When prompted, choose POP3 or IMAP4 and type in addresses for the sending (SMTP) and receiving servers.

Travel Assistance

Chapter 20 explores e-mail protocols, ports, and configuration.

FIGURE 11.36   Gmail app icon (top right) on the home screen

Android devices assume you'll have a Gmail account as your primary account, so you'll find Gmail on the home screen (see Figure 11.36), but there's a regular e-mail app for setting up Exchange, POP3, or IMAP4 accounts. Configure it with the port number and security type, such as SSL or TLS (see Figure 11.37).

Exam Tip

Be familiar with integrated commercial provider e-mail configuration settings for Google's Inbox (Inbox by Gmail), Yahoo!, Outlook.com, and iCloud. Use Chapter 20 as a reference for corporate and ISP e-mail configuration, including POP3, IMAP4, port and SSL settings, Exchange, and S/MIME.

FIGURE 11.37   Setting up a secure IMAP4 account

Synchronization

People generally want contacts and calendars to match across devices, so mobile devices need to synchronize data to maintain one set of contacts, one e-mail inbox, one calendar, and so forth. Smartphones and tablets use local machines or Internet servers to *synchronize,* or *sync,* personal documents, Internet bookmarks, calendar appointments, social media data, e-books, and even location data.

iOS devices use Apple iTunes software to sync iPhones, iPads, and iPods. Android and Windows devices also have an app store that can sync configuration settings, apps, software upgrades, and so on. In some cases, individual apps synchronize their parts of the device; an e-mail app, for example, may synchronize its e-mail and contacts.

Exchange ActiveSync

Exchange ActiveSync (EAS) is a Microsoft protocol used to synchronize Microsoft Exchange e-mail, contacts, and calendars, but you'll find it on Apple and Android devices. It has evolved to include device management features such as remotely wiping or locking a device as well as configuring network connectivity, secure e-mail settings, password policies, and so on.

Synchronization Methods

We used to sync to a desktop (uphill, in the snow!) with bundled software that only handled contacts—but it beat not syncing. Now, you can wirelessly sync contacts, media files, apps, and even OS updates. Each vendor has its own cloud technology to store personal data from your mobile device: Apple iCloud, Microsoft OneDrive, and Google Drive. Independent cloud providers such as Dropbox enable you to store and even share files.

Synchronizing your data to a computer gives you full control of storing, encrypting, and protecting your own data, but you must be able to connect to your computer. You can sync to the cloud from any wireless connection, but be wary of syncing over insecure public wireless networks. Finally, once your data is in the cloud, you no longer fully control it. You are at the mercy of the limits, security mechanisms, and privacy policies of your provider.

iTunes and iCloud

Apple iPhones and iPads can sync through Apple iTunes installed on a Mac or PC to locally store music, videos, contacts, pictures, e-mail, apps, and so on. This single backup source makes recovering from a lost or destroyed device simple: sync the new device to copy all of your files, contact information, and apps over. With iCloud, you can back up data (including iTunes media, calendars, contacts, and reminders) online and access it anywhere.

> **Exam Tip**
>
> Apple iTunes will run on just about any Mac OS X or Windows machine. To install the latest iTunes for Windows (64-bit), Apple suggests a Windows 7 (64-bit) or later PC with a 1GHz Intel or AMD CPU supporting SSE2, and 512MB RAM. You can play music with a 1GHz CPU and a 16-bit sound card, for example, but for complex media, such as HD video, you need a 2.4GHz CPU with two or more cores. For a Mac, the basic software requirements are OS X version 10.7.5 or later. For more information, visit https://www .apple.com/support/itunes/getstarted/.

Android and Gmail

Android doesn't have a central desktop application accomplishing what iTunes does for Apple devices; instead, they sync over the Internet. Synced data types depend on what apps and services you use, but they commonly include app data, contacts, calendars, e-mail, media purchased through Google Play, files in Google Drive or Google Pictures, and so on. For other files, you can still treat the device like a USB flash drive.

Mobile Device Communication and Ports

Mobile devices wouldn't be much use if not for all of the other devices and services they can interconnect with. Let's look at the mobile device connection technologies you need to know.

Micro-USB/Mini-USB   Unless your devices are manufactured by Apple, it's very likely they use either a micro- or mini-USB port to charge, connect to laptops or desktops, and sync between those devices. *Micro-USB* and *mini-USB* connectors are ubiquitous on Android and Windows devices.

FIGURE 11.38   Lightning connector

Lightning Connector   With the iPhone 5, Apple replaced its older 30-pin connector with its proprietary 8-pin *Lightning* connector (see Figure 11.38), which can be inserted in both up and down orientations—it's not "keyed" to a single orientation. Licensed Lightning connectors have a small verification chip, and knock-off cables without it may have limited use.

> ## Exam Tip
>
> The Apple Lightning standard is the poster child for *proprietary vendor-specific ports and connectors.* Only iOS devices use Lightning for communication and power. Android and Windows mobile devices typically use industry-standard, vendor-neutral ports and connectors.

USB Type-C   The newest *USB Type-C* connector (see Figure 11.39) isn't common on mobile devices yet, but expect to see it. Like the Lightning connector, the USB Type-C connector is not keyed, and with any luck it will be the standardized connector of the near future—even Apple may be moving in this direction—making it easier to buy interoperable cables.

> ## Exam Tip
>
> You will likely see micro- and mini-USB, USB Type-C, and Lightning mobile device connection types on the exams. Know their characteristics and differences.

FIGURE 11.39 USB Type-C connector

Bluetooth We'll discuss Bluetooth, including configuring and pairing, in Chapter 19, but let's outline the pairing process on a mobile device. First, enable Bluetooth (if it isn't already) via the mobile device's quick settings or full device settings menus. Next, ensure the Bluetooth device is powered on and has Bluetooth enabled. Use the mobile device to discover and select the Bluetooth device for pairing, enter or confirm the personal identification number (PIN) code (see Figure 11.40), and the devices should connect. Finally, confirm the new device works.

NFC *Near field communication (NFC)* uses chips that create and communicate with tiny electromagnetic fields, limiting range to a few inches. NFC can exchange contact information, small files, and even payment transactions with stored credit cards using systems such as Apple Pay and Android Pay.

Infrared The *Infrared Data Association (IrDA)* standard was once used for close-range line-of-sight wireless connections to transfer data between mobile devices and create the first real personal area networks (PANs). *Infrared (IR)* windows on modern mobile devices are almost certainly *infrared blasters* that emit (not receive) longer-range line-of-sight infrared signals to function as a remote control.

Hotspots and Tethering   A *mobile hotspot* device creates a Wi-Fi network to share its cellular data connection (3G, 4G, and 4G LTE) with other Wi-Fi devices. Wireless providers sell standalone hotspot devices for their network, but many smartphones and tablets can act as hotspots. Just enable the cellular data connection and toggle the hotspot setting to broadcast the Wi-Fi network and serve as a router between it and the cellular network (see Figure 11.41); configure a password to limit access.

Local Lingo

Tethering   Sharing a smartphone or tablet's data connection is also called *tethering*, a term you'll see carriers use to indicate different rules, rates, and restrictions on data consumed this way.

FIGURE 11.41 Configuring an Android phone as a portable hotspot

Mobile Device Accessories

There are tons of mobile device accessories, so let's focus on the ones CompTIA wants you to know for the exam:

- You can use Bluetooth *headsets* and *external speakers* for music and chatting.
- USB and Bluetooth *gamepads* can turn tablets into small gaming platforms; the Android-based NVIDIA SHIELD tablet is even designed as a gaming platform.
- Removable external storage, often *miniSD* or *microSD memory cards*, effectively upgrades the device's storage capacity; Apple hasn't quite embraced this.
- If your mobile device has a removable battery, *extra battery packs* can keep you going. Removable batteries can be directly charged with a *battery charger* while not in use.

- *Device chargers* either plug into a wall outlet or USB port and the mobile device. *Wireless device chargers* use a special pad you lay the device on to recharge.
- Much like those for portable computers, *docking stations* (typically for tablets) can adapt the device for purposes such as reading, writing, acting as a cash register, and so on.
- *Credit card readers* allow small businesses to process credit card payments on a mobile device.
- *Covers, cases,* and *screen protectors* protect all parts of the device from scratches and impacts, though fashion is also a factor. Special-purpose cases offer improved protection from threats such as water.

Objective 11.04 Troubleshooting Mobile Devices

Mobile device troubleshooting is a little different, but don't throw out what you already know. Let's look first at tools for troubleshooting general hardware, OS, and app issues, which will help you work through the troubleshooting process we looked at in Chapter 1. Then we'll apply these tools to common problems.

Troubleshooting Tools

Because hardware repairs require a specialist, mobile device troubleshooting focuses on ruling out software issues. The few things we can try are common to almost all mobile devices, and we start with options that inconvenience the user least. These might fix the problem, restore normal functionality until the problem recurs, or help you rule out causes. If these don't fix the problem or identify a cause you can resolve in-house, take the device to an authorized service center.

Travel Advisory

Most of these are guaranteed to erase data and customizations or have some risk of doing so. Communicate potential data loss with the user and give them a chance to back up data.

The steps to perform these operations depend on the device and its OS (including version). Be prepared to consult manufacturer and OS resources for exact steps.

Check and Adjust Configuration/Settings

Modern mobile operating systems have tons of configurable settings, as do some apps. Confirming relevant settings are not the "problem" that might keep you from reaching later steps that require backing up and restoring user data. If settings aren't a likely cause, don't waste tons of time toggling them until after you've tried a soft reset. Keep track of configuration changes.

Close Running Apps

Mobile operating systems enable you to close an app by swiping the app in a particular direction from the list of *recent apps*. Keep in mind that unsaved work can be lost, and features the app supports will stop working until you restart it. Avoid closing apps unless you suspect they are frozen, malfunctioning, or causing the device to misbehave; the OS does a good job of pausing and killing apps to free resources. Some can close all open apps at once (see Figure 11.42); it's a nice step on the way to trying a soft reset, but you won't know which app was causing trouble.

Some Android and Windows mobile apps can (intentionally or accidentally) leave background processes running after the GUI has closed and no longer appears in recent apps. You can use Android's Application Manager to *force stop* an app, killing its background processes. Control background tasks in Windows mobile OSs through application or battery settings.

Soft Reset

On a desktop, you initiate a soft reboot (where the machine never powers off) within the OS, and perform a hard reboot by holding down the system's power button until it powers off. On mobile devices, a *soft reset* is restarting the device from the OS or with hardware buttons (consult documentation for specifics). Much like a reboot, a soft reset can fix all kinds of strange app and hardware behavior.

Uninstall/Reinstall Apps

You can uninstall apps through the app store or *application manager*. If trouble started after installing a new app, uninstall it to see if the problem goes away. If the user has been successfully using the app, note important settings and back

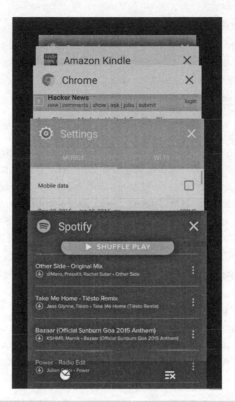

FIGURE 11.42 The overview screen on Android 5.1 with a button (at bottom right) to close all running apps

up data before you uninstall; if it started acting up after an update, removing and reinstalling the app may clear out the conflict—or you may have to wait for a fix from the app's developers.

Reset to Factory Default

A *hard reset* (also known as a *factory reset* or *reset to factory default*) clears user data and settings and returns the device software to a factory-fresh state. Don't confuse a hard reset with a hard reboot, and avoid documentation that mixes the terms unclearly. Back up user data first unless using a factory reset to clear user data before selling, recycling, or reassigning a device. If the problem survives a factory reset, send it for service; if the problem returns after restoring user data and apps, return to earlier steps for tracking down the troublemaking app.

Touchscreen and Display Issues

Display issues tend to be urgent for most devices, but the touchscreen's role in controlling a modern mobile device makes it all the more so. The mobile-centric issues in this section build on touchscreen troubleshooting issues in the "Input Problems" section at the end of Chapter 10.

Dim Display

Mobile devices have a *brightness control* that you set to automatic or control manually. A dim display might be a panel problem, but you need to rule out display settings. Disable auto-brightness and manually change from the dimmest to brightest setting. If it doesn't cover an appropriate range, suspect the display panel; if it does, suspect auto-brightness and try the following: ensure front-facing sensors and cameras are clean and unobstructed, check the environment for bright lights that may confuse the sensor, and perform a soft reset to clear up issues with apps that tinker with system brightness.

Touchscreen Responsiveness

When you find the *touchscreen nonresponsive* or get an *inaccurate touchscreen response,* there are a few simple things to rule out first: dirt, accidental touches, and performance issues. With those out of the way, we'll turn to more catastrophic causes:

- Touch sensors can register an accidental touch, often where you grip the device. Show the user how the sensors pick up an accidental touch, and how to hold the device to avoid them.
- Sometimes you can restore responsiveness by cleaning the touchscreen (see Figure 11.43) with a dry microfiber cloth to get rid of fingerprints, dust, dirt, grease, and so on.
- Performance issues can make a touchscreen inaccurate, sluggish, or inoperable. Be patient, and look for clues: incorrect time, jumpy lock screen or wallpaper animations, out-of-date weather or stock widgets, slow or no response to hardware buttons, doesn't receive texts or calls, and so on. If you can't regain control after a few minutes, perform a soft reset and see if the touchscreen works.
- Look online to see if the device has a hidden *diagnostics menu* or *service menu.* You reach these by typing a code into the device's dialer or holding specific buttons while the device boots. A touchscreen diagnostic makes hardware problems obvious. Some Android and Windows Phone devices may have a touchscreen calibration routine in either the primary OS settings menu or a hidden device menu.

FIGURE 11.43 Cleaning a smartphone

- If the touchscreen is still not responding properly, look for signs it has physical damage and needs service or replacement. You can ask, but don't expect much; the cause is often embarrassing. Even if the glass is fine, impacts can break internal connections, so check for scuffs and dings. Liquid can cause shorts and disorient sensors, so check for *liquid contact indicator (LCI)* stickers (see Figure 11.44) on the battery or in the battery compartment and external ports; look up additional locations online.

FIGURE 11.44 Pristine LCI sticker (top) and LCI sticker absorbing a drop of water (bottom)

App Not Loading

Start with a soft reset. If the app still won't load, it may be incompatible with some combination of the mobile device's hardware, OS, or vendor/carrier customizations to the OS. Confirm the device meets the app's hardware requirements, including RAM, storage space, processor type, specific sensors or radios, required camera features, and so on.

Overheating

We looked at most of what you need to troubleshoot overheating in Chapter 10. The big difference with mobile devices is that they are usually on and nestled near our bodies as we ride in hot summer cars or wear well-insulated winter clothing. Avoid very hot environments or turn the device off. If the device is hot to the touch in a cool environment, put it into airplane mode, close all running programs, and see if it cools. If not, turn it off until it cools and try again.

Beware if the device overheats for no obvious reason, or gets hot enough to burn someone. These problems are usually caused by a defective battery or other power circuit within the device. There's not much you can do other than turn it off to protect the device from further damage; keep it out of pockets, away from people, and take it to a service center.

Slow Performance

Add the following to what you already know about poorly performing devices. A mobile device with performance issues will often be running hot, but a hot device could be using *thermal throttling* to protect the device's CPU from heat damage; see if performance picks up as it cools. Performance issues can also be caused by struggling to efficiently save data or install apps to nearly full storage; free some space and see if the problem resolves.

A soft reset often resolves the immediate symptoms, and you can use the device settings or third-party apps to measure the device's performance, separate hardware from software causes, and decide whether you should take the device to an authorized repair facility.

Battery Life

Modern mobile devices also use Li-Ion batteries, and it's important to manage them well to ensure the device lives a long life. Before good management can help, you need to meet the user's power needs. Know how long a user's device needs to last on a charge, and shoot for 20 percent longer to account for dwindling capacity over the battery's life.

Mobile devices are rated in terms of "normal" duration, time between battery charges, and how much power the battery provides and needs to charge. Start with the device maker's numbers, and follow up with benchmarks on mobile device review sites. If no devices meet the user's needs, make sure they have a removable battery and spares, or a portable external battery recharger. You can plug a mobile device into a *portable battery recharger* (also called an *external battery, power pack,* or *portable charger*) to recharge.

There are two ways to think about battery life: how long it will last on each charge, and how long the battery can meet your needs before you have to replace it. When you waste battery life on unused device features, you shorten both. Here's a list of power-hungry components with tips for managing them, but there's no need to guess; check your device's battery usage monitor (see Figure 11.45).

- The fastest way to drain most modern mobile devices is leaving the screen on. Keep the display off when you can, and use the lowest acceptable brightness setting or automatic brightness. Other settings control how soon the screen turns off without input, whether notifications turn it on, and enable *power-saving modes*—some of which can even go grayscale. OLED displays, which use less power for darker colors, can reduce drain with black wallpapers and dark app themes.

- Another big battery drain is wireless communication. Cellular voice, cellular data, Wi-Fi, Bluetooth, NFC, and so on, all have a radio inside the device, and each draws power while enabled. Additionally, searching for a signal is expensive, and some apps will do more work when a radio is available. You may be able to dodge signal-search drain with settings to limit or disable device roaming and searching for new wireless networks. You can likewise restrict drain from overeager apps with app or OS settings.

- The power drain caused by location services can vary widely between an app occasionally checking low-accuracy location based on nearby cellular or Wi-Fi networks in the background, and one constantly requesting high-quality GPS updates. The simple solution is keeping location services off unless needed, but you may find a happy medium with per-app restrictions. An app should prompt you to turn location services on when it needs them.

Exam Tip
Be familiar with the factors that can reduce battery power and battery life.

FIGURE 11.45   Battery usage for a smartphone

Swollen Battery

Combine the handling and disposal steps from Chapter 10 with these mobile-specific tips. To avoid swelling, don't let batteries overheat (especially while charging) and prefer OEM chargers and batteries for your exact device. To protect from it, look for subtle changes in how the device's frame and screen or back cover come together, wobbling on a flat surface, weird creaking or popping, inexplicable heat, and so on. If the device lacks a removable cover, find a service center or mobile technician comfortable with taking the device apart.

Frozen System

The immediate goal is getting to a usable state. If the device isn't responding, follow the manufacturer's steps for performing a soft reset. If the device is partially responsive, close the offending app, save work in other open apps, and perform a soft reset. When the device is usable again, look for a solution.

If it froze when you opened a new or updated app, give it one more try before you uninstall and wait for an update or find a replacement app. OS issues can also cause a freeze, especially after an update; look for follow-up OS patches. If you haven't recently updated and the device starts freezing when you use any app that activates a component (such as the GPS or camera), your device needs service.

If the device is unusable after the soft reset, find documentation on how to boot into any special modes that enable you to remove an offending app, repair the OS installation, or reset the device to factory default. If this too fails, send it to a service center.

Cannot Broadcast to an External Monitor

Here are a few tried-and-true things to check when your device cannot broadcast to an external monitor:

- Is your input source correct on the external monitor?
- Do you have the right adapter for your device? Make sure you have an adapter known to work for your device.
- Does your adapter need its own power source?
- For HDMI: Did the HDMI recognize your device and your external monitor? Try resetting one or both devices to give the HDMI time to see connections and set up.

No Sound from Speakers

If you have no sound, check volume and mute settings in the OS and apps as well as hardware controls; expect the OS to have multiple settings for calls, music, notifications, and so on. Try a soft reset. If none of these steps works, the speakers have likely been damaged or disconnected inside the device; it needs service.

Connectivity and Data Usage Issues

The biggest connectivity problem is a weak signal caused by distance or interference; symptoms are dropped connections, delays, slow transmission speeds, and frequent no-signal indicators. There's not much you can do on the device end except move. Cellular signal boosters exist, but they're best in a fixed low-signal location.

Some tricky connectivity problems can occur despite a good signal. An *overloaded network* is common when large public events or emergencies cause a surge in network use, leaving users with a good signal unable to place calls,

FIGURE 11.46   Option to disable cellular data in iOS

texts, or transfer data. You may experience slow data speeds while roaming just because the carrier of the network you are roaming on limits data rates for nonsubscribers. Exceeding *data usage limits* your carrier sets can lead to slow data speeds, overage charges, or a hard data cap. To resolve this last problem, which CompTIA calls *data transmission overlimit*, pay to raise the data limits or monitor data use and disable cellular data (see Figure 11.46) as needed. Symptoms depend on how the carrier handles the overage, so check these limits when dealing with unexplained good-signal connection problems.

Synchronization Issues

A partial sync caused by connectivity, device, or remote infrastructure problems can result in duplicate messages, or just leave you stuck waiting for an important sync to complete. The common culprits are connectivity issues with Wi-Fi or cellular connections, upstream connectivity issues (somewhere between you and the sync server), problems with the sync server, authentication issues, incorrect OS or software versions, and incorrect configuration settings.

You can break these into issues that resolve on their own and those that won't—so we need to narrow it down. Try another networked activity, such as loading a few web pages; if this fails or is slower than usual, move closer to an access point or switch connection types and see if the problem resolves. If your connectivity is fine, many sync providers have a status page or post status updates that may save you from pointless troubleshooting. Confirm you are properly authenticated, and check your app store for updates to the sync app.

A separate sync issue occurs when multiple services try to sync the same data; a configuration change you made for one might prevent another from working—or the sources might be independently trying to sync to the same location. In an enterprise environment, the conflict is likely in the mobile device management software's configuration.

GPS and Location Services Problems

Location issue symptoms vary by app: photos tagged with the wrong location; you walk by a coffee shop on your way to the one your device said was closest; a navigation app calls out street names that don't match where you are; and explicit prompts (Figure 11.47), errors, and informational messages from the OS or apps that rely on location data.

Confirm services used to locate you (GPS, cellular data, and Wi-Fi) are turned on and functioning. Check if the app is configured not to access or use location services. Look for environmental causes; GPS won't work well or at all

FIGURE 11.47 GPS prompt

if you're underground, in a big building away from windows, or surrounded by tall buildings. When multiple apps have location issues unexplained by environment, consult manufacturer and carrier documentation to confirm OS settings.

Exam Tip

If you run into GPS error questions on the exam, remember that all apps will tell you if GPS is turned off and usually ask you if want to turn on GPS. Consider simple causes, such as your environment, before going complicated.

If the issues persist, the problem may be in GPS or network hardware, or in the OS. Look online to see if others report similar trouble on the same device software versions. If you don't see any, the device needs service; if you do, you're probably stuck waiting for a device update.

System Lockout

When too many consecutive login attempts fail, *system lockout* protects the device from attempts to guess the password by limiting how often you can try, requiring full account credentials, or wiping user data to be safe. Configure options like this on the device itself, or through the organization's central MDM software, but advise users to keep their devices away from criminals, snoops, and toddlers.

The company should securely store PINs and maintain current backups of all its own mobile devices, and hope those with their own devices keep backups. The MDM software can unlock the device, but it won't help if it has already been wiped. If no one can unlock a device, you'll have to restore from a backup or perform a reset to factory default.

Encryption Problems

The 902 exam expects you to troubleshoot mobile devices that are *unable to decrypt e-mail*, but encryption and how it secures e-mail are advanced topics you'll see on the CompTIA Security+ exam; let's focus on the basics. To secure an e-mail, we *encrypt* or scramble it with a unique key using some standard, such as *Pretty Good Privacy (PGP)* or *Secure/Multipurpose Internet Mail Extensions (S/MIME)*, so only the recipient can *decrypt* or unscramble it with software and a related unique key. Each *key* is a string of bits software uses to encrypt or decrypt data.

If the e-mail client doesn't support the encryption standard used, the fix is a plugin or a new client. Confirm the e-mail client supports this encryption method and follow steps to configure the client to do so. Finally, the e-mail client needs the decryption key. Some standards require manual key exchange; contact the sender to exchange keys. Other standards may exchange keys automatically if you meet certain criteria, such as being part of the same organization.

Objective 11.05 Securing Mobile Devices

Just like any computer we use to input or access sensitive data and network resources, we need to secure our mobile devices as well as protect our networks from compromised devices. Whether the device is company owned or personal, we should avoid preventable damage, theft, and malware infections, as well as the chance of important data being lost completely or falling into the wrong hands.

BYOD vs. Corporate-Owned Devices

A *Bring Your Own Device (BYOD)* policy covers if and how individually owned devices can be used within the organization. Some companies prohibit access to corporate data and resources with personal devices, particularly in high-security environments; others encourage personal devices to cut costs and keep employees happy. Most fall in the middle. The BYOD policy answers questions such as who pays for device service, who can own and access its data, and how privacy is handled.

Exam Tip
The two critical issues with BYOD are personal data privacy versus protection of corporate data as well as the level of organizational control versus individual control.

Profile Security Requirements

A *profile* collects configuration and security settings to apply to almost any user or device categories (see Figure 11.48) you could want. Profiles, created through the MDM software or a program such as Apple Configurator, are typically saved in eXtensible Markup Language (XML) format and pushed out to

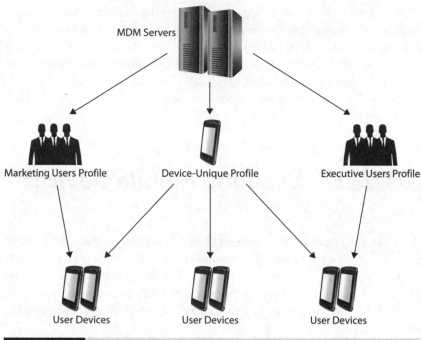

MDM Servers

Marketing Users Profile   Device-Unique Profile   Executive Users Profile

User Devices   User Devices   User Devices

FIGURE 11.48 Applying profiles to different device and user groups

the correct devices. A common use is to restrict or grant access to apps, connections, and servers based on whether the user is a manager, executive, external contractor, works in a given department, and so on. Profiles for a given device or OS can address device or platform-specific risks.

Preventing Physical Damage

Physical damage costs money, causes data loss, and creates chances for your data to be stolen during repair or recycling, so do the obvious to protect your devices. Don't get them anywhere near liquids or place heavy objects on them. Use the protective cover (see Figure 11.49) accessories discussed earlier; if your device is regularly exposed to threats such as dust or water, look for appropriate specialty cases.

Combating Malware

Tight controls on the OS and apps make traditional malware rare on iOS and Windows Phone devices, and third-party antivirus (see Figure 11.50) and anti-malware solutions try to plug this gap on Android. When malware strikes, the

FIGURE 11.49 Putting an Apple Smart cover on an iPad

FIGURE 11.50 Antivirus app for Android

OS maker boots the offending app from its store or pushes out a fix via automatic *patching/OS updates*. The foundation for protecting all of your devices is keeping the device software up to date.

| Travel Assistance |
Chapter 21 takes an in-depth look at malware.

Dealing with Loss

Say it to yourself: every mobile device will get lost and end up at the mercy, kindness, or ignorance of strangers. Protect data with a good *passcode lock* (see Figure 11.51) or *screen lock* that requires a password, PIN, pattern, fingerprint,

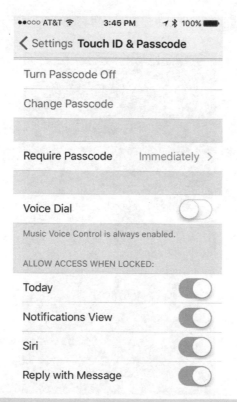

FIGURE 11.51   Passcode option in Settings

FIGURE 11.52   Locating a device in iCloud

or successful facial recognition to unlock the mobile device. Backstop the screen lock by limiting login attempts with system lockout, and configure a device locator service (see Figure 11.52). Configure your OS to encrypt the contents of built-in storage, protecting that content even if a "finder" dismantles the device to access the drive or data card.

Exam Tip
For the 902 exam, know the types of screen lock used to secure mobile devices: fingerprint lock, face lock, swipe lock, and passcode lock.

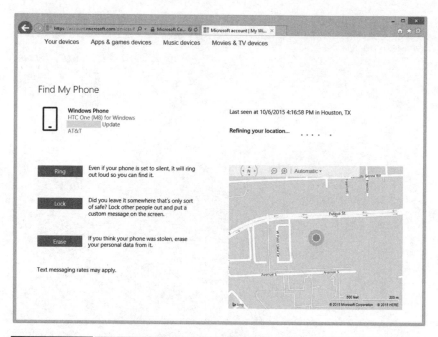

FIGURE 11.53   Select Erase to perform a remote wipe.

Recovering from Theft

Much like loss, dealing with theft effectively is more about what you do before it happens. If you keep your data backed up locally and remotely, you're free to *remotely wipe* (see Figure 11.53) your mobile device to safeguard data such as credit card numbers from a sustained attack.

With Windows Phone 8.1, for example, go into Settings and select items to back up with Microsoft's OneDrive cloud service (see Figure 11.54). For Apple devices, you back up and restore with services such as iCloud and iTunes, or use the Apple Configurator to handle a whole fleet. Android devices use Google Sync to back up and restore.

Securing Your Data

Aside from remote wipe, this discussion has been about protecting your device itself; let's turn to protecting your data.

Multifactor Authentication

Authentication (even at your front door) uses one or more *authentication factors*: something you know (a password, user name, or first childhood pet) is a *knowledge* factor; something you have (a smart card, key, or driver license) is

FIGURE 11.54 Cloud backup settings on Windows Phone

an *ownership* or *possession* factor; something you are (your voice, fingerprint, or retinal pattern) is an *inherence* factor.

Travel Advisory

Less common factors exist: somewhere you are is a *location* factor, and *temporal* factors may restrict authentication to given times, or specify time relationships between different steps (like in the movies, when two people must turn two keys simultaneously).

A user name and password are both knowledge factors, so we call this common authentication scheme *single-factor authentication*. *Multifactor authentication* aims for better security by using more than one factor; you may hear *two-factor authentication* used to describe common schemes that combine a user name and password with a code generated by or sent to your device.

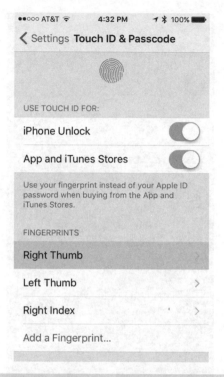

FIGURE 11.55   Touch ID options

Biometric Authentication

A common form of *biometric authentication* uses fingerprint readers to compare the current user's fingerprint to previous samples in order to unlock laptops and mobile devices. Starting with the iPhone 5s, for example, Apple's Touch ID (see Figure 11.55) can unlock the device with a fingerprint.

Authenticator Applications

Corporate networks may require you to authenticate with their own application to access a corporate VPN. Generic authenticator apps can provide a similar service for multiple sites or networks. Authenticator apps for multifactor authentication act as tokens or issue temporary session PINs. The key to these apps is proper initial configuration and setup.

Trusted Sources vs. Untrusted Sources

Getting software from *trusted sources*—legitimate app stores run by the major vendors, such as Apple, Google, Microsoft, and Amazon—is easy and mostly secure. App stores have their own requirements (including security) that developers must meet in order to get an app into the vendor's store. Remember that modified versions of Android can change which stores and sources a device will or won't trust.

Untrusted sources are a different beast, and have a higher risk of malware and spyware. Apple has strict controls to block untrusted sources (though organizations can deploy in-house apps to their own devices). Android blocks untrusted sources by default, but you can install apps from wherever you like with a simple settings change. Some apps are forced to use untrusted sources because they require elevated access to your OS or hardware that the trusted source forbids; see the upcoming "Unauthorized Root Access" section for the risks involved.

Firewalls

We'll examine firewalls in Chapter 21, so for now it's enough to know that software firewalls on individual devices protect them from network-based threats. Mobile devices generally don't use a firewall because they don't listen for the traffic a firewall blocks; think of them as having a firewall by design. Cellular and Wi-Fi networks also employ firewalls to protect networked devices. You can find firewall apps (see Figure 11.56) for individual or enterprise use to filter specific traffic coming into the host, which may also include anti-malware and basic intrusion detection.

FIGURE 11.56   An Android firewall app

Objective 11.06 Mobile OS and Application Security Issues

Security is complex and fast-changing. Much as with general troubleshooting, we'll begin with tools you can use to troubleshoot mobile OS and application security issues, and then turn to some of the common risks, symptoms, and clues related to mobile security issues.

Troubleshooting Tools

A good security foundation avoids giving attackers easy wins by keeping up with new threats and required patches, configuration updates, policy changes, anti-malware updates, and user re-education. Beyond this, security issues such as novel threats, insecure apps, and irresolvable vulnerabilities require constant vigilance. You'll need curiosity, instinct, persistence, and technical tools to troubleshoot mobile security issues.

Network Attacks

Network attacks exploit mobile devices that readily connect. We'll consider specific issues later in the "Unintended Connections" section, and focus now on tools for identifying and mitigating risks:

- Configure your device security settings (per device, or with device management software) to ensure your devices won't automatically connect to an open Wi-Fi network or nearby Bluetooth device.

- Configuration isn't worth much if your users still innocently select any open Wi-Fi network or agree to pairing requests. Your network will be at risk if your users don't notice clues that their connection to your organization's secure Wi-Fi network has been intercepted by an evil-twin wireless access point (WAP). Teach them to stop and report anything that seems out of place.

- In addition to using a *Wi-Fi analyzer* for tasks such as figuring out what channel a network should use, optimizing WAP placement, and finding dead spots, you can map out nearby networks (see Figure 11.57) to identify a malicious WAP.

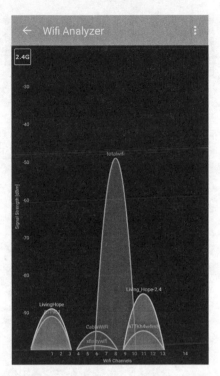

FIGURE 11.57   A Wi-Fi analyzer app on Android showing several SSIDs in the area

- A *cell tower analyzer* helps identify nearby cellular signals, estimate distance and direction (see Figure 11.58), measure signal strength, and collect information on the technologies they are using, network names, and more. Use one to confirm signal quality for a user with trouble connecting, map out access in the building, or spot an illegitimate tower operating nearby.

App Security

It won't take long to figure out malware is causing a device to run like it's full of molasses and redirect your searches to an announcement that you've won a round-trip to Mars. The "best" malware accomplishes its objective undetected,

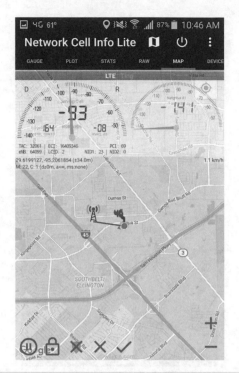

FIGURE 11.58   My Android-based cell tower analyzer estimating the location of a cell tower

so you should use tools to help you catch the easy stuff, freeing your attention to catch hints something is amiss.

- Mobile *anti-malware* apps use signatures to identify, block, remove, or warn about known malware. An *app scanner* looks through the permissions installed apps request to assess what security or privacy risks they pose. You can find separate or combined apps (see Figure 11.59); on iOS, similar features are available through the Settings app.

Travel Advisory

App scanners are useful because every feature and permission in every installed app is a risk. Even if the app isn't directly designed to spy on you, the app developer's server could be hacked, they could lose control of the app itself, or errors in its code could allow an attacker to use it against you.

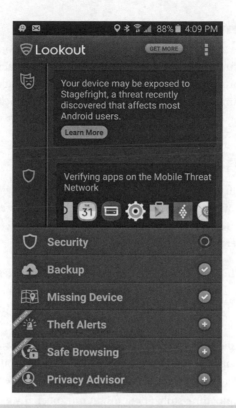

FIGURE 11.59 Combined anti-malware and app scanner

- Maintaining a current backup of your device gives you the confidence to focus on getting rid of malware instead of worrying about data loss. Different tools used to perform backups and restore data include MDM software, iTunes, and synchronization tools for Android and Microsoft devices; another option is to back up data to cloud storage such as Microsoft OneDrive or Apple iCloud.

- We've already looked at force stop, uninstalling and reinstalling apps, and using a factory reset for troubleshooting general app issues, but these also help pinpoint and address app security issues. When you see symptoms of malware or another app security issue, stop different apps until you isolate the cause and then uninstall it. If the app is reputable and the symptoms could be nonmalicious, reinstall to see if the problem returns. If you can't resolve the behavior, use a factory reset.

Risks, Symptoms, and Clues

The best malware and attacks are astonishingly creative, complex, and multi-faceted, so your curiosity, intuition, and persistence are crucial for identifying the risks, symptoms, and clues. The scenarios discussed here can be risks to understand and manage, symptoms of malware or an attack, or merely clues of an attack underway. They may appear alone or in groups whether an attack is present or not.

Unexpected Resource Use

Malware is just software that uses your device against your will, so a simple sign is unexpected resource use. Because many resource issues are benign problems fixed by a soft reset, it's easy to shrug them off; be suspicious, especially of unexplained patterns.

- A hot phone, *high resource utilization,* and excessive *power drain* might mean your device is doing a malware developer's bidding, such as uploading recorded audio in real time or smuggling networked files out.
- *Slow data speeds* can mean a device is busy uploading or downloading data without your knowledge, or a clue it is using an illegitimate WAP or cell tower with less capacity than its official counterpart.
- A device uploading stolen data might unexpectedly exceed cellular data transmission limits.

Unintended Connections

Unintended cellular connections aren't common because these are prepro-grammed into the phone by the carrier, but *tower-spoofing* equipment can trick devices into using it by imitating a carrier's tower and infrastructure. Once they connect, it can eavesdrop or even install malware. In addition to hackers and criminals, law enforcement agencies reportedly use land and aircraft-mounted spoofing devices.

Unintended Wi-Fi and Bluetooth connections enable malicious people to access, steal, or modify data. Configure your mobile device not to automatically connect or pair; doing these manually is worth the trouble. If the device is centrally managed, MDM software can enforce these protections via profile settings.

> **Exam Tip**
>
> The CompTIA A+ 902 exam objectives suggest using software or hardware *cell tower analyzers* and *Wi-Fi analyzers* to combat rogue connections. They can't help spot a rogue connection on the go, but they might help you notice a suspicious new WAP or tower near a fixed location you scan regularly.

In addition to their impact on battery life, power management, and running apps, *signal drop* and *weak signal* are some of the few clues you'll get that your device is interacting with a spoofed cell tower. If signal quality suddenly changes in either direction, be curious. See if the cellular provider has known tower issues nearby. Fire up a cell tower analyzer and compare nearby signals with what you've seen in the past, or with third-party resources online.

Unauthorized Data Access

Device locks and remote wipe can prevent unauthorized users from accessing data on a mobile device—if you wipe the device in time. Data can also leak out through apps and removable storage cards. Encrypt removable storage if it contains sensitive data. App and device security and privacy settings can protect personal data, but there's always risk here.

No matter the source, *leaked personal files and data* can pose a direct privacy or security risk, indicate an ongoing security issue, and suggest what that issue might be. A full audit of ways an important file could've leaked out of a networked environment is beyond what can be expected of a CompTIA A+ tech, but be curious—you may well get the first chance to escalate the issue, or write it off as a compromised login and make the user change passwords.

Unauthorized Account Access

For convenience, mobile devices are often set to automatically authenticate with networks, VPNs, e-mail servers, online services, and so on, granting unauthorized account access to anyone who can unlock the device. To keep sensitive accounts and connections secure, don't store credentials for automatic entry. When a device is lost, change the user's credentials. Unauthorized account access can also indicate an attack or malware has compromised a device, creating an ongoing threat to the organization.

Unauthorized Root Access

To protect against malware and attacks, each mobile OS limits the actions a user can perform. You can't install blocked software or unlock functionality for some purposes without degrading its security by going around these restrictions. To remove them, a user has to *jailbreak* (iOS), *root* (Android), or *unlock* (Windows Phone) the device.

Exam Tip
Know each term and the associated OS, but know it's common to see all of these used in relation to removing access restrictions from any given device.

- *Jailbreaking* is installing a program on the iOS device to change settings Apple didn't intend for users to change.
- *Rooting* is a similar procedure to grant the user full administrative access to the lower-level functionality of an Android device.
- Windows Phone devices have an official, security-conscious *unlocking* process for registered app developers; regular users, of course, can use tools to obtain the same access. Multiple unlocking layers grant additional freedom by peeling back a layer of protection.

Travel Advisory
These security-reducing methods have risks: bricking the device, voiding its warranties, and exclusion from service provider and organizational networks. You can use an MDM solution to exclude such devices from your networks.

Unauthorized Location Tracking

Depending on settings, the OS and apps may send a user's location to third parties. Prevent this by disabling GPS or location services until needed; otherwise, configure the OS and geotracking apps to prevent unauthorized tracking. Some apps or specific features won't work until geotracking is enabled (see Figure 11.60).

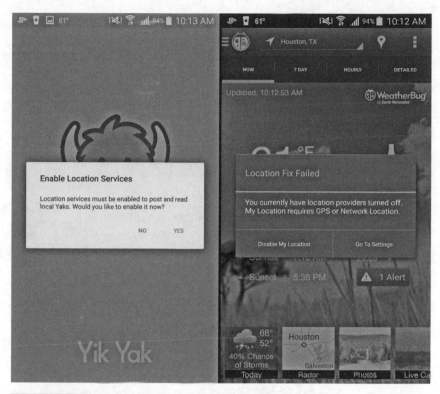

Both legitimate networks and some of the network attacks in the "Unintended Connections" section can also be used to locate or track a device. Tracking when devices cross invisible boundaries, or *geofencing*, is used for advertising, customer tracking, and employee tracking.

Travel Advisory

People tend to enjoy privacy, so tracking them can have legal consequences, especially if they didn't opt in.

Unauthorized Camera and Microphone Activation

App features, malware, and unauthorized network connections can potentially be used to toggle device features such as built-in cameras and microphones, enabling attackers to spy on anyone nearby. You can limit risk by restricting camera and microphone permissions in apps or OS settings, preventing unauthorized network connections, and using anti-malware solutions. With camera and microphone permissions, even popular apps (see Figure 11.61) by trustworthy developers could have a vulnerability that enables an attacker to listen in.

> **Travel Advisory**
>
> Sophisticated network attacks can reportedly *appear* to power down a device but leave its microphone active. Be on the lookout for strange behavior.

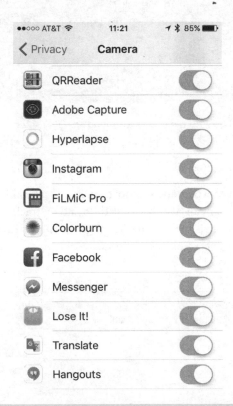

FIGURE 11.61 Apps with permission to access my iPhone's camera

CHECKPOINT

✔**Objective 11.01: Mobile Computing Devices** Mobile devices are small, lightweight computers that run a mobile operating system. They typically have a touchscreen that combines an LCD or OLED screen with a digitizer, and sensors such as a camera, microphone, and GPS. General-purpose tablet and smartphone mobile devices perform many tasks sufficiently, while purpose-built e-reader, smart camera, and GPS devices are tailored to performing a given task. Wearable devices typically pair with a smartphone, adding additional sensors and interfaces that collect useful data and enable more natural interaction.

✔**Objective 11.02: Mobile Operating Systems** Closed-source products follow the traditional practice of keeping how the product is made a secret, while open-source products have this information available but specify terms for how it may be used. Related terms *proprietary* and *vendor-specific* suggest technology that doesn't use common standards or interoperate with other products. The two most common mobile operating systems are Apple iOS and Google Android. Microsoft Windows Phone and Windows 10 Mobile lag far behind. The development model each uses is echoed throughout its ecosystem: Apple iOS is a strictly controlled closed-source OS installed only on (and designed for) Apple's own devices; Google Android is a loosely controlled open-source OS that device makers can modify as they see fit; Microsoft Windows Phone and Windows 10 Mobile are tightly controlled closed-source OSs but are licensed to other device makers for inclusion on their devices.

Mobile OSs have a primarily touch-driven graphical user interface, though users also interact with voice commands and gestures or movements. Devices come precalibrated, but some sensors or inputs may need recalibration. Common features include placing calls over Wi-Fi, voice-driven virtual assistants, a plethora of third-party apps enabled by open software development kits, emergency notifications, automatic location reporting to emergency dispatchers, and mobile payment services. They also support convenient connection features such as disabling radios with airplane mode, automatically updating radio firmware, and virtual private networking for improved security on Wi-Fi.

✔**Objective 11.03: Configuring Mobile Devices** Modern devices come preconfigured with the basics—except for your login credentials—but you'll inevitably end up configuring hardware enhancements, new apps, networking, e-mail, synchronization, ports, and other communications features.

Common hardware enhancements include USB devices, removable storage, external monitors, and Bluetooth headsets, mice, keyboards, and wearables. Networking settings dictate which Wi-Fi and cellular networks the device will connect to under what conditions. Devices come with integrated commercial e-mail service from the OS developer, though you can also add traditional POP3, IMAP4, and Microsoft Exchange Server accounts through device settings or e-mail apps. Sync settings control how and when the device is synchronized, including what kinds of data (contacts, apps, e-mail, pictures, music, videos, e-books, calendar, bookmarks, documents, location, and social media data) are synchronized.

Most devices have USB physical expansion and charging ports with micro-USB, mini-USB, or USB Type-C connectors, though current Apple devices use the Lightning connector. Other communications options include Bluetooth, near field communication, infrared, and creating Wi-Fi hotspots tethered to cellular data.

✔**Objective 11.04: Troubleshooting Mobile Devices** Troubleshooting mobile devices is about solving or ruling out software causes for common issues by applying simple tools and processes such as checking and adjusting configuration settings, closing running apps, performing a soft reset, uninstalling and reinstalling apps, and resetting the device to factory defaults.

These tools can be used to resolve device issues with display brightness, touchscreen responsiveness, apps that won't load, and power and performance issues such as overheating, slow performance, short battery life, swollen batteries, and a frozen system. They can also address connectivity issues with broadcasting to an external monitor, no audio output, poor connection or data limits, synchronization, GPS and location services. Finally, they can help address the side-effects of security settings such as system lockout and e-mail encryption.

✔**Objective 11.05: Securing Mobile Devices** Mobile device security can protect organizational resources from compromised devices, protect devices and data from physical threats and malware, and enable effective reaction to loss or theft. An organization's Bring Your Own Device policy and security profiles allow or exclude certain types of device on the network, and enforce settings to protect the devices and network. Cases, caution, and covers all protect from acute physical damage; staying on top of device software updates protects it from malware.

Start by assuming all devices will be lost: protect them with good screen locks, limit guesses with system lockout, configure a device location service, encrypt the device, and keep your data backed up; these steps delay an attacker and give you a chance to remotely wipe the device before it is compromised. Data can be further secured by using strong multifactor authentication enhanced with biometric authentication and authenticator applications, as well as only using apps from trusted sources. Although firewalls are available, mobile device design means they aren't a critical component.

✔**Objective 11.06: Mobile OS and Application Security Issues** Security issues with the mobile OS and its applications leverage the same troubleshooting tools we use to resolve general issues, though the increased complexity of security issues mandates a few additions: configuring devices not to connect automatically, training users how to identify and avoid risky connections, and mapping out nearby networks with Wi-Fi and cell tower analyzers to watch for suspicious connections.

Security issues can be subtle, and so are the symptoms—which occur alone or in groups, and occur whether or not a genuine security issue is present. These issues include unexpected use of resources, unintended connections to malicious networks, unauthorized data access, unauthorized account access, unauthorized root access, unauthorized location tracking, and unauthorized camera and microphone activation. Common symptoms of security issues are unexpected warmth, processing, or RAM use; congested data connections; data limit violations; excessive battery consumption; leaked data or files; compromised accounts; active recording lights, and so on.

REVIEW QUESTIONS

1. Which of the following would you need a specialty cover or case to protect the phone from?
   A. Scratches
   B. Impact
   C. A few drops of water
   D. Immersion in water

2. What is the difference between a hard reset, a factory reset, and a reset to factory default?

   A. A hard reset merely requires holding down a few buttons as directed by the manufacturer, while both factory resets are the same and require mailing the device to the manufacturer.

   B. A hard reset involves removing or disconnecting the battery for 20 seconds, but factory resets are performed by holding down a few buttons as directed by the manufacturer.

   C. Both of the above.

   D. None of the above.

3. John has a high-resolution image on his iPad of his two-year-old son and the family dog. The image initially displays smaller than the screen, so he wants to zoom in to get the details of his son's expression. How can he accomplish this task?

   A. Click the mouse in the middle of the picture to select it and then use the scroll wheel on the mouse to zoom in.

   B. Tap the picture with his index finger on his son's face.

   C. Right-click the picture with his index finger on his son's face.

   D. Touch his son's face on the screen with his thumb and finger, pinching outward to zoom in.

4. Which mobile device screen technology uses no backlight?

   A. CCFL

   B. LCD

   C. LED

   D. OLED

5. What can a government use to determine your location at a specific time as long as you're using your mobile device?

   A. Geocaching

   B. Geotracking

   C. Google Earth

   D. Gyroscope

6. What are the steps involved in pairing a Bluetooth keyboard with a tablet?

   A. Enable Bluetooth on the tablet; turn on the Bluetooth device; find the device with the tablet; enter a PIN code or other pairing sequence.

   B. Turn on the Bluetooth device; find the device with the tablet; enter a PIN code or other pairing sequence.

C. Search for a Bluetooth device from the tablet; select "pair" from the options to enable the device.

D. Enable Bluetooth on the tablet; turn on the Bluetooth device; find the device with the tablet; select "pair" from the options to enable the device.

7. Which of the following numbers uniquely identify the actual user associated with a SIM card?

A. IMEI

B. GSM

C. ICCID

D. IMSI

8. A client calls and is upset that he's misplaced his iPad. The mobile device has literally thousands of client records, including business addresses, e-mail addresses, phone numbers, and, in some cases, credit card information. What should he do first?

A. There's nothing he can do.

B. He should call his ISP and have them track his iPad.

C. He should access his iCloud account and remote wipe his iPad to erase all personal data.

D. He should purchase another iPad and sync with his iTunes account. This automatically erases the information on the old tablet.

9. Which of the following can improve battery life on an older mobile device with an LED display? (Select two.)

A. Turn down the display brightness setting.

B. Keep the device in airplane mode while you sleep.

C. Use a dark theme in any apps that support one.

D. Recalibrate the battery.

10. Which of the following authentication schemes uses three factors?

A. A door lock requiring a PIN code, an ID badge, and a key

B. A web application login process requiring your user name, password, social security number, and date of birth

C. A door lock requiring a fingerprint scan, a speech sample, and an ID badge

D. A door lock requiring a fingerprint scan, a PIN code, and an ID badge

REVIEW ANSWERS

1. **D** A standard cover will not protect your phone from being immersed in water, but a specialty cover can.

2. **D** There is no difference between a hard reset, factory reset, and reset to factory default.

3. **D** John can pinch outward with his fingers to zoom in on the image.

4. **D** OLED technology does not use a backlight.

5. **B** Geotracking can locate you and your GPS-equipped mobile device.

6. **A** To pair a Bluetooth keyboard with a tablet, enable Bluetooth on the tablet, turn on the Bluetooth device, find the Bluetooth device in the tablet's settings screen, and then enter a PIN code or finalize the pairing.

7. **D** The IMSI, included on the SIM card, uniquely identifies the user associated with the SIM.

8. **C** To protect his data, the client should log in to his iCloud account to remote wipe the iPad and erase all personal data.

9. **A B** Lowering display brightness and keeping device radios disabled will both improve battery life. LCD displays don't use less power for darker colors, and modern batteries don't need to be recalibrated.

10. **D** The fingerprint is an inherence factor, the PIN code is a knowledge factor, and the ID badge is a possession or ownership factor.

Operating System Fundamentals

	NEWBIE	SOME EXPERIENCE	EXPERT
ETA	3 hours	2 hours	1 hour

Computers have a lot of raw data-processing power and useful components, but it's up to the operating system to draw all these capabilities together into a useful platform. This chapter examines basic OS concepts and how they apply to common operating systems.

Objective 12.01 Operating System Concepts

Much like motherboards are the foundation of a system's hardware, operating systems are the foundation of its software. Desktop motherboards are well standardized, and even though the layouts and specifics differ a little, they have very similar features; likewise, any general-purpose OS you'd install on a desktop or portable computer will meet some basic needs. Carry this a little further: both the system board and OS embedded in smaller special-purpose devices are highly varied.

Common Operating System Functions

Because of its foundational role, any OS is responsible for certain functions:

- The OS provides an *application programming interface (API)* that programs use to communicate with hardware, while the OS itself talks to hardware directly (with *device drivers*) or through system BIOS.
- The OS provides a *user interface (UI)*—a framework enabling a human body to interact with a computer—that leverages input and output devices.
- The OS, via its UI, enables users to *discover* and use available programs or features. Almost every user-installed OS can also add, remove, and reorganize programs and data—but features of an embedded or special-purpose OS may be fixed.
- The OS should have a security framework appropriate for its capabilities, such as file access permissions on a multiuser OS or external attack protections on a networked OS.

From a basic user's perspective, the user interface *is* the OS, and knowing an OS is understanding how to manipulate its interface. As a tech, a little knowledge of basic interface concepts can help you support an OS you've never used, or support users who can't use a specific UI.

User Interface

We can't meet a modern computer on its own terms—imagine having to read and write binary (or even source code) in real time—so we build in a UI that translates between actions or metaphors we understand and a language the computer understands. A few of these metaphors are so deeply ingrained in computing that they are in almost every device, OS, and interface: files, folders, and programs.

A *file* collects related data; files have a *filename* so we can tell them apart and an *extension* that indicates what kind of data they contain. Some extensions let the system know the file is a *program* it should execute, but most indicate a specific data format—so the system checks its list of *file associations* to see which program it should load the data with.

For the benefit of all involved (even the computer), most operating systems use a hierarchical file system that organizes files with a deeply nested "tree" of *folders* (also called *directories*). A file or folder's *path* describes its location within this tree, and its *attributes* tell the OS to give it special treatment.

Travel Advisory

Available attributes depend on the OS and file system, but common options include hiding, compressing, archiving, and restricting who has access.

The *graphical user interface (GUI)* has dominated computer operating systems for decades, but it wasn't always this way. The previous dominant paradigm, the text-based *command-line interface (CLI)*, still plays an important role for power users such as programmers, researchers, server administrators, and—of course—techs. For now we'll look at these interfaces broadly; later we'll examine how each OS employs them.

Travel Advisory

These UI paradigms shape modern computing, but keep three things in mind: other types exist, real-world UIs often mix paradigms, and you'll likely have to work with other paradigms to support specific devices or users. Think about what sorts of UIs could support users who can't hear, see, speak, or use their hands; compare a GUI-based computer that turns voice commands into onscreen actions with a vocal interface on a screen-free device such as Amazon Echo.

Graphical User Interface

GUIs show visual metaphors for the computer's state and actions. For our benefit, the OS represents files and folders with tiny graphic *icons* that mimic paper files and folders, organized in a workspace called the *desktop*. You *point* at these metaphors with a *pointer* you control through a *pointing device* (mouse, touchpad, finger, and so on) to indicate which ones you'd like to *open, close, move,* or toss into the *recycling bin*.

Command-Line Interface

Mainframes and minicomputers of old used the classic CLI for years before the advent of the GUI, but the CLI didn't get eradicated like floppy drives; you can open a CLI program in all modern OSs—Windows, Mac OS X, and the many flavors of Linux—to reach a command *prompt* where you type and send text commands. It can be a surprise if you've been content with graphical interfaces, but many programs and utilities for technical users—even ones made this decade—*only* run from a CLI.

 **Objective 12.02** **Graphical User Interfaces**

In addition to creating the look-and-feel of modern OSs, the GUI also establishes many of the terms and names we use to talk about them. You need to know the names of these UI features and understand their functions for the exam, of course, but you'll also see them in the coming chapters and use them in the field.

Windows

All current Windows versions share some structural features; we'll look at these first, and then at specific versions.

- Windows boots to the welcome (or login) screen (see Figure 12.1), where you select a user account and provide credentials to log in.
- After logging in on most systems, you'll be taken to the primary interface for traditional desktop and laptop computers—the Windows desktop (see Figure 12.2). User accounts enable each user to personalize the interface with their own desktop icons and wallpapers, sound effects, color schemes, language and accessibility options, and so on.

FIGURE 12.1 Windows 7 Welcome screen

Application running in the foreground   Desktop with a few icons on it

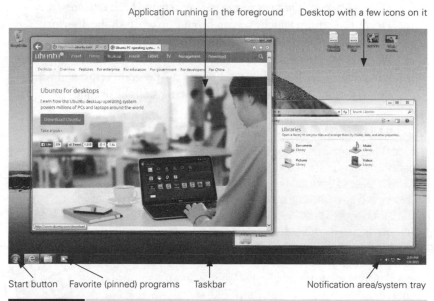

Start button   Favorite (pinned) programs   Taskbar   Notification area/system tray

FIGURE 12.2 Windows 7 with applications open

Travel Advisory

Windows Vista, 7, 8.1, and 10 all start at the desktop, but Windows 8 starts instead at the mobile-friendly Start screen. Since Windows 8 is the lone exception, we'll cover it in the Windows 8 section.

- The *taskbar,* at the bottom of the desktop by default, has a *Start button* for quick access to the *Start menu,* favorite programs, running programs, and the *notification area* or *system tray.*
- The Start menu provides compact access to most of your system's programs, settings, documents, and utilities, and enables you to search for other elements.
- The notification area or system tray contains icons for notifications, common settings, longer-running background programs, and a clock.
- You interact with an icon, button, and other interface element by moving the cursor to the element with your pointing device and clicking it. One left-click selects items on the desktop itself (open them with a double-click) and items on the taskbar; a right-click opens a *context menu* (see Figure 12.3) with options that depend on what you clicked.
- Folders open in *Windows Explorer,* later renamed *File Explorer* (see Figure 12.4), from which you can browse up or down the directory tree; copy, paste, move, create, and delete files and folders; view and modify file or folder properties and attributes; and access some other important *views.* File icons differ by extension and the program associated with that extension; Windows hides known extensions by default.

Exam Tip

Hidden files are made visible via *Folder options* or *View options* (along with general options to control whether folders open in their own window, how many clicks it takes to open an item, how the navigation pane opens and collapses folders, and so on). Microsoft tweaks View options from version to version, but the 902 objectives describe these with older terms: *view hidden files* and *hide file extensions.* Regardless, the effect is still to show or hide specific elements in a folder.

Right-click a file or folder, select Properties, and go to the General tab to change attributes that control whether it is hidden, read-only, compressed, encrypted, indexed, archived, and so on.

FIGURE 12.3 Context menu

FIGURE 12.4 File Explorer

FIGURE 12.5   Computer in Windows 7

- File Explorer's *Computer* view shows accessible storage volumes (see Figure 12.5) and devices. You can access this view directly from the desktop by choosing Start | Computer.

Travel Advisory

Microsoft changes UI options and features with *every* version of Windows and users can further customize the UI—having to hunt for specific files and folders is normal.

Windows Explorer and its ten default locations/folders are in Windows Vista's Start menu, but later versions pin File Explorer to the taskbar. The default locations/folders are consistent between Windows 7 and Windows 8: Favorites, Libraries, Homegroup (if in a home network), Computer, and Network. But Microsoft changed the lineup in Windows 8.1 and again in Windows 10, compressing Libraries and Computer into This PC, adding OneDrive, and more.

- The *Network* view shows devices connected to your network as well as available remote networked resources.
- Windows can assign *drive letters* to storage drives and volumes (the primary drive is traditionally assigned "C:"), giving each its own directory tree with the drive letter as the *root directory*. Windows creates a few special folders at the root (C:\) of the drive you install it on:

Windows, Program Files, and *Users.* As you might expect, the OS itself is installed in the Windows directory.

Local Lingo

SystemRoot   The Windows directory is also called *SystemRoot,* which you may see written as a variable (%SystemRoot%) at the start of a longer path, such as %SystemRoot%\Fonts.

- 32-bit versions of Windows have a single "C:\Program Files" folder where many applications install by default. 64-bit versions have a second folder, in order to store 32-bit and 64-bit programs separately. 64-bit programs use "C:\Program Files" whereas 32-bit programs use "C:\Program Files (x86)."

- The Users folder contains a folder for each user's files and programs as well as settings specific to the account. Windows creates a number of folders for my *personal documents* here; you'll need to know a few of them: Desktop, Documents, Downloads, Music, Pictures, and Videos. Windows Explorer/File Explorer changes the path view; it shows my user directory, for example, as "Local Disk (C:) > Users > Mike" instead of C:\Users\Mike (see Figure 12.6).

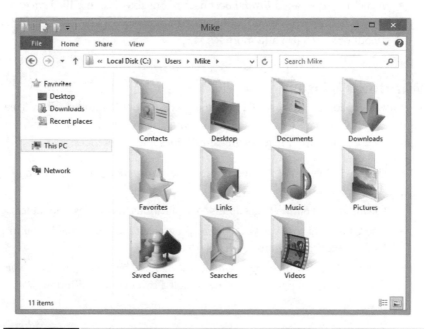

FIGURE 12.6   File Explorer viewing Mike's folders

Exam Tip

Know the personal directory paths (for example, C:\Users\Mike\Desktop).

- Windows sends a deleted file to the *Recycle Bin* folder until you empty the bin or restore the item (by right-clicking it and selecting Restore). Eventually, Windows will delete the file to make room for newly deleted files. If you need a deleted file that isn't in the Recycle Bin, a third-party recovery utility might work.
- Windows uses a portion of your hard drive space as *virtual memory,* a *slow* extension of system RAM that enables the size of loaded programs to exceed physical RAM capacity at the expense of performance.

Local Lingo

Virtual memory, swapfile, pagefile   All these terms refer to the same thing: space on the hard drive reserved as temporary storage for running programs.

- A caching tool called *ReadyBoost* uses removable flash media devices as virtual memory. SSDs and falling RAM prices have made ReadyBoost all but obsolete; just add more RAM.

Windows Vista/7

Windows 7 looks pretty similar to its predecessor, Windows Vista (see Figure 12.7). Compare this Vista desktop with the Windows 7 desktop from Figure 12.2 and identify the following similarities and differences:

- Open windows in each have an interface *transparency* feature called *Aero* or *Aero Glass.*
- Click the *Start button* to get access to applications, tools, files, and folders.
- The *Quick Launch* (Vista) or *pinned programs* (7 and up) enable you to launch favorite programs with a left-click.
- The *Sidebar,* which contains *Gadgets,* is enabled by default in Vista. The Sidebar is absent and Gadgets are disabled by default in Windows 7.

Gadgets in the Sidebar   Windows Vista Sidebar

Favorite (Quick Launch) programs

FIGURE 12.7   Windows Vista

Travel Advisory

Microsoft recommends disabling Sidebars and Gadgets on Windows Vista and Windows 7 systems due to security flaws. Later versions have neither.

Windows 8/8.1

The significant interface update in Windows 8 borrowed from the Windows Phone OS to create full-screen programs, called *apps*. The Windows 8 *Start screen* (see Figure 12.8) presents a grid of *tiles*, each representing a pinned app. This giant tablet-like interface was code-named *Metro UI*; Microsoft changed this to *Modern UI* for legal reasons, but the Metro name stuck.

It still has a classic desktop, accessed by pressing the WINDOWS LOGO KEY, though it lacks a visible Start button. Windows 8 also supports *side-by-side apps*, which streamline arranging windows to compare or reference documents.

Exam Tip

Windows 8 has a Start button on the Charms bar, discussed in a moment.

Start screen   Live Tiles (that update regularly)

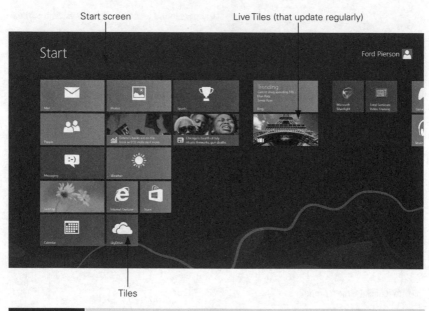

Tiles

FIGURE 12.8   Windows 8 Start screen

With the Windows 8.1 update (see Figure 12.9), Microsoft brought back features such as the Start button, easy access to a Close button for apps, and booting directly to the desktop.

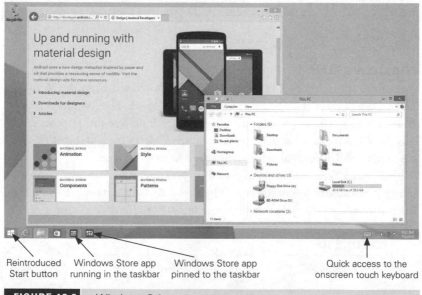

Reintroduced   Windows Store app   Windows Store app   Quick access to the
Start button   running in the taskbar pinned to the taskbar   onscreen touch keyboard

FIGURE 12.9   Windows 8.1

FIGURE 12.10 Charms accessed by moving the cursor to the upper- or lower-right corner

Windows 8 and 8.1 have some hidden interface components that activate when you move the cursor to certain locations:

- The bottom-left corner activates the Start button while on the Start screen in Windows 8.
- The top- and bottom-right corners reveal the *Charms bar* (see Figure 12.10), a location for tools called *charms*: the combined Search charm searches both the computer and the Internet; and the Share charm can share photos, e-mail messages, and more. We'll revisit the Settings charm in a moment.

Windows 10

Windows 10 (shown in Figure 12.11) blends the Windows 7 interface with some progressive features from the Metro/Modern UI. In particular, Microsoft refined the Start menu (see Figure 12.12), removed the much unloved Charms bar, incorporated essential tools such as Search into the taskbar, further streamlined side-by-side apps, and added *Task View* to create *multiple desktops* for grouping applications by task.

Exam Tip

Windows 10 isn't included on the current CompTIA A+ exams.

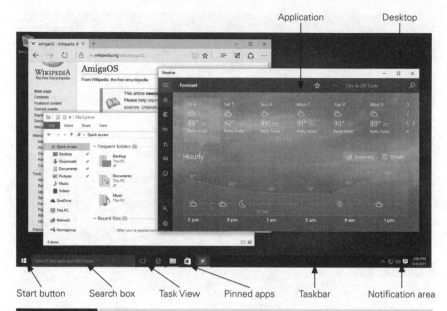

FIGURE 12.11   Windows 10 with a few applications open

FIGURE 12.12   Start menu in Windows 10

Mac OS X

The Mac OS X interface (shown in Figure 12.13) has a *Desktop,* as you'd expect, though you'll access frequently used, running, and pinned applications through the *Dock.* The interface features *Spaces*—essentially multiple desktops—that can have different backgrounds and programs. You can open *Spotlight* (COMMAND-SPACEBAR) to search for files and applications, and, Apple keyboards have a dedicated button (see Figure 12.14) to open *Mission Control* (see Figure 12.15), where you switch between desktops, applications, windows, and more.

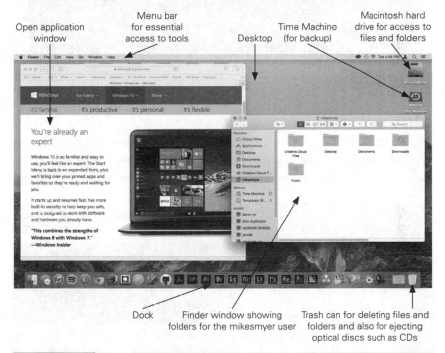

Open application window | Menu bar for essential access to tools | Desktop | Time Machine (for backup) | Macintosh hard drive for access to files and folders

Dock | Finder window showing folders for the mikesmyer user | Trash can for deleting files and folders and also for ejecting optical discs such as CDs

FIGURE 12.13 Mac OS X

FIGURE 12.14 Mission Control button on a keyboard

FIGURE 12.15 Mission Control showing four open apps and nine Desktops

Linux

There are many different distributions of Linux that offer a variety of graphical user interfaces, called *desktop environments (DEs)*. The popular Ubuntu Linux distro (see Figure 12.16) comes with the Unity DE; frequently used utilities and

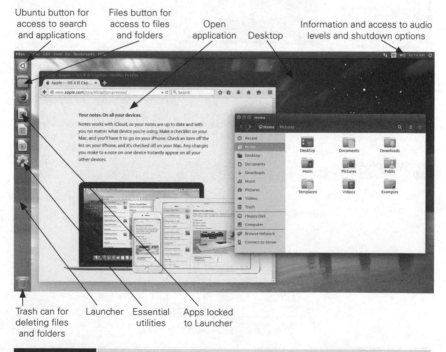

FIGURE 12.16 Ubuntu Linux

applications are locked on the Launcher on the left side of the screen. The top-left Ubuntu icon offers powerful system/network/Internet searching, while the next icon enables access to files and folders.

> **Travel Assistance**
>
> Chapter 17 takes a closer look at Linux and Mac OS X.

Objective 12.03 Command-Line Interfaces

In a modern graphical OS interface, the CLI opens in a window like any other program, but it contains something very different—a text-based interface where you type commands and send them to the *command interpreter,* also called the *shell*. On Windows, most techs reach the *cmd.exe* shell (see Figure 12.17) by typing **cmd** or **command** in the Start | Search box; Windows 7 and up also ship with the more advanced *PowerShell,* which includes *cmdlets* and advanced scripting. The equivalent program is called *Terminal* (which uses the *bash* shell by default) in Mac OS X (see Figure 12.18) and most Linux distros (see Figure 12.19). When you're done, you can use the **exit** command.

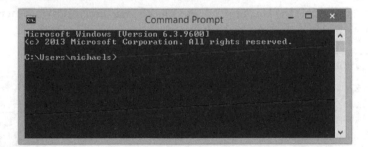

FIGURE 12.17 The Windows 8.1 command-line interface

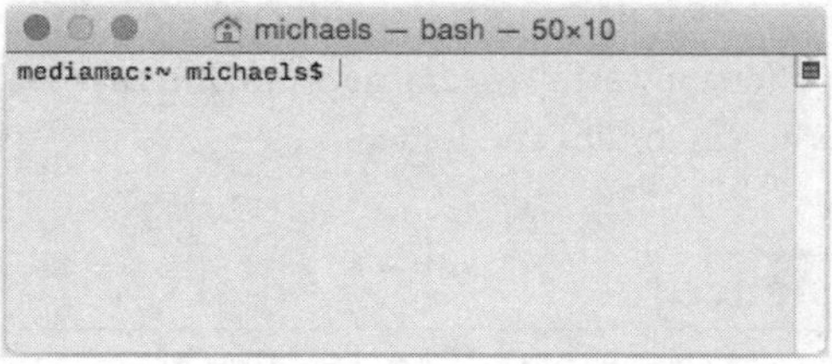

FIGURE 12.18 Mac OS X Terminal

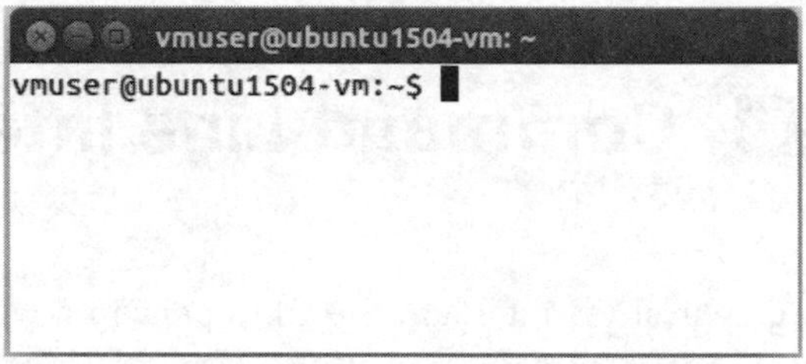

FIGURE 12.19 Linux Terminal

Issuing Instructions Using the Command Line

Working with the command line requires you to use commands recognized by the OS and to type in those commands correctly. Each OS can have different commands. To see the contents of a folder in Windows, for example, you type the **dir** command. To see the contents of a folder in Linux or Mac OS X, however, you type the **ls** command. You can change directories on either system with the **cd** command.

Exam Tip

In each OS, security settings will prevent you from running some commands at a basic prompt. In Windows, you'll need to right-click the cmd.exe icon and select *Run as administrator,* while you can use the *sudo* and *su* commands from within Terminal to respectively elevate a single command or entire session to *super user* or *root user privileges.*

Navigating the Command-Line Interface

The command prompt always *focuses* on a specific folder (see Figure 12.20), the *working directory,* and any commands you issue are performed on files in the working directory unless the commands specify another path. The prompt shows your working directory, but prompts differ by system. A Windows *C:\>* prompt focuses on the root directory of the C: drive.

Exam Tip
Know the default command prompt working directory. In current Windows versions, it's C:\Users\Username.

Information-dense Mac OS X and Linux prompts can be jarring to Windows users. There's a default—which contains the current user and the system's name—but it's common for power users to customize their prompt. Windows prompts end at the > character, but $ ends Terminal prompts. Slashes are reversed in Mac OS X and Linux (and drive letters don't exist) so an equivalent root-directory prompt is

```
mike@server:/$
```

Each of these systems has a user directory with similar default folders, but Terminal uses ~ as shorthand for the current user's directory. Windows and Terminal prompts focusing on the user's "Desktop" directory look like this:

```
C:\Users\mike\Desktop>
mike@server:~/Desktop$
```

You change the focus to another folder (but not another drive) by typing **cd** followed by the target folder's name relative to your current working directory. To see which files are contained in a particular folder, use the **dir** or **ls** command. Windows users can change focus to another drive or partition by typing the target drive letter followed by a colon and pressing ENTER. It isn't case sensitive, so **D:** and **d:** are equivalent. Linux typically *mounts* additional

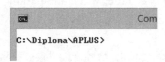

C:\Diploma\APLUS>

FIGURE 12.20 Command prompt indicating focus on C:\Diploma\APLUS\

drives to the directory tree in the */mnt* or */media/<username>* folders; Mac OS X uses the */Volumes* folder.

Travel Advisory

Windows and Mac OS X paths aren't case sensitive, but Linux paths are. On Linux, *~/desktop* and *~/Desktop* are different directories; Windows and Mac OS X can only make one of these; the other would fail.

Command-Line Concepts

The CLI is a really powerful tool if you take the time to learn it, and a few key concepts will light your way.

Syntax

Commands require proper *syntax*—the arcane combination of *arguments, switches,* and *parameters* that follow the command itself—but you can see syntax documentation for almost any command through the shell itself. Generally, Windows systems use the **help** command or the */?* switch, while Terminal uses the **man** (manual) command and the *-h* switch.

- Commands use *arguments* or *parameters* to gather basic input. The **help** and **man** commands both have a primary argument that requests documentation on some topic. For example, **help cd** and **man cd** both request information on the **cd** command.
- You modify how a command runs with switches. Each switch may have a short form with one hyphen or forward slash followed by another character (**-h** or **/?**), a long form with two hyphens followed by a name (**--help**), or both. Short forms are sometimes case sensitive.
- Switches may also have their own parameters. Typically, a short-form switch uses a space before any parameter, while long-form switches use the = character between the switch and parameter.

Travel Advisory

You can find individual commands that ignore these traditions, especially for software written to run on every OS.

- Short switches can often be combined to change multiple options at once, but if switches don't make sense together, the command may fail, or silently ignore some options. You may see short switches combined (for example, **ls -la**) in examples, but I don't recommend doing this while you learn.

Redirecting Command Output

It isn't in the objectives, but shells support a really powerful concept—redirecting command output—that creates much of the CLI's value. I'll leave researching the syntax up to you, but common *operators* let you write or append command output to a file, or *pipe* the output of one command into a second command (or more, if you like).

Running Applications from the CLI

In addition to CLI programs, you can also start GUI programs from the command prompt. Simply navigate to the folder containing the application, type the name of the executable file, and press ENTER. Valid Windows executable files have an extension of .exe or .com, but typically you don't need to enter the file extension, just the filename. On other platforms, executable files are indicated by the *executable* file attribute.

Exam Tip

This makes it easy to open useful GUI utilities (such as **notepad**, **explorer**, and **defrag**) without leaving the CLI, or to launch those programs with scripts. In fact, thanks to a variable called the *path*, you can open common utilities like this without changing your prompt to their directory. It's not the same as the path to a single file; it's actually a list of directories that your shell will search for a file or executable before giving up.

Common Commands

As you've seen, the two shell styles have minor but manageable differences. The hard part of hopping between the two styles is remembering which commands belong to which system. Some commands are universal, others have different names but the same result, and some concepts exist on only one system; commands with the same name or purpose may have different options per system.

TABLE 12.1	Common CLI Commands	
Windows	**Terminal**	**Purpose**
cd	cd	Change the focus of the command prompt.
chkdsk		Scan, detect, and repair file system issues and errors.
copy	cp	Copy files.
	dd	Create an exact (bit-by-bit) copy of a storage volume.
del	rm	Permanently delete files.
dir	ls	List files and folders in a directory.
exit	exit	Close the command shell.
format		Format data storage volumes.
	grep	Search text files or command output.
help	man	Display command documentation.
md	mkdir	Create a new folder.
move	mv	Move files.
	pwd	Show your *present working directory* path.
	passwd	Change a user account password.
	q	Quit the Terminal file/manual reader.
rd	rmdir	Delete (remove) a folder.
robocopy		Advanced file copying across a network.
shutdown	shutdown	Shut down or reboot a local or remote computer.
	su	Change authenticated user account (usually to root).
	sudo	Execute command with another account (usually root).
xcopy		Copy files and directories (including subdirectories).

Table 12.1 lists and compares common commands; advanced commands appear in subsequent chapters. Use the **help** commands to review basic syntax.

CHECKPOINT

✔**Objective 12.01: Operating System Concepts** The OS is in the middle of a conversation between the user, applications running on the system, and the system's hardware. It uses device drivers to interface with hardware, interfaces with applications through its own application programming interface, and interfaces with the user via the user interface. The graphical user interface and command-line interface are the dominant user interfaces. The GUI leverages visual metaphors such as icons to model system state and activity in a user-friendly visual language; the CLI, which is more oriented toward technical users, uses text commands and output for similar purposes.

✔**Objective 12.02: Graphical User Interfaces**   An operating system's GUI helps define many of the terms we use to discuss it. All current Windows versions share concepts such as a login screen, desktop, icons, folders, files, file extensions, wallpaper, taskbar, notification area (or system tray), Start menu, Windows/File Explorer, user accounts, personal document folders, and so on. Windows 8/8.1 moved the UI in a new direction, introducing mobile/tablet elements such as the touch-friendly Start screen, which Microsoft has refined over time. Operating systems such as Mac OS X and Linux have GUIs with similar concepts that often use different names.

✔**Objective 12.03: Command-Line Interfaces**   Modern CLIs run in a window within a graphical OS. There are some minor differences between command shells in Windows and Mac OS X/Linux systems, but for the most part you issue commands, navigate the directory structure, discover command syntax, redirect command output, and run applications in very similar ways. The biggest difference is between the commands they support.

REVIEW QUESTIONS

1. Which of these enables a program to activate a hardware device such as a webcam?
   A. Video user interface
   B. Device drivers
   C. Graphical user interface
   D. Application programming interface

2. What determines which program a data file will open in? (Select two.)
   A. Filename
   B. File extension
   C. File attributes
   D. File associations

3. Where in the CLI do you type and send text commands?
   A. Command-line link
   B. Command shell
   C. Command prompt
   D. Search box

4. Which of the following commands entered in the Start | Search dialog box will bring up the command-line interface in Windows? (Select two.)
   A. cmd
   B. command
   C. terminal
   D. shell

5. Which of these directories is created in the root directory when you install Windows?
   A. System32
   B. Fonts
   C. Users
   D. Documents

6. Which side of the desktop is the default location of the Windows taskbar?
   A. Top
   B. Right
   C. Bottom
   D. Left

7. Which of the following is a typical Windows command prompt?
   A. A:\\
   B. D:/>
   C. C:\>
   D. C://

8. What is the name of the Mac OS X search tool?
   A. Search
   B. Siri
   C. Spotlight
   D. Searchlight

9. Which term describes a Linux GUI?

   A. Desktop environment

   B. Desktop emulator

   C. Desktop experience

   D. Desktop elements

10. What type of memory stores running programs in a pagefile on a hard drive?

    A. Extended memory

    B. Flash memory

    C. Virtual memory

    D. Random access memory

REVIEW ANSWERS

1. **D**   An API enables an application to communicate with the hardware through the OS. The OS itself uses device drivers to control the hardware.

2. **B D**   The OS will open the data file using the program associated with the file's extension in the file association map.

3. **C**   You type and enter commands at the *command prompt*.

4. **A B**   Typing **cmd** or **command** at the Start | Search dialog box starts the command-line interface.

5. **C**   The Windows installation process creates C:\Users, which it uses to store user account directories.

6. **C**   The taskbar defaults to the bottom, but you can move it if you like.

7. **C**   C:\> is a typical command prompt.

8. **C**   The Mac OS X search tool is called Spotlight.

9. **A**   Linux distros use a desktop environment, or DE, to define the GUI.

10. **C**   Virtual memory holds the pagefile (or swapfile).

Windows in Detail

	NEWBIE	SOME EXPERIENCE	EXPERT
ETA	3 hours	2 hours	1 hour

This chapter picks up where the user-level tour of Windows left off: with the tools, features, and concepts a tech needs to know. We'll start with a roundup of available editions within Windows versions, and then you'll learn about tech utilities, basic Windows security, and the boot process.

Objective 13.01 Windows Versions and Editions

Microsoft offers multiple editions of each version of Windows to support a wide variety of user needs. When it comes to finding the tools you need to work effectively, there are a few trends to keep in mind. Microsoft likes to

- Add and remove tools with each version.
- Hide or simplify tools for working with features not included in an edition.
- Reorganize tools so newer users can better discover what they need.
- Add new shortcuts to tools from contexts where they're useful.

Unfortunately, a tech would need a photographic memory to keep everything straight while actively supporting multiple Windows versions and editions. From basic to full featured, here are the common versions of Windows and their various editions:

- **Windows Vista**   Home Basic, Home Premium, Business, Ultimate, Enterprise
- **Windows 7**   Starter, Home Premium, Professional, Ultimate, Enterprise
- **Windows 8**   Windows 8 (standard), Pro, Enterprise
- **Windows 8.1**   Windows 8.1 (standard), Pro, Enterprise

Windows 10 isn't included on the current exams, but it's worth knowing the common editions: Home, Pro, and Enterprise.

Exam Tip

Right-click Computer | Properties or use WINDOWS KEY-PAUSE to see the Windows version and edition in the System applet. You can also access this information through Control Panel, as discussed in a moment.

Modern Windows versions support 32- and 64-bit CPUs, but the builds are separate. 64-bit Windows needs a 64-bit CPU, but it can run 32-bit programs. 32-bit Windows should run on either a 32- or 64-bit CPU, but it won't run 64-bit programs (and you're limited to 4 GB of RAM). Make sure you get the right one—probably 64-bit, since new CPUs are almost inevitably 64-bit. The other issue is that you can't upgrade from 32-bit Windows to 64-bit Windows; you'll need a fresh install of the 64-bit OS, or a 32-bit version to upgrade.

Travel Assistance

We looked at 32-bit and 64-bit CPUs in Chapter 5.

Objective 13.02 Essential Tech Utilities

Windows offers a huge number of utilities you can use to configure the OS, optimize and tweak settings, install hardware, and more. The trick is finding them, so let's start with a few places to look:

- For many items, the right-click context menu will enable you to access properties as well as related tools and options. Furthermore, in Windows 8.1 and up, you can right-click the Start button (see Figure 13.1) to access the *quick links* menu for direct access to many tech tools.

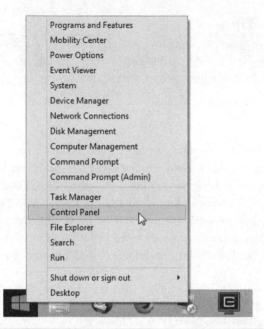

Programs and Features
Mobility Center
Power Options
Event Viewer
System
Device Manager
Network Connections
Disk Management
Computer Management
Command Prompt
Command Prompt (Admin)

Task Manager
Control Panel
File Explorer
Search
Run

Shut down or sign out   ▶
Desktop

FIGURE 13.1   Quick links menu

- The *Control Panel* (see Figure 13.2) contains a number of topical
  applets that, combined, enable you to configure most settings. You can
  use Category view to see applets by topic, and the Classic (Vista) or
  Large/Small icons view (Windows 7 and up) to see them alphabetically.
  Although applets do differ between versions, all versions have applets
  for managing appearance, installed programs and devices, and system
  settings. You can access Control Panel through the Start menu, Start
  screen | Apps view (down arrow) | Windows System, quick links, or
  search for it on the Start screen/menu.

Exam Tip

The 902 exam assumes you'll use the Classic or Large icons view.

All versions of Windows share many of the same applets, including
Display/Personalization, Add or Remove Programs/Programs and Features,
and System (all versions)—what I call the *Big Three* applets for techs. With

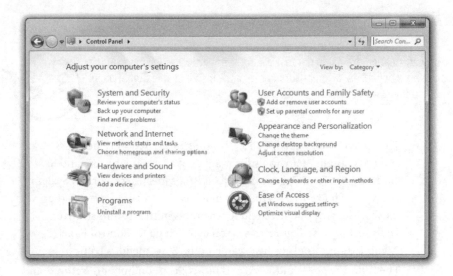

FIGURE 13.2   Two views of the Windows 7 Control Panel

Display/Personalization, you can make changes to the look and feel of your Windows desktop and tweak your video settings. Add or Remove Programs/ Programs and Features enables you to add or remove programs. The System applet gives you access to essential system information and tools, such as the Device Manager.

Exam Tip

Even common applets vary slightly among Windows versions. The CompTIA A+ certification exams do not test you on every little variance among the same applets in different versions—but you should know what each applet does.

- The *System Tools* (Vista, 7) and *Administrative Tools* (Windows 8 and up) contain many tools for managing a running system and its hardware. In Vista/7, go to Start | All Programs | Accessories | System Tools (see Figure 13.3). This gets much easier in Windows 8 and up; the Start screen's app list includes the tools in the Administrative Tools section (see Figure 13.4). You can also go to Control Panel | Administrative Tools or just search at the Start menu/screen.
- The *Settings app* (Windows 8 and up) collects a number of settings and tools in one handy interface (see Figure 13.5). It grows significantly in Windows 10, so Microsoft may continue adding to it. Access it via Start | Settings or the Settings charm.

FIGURE 13.3   System Tools

FIGURE 13.4 Administrative Tools section of the Apps list

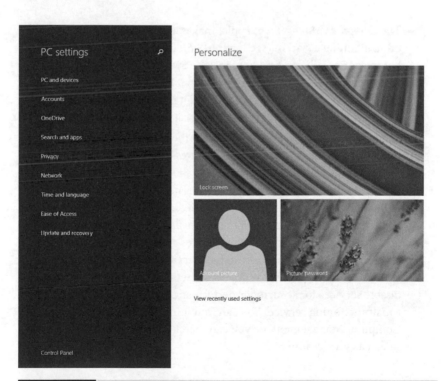

FIGURE 13.5 Windows Settings app

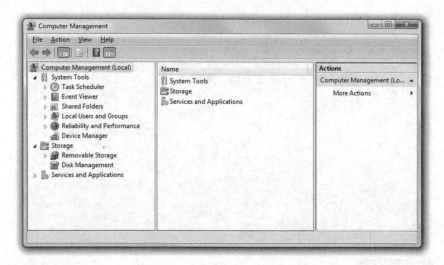

FIGURE 13.6   Computer Management applet

- The *Computer Management* applet makes a great dashboard for building or maintaining a system (see Figure 13.6). Its contents vary by version, but categories you can find here include System Tools, Storage, and Services and Applications. You can open it by right-clicking Computer and selecting Manage. You can also find it in Administrative Tools, in the quick links menu, or by searching for it on the Start menu/screen.

- Windows has many *services* that run in the background, providing support for many of your system's features. The *Services applet* (see Figure 13.7) lists available services and shows whether they are running as well as when they are allowed to run: *Automatic* services start early in the boot process, *Automatic (Delayed Start)* services start after everything else, *Manual* services must be launched by the user, and *Disabled* services won't run. The Services applet also allows you to start, stop, pause, restart, or resume a service. In general, you use the applet to enable services to support something that isn't working, to disable services for security or performance reasons, and to restart a malfunctioning service. You can find it in Administrative Tools or Computer Management, or you can search for it on the Start menu/screen as **services.msc**.

FIGURE 13.7 Services applet

Exam Tip

Don't memorize these services—just know how to manipulate them.

- *Task Manager* (shown in Figure 13.8) is your dashboard for day-to-day management tasks related to running applications, processes, and services—this is where you go to view what's running, to see how it is affecting system performance, and to end problem programs. Press CTRL-SHIFT-ESC to open Task Manager quickly. You can also go to Start | Search, type **taskmgr**, and press ENTER; or press CTRL-ALT-DELETE and select Task Manager.

We'll return to these locations again and again in the coming chapters to address many of the tools they contain and scenarios in which they're useful.

FIGURE 13.8 Task Manager in Windows 7

 **Objective 13.03** **Windows Security Basics**

We'll look at the *how* of security in coming chapters, but good security isn't magic you sprinkle on top once everything else is in place. Good foundational security is about assuming every layer of defense is vulnerable and then doing what you can to limit risk at every layer. When used with strong authentication and authorization, the *user account* becomes a foundational unit of security in modern Windows versions. *Authentication* is about denying access to anyone who can't supply valid credentials for a valid user account, and *authorization* is about limiting the actions an authenticated user can perform. What we really want, though, is *strong* authentication and authorization.

Local Lingo

Local user account   An account created on and local to a specific system, as opposed to domain accounts accessible at all systems on the same domain.

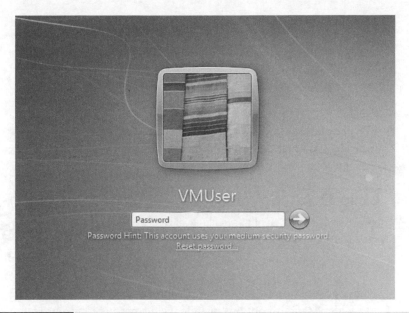

FIGURE 13.9 Password hint on the Windows 7 logon screen

Strong authentication means making sure only the authorized user has access to an account; this starts with *strong passwords* (but it doesn't end there—we'll revisit good security hygiene in later chapters). Windows enables you to create a *password hint* that appears after your first logon attempt fails (see Figure 13.9), but make sure it doesn't undermine password security.

Strong authorization limits the actions an account can perform to the bare minimum, and the *New Technology File System (NTFS)*, also called the NT File System, has a big role to play. NTFS has *tons* of features, but the 902 objectives zero in on security features: permissions and encryption.

Permissions

Folders and files on an NTFS partition have a set of *NTFS permissions* that define which users and groups can access them, and what actions those users or groups can take. Here are the important permissions:

- **Ownership** You're the *owner* of the files and folders you create on an NTFS partition, and owners have full permissions; they can even block administrators from accessing them.

- **Take Ownership permission**   There's a big asterisk on ownership; anyone with the *Take Ownership* permission—and administrator accounts have Take Ownership permission for everything—can take ownership and *then* access the file.
- **Change permission**   Enables an account to add or remove permissions for other users.
- **File permissions**   File permissions define what a user may do to an individual file. Standard options include Full Control, Modify, Read & Execute, Read, and Write.

Exam Tip

Windows Home editions do not have file-level permissions, and they only have one permission for folders: *Make this Folder Private.*

- **Folder permissions**   Folder permissions define what a user may do to a folder. Standard options include the file permissions plus List Folder Contents.

Now that you know what permissions are, you need to understand a few concepts related to how they work: inheritance, propagation, and groups.

- *Inheritance* determines which NTFS permissions apply to new files or subfolders. The default rule is that new files or folders get the NTFS permissions of the parent folder. You can technically disable inheritance in the file or folder properties, but don't. Inheritance is good (and expected). Inherited permissions are grayed out and can't be changed (see Figure 13.10), but you can override them as needed with the Deny checkbox. These permissions are additive: if you have Full Control on a folder and only Read on a file in it, you still get Full Control on the file.
- *Permission propagation* solves the related question of which permissions apply to files and folders you move or copy: their original permissions or those of their destination? Table 13.1 summarizes the results of moving and copying between NTFS volumes.

TABLE 13.1	Permission Propagation	
	Same Volume	**Different Volume**
Move	Keeps original permissions	Inherits new permissions
Copy	Inherits new permissions	Inherits new permissions

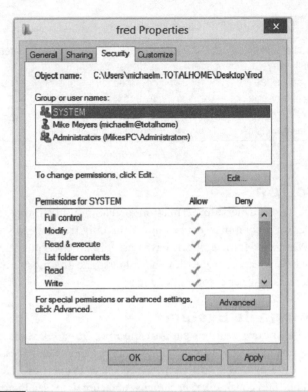

FIGURE 13.10 Inherited permissions

- A *group* collects users and permissions that apply to them. If you make an Accounting group and add all users in the accounting department, you can easily grant or deny the whole group access to a given file or folder. Windows provides built-in groups with predetermined access levels, but these are the only ones you need to know for the exam:
  - The *Administrators group* has complete control over a machine, and setting a user account's type to Administrator adds it to this group.
  - The *Power Users group* cannot install new devices or access other users' files or folders unless the file or folder permissions grant them access.
  - When you set an account's type to Standard user, it is added to the *Users group*. These standard users cannot edit the Registry or access critical system files; they can create groups, but can only manage ones they create.
  - The *Guests group* controls what actions the *guest account* can perform.

> **Travel Advisory**
>
> Protect yourself from *any* access you don't really need. Don't let someone hand you the keys to a permanent administrator account. Inform the system's administrator what you'll be doing and how long it will take. Have them create you a temporary account in the Administrators group and *make sure they delete the account* after you complete your work. If the physical location is secure, have someone else unlock the doors.

Encryption

Because the Take Ownership permission enables administrators to seize any file or folder on a computer, encryption is the only true way to secure sensitive data. Windows Home editions have basically no encryption features, but advanced editions can encrypt files and folders, and the most advanced editions feature full-drive encryption.

Encrypting File System

Professional Windows editions support the *Encrypting File System (EFS)*, an encryption scheme any user can use to encrypt individual files or folders. To encrypt a file or folder, just right-click | select Properties | General tab | Advanced and then check *Encrypt contents to secure data* (see Figure 13.11) in the Advanced Attributes dialog. Once you close out of the open dialogs, the file or folder is locked from other user accounts (unless you copy it to a non-NTFS drive).

> **Travel Advisory**
>
> Data you encrypt with EFS is secure from prying eyes, but access to your encrypted files is based on that specific installation of Windows. If you lose your password or an administrator resets it, you're locked out of your encrypted files permanently. If you use EFS, make a password reset disk.

BitLocker Drive Encryption

Windows Ultimate and Enterprise editions in Vista/7 and Pro edition in 8/8.1 feature *BitLocker Drive Encryption*, which encrypts the whole drive, including every user's files. If the system has a Trusted Platform Module (TPM) chip, it can enhance security by validating on boot that the computer has not changed. Create a recovery key or password when you enable BitLocker and keep it somewhere secure (like a safe). To enable BitLocker, double-click the BitLocker Drive Encryption icon in the Classic Control Panel and then click Turn on BitLocker (see Figure 13.12). *BitLocker to Go* enables you to encrypt removable media (such as a USB flash drive) and require a password to access its data.

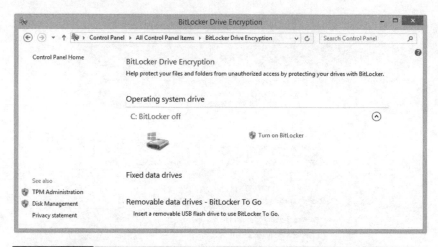

FIGURE 13.12 Enabling BitLocker Drive Encryption

Objective 13.04 Booting Windows

When you power on a Windows system, either the BIOS or the UEFI BIOS starts and then

- A traditional BIOS system scans each drive in its boot order for a master boot record (MBR) until it finds one. Boot code in the MBR scans the partition table for the system partition and loads its boot sector, which points the boot process toward the Windows Boot Manager, *bootmgr*.
- A UEFI system just loads bootmgr directly.

When bootmgr starts, it reads a *Boot Configuration Data (BCD)* file for information about installed operating systems and instructions for how to bootstrap (load) them. In a *multiboot* system, this is where it prompts you to pick an OS. Next, bootmgr loads winload.exe, which readies your system to load the operating system kernel (called ntoskrnl.exe) by loading the hardware abstraction layer, the system Registry, and the drivers for boot devices. Finally, the operating system process itself takes over.

CHECKPOINT

✔**Objective 13.01: Windows Versions and Editions** In addition to the Windows versions—Vista, 7, 8, 8.1, and 10—Windows is also available in editions that range from basic to full featured. Microsoft tends to reorganize tools for techs from version to version, and the location can vary between editions if a tool pertains to a feature in one but not the other. Most new Windows installs will be 64 bit, but you'll need a 32-bit version to upgrade an older 32-bit install; 32-bit programs will run in 64-bit Windows, but not vice versa.

✔**Objective 13.02: Essential Tech Utilities** Even though tech utilities get reorganized often, there are thankfully a limited number of places to look. The quick links menu offers direct access to some of the most common tools, while the Control Panel contains applets for almost everything you can configure on the system. The System Tools and Administrative Tools menus have some more advanced tools for managing a running system and its hardware. Beginning in Windows 8, the Settings app also collects a number of settings and tools in a single handy interface. The Computer Management applet is a great console for system building and maintenance, as it collects system tools, storage tools, and tools for managing services and applications—including the Services applet, where you can start/ stop and enable/disable services. Task Manager is an excellent dashboard for information and controls related to running processes and system performance.

✔**Objective 13.03: Windows Security Basics** Basic Windows security is about using authentication to limit user-account access to only authorized people, and limiting what actions an account is authorized to take to the bare minimum. The cornerstone of account authentication is the password, and the cornerstone of account authorization is NTFS permissions. These permissions enable us to specify what users or groups can take which actions on a file or folder; along with user groups, this makes it possible to administer many accounts efficiently. Account security alone can't always protect your files, but encryption, via the Encrypting File System or BitLocker, can.

✔**Objective 13.04: Booting Windows**   After the BIOS or UEFI BIOS loads, the boot process diverges. Traditional BIOS systems follow the boot order to scan hard drives for a master boot record, which leads them to the partition table. The partition table's system partition loads the boot sector and, subsequently, the Windows Boot Manager (bootmgr). UEFI, by contrast, jumps straight to this last step. Bootmgr also handles OS selection on multiboot systems.

REVIEW QUESTIONS

1. What's the easiest way to access the properties of an object in Windows?
   A. Right-click and select Properties.
   B. Left-click and select Properties.
   C. Double-click and select Properties.
   D. In the Control Panel, select the Properties applet.

2. Which Control Panel applet enables you to access essential system information and tools, such as Device Manager?
   A. Add or Remove Programs
   B. Display
   C. Program Options
   D. System

3. Which keyboard shortcut opens the System applet?
   A. WINDOWS-PAUSE
   B. WINDOWS-ENTER
   C. CTRL-PAUSE
   D. CTRL-ENTER

4. Which of the following are true of 32- and 64-bit versions of Windows? (Select two.)
   A. 32-bit Windows can run 64-bit programs.
   B. 64-bit CPUs can run 32-bit Windows.
   C. 32-bit Windows can upgrade to 64-bit Windows.
   D. 64-bit Windows can run 32-bit programs.

5. Which Windows version introduces the quick links menu?

   A. Windows 7

   B. Windows 8

   C. Windows 8.1

   D. Windows 10

6. Which view shows Control Panel icons listed alphabetically in Windows 7 and up?

   A. Small icons view

   B. Category view

   C. Classic view

   D. List view

7. Which of the following runs first after a Windows system is turned on?

   A. bootmgr

   B. BIOS

   C. boot.ini

   D. mbr

8. What do we call the tools in Control Panel?

   A. Apps

   B. Utilities

   C. Widgets

   D. Applets

9. Members of which account group can access anything on a Windows system?

   A. Administrators

   B. Power Users

   C. Super Users

   D. Users

10. What determines which NTFS permissions apply when you move or copy an object?

   A. Folder permissions

   B. Change permission

   C. Inheritance

   D. Permission propagation

REVIEW ANSWERS

1. **A**   Right-click any object in Windows and select Properties from the pop-up menu to see the properties for that object.

2. **D**   The System applet enables you to access essential system information and tools, such as Device Manager.

3. **A**   Use the WINDOWS-PAUSE keyboard combination to open the System applet.

4. **B D**   64-bit CPUs can run 32-bit versions of Windows, and 64-bit Windows can likewise run 32-bit programs.

5. **C**   The quick links menu was introduced along with the return of the Start button in Windows 8.1.

6. **A**   Small icons view, along with Large icons view, shows Control Panel applets in an alphabetical list.

7. **B**   After a Windows system is turned on, either the BIOS or UEFI runs first.

8. **D**   Control Panel tools are called applets.

9. **A**   Members of the Administrators group can access any object on a Windows system.

10. **D**   Permission propagation determines which permissions apply when you move or copy an object.

Installing and Upgrading Windows

	NEWBIE	SOME EXPERIENCE	EXPERT
ETA	4 hours	2 hours	1 hour

You can dive into most software installations and everything will turn out fine, but because the OS plays a foundational role for the system, a Windows installation takes homework and preparation. We'll start with preparing to install or upgrade Windows, walk through the installation on both physical and virtual machines, and wrap up with how to troubleshoot installation and upgrade issues. The procedures here are tedious at times, but they can help you pass the 902 exam and save your hide once you're a working tech tasked with upgrading your boss's computer to the latest Windows version.

Objective 14.01 Preparing for Installation or Upgrade

OS installs can be time-consuming even when everything goes right, so a little planning can save a lot of time. Let's look at the decisions you need to make.

Identify Hardware Requirements

The first thing you need is an OS your system can run, or a system that can run the Windows version you need to install. Luckily, the minimum hardware requirements (shown in Table 14.1) for modern Windows versions (including Windows 10) have leveled off, making your decision fairly simple. Just keep in mind that an OS update *could* change these requirements.

TABLE 14.1	Hardware Requirements for Windows

Component	Hardware Requirements
CPU[1]	1 GHz (gigahertz) or faster 32-bit (x86) or 64-bit (x64)
Memory[2]	1 GB (gigabyte) of RAM (32-bit) or 2 GB of RAM (64-bit)
Hard drive[3]	16 GB of available hard drive space (32-bit) or 20 GB (64-bit)
Graphics	DirectX 9 graphics device with WDDM driver
Network	Internet access

[1] Windows Vista can get by with an 800MHz processor.
[2] Windows Vista requires a minimum 512 MB of RAM for Vista Home Basic; 1 GB for all other editions.
[3] Windows Vista requires 15 GB of available hard drive space for all editions.

Travel Assistance

The minimums are published on the packaging and at Microsoft's website (www.microsoft.com).

Verify Hardware and Software Compatibility

Assuming your system meets the requirements, confirm that Windows supports any specific hardware and software you need to use. When you install Windows, the Setup Wizard automatically checks your hardware and software and reports any potential conflicts—but don't wait until you are installing to check this out. Microsoft used to run the *Windows Compatibility Center* website for this purpose, but it shuttered the site in late 2015. Now, your best bets are to trust the Windows compatibility logo on the package, check the device or software maker's website, or download and run the Windows Upgrade Advisor (see Figure 14.1) or Upgrade Assistant.

FIGURE 14.1   Upgrade Advisor

Confirm Upgrade Paths

By the time you add up available Windows versions, each with multiple editions, it's tricky to figure out if you can upgrade a client's computer from X to Y. If the upgrade options don't work out, remember that you can always do a clean install as long as the system meets the hardware requirements for the new OS; just back up everything important first. Keep in mind that 32- and 64-bit versions are incompatible; a 32-bit install can only use a 32-bit upgrade, and likewise for 64-bit installs. Table 14.2 outlines upgrade paths from Windows Vista to Windows 7.

If you have Windows 7 and you want to upgrade to a higher edition with more features—from Windows 7 Home Premium to Windows 7 Ultimate, for example—you can use the built-in Windows Anytime Upgrade option pinned to the Start menu. Table 14.3 outlines upgrade paths from Windows 7 to Windows 8.

TABLE 14.2	Upgrading from Windows Vista to Windows 7
From Windows Vista	**Upgrade to Windows 7**
Home Basic	Home Basic, Home Premium, Ultimate
Home Premium	Home Premium, Ultimate
Business	Professional, Enterprise, Ultimate
Enterprise	Enterprise
Ultimate	Ultimate

TABLE 14.3	Upgrading from Windows 7 to Windows 8
From Windows 7	**Upgrade to Windows 8**
Starter	Windows 8, Windows 8 Pro
Home Basic	Windows 8, Windows 8 Pro
Home Premium	Windows 8, Windows 8 Pro
Professional	Windows 8 Pro, Windows 8 Enterprise
Enterprise	Windows 8 Enterprise
Ultimate	Windows 8 Pro

TABLE 14.4	Upgrading from Windows 7/8/8.1 to Windows 8.1
From Windows 7/8/8.1	**Upgrade to Windows 8.1**
Windows 7[1]	Windows 8.1
Windows 8	Windows 8.1, Windows 8.1 Pro[2]
Windows 8 Pro	Windows 8.1 Pro, Windows 8.1 Enterprise
Windows 8 Pro with Media Center	Windows 8.1 Pro, Windows 8.1 Enterprise
Windows 8 Enterprise	Windows 8.1 Pro, Windows 8.1 Enterprise
Windows 8.1	Windows 8.1 Pro
Windows 8.1 Pro	Windows 8.1 Enterprise

[1] You can upgrade from Windows 7 to Windows 8.1, but you can only keep personal files, not applications.

[2] You can upgrade to Windows 8.1 with one of two methods: through the Windows Store or via upgrade media, such as a Windows disc. You can only change versions via upgrade media. Installing through the Windows Store locks you into the previous edition.

You can upgrade from Windows 8 to Windows 8.1 pretty easily, keeping all your applications and personal files. Upgrading from previous versions? I suggest you back up your stuff and do a clean installation. Table 14.4 outlines the upgrade paths from Windows 7/8/8.1 to various Windows 8.1 editions.

Select Installation Media

To begin installing Windows, you have to boot the system from the *installation media*. For a long time this meant booting from a Windows CD or DVD, but fewer and fewer installs actually go this route as optical media fade away. If you don't have an optical drive, you can boot to removable drives (flash media, hard drives, solid-state drives) via USB, FireWire, eSATA, or Thunderbolt ports. Any number of *external/hot-swappable drives* will do the job. You can use the Windows Media Creation Tool to make your own bootable installation media from a downloaded *ISO image* of the installer.

Travel Advisory

Some systems have a hotkey you can press to boot from a specific device; otherwise, you'll have to use the system setup utility to make the installation media boot first.

Choose Installation Types

Just as there are multiple types of installation media, there are also different installation processes for different purposes:

- A *clean installation* usually starts with an empty hard drive, but since the process partitions and formats the hard drive, it can also erase and install over an existing installation. A clean install won't carry over problems from the old OS, but you'll have to reconfigure the system and reinstall software. Begin by booting from installation media.
- An *upgrade installation* attempts to update the OS files but leave programs and files intact, but there's always some risk of problems. Insert and run the installation media while the OS you intend to upgrade is already running, and indicate that Windows should install into the existing directories (instead of removing the existing OS before installing).

Local Lingo

In-place upgrade Microsoft calls an upgrade installation an *in-place upgrade,* so be prepared for either on the 902 exam. Microsoft also applies this term to the separate *repair installation* process—read questions about this carefully for context.

- A dual-boot or *multiboot installation* configures your system with more than one OS to choose from, each in its own partition or volume. If you only have a single drive with one partition, you can use Disk Management to shrink your existing partition and create a new one in the reclaimed space. The recommended order is to install Windows versions from older to newer, and install Windows before any other OS, such as Linux.

Travel Assistance

We'll look at how multiboot works on Apple and Linux systems in Chapter 17.

- A *remote network installation* uses a network location as the installation media. Larger organizations may use this along with special scripts to automatically select options and answer all the prompts that us mere mortals have to deal with manually during the installation process. So-called *unattended installations* can even install applications once the OS is in place.

- *Image deployment* saves tons of time when you manage many systems. The *image*, like the ISO image you use to create your own bootable installation media, is a complete copy of a bootable operating system. If you configure the system and install needed software before you make the image, you can use special software to set up a fully loaded system by copying the image over from removable media or the network.

Travel Assistance

The 902 objectives mention some additional installation media and types. Chapter 16 looks at how to reinstall from the hidden recovery partitions some system builders include—called installing from an *internal hard drive (partition)* in the objectives—along with *repair installations* and *refresh/restore installations.* We'll look at how *PXE* works as installation media in a *remote network installation* later in this chapter.

Back Up and Restore Existing Data

There's no way around it: if you're installing to a drive that contains data you'd rather not lose, you need to make a backup. If the system runs fine, this may be as easy as copying it off to a network location or external/removable media. If the system doesn't work, you may be able to spare the trouble of moving the drives to a working system by booting to an OS on a USB thumb drive or other removable media (loaded up with tech tools, ideally). Finally, start a list of post-installation tasks, and put restoring this backed-up data on it.

Plan Partitions and File Systems

If you are performing a clean installation, you need to decide how to partition the hard drive, including the number and size of partitions and the file system(s) you will use (for modern Windows versions, this is almost inevitably NTFS). If you're making a multiboot system, this means researching how much room each OS will need to install and operate comfortably.

Avoid Upgrade Issues

If you plan to upgrade rather than perform a clean installation, a few extra steps can save you the stress of a failed upgrade:

1. Uninstall software you don't use or need, and delete old files.

2. Perform a disk scan (error-checking) and a disk defragmentation.

3. Uncompress all files, folders, and partitions.

4. Perform a malware scan, and then remove or disable all anti-malware (including in your system setup utility, if you have built-in protections).

5. Don't upgrade until you are completely prepared to start over and do a clean installation if it fails.

Objective 14.02 # Installing and Upgrading Windows on a Physical Machine

Clean OS installs are all fairly similar—just boot the installation media, and follow the installation wizard until you have everything completed. Along the way, you'll accept the *End User License Agreement (EULA)* and enter the product key.

Exam Tip
Successful installation results in a properly formatted boot drive with the correct partitions/formats.

The Windows Clean Installation Process

The installation methods for Windows Vista/7/8/8.1/10 are so similar—only the splash screens and the dialog for entering the product key change from Windows Vista to Windows 8—that separating them is a waste of paper.

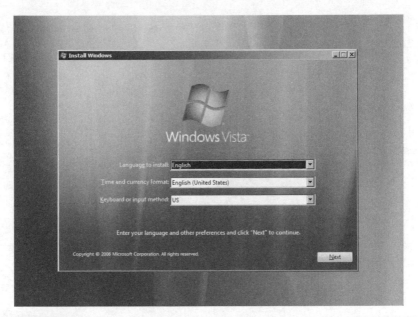

FIGURE 14.2 Windows Vista localization settings screen

Start by booting from your Windows installation media. Once you're in the installer, the first screen asks for your preferred localization (language, time/currency format, and keyboard) settings (see Figure 14.2).

Clicking *Repair your computer* on the next screen (see Figure 14.3) leads to the installation disc's repair tools, which we'll examine in Chapter 16. To continue, click *Install now.*

Next, a Vista installer will prompt you to enter your product key (see Figure 14.4) to determine which edition to install. In fact, if you don't enter a key, the next screen asks which edition of Windows Vista to install (see Figure 14.5). Starting with Windows 7, you can only install the edition named on the box or disc, so it doesn't prompt you for a product key until much later.

Travel Advisory

In Windows Vista and 7, installing without a key gives you a 30-day trial before the OS requires a product key valid for your edition, but Windows 8 and up require a product key during setup.

Next, you'll find Microsoft's EULA (see Figure 14.6), which you can read if you'd rather fall asleep than finish installing Windows.

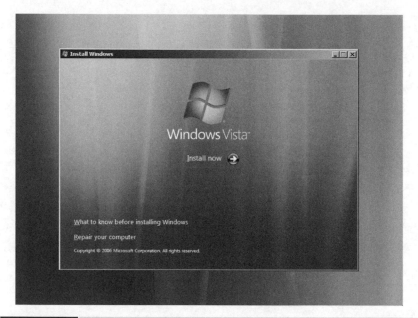

FIGURE 14.3 The Windows Vista setup welcome screen

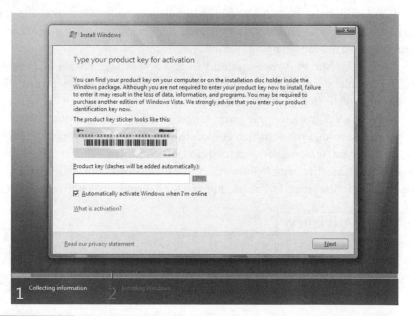

FIGURE 14.4 The Windows Vista product key screen

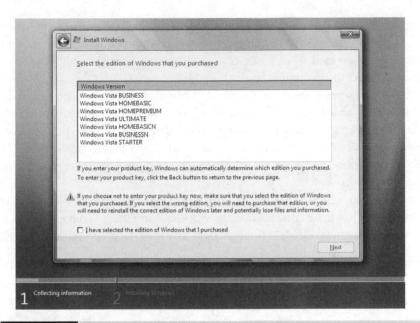

FIGURE 14.5   Choose the edition of Vista you want to install

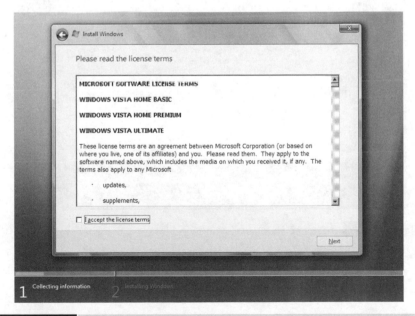

FIGURE 14.6   The Vista EULA

Now it's time to select an upgrade installation or a clean installation (see Figure 14.7), though the upgrade option will be dimmed if you booted from the installation media—in which case you have only been given the illusion of choice. Select the Custom (advanced) option.

The next screen (shown in Figure 14.8) prompts you to partition your hard drives and choose where to install Windows. The Drive options (advanced) link displays partitioning options, and Load Driver (see Figure 14.9) enables you to browse for alternative, third-party drivers to load. With luck, you'll never need this—and if you do, your drive should come with driver media and/ or instructions.

After you select a destination partition, the installation process starts churning (I like to imagine the installer whistles Daft Punk's "Technologic" as it works). This can take a while (though SSDs have sped the process considerably),

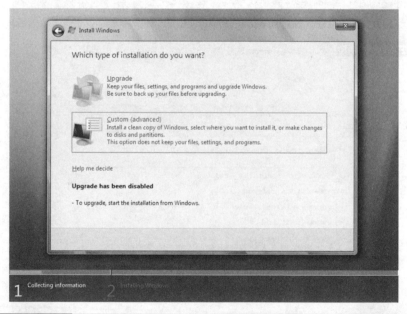

FIGURE 14.7   Choose your installation type.

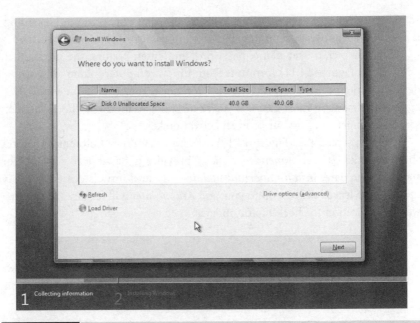

FIGURE 14.8 The partitioning screen

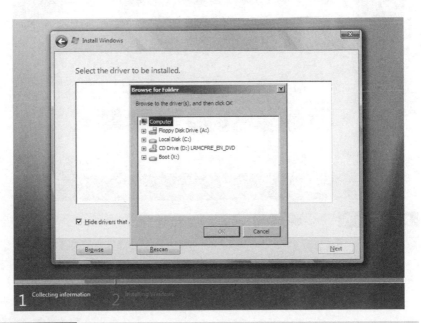

FIGURE 14.9 Browse for drivers.

so it's a good time for a break. When Windows finishes unpacking and installing, it asks you to choose a user name, picture, and password (see Figure 14.10).

After you pick a user name, password, and kitten picture, the next screen (shown in Figure 14.11) prompts you for a computer name and initial desktop background. The default computer name, your user name with "-PC" appended, is fine in most cases. If you're installing Windows 7/8/8.1, the next screen prompts you for your product activation key.

The next screen (see Figure 14.12) asks how Windows Automatic Updates should work: *Use recommended settings* provides a hassle-free method for staying up to date, *Install important updates only* auto-installs critical security updates and leaves the rest up to you, and *Ask me later* will require unrelenting weekly dedication to checking for updates.

FIGURE 14.10   Choose a user name and picture.

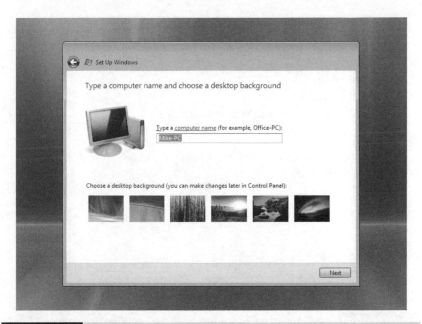

FIGURE 14.11 Choose your computer name.

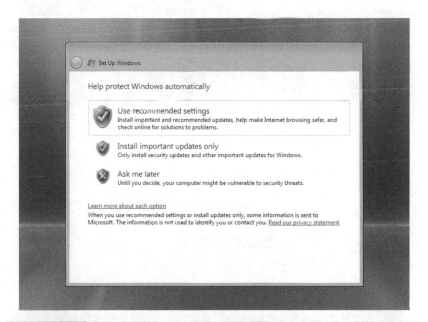

FIGURE 14.12 The automatic updates screen

FIGURE 14.13 Vista pities the fool who doesn't know what time it is.

Now you're on the home stretch. The next screens will ask for the date, time, and time zone (see Figure 14.13); ask whether you're on a trusted home or office network, or in an untrusted public location (see Figure 14.14); and

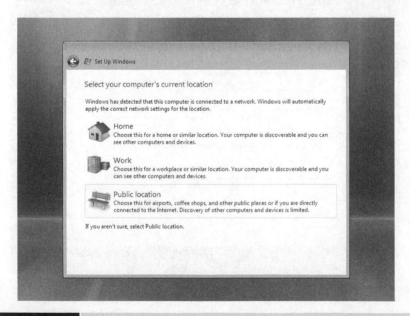

FIGURE 14.14 Tell Windows what kind of network you're on.

FIGURE 14.15 Aw, shucks, Microsoft Windows Vista. Don't mention it.

politely thank you for installing (see Figure 14.15). Afterward, Windows Vista and 7 want to test and rate your system's performance, but don't waste your time; skip this with the ALT-F4 (close program) shortcut.

Installing Windows over a Network

For machines to receive network installations, they (the clients) need to be connected to a server. That server could be another Windows desktop, or it might be a full server running some version of Windows Server—regardless, it hosts a default or custom Windows installation image. Setting up a server to deploy Windows installations and images goes beyond the CompTIA A+ exams, but let's take a closer look at the client side of things.

The *Preboot Execution Environment (PXE)* can boot from a network location using protocols such as IP, DHCP, and DNS. If your NIC supports PXE, you can enable it in the system setup utility from whichever screen has other options for your NIC. While you're there, move network locations to the top of the boot sequence.

Travel Assistance
Chapters 18, 19, and 20 explore IP, DHCP, DNS, and a host of other networking protocols.

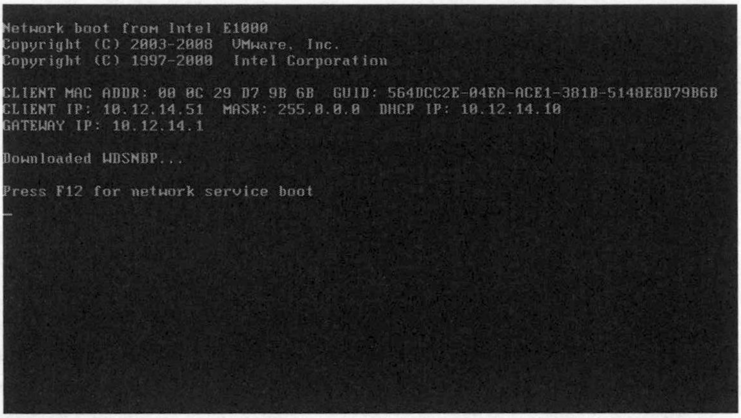

```
Network boot from Intel E1000
Copyright (C) 2003-2008  VMware, Inc.
Copyright (C) 1997-2000  Intel Corporation

CLIENT MAC ADDR: 00 0C 29 D7 9B 6B  GUID: 564DCC2E-04EA-ACE1-381B-5140E8D79B6B
CLIENT IP: 10.12.14.51  MASK: 255.0.0.0  DHCP IP: 10.12.14.10
GATEWAY IP: 10.12.14.1

Downloaded WDSNBP...

Press F12 for network service boot
_
```

FIGURE 14.16 Network boot

To enable PXE, you'll need to enter the system setup utility. Find the screen that configures your NIC, which changes depending on your particular BIOS. If there is a PXE setting, enable it and change the boot sequence so that the system boots from a network location first. If PXE isn't there, you can also create boot media that will boot from a network location.

When you reboot, somewhere along the familiar boot process you'll see the instruction "Press F12 for network boot." (It's almost always F12.) If the system can find and connect to a server, you'll be asked to press F12 again to continue booting from the network (see Figure 14.16), at which point you'll see a selection screen if there are multiple images, or be taken directly to the Windows installer if there's just one.

Post-Installation Tasks

Assuming the installation resulted in a bootable OS, you're ready to go through the post-installation checklist:

- Immediately after installing Windows, install available OS updates to obtain the latest features and *patches* for known bugs and vulnerabilities.

Exam Tip

Microsoft used to bundle updates and into cumulative *service packs,* but they haven't released one since the first for Windows 7. You may never have to install one, but know what it is for the 902 exam. We refer to them in shorthand such as SP1 or SP2 if the Windows version is obvious, or Windows 7 SP1 otherwise.

- Likewise, check for driver updates for important hardware (especially if you used default drivers during installation.)

- Remember when you backed up the user data files before installation? You don't? Good thing you already put it on your post-installation checklist. Restore this data.

- When it's time to *migrate* an OS and its users to new hardware, you can use the *User State Migration Tool (USMT)* or *Windows Easy Transfer* to quickly migrate user data. USMT is a business-grade tool for migrating many users on systems within a Windows Server Active Directory domain. Windows Easy Transfer enables you to migrate user data quickly. In Windows Vista/7, it is located in System Tools; in Windows 8/8.1, you can use Start | Search or find it in the Windows System category in the Apps list.

- When you're decommissioning hardware or otherwise migrating users off of it, the data it holds is at great risk. Not only do you need to safely wipe any data it contains after all users are migrated, but you need to make sure the drives are secure until the data can be destroyed. Don't leave them in common areas, or start a long copy operation and walk away.

- Data seems easy to lose, but intentionally destroying all of it is hard. Your options are to obliterate the hardware (with drive shredders, hammers, drills, and incinerators) or destroy data and render the platters physically useless with powerful electromagnets (a process called degaussing). Consider using a professional disposal service that issues a *certificate of destruction* confirming they have destroyed the drive.

- You can also attempt to sanitize the drive without rendering it unusable by overwriting data. While a standard format leaves data in place but inaccessible through the file system, a *low-level format,* also called a *zero-fill* or *overwrite* operation, fills the drive with zeros—but sensitive tools can still recover the data. A *drive wiping* utility fills the drive with junk data many times over; this is better, but not perfect.

- Many computer parts contain hazardous materials that pollute the environment, so it's important to ensure your old hardware doesn't end up in the landfill; either donate it to someone who needs it or recycle it. Many electronics retailers and cities have electronics recycling programs, and there are also companies that specialize in recycling computers.

Objective 14.03 ## Installing Windows into a Virtual Machine

Today's hardware is powerful enough to run multiple operating systems simultaneously on one physical machine. In the simplest terms, *virtualization* uses programs called *hypervisors* or *virtual machine managers (VMMs)* to create a complete *virtual* environment in which a *guest* OS can run as though it were installed on its own hardware. This environment is also called a *virtual machine (VM)*. Many hypervisors can run in an OS like Windows, but a *bare-metal* hypervisor is basically a lightweight, high-performance OS designed just to host VMs.

Purposes and Benefits of VMs

If you aren't familiar with virtualization, the idea can seem a little pointless at first. Why would you need to run an OS inside an OS? Is this secretly a plot for a film by Christopher Nolan? Here are a few of the biggest benefits:

- Going virtual enables companies to combine multiple servers onto fewer machines than in traditional computing. This offers tremendous savings on hardware purchases, electricity use, and the space used for computing.
- Because a VM is only a single file or two, a hacked system can rapidly be replaced with a snapshot (a backup) taken of the properly working VM. This is especially useful for getting critical servers back up quickly. Likewise, the minimal file numbers makes it easy to duplicate a VM.
- The capability to run many operating systems on a single physical machine makes multiplatform testing and research easier and cheaper than with traditional setups.

Emulation vs. Virtualization

Virtualization takes the hardware of the host system and segments it into individual virtual machines. If you have an Intel system, a hypervisor creates a virtual machine that acts exactly like the host Intel system. It cannot act like any other type of computer. For example, you cannot make a virtual machine on an Intel system that acts like a Nintendo 3DS. Hypervisors simply pass the code from the virtual machine to the actual CPU.

Emulation is very different from virtualization. An *emulator* is software or hardware that converts the commands to and from the host machine into an entirely different platform, such as the Super Nintendo Entertainment System emulator, Snes9X, running a game called *Donkey Kong Country* on a Windows system in Figure 14.17.

Exam Tip

Although the 902 objectives include emulation within virtualization, the concepts are not the same. For the sake of completeness, however, know that emulating another platform (using a laptop to run Sony PlayStation 4 games, for example) requires hardware several times more powerful than the platform being emulated.

FIGURE 14.17 Super Nintendo emulator running on Windows

Installation Process

The simplest form of virtualization—*client-side virtualization*—is literally just loading a virtual machine in a hypervisor running on your local system. The basic process is:

1. Verify and configure your system's hardware to support virtual machines.

2. Install a hypervisor on your system.

3. Create a new virtual machine that has the proper virtualized hardware required by the guest OS.

4. Start the new virtual machine and install the new guest OS exactly as you'd install it on a new physical machine.

Hardware Support

Any computer running Windows (and Linux and Mac OS X!) will support a hypervisor, but the hypervisor will run better if you have hardware virtualization support. If your CPU and UEFI/BIOS have this support, you can turn it on or off inside the system setup utility (see Figure 14.18).

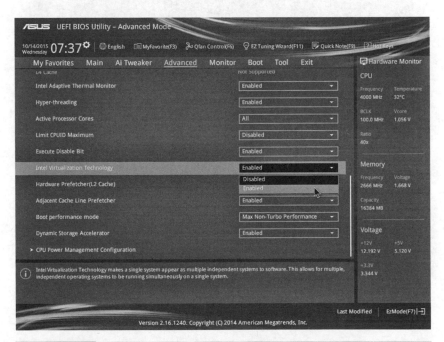

FIGURE 14.18 UEFI setting for CPU virtualization support

> **Local Lingo**
>
> **Hardware virtualization support** Both AMD and Intel have added extra features to their CPUs to enable better performance when the CPU is serving multiple operating systems.

The other big hardware requirements are RAM and storage space. Each virtual machine needs just as much RAM as a physical one, and you need enough left over for the hypervisor, host machine, and any other software the host machine needs to run. It takes some research to figure out. Likewise, VM files eat up tons of storage space because they include everything installed on the VM—anywhere from megabytes to hundreds of gigabytes.

Emulator Requirements

I lied: there are *some* situations where hypervisors do a little emulation. Instead of writing drivers so that every imaginable guest can use the hypervisor's virtual hardware, the hypervisor often emulates popular, widely supported hardware—devices every OS already has drivers for.

Installing a Hypervisor and Creating a Virtual Machine

Installing a hypervisor is like installing any other software. On a Windows 8/8.1/10 system, you can enable Microsoft's Hyper-V in the Windows Features dialog (see Figure 14.19), which you reach via Control Panel | Programs and Features applet | *Turn Windows features on or off*.

On pretty much any VMM, you create a new VM by clicking New | Virtual Machine and completing the wizard it opens (see Figure 14.20). Most hypervisors have presets to ensure your guest OS has the virtual hardware it needs.

Installing the Operating System

Once you've created the new guest VM, it's time to install a guest operating system. Would you like to use Microsoft Windows in your virtual machine? No problem, but know that Windows and any other licensed software you install require a valid license.

If you don't already have installation media, most VMMs can just treat any ISO file (such as the one you'd use to make your own installation media) as the virtual machine's optical drive. If the VMM recognizes your installation media

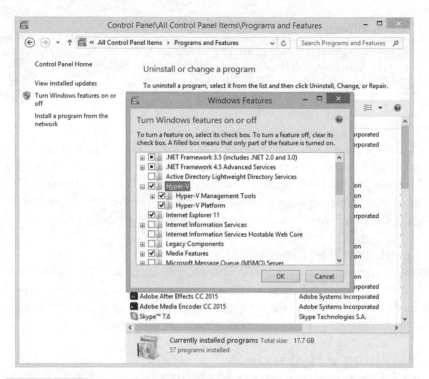

FIGURE 14.19 Installing Hyper-V in Windows

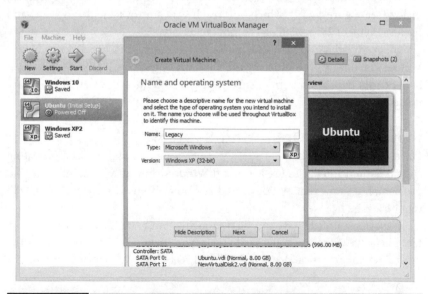

FIGURE 14.20 Creating a new VM in Oracle VirtualBox

FIGURE 14.21 Installer recognizing selected installation media

(see Figure 14.21), it may configure the virtual hardware settings (amount of RAM, virtual hard drive size, and so on) automatically; otherwise, you need to set sensible values for these (you can still change them after the virtual machine is created). Next, set the size of the virtual drive (see Figure 14.22).

FIGURE 14.22 Setting the virtual drive size

You'll also be prompted to name the VM and indicate where to store its data files. If you specified installation media, you'll also have some time to burn while the OS installs. After configuration and installation, you can stop, start, pause, or delete the VM, add or remove virtual hardware, or just interact with the OS and other software inside it.

Travel Advisory

Use descriptive names for virtual machines. This will save you a lot of confusion when you have multiple VMs on a single host.

It's almost exactly like using a real system, except it's contained in a window and some hotkeys differ. VMware Workstation, for example, replaces CTRL-ALT-DELETE with CTRL-ALT-INSERT by default (so you can still use CTRL-ALT-DELETE on your desktop). That, and you can adapt your *virtual desktop* to changing needs without a trip to the store: a good hypervisor can add and remove virtual hard drives, virtual network cards, virtual RAM, and so on.

Exam Tip

Virtualized operating systems use the same security features as real ones. You still need to keep track of user names, passwords, permissions, and so on, just like on a normal system.

Objective 14.04 # Troubleshooting Installations and Upgrades

The installation process itself almost never fails. Usually, something else fails during the process that is generally interpreted as an "installation failure." Let's look at some typical installation problems and how to correct them.

Travel Advisory

Even if the installation seems smooth, issues may surface over time. Especially with upgrades, be prepared to reinstall applications or deal with issues surrounding new, changed, and removed features. If things really fall apart, go back to the previous OS.

Media Errors

If you're going to have a problem, have a media error, such as a scratched DVD. It's always better to have the error right off the bat as opposed to when the installation is nearly complete. Here are some of the most common:

- If the destination *drive or RAID array is not detected,* Windows may not have the proper driver for the hard drive or RAID controller. If the hard drives show up fine in the RAID setup utility, it's almost certainly the drivers. Get a driver disc from the manufacturer and run setup again. Press F6 when prompted early in the Windows installation process; nothing happens immediately, but later you'll be prompted to install drivers.

- If the installation media is bad or the boot sequence is pointing to the wrong device, you may see a *no boot device* present error. Confirm the boot sequence in the system setup utility and then check the media for errors.

- Optical drives can fall behind, leading to a *not ready* error; it may just need a moment to catch up. Press R for retry a few times. You may also have a damaged installation disc, or the optical drive may be too slow for the system.

Graphical Mode Errors

Once the graphical part of the installation begins, errors can come from hardware or driver problems. Avoid these hardware detection errors by researching compatibility beforehand, or troubleshoot them at your leisure (typically by updating drivers) if the hardware isn't critical. With critical hardware, every Windows installation hinges on Windows Setup detecting the computer type (motherboard and BIOS in particular) and installing the correct *hardware abstraction layer (HAL)* to run on different hardware platforms.

Lockups During Installation

Lockups are challenging because they don't announce a cause. Here are two things to check:

- Bad media can keep an installation from getting off the ground, but localized damage or errors can cause trouble at any point in the process. Even if the media itself is fine, the ISO image—also part of the media—might not have downloaded perfectly. Check the media itself for obvious issues; if you find none, try creating another installation media from the same ISO. If this doesn't work, download the ISO again and start over.

- Windows generates text *log files* that track the progress of the installation phases, and each phase has a setuperr.log file to track errors. Windows stores these log files in the system root directory (where the OS is installed). The installers have powerful recovery options, so *you* probably won't have to read and understand these to fix something. Support people at Microsoft or a hardware manufacturer, however, would *love* to read these files.

> **Exam Tip**
>
> Don't try to understand these logs for the 902 exam; just make sure you know the names and location.

CHECKPOINT

✔**Objective 14.01: Preparing for Installation or Upgrade**   Identify hardware requirements, making sure that your computer meets the recommended minimums for CPU, RAM, free hard disk space, video adapter, display, and other components. Verify the Windows edition you're installing supports the hardware and application software you need. If you plan to upgrade, confirm you can upgrade to the Windows version you intend. Once you know what version of Windows you need, select the appropriate installation media and installation type. Back up existing data and plan out your partitions and file systems for the new install. If you are upgrading, go through the checklist of avoidable upgrade issues.

✔**Objective 14.02: Installing and Upgrading Windows on a Physical Machine** Installing modern Windows versions is pretty simple. Insert the installation media (or connect to it over the network), and then satisfy all of the prompts the installer throws at you. After installation, it's time to patch Windows, upgrade drivers, restore or migrate user data, destroy data on old hardware, and safely recycle any decommissioned hardware.

✔**Objective 14.03: Installing Windows into a Virtual Machine** Virtualization is a powerful technology that runs separate OS installs inside separate virtual machines, allowing organizations to consolidate hardware, save power, efficiently manage systems, and access many different platforms or operating systems on a limited number of physical systems. If your system meets the hardware requirements, you can install Windows into a virtual machine by downloading a hypervisor, creating the virtual machine itself, using the virtual machine manager to boot the VM from the installation media, and following a normal installation process.

✔**Objective 14.04: Troubleshooting Installations and Upgrades** Although the installation process itself rarely fails, other things can cause an installation failure. Media errors can include problems with drivers or a RAID controller, an incorrect boot sequence, damaged installation media, or errors in the ISO download. You can best avoid graphical mode errors, which typically come down to drivers or hardware compatibility issues, by researching compatibility beforehand. Lockups during installation can be frustrating. Check first for media errors, but if you can't identify any, it may be time to locate the Windows installation log files and contact support at Microsoft or your hardware manufacturer.

REVIEW QUESTIONS

1. Mary's Windows installation has failed. The error message says "RAID array not detected." Which of the following most likely is the problem?
   A. Windows doesn't have the proper driver for the RAID array.
   B. Windows doesn't support RAID arrays.
   C. The installation disc is bad.
   D. The network is not ready.

2. If you do not complete the activation process for Windows 7, what will happen to your computer?

    A. Nothing. Activation is optional.

    B. The computer will work fine for 30 days and then Windows will be disabled.

    C. Microsoft will not know how to contact you to provide upgrade information.

    D. It will revert to Windows Vista.

3. After you complete a Windows installation and verify the system starts and runs fine, what should you do?

    A. Do nothing. You're through.

    B. Install *World of Warcraft* and enjoy.

    C. Install productivity applications and restore data.

    D. Install the latest updates along with any updated drivers.

4. What version of DirectX do all versions of Windows from Vista to 10 require?

    A. DirectX 8

    B. DirectX 9

    C. DirectX 10

    D. DirectX 11

5. What happens if you upgrade from Windows 7 directly to 8.1?

    A. Windows transfers your files, preferences, and applications.

    B. Windows transfers your files and preferences, but not applications.

    C. Windows transfers your files, but not preferences or applications.

    D. You can't upgrade from Windows 7 to Windows 8.1; you have to upgrade to Windows 8 first.

6. How do you begin a Windows upgrade installation?

    A. Restart and boot to the Windows installation DVD.

    B. Restart and boot to any Windows installation media.

    C. Restart and boot directly to Microsoft's remote installation server.

    D. Run the Windows installation media's installer while Windows is running.

7. Which installation type does Microsoft refer to as an in-place upgrade? (Select two).

    A. Clean installation

    B. Upgrade installation

    C. Image deployment

    D. Repair installation

8. How often does Microsoft release a service pack?

    A. It releases three service packs over the life of each version, but not on a fixed schedule.

    B. Every two years.

    C. Every 18 months.

    D. Microsoft no longer releases service packs.

9. How does a professional hard drive disposal service confirm it has destroyed your drives?

    A. It issues a certificate of destruction.

    B. It returns a box containing the remnants of the destroyed drives for you to recycle.

    C. It sends you a link to a video of your drives being destroyed.

    D. It mails you tiny pieces of the drives each year on the anniversary of their destruction.

10. Which of these can you use less of by using virtual machines? (Select three.)

    A. Electricity

    B. Hardware

    C. Physical space

    D. Software licenses

11. Which tool is best for migrating many users from system to system in larger organizations?

    A. User Data Migration Tool

    B. User State Migration Tool

    C. Windows Easy Transfer

    D. Windows User Transfer

12. What process returns the drive to a state as close to like-new as possible by writing zeros to every location on the disk?

    A. Low-level format

    B. Degaussing

    C. Standard format

    D. Disk cloning

REVIEW ANSWERS

1. **A**   Windows doesn't have the proper driver for the RAID array.

2. **B**   If you do not complete the activation process for Windows 7 (or Vista), the computer will work fine for 30 days and then Windows will be disabled. Windows 8 and up require a product key during installation.

3. **D**   After you have completed a Windows installation and verified that the system starts and runs okay, you should install the latest updates along with any updated drivers.

4. **B**   Modern Windows versions have modest requirements; DirectX 9 is all you need.

5. **C**   Only your personal files can make the leap from 7 straight to 8.1. Preferences will need to be reconfigured, and applications will need to be reinstalled.

6. **D**   Booting to the installation media is only for clean installations; upgrade installations begin by running Windows from the installation you will upgrade.

7. **B D**   Upgrade installations are properly called in-place upgrades, but Microsoft has also used the term for repair installations.

8. **D**   Microsoft hasn't released a service pack since Windows 7 SP1.

9. **A**   Professional disposal services issue a certificate of destruction.

10. **A B C**   Virtual machines save power, hardware, and space, but each VM still requires licensed software.

11. **B**   The User State Migration Tool (USMT) helps manage migrations in a large organization.

12. **A**   The term *low-level formatting* is often used to describe a zero-fill or overwrite operation.

Maintaining and Optimizing Windows

	NEWBIE	SOME EXPERIENCE	EXPERT
ETA	4 hours	2 hours	1 hour

Much as your computer's case and components will accumulate a layer of dust over time, your OS accumulates the digital equivalent. This chapter opens with a look at the regular *maintenance* performed to keep Windows chugging along and then explores how *optimization* can improve its performance.

Objective 15.01   Maintaining Windows

Various system utilities enable you to maintain Windows properly. This section first looks at tools to prepare for problems, install patches and updates, and manage user accounts. We'll also look at utilities to schedule automatic maintenance, control startup programs, collect information about a system, and customize utility consoles.

> **Travel Assistance**
>
> We'll save specifics until we explore anti-malware software in Chapter 21, but your maintenance routine should include updating anti-malware software and definitions to catch the latest threats.

Preparing for Problems

System maintenance starts with preparation. Regular backups of critical system files and personal data protect the system and its users from accidents and hardware failures. They also protect you from problems that happen during maintenance. It's best if you're always positioned to restore both the OS and personal data quickly, but you can ultimately reinstall Windows and programs; personal data, on the other hand, is often irreplaceable. Let's look at backing this data up first.

Windows comes with a few backup utilities, but this is one of the areas where Microsoft changes things with almost every version. Here are the options:

- Windows Vista includes the simple *Backup and Restore Center* applet (see Figure 15.1) with two primary options: *Back up files* (see Figure 15.2) and *Back up computer*. The first enables you to select the types of user data to back up, but you'll have to use the latter to back up installed applications or Windows itself.

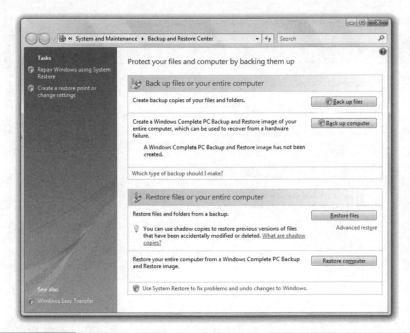

FIGURE 15.1   Backup options in Vista

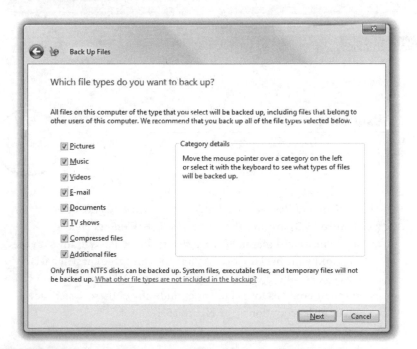

FIGURE 15.2   Types of files to back up

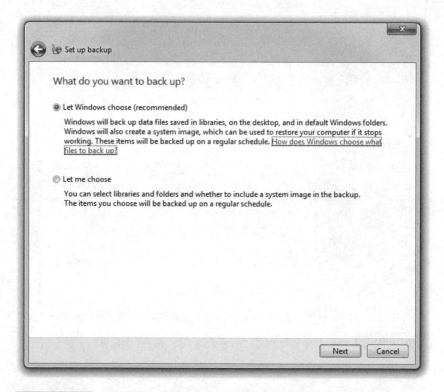

FIGURE 15.3 Who chooses what to back up?

Exam Tip

Windows will not back up content stored on non-NTFS volumes.

- The *Backup and Restore* applet in Windows 7 orients the options (see Figure 15.3) around the automatic *Let Windows choose (recommended)* and manual *Let me choose*. If you let Windows do the picking (and your backup location has enough space), it will back up each user's data and create a full system image. Alternatively, you can use granular controls to include or exclude any of these system-level and account-level options (see Figure 15.4).

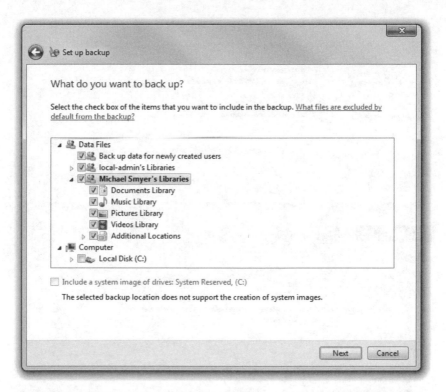

FIGURE 15.4 Granular backup options include libraries/folders for each account

- Windows 8/8.1/10 all have the *File History* applet (see Figure 15.5), where you can enable continuous backup of any personal files in your user account's libraries (both the default libraries and any custom libraries you add) to another storage volume. File History doesn't replace full-system backups, but it does link to the Backup and Restore tool.

These backup tools create a strong safety net for personal data and even full systems, but it can take a while to fully recover with them. In practice, it's best when restoring from a full system image is your last recourse. The Windows *System Restore* tool creates *restore points* (see Figure 15.6) that are lightweight *snapshots* of your computer's configuration at certain points in time, which you can return to quickly—without also rolling back personal files—when

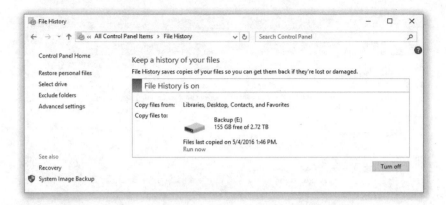

FIGURE 15.5 File History in Windows 10

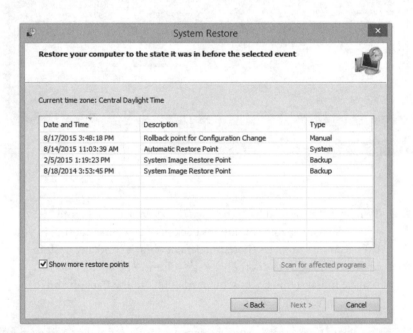

FIGURE 15.6 Restore points in Windows

something goes awry during common tasks such as system or driver updates. Most restore points are made automatically, but you can also make your own (see Figure 15.7) from the *System Protection* tab in the *System Properties* dialog box, which you can access via the System applet.

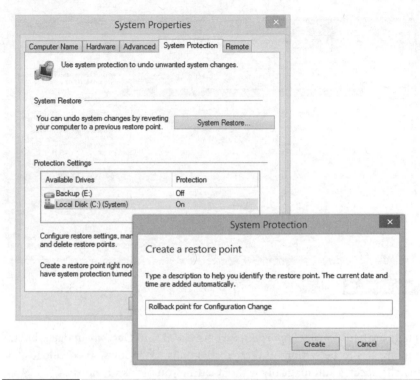

Patches, Updates, and Service Packs

Every OS has flaws, and the *Windows Update* applet is how Microsoft distributes updates to patch user systems easily and automatically. Microsoft makes unique patches available in Windows Vista/7/8/8.1; plus the company provided bundles of updates, called Service Packs, in Windows Vista and Windows 7. (Vista has two, SP1 and SP2; 7 has one, SP1.)

Local Lingo

Patch management The CompTIA A+ exam objectives describe keeping a computer up to date on patches and updates as *patch management*. Techs do the job of patch management.

Windows Update will check for available updates automatically, so you'll often see available updates as soon as you open the applet (see Figure 15.8).

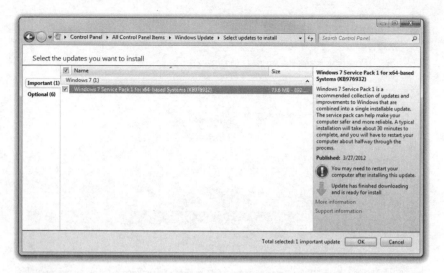

FIGURE 15.8   Important Windows 7 SP1 update in Windows Update

There are traditionally *Important*, *Recommended*, and *Optional* updates, but the sun appears to be setting on these distinctions—Windows 10 downloads and installs updates automatically without letting you pick and choose.

Travel Advisory

While Windows Update is accessible in the Control Panel for the Windows versions on the 902 exam, Windows versions 8 and 8.1 also provide access to it from within the Settings app. Windows Update is only accessible through the Settings app (under Update and Security) in Windows 10.

Managing User Accounts and Groups

In Chapter 13 we briefly looked at the role that user accounts and groups play in securing your system, and we supplied a user name and password for the administrator account during the installation process in Chapter 14. Unless you join the computer to a domain or create a new user account, this is the only usable account. To add more, you'll need to use an administrator account to manage users and groups with one of two tools: the simple *User Accounts* applet (shown in Figure 15.9) or the advanced *Local Users and Groups* tool (shown in Figure 15.10) in the Computer Management console.

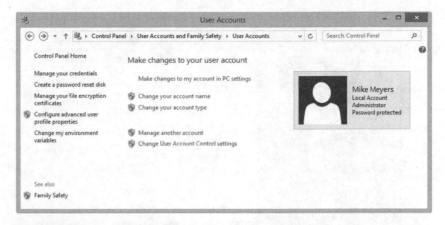

FIGURE 15.9   User Accounts

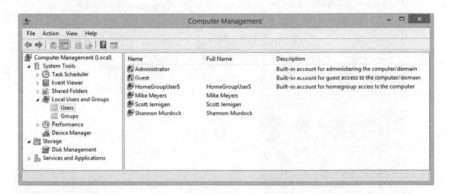

FIGURE 15.10   Local Users and Groups

Travel Assistance

Don't use weak passwords—especially on administrator accounts.
Chapter 21 explores password best practices.

User Accounts

The basics stay the same, but different versions and editions of Windows—and whether you're logged on to a workgroup or a domain—give you different versions of the User Accounts applet (see Figure 15.11). In any case, the applet collects links and information you need to change basic account settings and create users.

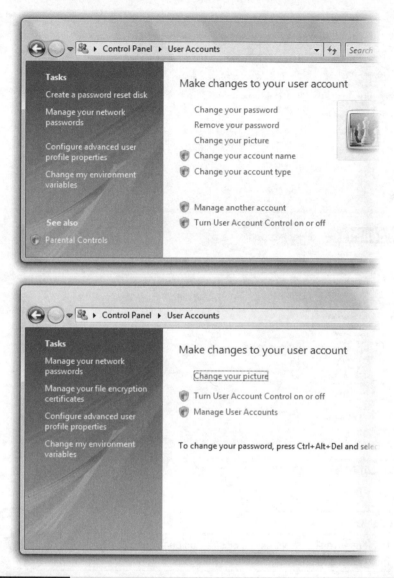

FIGURE 15.11 User Accounts in Windows Vista Business (bottom) and Home Premium (top)

To add a user, click *Manage another account* and select *Create a new account*. Give the account a user name and select a user account type; the account type is equivalent to a group, but User Accounts only lets you choose from administrator and standard user.

User Account Control

The more power a user account wields; the more damage the user with that account can do to the system. You can protect the system by limiting the user's ability to do things such as install programs or change security settings, but the system will be even less secure if the user finds the protections so stifling that they just use an administrator account.

With the release of Windows Vista, Microsoft tackled this problem at both ends with the *User Account Control (UAC)* feature that displays a permissions dialog box—the *UAC consent prompt*—when standard and administrative users do things that could harm the computer (such as install a program). Standard users don't have to switch accounts—they can just supply an administrator password to continue. Administrative users, for their part, are made aware of potentially dangerous actions in case they didn't intentionally initiate them.

UAC wasn't well received in Vista, in part because it aggressively requested permission to perform actions the user initiated by preventing the user from doing anything else until they answered the prompt. Many users went back to earlier versions of Windows, or defeated the purpose of UAC by disabling it entirely. You can configure UAC through the User Accounts applet.

In Windows 7, Microsoft introduced the kinder, gentler UAC we know and love, with four levels (see Figure 15.12):

- *Always notify me.* This is Vista-level strictness.
- *Notify me only when programs try to make changes to my computer.* This is the default option, which forces you to respond to the form before doing anything else.
- *Notify me only when programs try to make changes to my computer (do not dim my desktop).* Notification doesn't prevent you from taking other actions until you address it.
- *Never notify me.* UAC is effectively off.

Parental Controls

The *Parental Controls* (Vista/7) or *Family Safety* (8/8.1/10) applet enables administrator accounts to log and restrict the activities of any standard user (see Figure 15.13) based on ratings or explicit block/allow lists. It's also possible to limit when and for how long a user can log in. (Windows disables this feature for workstations in a domain.)

Settings Charm and App

In Windows 8, Microsoft shifted the focus with user accounts to Internet-wide Microsoft accounts. When you first set up Windows 8/8.1/10, you're prompted to sign in to your Microsoft global account or to create one with any valid

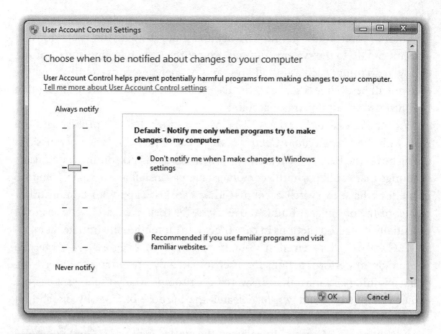

FIGURE 15.12   Four levels of UAC

FIGURE 15.13   Parental Controls

FIGURE 15.14   Accounts screen in Windows 8.1

e-mail address. You can still opt to create a local user account as on previous versions, but a global Microsoft account enables you to synchronize user settings and files. In fact, signing in with a global account also creates a local user account synchronized with the global account settings.

Starting in Windows 8, you can also change account settings through the *Accounts* option (see Figure 15.14) in the Settings charm (Windows 8/8.1) or app (Windows 10). The language is a little different than in the User Accounts applet, but creating an account is still very similar: select the *Other accounts* option (see Figure 15.15) and click *Add an account*.

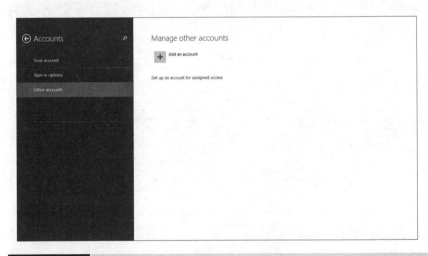

FIGURE 15.15   Manage other accounts

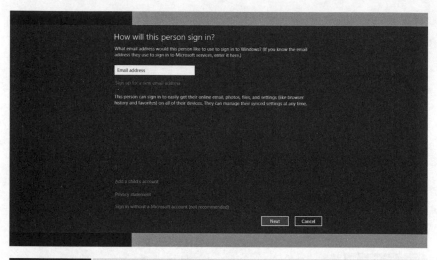

How will this person sign in?

What email address would this person like to use to sign in to Windows? (If you know the email address they use to sign in to Microsoft services, enter it here.)

Email address

Sign up for a new email address

This person can sign in to easily get their online email, photos, files, and settings (like browser history and favorites) on all of their devices. They can manage their synced settings at any time.

Add a child's account

Privacy statement

Sign in without a Microsoft account (not recommended)

Next   Cancel

FIGURE 15.16   Options for a new account

Next, you'll see options to use a valid Microsoft account, get a Microsoft account, add a child's account with parental controls enabled, and create a local account (see Figure 15.16).

Local Users and Groups

Professional editions of Windows include the Local Users and Groups tool (see Figure 15.17), a more powerful tool for working with user accounts—one that won't hold your hand like Control Panel applets do.

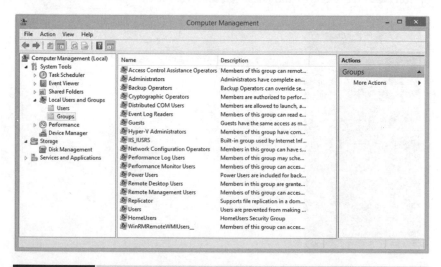

FIGURE 15.17   Local Users and Groups in Windows 8.1 Pro

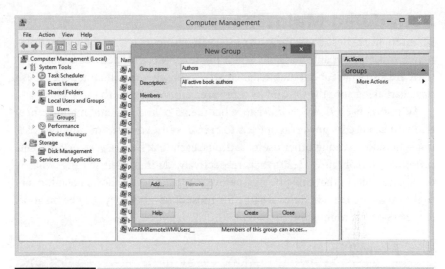

FIGURE 15.18 New Group dialog box in Windows 8.1 Pro

To add a group, right-click a blank spot in the Groups folder, select New Group, and enter a group name and description in the New Group dialog box (see Figure 15.18). Click Add below the member list to open a dialog box (shown in Figure 15.19) that you can use to add multiple *object* types, such as user accounts, computers, and even other groups.

You can also add or remove group membership through the user's properties. Just open the user's folder, right-click the user, select Properties, click the *Member Of* tab, and click *Add* below the group list.

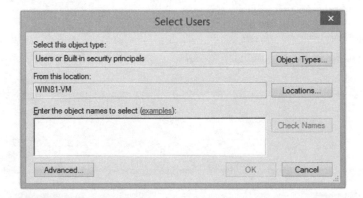

FIGURE 15.19 Select Users dialog box in Windows 8.1 Pro

Scheduled Maintenance

Maintenance is best done at regular intervals, so smart techs schedule maintenance tasks to run automatically when possible. Most modern operating systems are also smart about maintenance, so part of scheduled maintenance these days is making sure the OS and its users aren't interfering with each other.

Windows uses *Task Scheduler* to schedule its own automatic maintenance, and you can use its powerful options to create your own tasks or modify existing schedules. Among other useful settings, each task has *triggers*, *actions*, and *conditions* (see Figure 15.20) that, respectively, define when it runs, what it does, and criteria that must be met before it runs. The Windows default overnight maintenance schedules are fine for most of us—but they may be no good for users on the night shift.

Exam Tip

Task Scheduler illustrates why you need to know executable names and command-line options for common utilities—this is how a task action specifies the options a utility needs to run without user input.

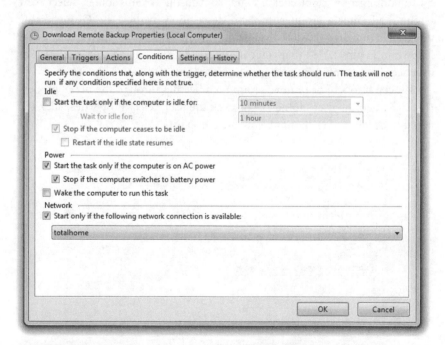

FIGURE 15.20 Conditions tab in Windows 7 Task Scheduler

The CompTIA A+ 902 exam lists two specific kinds of scheduled maintenance: *scheduled backups* and *scheduled disk maintenance*. Know how to modify these schedules from within Task Scheduler, but keep in mind that some applets include their own scheduler conveniently located alongside other configuration options. We've already looked at the basics of each process and the required tools, so we just need to bring it all together:

- The backup schedule can depend on the system's role. If its users just browse the Internet, monthly backups should suffice. If the users create important files on a daily basis, weekly backups are a good idea.

- While you should know about regularly scheduled disk or drive maintenance for the 902 exam, you shouldn't dogmatically schedule these tools to run on modern systems, which are trending away from the practice. For example, Windows 8/8.1/10 will periodically test hard drives and notify the user if it detects errors—the user doesn't need to run Error checking. Even on a Windows Vista/7 system, it's fine to run Error-checking when you suspect a problem. You should still defragment magnetic HDDs; let Windows handle defragmenting SSDs.

Travel Assistance

We looked at three tools commonly used for *scheduled disk maintenance*—Error checking, Defragmentation, and Disk Cleanup—in Chapter 8.

Controlling Autostarting Software

As you add applications and peripherals to your system, it accumulates software that loads automatically at startup. Most of the time these are welcome—but others cause trouble and need to be stopped, either temporarily or from loading at all.

In Windows Vista/7, techs use the *System Configuration utility* (also known by its executable name, *msconfig*) to edit and troubleshoot startup processes and services. From Windows 8 on, this functionality moves to the Startup tab in Task Manager, which you'll see later in the chapter.

To start the System Configuration utility, go the Start | Search bar, type **msconfig**, and click OK or press ENTER. The System Configuration utility

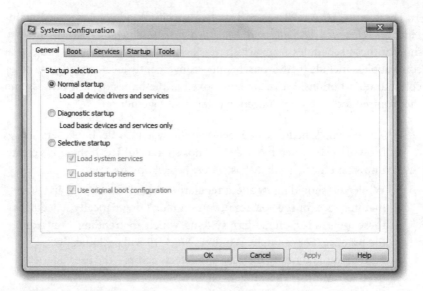

FIGURE 15.21 Windows Vista System Configuration utility

(shown in Figure 15.21) offers a number of handy features, distributed across the following tabs:

- **General** For the next boot, select a normal startup with all programs and services, a diagnostic startup with only basic devices and services, or a custom boot called Selective startup.

- **Boot** See every copy of Windows you have installed, set a default OS, or delete an OS from the boot menu. You can set up a safe boot, or adjust options like the number of cores or amount of memory to use. While selected, Safe boot will always start the system in *Safe mode* with minimal, generic, trusted drivers for troubleshooting purposes.

- **Services** Enable or disable services running on your system.

- **Startup** Enable or disable any startup programs that load when you launch Windows.

- **Tools** Lists many of the tools and utilities available elsewhere in Windows, including Event Viewer, Performance Monitor, Command Prompt, and so on.

System Information

The *System Information tool* (shown in Figure 15.22) collects information about hardware resources, components, and the software environment into a

FIGURE 15.22 System Information

nice report, enabling you to troubleshoot and diagnose any issues and conflicts. As with many other tools, you can access this tool from the Start | Search bar; simply enter **msinfo32**. The CompTIA A+ exams also refer to System Information by its executable, *msinfo32*.

Microsoft Management Console

Windows has so many utilities that it's hard to organize them all in a way that satisfies everyone, so *Microsoft Management Console (MMC)* is simply a shell program that enables you to build your own utility from individual *snap-ins*. To give you an idea of how powerful an MMC can be, the apps in Administrative Tools are just preconfigured MMCs. To start a blank MMC (see Figure 15.23), select Start | Search | type **mmc** and press ENTER.

You make a blank MMC console useful by adding as many snap-ins as you like, including utilities such as Device Manager. You can even buy third-party MMC snap-in utilities. To add one, select File | Add/Remove Snap-ins and then select one from the dialog box's list of available snap-ins (see Figure 15.24). Depending on the snap-in, you may need to configure some additional options before adding it. Once you've added the snap-ins you want, you can name the console (and put it somewhere accessible) by saving it.

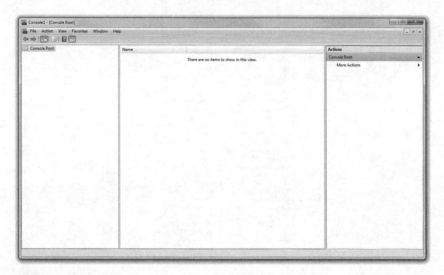

FIGURE 15.23 Blank MMC

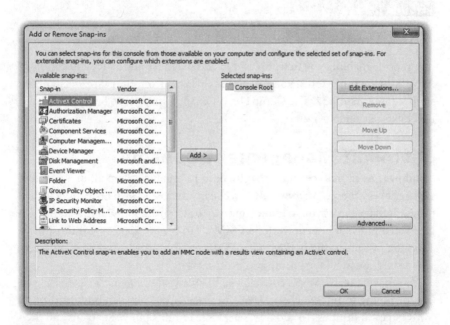

FIGURE 15.24 Available snap-ins

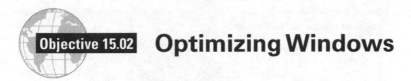

Objective 15.02 Optimizing Windows

Maintenance is about well-defined routines that keep the performance of Windows from degrading with time and use, but *optimization* is all about the art of getting as much out of your system as possible. Let's look at the tools of the trade.

Installing and Removing Software

More and more software is distributed online these days, but there's still a good chance you'll need to install software from removable optical or USB media. The removable media will almost inevitably *Autorun*, but if it doesn't, you'll need to open Windows/File Explorer and double-click the drive icon. Keep in mind that you'll probably have to satisfy a UAC consent prompt to install software.

If you don't see a prompt and the installer doesn't open, it may help to right-click the executable and select *Run as administrator*. When the installer opens, you'll typically have to accept the terms of its software license and make decisions about where to install it or what features to include.

Removing Software

At best, unused programs waste space that could be used for other purposes. At worst, they start up with your system and limit its performance; removing them can be an important piece of optimization.

You remove a program in much the same way that you install it: use the application's own uninstaller when possible. You normally find the uninstall program listed alongside the application in the All Programs section of the Start menu (see Figure 15.25).

If an uninstall program is not available, use the *Programs and Features* applet to remove the software (see Figure 15.26), including its files and Registry entries. Just select the program you want to remove, click the Uninstall/Change button or Change/Remove button, and answer the uninstaller's questions (such as whether to leave settings files in place, in case you reinstall later) to remove the program or modify its installed features. It may request approval to delete shared files that don't appear to be in use; this is typically safe, and the files may end up orphaned if you don't remove them.

FIGURE 15.25 Uninstall me

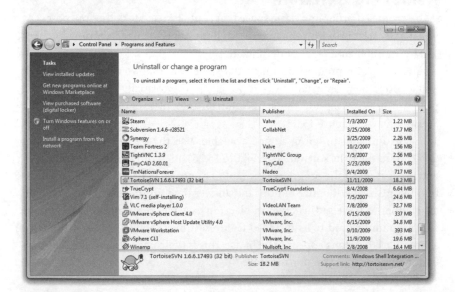

FIGURE 15.26 Programs and Features applet

FIGURE 15.27   Windows Features dialog box

Adding or Removing Windows Components/Features

Windows installs certain features by default, but you can add or remove Windows components from your system later. Just open the Programs and Features applet and click *Turn Windows features on or off* in the Tasks list. To toggle a feature on or off, simply check its box in the Windows Features dialog box (see Figure 15.27).

Device Driver Updates

Device manufacturers occasionally update device drivers to fix problems, improve performance, or add features. Windows Update can find updates for some drivers, and many other devices have software to check for updates; you can also check the manufacturer's website.

If the drivers don't update automatically, you can do it yourself through a tool you've already seen for installing and troubleshooting devices: Device Manager. Right-click a device in Device Manager to display the context menu, from which you can update or uninstall a driver, disable the device, scan for hardware changes, or display the Properties dialog box. Tabs in the Properties dialog box vary by device, but most include General, Driver, Details, and Resources. The Driver tab, which matters most for optimization, has these buttons:

- **Driver Details**   Lists the driver files and their locations on disk.
- **Update Driver**   Opens the Hardware Update Wizard.

FIGURE 15.28 Rollback dialog box

- **Roll Back Driver** Enables you to remove an updated driver and restore the previous driver version (see Figure 15.28). This is a lifesaver when a new driver doesn't work right.
- **Disable** Disables the device. Use this option for troubleshooting when trying to determine which device caused the problem.
- **Uninstall** Removes the driver completely.

Performance Options

Performance Options can configure CPU, RAM, and virtual memory (page file) settings. To access these options, right-click Computer or This PC and select Properties, and then click the Advanced system settings link in the Tasks list. On the Advanced tab, click the Settings button in the Performance section. The Performance Options dialog box has three tabs:

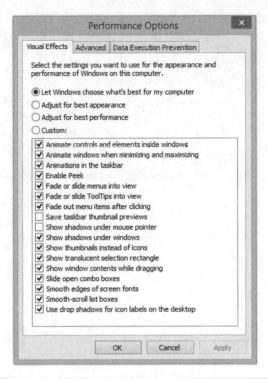

FIGURE 15.29 Windows 8.1 Performance Options dialog box

- The *Visual Effects* tab (shown in Figure 15.29) adjusts visual effects.
- You can adjust processor scheduling on the *Advanced* tab (shown in Figure 15.30) for the best performance of programs or background services, and to modify the size and location of virtual memory.
- The *Data Execution Prevention (DEP)* tab controls which programs are protected by DEP. DEP works in the background to stop viruses and other malware from taking over programs loaded in system memory.

Resource Tracking in Task Manager

Half of the optimization battle is knowing what needs to be optimized. Current versions of Windows rely on *Task Manager* to manage applications, processes, and services. Most users just use it to shut down troublesome programs, but it's a great tool for keeping tabs on how hard your system is working—and, if it's running slowly, what the cause may be. The quickest way to open Task Manager

FIGURE 15.30   Advanced tab of Performance Options dialog box

is pressing CTRL-SHIFT-ESC. Task Manager got a major update in Windows 8, so we'll look at the major variations separately.

Exam Tip

You can do a number of things you'd normally open Task Manager for from the command line, or even with scheduled tasks. You can start and stop services with **net start <service>** and **net stop <service>**, list processes with **tasklist**, and kill them with **taskkill**.

Task Manager Tabs in Windows Vista/7

The Task Manager in Windows Vista/7 enables you to control and review essential Windows components. It has six tabs: Application, Processes, Services, Performance, Networking, and Users.

FIGURE 15.31   Processes tab and context menu options

- The *Applications* tab shows all the running applications on your system. If you're having trouble getting an application to close normally, this is the place to go.
- The *Processes* tab (see Figure 15.31) shows you every running process and enables you to kill it.

Local Lingo

Process   Every program that runs on your system is composed of one or more process.

- The *Services* tab enables you to work directly with services, the small programs that control various components of Windows (such as printing, sharing files, and so on). Here, services can be stopped or started, and you can go to the associated process.

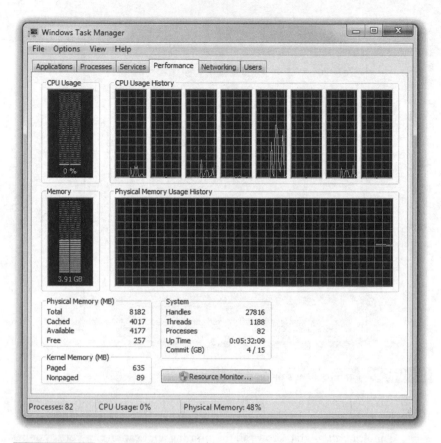

FIGURE 15.32 Task Manager Performance tab

- The *Performance* tab (see Figure 15.32) enables you to see CPU usage, available physical memory, the size of the disk cache, commit charge (memory for programs), and kernel memory (memory used by Windows).
- The other two tabs in the Task Manager, *Networking* and *Users,* enable you to see network use at a glance and see which users' accounts are currently logged on to the local machine, respectively. The Networking tab is a good first spot to look if you think the computer is running slowly on the network.

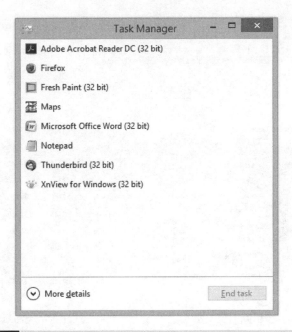

FIGURE 15.33 Fewer details view in Windows 8 Task Manager

Task Manager Tabs in Windows 8/8.1/10

With Windows 8 and later, Microsoft gave Task Manager a new look and feel and significantly improved its usefulness by reshuffling how it is organized, adding new information, and adding useful context menu options. Task Manager defaults to a simplified *Fewer details* view (shown in Figure 15.33) for listing and terminating running programs, but you can click *More details* to get the traditional tabbed view. Even here, much changed from previous versions.

- Task Manager's "more details" view opens on the *Processes* tab (see Figure 15.34). When sorted by the name column, it groups processes into three sections: Apps, Background processes, and Windows processes. Regardless of how you sort these processes, the view shows a color-coded breakdown of CPU, memory, disk, and network use.
- The *Performance* tab (shown in Figure 15.35) serves the same purpose as in previous versions, but it is easier on the eyes and folds in performance information about disk and network use.
- The *App history* tab collects recent performance statistics regarding how heavily processes are hitting the CPU and network.

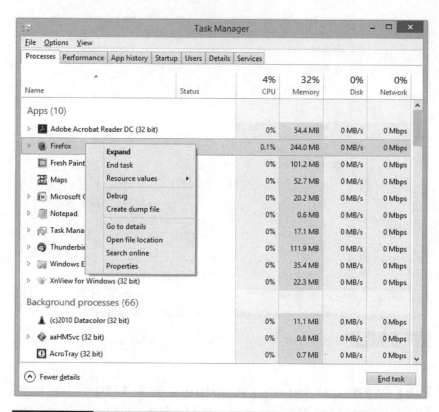

FIGURE 15.34 Processes tab context menu in Windows 8 Task Manager

- The *Startup* tab, which moved over to Task Manager from System Configuration, enables you to control which programs load when Windows does, and assess what impact each has on the startup process.

- The *Users* tab serves the same basic purpose as in previous versions, but it also makes it dead simple to see what impact other logged-in users are having on system performance.

- The *Details* tab has all of the details that used to be in the Processes tab in previous versions.

- The *Services* tab is virtually unchanged, but it did receive some nice polish, such as a context-menu option to search for a process online as well as to restart a service with a single click.

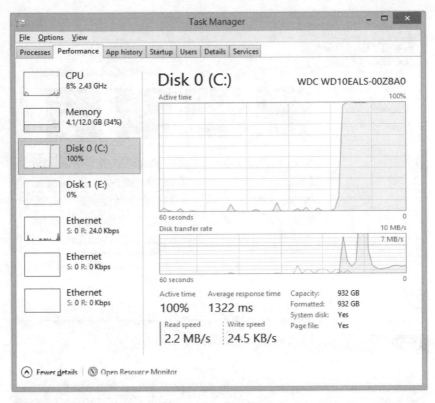

FIGURE 15.35 Performance tab in Windows 8 Task Manager showing a very active Disk 0

Performance Tools

Windows comes with tools to log resource usage so you can track metrics such as CPU and RAM usage over longer periods of time. In Windows Vista this was called *Reliability and Performance Monitor,* but in Windows 7 Microsoft pulled out the Reliability tool to make the remaining *Performance Monitor* tool smaller and tighter.

You can open Reliability and Performance Monitor/Performance Monitor in Windows Vista/7 via Control Panel | Performance Information and Tools | Advanced Tools. You can also open it by going to Start | Search, typing **perfmon.msc**, and pressing ENTER. You'll find the utility in Administrative Tools in Windows 8 and later.

Reliability and Performance Monitor in Windows Vista opens to a Resource Overview screen (see Figure 15.36), which is like an advanced version Task Manager's Performance tab. If you click one of the bars, such as Network, you get details on exactly which processes are using resources (see Figure 15.37).

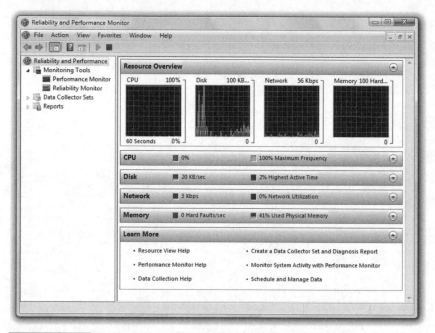

FIGURE 15.36 Resource Overview in Windows Vista

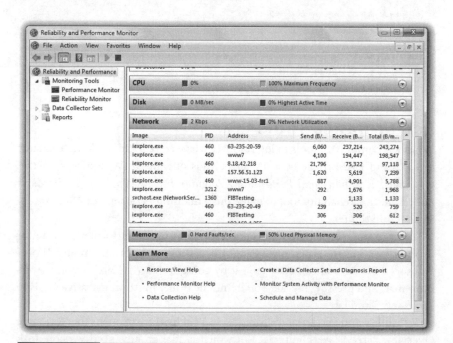

FIGURE 15.37 Network bar in Resource Overview

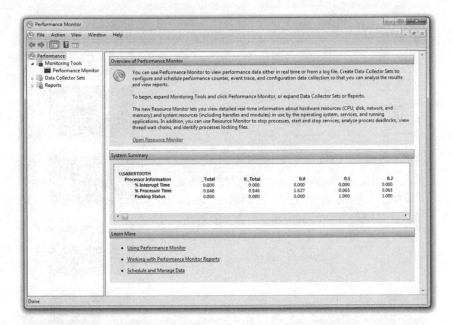

FIGURE 15.38 Initial Performance Monitor screen in Windows 7

Travel Advisory

The Reliability Monitor tool, in the Action Center Control Panel applet for Windows 7 and up, provides an overview of how a system behaves over time, showing events such as application or OS crashes.

Performance Monitor in Windows 7 and later opens to an introduction to the tool and a System Summary (see Figure 15.38). Aside from placing the graphs on the right rather than on the top (see Figure 15.39), the tool is the same as the Resource Overview in Windows Vista.

Performance Monitor gathers and graphs real-time data on *objects* (system components such as memory, physical disk, processor, and network). When you first open it, Performance Monitor shows a graph of data from the set of *counters,* which track a specific piece of information about an object, listed below the chart.

To add counters, click the Add (plus sign) button or press CTRL-I to open the Add Counters dialog box. Click the Performance object drop-down list and select an object to monitor. To make one counter to stand out (see Figure 15.40), select it in the list and press CTRL-H.

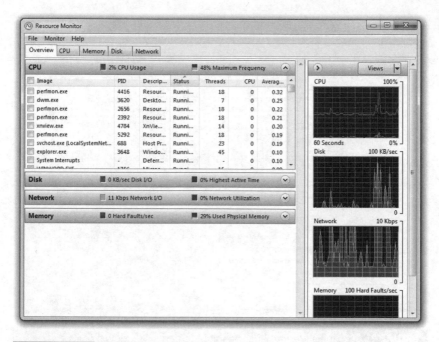

FIGURE 15.39   Resource Monitor displaying CPU usage

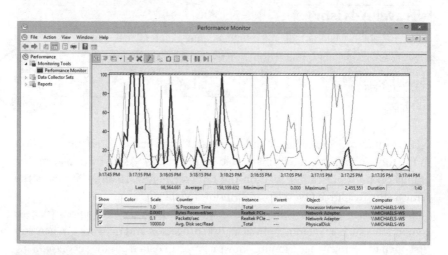

FIGURE 15.40   Pressing CTRL-H makes one set of data stand out.

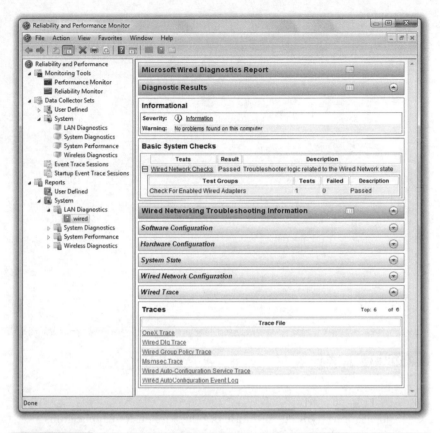

FIGURE 15.41   Sample report

Data Collector Sets are groups of counters you can use to make reports. Once you start a Data Collector Set, you can use the Reports option to see the results (see Figure 15.41). Data Collector Sets not only enable you to choose counter objects to track, but also enable you to schedule when you want them to run.

Tools for Programmers

Microsoft provides an assortment of tools in Windows that go well beyond what techs typically need, and the 902 exam includes two such tools (found in Administrative Tools) that programmers use to deal with some low-level functionality in Windows: Component Services and ODBC Data Source Administrator.

- *Component Services* (shown in Figure 15.42) is a tool administrators and developers use to configure systems to support specific

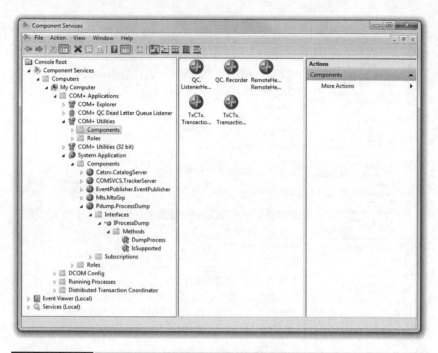

FIGURE 15.42 Component Services in Windows 7

applications (typically in-house or otherwise custom applications that take advantage of data-sharing tools with names such as COM, DCOM, and COM+). Professional software can typically handle all of this by itself. If you need to use this tool, you'll almost certainly have explicit directions for what to do with it.

- *ODBC Data Source Administrator* (shown in Figure 15.43) enables you to create and manage Open Database Connectivity (ODBC) entries called Data Source Names (DSNs) that point ODBC-aware applications to shared databases. Once again, you'll probably have explicit instructions if you need to use this.

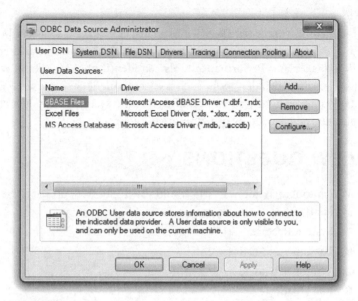

FIGURE 15.43 Data Source Administrator in Windows 7

CHECKPOINT

✔**Objective 15.01: Maintaining Windows** It is important that you are prepared to recover quickly from problems and keep Windows updated with the latest security patches from Microsoft. By managing user accounts, a system administrator can set permissions for users and audit their access to files and network resources. Automatic scheduled maintenance such as backups and drive scans can keep a system chugging along. From time to time, you may need to cull startup programs as they accumulate to keep the system performing well and starting quickly. The System Information utility enables you to audit system hardware for problems and conflicts, and the Microsoft Management Console helps you build custom utilities.

✔**Objective 15.02: Optimizing Windows** Removing applications that are no longer needed is an important part of housekeeping. When possible, use the uninstall program that came with the application. You can add or remove Windows components as needed. It's also important to keep device drivers up to date with Windows Update, the software that came with the device, or at the manufacturer's website; Device Manager is a good tool for checking and updating hardware, drivers, and resources. Resource tracking with Task Manager and Performance tools can identify bottlenecks to resolve. Windows also includes tools such as Component Services and ODBC Data Source Administrator for configuring the system to support custom applications developed by or for an organization.

REVIEW QUESTIONS

1. Which tool in Windows Vista would you use to back up your essential system files?
   A. System Restore
   B. Backup and Restore Center
   C. Windows Update
   D. File History

2. Phil receives a report when he arrives in the morning from a user recently assigned to the night shift. The report states that once a week the user's system slows to a crawl in the middle of the night. Which tools could help Phil fix this before it happens again? (Select two.)
   A. Performance Monitor
   B. Task Manager
   C. Task Scheduler
   D. Windows Update

3. Mary wants to get a quick snapshot of a system's performance after receiving a report that it is sluggish. How does she get to the appropriate tool?
   A. Start | Search | Perfmon.
   B. Start | Control Panel | Administrative Tools | Performance.
   C. Start | All Programs | Accessories | System Resources.
   D. Press CTRL-SHIFT-ESC once and click the Performance tab.

4. What tool should Bill use to set his computer's configuration back to a specific point in time?
   A. System Restore
   B. Resource Monitor
   C. Task Scheduler
   D. Task Manager

5. Mary didn't find any obvious performance problems when she checked before, but she keeps getting reports about the system. What utilities could she use to get a better picture of how it performs over time? (Select two.)

   A. Microsoft Management Console

   B. Performance Monitor

   C. Task Manager

   D. System Information

6. Which of these Task Manager tabs were added in Windows 8? (Select two.)

   A. Processes

   B. Details

   C. Services

   D. Startup

7. Which of the following should be your first choice to remove an application that you no longer need?

   A. Delete the program files.

   B. Use the uninstall program that came with the application.

   C. Use the Add or Remove Programs applet or the Programs and Features applet.

   D. Use the Registry Editor to remove references to the application.

8. Which command-line utility can you use to start or stop a service?

   A. service

   B. taskkill

   C. net

   D. msconfig

9. Which of the following commands opens the System Information tool?

   A. msconfig

   B. msinfo64

   C. msinfo32

   D. mscnfg32

10. When performing automatic updates, Windows uses which feature to download additional updates for other Microsoft products?

    A. Programs and Features

    B. msinfo32

    C. Windows Update

    D. Registry

REVIEW ANSWERS

1. **B** The Backup and Restore Center in Windows Vista is used for backing up essential files (or all files).

2. **C D** Task Scheduler can identify and reschedule most tasks that could slow the system. Phil can also adjust Windows Update settings to change when it occurs. Task Manager and Performance Monitor can't identify the problem until it happens again.

3. **D** Mary should press CTRL-SHIFT-ESC once and click the Performance tab.

4. **A** System Restore is the tool Bill needs.

5. **A B** Performance Monitor is preconfigured to help answer these sorts of questions, but she could also create her own MMC configuration for monitoring the system.

6. **B D** Details and Startup are both new tabs introduced to Task Manager in Windows 8.

7. **B** Use the uninstall program that came with the application.

8. **C** The **net** command can start or stop a service from the CLI.

9. **C** Type **msinfo32** in the Start | Search box to open the System Information tool.

10. **C** Windows uses Windows Update to download additional updates for other Microsoft products.

Troubleshooting Windows

	NEWBIE	SOME EXPERIENCE	EXPERT
ETA	4 hours	2 hours	1 hour

Now that we've been over how to install, maintain, and optimize Windows, it's time to dig into what you should do when things go awry. We'll start with the basics—how to fix problems booting the system. Then we'll turn to troubleshooting problems in the Windows GUI, and close with a look at application problems.

 **Objective 16.01** **Failure to Boot**

When Windows fails to boot, rule out obvious hardware problems. If you're staring at a dire error message such as *Operating System not found,* recall from Chapter 8 that a hard drive needs proper connectivity and power, and that the system setup utility must be configured correctly. If simple hardware and system settings don't appear to be the cause, it's time to roll up your sleeves and use the repair and recovery tools that come with Windows.

Hardware and System Setup

Hardware problems may leave you with little but a blank screen to go on, so you'll need to follow the tried-and-true hardware troubleshooting methods we've covered in previous chapters. Make sure everything is plugged in and powered. If the system or some hardware is very new, consider burn-in failure. Use your senses—rule out strange sounds and smells, or follow them to the source. If you've added new hardware, disconnect it. Try swapping in known-good components.

If the system powers on and the POST succeeds, the computer will try to load an OS. Some failures at this stage yield a simple message such as *Operating System not found* or *No boot device detected* that should lead you pretty swiftly to the cause, but there are a variety of ominous messages that are less clear.

There's a basic template—a critical boot file or component is missing, corrupt, damaged, invalid, can't be found, and so on. The specific critical files and components you should know for the exam are bootmgr, Boot Configuration Data (bcd), and ntldr, but this is far from a comprehensive list.

First, focus on what the message implies: the BIOS is unable to pass the baton to the OS. There are some dead simple causes, such as leaving a USB drive plugged in. Check your external ports (USB, Thunderbolt, eSATA, and so on) for errant drives; check optical drives and flash card readers as well.

Confirm your boot sequence is correct, and check settings to boot from USB or other sources. Check power and data cables for the OS drive. Check the appropriate settings if your system uses RAID or multiboot.

Exam Tip

The 902 objectives include *Missing NTLDR* (in all caps), but ntldr and boot.ini were replaced with bootmgr and bcd from Windows Vista on. It's possible CompTIA expects you to know to use the *Recovery Console* to repair old Windows XP installations, but the fact that they removed all other vestiges of Windows XP from the A+ exams makes this seem unlikely. They may have kept it around because there are reports from users of every modern Windows version who've seen this message. The common threads are boot sequence issues, upgrading the OS to a new version or attempting to install a new version to a volume that held an earlier one, and installs that are or have been part of a multiboot setup.

Windows Repair and Recovery

Windows needs two critical files to boot: bootmgr and bcd. If they are damaged, you can fix them with a tool called bcdedit. But bcdedit isn't just hanging out in Control Panel, so first we need to take a step back and look at where bcdedit lives and how you get there.

Local Lingo

BCD   Boot configuration data (BCD) contains information about installed operating systems. It serves the same role for bootmgr as boot.ini served for the older ntldr.

Windows Recovery Environment

In Windows Vista, Microsoft replaced the old 16-bit text mode environment used to install every previous version of Windows with a 32- or 64-bit environment that supports a full GUI. This *Windows Preinstallation Environment* (*WinPE* or *Windows PE*) supports booting a limited graphical OS directly from the Windows DVD—one that includes troubleshooting and diagnostic tools alongside the installer. These troubleshooting, diagnostic, and repair tools are collectively (and confusingly) called the *Windows Recovery Environment* (*WinRE* or *Windows RE*) or the *System Recovery Options* (see Figure 16.1).

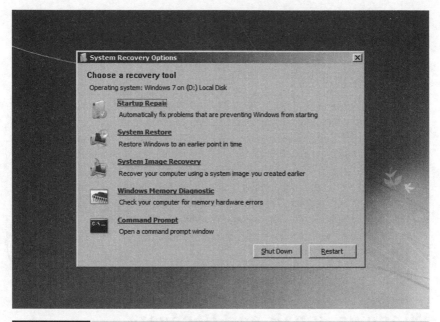

Travel Advisory

WinPE can also assist unattended installations, network installations, and booting diskless workstations on a network.

Depending on your Windows version, a few different paths lead to WinRE:

- In any version, boot from the Windows installation media and select *Repair*.
- Select *Repair Your Computer* on Windows 7's Advanced Boot Options (F8) menu (see Figure 16.2).
- Create a system *repair disc* before you have problems. In Windows Vista (SP1 or later) and Windows 7, go to Control Panel | System and Security | Backup and Restore and select *Create a system repair disc*. In Windows 8 and up, go to Control Panel | Recovery | Create a Recovery Drive.

```
████████████████████████████████████████████████████████████████████████
                          Advanced Boot Options

Choose Advanced Options for: Windows 7
(Use the arrow keys to highlight your choice.)

    ████████████████████████
    │ Repair Your Computer │
    ████████████████████████

      Safe Mode
      Safe Mode with Networking
      Safe Mode with Command Prompt

      Enable Boot Logging
      Enable low-resolution video (640x480)
      Last Known Good Configuration (advanced)
      Directory Services Restore Mode
      Debugging Mode
      Disable automatic restart on system failure
      Disable Driver Signature Enforcement

      Start Windows Normally

Description: View a list of system recovery tools you can use to repair
            startup problems, run diagnostics, or restore your system.

    ENTER=Choose                                              ESC=Cancel
████████████████████████████████████████████████████████████████████████
```

FIGURE 16.2   Selecting Repair Your Computer in the Advanced Boot Options menu

I recommend you access WinRE from the installation media because it works in each OS, doesn't require an administrator password, and isn't vulnerable to interference from malware or hard drive issues. No matter how you choose to access the Windows Recovery Environment, you have a few options:

- **Startup Repair**   Performs a number of repairs on the Registry, critical boot, system, and driver files. Rolls back or uninstalls incompatible drivers and patches. Runs chkdsk and a RAM test. Saves diagnostic and repair details to *srttrail.txt*.

- **System Restore**   Provides a simple way to return to an earlier *restore point* or snapshot.

- **System Image Recovery**   Enables you to select and restore from a full system image. This feature is called Windows Complete PC Restore in Windows Vista, but the result is the same. It includes an option to format and repartition disks so the restored system will get the same partitions that the backed-up system had.

> ### Exam Tip
>
> Most prebuilt systems come with a *factory recovery partition,* other recovery media, or the ability to create recovery media. These can restore the active system partition or the entire hard drive to fresh-from-the-factory condition from a *recovery image.*

- **Windows Memory Diagnostic**   During the next reboot, the diagnostic tool checks your RAM (see Figure 16.3) for the sorts of problems that can cause Blue Screens of Death (BSoDs), system lockups, and continuous reboots. After the tool runs and your system reboots, you can use Event Viewer to see the results.

> ### Travel Advisory
>
> You can also launch the Windows Memory Diagnostic Tool from Administrative Tools or as **mdsched** at an administrative command prompt.

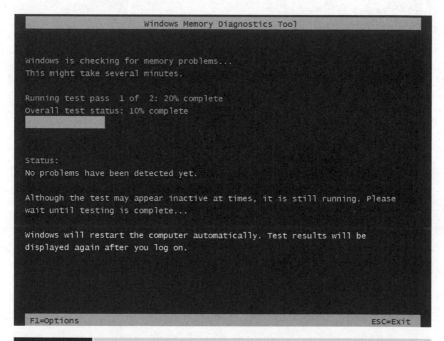

FIGURE 16.3   Windows Memory Diagnostic Tool running

- **Command Prompt** A true 32- or 64-bit command prompt with useful recovery and repair tools (though it lacks a number of commands you would have at a regular Windows command prompt).

Windows 8 reorganizes these menus a little and updates everything to Modern/Metro UI. First, it introduces a new Troubleshoot menu with two new options:

- **Refresh your PC** Rebuilds Windows; preserves user files, settings, and Windows Store apps (but deletes all other applications)
- **Reset your PC** Removes all apps, programs, files, and settings and freshly reinstalls Windows

The Troubleshoot menu also has an Advanced options button, which is where you'll find the utilities from the earlier version of WinRE. The Advanced options menu includes a link to your UEFI firmware settings if you have a UEFI motherboard.

Command-Line Recovery and Repair Tools

The CompTIA A+ exams won't expect you to know everything about these utilities—the goal is for you to use them with higher level support—but you should know roughly what the tools listed in Table 16.1 do, how to access them,

TABLE 16.1	Useful Recovery and Repair CLI Commands
Command	**Description**
bcdedit	See and edit the BCD store that controls how Windows boots.
bootrec /fixboot	Rebuild boot sector for active system partition.
bootrec /fixmbr	Rebuild MBR for the system partition.
bootrec /scanos	Find and report Windows installations not in the BCD store.
bootrec /rebuildmbr	Like scanos, but can optionally add found installs to the BCD store.
diskpart	Advanced drive partitioning tool (lacking most of Disk Management's safety features).
expand	Expand one or more compressed files.
fsutil	Perform advanced queries, changes, and repairs on the file system.
reg	Query, copy, change, and restore the Registry.
sfc	Scan, detect, and restore important Windows system files and folders. Short for System File Checker.

and some of the basic switches. Keep in mind that these commands are in addition to basic CLI commands such as copy, move, del, format, and so on.

Objective 16.02   Windows GUI Problems

Assuming Windows clears the boot stage, it will begin to load the Windows GUI. Several issues can cause Windows to hang during the GUI-loading phase, such as buggy device drivers, Registry problems, and problems with autoloading programs or services. The first step is to use an Advanced Startup option to get into Windows by skipping the problem spot.

Exam Tip

The 902 objectives include "Graphical Interface fails to load" and "Missing Graphical Interface." This section covers the former; the latter points to the sort of catastrophic failure you would troubleshoot with suggestions from the "Failure to Boot" section.

Advanced Startup Options

If Windows fails to start normally, press F5 at boot-up to boot directly to Safe Mode. Alternatively, in Windows Vista or Windows 7, you can use the Windows *Advanced Startup Options* menu to discover the cause. To get to this menu, restart the computer and press F8 after the POST messages but before the Windows logo screen appears.

Travel Advisory

Windows 8/8.1/10 have Startup Settings that mirror those of older versions of Windows, but getting there can be a chore. Ignore Startup Settings in Windows versions beyond Windows 7 and work with other tools.

Some options vary by Windows version. Here's an incomplete rundown of options that are most useful for troubleshooting:

- **Safe Mode**   Starts Windows with basic/default drivers, settings, and services. Screen resolution is limited to 800 × 600 (Vista/7) or 1024 × 768 (8/8.1). In Safe Mode, you can use Device Manager and other tools to locate and fix problems. If the system is repeatedly and unintentionally booting into Safe Mode, you may need to deselect the Safe boot or Boot to Safe Mode check box (see Figure 16.4) in System Configuration.

Exam Tip

The CompTIA A+ 902 exam objectives mention a scenario where Windows boots directly to Safe Mode. This can only happen if a tech specifically makes a change to the System Configuration utility.

- **Safe Mode with Networking**   Identical to Safe Mode, but with Networking support. If your system boots into regular Safe Mode fine but fails to boot into Safe Mode with Networking, check network devices for driver issues.
- **Safe Mode with Command Prompt**   Boots directly to a command prompt instead of the Explorer GUI, which may succeed even if you

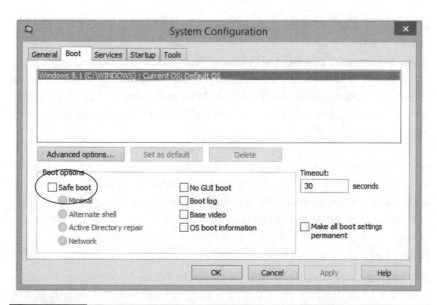

FIGURE 16.4   Uncheck Safe boot.

can't successfully boot into regular Safe Mode due to video drivers or corrupt Windows GUI files such as explorer.exe. You can load other GUI tools that don't depend on Explorer. All you have to do is enter the correct command. For instance, to load Event Viewer, type **eventvwr.msc** at the command prompt and press ENTER.

- **Enable Boot Logging**   Starts Windows normally and creates a log file as drivers load into memory. The log, named Ntbtlog.txt, is saved in %SystemRoot%. If the startup failed because of a bad driver, the last entry in this file may be the one that failed.
- **Enable Low-Resolution Mode**   Starts Windows normally, but in standard VGA mode, which may help if there are problems with your graphics settings.
- **Last Known Good Configuration**   Attempts to fall back to the previous driver configuration if installing a new driver causes failures on reboot.
- **Disable Automatic Restart on System Failure**   If the system reboots too quickly after an error for you to read the error message, this option gives you a chance to note it.
- **Return to OS Choices Menu**   Select a different OS on a multiboot system.

Device Drivers

Device driver problems that stop the Windows GUI from loading can either freeze the system or produce the infamous Windows *Stop error* (see Figure 16.5), better known as the *Blue Screen of Death (BSoD)*. The BSoD appears only when something causes an error from which Windows cannot recover, including device driver problems. The error screen typically indicates a cause and recommended action, but these aren't always helpful.

These device driver problems almost always take place immediately after you've installed a new device and rebooted. Take out the device and reboot. If Windows loads properly, head over to the manufacturer's website to look for updated drivers or to request a replacement device. If the system still won't boot, try one of the Advanced Startup Options.

Registry

The Registry files load every time the computer boots. Windows does a pretty good job of protecting your Registry from corruption, but if it happens,

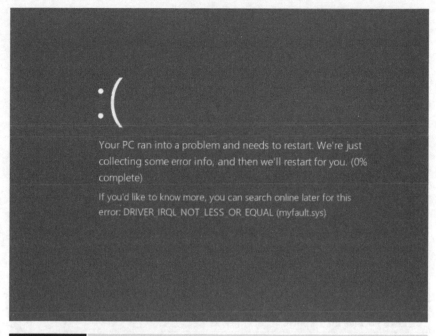

Your PC ran into a problem and needs to restart. We're just collecting some error info, and then we'll restart for you. (0% complete)

If you'd like to know more, you can search online later for this error: DRIVER_IRQL_NOT_LESS_OR_EQUAL (myfault.sys)

FIGURE 16.5   BSoD in Windows 8.1

the errors may show up as BSoDs that say "Registry File Failure" or text errors that say "Windows could not start." Try the Last Known Good Configuration boot option first (in Windows Vista/7); if this fails or you're in Windows 8 or later, you'll need to use WinRE to restore an earlier version.

Windows keeps a regular backup (every 10 days) of the Registry in \Windows\System32\config\RegBack for occasions like this, but it's a good idea to keep your own copies. To replace the Registry, boot to Windows RE and get to the command prompt. Run the **reg** command to get to a reg prompt. From there, you have numerous commands to deal with the Registry. You know the location of the backed-up Registry files. Just **reg copy** the files to the location of the main Registry files—up one level in the tree under the \config folder.

Exam Tip
If the GUI is usable, you can also launch the friendlier graphical Registry editor, **regedit**, from the CLI or Start | Search.

Troubleshooting Tools

Once you're able to load Windows through Safe Mode or another option, the whole gamut of Windows tools we've looked at previously are available. For example, know how to use Device Manager to troubleshoot driver issues as well as disable an autoloading program or service that fails to start with System Configuration, Task Manager, or the Services console in Administrative Tools. You can still attempt to roll back to better times with System Restore. This section focuses on additional useful tools.

Event Viewer

Your first stop after you hit the desktop should be *Event Viewer,* the default tattletale program in Windows. With a little tweaking, Event Viewer records almost any system event you might want to know about. Open Event Viewer (shown in Figure 16.6) via Administrative Tools | Event Viewer.

Travel Assistance

Event Viewer is for much more than troubleshooting; Chapter 21 shows how it's also a powerful security tool.

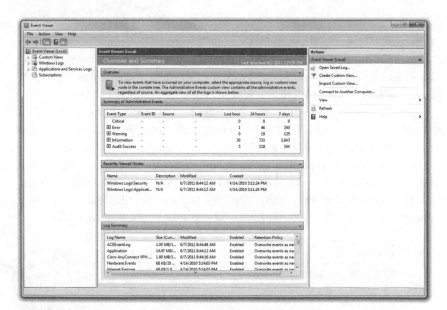

FIGURE 16.6   Windows 7 Event Viewer default screen

Note the four main bars in the center pane: Overview, Summary of Administrative Events, Recently Viewed Nodes, and Log Summary. The Summary of Administrative Events breaks down the events into different levels: Critical, Error, Warning, Information, Audit Success, and Audit Failure. You can click any event to see a description of the event.

Windows Event Viewer still includes classic Application, Security, and System logs, but leans heavily on filtering their contents through *Views* that enable custom reports by beginning/end times, error levels, and more. You can use the built-in Views or easily create your own. Administrators can configure log file location as well as maximum size and what to do when it's reached, as shown in Figure 16.7.

System Files

Windows lives on dynamic link library (DLL) files. Almost every program used by Windows—and certainly all of the important ones—call to DLL files to do

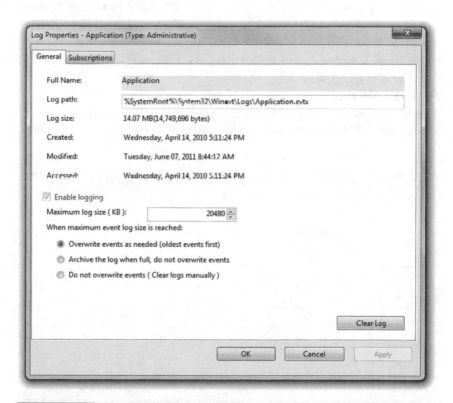

FIGURE 16.7 Log Properties dialog box in Windows 7

most of the heavy lifting that makes Windows work. Windows tries to protect all of the critical DLL files, but once in a while you may get an error (during boot or while Windows is running) saying Windows can't find or load one.

The *System File Checker (sfc)* can check a number of critical files, including the ever-important DLL cache, from a command prompt. The most important option is **sfc /scannow** to automatically check all critical files and replace any it sees as corrupted; it may ask for the Windows installation disc, so keep it handy.

> ### Exam Tip
>
> You can use **regsvr32** from the CLI to manually register .dll files as command components in the registry.

Problem Reports (and Solutions)

The applet *Problem Reports and Solutions* in Windows Vista and *Problem Reports* (see Figure 16.8) in Windows 7 and up lists all *Windows Error Reporting* issues (plus a few easy-to-check items such as firewall and anti-malware status). You click the solution and, in many cases, the problem is fixed.

Action Center

The *Action Center* (see Figure 16.9) introduced in Windows 7 improves on the concept behind Problem Reports and Solutions with a one-page aggregation of

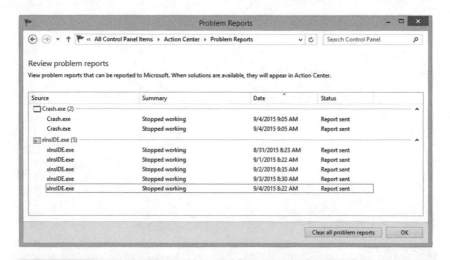

FIGURE 16.8   Problem Reports

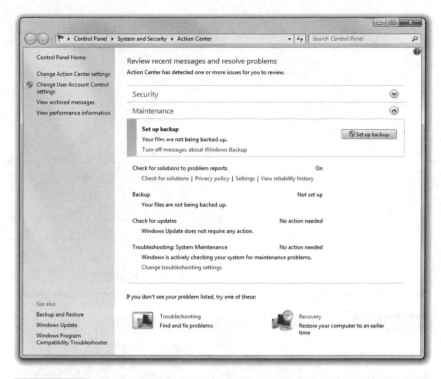

FIGURE 16.9   Action Center

event messages, warnings, and maintenance messages—and links to the utilities you need to address them—that, for many techs, could even replace Event Viewer as the first place to look for problems. Action Center separates issues into Security and Maintenance sections, making it easier to scan a system quickly.

Action Center compiles information from well-known utilities such as Event Viewer, Windows Update, Windows Firewall, and UAC. If you wish, you can tell Action Center where to look for information by selecting Change Action Center settings (see Figure 16.10). To address problems, you can follow links from Action Center to useful locations such as UAC settings, Performance Information and Tools, Backup and Restore, Windows Update, Troubleshooting, System Restore, and Recovery.

Troubleshooting

Windows 7 introduced the *Troubleshooting* applet (shown in Figure 16.11) to help the user fix a hodgepodge of issues in various parts of the system by using a number of troubleshooting wizards for issues with system maintenance, media devices, printers, networking, and more.

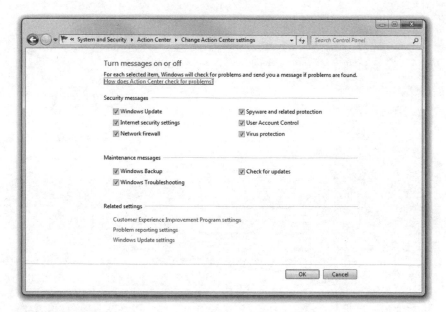

FIGURE 16.10 Change Action Center settings

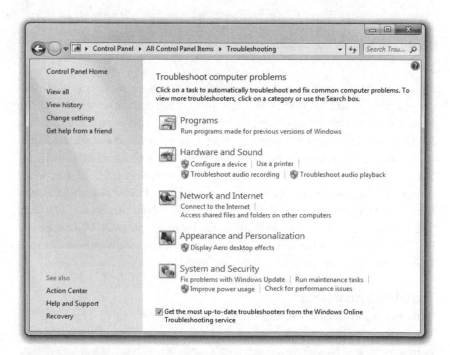

FIGURE 16.11 Troubleshooting applet in Windows 7

Objective 16.03 Windows Application Problems

Application problems are vague because applications do all kinds of different things and can have all sorts of problems. Common scenarios are failing to install or uninstall, compatibility problems, files that go missing or won't open, programming errors that cause the application or the OS to crash, and misbehaving applications corrupting the files they use. Some application problems stem from upgrading Windows or the application, and some persistent application issues can be fixed by uninstalling and reinstalling the program, or by using a repair feature if its installer has one.

Application Installation and Uninstallation Problems

Most Windows programs come with an installer. If you download the application, you'll just run the installer directly. If you're using installation media, autorun.inf tells Windows which file to *Autorun* (usually setup.exe). A well-behaved program should also make itself easy to uninstall from the program's Start menu area or from Control Panel via the Add/Remove Programs or Programs and Features applet.

Exam Tip
Remember that you need local administrator privileges to install applications in all versions of Windows.

Windows may prevent programs from installing if the system lacks some other software the program needs. For example, many programs take advantage of the popular Microsoft .NET Framework. If .NET is missing, the application installer should install it, but you can't count on this. Figure 16.12 shows the VMware vSphere client failing due to the wrong .NET version in Windows 7. Don't expect the error to tell you this—you'll often have to go search the message and application name online.

The single biggest uninstall problem is trying to run the uninstaller without administrator privileges. If you try to uninstall and get an error, log back on as an administrator or right-click the uninstaller and select *Run as administrator* to switch to administrator privileges.

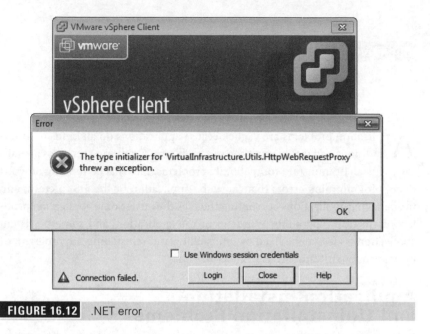

FIGURE 16.12   .NET error

Compatibility

Most applications are written for the most recent version of Windows, but as Windows versions change over time, older programs have difficulty running in more recent Windows versions, and vice versa. Windows provides *compatibility modes* to support older applications, which you can select from the Compatibility tab (shown in Figure 16.13) in every executable program's Properties dialog.

You can also set other options on the Compatibility tab, such as the following located under Display settings in the various versions of Windows:

- **Reduced color mode**   Support programs designed to run in 256 colors.

- **Run in 640 × 480 screen resolution**   Support programs that assume a 640 × 480 screen resolution.

- **Disable desktop composition (Windows Vista/7)**   Disable advanced Windows display features that may bog down older programs.

- **Disable display scaling on high DPI settings**   Fix programs with large fonts that look bizarre when resized.

- **Run this program as an administrator**   Always run the program as an administrator.

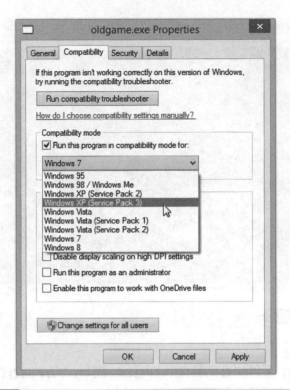

FIGURE 16.13 Compatibility mode options in Windows 8.1

- **Enable this program to work with OneDrive files (Windows 8/8.1/10)** Add networking support for applications that don't understand cloud-based file storage.
- **Change settings for all users** Apply compatibility settings for all users.

For 100 percent compatibility with Windows XP on a Windows 7 (Pro, Ultimate, or Enterprise) system, you can download *Windows XP Mode* (see Figure 16.14) to access a premade Windows XP SP3 virtual machine.

Travel Advisory

Windows XP support, including security patches, ended in April 2014.

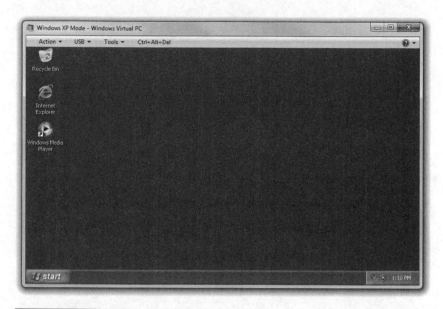

FIGURE 16.14 Windows XP Mode

Missing File or Incorrect File Version

Some applications will throw error messages such as "missing DLL" or "cannot open file *xyz*" when a common file they need is missing. You may have luck with an Internet search for the missing DLL or file that fails to open, along with the name of the program you're trying to use. DLLs can be infected with a virus, so if you need a replacement, don't indiscriminately download and install one from an untrusted source.

Crashing Programs

Some programs, often games rushed to market near the winter holidays, are released with code errors that render them unstable. These errors can produce symptoms such as a crash to desktop (CTD), freeze, or even an unexpected shutdown or restart. These improper shutdowns can cause other problems, including damage to open files and folders. Keep an open mind, because hardware or driver problems could also be the cause; think in terms of what the system is using.

Think about what could cause this scenario: your whole system freezes while you're playing a huge, graphically intensive game that eats RAM like candy. For starters, it could be an error in the game code, an overwhelmed video card, a problem with the video card driver, a hardware problem on the video card, or a bad section of RAM. But what if the system didn't freeze; what if it was just slow and jerky? It's more likely to be poor programming, or hardware that just can't cut the mustard.

Volume Shadow Copy Service and System Protection

A good backup or a restore point might save you from a corrupted or lost file, but these can be a hassle and there's a chance the data wasn't even included in the backup. Windows Vista introduced *System Protection,* a file backup feature powered by the Volume Shadow Copy Service (VSS).

VSS enables the OS to back up any file, even ones in use. To access previous versions of any data file or folder, right-click it and select *Restore previous versions* to open the Previous Versions tab (see Figure 16.15). Vista support is limited to the Business, Ultimate, and Enterprise editions, but all newer versions and editions of Windows support it.

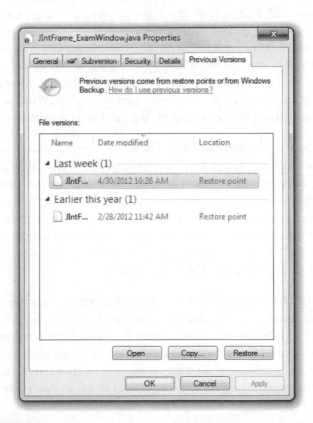

FIGURE 16.15 Previous Versions tab

If System Protection is enabled and any of the following criteria are met, you will have at least one previous version in the list:

- The file or folder was backed up using the backup program.
- You created a restore point.
- The file or folder was changed.

System Protection falls in the category generically called *file recovery software,* along with many third-party utilities such as Recuva from Piriform, which I've used many times to get "deleted" data off a hard drive or RAID array.

CHECKPOINT

✔**Objective 16.01: Failure to Boot**   If you see errors about a missing OS or critical boot files, you first want to check your drive cabling, boot sequence, expansion ports, and removable media drives. Otherwise, you can run the Windows Recovery Environment (also known as the System Recovery Options menu), where you can access Startup Repair, System Restore, System Image Recovery/Windows Complete PC Restore, Windows Memory Diagnostic (Tool), the Command Prompt, and other repair/recovery tools.

✔**Objective 16.02: Windows GUI Problems**   Several issues can cause Windows to hang during the GUI-loading phase, such as buggy device drivers, Registry problems, and even autoloading programs. Event Viewer in Window shows you all sorts of interesting happenings on the system. You can record application events, security events, and system events. You can repair system files with sfc, view aggregate information about problems and solutions in both Problem Reports and Action Center, and troubleshoot simple issues with the Troubleshooting applet.

✔**Objective 16.03: Windows Application Problems**   Programs that fail to install usually aren't to blame in and of themselves. In most cases, a problem with Windows prevents them from installing; a common cause is the absence of another prerequisite program. If you get an error while trying to uninstall a program, log back on as an administrator and try again or run the uninstaller as administrator. You can use compatibility modes to emulate older versions of Windows.

Windows Vista Business, Ultimate, and Enterprise and all versions and editions of Windows after use Volume Shadow Copy Service via System Protection, which enables the OS to make backups of any files (even one that is in use) and grants access to previous versions of any data file or folder.

REVIEW QUESTIONS

1. Your Windows system fails to boot up. You suspect that the boot sector has become corrupted. You start the system using the OS installation media and then launch the System Recovery Options Command Prompt. Which bootrec option should you use to write a new boot sector into the system partition?

    A. bootrec /fixboot

    B. bootrec /fixmbr

    C. bootrec /scanos

    D. bootrec /rebuildmbr

2. You've just installed a software update, rebooted, and now your system experiences random crashes. Which utility should you use first to try to fix the problem?

    A. Bootrec /rebuildmbr

    B. Device Manager

    C. System Restore

    D. Windows Recovery Environment

3. You suspect your system is failing to boot because of a corrupt master boot record. Which utility is the best to fix this?

    A. Event Viewer

    B. Refresh your PC

    C. Reset your PC

    D. WinRE Command Prompt

4. What command should you run to check and fix corrupt system files, DLLs, and other critical files?

    A. Bootrec /fixboot

    B. sfc /scannow

    C. chkdsk /r

    D. defrag –a

5. You get a tech call from a distraught Windows 7 user who can't get into Windows. He says he has a Recovery CD from the manufacturer and plans to run it. What would you suggest?

   A. Run the Recovery CD to restore the system.

   B. Run the Recovery CD to return the system to the factory-installed state.

   C. Try to get the computer to boot into Safe Mode.

   D. Reinstall Windows by using a Windows 7 disc.

6. You respond to a tech call and boot the problematic system. Windows flashes some error message, but makes it to the desktop. Which tool in Windows most likely will enable you to track down the error?

   A. Device Manager

   B. Event Viewer

   C. System Restore

   D. Task Manager

7. John's computer has an error that says bootmgr is corrupted. What tool can he use to fix this problem?

   A. bcdedit

   B. extract

   C. diskpart

   D. regedit

8. What does Microsoft call the 32- or 64-bit Windows Preinstallation Environment?

   A. WinEE

   B. WinPE

   C. WinRE

   D. WinPI

9. Ralph suspects a bad RAM stick is causing Windows to fail to boot. What default Windows tool can he use to check the RAM?

   A. Diskpart

   B. Bootrec /scanram

   C. Windows RAM Diagnostic

   D. Windows Memory Diagnostic

10. Ellen tries to boot into Windows, but the computer crashes at the logon screen. What tool should she use first to try to fix the problem?

    A. Windows Recovery Environment

    B. Startup Repair

    C. Safe Mode

    D. Safe Mode with Command Prompt

REVIEW ANSWERS

1. **A**   The command **bootrec /fixboot** writes a new partition boot sector to the system partition.

2. **C**   You should first try to fix the problem with a System Restore.

3. **D**   Of the options available, the best tool to fix a corrupt MBR is the Windows Recovery Environment's Command Prompt, via **bootrec /fixmbr**.

4. **B**   Run the **sfc /scannow** command to fix corrupt system files, DLLs, and other critical files.

5. **C**   Ack! Tell him to try Safe Mode first!

6. **B**   Of the options listed here, Event Viewer is most likely to reveal the details on the error message.

7. **A**   John can use the bcdedit tool to fix an error that says bootmgr is corrupted.

8. **B**   Microsoft calls the 32- or 64-bit installation environment in Windows the WinPE.

9. **D**   Ralph should run the Windows Memory Diagnostic if he suspects that a bad RAM stick is causing Windows to fail to boot.

10. **C**   Ellen should reboot the system into Safe Mode first. If the system still won't boot, Safe Mode with Command Prompt may work.

Linux
and Mac OS X

	NEWBIE	SOME EXPERIENCE	EXPERT
ETA	3 hours	2 hours	1 hour

Back in Chapter 12 we looked at modern OS interfaces, including Linux and Mac OS X, but since then it has been Windows, Windows, Windows. Now that you're familiar with Windows concepts, features, maintenance, optimization, and troubleshooting, it's time to explore the highlights of how these manifest in the other desktop operating systems you'll see on the 902 exam: Linux and Mac OS X.

Local Lingo

OS X The X is a Roman numeral; OS X is the tenth major version of the Mac OS. The 902 objectives specify only *Mac OS,* but OS X (pronounced "OS ten") was initially released in 2001. Since then, Apple has released named minor version updates at least every two years, though the last few have been yearly updates. As of this writing, the current version is 10.11, also known as OS X El Capitan.

 **Objective 17.01** Important OS Concepts

Modern desktop operating systems are all pretty similar from the user's perspective because each must support the core reasons people use computers in the first place. Behind the scenes, though, there are a number of stark philosophical, architectural, and practical differences.

Background

Linux and Mac OS X (for brevity, simply "OS X" for the rest of this chapter) have common roots as UNIX-based operating systems, so there are tons of functional similarities. That said, OS X is a closely guarded proprietary operating system used only on Apple's hardware, and Linux is more accurately an open-source OS kernel.

Travel Assistance

We discussed closed-source, proprietary, and open-source software in Chapter 11.

If you remember back to Chapter 12, we looked at the Unity desktop environment (DE), which is packaged with the Ubuntu distro. A Linux *distro,* or *distribution,* is a package of software that includes some version of the Linux *kernel*—the core of the operating system—along with any updates, customizations, and additional software needed to tailor it for some purpose, such as a server, desktop, tiny computer, and many more. Some popular distros are Linux Mint, Ubuntu, Debian, openSUSE, and Fedora, but distros are often related— Linux Mint is based on both Ubuntu and Debian, and Ubuntu is itself based on Debian.

CompTIA doesn't specify a distro, nor does it specify all that many explicit Linux features. We've chosen to explore Linux as it manifests in the popular, flexible Ubuntu distribution—but don't focus too closely on what features are called or how they look in a specific distro.

Hardware

One of the really big differences between OS X and both Linux and Windows is that Apple develops OS X for its hardware, and vice versa. Apple has also been trending toward fewer and fewer updatable components in recent years, especially in its laptops, meaning OS X has to support relatively little core hardware. Apple hardware tends to be more expensive and more restrictive as a result— especially since you have to pay today's prices for upgrades you might need in the future. The upside is fewer compatibility issues.

> ### Exam Tip
>
> Apple is also well known for decisively adopting new hardware and interfaces before they are mainstream, and ruthlessly removing older ones before everyone is quite ready to move on. A recent example is its decision to remove optical drives—though it gives users the option to purchase a USB optical drive, or borrow one from another system over the network via its *Remote Disc* feature.

As you might expect from the earlier description of Linux, hardware support varies greatly. Linux is more popular in the server market, and popular distributions intended for use on servers tend to *just work* quite well with common server hardware. If you're thinking about turning your old Windows box with a hodgepodge of hardware into a Linux desktop, however, you may run into trouble. Keep in mind that hardware support can vary by distribution, so you should research the components before you commit.

Permissions

Linux and OS X handle users, groups, and permissions a little differently than Windows does. If you go into Terminal on either system and enter the command **ls –l**, you'll see a detailed list of files and folders, including information about the file's owner, group, and permissions. Let's zero in on one line of this command's output:

```
-rwxrw-r-- 1 mikemeyers mi6   7624 Oct  2 18:39 launch_codes
```

First, consider the string -rwxrw-r--, where each letter and dash represents a permission for this file. Ignore the dash at the beginning, which tells us if this listing is a file, directory, or shortcut. What we have left are three groups of permissions (see Figure 17.1), which, in order, stand for:

- **Owner**   Permissions for the owner of this file or folder
- **Group**   Permissions for members of the group for this file or folder
- **Everyone**   Permissions for anyone for this file or folder

Each position in a group is a letter if the permission is enabled and a dash otherwise:

- **r**   Read the contents of a file
- **w**   Write or modify a file or folder
- **x**   Execute a file or list the folder contents

Travel Advisory

Executables aren't indicated by a file extension, but by the executable permission. To run an executable script or program from your current directory, you prepend it with **./** (called *dot-slash*), which keeps you from accidentally executing a malicious script named after a common command.

rwx|rwx|rwx

Owner   Group   Everyone

FIGURE 17.1   Linux file permissions

After the permissions, the numeral 1 indicates the number of hard links to the file (don't worry about knowing hard links for the exam). Next, you see the user name of the file owner, mikemeyers, and that the file is in the mi6 group. If you combine these with the permissions, mikemeyers can read, write, and execute the file; the mi6 group can read and write it; and all permissions are denied for other users.

You can modify these permissions from the CLI. The *chown* command changes the owner and group associated with a file, and *chmod* changes the individual permissions. Changing ownership is fairly simple; the command **chown m launch_codes** would set the owner to "m" while **chown m:users launch_codes** would set both the owner and the group.

Travel Advisory

These commands may require superuser privileges via the sudo or su command.

Permissions are trickier because of the unintuitive abbreviated syntaxes used to specify them. The most common numeric form, for example, uses a three-digit number with one digit representing each set of three permissions; each digit starts at 0 and then you add the permissions—read (+4), write (+2), and execute (+1). The permissions for *launch_codes* (rwxrw-r--) would be represented as 764, or (4+2+1, 4+2, 4). We could use **chmod 660 launch_codes** to remove execute permissions for mikemeyers and remove read permissions for everyone else. (Each "6" indicates read and write [4+2]; the "0" grants no permissions.)

Package Management and App Stores

One of the really impressive things about the Linux ecosystem (in large part because highly interoperable open-source software is one of its primary values) is that most significant applications are built on the shoulders of other applications or software packages; we call these *dependencies,* because the program depends on this other software to be present (and working!) to run.

Once upon a time, UNIX and Linux users largely downloaded and compiled their own software, which meant they were responsible for hunting down each dependency. This grew untenable, and long ago Linux distributions pioneered *package manager* programs that usually enable you to download and install a program and all its dependencies at once. Different distros have their own package managers and package-management interfaces, but the most common are the *advanced packaging tool (APT),* which is used on Debian-based distros, and *Red Hat Package Manager (RPM)*. Later in the chapter we'll look at how to use the *apt-get* CLI tool (included in the 902 objectives) to install and update software.

The other way of handling dependencies is to bundle them up with the application and distribute them together, which is generally what you get when you download an installer or use an *app store*. This applies to both the mobile device stores you saw in Chapter 11, and their desktop counterparts: the Apple App Store (OS X) and Windows Store (Windows 8 and up). This method is simpler for the user, but it can also be wasteful and less flexible. Imagine multiple apps on your system, all including their own copies of a few common dependencies—not only does this waste space, but each app's developers must also release a new version to include security patches to the dependency.

Exam Tip

App stores and package managers aren't synonymous, but they do share some important features, such as giving users a central place to discover, install, and update software.

Settings and Configuration

The differences between OS X and Linux really show when it comes to settings and configuration. Mac OS X creates a thoughtful user experience with two key launch points for techs:

- The *System Preferences* app contains most of the settings you need to administer an OS X system. To access it from anywhere, just click the Apple (top-left corner) and select System Preferences (see Figure 17.2).

- The *Utilities* folder contains important tools for techs and power users. It's located in the Applications folder, but these tools are powerful enough that Apple provides multiple shortcuts. The simplest is the COMMAND-SHIFT-U hotkey, but you can also open Finder (which we'll discuss further in a moment), click Go on the menu bar, and select Utilities (see Figure 17.3).

The trouble with configuring Linux is that the easy GUI settings and configuration tools are, well, part of the GUI. If you recall, the Linux GUI is dictated by the desktop environment you use. Some DEs handle settings much like

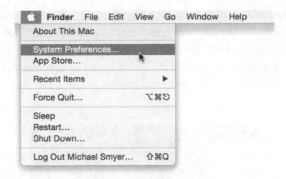

FIGURE 17.2 Accessing System Preferences

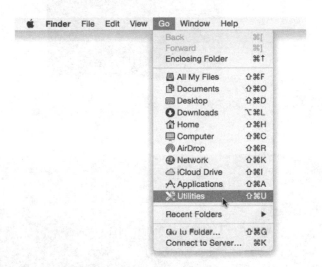

FIGURE 17.3 Accessing the Utilities folder

Windows, or much like OS X—but others blaze their own trail. The best advice is to familiarize yourself with any DE you'll need to support by using a tutorial or checking each corner and screen edge for icons, buttons, and menus.

The consistent (if intimidating) way to configure Linux is via the CLI, which you can reach in most distros by pressing CTRL-ALT-T to open Terminal. It's such an essential part of the Linux experience that you'll also typically find it on whatever version of a toolbar, dock, desktop, or quick-launch menu your DE uses.

Unity has a central *System Settings* application; just click the gear icon on the far right of the menu bar and select System Settings (see Figure 17.4). You can find other settings and utilities in the Dash. Click the Ubuntu button at the top of the Launcher (see Figure 17.5). From here you can search or browse for handy applications such as the System Monitor or the always critical Terminal.

FIGURE 17.4   Accessing System Settings

FIGURE 17.5   Dash applications

Objective 17.02 Useful Features

Now that we have reviewed some general concepts, you're ready to meet some of the specific tools and features you'll find in Linux and OS X. Because the 902 objectives don't list many specific Linux features or tools, this section includes the Ubuntu equivalent when appropriate but only italicizes terms that appear in the objectives. I've divided the features CompTIA includes into basic features your average user will need frequently and advanced features oriented toward power users and techs.

Basic Features

Much as in Windows—or even on a mobile device—users need to be able to customize their device's appearance, add and remove software, as well as browse, back up, and synchronize their data across devices.

Display Options

OS X and most modern Linux distros offer clear options for changing display settings. The OS X options are spread over a few menus in System Preferences (see Figure 17.6): General, Desktop & Screen Saver, and Dock.

Everything you can modify in Windows, you can modify in Linux, but you might have to do a little hunting. Look for one or more utilities in the System Settings. The Appearance applet in Ubuntu (see Figure 17.7) can alter the background, theme, and Launcher icon size.

Installing and Removing Software in OS X

In OS X, the simplest way to install software is through Apple's App Store. This works like downloading an app on a smartphone. Alternatively, you can download software from a third-party developer. This sort of installation requires one or two more steps. Unless these programs come with an installer (which is rare), installing is as simple as dragging them into the Applications folder. Many even present you with a screen that prompts you to do so. The uninstall procedure depends on how you installed the app; if you don't remember, step through the options listed here.

To remove App Store apps, open the Launchpad app from the Dock or Applications folder (it looks like a rocket ship) and then click and hold on any

FIGURE 17.6 System Preferences in Mac OS X

FIGURE 17.7 Appearance applet in System Settings

FIGURE 17.8 Uninstalling App Store–purchased applications using the Launchpad app

app icon until all the icons start to wiggle. An × in a circle will appear on the upper-left corner of any app that can be removed (see Figure 17.8). Click the × to remove the app. Otherwise, run the app's uninstaller if it has one or (more common) just drag the app to the Trash. Simply deleting an app can leave behind various files (such as user preferences) in the user's Library folder.

Installing and Removing Software in Linux

In Linux, you'll typically install software by directly downloading an installer, or using either a GUI or CLI interface to your system's package manager. When you download an installer, this should be as simple as double-clicking the installation file and selecting Install from the options.

On average, package managers aren't as commercial as app stores are, so the trick to using them is that you generally need to know what package (and maybe even what version) you need. The growing popularity of Linux on the desktop has led to a few easy-to-use graphical package managers that look a lot like app stores and even sell commercial software, including Ubuntu Software Center and the program slated to replace it, GNOME Software. Figure 17.9 shows a recent package manager interface in Ubuntu.

Let's look at a CLI version, *apt-get,* since it's less familiar. Let's say you want to replace the not-so-popular built-in text editor vi with a more popular editor

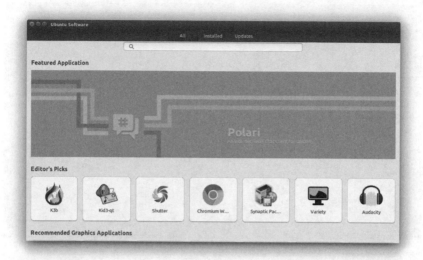

FIGURE 17.9   Ubuntu Software package manager

called Vim. You technically need just one command to install it, but it's a good idea to update the package manager first to ensure you get the latest version:

```
mike@server:~$ sudo apt-get update
mike@server:~$ sudo apt-get install vim
```

Removing software installed through the package manager in mainstream Linux distros is as easy as installing it. You can open a package manager GUI such as Ubuntu Software, find the app, and then click Remove (see Figure 17.10), but a simple **sudo apt-get remove <package>** from the CLI will also suffice.

Travel Advisory

The apt-get command just removes the stated packages. After you've removed them, you can use **sudo apt-get autoremove** to also remove unused dependencies.

Files and Data

Desktop operating systems are file driven, and they all have GUI programs for browsing your file tree and performing common file operations (such as copy, paste, and delete). In Windows we saw how Windows Explorer/File Explorer performs this task, and the programs for doing this in OS X and Linux are fairly similar. OS X uses *Finder* (shown in Figure 17.11) to browse files on hard

FIGURE 17.10 Removing an application in Ubuntu Linux

FIGURE 17.11 Finder

drives, removable media, and network locations. The trick with Linux is that, once again, this application varies. Rest assured that your distro or desktop environment comes with one—Ubuntu comes with Nautilus.

These days, the other half of the equation is keeping your files and data backed up and synchronized across all of your devices—typically with cloud data services. Apple devices have built-in support for *iCloud,* which can synchronize pictures, documents, music, e-mail, contacts, calendars, bookmarks, login credentials, credit card information, and more. Some of iCloud's features can be used through client applications on Windows, Linux, and other non-Apple platforms—but one of its more unique features, *iCloud Keychain,* can only securely manage passwords and credit card information for OS X and iOS devices.

> **Travel Assistance**
>
> You can of course use third-party cloud data services such as Dropbox with any OS that has an available client. You'll see how cloud services work in Chapter 20.

Advanced Features

Beyond the basic features many users will need, the 902 objectives also specify a few features that your average user may never use or even see.

Multiboot

We looked at creating a multiboot Windows system in Chapter 14, but Windows isn't the only game in town. Contemporary Linux systems use the GRUB bootloader, which has excellent multiboot support. Apple *Boot Camp* makes it pretty simple to install Windows on your Mac and choose which OS to load when you start the system; more recent versions of Boot Camp support only 64-bit versions of Windows.

> **Travel Advisory**
>
> You can still multiboot Linux on an Apple system, but Boot Camp isn't the tool for the job.

CLI File Editing

Learning to make meaningful edits to text files from the CLI (or even exit the editor without getting trapped) is a rite of passage for many techs.

FIGURE 17.12   New file open in vi

The traditional UNIX CLI editor, *vi,* is the one CompTIA wants you to know—probably because vi is ubiquitous on UNIX systems. When you open a new or existing file by entering **vi <filename>**, OS X and most Linux distros actually open your file in Vim (Vi Improved), which layers a number of features atop vi. Let's open a new text file called "fred" for editing in vi/Vim (see Figure 17.12):

```
mike@server:~$ vi fred
```

The editor is always in either *insert mode* or *command mode,* but it opens in the latter. Insert mode enables you to insert and edit text; command mode supports commands such as cut, paste, delete line, save, and so on. In command mode, press the I key to enter insert mode. Using ENTER to end a line and BACKSPACE if you make an error, enter a few lines of text (as shown in Figure 17.13) and then press ESC to return to command mode. Type **:q** and press ENTER to exit the program.

NetBoot

NetBoot enables a Mac to boot an OS X system image over the network, making it simple to bring up a bunch of identical OS X machines for use in a classroom or library. This has many of the advantages of the client-side virtualization you saw in Chapter 12, such as rolling out custom, preconfigured OS X images with necessary software preinstalled.

```
⊗ ⊜ ⊙   vmuser@ubuntu1504-vm: ~
#include <stdio.h>

int main(){
    printf("Hello World\n");
    return 0;
}▮
```

FIGURE 17.13   vi with a short "Hello World" program

Objective 17.03   # Maintenance and Optimization

The concepts behind maintaining and optimizing Linux and OS X systems are basically the same as the ones we applied to maintaining and optimizing Windows in Chapter 15: keep the system or at least its important data backed up, make sure it is updated promptly, maintain its hard drives, and manage programs to optimize performance. Because we don't need to add new concepts, we can focus on how to perform these same actions in Linux and OS X.

Preparing for Problems

OS X systems use *Time Machine* (along with an external or shared network drive) to create full system backups (see Figure 17.14) called *local snapshots*. These snapshots enable you to recover from a crash or even *restore* deleted files and previous versions. Configure it via Time Machine in System Preferences. You can also create and restore full disk images with Disk Utility, which we'll see later in the chapter.

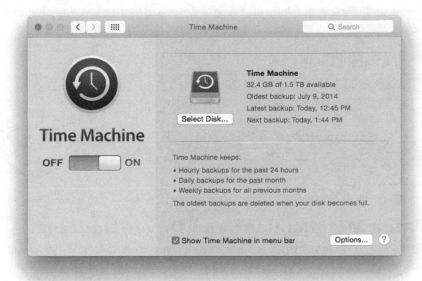

Time Machine

As you should expect by now, Linux backup tools can differ by distro. Ubuntu uses Déjà Dup, though it's called Backups in System Settings (see Figure 17.15). Déjà Dup covers a user's Home folder by default—just specify a location and it will permanently store file versions as long as the storage location has space.

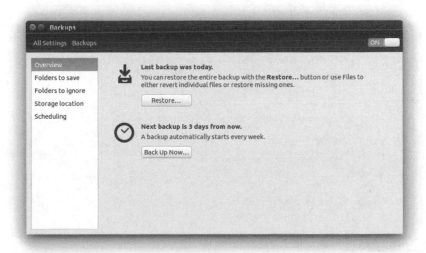

Backups under System Settings in Ubuntu

It isn't on the 902 exam, but you can also download a drive imaging program such as Clonezilla.

Exam Tip

You can technically image your OS drive in both OS X and Linux with the *dd* command at the Terminal, but the image will be as large as the drive's full capacity unless you compress it (ideally by piping it through a compression program before saving it). You can later use dd to apply this image to another drive (after decompressing it if necessary).

Patch Management and Driver Updates

Both OS X and Linux alert you when software needs an update. In OS X, you access updates through the App Store and configure update settings with the App Store menu in System Preferences (see Figure 17.16). Most Linux distros have an updating tool like the Software Updater in Ubuntu (see Figure 17.17).

As useful as package managers are for installing single applications, that's not where their real power lies. These package managers can manage *all* the

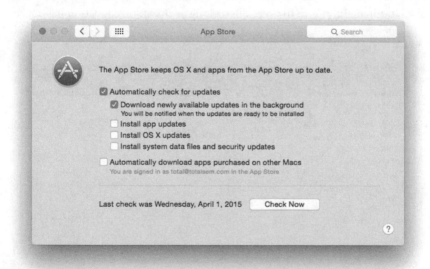

FIGURE 17.16 App Store update options

FIGURE 17.17   Software Updater in Ubuntu Linux

software (minus anything you compiled yourself) on the system, so you can upgrade installed packages from the CLI with two commands:

```
mike@server:~$ sudo apt-get update
mike@server:~$ sudo apt-get upgrade
```

> **Travel Advisory**
>
> *Dependency management* gets harder as you install more packages.

Disk Maintenance

OS X handles most chores automatically, and both OS X and Linux will occasionally run file system check (fsck) on reboot. Still, if you have reason to suspect a problem, it's worth running fsck from the CLI or using an included or third-party GUI tool. OS X includes *Disk Utility*, which can verify and repair

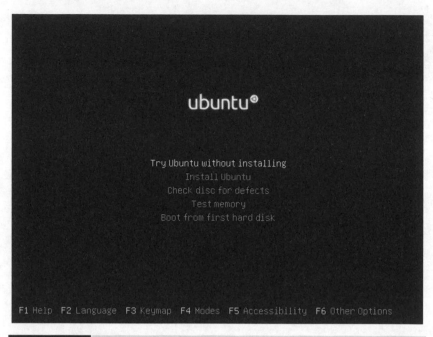

FIGURE 17.18 Ubuntu installation options, including one for disk diagnosis

file structures, partition and format drives, and even create disk images. Most Linux distros have one or more disk maintenance utilities, but if you keep the bootable installation media handy, you can just use its disk diagnostic (see Figure 17.18).

Travel Advisory

Linux and OS X don't include an equivalent to Disk Cleanup in Windows, but you can download third-party utilities for cleaning up junk files.

Scheduled Maintenance

Mac OS X and most Linux distributions use one of two scripting tools to run all sorts of tasks automatically in the background. Apple developed launchd for automation; most Linux distros use cron. You can create custom launchd and cron jobs, but actually doing so is beyond the CompTIA A+ exams.

> **Exam Tip**
>
> The 902 Linux and OS X objectives include *scheduled disk maintenance* and *scheduled backups,* but each OS checks disks and drives automatically. If you're using common GUI backup utilities, you'll schedule backups within the utility itself. You can, of course, use the task schedulers to run other utilities or even custom backup scripts.

Optimizing Performance

The first step to optimizing running programs is knowing what is running and what kind of impact it has on your system. The Activity Monitor (shown in Figure 17.19) utility provides both summary and detailed information on your OS X system's recent resource use, and Ubuntu's System Monitor (shown in Figure 17.20) serves a similar purpose.

The second step, of course, is fixing or closing programs that are causing problems. Activity Monitor has a *force quit* button (along with options for

FIGURE 17.19 OS X Activity Monitor

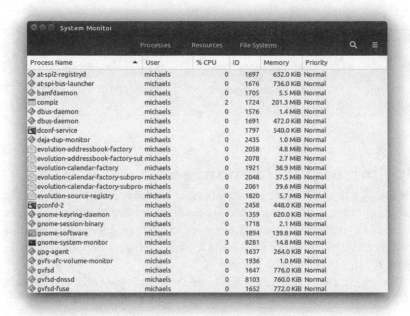

FIGURE 17.20 Ubuntu System Monitor

gathering more information on a process), and System Monitor likewise has an End Process button.

Exam Tip

You can do this from the CLI. The **top** command will bring up a CLI process monitor on OS X and most Linux distros, but the 902 objectives specify the older process status (*ps*) command. You can use **ps aux** to display detailed process information specified by the three switches: a = processes for all users, u = show process owner, x = process not attached to a terminal. You can use **kill <process_id>** to kill any process by its numeric ID.

It's also simple to control startup apps in both Linux and OS X with settings menus. In OS X you can readily select or deselect any application that might load with specific user accounts (see Figure 17.21) via the Users & Groups menu in System Preferences. Ubuntu Linux has a Startup Applications menu (see Figure 17.22) with a checkbox for each startup program.

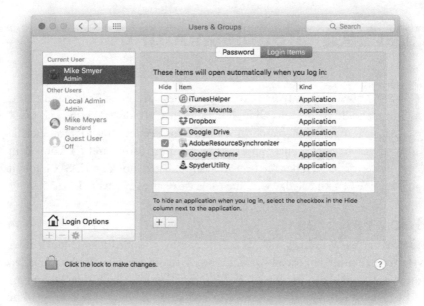

FIGURE 17.21 Options in Users & Groups pane

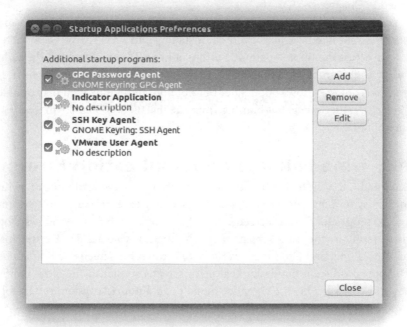

FIGURE 17.22 Disabling an autostarting program in Startup Applications

Objective 17.04   # Troubleshooting

The 902 objectives only mention a few issues specific to Linux and OS X, but it should be obvious enough by now that Windows, Linux, and OS X systems have most of the same problems. This section will look at specific issues related to boot failures and serious run-time errors and the equivalent Windows errors. You'll be able to troubleshoot basic Linux and OS X issues if you combine this knowledge with the tools we've already covered.

Boot Failures

Much as current Windows systems use the bootmgr bootloader and much older systems used ntldr, almost all current Linux systems use the GRUB bootloader. You aren't as likely to see the older LILO bootloader, which doesn't support UEFI systems and was discontinued in late 2015. If either gets corrupted or deleted, Linux won't start and you'll get a "Missing GRUB" or "Missing LILO" error message equivalent to the bootmgr, bcd, ntldr, and boot.ini errors discussed in Chapter 16.

The most reliable approach is to boot to the Ubuntu installation media and select the option to try Ubuntu without installing it to a hard drive. From there, you can access the Boot Repair GUI utility or open Terminal and run the **sudo grub-install** command (along with the location of the boot drive) to repair. If you can get to the GRUB bootloader but not boot into Linux, you may be able to select *recovery mode,* but booting from the installation media will give you more options.

Run-Time Failures and Application Errors

Linux and OS X systems can also have run-time and application errors with familiar symptoms, including applications that freeze or crash, full system freezes, proprietary crash screens, and spontaneous reboots. Windows stop errors result in the blue screen of death (BSoD), whereas UNIX systems, including Linux and OS X, have *kernel panic;* the error screen itself differs by OS. Some produce intimidating text error screens similar to the older BSoD; current OS X versions use a gentler method: an automatic system restart followed by a gray notification screen.

Exam Tip

The 902 objectives refer to these as *proprietary crash screens (BSOD/pin wheel),* but technically the spinning rainbow-colored pinwheel in OS X is just a wait cursor. Sometimes you'll see it while a program works, but other times you'll see it when a program is frozen (until you kill the process). Because it can appear during a full system freeze that requires a reboot, some users call it the "pinwheel of death."

Some of these errors are caused by driver issues or failing hardware; in the case of the former, you can check the manufacturer's website for updated drivers or kernel modules. If you suspect hardware is failing on a Linux system, apply the hardware troubleshooting techniques you've learned to test your theory—Apple systems, however, typically have tightly integrated hardware that is hard if not impossible to tear down and replace. If an application reliably causes errors, you may need OS or application updates, or have to uninstall the software until it is updated to address the stability issue.

Local Lingo

Kernel module Code that is inserted into the kernel to extend it—in this case, to add device support.

CHECKPOINT

✔**Objective 17.01: Important OS Concepts** Linux and OS X have many similarities because they're both UNIX-based operating systems. OS X is a complete proprietary OS used only on Apple hardware, whereas Linux is technically an open-source OS kernel included in a wide array of (often related) Linux distributions ("distros") such as Ubuntu, Debian, Linux Mint, openSUSE, Fedora, and so on. Files and folders in OS X and Linux belong to a user and a group, and each has three sets of permissions—for the owner, group members, and everyone else. Each set has three permissions: read, write, and execute.

OS X applications are typically installed through the Apple App Store or downloaded from the Web, whereas Linux systems use package managers in the place of app stores (though some package manager interfaces resemble app stores). Both typically handle configuration through a unified system settings app or preferences app.

✔**Objective 17.02: Useful Features**   OS X users have common appearance and display options located in System Preferences, the App Store to install applications, and the ability to remove software through the Launchpad, running an uninstaller, or simply dragging it to the Trash. They can also use Finder to browse the file system and iCloud to synchronize many kinds of data. Linux users can accomplish these same tasks, but built-in tools may vary by distro and desktop environment, and features such as cloud data sync may require third-party applications.

Linux's GRUB bootloader has good multiboot support, but OS X has limited built-in support to multiboot 64-bit copies of Windows via Boot Camp. It's worth knowing how to make basic text edits in the CLI text editors vi and Vim, which are ubiquitous on UNIX systems, including Linux and OS X. Techs can use NetBoot to boot networked Macs from system images stored on a server or to deploy preconfigured system images.

✔**Objective 17.03: Maintenance and Optimization**   The basic principles behind maintaining and optimizing Windows apply to Linux and OS X systems. To maintain them, use the appropriate utilities to create backups of user data or full system images, regularly update system and application software, and run disk/drive maintenance utilities if you suspect hardware or file system problems. CompTIA recommends scheduling backups and disk maintenance; you can schedule backups through most backup utilities, but systems will automatically run disk maintenance checks from time to time. Optimize system performance by disabling unnecessary startup programs and identifying/closing programs that hog resources with the appropriate utility.

✔**Objective 17.04: Troubleshooting**   Linux and OS X systems have most of the same problems you see on Windows, though they may have different names and screens. The Linux and OS X equivalent of the Windows stop error (which produces a BSoD) is kernel panic. The spinning pinwheel seen in OS X is a wait cursor that commonly indicates a busy or frozen application, though it sometimes appears when the system freezes and needs a reboot. Kernel panic errors related to devices can be fixed by updating device drivers or kernel modules; persistent errors related to application software may require an OS update or application update, or you may have to uninstall the application.

REVIEW QUESTIONS

1. Which of these operating systems is closed-source software?
   A. Debian
   B. Fedora
   C. OS X
   D. Ubuntu

2. What OS X program would you use to browse the file system?
   A. Dock
   B. Launchpad
   C. Mission Control
   D. Finder

3. Which CLI command can change a file's permissions?
   A. chperm
   B. chmod
   C. chgrp
   D. chown

4. What GUI program do you use to install software in Linux?
   A. Package Manager
   B. apt-get
   C. Ubuntu Software Center
   D. It depends on what distro you are using.

5. Which OS X feature enables users to boot into Windows on their Apple systems?
   A. Multiboot
   B. Boot Camp
   C. Launcher
   D. bootmgr

6. On which of these operating systems would the command **vi fred** open a file named "fred" for editing?
   A. OS X
   B. Ubuntu Linux
   C. Linux Mint
   D. All of the above

7. Which OS X feature creates backups called local snapshots?
   A. Time Machine
   B. Disk Utility
   C. dd
   D. Backup

8. When is the best time to schedule disk/drive maintenance utilities to run on your Linux or OS X system?
   A. Overnight, while the system is idle.
   B. Every time it reboots.
   C. Once a week, usually early Monday morning.
   D. Both systems periodically run these utilities on their own.

9. Which OS X and Linux CLI commands display process information similar to what's available in Task Manager's Processes tab? (Select two.)
   A. top
   B. ps
   C. stat
   D. ps aux

10. What is the current Linux bootloader with support for UEFI systems?
    A. bootmgr
    B. GRUB
    C. LILO
    D. ntldr

REVIEW ANSWERS

1. **C** Debian, Fedora, and Ubuntu are all distros of the open-source Linux OS, but Apple's OS X is a proprietary/closed-source OS.

2. **D** Finder, the OS X equivalent of File Explorer, is how you browse the file system.

3. **B** The chmod command can change file and folder permissions in OS X and Linux.

4. **D** While Ubuntu Software Center is a GUI tool for installing programs in Ubuntu Linux, the appropriate program depends on which distro you are using.

5. **B** Boot Camp allows OS X users to boot into 64-bit copies of Windows.

6. **D** The vi text editor is ubiquitous on UNIX-based systems, including OS X and Linux, though the vi command will often open files in Vi IMproved (Vim).

7. **A** Time Machine creates local snapshots of changes on an OS X system.

8. **D** You don't need to schedule them, because both OS X and Linux will periodically run disk/drive maintenance utilities on reboot.

9. **A D** You can monitor process information from the CLI with the more modern **top** command, or you can print information once with **ps**, though you'll need flags such as those present in **ps aux** to display information similar to what you would see in Task Manager.

10. **B** GRUB is the current Linux bootloader. The older LILO bootloader lacks UEFI support.

Networking

	NEWBIE	SOME EXPERIENCE	EXPERT
ETA	5 hours	4 hours	2 hours

It's hard to find computers that aren't connected to a network these days—unless they're intentionally disconnected for security or productivity. As a result, CompTIA has added quite a bit of networking to the A+ exams. This chapter focuses on networking concepts and wired networking—but you'll learn more about wireless networking and the Internet in the next two chapters.

Objective 18.01 Networking Concepts and Components

Networks are all about interconnecting computing devices (also called hosts) so they can communicate. More specifically, your *local host* can communicate with *remote hosts* in order to access the *resources* (such as printers, files, web pages, and so on) those systems share, and to share its own resources. In a given exchange, the system providing a resource is the *server,* and the system using the resource is the *client;* when we call an entire system a server, what we really mean is that the system's primary job is serving some resource(s) to clients.

> ### Exam Tip
>
> Some servers fulfill a very specific *role,* while others wear many hats. Of the roles CompTIA wants you to know for the 902 exam, DHCP, DNS, file, print, and authentication servers appear in this chapter, and web, proxy, and mail servers appear in Chapter 20.

In order for a variety of different devices to share resources over a network, the network components need a shared connectivity standard, an addressing method clients and servers can use to find and communicate with each other, and shared software protocols that each system in an exchange understands. Let's look at many of the concepts and components that come together to form a network.

> ### Exam Tip
>
> Networked devices don't necessarily look like computers. Many are, but you can find narrow-purpose computers or servers embedded in all sorts of machines and other equipment—CompTIA calls these *legacy/embedded systems.* It can be easy to overlook networked devices embedded in this equipment, but they may represent massive investments your network must remain compatible with.

FIGURE 18.1 A switch and two laptops connected by UTP cable

Ethernet

The dominant shared connectivity standard on modern networks, *Ethernet*, defines everything you need to get data from one system to another. Ethernet has evolved through hundreds of *Ethernet flavors* over the years—and most modern network speeds are expressed as *10BaseT*, *100BaseT*, and *1000BaseT*, which respectively run at 10, 100, and 1000 Mbps. Individual hosts have a network adapter that connects to a central switch with a segment of *unshielded twisted pair (UTP)* cable (see Figure 18.1), which is limited to 100 meters for most cable types.

> **Travel Advisory**
>
> Gigabit Ethernet (another name for 1000BaseT) is common on current desktops, but 10-Gigabit Ethernet is common for server-to-server links, and 40/100-Gigabit is approaching.

Each network adapter (or *NIC*) has a 48-bit built-in binary *media access control (MAC) address* that uniquely identifies it; before a NIC sends data out, it chunks it into transmission-friendly *frames* (see Figure 18.2) that are tagged with the MAC address of the sender and recipient and include information the receiver can use to detect errors. A *switch* will use the MAC address to send frames to the correct host.

> **Local Lingo**
>
> **Cyclic redundancy check (CRC)** A common mechanism for detecting data transmission errors.

Twisted-Pair Cabling

Most networks use UTP, but that doesn't mean there aren't other options. The wire pairs in *shielded twisted pair (STP)*, for example, are wrapped to shield

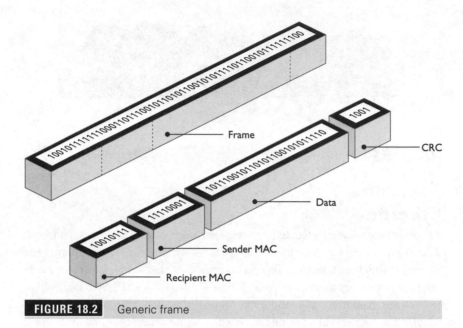

Frame

CRC

Data

Sender MAC

Recipient MAC

FIGURE 18.2   Generic frame

them from EMI. STP is rare because few cables run in EMI-heavy settings such as a shop floor crowded with electric motors.

UTP cabling consists of 22–26 AWG wire twisted into color-coded pairs. Each wire is insulated, and then the group is encased in a common jacket. The TIA/EIA 568 standards specify several UTP categories that define maximum data transfer speeds (or *bandwidth*); these are printed on the cable. Of these, installers currently use CAT 5e, CAT 6, or CAT 6a. The following is a list of the major categories.

Local Lingo

TIA/EIA   The Telecommunication Industry Association/Electronics Industries Alliance.

- **CAT 3**   Data speeds up to 10 Mbps (or 100 Mbps with a four-pair variant).
- **CAT 5**   Data speeds up to 100 Mbps.
- **CAT 5e**   Data speeds up to 1 Gbps.
- **CAT 6**   Supports 1 Gbps up to 100 meters; 10 Gbps up to 55 meters.

- **CAT 6a / CAT 6e** Supports 10 Gbps up to 100 meters. The current 901 objectives incorrectly list *CAT 6e*, which is a non-standard name for *CAT 6a*.

- **CAT 7** Supports 10 Gbps at 100 meters; individual wire shielding; not a recognized TIA/EIA standard.

> ### Exam Tip
> You'll only find CAT 3 installed for telephones and in very old networks, but CompTIA traditionally enjoys tripping up techs who don't know it can handle 100 Mbps.

Fiber Optic Cabling

Because *fiber optic cable* uses light to transmit Ethernet network frames, it's immune to electrical problems such as lightning, short circuits, and static. Fiber optic signals also travel 2000 meters (2 km) or more. Most fiber Ethernet networks use *62.5/125 multimode* fiber optic cable. Fiber optics are half-duplex; data flows only one way, so fiber connections require two cables.

> ### Local Lingo
> **Single mode vs. multimode** Fiber networks use laser or LED light sources. In single mode, lasers pulse single bursts over long distances at incredible speeds. Multimode fiber carries multiple simultaneous LED signals using different reflection angles within the core of the cable. These reflection angles disperse over long distances, limiting multimode to relatively short distances.

If you want to use fiber optic cabling, you need a fiber optic switch and fiber optic network cards. Regardless of fiber's impressive theoretical speed and range, real-world fiber networks are limited to the speed and distance specified by their respective Ethernet standard. The record single-mode transmission way back in 2011 was 100 *terabits* per second over 100 *miles*, but you won't find Ethernet standards anywhere near that (yet). Multimode networks run from 10 to 10,000 Mbps up to ~600 meters.

Coaxial Cabling

Early versions of Ethernet ran on *coaxial cable,* and coax lives on for cable modems and satellite connections. Coax consists of a core cable, surrounded by

FIGURE 18.3   Typical coax

insulation, covered with a *shield* of braided cable (see Figure 18.3) to eliminate interference and wrapped with a protective cover.

Exam Tip
Don't use a splitter to split a single segment of twisted pair or coax cable into more connections; splitters negatively affect signal quality.

There are hundreds of RG ratings for coax, but you just need to know *RG-59* and *RG-6* for the 901 exam; the RG rating is marked on the cable. Both have a 75-ohm impedance and are used in cable television (CATV), but RG-59 is thinner and can't carry data as far as RG-6. Coax generally tops out around 100 Mbps.

Connectors

There have been many connectors in networks past, but there are only a handful you're very likely to see in the real world or the 901 exam:

- **Twisted pair**   *RJ-45* is ubiquitous for UTP network connections, but you can also still find tons of *RJ-11* telephone connectors. Phones typically use a single wire pair, but *RJ-11* supports up to two pairs

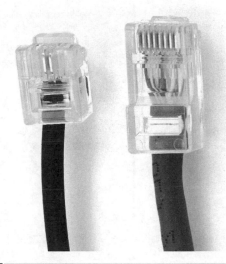

FIGURE 18.4   RJ-11(left) and RJ-45 (right)

so you can add another line; the wider *RJ-45* has up to four pairs (see Figure 18.4).

- **Fiber optic**   Older fiber optic setups use a pair of either *ST* or *SC* connectors, while newer setups use one *LC* connector (see Figure 18.5).

- **Coaxial**   Coax most often uses the screw-in *F-type connector* or the quarter-twist *BNC connector* (see Figure 18.6).

FIGURE 18.5   From left to right, fiber optic cables with ST, SC, and LC connectors

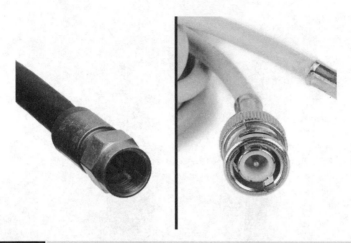

FIGURE 18.6   F-type connector (left) and BNC connector (right)

Network Architecture

Cabling is a critical part of network infrastructure, but we need a number of devices to control the relationships between hosts:

- **Hubs and switches**   Both connect hosts on a *local area network (LAN)* and pass signals between them. Hubs take a signal from one *port* and blindly repeat it out the others. Switches memorize the MAC address of each device to smartly repeat signals to the appropriate host. A group of computers connected by one or more switches is a *broadcast domain* (see Figure 18.7). We don't use hubs anymore because they waste bandwidth and other resources.

FIGURE 18.7   Two broadcast domains—two separate LANs

Local Lingo

LAN and WAN   A LAN is a group of networked computers within a few hundred meters of each other, whereas a wide-*area network (WAN)* is a group of computers on multiple LANs connected with long-distance technologies.

- **Router**   A box for connecting LANs into a WAN (see Figure 18.8). Hosts send signals for destinations outside of the LAN to the router, which routes traffic between networks.
- **Bridge**   Connects two different media types (such as UTP and fiber optic) and converts signals between them. This isn't just limited to traditional network media; an *Ethernet over Power (EoP)* bridge connects UTP to your building's power infrastructure, enabling you to have wired connections where it would be difficult to run new cable.
- **Modem**   True modems (short for modulator/demodulator) enable computers to communicate with digital signals over analog telephone lines. In common use, however, a modem is any device, expansion card, or box that connects a computer or network to an Internet service provider (ISP).

Travel Assistance

There are a few more network architecture devices on the 901 exam; we'll look at patch panels in the next section; access points, repeaters/extenders, and Power over Ethernet injectors in Chapter 19; and firewalls in Chapter 21.

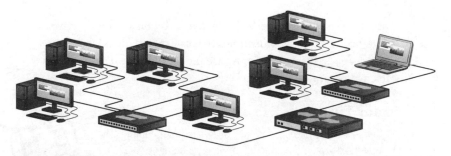

FIGURE 18.8   Two broadcast domains connected by a router—a WAN

Network Infrastructure

A typical wired office network has cables running above the drop ceiling from a central wiring closet or networking room. These cables drop down in the wall and terminate at an outlet near each workstation. This *structured cabling* is the playground of CompTIA Network+ techs and specialized cable installers, but the A+ exams still expect you to understand basic concepts and components to perform network troubleshooting and communicate with cable installers or network techs.

Travel Assistance
Wireless networks are also popular; we'll look at them in Chapter 19.

Structured cabling creates a safe, reliable cabling infrastructure for any devices that need to interconnect—but we'll focus on computer networks. You *could* place a switch in the middle of your office and run cable on the floor to each system, but in the real world people will hurt themselves, the cables, and connected equipment.

In structured cabling, *horizontal cabling* runs from the *work area* at individual workstations to a central *telecommunications room* (see Figure 18.9). The TIA/EIA has cabling standards that ensure cabling is reliable and easy to manage. Let's look at the components.

Horizontal Cabling

Each horizontal cabling *run* is usually CAT 5e or better UTP. Most of it runs in the *plenum* space above the ceiling, under the floors, or in the walls; this has two implications:

- The *PVC (polyvinyl chloride)* protective *jacket* on standard network cables produces dangerous fumes that can spread quickly via the plenum space. Instead, we must use more expensive *plenum-grade* cable with a fire-retardant jacket.

Exam Tip
The 901 lists *PVC* and *plenum* as types of twisted-pair cabling. They mean the same as the more specific terms used here.

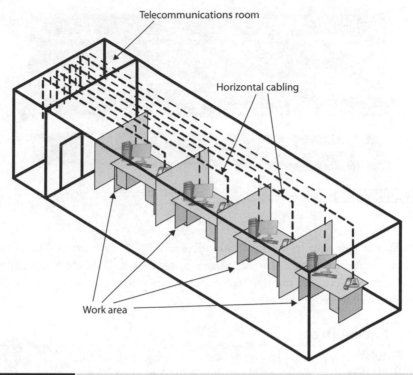

Telecommunications room

Horizontal cabling

Work area

FIGURE 18.9   Telecommunications room, horizontal cabling, and work areas

- The protection afforded by the plenum space means we can use faster *solid-core* UTP cable with a single fragile solid wire, instead of slower, damage-resistant *stranded-core* UTP with a bundle of tiny wire strands that don't conduct as well.

Telecommunications Room

The telecommunications room is where all of the horizontal runs come together, and it can become a mess over time if you don't use the right equipment to keep it organized. One or more *equipment racks* provide a stable platform for other hardware components (such as switches and servers). Racks are 19 inches wide, but they vary in height.

Because solid-core cable is fragile, it's best to install it once and not move it. A *patch panel* (shown in Figure 18.10) has a row of permanent connectors for horizontal cables on the back and a row of female port connectors on the

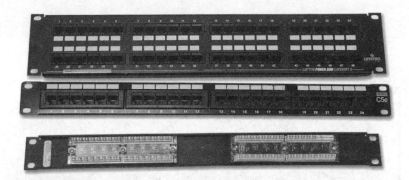

FIGURE 18.10 Typical patch panels

front, enabling you to use short stranded-core UTP *patch cables* (shown in Figure 18.11) to connect the patch panel to the switch. Premade patch cables make it simple to get multiple colors for organization and often come with booted (reinforced) connectors.

Local Lingo

Patch cable A specific length (usually short, but can be up to 100 feet) of cable terminated at each end with a plug or socket. Also called a patch cord.

FIGURE 18.11 Typical patch cable

Software Protocols

Protocols handle data transfer details, such as how to pack and unpack data with protocol-specific *packet* formats. The most famous is the *Transmission Control Protocol/Internet Protocol (TCP/IP)* used by most modern networks, including the Internet—though TCP/IP is technically a big group of protocols. Let's look at a simple example.

Local Lingo

Packet and frame The terms *packet* and *frame* get used interchangeably quite often, but they actually mean different things. A *frame* is used in Ethernet networks, and a *packet* is used in TCP/IP networks.

When data moving between systems must arrive in good order, we use the connection-oriented *Transmission Control Protocol (TCP)*. If it's not a big deal for data to miss a bit or two, then the connectionless *User Datagram Protocol (UDP)* is the way to go. Most TCP/IP applications use TCP (that's why we don't call it UDP/IP) because it transfers data reliably.

TCP accomplishes this with communication rules that require both machines to acknowledge each other to send and receive data. UDP is much faster because it lacks these checks—which is fine if your data can tolerate some errors or the chance of them is low. This speed might be more important than a few dropped frames for a Voice over IP call or video chat.

Travel Assistance

Chapter 21 explores many specific TCP/IP protocols in the 901 objectives.

Local Network Organization

Once everyone is connected to a network, users need to be able to share resources and solve common problems such as who can use which resources (and how). Microsoft designed three ways to organize Windows networks, but some have been adopted by the entire computer industry and apply to Mac OS X and other operating systems. Let's see how they compare.

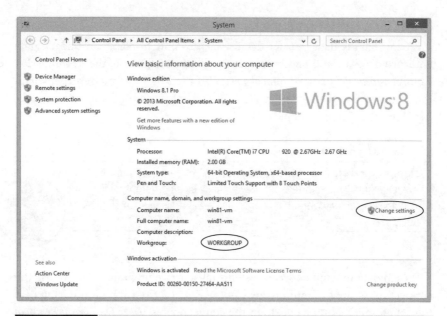

FIGURE 18.12   Default workgroup

Workgroups

By default, most new Windows installs are assigned to a generic *workgroup* (creatively named WORKGROUP) because only networked computers in the same workgroup can share resources. Workgroups lack central control; this is fine for small networks but isn't suitable for securing those with many users. You can see your system's workgroup (see Figure 18.12) by opening the System applet, and you can change it by clicking Change settings.

Because workgroups lack central control, you have to log on to each individual system to use its resources, which means you either need a password for a local account on each system or the system's administrator needs to set one up for you. All of these accounts quickly become an administrative chore as the workgroup grows.

Domains

Larger networks use *domains,* in which a server running Windows Server (see Figure 18.13) controls access to network resources. An administrator creates a domain on the Windows Server system, making it the *domain controller (DC)* and creates new *domain accounts* for the users.

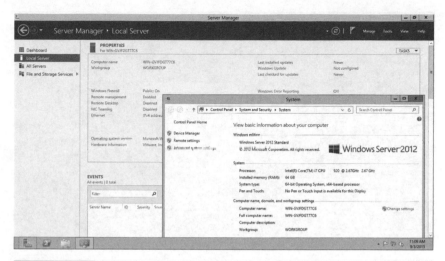

FIGURE 18.13 Windows Server

Exam Tip

The *netdom* command can manage a domain from the CLI. Administrators use netdom to join workstation computers to domains, manage computer accounts, and establish trust relationships between domains.

Each system needs to join the domain, which kicks it off the workgroup. When you log on to any computer in the domain, Windows prompts you for a user name (see Figure 18.14) to log on directly with the domain. All user accounts are stored on the domain controller, which functions as the *authentication server*, though each system still creates a local user directory when you log on. You can log on using <domain>\<domain user name>, so the user Mike on the domain totalhome.local would log on with totalhome.local\Mike.

Local Lingo

Single sign-on (SSO) Having a single account that can log on to any system on the domain. SSO permits a user to access multiple applications or resources with one user name and one password.

FIGURE 18.14   Domain logon screen

Homegroups

Workgroups provide almost no security and require lots of signing on to access resources; domains provide single sign-on and security at a cost. To split the difference, Microsoft introduced *HomeGroup* in Windows 7.

Travel Advisory

Homegroups are not available in Windows Vista, Mac OS X, or any Linux distro.

Most people just want to share types of data, such as music, so homegroups just share Windows libraries. A homegroup connects computers (which can only join one homegroup at a time) via a common password—no extra user names required.

You create homegroups from the HomeGroup applet. If you're in one already, you'll have options to edit relevant settings. If you're in a workgroup and not a homegroup, you can click the Create a homegroup button to bring up the Create a Homegroup dialog (see Figure 18.15), from which you select Library types. When you click Next, you'll see the generated homegroup password (see Figure 18.16).

If you go to another computer on the network and open the HomeGroup applet, it will prompt you to join the existing homegroup. Just click the Join

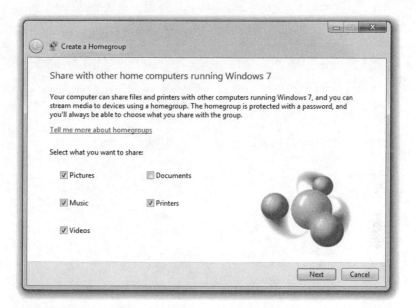

Create a Homegroup dialog

The homegroup's password

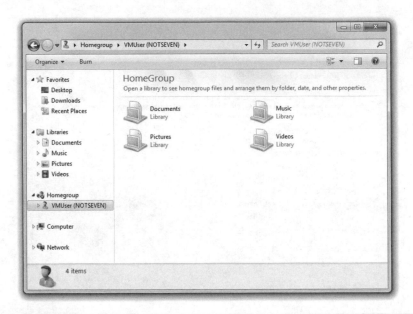

FIGURE 18.17   Using homegroups

now button, enter the password, and pick Libraries to share. You can browse your new homegroup through Windows Explorer or File Explorer (see Figure 18.17). To add additional folders or libraries, right-click either, select Share with (as shown in Figure 18.18), and choose a Homegroup option.

Network Addressing

A network address must uniquely identify the machine, and it must locate that machine within the larger network. In a TCP/IP network, an *IP address* identifies a device and the network on which it resides; what this address looks like depends on the Internet Protocol version.

IPv4 Address Notation

An *Internet Protocol version 4 (IPv4)* address is expressed in *dotted-octet notation*—four sets of eight binary numbers (octets) separated by periods. The binary form (11001010.00100010.00010000.00001011) isn't human-friendly, so we usually use a decimal form (202.34.16.11).

Part of an IP address identifies the network (the network ID), and the rest identifies the local computer (the host ID, or host). NICs use a *subnet mask* to indicate which part identifies the network ID and which identifies the host by

FIGURE 18.18 The Share with menu

blocking out (masking) the network portion. A 255 group is in the network ID, and zeros are in the host ID. Because the first three subnet mask octets in the following example are 255, the network ID is 192.168.4 and the host ID is 33:

IP address: 192.168.4.33
Subnet mask: 255.255.255.0

Computers on the same LAN must have the same network ID and unique host IDs. Two computers with the exact same IP address create an *IP conflict*; they won't be able to talk to each other, and other computers won't know where to send data. An IPv4 address can't end with 0 or a 255, so our sample network supports 254 addresses from 192.168.4.1 to 192.168.4.254.

Exam Tip

Know the basic differences between subnet mask notation formats.

Originally, subnet masks fell into A, B, or C "classes," where Class C was 255.255.255.0, Class B was 255.255.0.0, and Class A was 255.0.0.0. One Class B network ID left two full octets (16 bits) for 64,534 unique host IDs ($2^{16} - 2$).

TABLE 18.1	CIDR Subnets		
Binary	**Decimal**	**IDs**	**Shorthand**
11111111.11111111.11111111.00000000	255.255.255.0	254	/24
11111111.11111111.11110000.00000000	255.255.240.0	4094	/20

This system is long gone, but it's still common to see subnet masks expressed in one to three groups of 255.

The current *Classless Inter-Domain Routing (CIDR)* system works well in binary—where you make subnets with any number of 1s in the mask—but these octets tend to look odd to new techs when presented in decimal (see Table 18.1).

Local Lingo

Whack   With CIDR, techs write shorthand for how many binary 1s a mask has. A mask with 24 1s is /24 in shorthand—pronounced *whack twenty-four.*

IPv6 Address Notation

The 32-bit IPv4 standard offers 4 billion addresses; this seemed like plenty in the beginning, but the Internet Engineering Task Force (IETF) had to develop a replacement, *Internet Protocol version 6 (IPv6)*, to support enough addresses for the foreseeable future. IPv6 notation uses up to eight colon-separated groups (unofficially called *fields* or *hextets*), each containing a hexadecimal number between 0000 and FFFF.

Exam Tip

Homegroups require IPv6, though it's enabled by default.

It has "up to" eight groups because there are two ways to shorten the written form:

- Leading zeros can be dropped per group, so 00CF becomes CF and 0000 becomes 0.
- Once per address, you can omit any number of consecutive all-zero groups, leaving just the two colons at either end.

Here's a full address followed by a shorter form applying these rules:

2001:0000:0000:3210:0800:200C:00CF:1234
2001::3210:800:200C:CF:1234

IPv6 still has subnets, but we append the "/x" from CIDR with the IP address itself: FEDC::CF:0:BA98:1234/64.

Obtaining IP Addresses

With IPv4, IP addresses come from one of two places: either you type in a *static* IP address yourself or you receive a *dynamic* IP address from a pool of IP addresses that the network temporarily leases to connected systems via *Dynamic Host Configuration Protocol (DHCP)*. In DHCP, which Windows uses by default, systems receive their IP address, subnet mask, default gateway address, and DNS address from the *DHCP server*. If the system is configured to obtain an automatic address but can't do so, the OS will use *Automatic Private IP Addressing (APIPA)* to set a 16-bit subnet mask (255.255.0.0) and randomly choose an address from 169.254.0.1 to 169.254.255.254. The system will broadcast this random address on the subnet and use it if no other system responds.

Exam Tip	
Windows defaults to an APIPA address when it is configured for dynamic IP addressing but can't find a DHCP server.	

With IPv6, you can have multiple (usually three) IP addresses on a single NIC. When a computer running IPv6 boots, it gives itself a *link-local address,* the equivalent to IPv4's APIPA address. Because APIPA is a fallback in IPv4, the use of an APIPA address can indicate a loss of network connectivity or a problem with the DHCP server; IPv6 systems always have a link-local address. The first 64 bits of a link-local address are always FE80:0000:0000:0000 (which shortens to FE80::).

OS developers have two options for the last 64 bits of an IPv6 address. The method Windows uses is to generate a random value when you activate a NIC and never change it. Linux and Mac OS X use the other method: build it from the MAC address of the network card (called the *Extended Unique Identifier, 64-bit,* or *EUI-64*).

To get on the Internet, an IPv6 system needs a *global address,* and most systems have two; one is static, while the other changes to make tracking your system by IP address harder. To get a global address, your system locates the default gateway router by sending a router solicitation (RS) message; the router responds with a router advertisement (RA) containing the network ID, subnet, and DNS server. The system combines the network ID and subnet into the *prefix* and then generates the rest of the address.

Travel Advisory

A global address is a true Internet address. Another system with a global address can directly communicate with your system unless you have some form of firewall.

Interconnecting Networks with Routers

One of the big reasons to make a network is to communicate with computers on other networks; this is what routers do. Routers have at least two IP addresses: one on your LAN and another on the "next" network—usually your ISP or another router at your company. The LAN-side address, called the *default gateway,* is where your computer sends traffic bound for locations outside of your network ID.

You'll rarely actually type an IP address outside of your network ID—*Domain Name Service (DNS)* servers keep databases of IP addresses and corresponding human-friendly *domain names.* These *DNS servers* translate an address such as www.google.com or www.totalsem.com into the IP address your system needs to send packets to the right place.

Objective 18.02 # Installing and Configuring a LAN

Now that we've covered the concepts and components, let's install a network. For network connectivity, you need four things in place:

- **Network architecture and infrastructure**   This is the cabling in the walls, the switch for the LAN, and other devices.

- **NIC**   The physical network adapter connecting the computer to network infrastructure.
- **Protocol**   A format the computer systems use to communicate.
- **Network client**   The interface that allows the computer system to speak to the protocol.

Modern Windows versions install TCP/IP, the Client for Microsoft Networks, and File and Printer Sharing for Microsoft Networks when you install the NIC. If you want to share resources with other network users, you still need to *enable* Microsoft's File and Printer Sharing.

Installing Network Infrastructure

Almost all of the networking a CompTIA A+ tech does will be outside of the wall outlet in the work area. The 901 exam doesn't expect you to install the full structured-cabling setup behind that outlet, but it does expect you to know the tools and processes.

Structured cabling doesn't start with a trip to the electronics store where you buy retail cables in the exact length you need to reach every work area—you buy cable on spools, run it to the right length, cut it, and add the connectors (such as a female wall outlet) yourself. You can use the same basic process to make your own patch cables with male connectors on each end, so let's look at how you make a UTP patch cable.

Preparing the Cable

For a patch cable, use stranded UTP cable matching the CAT level of your horizontal cabling. The basic tool is a RJ-45 *crimper* (Figure 18.19) with built-in *wire stripper* and *wire snips*. Stranded and solid-core cable require different crimps; make sure you have the right kind. First, cut the cable square with the RJ-45 crimper or scissors; then use the built-in wire stripper to strip a half inch of plastic jacket off the end of the cable (see Figure 18.20). Once the cable is stripped, you're ready to wire the connector.

Wiring Male Connectors

If you wire your own connectors, you can technically order the wires however you like if you use the same pairings on each end, but you should pick either the TIA/EIA 568A *(T568A)* or the TIA/EIA 568B *(T568B)* standard—and save yourself time later by keeping good records. The pins in UTP are numbered

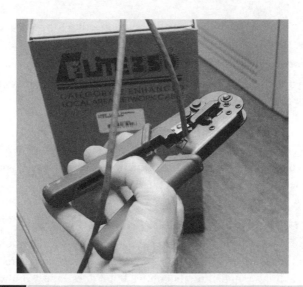

FIGURE 18.19   Crimper and snips

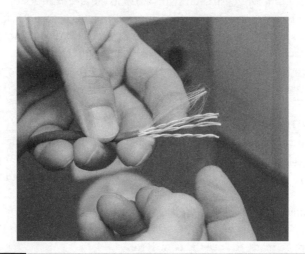

FIGURE 18.20   Properly stripped cable

(as shown in Figure 18.21), but each wire just has a standardized color, as detailed in Table 18.2.

Travel Advisory

UTP connectors have CAT levels, too. Don't even try to use a CAT 5e RJ-45 connector with a CAT 6 cable.

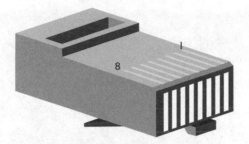

FIGURE 18.21 RJ-45 pin numbers

TABLE 18.2 UTP Cabling Color Chart

Pin	T568A	T568B	Pin	T568A	T568B
1	White/ Green	White/ Orange	5	White/ Blue	White/ Blue
2	Green	Orange	6	Orange	Green
3	White/ Orange	White/ Green	7	White/ Brown	White/ Brown
4	Blue	Blue	8	Brown	Brown

To wire your connector or *crimp,* carefully insert each individual wire (as shown in Figure 18.22) into the correct location according to either TIA/EIA 568A or B. Unravel as little as possible. Next, insert the crimp into the crimper and press (see Figure 18.23). The crimper has a stop to keep you from pressing too hard.

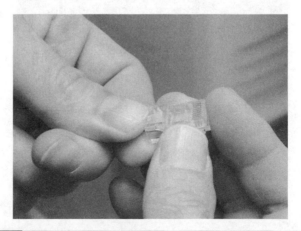

FIGURE 18.22 Inserting the individual strands

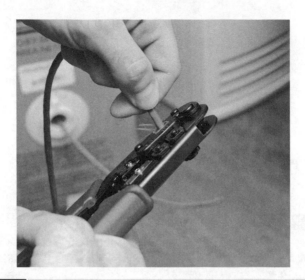

FIGURE 18.23 Crimping the cable

On a nicely crimped patch cable, the plastic jacket should extend into the crimp, and the joint should be protected with a boot (see Figure 18.24). Don't forget to slide each boot onto the patch cable before you crimp both ends. Next, use a *cable tester* (shown in Figure 18.25) to verify the individual wires are properly located and connected.

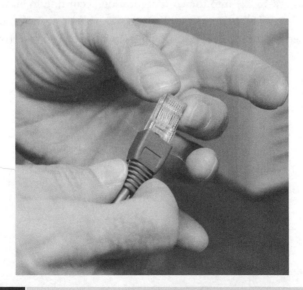

FIGURE 18.24 Adding a boot

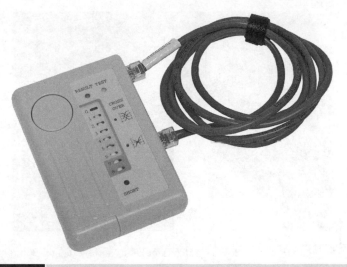

FIGURE 18.25 Typical tester

Wiring Female Connectors

With a typical horizontal cabling run, you'll connect the work-area end to the back of a wall outlet with a female connector, and the telecommunications-room end will connect to the back of a patch panel's female connector. You typically use a *punchdown tool* (see Figure 18.26) to connect the cable to a *110 block* (also called a *110-punchdown block*) which is wired to the female connector. The punchdown tool forces each wire into a small metal-lined groove (shown in Figure 18.27), where the metal lining slices the cladding to contact the wire.

FIGURE 18.26 Punchdown tool

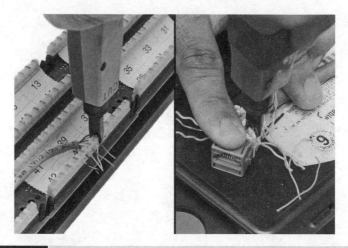

FIGURE 18.27 Punching down a patch panel (left) and modular jack (right)

A work-area wall outlet (see Figure 18.28) consists of one or two female jacks, a mounting bracket, and a faceplate.

FIGURE 18.28 Typical work area outlet

Installing a NIC

The NIC links your system to the network infrastructure. If you aren't using a NIC built into the motherboard, you'll need to install a USB or expansion-card NIC by following the manufacturer's instructions. Windows will automatically detect, install, and configure most NICs—you almost never need to configure one manually.

The 902 exam still expects you to know some manual configuration options. To get to these settings, open the Network Connections applet, right-click Local Area Connection, select Properties, and click the Configure button just below the NIC listing in the Local Area Connections Properties dialog. Here are the options you should know:

- Modern NICs in *full-duplex* mode send and receive data at the same time, but most NICs and switches have an *autosensing* option to accommodate very old *half-duplex* devices that can't send and receive simultaneously, as well as explicit (manual) duplex settings.
- Manually reduce the NIC's speed for compatibility with older networks.
- *Wake-on-LAN (WoL)* settings (see Figure 18.29) enable a NIC to wake the computer (from a sleep state) when it receives a "magic packet" telling the system to wake up.

FIGURE 18.29 Wake-on-LAN settings on the Power Management tab

Exam Tip

CMOS system settings control Wake-on-LAN for on-board NICs.

- *Quality of Service (QoS)* enables you to specify a priority for particular kinds of network traffic. The switch or router enforce the priorities, but the NIC helps by properly tagging its packets according to settings in the Advanced tab of its Properties dialog (see Figure 18.30).

Travel Advisory

We will look at how QoS helps busy networks in Chapter 20. A VLAN is an advanced feature in better switches. You won't see VLANs on the CompTIA A+ exams.

Once the NIC is installed, connect it to the wall outlet with a patch cable that can take typical work-area abuse, such as moving equipment and an

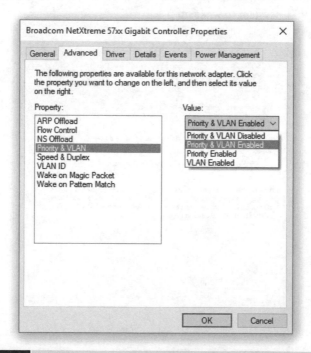

FIGURE 18.30   Network adapter Priority (QoS) & VLAN setting

occasional kick. The work area may seem relatively simple, but the extra abuse makes it the source of most network failures. When a user can't access the network and you suspect a broken cable, start in the work area.

Travel Advisory

Both NICs and switches have LED *status indicators* called *link lights* that can confirm your new connection. There are no real standards, but it's a safe bet that one indicates connection status; if all of them are unlit, there's no physical connection. Consult the motherboard or NIC manual to decipher other meanings.

Configuring a Network Client

For your system to see others and be seen on the network, you need a network client installed and configured properly. However, the Client for Microsoft Networks installed with the OS rarely needs manual configuration—the Properties button is even disabled in Windows 7 and later. Unless you're told to do something particular by a network administrator, leave this alone.

If you do need to reach it, it's in the adapter's Properties dialog. In Windows Vista, click Start, right-click Network, and select Properties | Manage network connections. In Windows 7 and later it's in Control Panel | Network and Sharing Center | Change adapter settings. From here, right-click your adapter and select Properties.

Manually Configuring TCP/IPv4

By default, TCP/IP will fetch the IP address, subnet mask, default gateway, and DNS servers from the network's DHCP server. As far as the CompTIA A+ certification exams are concerned, if your systems need static values, Network+ techs and administrators will give them to you. The following steps describe how to do it manually.

Exam Tip

The 901 objectives refer to these as *client-side DNS settings* and *client-side DHCP*.

---

1. Open the Properties dialog for the appropriate network adapter.
2. Highlight Internet Protocol Version 4 (TCP/IPv4) and click the Properties button.

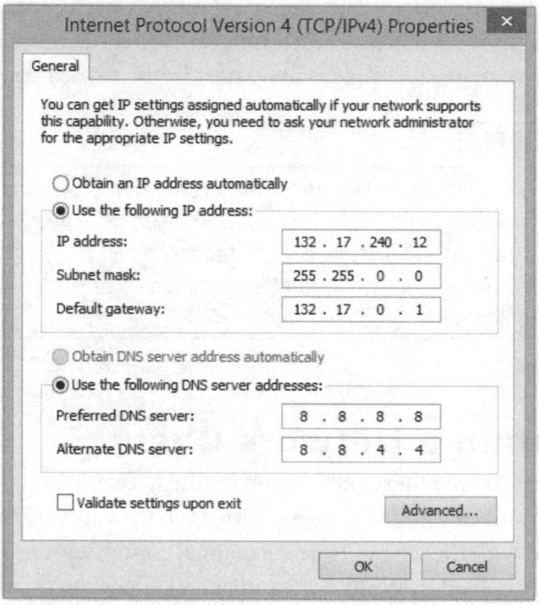

Internet Protocol Version 4 (TCP/IPv4) Properties ☒

General

You can get IP settings assigned automatically if your network supports
this capability. Otherwise, you need to ask your network administrator
for the appropriate IP settings.

○ Obtain an IP address automatically

◉ Use the following IP address:

IP address: 132 . 17 . 240 . 12

Subnet mask: 255 . 255 . 0 . 0

Default gateway: 132 . 17 . 0 . 1

○ Obtain DNS server address automatically

◉ Use the following DNS server addresses:

Preferred DNS server: 8 . 8 . 8 . 8

Alternate DNS server: 8 . 8 . 4 . 4

☐ Validate settings upon exit   Advanced...

            OK   Cancel

FIGURE 18.31 IP settings

3. In the Properties dialog box (shown in Figure 18.31), click the radio
   button next to Use the following IP address.

4. Enter the IP address in the appropriate fields.

5. Press the TAB key to skip to the Subnet mask field and type over the
   automatic value.

6. Optionally, enter the IP address for a default gateway.

7. Optionally, enter DNS server IP addresses; Figure 18.31 uses Google's
   public DNS servers.

TCP/IP Tools

Every modern OS comes with tools to test and configure TCP/IP. Those that
you're most likely to use in the field are the CLI utilities ping, ipconfig/ifconfig,
nslookup, and tracert/traceroute.

- You can *ping* an IP address or DNS name to determine if (and how
  quickly) your system can talk to it, as long as it isn't configured to
  ignore ping requests. For example, **ping wc3.org** tests if and how
  quickly the World Wide Web Consortium (WC3) server responds.

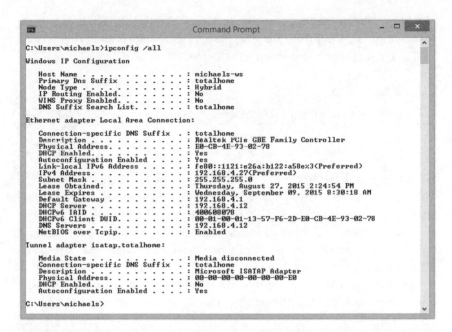

```
                              Command Prompt                      - □  ×

C:\Users\michaels>ipconfig /all

Windows IP Configuration

    Host Name . . . . . . . . . . . . : michaels-ws
    Primary Dns Suffix  . . . . . . . : totalhome
    Node Type . . . . . . . . . . . . : Hybrid
    IP Routing Enabled. . . . . . . . : No
    WINS Proxy Enabled. . . . . . . . : No
    DNS Suffix Search List. . . . . . : totalhome

Ethernet adapter Local Area Connection:

    Connection-specific DNS Suffix  . : totalhome
    Description . . . . . . . . . . . : Realtek PCIe GBE Family Controller
    Physical Address. . . . . . . . . : E0-CB-4E-93-02-78
    DHCP Enabled. . . . . . . . . . . : Yes
    Autoconfiguration Enabled . . . . : Yes
    Link-local IPv6 Address . . . . . : fe80::1121:e26a:b122:a58e%3(Preferred)
    IPv4 Address. . . . . . . . . . . : 192.168.4.27(Preferred)
    Subnet Mask . . . . . . . . . . . : 255.255.255.0
    Lease Obtained. . . . . . . . . . : Thursday, August 27, 2015 2:24:54 PM
    Lease Expires . . . . . . . . . . : Wednesday, September 09, 2015 8:30:18 AM
    Default Gateway . . . . . . . . . : 192.168.4.1
    DHCP Server . . . . . . . . . . . : 192.168.4.12
    DHCPv6 IAID . . . . . . . . . . . : 400600078
    DHCPv6 Client DUID. . . . . . . . : 00-01-00-01-13-57-F6-2D-E0-CB-4E-93-02-78
    DNS Servers . . . . . . . . . . . : 192.168.4.12
    NetBIOS over Tcpip. . . . . . . . : Enabled

Tunnel adapter isatap.totalhome:

    Media State . . . . . . . . . . . : Media disconnected
    Connection-specific DNS Suffix  . : totalhome
    Description . . . . . . . . . . . : Microsoft ISATAP Adapter
    Physical Address. . . . . . . . . : 00-00-00-00-00-00-00-E0
    DHCP Enabled. . . . . . . . . . . : No
    Autoconfiguration Enabled . . . . : Yes

C:\Users\michaels>
```

FIGURE 18.32 An ipconfig /all command on Windows 8.1

Windows systems ping four times by default, but Mac OS X and Linux ping until you issue the break hotkey (CTRL-C).

- In Windows, **ipconfig /all** displays all of your TCP/IP settings (see Figure 18.32), while a bare **ifconfig** accomplishes the same in Mac OS X and Linux. In Windows, ipconfig can also release or renew dynamic IP addresses.

- To check what your DNS server reports for the WC3 host name, use **nslookup wc3.org**, or use a bare **nslookup** command to enter an interactive prompt where you type a host name and press ENTER to look it up (enter **exit** at the prompt or use CTRL-C to quit).

- Discover the route a packet takes the WC3 server with **tracert wc3.org** in Windows or **traceroute wc3.org** in Mac OS X and Linux. If there's a failure between your network and a remote system, this is how you identify where it fails.

Sharing and Security

Windows systems can share files, folders, entire drives, printers, faxes, Internet connections, and much more—but the CompTIA A+ exams limit their interest to folders, printers, and Internet connections. We've already seen how to share with homegroups, but there are other ways to share folders and printers; we'll look at Internet connection sharing in Chapter 21.

Exam Tip

A regular computer sharing its files is a basic *file server*.

Sharing a Folder

The manual way to share a folder is to just right-click it and select Properties | Sharing tab | Advanced Sharing. From here, tick the Share this folder checkbox and name the network share (see Figure 18.33). By default, new Windows shares only have Read permission; click the Permissions button to set your share to Full Control (see Figure 18.34).

You add users and groups or change NTFS permissions from the Security tab of the file/folder Properties dialog. The top section lists users and groups

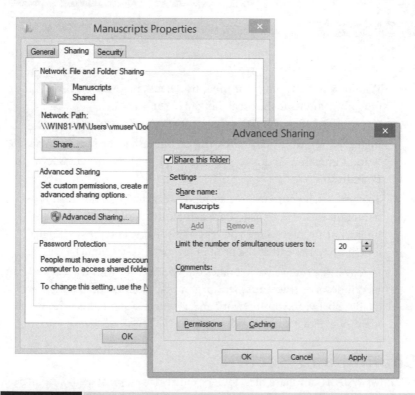

FIGURE 18.33   Advanced Sharing dialog

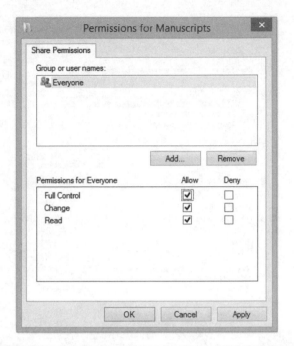

FIGURE 18.34   Setting the share to Full Control

that currently have NTFS permissions for the file/folder, and the bottom section lists NTFS permissions for the selected user or group (see Figure 18.35). Just click the Edit button to make changes.

A simpler (less powerful) method is to right-click a file or folder and select Share (or Share with) | Specific people. This opens the File Sharing dialog, where you can select user accounts from a drop-down list. These will be local accounts unless your system is in a workgroup or domain, in which case you can respectively select or search for remote accounts. When you select one, you can choose Read or Read/Write permissions (see Figure 18.36).

Verifying Shared Folders

Part of sharing securely is verifying that you aren't sharing anything unintentionally. Check what your system shares via Administrative Tools | Computer Management console | System Tools | Shared Folders. The tool has three options: Shares, Sessions, and Open Files. Select Shares to reveal all of your shared folders (see Figure 18.37). Double-click a share to open its Properties dialog for editing.

FIGURE 18.35 Folder Security tab

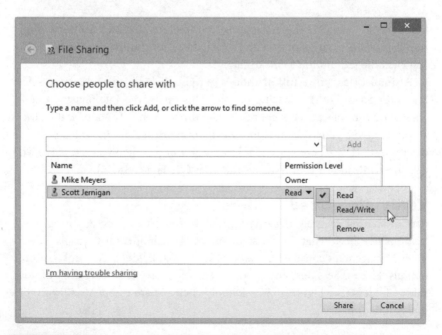

FIGURE 18.36 File Sharing dialog permissions options

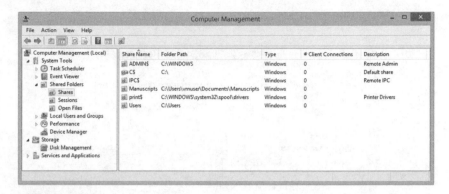

Share Name	Folder Path	Type	# Client Connections	Description
ADMIN$	C:\WINDOWS	Windows	0	Remote Admin
C$	C:\	Windows	0	Default share
IPC$		Windows	0	Remote IPC
Manuscripts	C:\Users\vmuser\Documents\Manuscripts	Windows	0	
print$	C:\WINDOWS\system32\spool\drivers	Windows	0	Printer Drivers
Users	C:\Users	Windows	0	

FIGURE 18.37 Shared Folders tool in Computer Management

NTFS vs. Share Permissions

Each OS uses separate network sharing permissions to grant or restrict access to shared resources. Beyond these, file- or folder-level permissions (such as NTFS) also affect network shares. Windows uses NTFS to authorize local and network users: even if you grant access via network share permissions, NTFS permissions still say what users can do with the resource.

If you share from an NTFS drive, you must set *both* network and NTFS permissions to grant access. The shortcut is to give everyone Full Control network permissions, and then use NTFS permissions to precisely control who has what access.

Administrative Shares

Windows has default shares: all hard drives, *%systemroot%*, and others depending on Windows version. These *administrative shares* grant local administrators access to these resources only when they log in remotely. You can't change permissions on these shares, and Windows will re-create them on reboot if you delete them.

Sharing Printers

If printer-sharing services are loaded and enabled, you can share printers with the same process you use to share drives and folders. In Windows Vista, go to the Printers folder in the Control Panel or Start menu and right-click the printer you wish to share. Select Sharing and then click *Share this printer* and give it a name. In Windows 7/8/8.1/10, open Devices and Printers in the Control Panel, right-click the printer you wish to share, select Printer properties, and then select the Sharing tab (see Figure 18.38), where you can check *Share this printer* and give it a name.

FIGURE 18.38 Giving a name to a shared printer on Windows 8.1

Exam Tip

A computer sharing its printer over the network is a simple *print server*.

 **Objective 18.03** **Troubleshooting Networks**

The secret to network troubleshooting on the CompTIA A+ exams is that the focus is on getting a single computer back on the network. You might need to check a switch or verify another system's connectivity in the process, but answers will focus on getting a single system up and running.

> **Travel Advisory**
>
> This section troubleshoots the LAN. Chapter 20 builds on what you've learned here to troubleshoot Internet connectivity.

CompTIA likes to ask questions about "no connectivity" or "intermittent connectivity," which could be physical connectivity problems, and trouble accessing a particular resource over an otherwise working connection.

Physical Connections

Quality, professionally installed cabling rarely fails, but you need to know what to do if it does. Let's start with simple symptoms of a physical problem:

- Physical interruptions stand out in Windows—a red X displays over the network icon in the notification area (as shown in Figure 18.39).
- Errors such as "No server found" or the inability to see other systems on the network.

If you suspect a physical connection problem, start with obvious possibilities in the work area, and work toward problems that are less obvious or located elsewhere.

- Check link lights on the NIC. If none are lit, there's no connection; confirm both ends of the patch cable are connected. Swap the patch cable for one you know is good. Plug the system into a known-good outlet.
- Confirm the NIC is enabled in Device Manager. See if nearby systems can access the network or resource. If all the systems on a switch can't see the network, you have a suspect—the switch or its connection to the larger network.

FIGURE 18.39 Windows 7 red X error notification icon

- Before you blame the structured cabling, confirm the other end of the horizontal run connects to a running switch. If it doesn't, connect it properly and check the link lights.

Now that you have the simplest problems out of the way, let's consider how to test for damage in the NIC itself or the horizontal cabling run, and how to confirm we're testing the right cable in case it is mislabeled.

Check the NIC

A bad NIC can cause these problems. The NIC's female connector is easy to damage, but diagnostics provided by the OS or NIC manufacturer may include a *loopback test* that sends data out of the NIC to see if it comes back. A true external loopback test with a *loopback plug* (see Figure 18.40) tests the connecting pins; an internal loopback test only checks the circuitry that sends and receives. If a NIC is bad, replace it.

Cable Testing

Anyone with a network should own a midrange time-domain reflectometer (TDR) tester such as the Fluke MicroScanner. A TDR measures impedance in network cabling; if it finds any, the cable is damaged. When you test a cable run, always include patch cables. If a horizontal run is bad, I call my installer to replace it.

FIGURE 18.40   Loopback plug

> ### Exam Tip
>
> The 901 objectives include multimeters in networking tools. Multimeters are a bit of a Swiss Army knife for testing anything that carries a current. You can certainly use a multimeter to test whether a dead switch is connected to a good outlet, for example. In a pinch, you can use one to test cables you don't have a regular tester for—but this is often tedious; a multimeter should be your last resort for testing network cable.

Toners

Even in well-planned networks that don't turn into a rat's-nest of cable, labels fall off and people miscount which port to label. In the real world, you may have to locate or *trace* cables and ports to test them.

Network techs use a *toner* (see Figure 18.41) with two components. The *tone generator* connects to the cable with alligator clips, tiny hooks, or a network

FIGURE 18.41   Fox and Hound, a toner made by Triplett Corporation

jack, and it sends an electrical signal along the wire. The *tone probe* emits a sound when it is placed near the cable carrying this signal.

Other Connection Failures

If you can't connect to a resource on the first try, these configuration issues could be the culprit:

- Did your system receive an appropriate address from the network, or does it just have an APIPA/link-local address? Confirm the router or DHCP server are working and reachable.
- Do you have the right share name? Go check at the serving system.
- Do you have the required user name/password? Ask someone who might have this knowledge, or double-check that your account has access.
- Do you have permission to use/access/connect to the shared resource? Confirm you have the correct permissions.
- Are you on the right homegroup/domain/workgroup? Check your system and the sharing system to verify the workgroup/domain, and double-check your homegroup password.
- Is the folder or printer shared? Share it!
- Does the folder or printer exist? Make sure the serving system still hosts the folder or printer you want. Try installing the network printer if you haven't yet.

If you suddenly can't use or connect to a resource you've used before, make sure:

- You can see the resource using Network.
- The serving system is on.
- The computer is physically connected to the serving system.

CLI Troubleshooting Tools

The 901 objectives include two Windows CLI commands you can use to gather information about your network.

The net Command

If you don't know the names of computers on a network, **net view** will show you a list. If you discovered one named "server1," **net view server1** will show shares on that machine and whether they are mapped drives:

```
C:\>net view server1
Shared resources at SERVER1
Share name  Type  Used as  Comment
-------------------------------------------------------------
FREDC       Disk
Research    Disk  W:
The command completed successfully.
```

The net command can also map a share; for example, **net use x: \\server1\ research** would map drive X: to the SERVER1's Research share.

The nbtstat Command

The *nbtstat* command, which predates Windows, is short for NetBIOS over TCP/IP Statistics. Long ago, Windows used NetBIOS for many aspects of LAN file sharing; now, bits of NetBIOS hang on as a way for Windows to resolve host names when a DNS server is not available.

Although not as useful as it once was, nbtstat can still help troubleshoot naming issues in small workgroups. Specifically, you can use it to see your system's NetBIOS name, look up the name of another system by IP address, and list the name and IP address of systems in your local NetBIOS cache.

CHECKPOINT

✔**Objective 18.01: Networking Concepts and Components** In order for networks to interconnect hosts that share and access each other's resources, the networks need shared connectivity standards, addressing methods that enable clients and servers to find each other, and shared protocols that hosts can use to communicate. Most local area networks use Ethernet standards that connect a NIC in each host to a switch with UTP cabling runs of up to 100 meters; the switch uses each NICs MAC address to repeat frames to the correct host.

LANs connect to wide area networks such as the Internet via a router. Most LAN and WAN networks use the TCP/IP protocol stack, and LANs are commonly organized into workgroups, domains, or home-groups. When TCP/IP is in use, each system on the LAN has one or more IPv4 or IPv6 addresses that enable routers to direct packets between interconnected LANs.

✔**Objective 18.02: Installing and Configuring a LAN**   A functioning network connection requires a link to the network infrastructure, as well as a properly installed and configured NIC, network client, and protocol stack. If you have to manually configure static IPv4 settings, you'll enter the IP address, subnet mask, default gateway, and DNS servers provided by a network tech or administrator. You can use CLI tools ping, ipconfig/ifconfig, nslookup, and tracert/traceroute to investigate issues with your TCP/IP configuration.

Share individual folders or printers by right-clicking and navigating to the Sharing tab of the Properties dialog; you can also share folders by right-clicking and selecting Share with | Specific people. Sharing securely requires verifying you are only sharing what you intend, confirming your NTFS and share permissions are in harmony, and guarding your administrative shares by keeping administrator passwords secure.

✔**Objective 18.03: Troubleshooting Networks**   Look for errors that point to physical disconnection. Check the link lights on the NIC and switch. Check the cabling from the work area to the horizontal run. Check the NIC with a true external loopback using a loopback plug if possible. Tools for testing cables and connectivity include cable testers and tone probes. If the problem isn't physical, check common configuration issues such as the share name, user name and password, network share and NTFS permissions, and correct homegroup/domain/workgroup membership. Make sure the resource exists and is still shared. If you suddenly lose access or connectivity, confirm you can see the resource in Network, and verify that the serving system is on and both systems have good connectivity.

REVIEW QUESTIONS

1. To provide a physical connection from a computer to a network, what must be installed?
   A. A switch
   B. A router
   C. A NIC
   D. A crossover cable

2. What is the maximum distance for a 10/100/1000BaseT segment?
   A. 1000 meters
   B. 330 meters
   C. 185 meters
   D. 100 meters

3. Brad has three Windows 7 computers that he wants to use to share media libraries, such as movies and pictures. One is in the upstairs study, one is in his bedroom, and third is a laptop that he'll use primarily in the kitchen. His house is professionally wired, so it has RJ-45 jacks available in the appropriate places. How should he set up his network to share most easily?

   A. Turn one of the computers into a domain controller and join the other two to the same domain.

   B. Have all three computers join the same workgroup.

   C. Have all three computers join the same homegroup.

   D. Replace his Windows PCs with Mac OS X systems.

4. Which CLI tool enables you to see the computers connected to a workgroup or domain?

   A. net use

   B. net view

   C. net see

   D. net scan

5. Which tool would you use to attach a female connector to a UTP cable?

   A. Wire stripper

   B. RJ-45 crimper

   C. 110-punchdown block

   D. Punchdown tool

6. Simon's Windows system can't contact a DHCP server to obtain an IP address automatically, but he can still communicate with other systems on his subnet. What makes this possible?

   A. Subnet masking

   B. Windows Internet Naming Service

   C. Automatic Private IP Addressing

   D. Client for Microsoft Networks

7. Everything worked fine on your 10/100/1000BaseT network yesterday, but today no one can connect to the server. The server seems to be in good running order. Which of the following is the most likely problem?

   A. A switch is malfunctioning.

   B. Someone changed all the passwords for server access.

   C. Someone's NIC LED is flashing amber.

   D. The server's cable is wired as TIA/EIA 568A, and all the others are wired as TIA/EIA 568B.

8. How far apart can two devices that share the same 10/100/1000BaseT switch be placed?
   A. 1000 meters
   B. 330 meters
   C. 200 meters
   D. 100 meters

9. In a TCP/IPv4 network, the two parts of an IP address are the _____ and the _____.
   A. Network ID, host ID
   B. IP address, subnet mask
   C. Client, server
   D. TCP address, IP address

10. What is special about plenum-grade network cabling?
    A. Plenum-grade cabling doubles the bandwidth throughput speed.
    B. Plenum-grade cabling increases the maximum length of Ethernet network segments from 100 meters to 185 meters.
    C. Plenum-grade cabling does not give off toxic fumes when burned.
    D. Plenum-grade cabling has no special qualities: it is simply a marketing term.

11. Which device emits a sound when near a cable carrying a specific signal?
    A. Tone generator
    B. Cable tester
    C. Tone probe
    D. Patch cable

REVIEW ANSWERS

1. **C** A system must have a network interface card (NIC) to join any type of network.

2. **D** 10/100/1000BaseT has a maximum segment distance of 100 meters.

3. **C** Because all three computers run Windows 7, putting them in the same homegroup is the easiest way to share libraries. A workgroup would work, of course, but require that he also create user accounts on each computer and share folders with those specific user accounts.

4. **B**   The **net view** command quickly shows computers connected to a workgroup or domain.

5. **D**   You use a punchdown tool to secure individual wires to the 110-punchdown block in the female connector.

6. **C**   Automatic Private IP Addressing is the Windows feature that makes it possible for Simon's system to communicate with other systems on his subnet, even though he can't contact a DHCP server to obtain an IP address.

7. **A**   Although someone might have changed all the passwords or the cables during the night, a bad switch is the most probable answer.

8. **C**   Because each system can be 100 meters from the switch, any two systems can be up to 200 meters apart.

9. **A**   The two parts of an IP address are the network ID and the host ID.

10. **C**   Unlike normal network cabling, plenum-grade cabling doesn't give off toxic fumes when burned. It is usually required by law when stringing cable into a building's plenum space.

11. **C**   The tone probe emits a sound when near a cable carrying a signal from the tone generator.

Wireless Networking

	NEWBIE	SOME EXPERIENCE	EXPERT
ETA	3 hours	2 hours	1 hour

For most users, wireless networks are a simple, attractive alternative to running cable for a wired network—especially in buildings where construction style or historical landmark status make installing cable impractical or impossible.

Objective 19.01   Wireless Networking Basics

Instead of physical wires strung between network *nodes*, wireless networks use either radio waves or beams of infrared light to communicate with one another. The wireless radio wave networks you'll support these days are either based on the *IEEE 802.11* wireless Ethernet standard—known as *Wi-Fi*—or on *Bluetooth* technology. Wireless networks using infrared light via the aging *Infrared Data Association (IrDA)* protocol are vanishingly rare. Finally, cell phone companies also offer Internet access through cellular networks.

Local Lingo

Wi-Fi   Some folks think Wi-Fi stands for *wireless fidelity,* a play on high fidelity audio, but it isn't short for anything; Wi-Fi is just a trademark of the Wi-Fi Alliance, which determines Wi-Fi specifications.

Most modern computing devices come with some form of wireless communication, and these wireless devices use the same protocols and clients as their wired counterparts, but the basic networking scheme differs. Wired Ethernet devices use *carrier sense multiple access/collision detection (CSMA/CD)* to communicate on the same network media without stepping on each other's frames; if they try to transmit at the same time and create a collision, each device picks its own random time to wait before retrying in the hope that they won't collide again.

Wireless devices use a variation, called *carrier sense multiple access/collision avoidance (CSMA/CA)*, in which they can take proactive steps to avoid collisions. They still use the detect-and-retry method, but they can also use the *Request to Send/Clear to Send (RTS/CTS)* protocol. When the wireless medium is clear, the sending node shoots an RTS frame to the receiving node and waits to transmit until the receiving node responds with a CTS frame. The transmitting node also waits for an acknowledgment (ACK) before sending the next frame. It's elegant, but it can hurt performance.

Wireless Networking Components

Wireless networking capabilities of one form or another are built into many modern computing devices. IrDA *transceiver* ports (see Figure 19.1) that could network with nearby devices were once common, but the infrared ports on modern devices enable them to be controlled with a remote or serve as a remote to control other devices. Wi-Fi and Bluetooth, however, are common integrated components, and you can easily add them via PCIe (see Figure 19.2) or USB (see Figure 19.3).

FIGURE 19.1   Infrared transceiver ports on a laptop and PDA

FIGURE 19.2   Wireless PCIe add-on card

FIGURE 19.3   External USB wireless NIC

Wi-Fi devices can communicate directly, but what most of us really want is to integrate them with the rest of our wired network and its high-speed Internet connection with a *wireless access point (WAP).* A WAP centrally connects wireless network nodes into a wireless LAN (WLAN) in the same way a switch connects wired devices into a LAN. Many WAPs also act as high-speed switches and Internet routers (see Figure 19.4).

FIGURE 19.4	Linksys device that acts as wireless access point, switch, and router

Exam Tip

Most network hardware—including WAPs—draw power from an electrical outlet. Advanced WAPs and networked devices such as security cameras can instead run on electricity supplied by a *Power over Ethernet (PoE) injector*. Don't confuse PoE with the inverse technology—Ethernet over Power—which uses electrical lines to transmit Ethernet signals.

Wireless Networking Software

In terms of configuring wireless networking software, you need to do very little. Wireless network adapters are plug and play, so any modern version of Windows immediately recognizes one when you install it, prompting you to load any needed hardware drivers. You will, however, need a utility to set parameters such as your network name.

Each OS includes built-in tools for configuring these settings (see Figure 19.5), or the wireless network adapter vendor may provide one. Using this utility, you can determine link state and signal strength, configure the wireless networking *mode* (discussed next), and set options for security, encryption, power use, and so on.

FIGURE 19.5   Wireless configuration utility in Mac OS X

Wireless Network Modes

The simplest *ad hoc* or *peer-to-peer* wireless network consists of two or more devices communicating directly without cabling or any other intermediary hardware. *Infrastructure mode* wireless networks use a WAP to centralize wireless communication and bridge wireless and wired nodes. Infrastructure is technically more complicated, but it's the default mode and it enables the security, central control, and stability you want in a modern *small office/home office (SOHO)* network. The decentralized free-for-all of ad hoc networks doesn't scale well beyond a few systems, but it does make sense for limited impromptu networks at a study group or meeting, or just to share a file or printer.

Wireless Networking Security

A major complaint against wireless networking is weak security, but the industry has trended toward some type of security by default in recent years. Still, problems with these well-intentioned defaults are common, so it's still important to take a critical look at the settings on new equipment. If frames are floating through the air instead of safely wrapped up inside network cabling—how do you stop an unscrupulous person with the right equipment from reading the data as it passes?

Wireless networks use three methods to secure access to the network itself and secure data in flight: MAC address filtering, authentication, and data encryption. There are also measures we can take to reduce the likelihood our network will be targeted in the first place. Let's take a look at these practices first, followed by the methods for securing the network itself.

SSID

Wireless devices want to be heard, and WAPs broadcast their *service set identifier (SSID)* or *network name* to announce their presence. Unfortunately, this default SSID can give away important clues about the WAP's manufacturer (and maybe even model) that make it easier for attackers to exploit known vulnerabilities in the hardware.

Always change the default SSID to something unique, and change the password right away. Older default SSID names and passwords are well known and widely available online. When you pick a unique SSID, think about whether the name makes your network a more interesting target or gives away information an attacker could use to physically locate the WAP. Most newer WAPs require you to create a unique SSID, user name, and password.

> **Exam Tip**
>
> CompTIA lists changing the default SSID and disabling SSID broadcast on the WAP as steps for securing a new wireless network. These practices for managing your SSID don't secure your network, but they help avoid the attention of someone targeting known vulnerabilities with specific hardware and default settings.

Access Point Placement and Radio Power

You can hide your network from outsiders to limit risk by keeping your signal from extending outside your home or office. Place omni-directional antennas that send and receive in all directions near the center of the physical space. If your WAP can adjust the radio power levels of the antenna, decrease radio power until you can get reception inside the target network space, but not outside.

Exam Tip	
Most WAPs have physical Ethernet ports that are not password-protected or encrypted. Place the WAP where unscrupulous folks can't get to it.	

MAC Filtering

Most WAPs support MAC address filtering to limit access to your wireless network using the physical, hard-wired address of each wireless network adapter. A table stored in the WAP—the *access control list (ACL)*—lists MAC addresses permitted (*white list*) or excluded (*black list*) from the wireless network.

WEP

WEP encryption was meant to secure wirelessly transmitted data with standard 40-bit encryption; many vendors also support 104-bit encryption (which some advertise as 128-bit). Unfortunately, WEP contains some serious security flaws. Shortly after it was released, hackers demonstrated that WEP could be cracked in a matter of minutes using readily available software. It's better than nothing, but it only stops casual snooping; it will not deter a serious attacker. Because WEP uses one key for all clients, other members of the network can read your packets.

WPA

WPA is a sort of interim security protocol upgrade for WEP-enabled devices. WPA uses the *Temporal Key Integrity Protocol (TKIP)* to protect from many attacks WEP was vulnerable to by providing a new encryption key for every packet sent. Other security enhancements include encryption key integrity-checking and user authentication through the industry-standard *Extensible Authentication Protocol (EAP)*.

WPA2

The full IEEE 802.11i standard, WPA2, is the preferred way to lock down wireless networks. WPA2 uses the *Advanced Encryption Standard (AES)*, among other improvements, to secure the wireless environment. Current WAPs and wireless clients support (and require) WPA2, and most access points have a "backward compatible" mode for the handful of devices that still need WPA.

FIGURE 19.6 WPS button on an e2500 router

WPS

The developers of Wi-Fi created *Wi-Fi Protected Setup (WPS)* to make secure connections easier for novice users to configure with a button (see Figure 19.6), password, or code. For example, you could connect a WPS-capable WAP and wireless printer by pressing the WPS button on the printer and then on the WAP within a set time. Sadly, WPS codes are very easy for a program to guess. The only protection is disabling WPS; check the WAP manufacturer's website for instructions.

Exam Tip
Be familiar with WEP, WPA, WPA2, TKIP, and AES.

Wireless Speed and Range

Wireless networking bandwidth speeds depend on the networking standard, the distance between the node and WAP, and on interference from solid objects and other wireless devices. Standards range from a measly 2 Mbps to a snappy 1+ Gbps, but this maximum throughput is usually only achieved within about 25 feet; speed will slowly fall until signal drops altogether beyond the device's effective range.

Most devices and standards list range with qualifiers such as "*around* 150 feet" or "*about* 300 feet" because, like speed, range is greatly affected by other factors. Wireless manufacturers list theoretical maximums, but real-world effective range is probably about half of this. Walls and large objects such as appliances can destroy speed and range, or even create *dead spots,* but wireless devices in the same frequency range—such as cordless phones and baby monitors—can be just as lethal.

To increase range, you can install extra WAPs for devices to roam between, replace stock antennas with higher-gain versions, use a signal booster, or use *wireless repeaters/extenders* to receive and rebroadcast the Wi-Fi signal.

Objective 19.02   Wireless Networking Standards

Wireless networking is dominated by *radio frequency (RF)* technologies, in particular the 802.11 (Wi-Fi) standards, but you still need to be familiar with infrared, Bluetooth, and cellular standards.

IEEE 802.11 Wi-Fi

The IEEE 802.11 wireless Ethernet standard, better known as *Wi-Fi,* defines how devices can communicate with data broadcast in small chunks spread over available frequencies within the 2.4GHz and/or 5GHz bands (which are further divided into discrete *channels*). The original 802.11 standard has been extended to the 802.11a, 802.11b, 802.11g, 802.11n, and 802.11ac variations—newer standards (except for 802.11a) have been backward compatible.

First, let's look at the important technological differences:

- **802.11a**   Despite the "a" on the end, it's newer than 802.11b. It runs in the faster 5GHz band, but its range suffered, and the use of the 5GHz band makes it incompatible with both older and newer Wi-Fi devices unless they support 5 GHz (802.11n and 802.11ac).

- **802.11b**   The first wireless networking standard to take off; uses the 2.4GHz band already crowded with baby monitors, garage door openers, microwaves, and wireless phones.

- **802.11g**   Achieved the range of 802.11b, the speed of 802.11a, and maintained backward compatibility with 802.11b.

- **802.11n**   Brought two new antenna technologies: *multiple in/multiple out (MIMO),* which increases speed by requiring all but handheld devices to use more than one of up to four antennas; and *transmit beamforming,* which adjusts the signal based on each client's location. Also introduced optional *dual-band* support for both 2.4 GHz and 5 GHz, which means some 802.11n devices were backward compatible with 802.11a.

- **802.11ac**   Expands on 802.11n technology by adding more streams, speed, and wider bandwidth. Technically, 802.11ac only uses the 5GHz band, but it too includes optional dual-band support. It introduces an updated MIMO called *Multiuser MIMO (MU-MIMO)* that enables a WAP to broadcast to multiple users simultaneously.

TABLE 19.1	Comparison of 802.11 Standards				
	802.11a	**802.11b**	**802.11g**	**802.11n**	**802.11ac**
Max. Throughput	54 Mbps	11 Mbps	54 Mbps	100+ Mbps	1+ Gbps
Max. Range	150 feet	300 feet	300 feet	300+ feet	300+ feet
Frequency	5 GHz	2.4 GHz	2.4 GHz	2.4 and 5 GHz	5 GHz
Security	SSID, MAC filtering, industry-standard WEP, WPA, WPA2	SSID, MAC filtering, industry-standard WEP, WPA, WPA2 (later hardware)	SSID, MAC filtering, industry-standard WEP, WPA, WPA2	SSID, MAC filtering, industry-standard WEP, WPA, WPA2	SSID, MAC filtering, industry-standard WEP, WPA, WPA2
Compatibility	802.11a	802.11b	802.11b, 802.11g	802.11b, 802.11g, 802.11n, (802.11a in some cases)	802.11a, 802.11b, 802.11g, 802.11n
Communication Mode	Ad hoc or infrastructure	Ad hoc or infrastructure	Ad hoc or infrastructure	Ad hoc or infrastructure	Ad hoc or infrastructure

Table 19.1 compares the important characteristics of the 802.11 versions.

Exam Tip
Be very familiar with the 802.11 wireless standards speeds, distances, and frequencies.

Other Wireless Standards

While Wi-Fi dominates the wireless networking market, it isn't the only standard. Mobile devices, such as smartphones, wearables, and tablets, connect wirelessly via cellular networks and use other standards to connect with other portables, car stereos, GPS devices, smart televisions, flying drones, and an endless litany of wireless-enabled products.

> ## Travel Assistance
>
> The cellular networks discussed in Chapter 11 can be used by non-cellular devices, either by tethering to a *wireless hotspot* or smartphone, or by adding direct cellular support with an expansion card or USB device.

Infrared Wireless Networking

Half-duplex *infrared (IR)* networking via the *Infrared Data Association (IrDA)* protocol has been largely eclipsed by newer, faster wireless and cellular standards. However, it is still a viable method to transfer files on some older devices. Infrared links require unbroken line-of-sight within about a meter and are susceptible to interference from other light sources. An infrared access point can enable Ethernet networking over IrDA, but beware that the connection isn't secure or encrypted.

Here are the important characteristics of IrDA:

- **Max. throughput**   Up to 4 Mbps
- **Max. range**   1 meter (39 inches)
- **Security**   None
- **Compatibility**   IrDA
- **Communication mode**   Point-to-point ad hoc

Bluetooth

Bluetooth creates small wireless networks ideal for wearable devices, audio headsets, and automotive entertainment systems that connect to your smartphone; linking two computers in a quick-and-dirty wireless *personal area network (PAN)*; and input devices such as keyboards and mice (see Figure 19.7). Most connections are ad hoc, but Bluetooth access points also exist.

> ## Local Lingo
>
> **Bluetooth**   This technology, which promised to allow cross-industry collaboration, was named after Harald Blåtand (Bluetooth in English), a tenth-century Danish king, because the king had been instrumental in uniting warring factions in parts of present-day Norway, Sweden, and Denmark.

FIGURE 19.7 External USB Bluetooth adapter, keyboard, and mouse

Bluetooth has grown faster and more secure over the years, but speed isn't Bluetooth's big selling point—reliable low-power communication is. Bluetooth resists interference by hopping between 79 frequencies in the 2.45GHz range around 1600 times a second. Bluetooth enables wearables and peripherals to save much-needed power with three power-use classes:

	Max. Power	Max. Range
Class 1	100 mW	100 meters
Class 2	2.5 mW	10 meters
Class 3	1 mW	1 meter

Let's look at what has changed over the years:

- The first generation (versions 1.1 and 1.2) supports speeds around 1 Mbps.
- The backward-compatible second generation (2.0 and 2.1) increases speed to around 3 Mbps with Enhanced Data Rate (EDR).
- With the optional High Speed (+ HS) feature, the third generation (3.0) tops out at 24 Mbps by transferring data over an 802.11 Wi-Fi connection after initial Bluetooth negotiation.
- Called Bluetooth Smart, the fourth generation (4.0, 4.1, 4.2) focuses on better support for "smart" devices by reducing cost and power use, and improving speed and security. The most interesting addition is IP connectivity so Bluetooth devices can skip the smartphone and talk directly to a Bluetooth-enabled WAP.

Travel Advisory

As you saw in Chapter 11, most mobile devices can also use near field communication (NFC) to wirelessly exchange contacts, small files, or payment information over small distances.

Objective 19.03 Installing and Configuring Wireless Networking

Wireless network adapters are as simple to install as their wired counterparts—just insert the plug-and-play device and let the OS handle the rest. Install any supplied driver when prompted and you're practically finished. The trick is configuring the wireless network to keep out unauthorized users and secure all of the data flying through the air.

Wi-Fi Configuration

Wi-Fi networks support ad hoc and infrastructure operation modes. Which mode you choose depends on the number of wireless nodes you need to support, the type of data sharing they'll perform, and your management requirements.

Ad hoc mode Wi-Fi networks (see Figure 19.8) don't need a WAP; just configure each node with the same SSID and a unique IP address, enable the File and Printer Sharing service, and share the desired resources. Unfortunately, Windows 8.1 and up can't create ad hoc networks, and require a CLI workaround just to connect to one.

Infrastructure mode is similar on the client (see Figure 19.9)—make sure all clients use the right SSID, security type, and password.

The whole "infrastructure" part can be complex, though. These networks employ one or more WAPs connected to a wired network segment, such as a corporate intranet, the Internet, or both. Each WAP includes a web server that hosts a browser-accessible configuration utility (see Figure 19.10) at the WAP's default IP address (often 192.168.1.1). It will prompt you to log in with an administrator password, which you create during installation or find in the WAP's documentation.

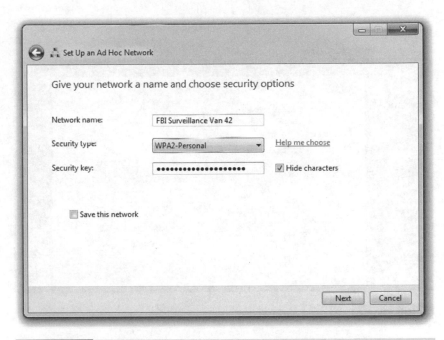

FIGURE 19.8   Setting up an ad hoc network in Windows 7

FIGURE 19.9   Infrastructure mode is set in a wireless configuration utility.

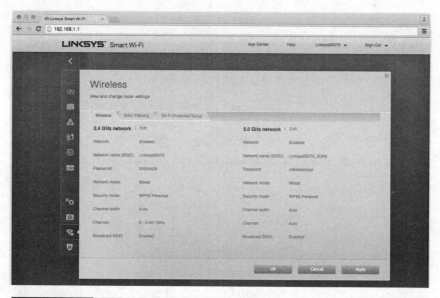

FIGURE 19.10   Linksys WAP setup screen

Travel Advisory

These configuration utilities vary by vendor and model.

Current WAPs come with web-based utilities that guide you through the initial setup, but manual setup isn't too hard. Here's a checklist:

- Install available firmware updates (see "Software Troubleshooting" for more).
- Give the configuration utility a secure administrator password.
- Configure a unique SSID and consider disabling SSID broadcast.
- Modern WAPs should select a channel/frequency automatically (see Figure 19.11), but you may still need to configure it to match other WAPs or use a quieter channel, based on a survey with a wireless analyzer (which you saw in Chapter 11).
- Dual-band WAPs can separately enable or disable the 2.4GHz and 5GHz networks (see Figure 19.12). Most setups use both for

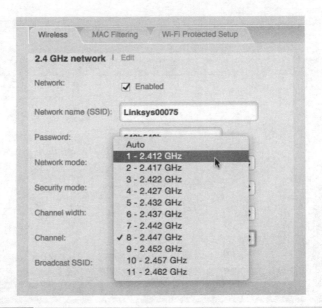

FIGURE 19.11 Changing the channel

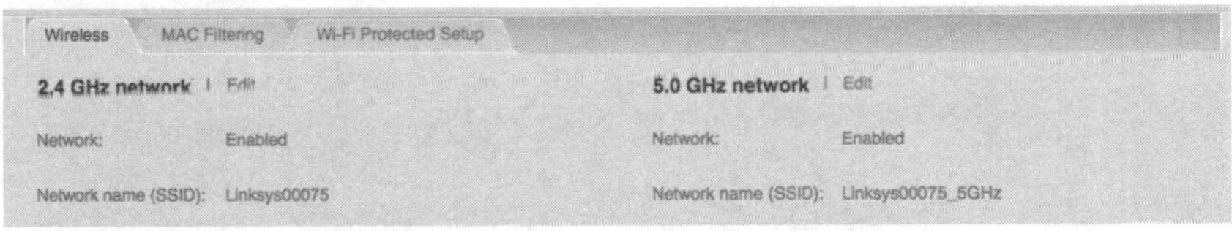

FIGURE 19.12 Linksys router sporting dual bands

compatibility, but you can disable one if interference makes it unreliable and all of your devices support the other band.

- Configure MAC filtering (see Figure 19.13) if you have known MAC addresses to allow or deny.
- Enable the best available security/encryption mode on the WAP and generate or enter the security key or password (see Figure 19.14).
- If you absolutely must use older equipment that only supports WEP, it should have an option to generate encryption keys; select the highest available encryption level, enter a unique *passphrase,* and click the Generate button or its equivalent. Document these settings and either export the encryption keys to removable media or write them down as well; wireless clients will need this information to connect.

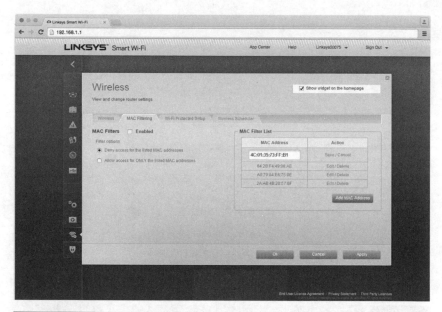

FIGURE 19.13   MAC filtering configuration screen for a Linksys WAP

FIGURE 19.14   Basic properties panel for a Linksys WAP

Exam Tip

WEP is easily cracked. Use WPA2 or, if you have older equipment, settle for WPA until you can upgrade.

- WPA and WPA2 are configured similarly. Use WPA/WPA2 Personal for SOHO networks (see Figure 19.15). WPA/WPA2 Enterprise requires a special server (called a *RADIUS server*) for serious security in larger business environments. Mixed network mode supports WPA clients on a WPA2-encrypted WAP; only use it if you must support WPA devices.

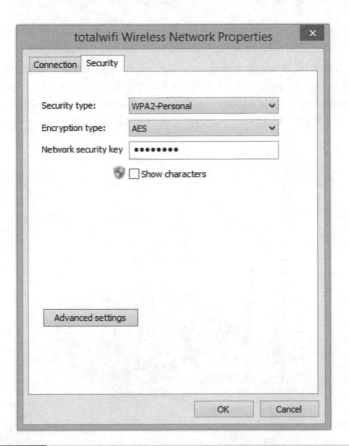

FIGURE 19.15 Encryption screen on client wireless network adapter configuration utility

Local Lingo

Pre-Shared Key (PSK) A more technical name for WPA/WPA2 Personal.

Another important part of installation and configuration is managing signal coverage to avoid: interference, congestion, dead spots where you need access, and leaking signal into insecure areas. A formal *site survey*—a complex job where a team of specialists interview stakeholders, evaluate your space, and use special equipment to survey sources of interference—results in a set of plans detailing the WAPs, channels, and antennas you need. If you have to make do without a formal site survey, here are some pointers:

- You can perform your own rudimentary survey of nearby networks with a smartphone or laptop and a Wi-Fi analyzer program.
- Antennas strengthen and focus RF output; we measure the ratio of increase or *gain* in decibels (dB). Many WAPs (and some NICs) have small removable antennae with a gain of 2 dB; larger replacements (see Figure 19.16) can vastly improve on this.

FIGURE 19.16 WAP with replacement antenna

- Most networks need blanket coverage, which is best achieved with omni-directional antennas—such as a stick-shaped *dipole antenna*—so this is what most devices come with. You can also use directional parabolic dish or multi-element Yagi antennas.

- Reception is best when the signal and receiving antenna have the same *polarization* or orientation in physical space (the polarization of the signal matches the orientation of the *broadcasting* antenna). You can optimize this if all of your devices are stationary and have adjustable antennas, but the fixed antennas in portable and mobile devices make this rare; 45-degree angles are a good compromise.

Exam Tip
Linux users can use the *iwconfig* CLI command to list detailed information about their wireless connections and tweak low-level settings.

Bluetooth Configuration

Once your plug-and-play Bluetooth device is installed, the *pairing* process (see Figure 19.17) securely connects devices. Start by enabling Bluetooth (it may

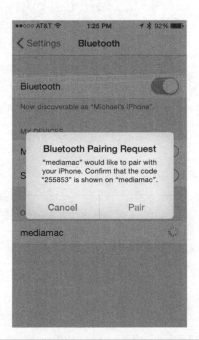

FIGURE 19.17 iPhone receiving a pairing request from "mediamac"

always be enabled on single-purpose devices); in Windows, enable or disable it in the Network and Sharing Center.

Next, place both devices into pairing (or discovery/discoverable) mode; once again, some devices will always be listening or discoverable. The devices in pairing mode will discover each other and agree on what Bluetooth version, speed, and features to use. Some devices will connect without further input when you initiate the pairing request, but most have a security component that requires you to input a short code, confirm two codes match, or similar.

Finally, make sure everything works. If not, delete the paring and re-pair. If this doesn't help, check relevant settings (such as microphone and audio settings, for a Bluetooth headset or speaker). Use any vendor-provided testing and troubleshooting utilities.

If you're pairing to share network access via a Bluetooth PAN, you'll also need to set the network connection up within your OS (see Figure 19.18).

FIGURE 19.18   Mac OS X Bluetooth PAN ready to connect using "Michael's iPhone"

FIGURE 19.19 Verizon's connection application, VZAccess Manager

Cellular Configuration

There's no standard way to configure cellular network cards because each provider does its own thing; make sure to consult their instructions. Fortunately, most make this dead simple: plug in the card, install the software, and launch the connection application (see Figure 19.19).

Objective 19.04 Troubleshooting Wi-Fi

Misbehaving wireless networks can be one of the most vexing things to troubleshoot. Your first goal is to understand who is affected, the nature of their problem, and when it started.

If all systems—wired and wireless—have lost connectivity, you obviously have bigger problems than Wi-Fi. Troubleshoot this situation the way you'd troubleshoot any network failure: determine which wireless nodes are affected and what they have in common. A problem with one node is likely the client configuration; a problem at many nodes may point to a down WAP; intermittent trouble for a few nodes in the same room could point to interference.

Next, explore the nature and full extent of the problem the users are experiencing. If they can browse the Internet but can't access shared files on a server, they're probably experiencing a permissions-related issue rather than a wireless one.

The last bit of gathering information for this issue is to determine when the problem started. Did someone change the WAP? Did your office experience a power outage, sag, or surge? All could cause a WAP to fail.

The answers to these questions feed into the next step of the troubleshooting process—establishing a theory. Most of your theories will point to hardware, software, connectivity, and configuration issues; you've already seen how to troubleshoot hardware in earlier chapters—wireless networking hardware isn't special, so we'll focus on software, connectivity, and configuration issues specific to wireless networking.

Travel Advisory

Don't forget to try a reboot before you make configuration or hardware changes.

Software Troubleshooting

Because you've already checked to confirm your hardware is using the correct drivers, what kind of software-related problems are left? Two things come immediately to mind: the wireless adapter configuration utility and the WAP's firmware version.

- Some wireless adapters—especially USB ones—won't work correctly unless you install the vendor-provided drivers and configuration software before plugging in the device. Uninstall the device in Device Manager, remove it, and start fresh.
- By the time you unpack your new WAP, there's a good chance its firmware is already out of date—and this can manifest in strange ways: clients may connect fine, but experience frequent timeout errors; every week or so, your clients may lose Internet access until you reboot

the WAP; Apple devices may have trouble connecting or running at
advertised speeds.

- Some WAPs can check for (and install) firmware updates from
  the configuration utility. With others, you'll need to look for
  updates—using your exact model number, hardware version, and
  current firmware version—on the manufacturer's website. Once you
  download the update, you'll either upload the new firmware from the
  configuration utility or run special software to flash the new firmware.

Travel Advisory

Installing the wrong firmware can brick your WAP; follow the
manufacturer's instructions to the letter.

Connectivity Troubleshooting

Assuming the client and WAP support the same bands, properly configured
wireless clients should quickly connect to the desired SSID; if this isn't taking
place, it's time for some troubleshooting. Most wireless connectivity problems
come down to either an incorrect configuration (such as an incorrect password) or low signal strength.

- Without a strong signal, even a properly configured wireless client isn't
  going to work. You can check link lights if your wireless NIC has them,
  but it's usually best to check signal strength in the connection status or
  configuration utilities (see Figure 19.20).

- If your signal registers but is low, you may be experiencing slow
  transfer speeds on the edges of your equipment's effective range, which
  can cause intermittent connectivity, failures, and other inconsistent
  behavior.

Exam Tip

A small light-up *Wi-Fi/wireless locator* can let you know you're in
range of an access point without having to walk around with your
phone or laptop out.

- If you're experiencing what the 901 objectives call "low RF signal,"
  you may be out of range, experiencing interference, or in a dead spot.
  If reasonable, move closer to the WAP and retry. If not, repositioning

FIGURE 19.20 Windows 8.1 Pro's wireless configuration utility

antenna on the WAP and NIC may help, as may moving the WAP
entirely. Look for and move or disable potential interference sources.
Try changing channels. If none of these work, you may need to use
previously discussed options for enhancing signal strength or reception.

- If your link state shows no signal, confirm the WAP is on and double-
  check the SSID you're using. The next list considers additional
  SSID issues.

All it takes is one slip of the typing finger to throw off your configuration completely. The things you're most likely to get wrong are the SSID and
security configuration, though dual-band routers have introduced some
additional complexity.

- Verify SSID configuration on your access point first, and then check
  on the affected wireless nodes. You can often use any characters in the
  SSID—watch for leading or trailing spaces.

- Clients that have always connected to a WAP with a particular SSID may give an "SSID not found" message if the WAP is down or its SSID has changed.

- If you use MAC address filtering, make sure the MAC address of the client attempting to access the wireless network is on the list of accepted users. You'll have to manually add the MAC for new systems or old systems with new NICs. If you find the correct MAC, double-check that it is configured to *allow* users on the list—not block them.

- Double-check the security settings, including security type and encryption key or password.

CHECKPOINT

✔**Objective 19.01: Wireless Networking Basics**   Wireless networks operate much like their wired counterparts, except they eliminate the network cabling by using either radio waves or infrared light as a network medium. Wireless networks operate in ad hoc (decentralized) or infrastructure (centralized) fashion. Ideally, the WAP should use WPA2 for security and encryption, though additional security practices include MAC address filtering and tuning the signal coverage to keep it from leaking into uncontrolled areas. Using a unique SSID that doesn't leak information about your WAP hardware and disabling SSID broadcast can additionally help avoid being targeted by attackers looking for hardware with well-known weaknesses. The range and speed of wireless networks depend greatly on the environment, distance from the access point, interference, and networking standard.

✔**Objective 19.02: Wireless Networking Standards**   Wireless networks are based around several standards: IEEE 802.11*x*, Infrared Data Association (IrDA), Bluetooth, and cellular. Of these, 802.11ac (1+ Gbps throughput) is the fastest. Infrared is line-of-sight only and tops out at 4 Mbps. Bluetooth creates efficient wireless networks that can be tailored to the needs of a given device.

✔**Objective 19.03: Installing and Configuring Wireless Networking**   Ad hoc mode is the simplest way to network computers without wires, but it lacks central control and security. Infrastructure mode requires more planning and wireless access point (WAP) hardware. WAPs are configured using built-in browser-based utilities where you set the SSID, select channels and dual-band support, configure MAC filtering, and enable security/ encryption such as WPA2. To connect Bluetooth devices, turn Bluetooth on, put devices in pairing/discovery/discoverable mode, initiate pairing, and confirm the security prompt. Cellular devices are generally plug and play, though you often need to run the included software to connect.

✔**Objective 19.04: Troubleshooting Wi-Fi**   Regular hardware installation and troubleshooting procedures should be used for wireless network adapters. Otherwise, look for WAP firmware updates if you experience strange or inconsistent behavior—but follow manufacturer instructions carefully. Wireless connectivity problems often come down to poor signal quality or incorrect configuration. Check signal quality in connection status or configuration utilities; reposition the client or WAP, or try to adjust their antennas; search for and move or disable potential sources of interference; try changing channels. Common configuration problems include an incorrect SSID at the client or WAP end, an SSID changed on the WAP but not the client, incorrect MAC address filter entries, and incorrect security settings.

REVIEW QUESTIONS

1. How does TKIP protect WPA/WPA2 from attacks that WEP is vulnerable to?
   A. It forces the user to change the password once every 90 days.
   B. The encryption key changes once a minute.
   C. It forces the user to change the password every time they connect.
   D. The encryption key changes for every packet.

2. Which wireless security standard uses AES?
   A. WEP
   B. WPA
   C. WPA2
   D. B and C

3. The 802.11g wireless specification enables what maximum throughput speed?
   A. 2 Mbps
   B. 11 Mbps
   C. 54 Mbps
   D. 4 Mbps

4. What is the maximum range of a Class 3 Bluetooth device?

   A. 1 meter

   B. 30 feet

   C. 10 meters

   D. 300 feet

5. What function does CSMA/CA provide that CSMA/CD does not?

   A. Data packet collision detection

   B. End-to-end data packet encryption

   C. Data packet collision avoidance

   D. Data packet error checking

6. Which of these would be the easiest to implement in helping a wireless network avoid interference?

   A. Replace the stock antenna with a higher-gain antenna.

   B. Replace the 802.11n WAP with an 802.11ac WAP.

   C. Change the channel.

   D. Add another WAP to the network.

7. What is the maximum speed of IrDA?

   A. 115 Kbps

   B. 2 Mbps

   C. 4 Mbps

   D. 11 Mbps

8. Which encryption method offers the best security?

   A. SSID

   B. WEP

   C. WPA

   D. WPA2

9. What hardware do you need to enable wireless devices to connect to resources on a wired network segment in infrastructure mode?

   A. A wireless access point

   B. A wired router

   C. A wireless hub

   D. A wireless bridge

10. Which Bluetooth version introduced the optional High Speed feature that increases maximum throughput by transferring data via Wi-Fi?

   A. Bluetooth 3.0

   B. Bluetooth 4.2

   C. Bluetooth Smart

   D. Bluetooth 4.0

REVIEW ANSWERS

1. **D** TKIP changes the encryption key for every packet.

2. **C** WPA2 is the only one of these wireless security standards to use AES encryption.

3. **C** The 802.11g wireless networks run at a maximum of 54 Mbps.

4. **A** A Class 3 Bluetooth device has a maximum range of 1 meter (~3 feet).

5. **C** CSMA/CA uses the RTS/CTS protocol to provide data packet collision avoidance.

6. **C** Changing the channel can help avoid interference. Most 802.11n/ac WAPs support both the 2.4GHz and 5GHz bands, so neither offers a substantive advantage.

7. **C** The maximum data throughput speed of IrDA is 4 Mbps.

8. **D** No contest! WPA2 offers the best security.

9. **A** A wireless access point enables you to connect wireless devices to a wired network segment.

10. **A** Bluetooth 3.0 introduced High Speed (+ HS), which creates a Wi-Fi connection after Bluetooth negotiation to transfer data at higher speeds.

The Internet

	NEWBIE	SOME EXPERIENCE	EXPERT
ETA	3 hours	2 hours	1 hour

Internet access profoundly benefits users and is one of the primary reasons we network. We've already talked about the Internet as a WAN interconnecting LANs all over the world, but the goal isn't sharing a printer or documents directory with billions of your closest friends—there's obviously more to the Internet. People really want to access the software available through this global network. We'll start with a look at what the Internet—all of this software—is, and then explore how you connect to it. The chapter wraps up with a look at troubleshooting Internet issues.

 **Objective 20.01** What Is the Internet?

The Internet interconnects many networks, but individual LANs don't actually make up the Internet's infrastructure. The networks that *do* make up this infrastructure are roughly divided into three conceptual tiers—Tier 1 through Tier 3—which reflect how central or critical they are to the Internet's operation.

A small number of Tier 1 providers own (and charge lower-level networks for the use of) the long-distance high-speed fiber-optic *backbone* networks that interconnect the earth's major cities at special network access points (NAPs). Most of the regional *Internet service providers (ISPs)* with names recognizable by the general public are Tier 2 providers, while Tier 3 providers operate smaller regional and local ISPs and networks.

Routers at multiple stops along these many interconnected networks use the IPv4 and IPv6 addressing schemes you saw in Chapter 18 to shepherd packets to their destination—and even route them around network or power failures. TCP/IP not only allows packets to find their way between our IP address to one clear around the world, but it provides the framework and common language for the Internet, enabling programmers to build applications atop its features.

Internet Application Protocols

The Internet is all about what we do with the layers of software that TCP/IP supports. If you want to surf the Web, you need a *web browser* such as Mozilla Firefox, Google Chrome, or Microsoft Edge. If you want to make a VoIP phone call, you need an application such as Skype or Google Voice. These applications in turn use clearly designed TCP/IP application protocols; there are tens of

TABLE 20.1	Application Protocols	
Application Protocol	**Function**	**Port Number**
HTTP	Web pages	80
HTTPS	Secure web pages	443
FTP	File transfer	20, 21
SFTP	Secure file transfer	22
IMAP	Incoming e-mail	143
POP3	Incoming e-mail	110
SMTP	Outgoing e-mail	25
Telnet	Terminal emulation	23
SSH	Encrypted terminal emulation	22
RDP	Remote Desktop	3389

thousands of these—each with its own rules and port numbers—but CompTIA only wants you to know some of the most common.

In addition to the application protocols we see and use daily, others handle important jobs behind the scenes to ensure the application protocols we do see run well—think of the near-invisible role DNS and DHCP play in your LAN (when they work). I'll use "utility protocols" to distinguish these.

We'll begin with a quick overview of the application protocols (detailed in Table 20.1) and utility protocols (detailed in Table 20.2) CompTIA would like you to know, and then look at the applications they support.

TABLE 20.2	Utility Protocols		
Utility Protocol	**Function**		**Port Number**
DNS	Allows the use of DNS naming	UDP	53
DHCP	Automatic IP addressing	UDP	67, 68
LDAP	Querying directories	TCP	389
SNMP	Remote management of network devices	UDP	161
SMB (NetBIOS/NetBT)	Windows naming/folder sharing; also CIFS	TCP	445
		UDP	137, 138, 139
AFP	Mac OS X file services	TCP	548
SLP	Services discovery protocol	TCP/ UDP	427

If you're like me, being told to remember port numbers is a lot like being told to remember what day the Thirty Years' War ended. But imagine the company executive you're supporting can't send e-mail with her company account from hotel Wi-Fi because your corporate network routers block external connections on port 25—how quickly could you get from "I can't send e-mail" to this conclusion if you aren't aware of the ports and protocols involved?

The World Wide Web

For many, the Web is synonymous with the Internet. For the average user, a web browser on their device uses the *Hypertext Transfer Protocol (HTTP)* or *Hypertext Transfer Protocol Secure (HTTPS)* to request a web page (such as http://www.totalsem.com) from a given site's *web servers* (servers running software designed for serving websites).

As the existence of HTTPS implies, HTTP isn't secure; an attacker can read any HTTP packets they intercept. Traditionally, you can tell if a website is using HTTPS because the web address starts with *https* (as shown in Figure 20.1). Unless you develop applications, you don't work directly with these protocols; your browser just uses them on your behalf.

| **FIGURE 20.1** | A secure web page |

Local Lingo

Attacker   Attacker is a generic term for someone or something attempting to compromise your systems, networks, or data. The attacker could be a lone hacker trying to breach your system, a state surveillance agency monitoring traffic at your ISP, or a malware-compromised router with opportunity to modify or redirect your packets. Chapter 21 explores attacks and security.

The web browsers using these protocols on your behalf are highly configurable, though the 902 objectives conspicuously focus on just settings in the Internet Options applet, which only apply to Microsoft Internet Explorer (IE).

Travel Advisory

Microsoft announced that IE11 (the current version) is the last. Microsoft Edge replaces it on Windows versions beyond 8.1. Because Internet Options has no effect on other browsers, its days are likely numbered.

Before we dive in, you can access equivalent options through the menu icon in Google Chrome and Mozilla Firefox—it looks like a stack of three lines in the top-right corner; from here, select Settings (Chrome) or Options (Firefox). Controls in Firefox (see Figure 20.2) are laid out similar to IE; Chrome's settings (shown in Figure 20.3) look like a web page (because they are one!).

When you open the Internet Options applet (shown in Figure 20.4), you'll see these tabs along the top:

- **General**   This tab controls basic features: home page, tab management, browsing history, searching, and other appearance controls. This is where you delete or change how Internet Explorer stores the websites you've visited.
- **Security**   This tab enables you to relax or tighten web browsing safeguards. You can configure websites into zones and then control the security level for each.
- **Privacy**   This tab works a lot like the Security tab, but for privacy risks such as cookies, location tracking, pop-ups, and whether browser extensions will run in private browsing mode.

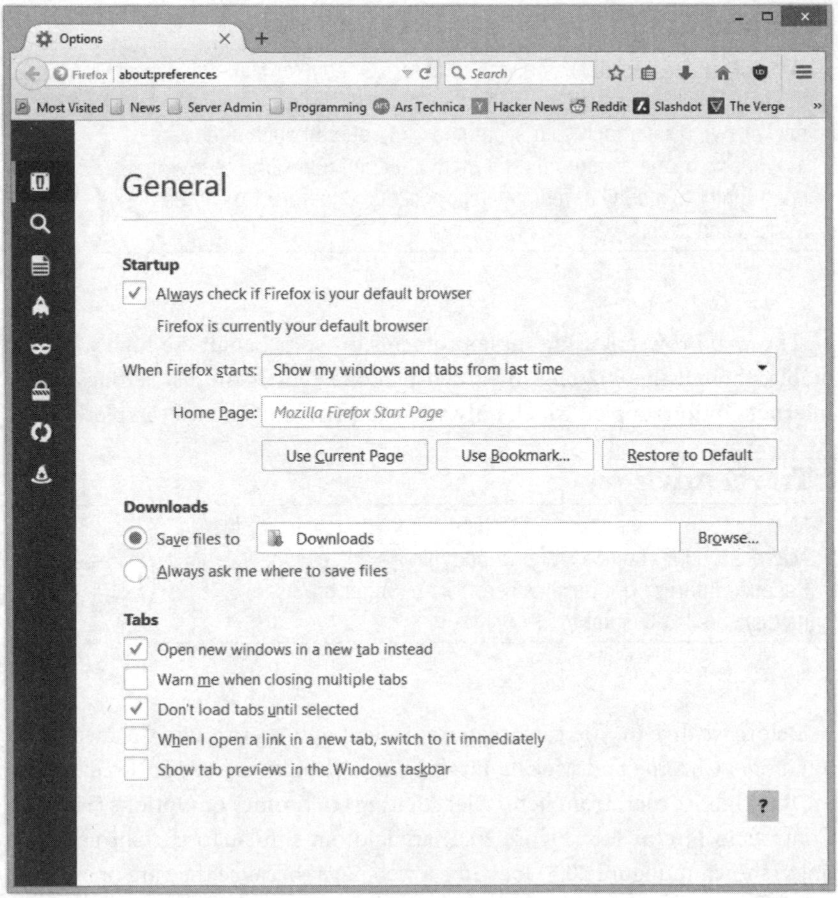

FIGURE 20.2   Mozilla Firefox Options

- **Content**   This tab enables you to gate access to insecure or objectionable sites—*content filtering*—via certificates and a *parental-control* tool called Family Safety (which you saw in Chapter 15). The Content tab also adjusts AutoComplete and settings for web page content update subscriptions.
- **Connections**   This tab can set up Internet connections and adjust some LAN settings that you probably won't use, except perhaps to configure a proxy server connection.

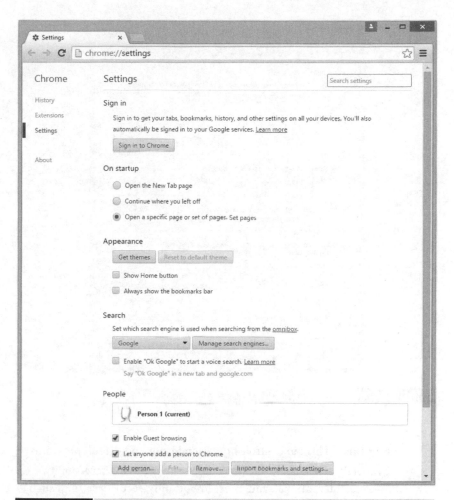

FIGURE 20.3 Google Chrome Settings

Exam Tip

A *proxy server* is an intermediary between its users and the resources they request. Applications send requests to the proxy server instead of trying to access the Internet directly, and the proxy server fetches the resources on behalf of the users. This enables the proxy server to monitor usage; restrict access to or modify insecure or objectionable content; cache, compress, or strip out resources to improve performance; and more.

FIGURE 20.4   Internet Options applet

- **Programs**   This tab controls browser add-ons and default programs.
- **Advanced**   This tab lists advanced option toggles for accessibility, browsing, international, and, most importantly, security settings such as how IE checks website certificates. It also has a button to reset settings for a fresh start.

Exam Tip

Given a specific scenario, be sure you know how to use the settings in Internet Options.

E-mail

It can seem like there are tons of ways to access e-mail, but they all boil down to generic e-mail client applications that can be configured to check one or many accounts, and clients tailored around a single e-mail service. Tailored clients, whether in an app or on a website, are preconfigured for access.

Exam Tip

Most modern operating systems support a global account login (such as Microsoft Account, Apple ID, or Google Account) that can synchronize your settings across devices. The 902 objectives call this *Live sign in* (after the older name for Microsoft Account—Microsoft Live ID). Signing in with a global account automatically configures the default client to check the global account's e-mail.

You have to manually configure generic clients with the address of your incoming and outgoing *mail servers;* incoming servers (where you check for new mail) typically use *Post Office Protocol version 3 (POP3)* or *Internet Message Access Protocol version 4 (IMAP4),* while outgoing servers (where you send mail) use *Simple Mail Transfer Protocol (SMTP).* These addresses come from your e-mail provider (usually your ISP, company, school, or other organization).

Exam Tip

Microsoft Exchange servers provide e-mail, calendars, and instant messaging for larger organizations. Generic clients can access Exchange accounts with the underlying e-mail protocols, but the client needs Exchange support to use other features. As long as they can use your e-mail address to find your Exchange server, Exchange-compatible clients self-configure; just enter your e-mail address and password.

In most cases, you open the client and access Setup or Preferences (the option varies among the many applications) to add an account. Outlook (like IE) is an odd duck; you add accounts via the Mail applet (see Figure 20.5). Click Add to get started.

By default, some clients (including Microsoft Outlook and Windows Live Mail) present a user-friendly account setup that attempts to guess mail servers from your address (even for non-Exchange accounts), in which case there is usually a secondary manual configuration option (as shown in Figure 20.6) for entering explicit server addresses.

The basic e-mail protocols, much like basic HTTP, are insecure—messages sent this way are readable by anyone who can intercept them. In Chapter 11, we

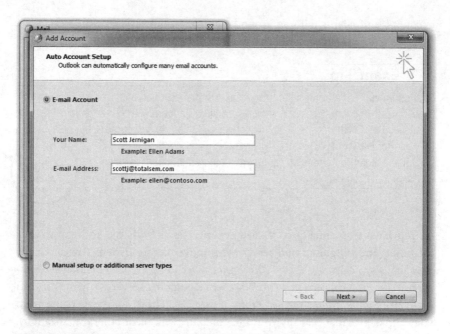

FIGURE 20.5 Adding an account with the Mail applet in Control Panel

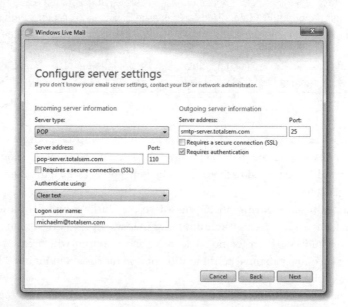

FIGURE 20.6 Adding POP3 and SMTP information in Windows Live Mail

briefly discussed options such as PGP and S/MIME for encrypting the text of a message so that the receiver must decrypt it before reading. This is a kind of *end-to-end encryption*: the message is encrypted from your system at one end to the recipient at the other.

Many modern e-mail servers use Secure Sockets Layer (SSL) or the stronger Transport Layer Security (TLS)—these are the options related to authentication and secure connections visible in Figure 20.6. These settings are for *transit encryption*, which just secures your message between your system and the mail server; an attacker who compromises the mail server itself has access to the unencrypted mail. Ideally, your mail server will use TLS to pass your message on, but it doesn't have to; messages you send with transit encryption can arrive at their destination without it!

File Transfer Protocol (FTP)

True to its name, the *File Transfer Protocol (FTP)* is for uploading and downloading files from a remote *FTP server*. Some web browsers have at least partial support built in (see Figure 20.7), but dedicated FTP client programs such as FileZilla have many useful features.

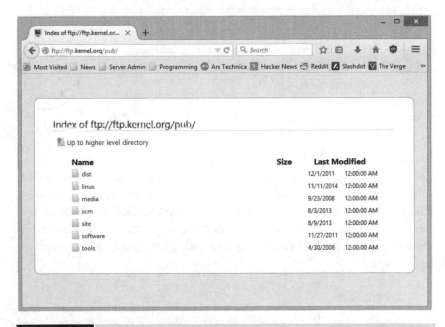

FIGURE 20.7 Accessing an FTP site in Firefox

Public FTP sites support anonymous logins, which is what your browser will attempt by default. Full clients have fields to enter (and remember) your user name and password, but if you want to log on as a specific user with your browser, you have to add your user name to the URL. Instead of typing **ftp://ftp.example.com**, you would type **ftp://mikem@ftp.example.com**. As with the other basic protocols, FTP is insecure; secure versions such as SFTP and FTPS are conspicuously absent from the 901 objectives.

Telnet and SSH

Telnet is a terminal (as in CLI) emulation program that enables authenticated users to run commands on a remote system (such as a server or router). Telnet, which is also insecure, sends passwords and user names as clear text, so you should use it only within your own LAN.

Secure Shell (SSH) has largely replaced Telnet because it encrypts the entire connection to prevent eavesdropping. SSH has one other trick up its sleeve: it supports *tunneling* files or any type of TCP/IP network traffic through its secure connection, enabling SSH to secure an insecure protocol such as FTP.

> ### Exam Tip
>
> The CompTIA A+ 902 exam tests your knowledge of a few networking tools, such as Telnet, but only enough to let you support a Network+ tech or network administrator. If you need to run Telnet or SSH, you will get details from a network administrator. Implementation of Telnet and SSH falls well beyond CompTIA A+.

Remote Desktop

Much as SSH and Telnet enable you to issue commands from a remote CLI, remote desktop software enables you to use another system's GUI as if you were sitting at it. Most of these use of either *Remote Desktop Protocol (RDP)* or *Virtual Network Computing (VNC)*. Microsoft's *Remote Desktop Connection* can connect to and control a Windows system with a fully graphical interface (see Figure 20.8).

> ### Exam Tip
>
> Because the Remote Desktop Connection executable is mstsc.exe, you can also open it from the CLI or search bar by typing **mstsc** and pressing ENTER.

Windows Remote Desktop Connection dialog box

Similar programs enable techs to see what a client sees, and use the client's system to resolve the issue. *Windows Remote Assistance* (shown in Figure 20.9) enables you to grant or assume control, enabling a user to request support directly from you. Upon receiving the support-request e-mail, you can log on to the user's system and, with permission, take the driver's seat.

Exam Tip

Apple sells a Remote Desktop program marketed to business customers that includes remote assistance features, but more modest *screen sharing* is built into Mac OS X. Enable screen sharing in System Preferences for general remote access, collaboration, and light remote troubleshooting.

In all these methods, the connecting system is a client and the remote system is a server providing access to its desktop. To configure whether your Windows system can act as a Remote Assistance or Remote Desktop server, go to the System applet and select the Remote settings link on the left. The Remote tab

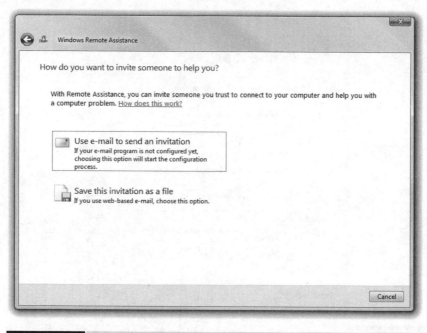

FIGURE 20.9 Remote Assistance in action

in System Properties has checkboxes for both Remote Assistance and Remote Desktop, along with some detailed settings.

> **Exam Tip**
>
> Windows can also run applications hosted on another machine. Think of it as Remote Desktop without the desktop—a single application runs on one machine (a server) but the GUI appears on another desktop (a client). Set it up in the RemoteApp and Desktop Connections applet.

Virtual Private Networks

A *virtual private network (VPN)* sets up endpoints at each end of an encrypted tunnel between computers or networks to join them into a private network as if they were on a directly connected LAN (though they obviously won't perform like it). In order to pull this trick off, the endpoint on each LAN gets its own LAN IP address and is responsible for handling traffic addressed to and from the remote network (see Figure 20.10).

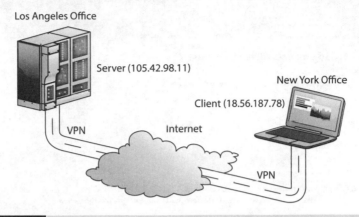

Los Angeles Office

Server (105.42.98.11)

New York Office

Client (18.56.187.78)

VPN

Internet

VPN

FIGURE 20.10 Typical tunnel

Travel Advisory

When your mobile or portable device connects to an untrusted Wi-Fi hotspot, you can connect to another network with a VPN and do all of your browsing (or other work) through the secure tunnel.

You can use Start | Search | VPN and press ENTER (Windows Vista and 7) or select *Manage virtual private networks* (Windows 8 and up). Enter your VPN server information, which your network administrator will most likely provide, in the resulting dialog (see Figure 20.11). This creates a virtual NIC that gets an IP address from the DHCP server back at the office.

Utility Application Protocols

The 902 objectives list five protocols that you may rarely if ever work with directly:

- The *Lightweight Directory Access Protocol (LDAP)* enables operating systems and applications to access directories. Windows Server uses LDAP to do anything with Active Directory. If you add a computer to an Active Directory domain, Windows uses LDAP commands to update Active Directory with the computer's information.

- The *Simple Network Management Protocol (SNMP)* enables remote query and configuration of just about anything on a network. Network+ techs can query SNMP-compatible network hardware for an unimaginable amount of data.

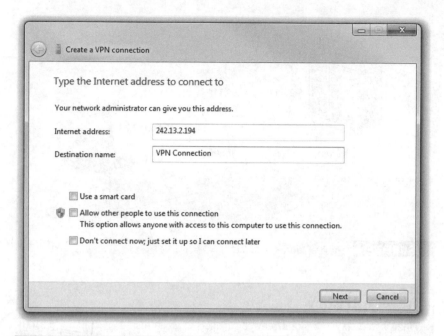

FIGURE 20.11 VPN connection in Windows

- *Server Message Block (SMB)*, the file and print sharing protocol in Windows, is the protocol of choice for LAN file servers. UNIX and Linux used the competing *Network File System (NFS)*, but every major OS uses SMB now (Linux does so via *Samba*).

Exam Tip

Over the years, Microsoft has introduced several versions (dialects) of SMB, including *Common Internet File System (CIFS)*, which is deprecated but still widely supported.

- Apple developed the *Apple Filing Protocol (AFP)* in the late 1980s to support file sharing on early LANs. Just like SMB, AFP survives for Mac OS X machines to share files and for Time Machine to back up OS X over the network. Windows lacks out-of-box support for AFP, but Linux has solid support.
- Devices use the *Service Location Protocol (SLP)* to advertise and discover network services (such as print or file shares).

Internet Applications

The software we come to the Internet for is built atop these application protocols, and the 902 objectives expect you to know some very basic information about how. In the early days, web servers served rudimentary static web pages that were cobbled together into websites; if anything changed between visits, it meant someone had directly edited or uploaded a file to the server. We didn't really think about these sites as software or applications, and early web servers were basic server programs that responded to HTTP requests by sending files stored locally.

On the modern Internet, most of us access *web apps* that are a complex collaboration between *front-end* code running in our web browser to create the interface we use and custom *back-end* software running on tens or hundreds of servers to do the heavy lifting. When these web apps are busy, they launch new servers to handle the additional traffic; when traffic dies down, they destroy the excess servers. Not with a hammer, of course—most of these servers are virtual machines, which you saw in Chapter 14.

Virtual Servers

The primary requirement for a VM you intend to use as a server is network connectivity—and one of the coolest features of VMs is the many different ways you can "virtually" network them. I don't mean just connecting them to the Internet—every hypervisor has the capability to connect each of its virtual machines to a network in a number of different ways. The combinations are infinite, but here are the basic options:

- Virtual machines on the same hypervisor can be internally networked (see Figure 20.12)—connected to a *virtual switch* (see Figure 20.13) inside the hypervisor—with none of their network traffic leaving the host machine.
- You can bridge the VM's NIC to the host system's NIC (connecting it to the Internet, if the LAN is connected), enabling it to get an IP address on the LAN from DHCP.

Travel Advisory

A VM connected using bridged networking is subject to all the same security risks as a real computer on the Internet, but it's also able to serve resources to any LAN or WAN nodes allowed to reach it.

- Just because you make a VM doesn't mean you need any kind of network. A no-network VM can be a simple place to test something quickly—or to test software that may pose a risk to your network.

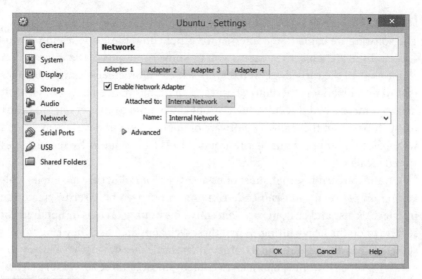

FIGURE 20.12   Configuring a VM for an internal network in VirtualBox

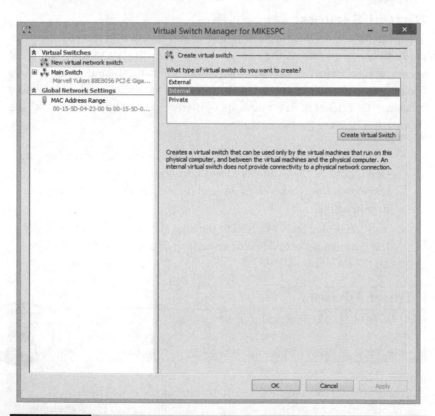

FIGURE 20.13   Hyper-V's Virtual Switch Manager

The ability to network these servers on the fly means you can create a virtual LAN with a whole team of servers performing different jobs or sharing a workload. Need to add new servers, or rearrange the network to try something new? No problem—you don't even have to re-cable—just reconfigure the virtual network settings.

Server-Side Virtualization

When it comes to servers, virtualization has taken over. In Chapter 14 we considered some of the reasons virtualization is so popular—such as the power and hardware savings, and the fact that VMs are stored in files—but these were from the perspective of the hardware owner. Virtualization is important to hardware owners because *resource pooling* enables them to purchase less hardware and use what they buy more efficiently.

For simplicity, I left a big piece of the story out. Because VMs are just files (big ones, but files nonetheless), you can move or copy them around. Someone who owns servers can easily move the VM files from one physical system to another, or from one data center to another. In fact, you could copy the VM to data centers around the world and run an instance of your web server on every continent. You can even run Australia's copy of your web server on a VM with minimal resources while most of Australia is sleeping, but then load the same server image on VMs with more RAM and CPU cores as traffic picks up during the day, and unload them again in the evening.

If you own these servers, shutting down the VMs at night is mostly just about saving power—turn off enough VMs and you can consolidate the remaining ones onto fewer physical machines and power down idle servers. Those of us who don't own servers, though, can just pay someone who does (by the minute, hour, month, and so on) to create a VM and hand us the keys. When we're done using it, we can shut it down and stop paying. We don't need a server room, or people to look after the hardware. This isn't so different from how you pay for utility services such as water and electricity—it's servers *as a service*, but there's a more popular name for it: *cloud computing*.

Cloud Computing

Most people associate "The Cloud" with friendly file-storage services such as Dropbox and Google Drive—but cloud computing is about simple interfaces to a vast array of on-demand computing resources sold by Amazon (see Figure 20.14), Microsoft, Google, and many other companies over the open Internet. We use the servers and networks of the cloud through layers of software that make it simple to perform complex tasks and manage powerful hardware.

FIGURE 20.14 Amazon Web Services Management Console

These companies use an overlooked innovation to charge for their cloud resources: a *measured service* model that encourages customers to use only what they need. The ability to request and release resources *on demand* empowers customers to handle spikes or sags in their own demand with *rapid elasticity*. VMs and other processing resources are billed by their computing power and how long they run; storage space is billed by how much you store per unit of time. Other common measurements are bandwidth used, and how many times you perform certain actions.

Measured service outright enables certain kinds of app, business, and research that have short periods of very high demand. These are prohibitively expensive under the old model where you must pay flat monthly or yearly rates for fixed resources (with overage charges or strict caps). These days, a researcher can fire up scores of temporary cloud VMs overnight to perform a complex one-off data-processing job.

As end users, the web applications such as Dropbox that we associate with the cloud are actually the sweet icing atop a novel layer cake of cloud services (see Figure 20.15) that support web applications and their developers. Let's slice it open and start at the bottom:

FIGURE 20.15   A tasty three-layer cake

- Large-scale global *Infrastructure as a Service (IaaS)* providers combine virtualization's ability to minimize idle hardware, protect against data loss and downtime, and respond to spikes in demand with the power of vast data centers and massive networks. Providers such as Amazon Web Services (AWS) enable everyone from you to large multinational corporations to launch new virtual servers using a given OS, on demand (see Figure 20.16), for pennies an hour. AWS provides many of the services needed to drive popular, complex web applications—unlimited data storage, database servers, caching, media hosting, and more—all billed by usage. IaaS frees us from managing hardware, but we're still responsible for configuring each VM and keeping its software up to date.

- A *Platform as a Service (PaaS)* provider such as Heroku (see Figure 20.17) gives programmers the tools they need to deploy, administer, and maintain a web application. The PaaS provider starts with some form of infrastructure, which could be provided by an IaaS, and on top of that infrastructure the provider builds a *platform:* a complete deployment and management system to handle every aspect of a web application. The infrastructure underneath the PaaS is largely invisible to the developer—a PaaS service saves you even more time on setup, configuration, and maintenance (at the expense of flexibility).

- *Software as a Service (SaaS)* sits at the top of the cake, accessible as the web applications we've been discussing. Users of these web apps don't own the software—there's no installer. You use a web

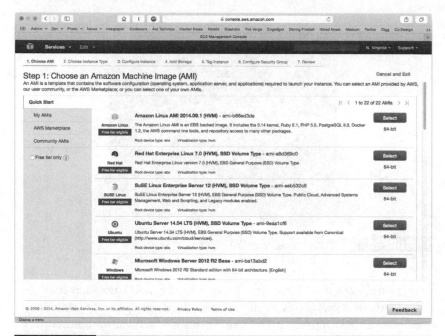

FIGURE 20.16 Creating an instance on AWS

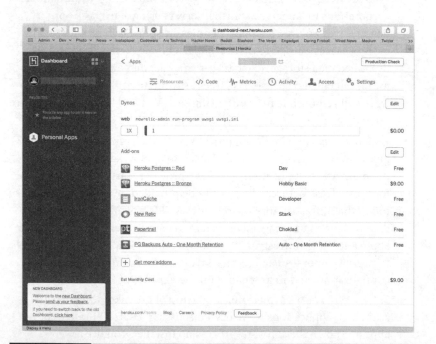

FIGURE 20.17 Heroku's management console

application through its website or native device apps. This may sound like a disadvantage, but the SaaS model provides access to necessary applications wherever you have an Internet connection without having to carry data or install regular updates. The monthly or yearly subscription model of many SaaS offerings makes it easier to budget and keep hundreds or thousands of computers up to date. The tradeoff is giving control of your data to the SaaS provider.

Local Lingo

SaaS The trouble with defining SaaS is an argument that almost everything on the Internet is SaaS. In the early 2000s, we called the Google search engine a *website*—but it provides a search service you don't own and must access on the Internet. If you're online, you're arguably always using SaaS.

When it comes to security concerns like these (among other factors), different organizations come to different conclusions. The result is a number of terms we use to describe who owns and controls given cloud resources:

- Out on the open, public Internet, cloud services that anyone can pay for are the *public cloud*. When we talk about *the* cloud—we mean the public cloud. The public doesn't own it—companies such as Amazon, Google and Microsoft do—but any individual or company can use public IaaS, PaaS, and SaaS offerings.

- Organizations that want some of the flexibility the cloud offers but need complete ownership of their data (and can afford both) can build (or contract a third party to build) an internal *private cloud*. A business could build a private IaaS that departments use to create and destroy VMs as needed, and a private PaaS to support the quick development of internal web apps such as private SaaS to meet the collaboration, planning, or time management needs of their employees.

- A *community cloud* is basically a private cloud paid for by a "community" of organizations in the same industry or with similar challenges. Imagine, for example, a community cloud for hospitals that meets the special regulatory requirements of dealing with patient data—or a cloud for military contractors that enables them to share the burden of defending against attackers sponsored by foreign states. This could be as simple as a SaaS application for tracking patient charts, or complex IaaS and PaaS offerings.

- A *hybrid cloud* isn't really a type of cloud—it just describes blending IaaS, PaaS, and SaaS resources from the other types. For example, you could maintain your own private cloud to satisfy average demand, then launch new VMs in the public cloud as you approach your own cloud's capacity—which we call *cloud bursting.* Hybrid cloud can also mean integrating specific services across cloud types—a hotel chain, for example, could build a private/internal SaaS app to enable each manager to predict which bookings will likely miss because their flights got delayed or cancelled. To accomplish this, they could integrate with a third-party weather forecasting application in the public cloud and a flight-tracking application in a community cloud for the aviation industry.

Exam Tip

You're expected to know the differences among the various cloud computing standards. Know your PaaS from your SaaS, IaaS, and definitely your sass.

 **Objective 20.02   Internet Connection Technologies**

In Chapter 18 we briefly discussed the concept of a bridge that translates signals from one network media to another. When you want to connect a LAN to the Internet, what you're looking for is a bridge between that LAN and one of the data transmission media available in your house or building. No matter how you slice it, you need hardware that can connect your computer, LAN, or WLAN to this other media and software that speaks to this hardware—but where these components are located varies.

In general use we call this hardware a modem, even though vanishingly few of them are true modulator/demodulators that create a bridge to *analog* transmission media. Sometimes we install the hardware and software both into a host computer (in which case the computer itself serves as part of the bridge); other times, the software is built into the hardware device which itself connects directly to a standard RJ-45 jack on our computer or router. Let's look at the many variations on this theme.

> **Travel Advisory**
>
> Each OS has settings to share a direct Internet connection with the LAN or other systems; Windows systems use Internet Connection Sharing (ICS).

Dial-Up

Dial-up Internet links use the first ubiquitous data network—the telephone system:

- In traditional dial-up, connection software on a computer uses an internal modem (see Figure 20.18) or external modem (Figure 20.19) to dial (as in, dial a phone) the ISP, where it begins translating between digital information and analog sound to negotiate a connection. At 56 Kbps download and up to 48 Kbps upload, dial-up is glacial when compared to the newest connection standards.

- On all-digital telephone lines you may be able to get *integrated services digital network (ISDN)* dial-up, which uses a terminal adapter (TA) that closely resembles a dial-up modem. ISDN is uses 64 Kbps channels in two common configurations: basic rate interface (BRI), which combines two channels for 128 Kbps bandwidth, and primary rate interface (PRI), which combines 23 channels for 1.544 Mbps.

FIGURE 20.18   An internal modem

FIGURE 20.19   A external USB modem

You can create a new connection from within the OS; you'll need to provide one or more dial-up telephone numbers for the ISP as well as your user name and password; the ISP should give you this information along with any configuration options specific to their system. In Windows 7, for example, you can click *Set up a new connection or network* from the Network and Sharing center applet, select Connect to the Internet, and enter the dial-up connection details (as shown in Figure 20.20).

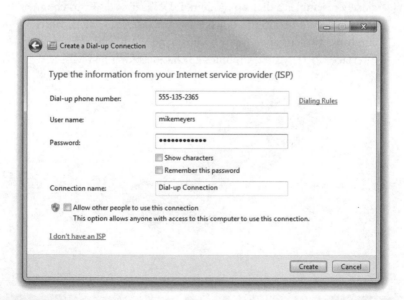

FIGURE 20.20   Creating a dial-up connection in Windows 7

If you have to troubleshoot a traditional modem, keep what it is and how it works in mind. The user needs a dial tone, and they may need to configure a prefix to "dial out" if they're in an office or hotel. They may not be able to test their connection while they speak with you. They can manually dial the number (or listen in) and confirm another computer answers it. If you've double-checked everything, including connection numbers and user credentials, it's time to call the ISP to troubleshoot Dial-up Networking settings.

DSL

Digital subscriber line (DSL) connections use standard telephone lines, but special equipment on each end creates always-on Internet connections at much greater speeds than dial-up. To set up a DSL connection, connect a DSL receiver (shown in Figure 20.21) from the ISP to the telephone line. A tech or knowledgeable user then configures the DSL modem and router with settings from the ISP.

FIGURE 20.21 A DSL receiver

Local Lingo

ADSL and **SDSL** The most common forms of DSL are *asynchronous (ADSL)* and *synchronous (SDSL)*. ADSL lines differ between slow upload speed (such as 384 Kbps, 768 Kbps, or 1 Mbps) and faster download speed (usually 3 to 15 Mbps). You can pay more for SDSL to get the same upload and download speeds. DSL encompasses many such variations, so you'll often see it referred to as *x*DSL.

Service levels for DSL can vary widely. At the low end of the spectrum, speeds are generally in the single digits—less than 1 Mbps upload and around 3 Mbps download. Where available, more recent *x*DSL technologies can offer competitive broadband speeds measured in tens of megabits per second.

Cable

Cable uses regular RG-6 or RG-59 cable TV lines to provide upload speeds from 1 to 20 Mbps and download speeds from 6 Mbps to 1+ Gbps. *Cable Internet* connections are theoretically available anywhere you can get cable TV. The cable connects to a cable modem that itself connects (via Ethernet) to a small home router or your network interface card (NIC).

Fiber

DSL providers have developed very popular fiber-to-the-node (FTTN) and fiber-to-the-premises (FTTP) services that provide Internet (and more). FTTN connections run from the provider to a box in your neighborhood, which connects to your home or office via normal coaxial or Ethernet cable. FTTP runs from the provider straight to a home or office, using fiber the whole way.

AT&T's U-verse (see Figure 20.22) FTTN service generally offers download speeds from 1 to 75 Mbps and upload speeds from 384 Kbps to 8 Mbps. A few locations currently have AT&T's GigaPower service with 1 Gbps download and upload speeds. Verizon's Fios FTTP service provides upload and download speeds from 25 Mbps to 500 Mbps. Google Fiber offers a 1 Gbps upload/download service. Service at this end of the scale is currently limited.

802.11 Wireless

Wi-Fi (or 802.11 wireless), which we covered in Chapter 19, is so prevalent that it's how many of us get to the Internet in public places such as coffee shops, airports, fast-food chains, and bars. Some cities even provide partial to full Wi-Fi coverage.

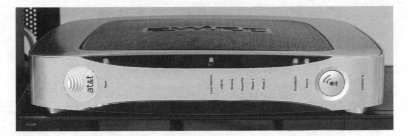

FIGURE 20.22 U-verse gateway

Local Lingo

MAN An 802.11 network that covers a single city is an excellent example of a *metropolitan area network (MAN)*.

Wi-Fi is convenient in densely populated areas, but short range makes it impractical in areas where it's hard to place new access points—though high-powered, directional antennas can create a *line-of-sight wireless Internet connection* to fixed locations up to about eight miles away. Keep in mind that open hotspots aren't encrypted, so attackers can monitor your connection.

Travel Advisory

Secure your public hotspot web browsing with HTTPS-secured sites, *HTTPS Everywhere* from the Electronic Freedom Federation (EFF), or the VPN connections discussed earlier in the chapter.

Cellular

Cellular data services have used an intimidating number of different standards over the years, so the cellular industry markets them in generations: first-generation devices were called 1G, second generation were 2G, and so on; some technologies even used terms like 2.5G to show they weren't 2G but not quite 3G. As a rule, don't trust these marketing terms; look into the exact standards in use.

Exam Tip

The CompTIA A+ exams will not ask you to define a G level for a particular cellular technology.

| **FIGURE 20.23** | Real-world LTE speed test |

Two competing digital cellular standards, Global System for Mobile Communications (GSM) and code division multiple access (CDMA), emerged in the early 1990s and have continued to evolve since. We're well into the fourth generation (*4G*); *Long Term Evolution (LTE)* technology rolled out worldwide in the early 2010s now dominates (on both GSM and CDMA networks). LTE features *theoretical* speeds (see Figure 20.23) up to 300 Mbps download and 75 Mbps upload. LTE coverage isn't universal, though, so carrier networks still use older technologies with more modest download speeds (generally under 10 Mbps).

Travel Advisory

Chapter 11 discusses how a smartphone or standalone hotspot device can share its cellular Internet connection via *tethering*.

Satellite

Satellite connections beam data to a professionally installed satellite dish at your house or office (with line-of-sight to the satellite). Coax connects the satellite to a receiver or satellite modem that translates the data to Ethernet, which can connect directly to your router or the NIC in your computer.

Real-world download speeds in clear weather run from a few to about 20 Mbps; upload speeds vary, but are typically a tenth to a third of the download speed. They aren't stunning, but satellite can provide these speeds in areas with no other connectivity.

> **Travel Advisory**
>
> Keep in mind *satellite latency*—usually several hundred milliseconds (ms). It isn't highly obvious for many purposes, but can affect real-time activities like gaming or video/voice calls.

Objective 20.03 Connecting to the Internet

O nce you sign up for an Internet connection, it's time to connect your computer or LAN. If you're connecting a single computer, you'll either install an expansion card or USB network adapter or modem, or you'll use an Ethernet patch cable to connect to an external modem/adapter box. You may need to follow instructions from your ISP to configure the connection (often with a browser-based utility for external boxes).

> **Exam Tip**
>
> A lot of networking devices designed for the residential space use a feature called *universal plug and play* (*UPnP*) to find and connect to other UPnP devices. This feature enables seamless interconnectivity at the cost of somewhat lower security, so disable it if you don't need it.

Direct connections are rare these days, in part because Wi-Fi is so popular. As you saw in Chapter 18, if you want to connect your entire LAN or WLAN, you need a router. In the consumer space, most are easy-to-configure "SOHO wireless routers" (see Figure 20.24) that combine a router, switch, and WAP. Simply plug your computer into any of the LAN ports on the back and then plug the cable from your Internet connection into the port labeled Internet or WAN.

FIGURE 20.24   Common home router with Wi-Fi

All of these routers use *Network Address Translation (NAT)* to present an entire LAN of computers to the Internet as a single machine. All anyone on the Internet sees is the *public* IP address your ISP gives you—not private addresses assigned to devices on your LAN—effectively firewalling LAN nodes from malicious users on the vast untrusted WAN that is the Internet.

Local Lingo

Dynamic NAT (DNAT)   Can share more than one routable IP address among devices on your LAN. Also called *pooled NAT*.
Firewall   Firewalls, discussed further in Chapter 21, are security barriers that restrict traffic between hosts or networks.

Basic Router Configuration

Most of the configuration concepts for these SOHO routers carry over from what we looked at in Chapter 19; most have built-in configuration web pages accessible by IP address (which differs by maker) that prompt you for an administrative user name and password. You'll reach the router's configuration pages (see Figure 20.25) after authenticating.

FIGURE 20.25   Configuration home page

Travel Advisory

Default administrative credentials were once common, but modern devices try to protect users who don't change the defaults. They'll include a generated password or prompt you for one on install. Protect yourself from flaws in the generation scheme—change your default user name and/or password.

The 902 exam objectives expect you to know how to change a number of settings. We looked at firmware updates, MAC filtering, and a number of wireless-specific settings in Chapter 19. You'll also see several more security-specific settings in Chapter 21. Aside from changing your default administrative credentials, there's an important organizational task you may need to perform—setting static IP addresses. This can mean one of two things:

- When you connect to your ISP, you'll receive a dynamic IP address using DHCP just like the computers on your LAN get. For some users, these occasional IP address changes cause trouble, so most ISPs enable you to pay for a static IP. You may need to change your connection type from Automatic/DHCP to Static IP and manually enter this information into your router (see Figure 20.26).

- Likewise, some devices—servers in particular—may need a static IP address within your LAN. You can manually configure the device's TCP/IP settings to use a static address, but it isn't ideal—it doesn't, for example, guarantee the DHCP server won't give its address out to another system. Some routers have DHCP settings that enable you to reserve IP addresses and assign specific hosts to them via DHCP; in other cases, you may just need to turn DHCP on or off depending on your needs (but turning DHCP off is rare).

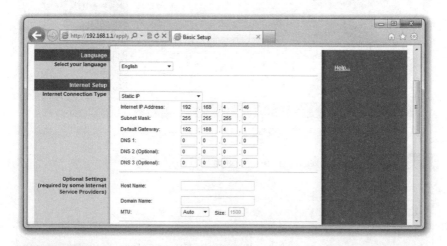

FIGURE 20.26 Entering a static IP address

 **Internet Troubleshooting**

The dominant Internet setup for a SOHO environment consists of some box from your ISP—a cable or fiber modem, a DSL modem, and so on—that connects via Ethernet cable to a home router. This router is usually 802.11 capable and includes four Ethernet ports. The network has a mix of wired and wireless nodes (see Figure 20.27). CompTIA likely has a setup like this in mind, so we'll use it as a frame of reference to review common Internet connectivity symptoms in the 901 objectives.

Travel Advisory
Most Internet connection problems are actually problems on your LAN or WLAN; we won't rehash them, but much of what you saw in Chapters 18 and 19 still applies. 

FIGURE 20.27 Typical SOHO setup

No Connectivity

Chapters 18 and 19 already covered wired and wireless connectivity issues, so let's look at a lack of connectivity to a specific website:

- Can you get to other websites? If not, go back and triple-check your local connectivity. If so, double-check the address you're using.
- Can you ping the site? Go to a command prompt and try pinging the URL as follows:

```
C:\>ping www.cheetos1.com
Ping request could not find host www.cheetos1.com.
Please check the name and try again.
```

The ping fails, but we learn a lot from it. The ping indicates that your computer can't get an IP address for that website. This points to a DNS failure, which is a very common problem. To fix DNS failures, follow these steps:

1. In Windows, go to a command prompt and type **ipconfig /flushdns**:

```
C:\>ipconfig /flushdns
Windows IP Configuration
Successfully flushed the DNS Resolver Cache.
```

Travel Advisory

Despite the similarity, ifconfig and iwconfig aren't suitable for flushing the DNS cache, if it exists, in Mac OS X or Linux.

2. In Windows, go to the Network and Sharing Center and click *Change adapter settings*. Right-click your network connection and select Diagnose to run the troubleshooter (see Figure 20.28).
3. Try using a reputable public DNS server, such as Google's: 8.8.8.8 and 8.8.4.4.

Limited Connectivity

Assuming you're connected to a DHCP server, limited connectivity points to a DHCP problem. Run **ipconfig** and see if you have an APIPA address (or, for IPv6, you lack a global address):

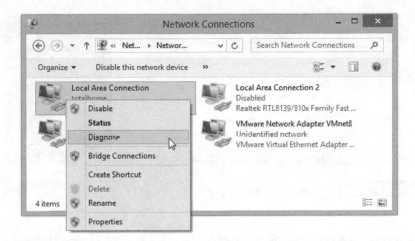

FIGURE 20.28 Diagnosing a network problem in Windows 8.1

```
C:\>ipconfig
Windows IP Configuration
Ethernet adapter Local Area Connection:
        Connection-specific DNS Suffix   . :
        IP Address. . . . . . . . . . . : 169.254.0.16
        Subnet Mask . . . . . . . . . . : 255.255.0.0
        Default Gateway . . . . . . . . :
```

Uh-oh! No DHCP server! If your router is your DHCP server, try restarting the router. If you know the network ID for your network and the IP address for your default gateway (something you should know—it's your network!), try setting up your NIC statically.

Local Connectivity

Local connectivity means you can access network resources but not the Internet. This can point to DHCP trouble, but you might also have a problem with your router. Ping its default gateway and, if successful, ping the other (WAN) port. You can access the router's configuration web page to find the WAN IP address (see Figure 20.29).

If your router doesn't have a WAN IP address, this also points to DHCP trouble—but this time the DHCP server is at your ISP. Some router configuration pages have a button to renew your IP address via DHCP; if not, try resetting the cable/fiber/DSL modem. If that doesn't work, call your ISP.

FIGURE 20.29 Router's WAN IP address

Slow Transfer Speeds

We all wish our Internet connection was faster, but some slowdowns can be resolved without changing your ISP or service tier. To see what's happening on a sluggish network, open a command prompt and type **netstat** to see connections between your computer and others:

```
C:\>netstat
Active Connections
   Proto  Local Address          Foreign Address        State
   TCP    10.12.14.47:57788      totalfs3:microsoft-ds  ESTABLISHED
   TCP    192.168.15.102:139     Sabertooth:20508       ESTABLISHED
   TCP    192.168.15.102:50283   Theater:netbios-ssn    ESTABLISHED
   TCP    192.168.15.102:60222   dts1.google.com:https  ESTABLISHED
   TCP    192.168.15.102:60456   www.serve2.le.com:http  ESTABLISHED
   TCP    192.168.15.102:60482   64.145.92.65:http      ESTABLISHED
   TCP    192.168.15.102:60483   12.162.15.1:57080      TIME_WAIT
```

I recognized many of these as web pages or resources I was using, but not 12.162.15.1:57080; I looked it up on Google, which led me to the background torrent program I had left open. Oops!

When everyone on the network is getting slow Internet connectivity, it's time to check your router's options. You may simply have too many people sharing too little bandwidth—but getting more bandwidth isn't always something you can do. You can configure *Quality of Service (QoS)* on your router (see Figure 20.30) to prioritize or limit access for certain users, applications, or services when there isn't enough bandwidth to go around.

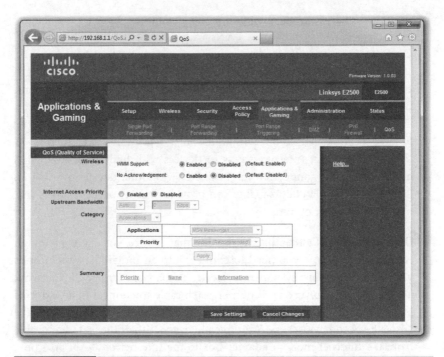

FIGURE 20.30 QoS

CHECKPOINT

✓**Objective 20.01: What Is the Internet?** Structurally, the Internet is a multi-tier network of networks that interconnect the world with high-speed backbone lines. What we think of as the Internet, however, is all of the software running atop this network. Internet application protocols support the World Wide Web, e-mail, file transfers, remote access to CLI and GUI interfaces, securely connecting to remote LANs, and more. Internet applications such as web apps are built on top of these application protocols and run primarily on virtual servers (that is, servers running in VMs) located in the cloud. Popular cloud services include Infrastructure as a Service, Platform as a Service, and Software as a Service—all of which can be found running in the public cloud or in private, community, and hybrid clouds.

✔**Objective 20.02: Internet Connection Technologies**   Internet connection technologies bridge individual LANs with the vast WAN of the Internet. Older traditional and ISDN dial-up technologies use the telephone network, as do faster DSL services. Cable and fiber Internet can provide direct high-speed Internet connections over cable TV lines or fiber optic connections. Beyond connecting individual machines in our homes or public places, line-of-sight Wi-Fi with large directional antennas can provide connectivity to fixed locations within a few miles. Cellular data connections such as 4G LTE provide direct Internet access to devices with built-in or expansion hardware, but the connection can be shared with other devices over Wi-Fi. Despite the high latency, satellite can provide decent speeds in areas that may have no other options.

✔**Objective 20.03: Connecting to the Internet**   Once you sign up for an Internet connection, you need to connect it to an individual system or to your LAN. Individual systems may need an expansion card or USB network adapter/modem, or use an Ethernet patch cable to connect to an external modem/adapter; these direct connections are rare, as we usually want the whole LAN to have access. We typically connect the Ethernet patch cable from the Internet modem/adapter box to the Internet or WAN port on a SOHO wireless router (a combined router, switch, and WAP).

✔**Objective 20.04: Internet Troubleshooting**   Internet-specific connectivity troubleshooting is largely about confirming that you are using the correct address, that the site's host name is properly resolving via DNS, and that your system and your router have properly received an IP address—typically from DHCP. Slow transfer speeds can be addressed by identifying unintentional bandwidth-consuming programs on individual systems, and by using QoS on the router to prioritize or limit access for certain users, applications, and services when there isn't enough bandwidth to go around.

REVIEW QUESTIONS

1. What is the port number for the HTTPS service?
   A. 440
   B. 445
   C. 427
   D. 443

2. The delay caused by the distance a signal must travel to a satellite dish is called the satellite _____.

   A. slow down

   B. latency

   C. interdiction

   D. proxy

3. Ethan connects to the Internet through a dial-up connection. He has multiple computers and wants to be able to get online from each of them. Which Windows solution would help him the most?

   A. Windows Firewall

   B. Internet Explorer

   C. Device Manager

   D. Internet Connection Sharing

4. Where can anyone pay to create a VM to run their very own server?

   A. Public cloud

   B. Private cloud

   C. Community cloud

   D. Hybrid cloud

5. A more secure alternative to the Telnet remote terminal is

   _____.

   A. PPP

   B. TCP/IP

   C. HTTP

   D. SSH

6. John wants to log in to a server remotely and take full control over the remote machine without an invitation, but he wants to have graphical control, not command line only. What tool should he use?

   A. Remote Assistance

   B. Remote Desktop

   C. SSH

   D. Telnet

7. Which term applies to Dropbox and similar file storage and synchronization services?

   A. Software as a Service

   B. Storage as a Service

   C. File System as a Service

   D. Synchronization as a Service

8. Which creates encrypted tunnels between computers or networks over the Internet?

   A. Telnet

   B. Tethering

   C. Port 548

   D. VPNs

9. What can greatly improve the performance of a VPN or VoIP connection?

   A. SSH

   B. SNMP

   C. QoS

   D. LDAP

10. Liz can receive her e-mail, but she cannot send e-mail. Which of the following is most likely causing her problem?

   A. POP3

   B. SMTP

   C. IMAP4

   D. Port 3389

REVIEW ANSWERS

1. **D**   HTTPS uses port 443.

2. **B**   The delay caused by the distance a signal must travel to a satellite dish is called satellite *latency*.

3. **D**   Ethan could use Internet Connection Sharing to share his connection with the other computers.

4. **A**   The public cloud is where anyone can create a VM, among other computing and storage resources.

5. **D**   The more secure remote terminal is called SSH, or Secure Shell.

6. **B**   All four choices enable you to control a remote computer, but Remote Desktop is the best answer here. Remote Desktop gives you full graphical control and doesn't require an invitation.

7. **A**   Software as a Service describes end-user Internet-based applications.

8. **D**   Encrypted tunnels between computers or networks through the Internet are called virtual private networks (VPNs).

9. **C**   Quality of Service (QoS) can greatly improve the performance of a VPN or VoIP connection.

10. **B**   Liz can receive her e-mail, but she cannot send e-mail. SMTP is the most likely cause of her problem. Remember that SMTP is used to send e-mail, whereas POP3 and IMAP4 are used to receive e-mail.

Securing Computers

	NEWBIE	SOME EXPERIENCE	EXPERT
ETA	3 hours	2 hours	1 hour

Sound computer security is a combination of strategy and tactics. Strategy is about understanding the threats your systems and networks face and deciding what policies, software, and hardware you should put in place to stop or limit them. Even the best security plans aren't perfect—there are always new vulnerabilities—but the foundation of good security is having the tactical discipline to implement your plans correctly. This is how you avoid giving away easy wins, such as letting hackers steal a database of customer information with a vulnerability published and patched years ago.

Many of the terms, metaphors, analogies, and methods in computer security make it tempting to imagine you're defending a military fort. There are certainly parts of computer security where this approach makes sense, but most computer security threats won't blow a smoking hole in your defenses—they're about quietly slipping in unnoticed to establish and maintain surveillance or control.

Instead, try to view computer security in terms of managing a restaurant kitchen. You might think the top priority is making sure the food tastes good, but the entire business and health of its customers hinge on good hygiene. To send safe food out of a kitchen dozens of people and tons of food pass through—many bearing germs and allergens capable of sending someone to the hospital—restaurants must practice good hygiene with care and vigilance.

 **Objective 21.01** **Security Hygiene**

When you start with the fact that threats will pass through your computers, networks, and physical space, it's obvious that you can't just focus all of your efforts on building an impenetrable digital wall. In an ideal world, physical and digital walls could prevent all *unauthorized access* to your hardware, software, and data. In the real world, we leave doors open and computers unlocked, or even hand out the wrong keys and permissions.

These unforced errors are opportunities for the naïve, curious, and malicious to access things they aren't supposed to—opportunities to copy, steal, change, or destroy data and hardware. You need a thoughtful system of overlapping *security hygiene* practices to protect your data and systems from accidents and attacks.

Restricting Access

Rigorous access controls make your organization a much tougher target; the goal is identifying the kinds of access that pose a risk for your organization, and establishing practices to minimize that risk. Here are two principles to keep in mind:

- Increased access poses greater risks. Just like a lost master key is a bigger threat than one for a single office, accounts with administrator, supervisor, or root user access can do vastly more damage if compromised by malware or a malicious user. Limit how many accounts have full control and the time they spend logged in.
- Attackers look for weak links; don't fall into the trap of focusing all your effort on technical threats you find interesting. An attacker won't notice the time you spent implementing the perfect password policy when they walk in dressed as a messenger and walk out with a laptop that automatically connects with saved credentials.

Physical Security

Access control begins with *physical security* to keep unauthorized people away from sensitive areas, devices, and information.

- Use a *mantrap* to keep intruders from *tailgating* in behind authorized entrants. Physically and electronically verify employee identity (and their permission to access an area or resource) with *radio frequency ID (RFID)* or smart card employee *ID badges* (see Figure 21.1).

FIGURE 21.1 Typical employee badge/smart card

Local Lingo

Mantrap   A small room with a door to an outer unsecured area as well as a door to a secure inner area. The mantrap's outer door must be closed before the inner door can be opened, and the entrant must present authentication. The mantrap is often controlled by a security guard who records comings and goings on an *entry control roster*.

- Lock doors and unattended computers. Password-protected screensavers are a good backstop if someone forgets to lock a system, but they can't replace explicitly locking unattended systems. Even a minute alone with an unlocked system is enough to install malware.
- Position desks and screens where snoops can't see them without the user's knowledge; where this is hard, you can use *privacy filters* (see Figure 21.2) to reduce the monitor viewing angle. For additional security, restrict access to a space or resource to just those that need it.

Local Lingo

Shoulder surfing   Observing a user's screen or keyboard for information such as a password—usually over the user's shoulder.

- Don't leave passwords, sensitive documents, or hardware containing sensitive data sitting out. Use data, drive, or full-device encryption to limit an attacker's ability to obtain sensitive information by

FIGURE 21.2   Privacy filter

stealing hard drives. Sanitize retired data storage devices with the data destruction practices discussed in Chapter 14, and make sure unneeded documents are immediately shredded to reduce your vulnerability to dumpster diving.

Travel Assistance

Your organization's data and operational capabilities can be threatened by attackers, malware, fire, power outages, storms, intentional vandalism, or even a failed air conditioner; therefore, it's important to have redundancy to keep the operation running as well as backups to recover from loss. Chapter 3 looks at protecting equipment from environmental threats, and Chapter 15 explores data backup and recovery.

- Whereas wireless access to properly secured networks requires a password, wired ports and infrastructure generally do not. An unattended switch, SOHO router, or connected outlet is all an attacker with a laptop and a patch cable needs to hop on your network.
- Don't leave passwords or sensitive documents lying around, and make sure unneeded documents are immediately shredded.

Local Lingo

Dumpster diving   *Dumpster diving* is the generic term for searching through refuse for information. This is also a form of intrusion.

- Likewise, physical expansion ports or removable media slots can be used to install malware on a system.

Social Engineering

While you're busy preparing to catch or deter intruders, the attacker may be using *social engineering* to trick or manipulate insiders into giving up access. Social engineering attacks are rarely used in isolation.

- Attackers may infiltrate by posing as cleaning personnel, repair technicians, or messengers. Once inside, they may snoop around or talk with people to gather more information. Passwords are obvious, but information such as employee names, office numbers, and department names could all be useful later.

- The attacker in a *telephone* scam attempts to come across as someone inside the organization to gain information (such as a phone number, user name, blackmail material, or schedule) or help (perhaps a password reset or wire transfer).

- *Phishing* has the same goals as telephone scams but uses online methods, including e-mail and messages through social networks such as Facebook. The more dangerous form, *spear phishing,* uses details from the target's life to make the bait harder to resist.

Authentication

Speaking of passwords and ID badges, good security (both physical and digital) requires strong authentication. We explored multifactor authentication in Chapter 11—but it is just as important for securing desktops, portable computers, servers, and physical space. Let's look at some practical recommendations for passwords (a knowledge factor), some useful possession factor devices, and hardware for authenticating with inherence factors.

Many people choose passwords that are easy to hack—often including the name of a relative or pet—and use poor security hygiene that exposes your systems and networks to risk. In an ideal world, all of your users have impossible-to-guess passwords that they change often and never write down or re-use elsewhere.

> **Exam Tip**
>
> The 902 exam objectives outline CompTIA's opinion on password *best practices*: always change default user names/passwords, require your users to use strong passwords that expire (and thus get changed) regularly, and password-protect the BIOS/UEFI and screensaver for additional security.

In the real world, good password hygiene is a compromise between security and usability:

- Use *strong passwords* that are reasonably resistant to a calculated attack by password-guessing programs—a good starting point is a minimum of eight characters, including letters (both upper- and lowercase), numbers, and symbols—but keep in mind that "strong" evolves along with processing power and password-guessing strategies. The catch is that users react predictably to complex requirements by tacking punctuation and numbers onto either end or writing the password down.

- Setting passwords to expire regularly reduces how long a compromised password is useful, but users tend to cope with frequent change requirements by using a predictable template or formula. Assume an attacker who recovers an old password like #1SportsFan5 will try #1SportsFan6, and several more increments if it doesn't work.

- To someone with physical access to the workspace, the accounts of users who write passwords down and leave them on their desk, monitor, or mouse pad are barely more secure than no-password accounts. You typically don't want your users to do this, but it is situational: a strong password on a sticky note in an office with strong physical security may do vastly more to protect you from hackers in another country than a weak, memorable password that never gets written down.

- Passwords can also restrict access to internal resources to users who understand or need to use them. The BIOS/UEFI passwords discussed in Chapter 7 are a great way to keep low-knowledge users from fiddling with the CMOS system setup utility.

You can greatly improve on password security, regardless of password quality, by adding a possession factor. *Smart cards* (see Figure 21.3) are credit-card-sized cards with circuitry that can identify the bearer of the card, and a *security token* (often in the form of a *key fob*) stores digital certificates, passwords, biometric data, and so on. *RSA tokens* (see Figure 21.4) and compatible authentication servers use an initial random seed to regularly generate a time-based number the user must enter to authenticate.

People can guess or discover passwords and steal possession factors, but it's much harder to forge someone's fingerprints. *Biometric devices* such as

FIGURE 21.3 Keyboard-mounted smart card reader being used for a commercial application (photo courtesy of Cherry Corp.)

RSA key fob (photo courtesy of EMC Corp.)

fingerprint scanners (see Figure 21.5) and *retinal scanners* require some sort of physical, flesh-and-blood authentication.

Users and Groups

User accounts and groups are the bedrock of access control. We looked at these concepts in Chapters 13 and 18, but let's review some specific recommendations:

- Access to user accounts should be restricted to the assigned individuals, and unused accounts (including default/guest accounts) should be promptly deleted or disabled.
- Groups are a great way to achieve (and understand) increased complexity without increasing the administrative burden.
- When assigning permissions to accounts and groups, follow the *principle of least privilege*: accounts should have permission to only resources they need.
- Find a user's *effective permissions* by adding up permissions from each group.

FIGURE 21.5 Microsoft keyboard with fingerprint accessibility

Travel Advisory

File-system security only extends to drives/cards formatted with modern file systems such as NTFS, HFS+, and ext3/4. If you copy a file to removable media formatted with an older file system such as FAT32, the OS will strip all permissions!

Security Policies

On each OS, *policies* can further restrict the actions a group or account can perform (such as opening a command prompt, installing software, or logging on at a given time of day). Every Windows client has its own *Local Security Policy* program (see Figure 21.6), but local policies are a pain if you want the same settings on multiple systems. If you want to apply *granular* policy settings *en masse,* you need to step up to Windows Active Directory domain-based *Group Policy* (see Figure 21.7).

Group Policy settings are a big topic on most of the Microsoft certification tracks, but for the purposes of the CompTIA A+ exams, you simply have to be comfortable with the concept behind Group Policy. To give you a taste, policies can: keep users from editing the registry, accessing the command line, or installing software; define who can log on to or shut down a system; enforce minimum password length; configure account lockout after a number of failed logon attempts; and enable users to browse for printers on the network.

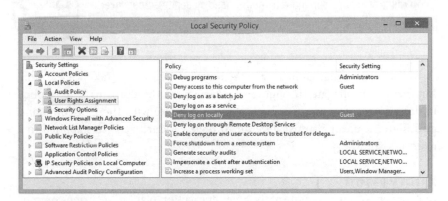

FIGURE 21.6 Local Security Policy

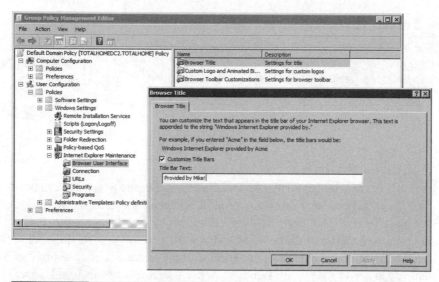

FIGURE 21.7 Using Group Policy to make the IE title bar say "Provided by Mike!"

Exam Tip

The 902 exam objectives specify some account management and workstation security best practices that you can accomplish with security policies and the principle of least privilege: restrict user permissions and login times; disable guest and default accounts; configure account lockout based on failed attempts; configure timeout-based screen or screensaver locks; and disable AutoRun or AutoPlay features.

When you change policies at the domain level, it can take a little time for them to propagate through every system on the domain. If the policy update is urgent, you can force systems to update with the CLI command **gpupdate**. You can also use *gpresult* to review security policies applied to a user or system.

Encryption

In Chapter 20 you saw some of the roles encryption plays in securing communications that pass through the open Internet, but there's a little more you need to know about these technologies when it comes to maintaining good security hygiene.

In order for a client and server—such as a web browser and web server—to encrypt data that the other can decrypt, they need to exchange the encryption keys they'll use. To do this, the server sends a public key to your browser in the form of a *digital certificate* that was previously signed by a trusted *certificate authority (CA)* to guarantee the public key it holds is actually from the web server and not from an attacker impersonating the web server.

Your web browser comes with a built-in list of *trusted root CAs* (see Figure 21.8), and if your browser receives a certificate signed by one of these highly respected root CAs from a website, the browser will seamlessly load the web page and display a small (usually green) secure-connection lock in the address bar. If your browser receives a fishy certificate—perhaps it's expired or doesn't use a trusted root CA—the browser will warn you (as shown in Figure 21.9).

What you do here is up to you. There are a number of boring reasons you could see certificate warnings for a site that is secure, but the safe thing to do is to go back instead of entering the site—and you certainly don't want low-knowledge users naively clicking past certificate warnings. If the invalid certificate warning exists because a secure site on your corporate intranet uses a self-signed certificate instead of one from a trusted root CA, you may have to do additional user education about why they can ignore the certificate warning on the intranet, but not on the Internet.

FIGURE 21.8   Trusted authorities built into Firefox

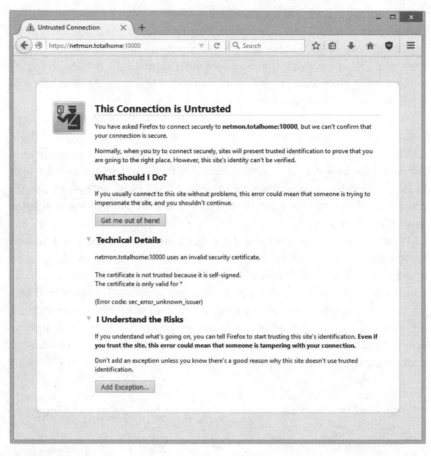

FIGURE 21.9	Untrusted certificate

Another issue you may run into is that a browser may refuse to trust a site if its certificate suddenly differs from the one cached on a previous visit. If this is the problem, you can remedy it by clearing the SSL cache. The process varies by browser, but Internet Explorer and Chrome both use the Windows cache, which you clear by clicking the Clear SSL state button on the Content tab of the Internet Options applet.

Data Classification and Compliance

Larger organizations, such as government entities, benefit greatly from organizing their data according to its sensitivity and minimizing surprises by keeping computer hardware and software as uniform as possible. This also helps maintain *compliance* with government and internal regulations; common examples are rules on approved software and regulations on how you must handle *personally identifiable information (PII)* such as health or academic records.

Exam Tip

The CompTIA A+ 902 objectives use specific language for compliance. People must *follow corporate end-user policies and security best practices*. Follow the rules, in other words.

A common *data classification* scheme that flags documents as public, internal use only, highly confidential, top secret, and so on, helps employees (including techs) know what to do with documents and hardware containing them (such as using different rules to recycle hard drives that hold top secret data). Your strategy for recycling a computer system left from a migrated user, for example, will differ a lot if the data on the drive was classified as internal use only or top secret.

Software compliance is simple enough if you have an explicit list of allowed software and strict controls on who can install programs, but less restrictive regimes have to stay in compliance with software licenses. Like other creative acts, programmers are granted copyright to software they create and decide how or if others can obtain a license to use the software. The licensing can be commercial or noncommercial, personal or enterprise. The software can be closed source or open source. You have a legal obligation to use the software in compliance with its license, which typically entails:

Exam Tip

Noncompliant systems are also at increased risk of malware infections or other vulnerabilities introduced by the unapproved software.

- Paying money for software released under a *commercial license* and complying with terms that indicate whether the license supports personal or private use.
- Complying with any *End User License Agreement (EULA)* you agree to when you open or install software, which typically specifies how you may use the software and whether you may share it. If the software uses *digital rights management (DRM)* techniques to protect the application or its files, the EULA typically forbids you from breaking, reverse-engineering, or removing these protections (or helping anyone else do so).

- Observing stipulations in noncommercial software licenses that specify whether the software is free for all uses, free only for personal/educational use, or requires a special commercial license for commercial use.

- Complying with additional stipulations in *open source software* licenses that specify how you may use the source code. These licenses commonly give you the right to modify the source, but may require you to release your modifications for free as well.

Exam Tip

The 902 objectives include an "open source vs. commercial license" distinction that does not exist in the real world. There are plenty of open source programs with licensing fees, such as server versions of Linux. Many "free" programs are likewise closed source.

- Observe stipulations in *closed source software* licenses regarding whether you may modify the software and whether you may include it in or distribute it with one of your own products.

Audits and Reports

Because security is a process and not a destination, we audit our systems and networks for events or conditions and report security issues for a network administrator or technician to resolve. The security policies you just saw can also enable logging, which you can view in Event Viewer. You won't be responsible for writing a brilliant auditing policy from scratch, but you need to know what it does and how to turn it on or off.

To turn on auditing at a local level, go to Administrative Tools | Local Security Policy | Local Policies | Audit Policy. Double-click one of the policy options and select one or both of the checkboxes in the resulting Properties dialog box (see Figure 21.10).

The Security section of Event Viewer doesn't show much until you've set up auditing. *Event auditing* tells Windows to create an entry in the Security Log when certain events such as a user login occur (see Figure 21.11). *Object access auditing* logs attempts to access an object such as a file or folder.

Incident Reporting

Once you've gathered data about a particular system or you've dealt with a computer or network problem, complete the mission by giving your supervisor an *incident report*. Many companies have pre-made forms; others may just

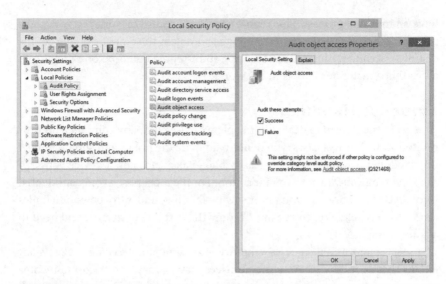

FIGURE 21.10 Audit object access Properties dialog box, with Local Security Policy open in the background

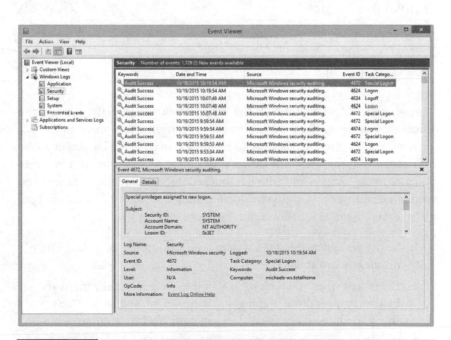

FIGURE 21.11 Event Viewer displaying security alerts

have an informal process. This report provides a record of work you've accomplished and may reveal a pattern or bigger problem to someone higher up the chain. A seemingly innocuous security audit report could be one of a dozen clues that a malicious plan is in the works.

Evidence Handling

As a tech, you'll need to deal with people who use company computers in prohibited ways. In most cases, you're not paid to be the police and should not get involved, but if something bad—really bad—takes place on a device you support, everyone may turn to you for action. For the most part, avoid confidential information and pretend you never saw it—but if you identify obvious felonies or dangerous behavior, you've just become the first line of defense and need to act accordingly.

Most organizations require employees to sign an *Acceptable Use Policy (AUP)* that defines what actions employees may or may not perform on company equipment, including computers, phones, printers, and even the network itself. This policy will define the handling of passwords, e-mail, and many other issues—and it guides what actions or content you should identify as prohibited.

Travel Assistance

The SANS Institute provides a boilerplate AUP at www.sans.org/security-resources/policies/Acceptable_Use_Policy.pdf.

You report violations through the proper channels: directly to a security officer or *incident response leader* if your organization has one, and to your supervisor otherwise. Do *not* speak to the person making the infraction unless your supervisor approves it. A device's data must be preserved if it becomes evidence, so its location and who has touched it may come into question; you need to establish a *chain of custody* documenting this history. You should have a legal expert to guide you, but common rules are:

1. Isolate the system. Shut the system down and store it in a place where no one else can access it.

2. Document when you took control of the system and the actions you took: shutting it down, unplugging it, moving it, and so on. Don't worry about too much detail, but you must track its location.

3. If another person takes control of the system, document the transfer of custody.

Objective 21.02 Network Security

Networks are under threat from the outside as well, so this section looks at issues involving Internet-borne attacks, firewalls, and wireless networking. This is the security bread and butter for a CompTIA A+ technician, so you need to understand the concepts and procedures and be able to implement them properly.

Malware Forms and Features

Malware is software designed to do something on a system or network that you don't want done. Let's examine the forms and features of malware, look at the symptoms of infection, and then examine how to protect against and remove malware.

Since the 1980s, malware has been an ever-changing threat to systems, data, and users. To better understand these threats, you need to understand the different forms and features malware can have:

- When executed, a *virus* copies itself into existing executables or data files. A user action (such as opening a file or inserting infected auto-run removable media) triggers the initial infection. Most have a malicious payload capable of damaging the system or stealing data, but it may not trigger until the virus has had time to quietly spread.

- More sophisticated *worms* are freestanding programs that run on the host system and exploit vulnerabilities to replicate themselves to other network nodes and even into the firmware of connected devices.

- A *Trojan horse* doesn't replicate—it tricks users into installing it by appearing to do something useful (such as scan for malware) while it does something malicious.

- *Rootkits* exploit root-level access to burrow deep into the system's OS or hardware where they can often hide from all but the most aggressive anti-malware tools.

- Most *stealth virus* programs are boot sector viruses that use various methods to hide from anti-malware software. The AntiEXE stealth virus hooks on to a little-known but often-used software interrupt, for example, running only when that interrupt runs. Others make copies of innocent-looking files.

- A *polymorphic virus* changes its signature (often by scrambling an unused part of its own code) to elude anti-malware programs.

The form malware takes is important for locating and uninstalling it, but what matters more is how "mal" the malware will be when it runs rampant on a system. Let's review some of the more common behaviors:

- *Spyware*, which often sneaks in alongside legitimate software, collects information on the system and its users. Many associate it with a subtype, *adware,* that attempts to make money by explicitly showing ads, redirecting searches, or replacing ads from other providers with its own—but this association is largely because most adware is obvious. The most dangerous spyware quietly collects private information without detection.

- *Ransomware* encrypts data it can access on the system and its mapped network drives and then demands a payment (often in Bitcoin) in exchange for the encryption keys. It may present a countdown to the deletion of the encryption keys to encourage fast payment.

Local Lingo

Bitcoin   An early digital currency that supports global transactions and lacks the governmental control of most other currencies.

- Some malware enables remote control of infected *zombie* systems, which collectively become a *botnet* that the operators use (or rent out) to send spam, attack other systems and networks, or do processing work such as mining Bitcoin and breaking encryption keys.

Malware needs what security people call an *attack vector*—the route the malware takes to enter and infect the system. Here are some of the most common vectors:

- *Zero-day attacks* exploit vulnerabilities that were previously unknown—the software's developers have had zero days to fix it. Systems running the software will be vulnerable until the developers release a patch and it is installed.

- Attackers pretend to be another entity by *spoofing* information such as a user name or MAC, IP, e-mail, or web address in order to trick other systems or users into aiding the attack.

- *Man-in-the-middle (MITM)* attacks occur when the attacker successfully positions themselves between communicating systems in order to observe or even change the data before sending it on to the intended recipient, often leaving both parties unaware of the intermediary.

- When you log in to a service, it responds with a session key that your system can send with each request (in place of your full account credentials). *Session-hijacking* intercepts or recovers this key to impersonate you.

- *Brute force* is technically any attempt to find a useful value by trying many or all possibilities (typically with a program), but it most often refers to discovering a password by trying many possibilities. You can also use a brute-force search to find open ports, network IDs, IP addresses, user names, or even to try a long list of known vulnerabilities.

Local Lingo

Dictionary attack   A form of brute-force attack that essentially guesses every word in a dictionary. Don't think Webster's dictionary—a dictionary used to attack passwords might contain every password ever leaked online.

- *Pop-ups,* or browser windows that pop up when you visit a site or click elements, used to be very common on websites. Many of these were simple ad windows, but others emulate alerts from the OS (see Figure 21.12) or attempt to circumvent efforts to close them. Abuse of automatic pop-ups led to the use of pop-up blockers, which have since been integrated directly into browsers; sketchy modern pop-ups need to trick the user into clicking something to open the pop-up. Press CTRL-W to close the browser tab/window or ALT-F4 to close the whole browser—even if navigational aids appear to be present, they may be dummy links designed to open additional pop-ups when you click them.

Travel Advisory

Browser extensions such as uBlock Origin and Ghostery combat many online annoyances such as pop-ups, cookies, tracking, and ads.

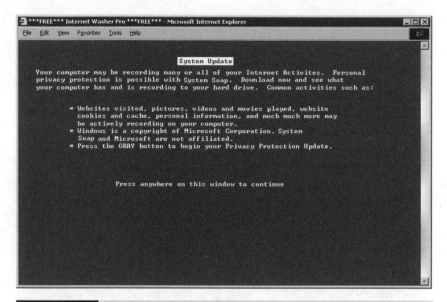

FIGURE 21.12 An old-school pop-up emulating a Windows alert

- When you click a legitimate download link, you're often taken to an informational page and the download begins automatically after a short delay. Malicious sites and pop-ups can use this same technique to automatically initiate unexpected *drive-by-downloads* that contain malware. Don't click or install these.

- Attackers and other forms of human pond-scum send tens or hundreds of millions of *spam* e-mails (often from a botnet or compromised servers) just to exploit the fraction of a fraction of a percent of recipients who fall for the bait. Some of these are simple ads for real products of questionable value, but many are outright attempts to scam, steal personal information, or deliver malware. Limit spam by not posting your e-mail address and using an e-mail service with robust spam filtering.

Travel Advisory

Most spam is from addresses you won't recognize, but some of the more dangerous spam spoofs an entity you recognize, or uses the compromised system/account of a friend to send spam—perhaps claiming your friend has run into trouble abroad and urgently needs you to wire cash.

Malware Signs and Symptoms

It would be great if the only malware signs and symptoms you needed to know were security alerts from built-in security tools or third-party anti-malware programs, but malware's biggest strength is its flexibility: it can look like anything. In fact, a lot of malware symptoms align with normal program misbehavior. If you're suspicious that malware is afoot, run a malware scan and look into what programs are currently running or start with Windows. Here are some symptoms that should get your malware sense tingling:

- A system is abnormally slow, sluggish, or prone to crashes and lockups given the programs you have open, especially if it persists after you close busy programs or reboot.
- An application or OS crash or error that cites unfamiliar programs or missing/corrupt system files.
- Renamed system files or user files, and files that go missing or have unexpected permission changes, may indicate that malware is modifying or destroying files and data.
- You receive e-mail responses from contacts or undeliverable mail notifications referencing messages you didn't send. CompTIA describes these symptoms of *hijacked e-mail* accounts with two unwieldy phrases: *responses from users regarding e-mail* and *automated replies from unknown sent e-mail*.

Travel Advisory

These symptoms of a hijacked e-mail account don't guarantee a device with access to the account is compromised; there are tons of potential causes. Other explanations include the following: you leave your system unlocked, lose a device configured with account credentials, or leave your account logged in on a public system; someone spoofs your e-mail address, hijacks your Webmail session, or discovers your account credentials; an app or extension you have granted permission to manage e-mail on your behalf is compromised; or you use a browser with a malicious extension installed.

Additionally, some malware defends itself by interfering with ways you might discover or remove it. Most of the time you won't notice this until you suspect an infection, but be suspicious if you find firewalls or automatic malware scanners disabled, or find that utilities to patch/update software or scan for malware fail to open, run, or update.

It may also try to narrowly block access to useful anti-malware sites, resources, and downloads by installing browser extensions/add-ons, or it may modify your HOSTS file to override DNS resolution for these sites. The result is usually the same: it redirects you to sites that fail to load, are explicitly malicious, or cleverly emulate your intended destination to trick you into downloading and installing a *rogue anti-malware* program that is itself malware.

Malware Prevention and Recovery

The only surefire way to protect a device from malware is to never turn it on. Even with the best anti-malware tools, there are times when malware still manages to strike. When you discover infected systems, you need to know how to stop the spread of the malware to other computers, how to fix infected computers, and how to remediate (restore) the system as close to its original state as possible.

Anti-Malware Programs

An *anti-malware program* such as a classic *antivirus program* can actively scan for lurking malware or operate as a *virus shield* that passively monitors your computer's activity, checking for viruses in real time as your system runs programs or downloads files.

Local Lingo
Antivirus　The term *antivirus* (and *antispyware,* or anti-anything) is becoming obsolete. Viruses are only a small component of the many types of malware. Many people continue to use the term as a synonym for anti-malware.

Anti-malware programs use different techniques to combat different types of viruses:

- Because most boot sectors are the same, anti-malware programs detect boot sector viruses simply by comparing the drive's boot sector to a standard boot sector. If they detect a virus, most replace the infected boot sector from a copy.
- Executable viruses are difficult to find because they can lurk in any file, so the anti-malware program compares files against a library of signatures identifying the code pattern of a known virus. From time

to time a perfectly clean program will match a signature, in which case the anti-malware program usually issues a patch to prevent further alarms.

- Anti-malware programs search for polymorphic malware by computing and storing a *checksum* from the contents of each executable file. Every time a program runs, the anti-malware program calculates a new checksum to see if the executable has changed.

Windows comes with a basic anti-malware program, Windows Defender (see Figure 21.13), but you can always supplement it with a third-party program such as Malwarebytes Anti-Malware (see Figure 21.14). It also includes the Action Center (Security Center in Windows Vista) applet to alert you of problems with your software firewall (see Figure 21.15), automatic updates, malware protection, and more.

User Education

Even the best anti-malware suite is imperfect—ideally it forms a rarely tested second line of defense. The first line of defense is educating your users— nobody wants their system infected with malware. Teach users to be cautious with e-mail from senders they don't recognize and to never click an attachment

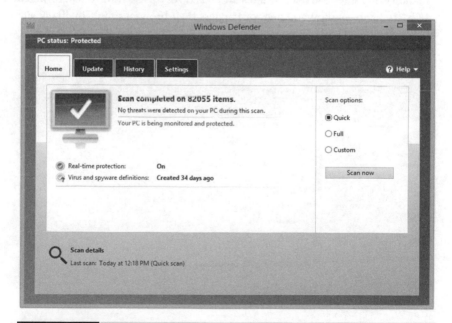

FIGURE 21.13 Windows Defender

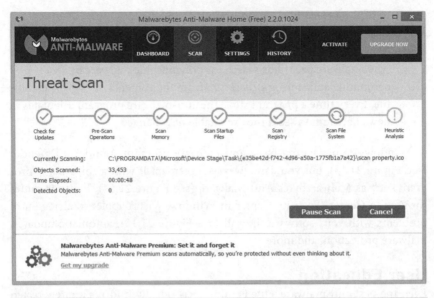

FIGURE 21.14   Malwarebytes

or URL in an e-mail unless they are 100 percent certain of the source. Explain the dangers of questionable websites and teach your users how to react when a site is trying to manipulate them or triggers their browser's built-in attack site warning (see Figure 21.16).

FIGURE 21.15   Windows 7 Action Center indicating Windows Firewall is disabled

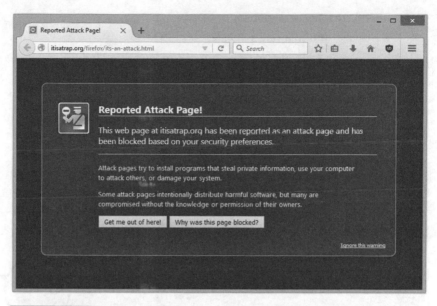

FIGURE 21.16 Attack site warning

Depending on how much say your users have over their systems, you may need to reinforce the importance of having an anti-malware program, scanning regularly, and enabling the virus shield that automatically scans e-mail, downloads, running programs, and so on. Tell your users to only install apps from trusted sources, such as the manufacturer's website, or well-known app stores, such as Valve's Steam service—and teach them how to both identify and avoid untrusted software sources, such as free registry cleaners from some .support domain.

Likewise, if your users have a say in whether their anti-malware software and its definitions automatically update, make sure they know how to enable these automatic updates to defend against new malware.

Malware Recovery Tips

When the inevitable happens, you need to follow certain steps to stop the malware from spreading and get the computer back into service safely. The 902 exam outlines the following multistep *best practice procedure for malware removal*:

1. Identify malware symptoms.
2. Quarantine infected system.
3. Disable System Restore (in Windows).

4. Remediate infected systems.

    a. Update anti-malware software.

    b. Use scan and removal techniques (Windows Safe Mode, Preinstallation Environment).

5. Schedule scans and run updates.

6. Enable System Restore and create a restore point (in Windows).

7. Educate the end user.

CompTIA considers removing malware as part of remediation. Because you can't actually remediate the system until the malware is gone, I approach this a little differently with a four-stage process: recognize and quarantine, search and destroy, remediate, and educate.

> **Exam Tip**
>
> Make sure you know CompTIA's malware removal process for the 902 exam.

Recognize and Quarantine   The first step is to recognize (identify) a potential malware outbreak and act swiftly to keep it from spreading. Network monitoring, security event logs, and user reports may all tip you off to the malware symptoms we looked at earlier. Many networks employ software such as the open source PacketFence to monitor network traffic and automatically isolate systems that start sending suspicious packets. You can also quarantine a computer manually by disconnecting the network cable. Depending on how the malware spread, you may need to take additional steps to keep others from contracting it.

Once you're sure the machine isn't capable of infecting others, disable System Restore to keep the malware from being included in (and potentially restored later from) saved restore points. To turn off System Restore in Windows, go to Control Panel | System applet | System protection. In the Protection Settings section, you'll need to individually select each drive, click Configure to open the System Protection dialog, and select Turn off system protection.

Search and Destroy   Once you've isolated the infected computer(s), you want to get to a safe boot environment and run anti-malware software; try Windows Safe Mode in Windows Vista/7 or the Windows Recovery Environment in Windows 8/8.1/10 first. If that doesn't work, or you suspect a boot sector virus, you need to boot to a clean OS—one you know is free of boot sector malware—on removable media.

Once you get to a clean boot environment, update your anti-malware software and definitions, run its most comprehensive scan, and remove any malware it discovers. Next, repeat this process for all removable media exposed to the system, and any other machine that might have received data from it.

Remediate You might need to *remediate* formerly infected systems to fix damage done by the malware. If you can't start Windows after the malware scan is finished, you need to boot to the Windows Preinstallation Environment and use the Windows Recovery Environment/System Recovery Options.

These recovery options, which you saw in Chapter 16, include useful remediation utilities such as Startup Repair, System Restore, Windows Complete PC Restore (System Image Recovery in Windows 7 and later), Refresh, Reset, and the command prompt. Run the appropriate option for the situation, and you should have the machine properly remediated in a jiffy.

Educate The malware-afflicted users may have learned their lesson, especially if they knew they were taking a risk and lost important work, data, or time in the process. It's also possible they've helpfully pointed out a hole in your organization's user education or lack thereof. If so, you may need to improve the user education program and make sure to go over it with everyone.

If not, you should review risks and threats with the user, using examples when possible, and make sure they understand how to stay away from malware in the future. Finally, make sure they have anti-malware updates and scans scheduled before you leave.

Firewalls

Firewalls generally protect an internal network from unauthorized access to and from the Internet at large with methods such as hiding IP addresses and blocking TCP/IP ports, but firewalls at internal boundaries can also help limit the damage a compromised node can do to important resources. *Hardware firewalls* are often built into routers (or standalone devices), whereas *software firewalls* run on individual systems.

Hardware Firewall Settings

Hardware firewalls protect a LAN from outside threats by filtering packets before they reach your internal machines. You can configure a SOHO router's firewall from the browser-based settings utility (see Figure 21.17). Hardware firewalls use *Stateful Packet Inspection (SPI)* to inspect individual packets and block incoming traffic that isn't a response to your outgoing traffic. You can even disable ports entirely, blocking all traffic in or out.

FIGURE 21.17   SPI firewall settings

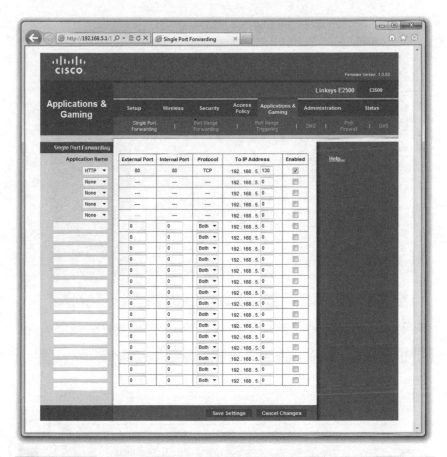

FIGURE 21.18 Port forwarding configured to pass HTTP traffic to a web server

Since Network Address Translation (NAT) hides the true IP address of internal systems, a common configuration task is enabling devices outside of your LAN to reach a server inside it.

Port forwarding (see Figure 21.18) enables you to open a port in the firewall and direct incoming traffic on that port to a specific IP address on your LAN.

Port triggering (see Figure 21.19) automatically opens incoming connections to one computer based on its outgoing connections. If you set the outgoing *trigger port* to 3434 and the incoming *destination port* to 1234, a system sending outgoing traffic on port 3434 will trigger the router to open port 1234 and send received data back to the same system.

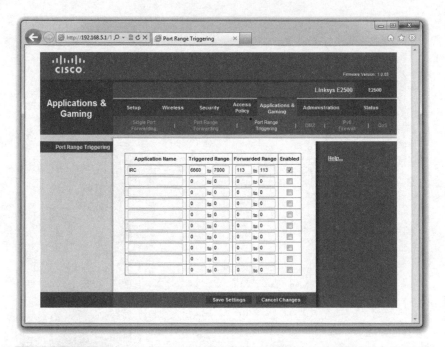

FIGURE 21.19 Port triggering for an Internet Relay Chat (IRC) server

Exam Tip

The incredibly dangerous demilitarized zone (DMZ) setting excludes specific devices from firewall protection, enabling all incoming traffic (and any attacks therein). Don't use it.

Software Firewalls

Software firewalls such as Windows Firewall (shown in Figure 21.20) handle port blocking, security logging, and more. The Windows Firewall applet enables you to turn the firewall on or off as well as create *exceptions* for programs and services to pass through the firewall. Most programs that need exceptions add themselves to this list on install; otherwise, Windows Firewall prompts you the first time you run the program and asks if you want to add an exception for it.

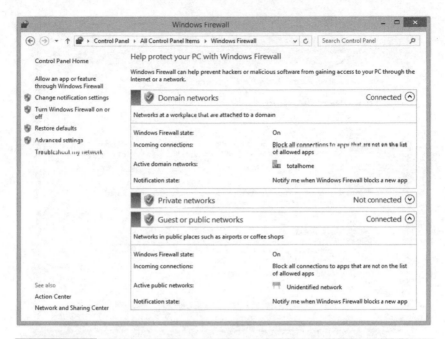

FIGURE 21.20 Windows 7 Firewall applet

Exam Tip

To turn Windows Firewall off (which I don't recommend), open the Windows Firewall applet. In Windows Vista, click *Turn Windows Firewall on or off* and then select *Off (not recommended).* In Windows 7 and later, select *Turn Windows Firewall on or off* and then select *Turn off Windows Firewall (not recommended)* for each network type you use.

When Windows 7 or later connects to a non-domain network for the first time, the OS will prompt you to choose the network type: Home, Work, or Public location (see Figure 21.21). When your computer joins a domain, Windows sets the network location to Domain by default. It asks because Windows Firewall enables exceptions for Network Discovery and File and Printer Sharing when you select a Private (Home or Work) location. Windows Vista has the

FIGURE 21.21   Set Network Location in Windows 7

same basic scheme, with a big flaw (at least for laptops): the firewall configuration and network type are the same for every connection.

> **Exam Tip**
>
> Network Discovery governs whether a computer can find devices on a network, and vice versa. Even with it activated, firewall settings may overrule certain connections.

If you click the Advanced Settings option in the Windows Firewall applet, you'll discover a much deeper level of firewall configuration (see Figure 21.22). In fact, it's an entirely different tool (an MMC snap-in) called Windows Firewall with Advanced Security, which can set complicated custom rules for inbound and outbound traffic (see Figure 21.23). Stick to the simpler Windows Firewall applet unless you need custom rules.

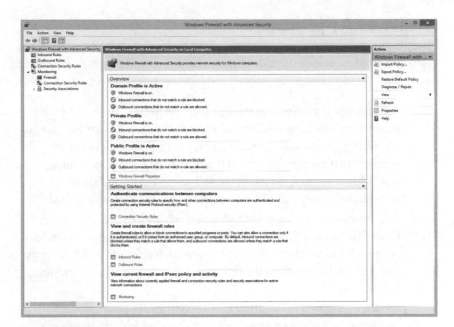

FIGURE 21.22 Windows Firewall with Advanced Security

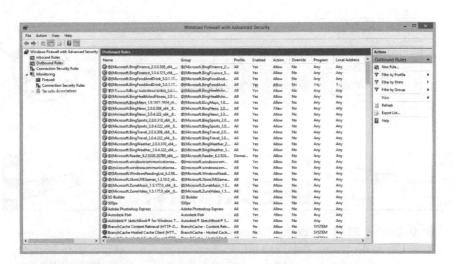

FIGURE 21.23 Outbound Rules list

Internet Appliances

Enterprise networking is generally beyond the scope of an A+ tech's duties, but the 902 objectives include some devices and concepts used to secure these large networks:

- An *intrusion detection system (IDS)* inspects packets from within the network to look for active intrusions or threats (such as viruses, illegal logon attempts, or a disgruntled employee running a vulnerability scanner) that are already behind the firewall. If it finds something, it will do some combination of the following: log it, contact an administrator, and enlist help from other devices such as a firewall.

- The more powerful *intrusion prevention system (IPS)* sits directly in the flow of traffic, enabling it to stop an ongoing attack dead in its tracks (or even fix packets on the fly), but network bandwidth and latency take a hit. Additionally, if the IPS goes down, it may take the network link with it.

- Modern dedicated firewall/Internet appliances are built around providing *unified threat management (UTM)*, which bundle other security services such as IPS, VPN, load balancing, anti-malware, and more.

Exam Tip

Many security appliances include context-based rules called Data Loss Prevention (DLP) to avoid data leaks. DLP scans outgoing packets and stops the flow if they break a rule.

CHECKPOINT

✔**Objective 21.01: Security Hygiene** Restricting physical and electronic access to programs, data, and other computing resources is both important and hard. Access controls include physically securing the workspace, resisting social engineering efforts, establishing strong authentication practices, limiting file permissions with users and groups, and limiting available actions with security policies to reinforce other protections.

Incident reporting means telling your supervisor about the data you've gathered regarding a computer or network problem to provide a record of what you've done and accomplished and help reveal larger patterns or problems to someone higher up the chain. Try to avoid personal information on a computer, but if you find something illegal, you must follow the proper procedures. If a device becomes evidence, isolate the system and document everything that happens going forward. Pay special attention to the chain of custody of the device.

✔**Objective 21.02: Network Security** Malware has many forms and features, all of which use your devices against your wishes. To help protect individual devices from malware, make sure to run up-to-date anti-malware software and keep up with all security patches for your software and OS. Some of the common symptoms of a malware infection include slowdowns, unresponsiveness, crashes, missing system files, disabled or malfunctioning security features, and browser redirections. When the inevitable happens, follow a process to halt the spread and get affected devices back into service safely: recognize and quarantine, search and destroy, remediate, and educate.

Hardware firewalls protect networks by hiding IP addresses and blocking TCP/IP ports. Port forwarding and port triggering enable traffic to pass through the firewall on specific ports to specific machines. Software firewalls such as Windows Firewall also enable strong protection against network attacks. In larger or enterprise networks, Internet security appliances further improve security by monitoring traffic for suspicious activity and even automatically stopping it.

REVIEW QUESTIONS

1. What is the process of using or manipulating people to gain access to network resources?
   A. Phishing
   B. Hacking
   C. Network engineering
   D. Social engineering

2. Which of the following might offer good hardware authentication?
   A. Strong password
   B. Encrypted password
   C. NTFS
   D. Smart card

3. What needs to be done before security event logs are available through Event Viewer?

    A. Event Viewer needs to be granted the proper file permissions to view system logs.

    B. Auditing must be enabled in the security policies.

    C. You must be logged in as an administrator.

    D. Privacy options must be updated to enable logging that may capture sensitive data.

4. Which of the following tools would enable you to require a minimum password length for all users of a workstation?

    A. AD Policy

    B. Group Policy

    C. Local Security Policy

    D. User Settings

5. Which of the following offers the best file system security?

    A. NTFS

    B. FAT32

    C. Privacy filter

    D. Local Security Policy

6. Why are unexpected ads a hallmark of spyware?

    A. Spyware collects data about the user in order to advertise to them.

    B. Spyware overrides browser protections that normally block these ads and pop-ups.

    C. Spyware that shows ads is more obvious than spyware that quietly collects data.

    D. Websites detect installed spyware to show more ads to gullible users.

7. A user account is a member of several groups, and the groups have conflicting rights and permissions to several network resources. The culminating permissions that ultimately affect the user's access are referred to as what?

    A. Effective permissions

    B. Culminating rights

    C. Last rights

    D. Persistent permissions

8. Which statement is true about virus shields?
    A. They automatically scan e-mails, downloads, and running programs.
    B. They protect against spyware and adware.
    C. They are effective in stopping pop-ups.
    D. They can reduce the amount of spam by 97 percent.

9. Which threat is a form of social engineering?
    A. Telephone scams
    B. Shoulder surfing
    C. Trojan horse
    D. Spyware

10. A user calls to complain that his computer seems awfully sluggish. All he's done so far is open his e-mail. What should the tech do first?
    A. Educate the user about the dangers of opening e-mail.
    B. Quarantine the computer so the suspected virus does not spread.
    C. Run antivirus software on the computer.
    D. Remediate the infected system.

REVIEW ANSWERS

1. **D** Social engineering is the process of using or manipulating people to gain access to network resources.
2. **D** A smart card might offer good hardware authentication.
3. **B** Event auditing or object access auditing must be enabled in Local Security Policy or via the domain.
4. **C** Local Security Policy enables you to require a minimum password length for all user accounts on a workstation.
5. **A** NTFS offers the best file system security through encryption.
6. **C** A more visible type of spyware, adware, shows ads; the most dangerous spyware quietly collects data while eluding notice.
7. **A** Effective permissions are the result of combined permissions, and they determine access to resources.
8. **A** Virus shields automatically scan e-mails, downloads, and running programs.
9. **A** Telephone scams are a form of social engineering.
10. **B** Quarantine the computer immediately.

Printers and Multifunction Devices

	NEWBIE	SOME EXPERIENCE	EXPERT
ETA	6 hours	4 hours	2 hours

In the past, your average office had many devices dedicated to performing some task with paper documents—think printers, copiers, scanners, and fax machines. Back in the 1990s, the *multifunction device (MFD)* or multifunction printer (MFP) consolidated multiple functions (often printing and scanning) into a single device. At first these devices weren't great at anything, but today the MFD is more common than its single-function counterparts.

The CompTIA A+ certification expects a high degree of technical knowledge of the function, components, maintenance, and repair of all types of printers and MFDs. This chapter examines the common printer and scanner varieties and then explores how laser printers work. The chapter continues with the steps for installing a multifunction device in a typical personal computer and then concludes with troubleshooting issues.

Objective 22.01 Printer and Multifunction Device Components and Technologies

When most of us imagine a printer or MFD, we tend to picture a small desktop *all-in-one* device (which can usually be used as a printer, scanner, copier, and fax machine) connected to a nearby computer (see Figure 22.1). Enterprise or commercial MFDs, however, look like the descendants of copy machines and even small printing presses—but they still share a set of core components with the all-in-ones we're familiar with. Let's review the components you'll find in MFDs—keep in mind that you can also find these components as standalone devices.

FIGURE 22.1 All-in-one printer/scanner/fax machine/copier/iPod dock

Printers

No other piece of your computer system is available in a wider range of styles, configurations, and feature sets than a printer, or at such a wide price variation. What a printer can and can't do is largely determined by the type of printer technology it uses—that is, how it gets the image onto the paper. Modern printers can be categorized into several broad types: impact, inkjet, dye-sublimation, thermal, laser, and solid ink.

Exam Tip
The 901 exam looks at only four types of printers: impact, inkjet, thermal, and laser. I've include dye-sub and solid ink printers here because real-world techs need to know about these technologies.

- *Impact* printers create an image by physically striking an *ink ribbon* against the paper's surface, making them relatively slow and noisy. Impact printers are largely gone from our homes, but one kind— *dot-matrix* printers—are still common in businesses because they can print to multipart forms. *Point-of-sale (POS)* machines, for example, use special *impact paper* that can print two or more copies of a receipt. Dot-matrix printers (see Figure 22.2) have a *printhead* holding pins or *printwires* that strike the inked ribbon, and many use tiny sprockets to advance *tractor-feed* impact paper. *Draft-quality* printheads use 9 pins, whereas *near-letter-quality (NLQ)* printheads use 24 pins.

- *Inkjet* (or ink-dispersion) printers use a *printhead* connected to a *carriage* containing the *ink cartridges* (see Figure 22.3) to print on a staggering array of paper types. A *belt* and motor move the assembly

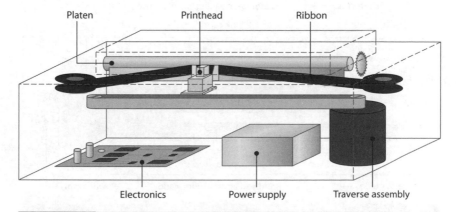

Platen   Printhead   Ribbon

Electronics   Power supply   Traverse assembly

FIGURE 22.2   Inside a dot-matrix printer

FIGURE 22.3   Inkjet ink cartridges

back and forth to cover the page. A *roller* grabs paper from a paper tray (usually under or inside the printer) or *feeder* (on the top or back of the printer) and advances it through the printer (see Figure 22.4). The printhead uses tiny tubes with resistors or electroconductive plates at the end to boil the ink, creating a tiny air bubble that ejects a droplet onto the paper (see Figure 22.5). *Print resolution*, measured in *dots per inch (dpi)*, indicates how densely the printer lays these droplets down, and high resolution is particularly important for images. Print speed is measured in *pages per minute (ppm)*, and printers with monochrome and full-color modes typically indicate two speeds.

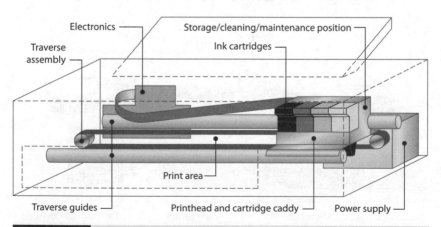

FIGURE 22.4   Inside an inkjet printer

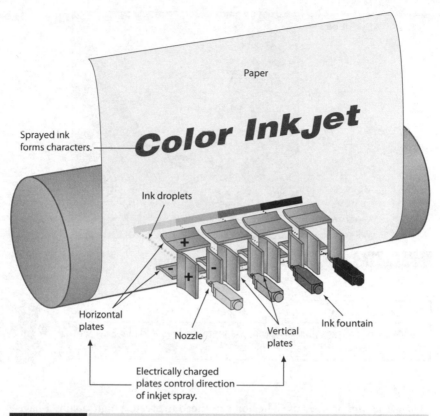

Paper

Sprayed ink forms characters.

Color InkJet

Ink droplets

Horizontal plates

Nozzle

Vertical plates

Ink fountain

Electrically charged plates control direction of inkjet spray.

FIGURE 22.5 Detail of the inkjet printhead

Local Lingo

Duplex assembly Built-in or add-on device that flips paper to enable automatic two-sided prints.

- *Dye-sublimation* or *thermal dye transfer* printheads vaporize CMYK dyes embedded in a roll of heat-sensitive plastic film (see Figure 22.6), causing them to soak into specially coated paper underneath; its high quality is suitable for photo printing (including small *snapshot* photo printers), high-end desktop publishing, medical and scientific imaging, and so on. This process requires one pass per color (and sometimes a final laminating pass) to produce *continuous-tone* images with blended colors as opposed to *dithered* images composed of closely packed dots of different colors.

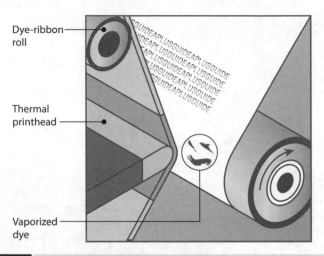

Dye-ribbon roll

Thermal printhead

Vaporized dye

FIGURE 22.6   The dye-sublimation printing process

Local Lingo

CMYK   Processes that mix **c**yan, **m**agenta, **y**ellow, and blac**k** ink for color printing.

- *Thermal* printers use a heated printhead to create a high-quality image on special or plain paper. *Direct thermal* printers use a heating element to burn dots into the surface of *special thermal paper*; these are often seen in retail receipt printers with large rolls of thermal paper housed in a *feed assembly* that automatically draws the paper past the *heating element*. *Thermal wax* printers work like dye-sublimation printers, but the film is coated with colored wax—no special paper required (though quality suffers because they use dithering, unlike dye-sublimation printers).

- *Laser* printers (see Figure 22.7), which we'll explore further in the "Laser Printing" section, use *electro-photographic imaging* for quick high-quality prints. The process leverages *photoconductive* compounds that conduct electricity when exposed to precise laser (or cheaper LED) light.

- As the name implies, *solid-ink* printers use solid sticks of nontoxic "ink" to produce more vibrant colors. The solid ink is melted into the paper fibers, where it solidifies to produce continuous-tone output.

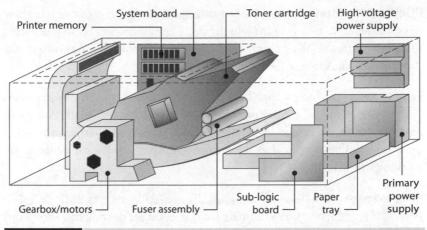

Printer memory — System board — Toner cartridge — High-voltage power supply

Gearbox/motors — Fuser assembly — Sub-logic board — Paper tray — Primary power supply

FIGURE 22.7 Components inside a laser printer

Unlike with dye-sublimation, all colors are applied in a single pass, and the cartridge-free solid ink sticks can be "topped off" *during* a print job by inserting additional color sticks. These quick, high-quality printers are expensive, but the solid ink sticks are cheaper in the long run.

Virtual Printers

The *virtual* printer doesn't look like much, but it's still pretty similar to "real" printing. When you print to one, your system goes through all the steps to prepare the document for printing and then sends it off to a virtual printer program that converts the output from your computer into some other format and saves the result to a portable file that looks like the printed page would. It's a quick way to save anything you can print. Let's look at some of the most popular virtual printers.

Exam Tip

The CompTIA A+ 901 exam objectives include *Print to file*, which produces a file that can be later printed without access to the program that created it, but this is a legacy option (you'll often see it as a checkbox on your print screen) that may not work well with USB printers and produces files that are hard to work with. Use one of the other options instead.

Print to PDF   Almost every OS can print to PDF files out of the box these days. However, Windows didn't join the party until Windows 10, so you'll need to install a virtual PDF printer on older versions of Windows. You can get one through official Adobe software or a third party.

Print to XPS   You'll see what XPS is in the next section, but Windows versions since Vista include the Microsoft XPS Document Writer, which creates an .xps file you can later open with the included XPS Viewer. Support in other operating systems varies, but most have third-party software available for working with XPS files.

Print to Image   This lets you save a regular image file, such as BMP, GIF, JPG, PNG, TIFF, and more. Image formats aren't the best for documents—text won't scale well and can't be easily searched/selected/copied, for example—but they are *very* portable. You will generally need a third-party virtual printer to print to the desired image format on a given OS.

Cloud and Remote Printing   A variety of applications such as Google Cloud Print blur the line between traditional and virtual printing. These install a virtual printer on your system that wraps up your document and sends it out over the Internet or other network to a cloud server that eventually routes it to a real printer for printing—all without your system needing a driver for the target printer.

Printer Languages

Printers are designed to accept predefined printer languages for indicating what characters and graphics to print and how to print them. Here are the more common printer languages:

- If you're familiar with *ASCII*, you may just think of it as a basic, outdated English-language-only plaintext character set—but ASCII also includes some control codes that modern printers still support—if they didn't, PRT SCR (print screen) would not work with every printer. Despite this universal support, ASCII is extremely limited and can't handle modern graphics or fonts.

> ### Local Lingo
>
> **ASCII**   The *American Standard Code for Information Interchange* was developed in the early 1960s, became a U.S. government standard by the end of the decade, and went on to play a huge role on the early Internet. In other words, it's been around so long you may never hear anyone call it anything but ASCII.

- Adobe Systems' *PostScript* is a device-independent printer language supporting high-resolution graphics and scalable fonts. PostScript interpreters are embedded in the printing device, so it does most of the image processing. Highly portable PostScript files define the page as a single raster image that can be reliably printed on another system or even a high-end typesetter.

- Hewlett-Packard's text-centric *printer control language (PCL)* features a set of printer commands greatly expanded from ASCII. The most recent version, PCL6, features scalable fonts and additional line-drawing commands. PCL files are less portable than PostScript, because a printer must support the commands they contain to print them.

- Although you *can* use an external printer language such as PostScript, most Windows users just install printer drivers and let Windows do all the work via the *graphical device interface (GDI)*, which uses the CPU to process a print job and sends the completed job (as a rasterized image) to the printer. When you do it this way—as long as the printer's raster image processor (explained later) and RAM are sufficient—you don't need to worry about the printer language.

Local Lingo

Rasterize   Most printers compose printed pages with many tiny dots, so the page must be turned into a compatible *raster image* composed, of course, of tiny dots.

- Windows Vista also introduced the *XML Paper Specification (XPS) print path,* which improves on GDI with enhanced color management (compatible with Windows Color System) and better print layout fidelity. The XPS print path requires a compatible driver or a printer with native XPS support (which, once again, eliminates converting output to a device-specific printer control language before printing).

Scanners

You can use a scanner to make digital copies of existing photos, documents, and drawings; better scanners also handle photographic negatives or slides. *Flatbed* scanners (see Figure 22.8), the most common variety, are pretty simple: lift the lid to reveal the glass or *platen* where you place an item face down and then use software or a hardware button to initiate the scan. The scanner runs a bright light along the length of the platen to capture the image.

FIGURE 22.8 Scanner open with photograph face down

Travel Advisory

Scanners and MFDs with an automatic document feeder (ADF) tray to automate scanning multipage documents are a little more expensive but well worth the investment if you scan such documents even occasionally.

Nearly every manufacturer includes drivers and scanning software (see Figure 22.9) that will, at worst, allow you to set basic configurable variables (detailed in the next section) and save scans, but many image-editing programs can directly import an image from a scanner (see Figure 22.10).

Local Lingo

TWAIN Most scanners support traditional TWAIN drivers; the acronym stands for (you can't make this stuff up) *Technology Without an Interesting Name*.

FIGURE 22.9 Epson scanner software

How to Choose a Scanner

Scanners have four primary variable qualities: resolution, color depth, gray-scale depth, and scan speed. You can adjust the first three down from the supported maximum; scan speed is influenced by the other settings.

Local Lingo

OCR *Optical character recognition* software, which comes with many scanners, can create editable text from the image of a scanned document. If you want OCR, make sure OCR software comes with your scanner or find a standalone program. All OCR software is not created equal, either—if OCR is a critical feature, compare the bundled program with other options.

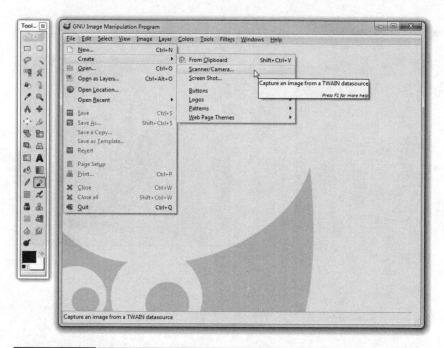

FIGURE 22.10 GNU Image Manipulation Program (GIMP) support for importing from a scanner

Configurable Variables Scanners convert the scanned image into a grid of pixels (or dots). The maximum number of pixels (or *resolution*) determines how much fine detail the scanner can capture and how large the resulting image be made before it appears blurry.

Older scanner resolutions commonly topped out at 600 × 600 dpi, but newer models often achieve four times that, and high-end devices go even higher. Manufacturers may cite two resolutions, but only the *optical* resolution indicates what the scanner supports at full quality—ignore the other number. I recommend at least 2400 × 2400 dpi optical resolution.

The number of bits of information the scanner can use to describe each individual pixel is its *color depth*, and it makes a dramatic difference in how easily you can adjust the color and tone of the scan. The most common color depths are 24- and 48-bit; 48-bit is common enough that you shouldn't settle for less. A 24-bit scan can save up to 256 shades per red, green, and blue subpixel, or 16,777,216 total color variations per pixel, so this option says "millions of colors" in some scanner settings. A 48-bit scan can save up to 65,536 shades per subpixel, so each pixel supports a massive 281,474,976,710,656 color variations. Unfortunately, 48-bit scans are twice as big and can easily be hundreds of megabytes per file.

Scanners also differ in *grayscale depth,* or how many shades of gray the scanner can save per pixel. Grayscale images only need a third of the information, so consumer-level scanners come in 8-bit, 12-bit, and 16-bit grayscale varieties. I recommend 16-bit.

Scanning Speed Scanners have a maximum scanning speed defined by the manufacturer, and scan times rise as you capture more detail. A low-end 24-bit scanner may take 30 seconds to scan a 4 × 6 photo at 300 dpi. A faster scanner might crank out the same scan in 10 seconds, yet take a full minute for a 48-bit scan of the same photo at 600 dpi. Don't waste time on the highest possible quality if you don't need the resolution and color depth for a given project.

Scanning Tips

As a general rule, make the highest quality scan you can justify, and adjust the size and image quality when it's time to print or share the scan over the Web. However, your system's RAM—and to a lesser extent processor speed—limit how big a file you can work with. If you travel a lot, get a smaller sheet-fed scanner, or make sure you get a scanner with a locking mechanism for the scanner light assembly. Just be sure to unlock it before scanning.

Copy and Fax Components

The scanning and printing capabilities of a multifunction device enable manufacturers to program a simple Copy button that initiates a combined scan-and-print. Because true faxes require a traditional analog phone line and an interface for dialing, fewer MFDs support it. Assuming you have a line with service connected, the process is simple: put a document in the feeder, plug in the fax number, and press the Send button.

Connectivity

Let's look at how you can connect printers, scanners, and MFDs:

- Most new printers and multifunction devices use USB connections that you can plug into any USB port on your computer. Leaving out the USB cable is common, so you'll probably need to pick up a cable with a type A connector for your computer and type B for the printer (though some also use type A).

- More and more homes and small offices are enjoying the benefits of network printing, such as not having to leave a computer on to ensure its printer is available. The typical *network printer* comes with its own built-in Wi-Fi adapter to enable wireless printing over infrastructure or ad hoc network connections (avoid the latter for security reasons). Others have a standard RJ-45 port to connect directly to a router. Once connected to the network and given a static or dynamic IP address, the printer is independent of any single computer.

Travel Advisory

Printers tend to have longer lives than most other computing devices, so they may have older ports (such as parallel, serial, or SCSI) or use older built-in Wi-Fi and Bluetooth standards than you're used to encountering.

- You can purchase a standalone *print server* device to network one or more traditional wired printers—but you may not be able to use all features of an MFD connected this way. First, see if your router has an *integrated print server*, in which case you can plug your printer into the router's USB port.

Exam Tip

Any time you plug a printer into a computer and share the printer over the network, the sharing system functions as a print server.

- Less common connectivity options include wireless Bluetooth, and you can also find some scanners that support wired Thunderbolt.

Objective 22.02 Laser Printing

The 901 exam takes a keen interest in the particulars of the laser printer's *imaging process*—but first you need to know your way around a laser printer. Here are the most important laser printer components and their functions:

- The *toner cartridge* (see Figure 22.11) holds the toner that creates the image and, to simplify maintenance, most of the parts that suffer "wear and tear" and need regular replacing.

- The aluminum *imaging drum* or *photosensitive drum* is a grounded cylinder with an ungrounded coat of photosensitive compounds. When light hits these particles, their electrical charge "drains" out through the grounded cylinder.

- The *erase lamp* lights the surface of the imaging drum, making the photosensitive coating conductive. Any electrical charge in the particles bleeds away into the grounded drum, leaving the surface particles electrically neutral.

- The *primary corona* wire (or *primary charge roller,* in newer laser printers) is so close to the photosensitive drum that charging it with an extremely high voltage forms an electric field (corona) that enables voltage to pass to the drum and charge the drum's photosensitive coating. The *primary grid* regulates this voltage transfer, ensuring the surface of the drum receives a uniform negative charge between ~600 and ~1000 volts.

- Any particle on the drum struck by the *laser* becomes conductive, draining its charge into the grounded drum, leaving the particle with a ~100-volt negative charge. This enables the laser to write a positive image to the drum.

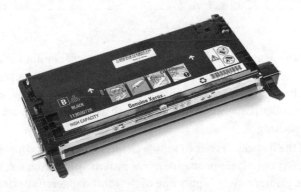

FIGURE 22.11 Laser printer's toner cartridge

- *Toner* is a fine powder made up of plastic particles bonded to pigment particles. The *toner cylinder* gives the toner a negative charge between ~200 and ~500 volts. Because this falls between the original negative charge of the photosensitive drum (~600 to ~1000 volts) and the charge of the particles on the drum's surface hit by the laser (~100 volts), areas of the photosensitive drum hit by the laser attract toner particles.

Exam Tip

The black toner used in laser printers is typically carbon melt mixed with a polyester resin, while color toner trades carbon for other pigments.

- The *transfer corona* (*transfer roller* in newer printers) applies a positive charge to the paper, so it in turn attracts toner particles from the drum. This positive charge also attracts the paper to the negatively charged drum, so a *static charge eliminator* removes the charge to keep the paper from wrapping around the drum.

Travel Advisory

The transfer corona/roller, which is commonly outside of the toner cartridge, is prone to attracting dirt, toner, and other debris. If it's not in the cartridge, most printers include a special tool to clean it; you can also (delicately) use a cotton swab soaked in 90 percent denatured alcohol (*not* rubbing alcohol).

- The *fuser assembly* is usually near the bottom of (but not included with) the toner cartridge where most use two rollers (a pressure roller and a heated roller) to permanently fuse the toner to the paper. The heated roller has a nonstick coating such as Teflon to prevent toner from sticking.
- All of the devices described in this chapter have power supplies, but the corona in a laser printer requires extremely high voltage, making a laser printer power supply one of the most dangerous devices in computing! Turn off and unplug the printer as a safety precaution before performing any maintenance.
- A laser printer also has many mechanical parts. Paper is grabbed by the *pickup roller* and passed over a *separation pad* (CompTIA says *separate pad*) to separate a single sheet. Next, imaging components

must roll, slide, and move to evenly distribute toner and write the laser image. Finally, the printer kicks out the paper and cleans its assembly to prepare for the next page. These components are typically bundled into two or three *gear packs* or *gearboxes* (often including a motor or solenoid) that can be separately replaced when they wear out.

- Laser printers contain one or more electronic boards that hold the main processor, the printer's ROM, and the RAM used to store images before printing. An older printer may also have an extra ROM chip and/or a special slot where you can install one to add special functions such as PostScript. Some models support upgrading or flashing the firmware stored in ROM, as we've seen with other devices such as SOHO routers. Some printers also have upgradeable RAM; if so, adding RAM is usually a simple job—just snap in a SIMM or DIMM stick or two—but check the printer manufacturer's website to confirm what type of RAM you need.

- Even tiny concentrations of ozone (O_3) will damage printer components, and because the coronas inside laser printers conveniently generate small amounts of ozone, they have special ozone filters that need occasional cleaning or replacement.

- Every laser printer has a large number of sensors and switches spread throughout the machine to detect paper jams, empty paper trays, low toner levels, and so on. Occasionally they break or get dirty and send false signals to the printer. Inspect the printer; if you can't find the reported problem, suspect the sensor or switch.

Now that you're familiar with the parts, we can dive into *imaging process*— knowing it helps you troubleshoot printing problems. If an odd line is printed down the middle of every page, for example, you know there's a problem with the photosensitive drum or cleaning mechanism, and the toner cartridge needs to be replaced. Here is the seven-step process you need to know for the 901 exam:

1. Processing
2. Charging
3. Exposing
4. Developing
5. Transferring
6. Fusing
7. Cleaning

Processing

When you click Print in an application, the CPU processes your request and queues the print job with the *print spooler*, causing the spooler's printer icon to appear in the notification area. Windows sends these jobs sequentially as the printer becomes available. Larger jobs must be broken into chunks first (which can take a while for huge documents), leaving documents further back in the queue waiting. The notification icon will go away when all jobs have gone to the printer—but you aren't out of the woods yet.

Raster Images

Impact printers receive data one character or one line at a time, but laser printers receive complete pages. If the page isn't already a raster image, the printer's *raster image processor (RIP)* rasterizes it to obtain a format the laser imaging unit can "paint" on the photosensitive drum. To accomplish this, the RIP needs enough memory (RAM) to process a full page.

> **Travel Advisory**
>
> Insufficient memory usually causes memory overflow ("MEM OVERFLOW") errors, in which case you can try reducing the resolution, printing smaller graphics, or turning off RET (see the following section for more on RET). Of course, the best solution is adding RAM to the printer.

Adding more RAM won't solve every laser printer memory problem. Some data is just too complex for a RIP, as with a "21 ERROR" on an HP LaserJet, which indicates "the printer is unable to process very complex data fast enough for the print engine." If the RIP is the limiting factor, reduce the complexity of the page image (use fewer fonts, less formatting, lower-resolution graphics, and so on).

Resolution

Just like monitors, laser printers support different resolutions (adjusted down from the maximum it physically supports), with higher resolutions improving quality but requiring more memory. Common resolutions are 600 × 600 dpi and 1200 × 1200 dpi. The first number (horizontal resolution) reflects how finely the laser can focus, while the second number (vertical resolution) reflects the smallest increment the drum can turn.

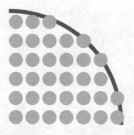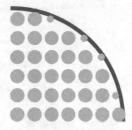

FIGURE 22.12 RET fills in gaps with smaller dots to smooth out jagged characters.

Even at 300 dpi, laser printers produce far better quality than dot-matrix printers by using resolution enhancement technology (RET) to insert smaller dots that smooth out jagged curves (see Figure 22.12). RET uses more of the printer's RAM, so disabling RET may free enough memory to complete the print job if you get a MEM OVERFLOW error.

Travel Advisory

Printers may convert complex memory-intensive images to lower resolutions.

Printing

Once processing is complete, the physical printing process can begin:

- **Charging** The primary corona wire or primary charge roller applies a uniform negative charge (usually between ~600 and ~1000 volts) to the entire surface of the drum (see Figure 22.13) so it can receive a new image.

- **Exposing** A laser (or LED) writes a positive image on the surface of the drum by forcing the photosensitive particles to release most of their negative charge.

- **Developing** These less-negative particles attract toner because they are relatively more positive than the toner particles (see Figure 22.14).

- **Transferring** The transfer corona or transfer roller gives the paper a positive charge so that the negatively charged toner particles will leap from the drum to the paper.

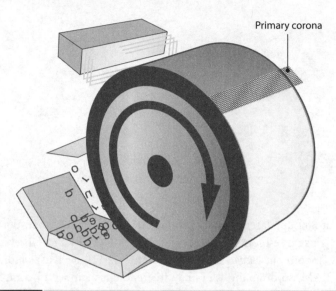

FIGURE 22.13 Charging the drum with a uniform negative charge

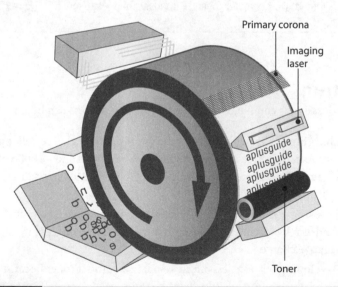

FIGURE 22.14 Writing the image and applying the toner

- **Fusing** The mostly plastic toner particles are only attracted to the page—they still need to be fused to it. Two rollers—a heated nonstick roller and a pressure roller—melt the toner permanently into the paper. At this point, a static charge eliminator removes the paper's positive charge (see Figure 22.15) so the printer can eject the page.

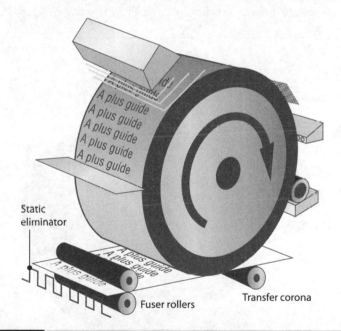

FIGURE 22.15 Transferring the image to the paper and fusing the final image

- **Cleaning**   Before a new page can be printed, the drum must be returned to a clean, fresh (physical and electrical) state (see Figure 22.16). A rubber cleaning blade *carefully* scrapes residual toner from the drum and deposits it in a debris cavity or returns it to the toner cartridge, and one or more erase lamps bombard the drum with light to neutralize all surface particles by draining any remaining charge into the drum.

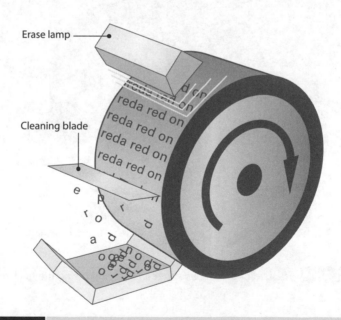

FIGURE 22.16   Cleaning and erasing the drum

Installing a Multifunction Device

M FD installations can be messy because of the complexity of the devices. Here are a few things that can go wrong:

- You excitedly plug in your new toy without consulting the manufacturer's instructions, which often require connecting the printer at a specific stage in the process.
- The drivers may be outdated.
- Manufacturers often add absurdly bad support applications (such as photo organizers) that bog down the system and fall far short of readily available tools.
- Maintaining, troubleshooting, and even using the device are all complicated by the sheer number of technologies, features, and options rolled into one package.

Although there's usually a unified installer for the device, it inevitably installs multiple drivers and programs. Sometimes this all works perfectly, but if you run into trouble it can help to conceptualize each function as a separate device to simplify troubleshooting. If printing is your problem, focus on the print hardware and drivers and ignore the other features.

Because the CompTIA A+ exams focus intently on printers, and that's what you'll have to deal with as a tech for the most part, the following sections look directly at installing standalone printers; the process for installing an MFD (if it goes cleanly) is virtually the same, except that the installer may give you a few extra options and take a little longer to install additional software.

Setting Up Printers in Windows

To Windows, a printer is a *program* that controls one or more physical *print devices;* the printer drivers and spooler are part of this software printer (see Figure 22.17). This flexible arrangement means one software printer can use multiple print devices and redirect output if a print device is busy or down for maintenance.

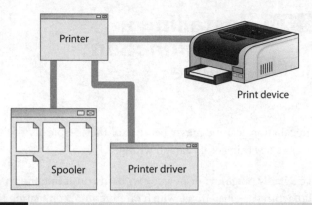

FIGURE 22.17 Printer driver and spooler in Windows

Most printers are plug-and-play devices; just plug it in and let Windows automatically detect and install the driver. If the system does not detect the printer, open the Printers (Vista) or Devices and Printers (Windows 7 and up) applet and click Add a Printer to open the Add Printer Wizard, which enables you to install a local printer or a network printer. This distinction isn't perfect; you can use the local printer option to add network printers manually—it just doesn't automatically search for them.

Installing a Local Printer

Unless your printer is very new, or very old, you'll probably never use this option except, surprisingly, to install standalone network printers by IP address or hostname. Even here, Windows will detect most modern printers on its own, so you'll just use this if it refuses to detect yours.

In Windows Vista and Windows 7, click *Add a local printer*. In the *Create a new port* drop-down box, select Standard TCP/IP Port. Click Next. Type the IP address here. Windows 8/8.1/10 is even simpler: if Windows doesn't automatically detect your new printer, click *The printer that I want isn't listed* and select *Add a printer using TCP/IP address or hostname*.

You'll need to manually select the proper driver (see Figure 22.18). Windows includes a lot of printer drivers, but you can use the Have Disk option to install from the printer's driver disc (Windows will require administrator privileges to proceed). The Windows Update button enables you to grab the latest printer drivers via the Internet.

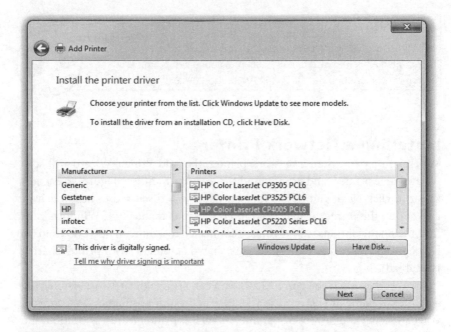

Travel Advisory

Using a driver not designed for your device is usually a bad idea, but some printers don't come with their own—they're designed to emulate a well-known printer (such as an HP LaserJet 4) and run on its driver. Some printers have emulation modes to run on non-native drivers (enabling them to use software written for the emulated printer). If you can't find a driver for a printer, drivers for another well-known printer may get you up and printing.

After you click Next, Windows asks if you want to use the new printer by default and share it with the network (resist the temptation to share an already-networked computer; anyone who installs it will lose access if you turn off your computer, and it will show up as *your* printer, potentially confusing them about where to pick up the print job). If you aren't sure, you can change the default later from the Printers or Devices and Printers applet; just right-click the desired printer and select Set as default printer (the current default will have a checkmark on its icon). Finally, print a test page to make sure everything works.

Exam Tip

A Windows system can use Apple's *Bonjour Print Service* (installed alone or with iTunes) to share a connected printer with *AirPrint*-compatible Mac OS X and Apple iOS devices.

Installing a Network Printer

When you try to install a network printer, the Add Printer Wizard will scan for available printers and usually find the one you want (see Figure 22.19). Just select it, click Next, and follow the procedure just discussed to install drivers and set up the printer. You'll need to configure it manually if Windows can't find it, and the options vary if you are connected to a domain or workgroup (in homegroups, all connected printers are shared automatically if printer sharing is enabled).

In a workgroup (see Figure 22.20), you can browse the network, connect to a printer by name or URL, or use a TCP/IP address or hostname. On a domain, you can search and browse by parameters such as printer features, location, and so on. Once you select a printer, you may be prompted to provide drivers using the method described earlier.

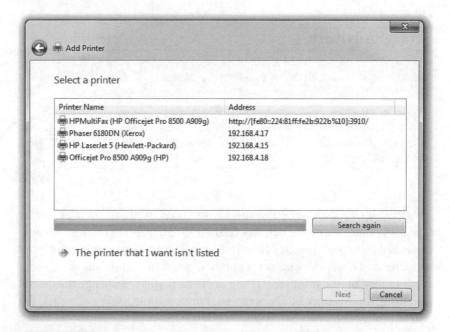

FIGURE 22.19 List of available shared printers on a network

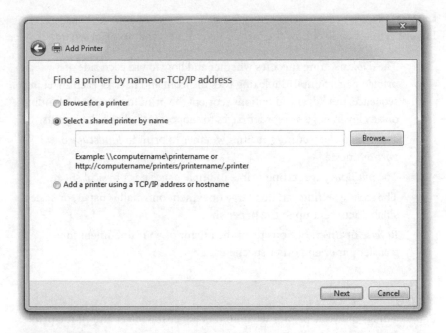

FIGURE 22.20 Options for finding network printers

Exam Tip

Windows 7 and newer (excluding Home/basic editions) also include the Print Management console in Administrative Tools. It enables you to view and manage printers, drivers, and Windows print servers on your system or network. Print Management's advanced features go beyond the CompTIA A+ exams, but know it centralizes (and sometimes enhances) standard Windows printer controls.

Configuring Print Settings

Once the printer is installed, find it in the Printers or Devices and Printers applet, right-click it, and select Printing preferences to configure how your printer will print documents. Options vary by device and features, but let's review the more common ones.

Layout

Layout settings control how the printer determines what to print where:

- The *duplex* setting specifies whether and how to use each side of a printed page. Simple duplexing uses the front and back of each sheet in sequence, but advanced options reorient the print to account for binding on any given edge or reorder pages to support folded booklet layouts.
- The *orientation* setting specifies whether to print in *landscape* or *portrait* mode.
- The *multiple page* setting prints multiple pages per physical sheet.
- The *scaling* setting can fit a large document on smaller paper, or scale a small document up to the paper size.
- *Reverse* or *invert* options print the mirror of your document for transfer paper and other special uses.

Paper

Paper settings tell your printer what kind of paper it will get and (if the printer has multiple paper trays) where to find it:

- Set the *paper size* to a predefined common paper size or define a custom one.
- Specify the *paper type*, which may involve setting thickness, coating, and special formats such as envelopes and labels.
- A *paper source* setting selects an available paper tray (or *manual feed*, so the printer knows to wait for you to feed oversized or one-off sheets individually).

Quality

These settings enable you to manage the tradeoffs between quality and speed, ink use, and memory use:

- The most obvious of these, *resolution*, specifies what DPI the document should be printed at.
- Some printers may let you choose some mode or quality presets that optimize printing for graphics or text, or choose to manually configure your own advanced settings.
- Some printers may have settings that reduce ink or toner used, for economic and environmental reasons.

Travel Advisory

The names and descriptions of settings that influence quality might discuss quality itself, ink or toner use, environmental friendliness, or even cost savings. As a result, quality-reducing settings may be scattered around multiple menus.

Other

These common settings are useful in specific but limited scenarios:

- The *apply a watermark* setting lightly prints a predefined or custom mark across every page, often to designate that a document is a draft or contains classified information.
- *Header/footer* settings typically add when a document was printed and who printed it.
- The *collate* option prints a full copy of a multipage document before starting the next copy. Otherwise, it prints all copies of a page before moving to the next page.

Other Print Quality Factors

Beyond your printer's quality and preferences, output quality also depends on factors such as maintenance, printer driver, paper, ink/toner, and color calibration. Most maintenance issues are covered in the upcoming troubleshooting section and we've already looked at installing appropriate drivers, but make sure you use paper suitable for both your printer and the intended quality. Third-party ink and toner sources may save money, but it's worth comparing prints made with them directly to prints made with ink/toner from the manufacturer if quality is more important than cost.

When what you see on your monitor and what prints differ significantly, monitor *calibration* hardware generates an International Color Consortium (ICC) color profile that defines the color characteristics of the hardware so the OS can correct for any difference between the intended and displayed colors. Color profiles can also document the quirks of a specific printer; you can find them on the installation media, purchase one separately, or generate your own. Combined, calibrating all of your imaging devices helps harmonize what you see onscreen and on paper with the file's image data.

Local Lingo

WCS   Windows includes *Windows Color System (WCS)* to help build color profiles for use across devices. WCS is based on a newer standard Microsoft calls *color infrastructure and translation engine (CITE).*

Managing Shared/Public/ Networked Devices

You need to know about two big privacy issues to effectively manage printers and MFDs:

- The ease of access that make network printers and MFDs so useful is also a big risk; they may be open to attack via the LAN or even the whole Internet. You don't need to know how to harden these devices, but you do need to know the risks they present. A compromised printer or MFD is obviously a risk to the data and documents flowing through the device, but because security is often overlooked on these devices, they are also common starting points for an attack on the broader network.

- A lot of sensitive information gets printed, especially in places like schools and hospitals where strict privacy regulations apply, and we have to make sure it isn't leaking out. Unfortunately, it's common for modern devices to cache documents the device prints, scans, copies, or faxes to a hard drive or other storage media. You may be able to disable this feature, schedule regular deletion of the cache, or manually clear the cache regularly to limit the damage a compromise could cause. It's also critical to clear this cache before disposing of the device.

Exam Tip

The 901 objectives call this *hard drive caching.*

- It wouldn't do much good to change these settings if anyone who could use the device could also change them, so enterprise models support *user authentication* and authorization on the device to control which users can take which actions.

- Because printers make a physical document copy, there's a risk someone will see, copy, or steal a document they couldn't otherwise access. User authentication can help by waiting to print received documents until the user authenticates at the device, and by restricting the ability of less-trusted users to use the device itself to scan/copy/e-mail an unattended document from the device and leave the original (this is just a speed bump; anyone with a smartphone can "scan" a document).

Objective 22.04 Troubleshooting Printers

Once set up, printers tend to run with few issues, assuming that you install the proper drivers and keep the hardware well maintained. But printer errors do occasionally develop. Let's take a look at the most common print problems, as well as problems that crop up with specific printer types.

> **Exam Tip**
>
> Every printer is different. Many include tiny displays that can clue you in to what's wrong with *error codes*. Check the manual or the manufacturer's website to translate codes and confirm device-specific steps for performing tasks in this section.

Tools of the Trade

Before you jump in and start to work on a printer that's giving you fits, you'll need a *maintenance kit*. You can use the standard computer tech tools in your toolkit, plus a couple of printer-specific devices. Here are some that will help you jump in to work on a printer that's giving you fits:

- A multimeter for troubleshooting electrical problems such as faulty wall outlets
- Cleaning solutions, such as denatured alcohol
- An extension magnet for grabbing loose screws and cleaning up iron-based toner

- Removable media with test patterns for checking print quality
- A Phillips-head and flat-head screwdriver

Print Job Never Prints

Start with the obvious: confirm the printer is on, connected, online, has paper, and any computer needed to share it is on. Check all involved cables and ports. Confirm your printer appears in the appropriate printer applet for your version of Windows and reinstall it with the Add Printer Wizard if not. With the basics out of the way, here are some more specific scenarios:

- If a shared printer produces "Access Denied" errors, confirm your account has access in the Security tab of the Printer Properties dialog on the host system.
- Check the printer to make sure it has the correct paper. If the print job specifies a different paper size than what's in the tray, the printer may pause the queue until someone switches out the tray or manually feeds the paper. You can usually override this pause by pressing an OK or GO button on the printer.
- Check the spooler's print queue (see Figure 22.21) for problems. Double-click the printer icon in the notification area, or right-click the printer in the appropriate Control Panel applet and select See what's printing. The spooler or specific jobs can have a number of problems; look for errors in the Status column, and then delete and resubmit affected jobs.

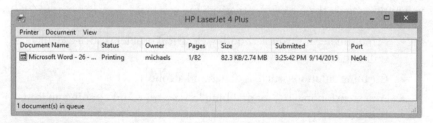

FIGURE 22.21 Print spooler's print queue

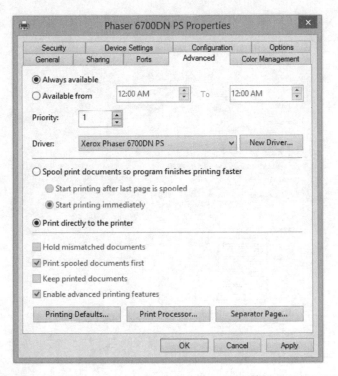

FIGURE 22.22 Print spool settings

- You can change how a given printer uses the spooler from the Advanced tab (see Figure 22.22) of its Printer Properties dialog. If the spooler isn't advancing, try skipping the spooler altogether: select *Print directly to the printer*, click OK, and resend your print job. You can also adjust the point of the spooling process when printing begins. You can also try restarting the Print Spooler service using the Services applet or Task Manager, as you saw in Chapter 13.

Misprints

A number of issues can render the printer output worthless. Here are a few:

- Print jobs may come out in unusual sizes or proportions if the Page Setup interface (see Figure 22.23) for the appropriate application is misconfigured. If these settings look correct, confirm the printer preferences aren't configured to scale the document unexpectedly

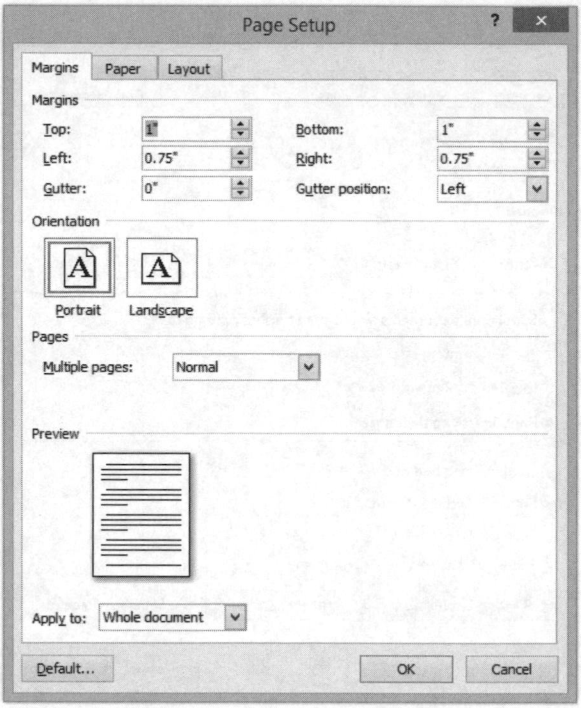

FIGURE 22.23 Page Setup options for Microsoft Word

and see if documents printed by other applications have the same problem. Uninstalling and reinstalling the printer drivers may help, but if the problem persists across multiple applications despite having the correct settings, the print engine may have a serious problem that requires service or replacement.

- When printing to smaller paper, misalignment can indicate the paper was fed at an angle or at the wrong horizontal position (this can happen with full-sized paper as well, but it usually creates obvious damage or jams the printer).

- Vertical misalignment can indicate the printer pulled multiple sheets at once; see if the next or previous page is blank or partially printed. Humidity can cause sheets to cling to each other; check for this by opening and loading a fresh ream (fan the sheets of the paper stack first). The paper may also not be appropriate for the printer. The upcoming printer-specific sections have some additional tips.

- Color printers often have an automatic alignment or calibration routine (typically using the scanner and a test page on an MFD) to fix misalignment of different colors.

- Persistent misalignment or garbage printouts invariably point to a corrupt/incorrect driver. Confirm you have the correct driver and either install or uninstall/reinstall the correct one.

- Garbled characters on a printed page can be caused by miscommunication between computer and printer. This applies to all types of print devices.

Dealing with Consumables

All printers have *consumables* such as paper, ribbons, and cartridges that should be disposed of or recycled properly; check with the local sanitation department or disposal services company before throwing away any component (except toner cartridges—certain companies will *pay* you for used cartridges).

Display Screen Malfunction

The small screens on many modern printers and MFDs can freeze, go out, and show artifacts such as lines or discoloration, but there's not much you can do. Turn the device off and on—some manufacturers even recommend completely unplugging it for a few minutes. If the device is otherwise functional and the problem didn't appear after a firmware update, take the device to a service center.

Troubleshooting Impact Printers

Impact printers are near-immortal with diligent regular maintenance:

- Keep the platen (the roller or plate the pins strike against) and printhead clean with denatured alcohol.
- Lubricate gears and pulleys (but never the printhead) to specification.
- Replace the ink ribbon every so often.

Most impact printer paper feeds continuously from a roll or ream, so you'll need to swap out the rolls or move the new ream into position, feed out any remaining paper, and feed in the new paper. Paper quality, debris, and improper feeding can lead to jams, which you typically clear by feeding the paper one way or the other.

Travel Advisory

Check the printer's documentation first; steps to feed paper on one impact printer can easily break the feeding system on another.

Other problems you may run into include:

- White bars through the text point to a dirty or damaged printhead. Replace it if cleaning it with denatured alcohol doesn't help.
- Chopped-off characters indicate the printhead needs to be adjusted according to manufacturer instructions.
- Characters degrade and grow faint over time as the printhead wears out—replace it.
- If the page is covered with peppery dots and small smudges, clean the platen with denatured alcohol.
- If the image is faded and you know the ribbon is good, adjust the printhead closer to the platen.
- If the image fades from one edge to the other, the platen is out of adjustment; they are difficult to adjust, so the manufacturer's local warranty/repair center is your best bet.

Troubleshooting Thermal Printers

Direct thermal printers only need occasional cleaning and paper replacement. Turn off the printer and open it according to the manufacturer's instructions; then use denatured alcohol and a lint-free cloth to clean the heating element. Clean the rollers with a cloth or compressed air so they can properly grip the paper. To replace the paper, slide off the old roll, slide on the new one, and feed the paper through the heating element. Thermal wax printers also need wax ribbon replacement, which is similar to replacing the roll of paper; make sure to feed it past the heating element. Your printer should include instructions for installing a new ribbon.

Troubleshooting Inkjet Printers

If you perform even the most basic maintenance tasks, most inkjets will soldier on for years without a whimper (or much expense). Here are the most common tasks:

- Unless your manufacturer explicitly tells you to do so, don't vacuum an inkjet.

- Inkjets generally have built-in maintenance programs that you should run from time to time to keep your inkjet in good operating order (see Figure 22.24). It may be hard to find; check Printing Preferences, the Start menu, and any printer management web page.

- Inkjets typically have a routine to align or calibrate the printheads, which can fix poor output; the printer spits out a test page, and you either manually select the best result or, on an MFD, place it on the scanner as instructed.

- Inkjet cartridge replacement varies widely from printer to printer— refer to the printer's documentation. Typically you'll open a compartment on the printer and see one or more cartridges attached to the printhead. If you can't reach them, the printhead should move into an accessible position if the printer is on (don't try to force it out). They may just slide into place, but many printers have clips or slots (along with indicators for which cartridge goes where). Check the new cartridge for a piece of tape or other covering on its nozzles and

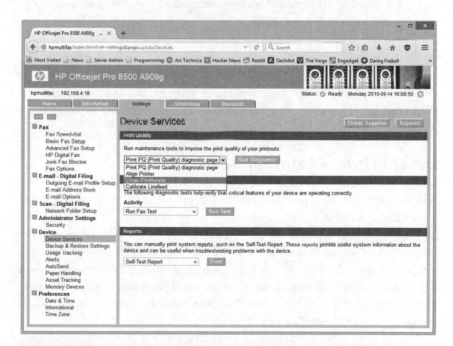

FIGURE 22.24 Inkjet printer maintenance screen

contacts. Make sure you have everything properly seated and clipped before you close the lid—these parts can catch on other components when the printhead moves.

- Ink inside the printhead nozzles has a tendency to dry out and plug them. If your printer is telling Windows that it's printing and feeding paper through, but either nothing is coming out (usually the case if you're just printing black text) or only certain colors are printing, the culprit is almost certainly dried ink clogging the nozzles. You can initiate a cleaning routine by pressing hardware buttons or through the printer preferences menu—but just do this as needed because it uses a lot of expensive ink.

- Aside from the usual suspects, an inkjet may pick up too many sheets if it is overheating, so let it cool down if you have been cranking out documents.

- If your printer has an ink overflow tank or tray to catch excess ink from the cleaning process, check it from time to time—an overflow onto electrical components is predictably bad. Put on some latex or vinyl gloves and stick a twisted paper towel into the tank to soak up most of the ink. The ink is water based, so dampen a paper towel with distilled water to clean any spilled ink.

Troubleshooting Laser Printers

Quite a few problems can arise with laser printers, but before getting into those details, let's review some recommended procedures for *avoiding* those problems.

Laser Printer Maintenance

Unlike computer maintenance, laser printer maintenance follows fairly well established procedures oriented around keeping it clean and following the maintenance schedule.

Over time, your laser printer builds up excess toner and paper dust or *paper dander*. Toner is hard to see—so the amount of paper dust is the best indicator a printer needs cleaning. If you can, take the printer outdoors and blow it out with a can of compressed air. If you must do it indoors, use a low-static vacuum (which the 901 objectives call a *toner vacuum*) designed for electronic components (see Figure 22.25).

The printer's manual will specify a cleaning process, but it often leaves out the rubber rollers that guide paper through the printer; these can slip and

FIGURE 22.25 Low-static vacuum

cause jams as they build up dirt and dust. Clean them with a small amount of 90 percent or better denatured alcohol on a fibrous cleaning towel. You can also re-texture slipping rollers and separator pads by rubbing them with a little denatured alcohol on a nonmetallic scouring pad.

Travel Advisory

The photosensitive drum, usually inside the toner cartridge, can be wiped clean if dirty, but be very careful—a scratch will appear on every page printed until you replace the toner cartridge.

Replacing parts according to the manufacturer's maintenance guidelines will help to ensure years of trouble-free, dependable printing from your laser printer; here are the common tasks:

- Many have *maintenance kits* that include everything you should replace on the same regular schedule, such as a fuser and one or more rollers or pads. You'll typically reset the page counter so the printer can prompt you when it's time again.
- Depending on the printer, you may clean (with an anti-static vacuum) or replace the ozone filter.
- Clean the fuser assembly with 90 percent or better denatured alcohol.
- A number of conditions require replacing the fuser assembly: pits or scratches on the heat roller (the Teflon-coated one containing a light bulb), an error code indicating the fuser is damaged or overheating (or merely that you've hit a preset replacement copy count), and failure of the thermal fuse that prevents overheating.

> **Travel Advisory**
>
> The fuser assembly melts stuff for a living; *always* let it cool down first.

- Clean the transfer corona with a 90 percent denatured alcohol solution on a cotton swab. If the wire is broken, you can replace it; most snap in or are held in by screws.
- Paper guides can also be cleaned with alcohol on a fibrous towel.

Laser Printer Problems

One of the most important tests on any printer is printing a *diagnostic print page* or an *engine test page*. You do this either by holding down the On Line button as the printer starts or via the printer's maintenance software. If print quality is poor, check for and run any calibration routine. Beyond this general step, let's look at specific technical and quality problems.

Crashes on Power-Up   Both laser printers and computers require more power during their power-on sequences than once they are running. Turning on one device and letting it finish initializing before starting the other can keep them from drawing too much power and crashing one or both devices.

Blank Pages   Blank pages usually mean the printer is out of toner, but if you know it's not out, print the diagnostic page. If that's also blank, remove the cartridge and check its imaging drum to see if the image (toner) is still there—if so, the transfer corona or power supply has failed.

Ghosting   Ghost images can have several causes. Dark ghosting can be caused by a damaged drum; replace the toner cartridge. A worn or damaged cleaning blade can cause light ghosting, but the most common direct cause is *developer starvation,* which is when a dark image uses so much toner that the toner cartridge is unable to charge enough for the next. There are a number of ways you can use less toner or give the cartridge recovery time:

> **Travel Advisory**
>
> Low temperature and low humidity can aggravate ghosting—check your user's manual for environmental recommendations.

- Lower the resolution (print at 300 dpi instead of 600 dpi).
- Change the image/pattern completely.
- Avoid 50 percent grayscale and "dot-on/dot-off patterns."
- Change the layout so that grayscale patterns do not follow black areas.
- Make dark patterns lighter and light patterns darker.
- Print in landscape orientation.
- Adjust print density and RET settings.
- Insert a blank page in the print job before the page with ghosting.

Toner Cartridge Symptoms   A number of toner cartridge problems typically require replacement. Let's review symptoms to look for and what to try before replacing the cartridge:

- Vertical white lines indicate a clog is preventing the proper dispersion of toner on the drum. Try shaking the toner cartridge to dislodge the clog.
- Blotchy prints indicate toner is unevenly dispersed, which is common as toner runs low. Shake the cartridge from side to side, and confirm the printer is level and the paper is dry. If the blotches always appear in a pattern or regular spot, check the fusing rollers and photosensitive drum for foreign objects.
- Spots at regular intervals point to a damaged drum or toner on the fuser rollers; try wiping off the fuser rollers. If that doesn't help, confirm the drum is damaged before replacing the cartridge.

Other Hardware Symptoms   Toner cartridges hold enough of the regularly replaced hardware that replacing them fixes a number of print issues, so it is still often the fallback fix for a number of other hardware issues that can cause poor print quality:

- Random black spots and streaks indicate the cleaner blade isn't properly cleaning the drum; the blade may be worn or damaged, especially if you have refilled the cartridge to re-use it. You'll need to replace the blade or cartridge.
- Foreign objects on a roller can cause a localized embossed effect (like putting paper over a coin and rubbing it with a lead pencil). Use 90 percent denatured alcohol or plain water with a soft cloth to try to remove one. If the foreign object is on the photosensitive drum, replace the toner cartridge.

- An embossed effect can also be caused by the contrast control being set too high (this is often a knob inside the unit—check your manual for specifics).
- A dirty fuser will leave a light dusting of toner on the paper, particularly on the back of the page; clean the printer. If the printout looks smudged, the toner isn't fusing properly; you may need to replace the fuser, but this can also happen when the fuser can't heat the toner through thick paper—try using a lighter-weight paper.
- Poorly formed (warped, overprinted, and so on) characters occasionally result from hardware problems. See if the diagnostic page prints cleanly. If so, try disabling advanced printer features and printing a very simple document from another application. If this works, advanced functions may not be working or properly configured at the printer or within the OS and its programs. Otherwise, check the data cable for anything that could harm connectivity: bends, crimps, pinches, and objects sitting on it. Replacing the toner cartridge may help, especially if you hear popping noises, but the problem may require service.

Media Issues   A number of poor output issues come down to what media you're loading into the printer (or how). Let's review the most common:

- Low print density can cause incompletely printed characters on laser-printed transparencies.
- The printer's rollers may crease paper to avoid jams caused by curling. Cotton bond paper is often more susceptible to noticeable creasing, so a different paper type may help. Try using a face-up paper tray if your device has one—it skips one roller.
- All printers jam sometimes—consult the manufacturer's jam removal procedure before you risk damaging components by tugging on the paper. When jams become frequent, there's a problem with your media or the components that guide it through the printer. Confirm you're using the right paper and check the pickup rollers, separation pads, and guide rollers, as discussed previously. If the printer reports a jam when none is present, a jam or paper feed sensor is malfunctioning—take the printer to a repair center.
- The printer may grab multiple sheets if the separation pad isn't doing its job. Check the pad for wear (a worn pad is typically shiny) and either use the earlier process for adding texture with a scouring pad or replace it.

- Poorly formed (warped, overprinted, and so on) characters can occur when the paper is either too rough or too smooth. Characters may not sit or fuse well on rough paper, and very smooth (usually coated) papers may not feed well. Don't let the paper get wet and don't open reams until you're ready to use them. Also, fan paper before loading it.

CHECKPOINT

✔**Objective 22.01: Printer and Multifunction Device Components and Technologies** There are several types of physical printer—impact, inkjet, dye-sublimation, thermal, laser, and solid-ink—as well as virtual printers capable of printing to a number of file formats or even to the cloud. Printer languages describe the characters, graphics, and layout of a printable page, and the printer language in use can limit the available features. Standalone flatbed or sheet-fed scanners enable scanning documents, images, negatives, slides, and so on. Scanners built into MFDs support these uses as well, and enable the device to act as a copy or fax machine.

✔**Objective 22.02: Laser Printing** Laser printers are complex devices, and the CompTIA A+ exams require knowledge of the laser-printer imaging process and the hardware devices that enable it. The seven steps of the process are: processing, charging, exposing, developing, transferring, fusing, and cleaning. This process produces a rasterized image, electrically draws this image, lays down toner that is attracted to the electrical image, transfers and fuses this toner to the paper, and cleans the printer for the next page.

✔**Objective 22.03: Installing a Multifunction Device** In no particular order, you install a printer by connecting it to your computer or network and installing the appropriate drivers and other software on systems you intend to use it. Typically you can just plug in a directly connected printer via USB and let Windows do the rest—but consult the manufacturer's installation process. After installing it, you'll need to configure the print settings and achieve optimal performance by ensuring it has appropriate paper and ink and is properly calibrated. In an office setting, you may also need to configure user authentication and establish restrictions and policies to protect the printer, documents, and data from unauthorized access.

✔**Objective 22.04: Troubleshooting Printers** The CompTIA A+ certification exams expect you to know the proper maintenance and cleaning procedures for each printer type, including impact, thermal, inkjet, and laser. In general, you will vacuum up small particles, clean appropriate surfaces and mechanisms, and, where needed, replace certain parts such as ribbons, belts, pads, rollers, and filters. You'll also need to know how to troubleshoot common issues such as jobs that never print, crashes, display issues, paper jams, and a huge variety of print-quality issues such as misprints, hardware problems that require service, and signs of regular wear and tear that require replacement.

REVIEW QUESTIONS

1. What are the seven steps of the laser printer imaging process?
   A. Paper in, cleaning, charging, developing, transferring, fusing, paper out
   B. Processing, charging, exposing, developing, transferring, fusing, cleaning
   C. Charging, cleaning, exposing, transferring, printing, fusing, processing
   D. Cleaning, processing, charging, developing, transferring, exposing, fusing

2. What type of feed mechanism do impact printers use?
   A. Tractor feed
   B. Friction feed
   C. Paper feed
   D. Spoke feed

3. What printer setting would enable you to properly arrange pages to print a small booklet?
   A. Orientation
   B. Multiple page
   C. Invert
   D. Duplex

4. Garbled characters are appearing in a printout. What's the most likely problem?
   A. The printer is old and needs to be replaced.
   B. You have the wrong language set up for the printer.

    C. The printer needs to be cleaned.

    D. The computer isn't communicating correctly with the printer.

5. What does the primary corona wire or primary charge roller in a laser printer do?

    A. Cleans the drum

    B. Charges the drum

    C. Creates the image on the drum

    D. Transfers the image from the drum to the paper

6. What role does hard drive caching play in the printing process?

    A. If a document is too large for RAM, the printing computer will build it in chunks, cache each chunk to its hard drive or storage device, and then send the completed copy to the printer.

    B. Individual computers cache a print-ready copy of recently printed documents to an internal hard drive or storage device in case the document is printed again.

    C. Individual printers cache print-ready copies of recently printed documents to an internal hard drive or storage device in case the document is printed again.

    D. Individual enterprise printers optimize the printing of frequently used images such as logos and letterhead graphics by caching print-ready copies to an internal hard drive or storage device.

7. Dye-sublimation printers use what to transfer ink to the paper surface?

    A. Impact print head

    B. Thermal print head

    C. Electrically charged plates

    D. Print nozzles

8. Which part of a laser printer is the most dangerous?

    A. Laser

    B. Primary corona

    C. Fuser

    D. High-voltage power supply

9. Which type of printer can create multipart copies?

    A. Laser

    B. Inkjet

    C. USB

    D. Impact

10. What component of a laser printer transfers the image from the drum to the paper?

    A. Primary corona

    B. Fusing rollers

    C. Transfer corona

    D. Friction feed

REVIEW ANSWERS

1. **B** The steps of the laser printer imaging process are as follows: processing, charging, exposing, developing, transferring, fusing, and cleaning.

2. **A** Impact printers use a tractor-feed mechanism.

3. **D** Duplex settings control how the printer uses multiple sides of the paper and sometimes account for binding or folded booklet layouts.

4. **D** Garbled characters in a printout mean the computer isn't communicating correctly with the printer. One possible reason for this is incorrect or corrupted drivers.

5. **B** The primary corona wire charges the drum.

6. **C** Printers use hard drive caching to save a local copy of recently printed documents.

7. **B** Dye-sublimation printers use a thermal print head to vaporize dyes and transfer them to paper.

8. **D** The high-voltage power supply inside the laser printer can pack a lot of punch and give you a terrible shock. Be very careful inside a laser printer!

9. **D** Impact printers can create multipart copies.

10. **C** The transfer corona in laser printers transfers the image from the drum to the paper.

Career Flight Path

The CompTIA A+ certification generally serves as the foundation for any number of career paths. Most IT companies, big and small, see CompTIA A+ certification as the entry point to IT. From CompTIA A+, you have a number of certification options, depending on whether you want to focus more on hardware, network administration, security, mobile devices, or cloud computing (although these are not mutually exclusive goals). Take a look at these four options in particular:

- CompTIA Network+ certification
- CompTIA Security+ certification
- Microsoft Technical Series certifications
- Cisco certifications

CompTIA Network+ Certification

If you haven't already taken the CompTIA Network+ exam, make it your next certification. Just as CompTIA A+ certification shows you have solid competency as a PC technician, CompTIA Network+ certification demonstrates your skill as a network technician, including your understanding of network hardware, installation, and troubleshooting. CompTIA's Network+ certification is a natural fit for continuing toward your Microsoft or Cisco certifications.

CompTIA Security+ Certification

The CompTIA Security+ certification is considered a benchmark for IT security best practices and essential security principles for risk management and network security. It's the first step into a lucrative career in keeping data safe. Security is top on the list of priorities for many companies, so demonstrating that you know how to protect systems and data by becoming CompTIA Security+ certified will make you more competitive in the job market. If you pass the CompTIA Security+ exam, you may want to consider even more advanced security-related certifications such CompTIA CASP or CISSP.

Microsoft Technical Series Certifications

Microsoft provides a series of exams and certifications geared for computer specialists. Most new techs start with a Microsoft Specialist exam, such as Exam 70-697: Windows 10, Configuring Windows Devices, to get deeper information on supporting Windows operating systems. After a Microsoft Specialist exam, your next step is to get one of the Microsoft Technology Associate (MTA) certifications. These provide you with the knowledge to administer and support Windows in higher-end business and home environments.

If you plan a career focused more on networking at an enterprise level, you can pursue Microsoft's cloud-focused Microsoft Certified Solutions Associate (MCSA) and Microsoft Certified Solutions Expert (MCSE) certifications. These deal with virtual machines, remote access, Windows Server in the enterprise, and more.

Cisco Certifications

Cisco routers pretty much run the Internet, and most intranets in the world, so Cisco provides several levels and paths of certification for folks who want to show their skills at handling Cisco products. Most everyone interested in Cisco certification starts with the Cisco Certified Entry Networking Technician (CCENT). CCENT shows basic competence with networking and routers as well as configuration and setup of a small network. From there, go for the Certified Cisco Network Associate (CCNA), to demonstrate proficiency as a network administrator on Cisco-specific systems. After attaining CCNA, you should consider the CCNP (Certified Cisco Networking Professional) certification.

As with the Microsoft certifications, each level of certification offers different career paths. You can specialize in routing and switching, for example, or network security. After CCENT, either path would take you to CCNA and then to CCNP.

See the Cisco certification website for more details: www.cisco.com/c/en/us/training-events/training-certifications/certifications.html.

About the CD-ROM

The CD-ROM included with this book comes with:

- A video from author Mike Meyers introducing the CompTIA A+ certification exam
- A link to the Total Tester practice exam software, which includes practice exam questions for exam 220-901 and exam 220-902
- A link to more than 20 sample TotalSims interactive simulations from Total Seminars
- A link to more than an hour of video training episodes from Mike Meyers' CompTIA A+ Certification Video Training series
- A link to a collection of Mike's favorite tools and utilities for computer troubleshooting
- PDF copies of the CompTIA A+ 220-901 and 220-902 exam objectives
- An electronic copy of the book in secure PDF format

System Requirements

The software requires Windows Vista or higher, in addition to a current or prior major release of Chrome, Firefox, or Internet Explorer. To run, the screen resolution must be set to 1024 × 768 or higher. The PDF files require Adobe Acrobat, Adobe Reader, or Adobe Digital Editions to view.

Playing the Mike Meyers Introduction Video

If your computer's optical drive is configured to auto-run, the menu will automatically start up upon inserting the disc. If the auto-run feature did not launch the disc, browse to the disc and click the Launch.exe icon.

From the opening screen you can launch the video message from Mike by clicking the **Mike Meyers Introduction Video** button. This launches the video file using your system's default video player.

Total Tester Exam Software

Total Tester provides you with a simulation of the CompTIA A+ exams. You may select practice exams for CompTIA A+ exam 220-901 or CompTIA A+ exam 220-902. The exams can be taken in either Practice mode or Exam mode. Practice mode provides an assistance window with hints, references to the book, explanations of the correct and incorrect answers, and the option to check your answers as you take the test. Exam mode provides a simulation of the actual exam. Both Practice mode and Exam mode provide an overall grade and a grade broken down by certification objectives.

The link on the CD-ROM takes you to a web download page. On the main page of the CD, click the **Software and Videos** link, then select **Total Tester A+ Practice Exams Online**. Click the download and follow the prompts to install the software. To take a test, launch the program and select A+ Demo from the Installed Question Packs list. Select either exam 220-901 or 220-902. You can then select Practice Mode, Exam mode, or Custom Mode. In Custom mode, you can select the number of questions and the duration of the exam. After making your selection, click Start Exam to begin.

Pre-assessment Test

In addition to the sample CompTIA A+ exam questions, the Total Tester also includes a CompTIA A+ Pre-assessment test option to help you assess your understanding of the topics before reading the book. To launch the Assessment test, click A+ Assessment from the Installed Question Packs list. Select either exam 220-901 or 220-902. Each A+ Assessment test includes 50 questions and runs in Exam mode. When you complete the test, you can review the questions with answers and detailed explanation by clicking See Detailed Results.

TotalSims for CompTIA A+

 The CD-ROM contains a link that takes you to Total Seminars Training Hub. On the main page of the CD, click the **Software And Videos** link and then select **TotalSims for A+ Online**. The simulations are organized by chapter, and there are more than 20 free simulations available for reviewing topics referenced in the book, with an option to purchase access to the full TotalSims for A+ 220-901 and 220-902 with more than 250 simulations.

Mike's Video Training

The CD-ROM comes with links to training videos, starring Mike Meyers, for the first four chapters of the book. On the main page of the CD, click the **Software And Videos** link and then select **Mike Meyers Video Training Online**. Along with access to the videos from the first four chapters of the book, you'll find an option to purchase Mike's complete video training series.

Mike's Cool Tools

Mike loves freeware/open-source networking tools! Most of the utilities mentioned in the text can be found via the CD-ROM. On the main page of the CD, click the **Software And Videos** link and then select **Mike's Cool Tools Online**. This will take you to the Total Seminars website, where you can download Mike's favorite tools.

Viewing the CompTIA Exam Objectives

To view the CompTIA A+ exam objectives, select the **CompTIA Exam Objectives** button from the main menu of the disc. On the next page, clicking either the **CompTIA A+ (220-901) Objectives** or the **CompTIA A+ (220-902) Objectives** buttons will open a PDF of the appropriate objectives. The objectives are the actual exam objectives from CompTIA as of the date of publication. Please visit the CompTIA website for the most up-to-date exam objectives.

PDF Copy of the Book

The entire contents of the book are provided as a PDF file on the CD-ROM. This file is viewable on your computer and many portable devices.

- **To view the PDF on a computer**, Adobe Acrobat, Adobe Reader, or Adobe Digital Editions is required. The CD-ROM includes a link to Adobe's website, where you can download and install Adobe Reader.

Note
For more information on Adobe Reader and to check for the most recent version of the software, visit Adobe's website at www.adobe.com and search for the free Adobe Reader or look for Adobe Reader on the product page. Adobe Digital Editions can also be downloaded from the Adobe website.

- **To view the PDF on a portable device**, copy the PDF file to your computer from the CD-ROM, and then copy the file to your portable device using a USB or other connection. Adobe offers a mobile version of Adobe Reader, the Adobe Reader mobile app, which currently supports iOS and Android. For customers using Adobe Digital Editions and an iPad, you may have to download and install a separate reader program on your device. The Adobe website has a list of recommended applications, and McGraw-Hill Education recommends the Bluefire Reader.

Technical Support

Technical support information is provided in the following sections by feature.

Total Seminars Technical Support

For questions regarding the Total Tester software, the operation of the CD-ROM, the Mike Meyers videos, TotalSims simulations, or Mike's Cool Tools, visit **www.totalsem.com** or e-mail **support@totalsem.com**.

McGraw-Hill Education Content Support

For questions regarding the PDF copy of the book, visit **http://mhp .softwareassist.com** or e-mail **techsolutions@mhedu.com**.

For questions regarding book content, e-mail **customer.service@ mheducation.com**. For customers outside the United States, e-mail **international_cs@mheducation.com**.

Glossary

%SystemRoot% The path where the operating system is installed.

4G Most popularly implemented as Long Term Evolution (LTE), a wireless data standard with theoretical download speeds of 300 Mbps and upload speeds of 75 Mbps.

10BaseT Ethernet LAN designed to run on twisted pair cabling. 10BaseT runs at 10 Mbps. The maximum length for the cabling between the NIC and the switch (or hub, repeater, etc.) is 100 meters. It uses baseband signaling. No industry-standard naming convention exists, so sometimes it's written 10BASE-T or 10Base-T.

100BaseT Ethernet cabling system designed to run at 100 Mbps on twisted pair cabling. It uses baseband signaling. No industry-standard naming convention exists, so sometimes it's written 100BASE-T or 100Base-T.

1000BaseT Gigabit Ethernet on UTP.

10 Gigabit Ethernet (10GbE) Ethernet standard that supports speeds of up to 10 Gbps. Requires CAT 6 or better twisted pair or fiber optic cabling.

110 block The most common connection used with structured cabling, connecting horizontal cable runs with patch panels.

16-bit (PC Card) Type of PC Card that can have up to two distinct functions or devices, such as a modem/network card combination.

2.1 speaker system Speaker setup consisting of two stereo speakers combined with a subwoofer.

3.5-inch floppy drive Size of all modern floppy disk drives; the format was introduced in 1986 and is one of the longest surviving pieces of computer hardware.

34-pin ribbon cable Type of cable used by floppy disk drives.

3-D graphics Video technology that attempts to create images with the same depth and texture as objects seen in the real world.

40-pin ribbon cable PATA cable used to attach EIDE devices (such as hard drives) or ATAPI devices (such as optical drives) to a system. (*See* PATA.)

5.1 speaker system Speaker setup consisting of four satellite speakers plus a center speaker and a subwoofer.

7.1 speaker system Speaker setup consisting of six satellite speakers (two front, two side, two rear) plus a center speaker and a subwoofer.

64-bit processing A type of processing that can run a compatible 64-bit operating system, such as Windows 7, 8, 8.1, or 10, and 64-bit applications. 64-bit PCs have a 64-bit-wide address bus, enabling them to use more than 4 GB of RAM.

8.3 naming system File-naming convention that specified a maximum of eight characters for a filename, followed by a three-character file extension. Has been replaced by LFN (long filename) support.

80-wire ribbon cable PATA cable used to attach fast EIDE devices (such as ATA/100 hard drives) or ATAPI devices (such as optical drives) to a system. (*See* PATA.)

802.11a Wireless networking standard that operates in the 5-GHz band with a theoretical maximum throughput of 54 Mbps.

802.11ac Wireless networking standard that operates in the 5-GHz band and uses multiple in/multiple out (MIMO) and multi-user MIMO (MU-MIMO) to achieve a theoretical maximum throughput of 1 Gbps.

802.11b Wireless networking standard that operates in the 2.4-GHz band with a theoretical maximum throughput of 11 Mbps.

802.11g Wireless networking standard that operates in the 2.4-GHz band with a theoretical maximum throughput of 54 Mbps and is backward compatible with 802.11b.

802.11n Wireless networking standard that can operate in both the 2.4-GHz and 5-GHz bands and uses multiple in/multiple out (MIMO) to achieve a theoretical maximum throughput of 100+ Mbps.

A/V sync Process of synchronizing audio and video.

AC (alternating current) Type of electricity in which the flow of electrons alternates direction, back and forth, in a circuit.

AC'97 Sound card standard for lower-end audio devices; created when most folks listened to stereo sound at best.

accelcrometer Feature in smartphones and tablets that rotates the screen when the device is physically rotated.

access control Security concept using physical security, authentication, users and groups, and security policies.

access control list (ACL) A clearly defined list of permissions that specifies what actions an authenticated user may perform on a shared resource.

ACPI (Advanced Configuration and Power Interface) Power management specification that far surpasses its predecessor, APM, by providing support for hotswappable devices and better control of power modes.

Action Center A one-page aggregation of event messages, warnings, and maintenance messages in Windows 7.

activation Process of confirming that an installed copy of a Microsoft product (most commonly Windows or a Microsoft Office application) is legitimate. Usually done at the end of software installation.

active matrix Type of liquid crystal display (LCD) that replaced the passive matrix technology used in most portable computer displays. Also called *TFT (thin film transistor)*.

active partition On a hard drive, primary partition that contains an operating system.

active PFC (power factor correction) Circuitry built into PC power supplies to reduce harmonics.

actively listen Part of respectful communication involving listening and taking notes without interrupting.

activity light An LED on a NIC, hub, or switch that blinks rapidly to show data transfers over the network.

ad hoc mode   Decentralized wireless network mode, otherwise known as peer-to-peer mode, where each wireless node is in meshed contact with every other node.

Add or Remove Programs   Applet allowing users to add or remove a program manually to or from a Windows system.

address bus   Set of wires leading from the CPU to the memory controller chip (traditionally the northbridge) that enables the CPU to address RAM. Also used by the CPU for I/O addressing. On current CPUs with built-in memory controllers, the address bus refers to the internal electronic channel from the microprocessor to RAM, along which the addresses of memory storage locations are transmitted. Like a post office box, each memory location has a distinct number or address; the address bus provides the means by which the microprocessor can access every location in memory.

address space   Total amount of memory addresses that an address bus can contain.

administrative shares   Administrator tool to give local admins access to hard drives and system root folders.

Administrative Tools   Group of Control Panel applets, including Computer Management, Event Viewer, and Reliability and Performance Monitor.

administrator account   User account, created when the OS is first installed, that is allowed complete, unfettered access to the system without restriction.

Administrators group   List of members with complete administrator privileges.

ADSL (asymmetric digital subscriber line)   Fully digital, dedicated connection to the telephone system that provides average download speeds of 3–15 Mbps and upload speeds of 384 Kbps to 15 Mbps. *Asymmetric* identifies that upload and download speeds are different, with download usually being significantly faster than upload.

Advanced Encryption Standard (AES)   A block cipher created in the late 1990s that uses a 128-bit block size and a 128-, 192-, or 256-bit key size. Practically uncrackable.

Advanced Host Controller Interface (AHCI)   An efficient way for motherboards to work with SATA host bus adapters. Using AHCI unlocks some of the advanced features of SATA, such as hot-swapping and native command queuing.

Advanced Startup Options menu   Menu that can be reached during the boot process that offers advanced OS startup options, such as to boot to Safe Mode or boot into Last Known Good Configuration.

adware   Type of malicious program that downloads ads to a user's computer, generating undesirable network traffic.

Aero   The Windows Vista/7 desktop environment. Aero adds some interesting aesthetic effects such as window transparency and Flip 3D.

AGP (Accelerated Graphics Port)   An older 32/64-bit expansion slot designed by Intel specifically for video that ran at 66 MHz and yielded a throughput of at least 254 Mbps. Later versions (2×, 4×, 8×) gave substantially higher throughput.

air filter mask   A mask designed to keep users from inhaling particulate matter, as when cutting drywall.

airplane mode   Mode for mobile devices that disables all wireless and cellular communication for use on airplanes.

algorithm   Set of rules for solving a problem in a given number of steps.

ALU (arithmetic logic unit)   CPU logic circuits that perform basic arithmetic (add, subtract, multiply, and divide).

AMD (Advanced Micro Devices)   CPU and chipset manufacturer that competes with Intel. Produces FX, A-Series, Phenom II, Athlon, Sempron, and Opteron CPUs and APUs. Also produces video card processors under its ATI brand.

AMI (American Megatrends, Inc.)   Major producer of BIOS and UEFI software for motherboards, as well as many other computer-related components and software.

amperes (amps or A)   Unit of measure for amperage, or electrical current.

amplitude   Loudness of a sound card.

analog Device that uses a physical quantity, such as length or voltage, to represent the value of a number. By contrast, digital storage relies on a coding system of numeric units.

AnandTech (anandtech.com) Computer, technology, and Internet news and information site.

Android Smartphone and tablet OS created by Google.

Android application package (APK) Installation software for Android apps.

anti-aliasing In computer imaging, blending effect that smoothes sharp contrasts between two regions—e.g., jagged lines or different colors. Reduces jagged edges of text or objects. In voice signal processing, process of removing or smoothing out spurious frequencies from waveforms produced by converting digital signals back to analog.

antistatic bag Bag made of antistatic plastic into which electronics are placed for temporary or long-term storage. Used to protect components from electrostatic discharge.

antistatic mat Special surface on which to lay electronics. These mats come with a grounding connection designed to equalize electrical potential between a workbench and one or more electronic devices. Used to prevent electrostatic discharge.

antistatic wrist strap Special device worn around the wrist with a grounding connection designed to equalize electrical potential between a technician and an electronic device. Used to prevent electrostatic discharge.

antivirus program Software designed to combat viruses by either seeking out and destroying them or passively guarding against them.

AOL You've got mail!

API (application programming interface) Software definition that describes operating system calls for application software; conventions defining how a service is invoked.

APIPA (Automatic Private IP Addressing) Feature of Windows that automatically assigns an IP address to the system when the client cannot obtain an IP address automatically.

APM (Advanced Power Management) BIOS routines (developed by Intel in 1992 and upgraded over time) that enable the CPU to turn on and off selected peripherals. In 1996, APM was supplanted by Advanced Configuration and Power Interface (ACPI).

app A program for a tablet or smartphone. Also, a program written for the Windows 8 Metro interface.

App Store Apple's mobile software storefront, where you can purchase apps for your smartphone, tablet, or other Apple products.

applet Generic term for a program in the Windows Control Panel.

Applications Name of the tab in Task Manager that lists running applications.

apt-get Linux command for installing or updating a program using the advanced packaging tool.

archive To copy programs and data onto a relatively inexpensive storage medium (drive, tape, etc.) for long-term retention.

archive attribute Attribute of a file that shows whether the file has been backed up since the last change. Each time a file is opened, changed, or saved, the archive bit is turned on. Some types of backups turn off this archive bit to indicate that a good backup of the file exists on tape.

ARM Energy-efficient processor design frequently used in mobile devices.

ARP (Address Resolution Protocol) Protocol in the TCP/IP suite used with the command-line utility of the same name (arp) to determine the MAC address that corresponds to a particular IP address.

Ars Technica (arstechnica.com) Internet technology news site.

ASCII (American Standard Code for Information Interchange) Industry-standard 8-bit characters used to define text characters, consisting of 96 upper- and lowercase letters, plus 32 nonprinting control characters, each of which is numbered. These numbers were designed to achieve uniformity among computer devices for printing and the exchange of simple text documents.

aspect ratio Ratio of width to height of an object. Standard television has a 4:3 aspect ratio. High-definition television is 16:9. Desktop computer monitors tend to be either 16:9 or 16:10.

ASR (Automated System Recovery) Windows XP tool designed to recover a badly corrupted Windows system; similar to the ERD in Windows 2000.

assertive communication Means of communication that is not pushy or bossy but is also not soft. Useful in dealing with upset customers as it both defuses their anger and gives them confidence that you know what you're doing.

AT (Advanced Technology) Model name of the second-generation, 80286-based IBM computer. Many aspects of the AT, such as the BIOS, CMOS, and expansion bus, have become de facto standards in the PC industry. The physical organization of the components on the motherboard is called the AT form factor.

ATA (AT Attachment) Type of hard drive and controller designed to replace the earlier ST506 and ESDI drives without requiring replacement of the AT BIOS—hence, AT attachment. These drives are more popularly known as IDE drives. (*See* IDE.) The ATA/33 standard has drive transfer speeds up to 33 MBps; the ATA/66 up to 66 MBps; the ATA/100 up to 100 MBps; and the ATA/133 up to 133 MBps. (*See* Ultra DMA.)

ATA/ATAPI-6 Also known as ATA-6 or "Big Drive." Replaced the INT13 extensions and allowed for hard drives as large as 144 petabytes (144 million GB).

ATAPI (ATA Packet Interface) Series of standards that enables mass storage devices other than hard drives to use the IDE/ATA controllers. Popular with optical drives. (*See* EIDE.)

ATAPI-compliant Devices that utilize the ATAPI standard. (*See* ATAPI.)

Athlon Name used for a series of CPUs manufactured by AMD.

ATM (Asynchronous Transfer Mode) A network technology that runs at speeds between 25 and 622 Mbps using fiber-optic cabling or CAT 5 or better UTP.

attrib.exe Command used to view the specific properties of a file; can also be used to modify or remove file properties, such as read-only, system, or archive.

attributes Values in a file that determine the hidden, read-only, system, and archive status of the file.

ATX (Advanced Technology Extended)   Popular motherboard form factor that generally replaced the AT form factor.

audio interface   High-end external sound device used by audio engineers and recording artists.

AUP (Acceptable Use Policy)   Defines what actions employees may or may not perform on company equipment, including computers, phones, printers, and even the network itself. This policy defines the handling of passwords, e-mail, and many other issues.

authentication   Any method a computer uses to determine who can access it.

authorization   Any method a computer uses to determine what an authenticated user can do.

autodetection   Process through which new disks are automatically recognized by the BIOS.

Automatic Updates   Feature allowing updates to Windows to be retrieved automatically over the Internet.

AutoPlay   Windows setting, along with autorun.inf, enabling Windows to detect media files automatically and begin using them. (*See* autorun.inf.)

autorun.inf   File included on some media that automatically launches a program or installation routine when the media is inserted/attached to a system.

autosensing   Used by better-quality sound cards to detect a device plugged into a port and to adapt the features of that port.

auto-switching power supply   Type of power supply able to detect the voltage of a particular outlet and adjust accordingly.

Award Software   Major brand of BIOS and UEFI software for motherboards. Merged with Phoenix Technologies.

backlight   One of three main components used in LCDs to illuminate an image.

backside bus   Set of wires that connects the CPU to Level 2 cache. First appearing in the Pentium Pro, all modern CPUs have a backside bus. Some buses run at the full speed of the CPU, whereas others run at a fraction. Earlier Pentium IIs, for example, had backside buses running at half the speed of the processor. (*See also* frontside bus *and* external data bus.)

Backup and Restore Center   Windows Vista/7's backup utility (Windows 7 drops "Center" from the name). It offers two options: create a backup or restore from a backup.

Backup or Restore Wizard   Older Windows utility that enables users to create system backups and set system restore points.

bandwidth   Piece of the spectrum occupied by some form of signal, such as television, voice, or fax data. Signals require a certain size and location of bandwidth to be transmitted. The higher the bandwidth, the faster the signal transmission, allowing for a more complex signal such as audio or video. Because bandwidth is a limited space, when one user is occupying it, others must wait their turn. Bandwidth is also the capacity of a network to transmit a given amount of data during a given period.

bank   Total number of DIMMs that can be accessed simultaneously by the chipset. The "width" of the external data bus divided by the "width" of the DIMM sticks. Specific DIMM slots must be populated to activate dual-, triple-, or quad-channel memory.

bar code reader   Tool to read Universal Product Code (UPC) bar codes.

basic disk   Hard drive partitioned in the "classic" way with a master boot record (MBR) and partition table. (*See also* dynamic disks.)

baud   One analog cycle on a telephone line. In the early days of telephone data transmission, the baud rate was often analogous to bits per second. Due to advanced modulation of baud cycles as well as data compression, this is no longer true.

bcdedit   A command-line tool that enables you to view the BCD store, which lists the Windows boot options.

BD-R (Blu-ray Disc-Recordable)   Blu-ray Disc format that enables writing data to blank discs.

BD-RE (Blu-ray Disc-REwritable)   Blu-ray Disc equivalent of the rewritable DVD, allows writing and rewriting several times on the same BD. (*See* Blu-ray Disc.)

BD-ROM (Blu-ray Disc-Read Only Media)   Blu-ray Disc equivalent of a DVD-ROM or CD-ROM. (*See* Blu-ray Disc.)

beep codes   Series of audible tones produced by a motherboard during the POST. These tones identify whether the POST has completed successfully or whether some piece of system hardware is not working properly. Consult the manual for your particular motherboard for a specific list of beep codes.

binary numbers   Number system with a base of 2, unlike the number systems most of us use that have bases of 10 (decimal numbers), 12 (measurement in feet and inches), and 60 (time). Binary numbers are preferred for computers for precision and economy. An electronic circuit that can detect the difference between two states (on–off, 0–1) is easier and more inexpensive to build than one that could detect the differences among ten states (0–9).

biometric device   Hardware device used to support authentication; works by scanning and remembering a unique aspect of a user's various body parts (e.g., retina, iris, face, or fingerprint) by using some form of sensing device such as a retinal scanner.

BIOS (basic input/output services) (basic input/output system)   Classically, software routines burned onto the system ROM of a PC. More commonly seen as any software that directly controls a particular piece of hardware. A set of programs encoded in read-only memory (ROM) on computers. These programs handle startup operations and low-level control of hardware such as disk drives, the keyboard, and monitor.

bit   Single binary digit. Also, any device that can be in an on or off state.

bit depth   Number of colors a video card is capable of producing. Common bit depths are 16-bit and 32-bit, representing 65,536 colors and 16.7 million colors (plus an 8-bit alpha channel for transparency levels), respectively.

BitLocker Drive Encryption   Drive encryption software offered in high-end versions of Windows. BitLocker requires a special chip to validate hardware status and to ensure that the computer hasn't been hacked.

Bluetooth   Wireless technology designed to create small wireless networks preconfigured to do specific jobs, but not meant to replace full-function networks or Wi-Fi.

Blu-ray Disc (BD)   Optical disc format that stores 25 or 50 GB of data, designed to be the replacement media for DVD. Competed with HD DVD.

boot   To initiate an automatic routine that clears the memory, loads the operating system, and prepares the computer for use. Term is derived from "pull yourself up by your bootstraps." Computers must do that because RAM doesn't retain program instructions when power is turned off. A cold boot occurs when the PC is physically switched on. A warm boot loads a fresh OS without turning off the computer, lessening the strain on the electronic circuitry. To do a warm boot, press the CTRL-ALT-DELETE keys twice in rapid succession (the three-fingered salute).

Boot Camp   Apple tool used to install and boot to versions of Windows on a Mac OS X computer.

Boot Configuration Data (BCD) file   File that contains information about the various operating systems installed on the system as well as instructions for how to actually load (bootstrap) them.

boot sector   First sector on a PC hard drive or floppy disk, track 0. The boot-up software in ROM tells the computer to load whatever program is found there. If a system disk is read, the program in the boot record directs the computer to the root directory to load the operating system.

boot sequence   List containing information telling the bootstrap loader in which order to check the available storage devices for an OS. Configurable in CMOS setup.

bootable disk   Disk that contains a functional operating system; can also be a floppy disk, USB thumb drive, or optical disc.

boot.ini   Text file used during the boot process that provides a list of all OSs currently installed and available for ntldr (NT Loader). Also tells where each OS is located on the system. Used in Windows XP and earlier Microsoft operating systems.

bootmgr   Windows Boot Manager for Vista and later versions.

bootrec   A Windows Recovery Environment troubleshooting and repair tool that repairs the master boot record, boot sector, or BCD store. It replaces the fixboot and fixmbr Recovery Console commands used in Windows XP and earlier operating systems.

bootstrap loader   Segment of code in a system's BIOS that scans for an operating system, looks specifically for a valid boot sector, and, when one is found, hands control over to the boot sector; then the bootstrap loader removes itself from memory.

bps (bits per second)   Measurement of how fast data is moved from one place to another. A 56K modem can move ~56,000 bits per second.

bridge   A device that connects two networks and passes traffic between them based only on the node address, so that traffic between nodes on one network does not appear on the other network. For example, an Ethernet bridge only looks at the MAC address. Bridges filter and forward packets based on MAC addresses and operate at Level 2 (Data Link layer) of the OSI seven-layer model.

broadband   Commonly understood as a reference to high-speed, always-on communication links that can move large files much more quickly than a regular phone line.

broadcast   A network transmission addressed for every node on the network.

browser   Program specifically designed to retrieve, interpret, and display web pages.

BSoD (Blue Screen of Death)   Infamous error screen that appears when Windows encounters an unrecoverable error.

BTX (Balanced Technology eXtended)   Motherboard form factor designed as an improvement over ATX.

buffered/registered DRAM   Usually seen in motherboards supporting more than four sticks of RAM, required to address interference issues caused by the additional sticks.

bug   Programming error that causes a program or a computer system to perform erratically, produce incorrect results, or crash. The term was coined when a real bug was found in one of the circuits of one of the first ENIAC computers.

burn Process of writing data to a writable optical disc, such as a DVD-R.

burn-in failure Critical failure usually associated with manufacturing defects.

bus Series of wires connecting two or more separate electronic devices, enabling those devices to communicate. Also, a network topology where computers all connect to a main line called a bus cable.

bus mastering Circuitry allowing devices to avoid conflicts on the external data bus.

bus topology Network configuration wherein all computers connect to the network via a central bus cable.

BYOD (bring your own device) An arrangement in some companies' IT departments where employees are permitted to use their own phones or other mobile devices instead of company-issued ones. Also, a feature of some wireless carriers where you can buy an unsubsidized device and use it to get cheaper wireless rates.

byte Unit of 8 bits; fundamental data unit of personal computers. Storing the equivalent of one character, the byte is also the basic unit of measurement for computer storage.

CAB files Short for cabinet files. These files are compressed and most commonly used during OS installation to store many smaller files, such as device drivers.

cache (disk) Special area of RAM that stores the data most frequently accessed from the hard drive. Cache memory can optimize the use of your systems.

cache (L1, L2, L3, etc.) Special section of fast memory, usually built into the CPU, used by the onboard logic to store information most frequently accessed by the CPU.

calibration Process of matching the print output of a printer to the visual output of a monitor.

capacitive touchscreen Type of touchscreen that uses electrical current in your body to determine movement of your fingers across the screen.

CAPTCHA (Completely Automated Public Turing Test to tell Computers and Humans Apart) Authentication challenge using images, videos, sounds, or other media to be identified by a user. Computers have a much more difficult time discerning the content of these tests than humans, making the challenge useful in determining if a human or a computer is attempting access.

card reader   Device with which you can read data from one of several types of flash memory.

CardBus   32-bit PC cards that can support up to eight devices on each card. Electrically incompatible with earlier PC cards (3.3 V versus 5 V).

CAT 5   Category 5 wire; a TIA/EIA standard for UTP wiring that can operate at up to 100 Mbps.

CAT 5e   Category 5e wire; TIA/EIA standard for UTP wiring that can operate at up to 1 Gbps.

CAT 6   Category 6 wire; TIA/EIA standard for UTP wiring that can operate at up to 10 Gbps.

CAT 6a   Category 6a wire; augmented CAT 6 UTP wiring that supports 10GbE networks at the full 100-meter distance between a node and a switch.

CAT 7   Supports 10-Gbps networks at 100-meter segments; shielding for individual wire pairs reduces crosstalk and noise problems. CAT 7 is not a TIA/EIA standard.

catastrophic failure   Describes a failure in which a component or whole system will not boot; usually related to a manufacturing defect of a component. Could also be caused by overheating and physical damage to computer components.

CCFL (cold cathode fluorescent lamp)   Light technology used in LCDs and flatbed scanners. CCFLs use relatively little power for the amount of light they provide.

cd (chdir)   Shorthand for "change directory." Enables you to change the focus of the command prompt from one directory to another.

CD (compact disc)   Originally designed as the replacement for vinyl records, has become the primary method of long-term storage of music and data.

CD quality   Audio quality that has a sample rate of 44.4 KHz and a bit rate of 128 bits.

CDDA (CD-Digital Audio)   Special format used for early CD-ROMs and all audio CDs; divides data into variable-length tracks. A good format to use for audio tracks but terrible for data because of lack of error checking.

CDFS (compact disc file system)   File structure, rules, and conventions used when organizing and storing files and data on a CD.

CD-R (CD-recordable)   CD technology that accepts a single "burn" but cannot be erased after that one burn.

CD-ROM (compact disc/read-only memory)   Read-only compact storage disc for audio or video data. CD-ROMs are read by using CD-ROM drives and optical drives with backward compatibility, such as DVD and Blu-ray Disc drives.

CD-RW (CD-rewritable)   CD technology that accepts multiple reads/writes like a hard drive.

Celeron   Lower-cost brand of Intel CPUs.

cellular wireless networks   Networks that enable cell phones, smartphones, and other mobile devices to connect to the Internet.

certification   License that demonstrates competency in some specialized skill.

Certified Cisco Network Associate (CCNA)   One of the certifications demonstrating a knowledge of Cisco networking products.

CFS (Central File System)   Method to unify all storage devices within a network or organization to facilitate a single management point and to provide user access to any file or data within the organization.

CFS (Command File System)   Along with CFS (**Common** File System), this term is found in the Acronym List of the CompTIA A+ learning objectives, and nowhere else. After diligent research, your intrepid author has not found a satisfactory reference to this alleged technology and believes that your ability to recognize that CFS can stand for Command File System will be sufficient knowledge to pass any exam questions about this topic on the corresponding test. —Mike Meyers

CFS (Common File System)   Along with CFS (**Command** File System), this term is found in the Acronym List of the CompTIA A+ learning objectives, and nowhere else. After diligent research, your intrepid author has not found a satisfactory reference to this alleged technology and believes that your ability to recognize that CFS can stand for Common File System will be sufficient knowledge to pass any exam questions about this topic on the corresponding test. —Mike Meyers

chain of custody A documented history of who has been in possession of a system.

CHAP (Challenge Handshake Authentication Protocol) Common remote access protocol; the serving system challenges the remote client, usually by means of asking for a password.

charms In Windows 8 and 8.1, tools located in the hidden Charms bar, such as a search function, a sharing tool, a settings tool, and more.

Charms bar The location in Windows 8 and 8.1 of the charms tools. Accessed by moving the cursor to the upper-right corner of the screen.

chassis intrusion detection Feature offered in some chassis that trips a switch when the chassis is opened.

chipset Electronic chips, specially designed to work together, that handle all of the low-level functions of a PC. In the original PC, the chipset consisted of close to 30 different chips; today, chipsets usually consist of one, two, or three separate chips embedded into a motherboard.

chkdsk (CheckDisk) Hard drive error detection and, to a certain extent, correction utility in Windows, launched from the command-line interface. Originally a DOS command (chkdsk.exe); also the executable for the graphical Error-checking tool.

chmod Linux command used to change permissions.

chown Linux command used to change the owner and the group to which a file or folder is associated.

CIFS (Common Internet File System) The protocol that NetBIOS uses to share folders and printers. Still very common, even on UNIX/Linux systems.

clean installation Installing an operating system on a fresh drive, following a reformat of that drive. Often it's the only way to correct a problem with a system when many of the crucial operating system files have become corrupted.

client Computer program that uses the services of another computer program. Also, software that extracts information from a server; your auto-dial phone is a client, and the phone company is its server. Also, a machine that accesses shared resources on a server.

client/server Relationship in which client software obtains services from a server on behalf of a person.

client/server network Network that has dedicated server machines and client machines.

clock (CLK) wire A special wire that, when charged, tells the CPU that another piece of information is waiting to be processed.

clock cycle Single charge to the clock wire of a CPU.

clock speed Speed at which a CPU executes instructions, measured in MHz or GHz. In modern CPUs, the internal speed is a multiple of the external speed. (*See also* clock-multiplying CPU.)

clock-multiplying CPU CPU that takes the incoming clock signal and multiples it inside the CPU to let the internal circuitry of the CPU run faster.

closed source Software that is solely controlled by its creator or distributor.

Cloud computing A model for enabling and accessing computing storage and other shared (or not shared) resources on-demand. The "cloud" is based on servicing models that include IaaS, PaaS, and SaaS, or hybrid mixtures of these services.

cluster Basic unit of storage on a floppy or hard disk. Multiple sectors are contained in a cluster. When Windows stores a file on a disk, it writes those files into dozens or even hundreds of contiguous clusters. If there aren't enough contiguous open clusters available, the operating system finds the next open cluster and writes there, continuing this process until the entire file is saved. The FAT or MFT tracks how the files are distributed among the clusters on the disk.

CMOS (complementary metal-oxide semiconductor) Originally, the type of nonvolatile RAM that held information about the most basic parts of your PC, such as hard drives, floppies, and amount of DRAM. Today, actual CMOS chips have been replaced by flash-type nonvolatile RAM. The information is the same, however, and is still called CMOS—even though it is now almost always stored on Flash RAM.

CMOS clear   A jumper on the motherboard that, when set, will revert CMOS settings to the factory defaults.

CMOS setup program   Program enabling you to access and update CMOS data. Also referred to as the *System Setup Utility* or *BIOS setup.*

CNR (communications and networking riser)   Proprietary slot used on some motherboards to provide a sound interference–free connection for modems, sound cards, and NICs.

coaxial cable   Cabling in which an internal conductor is surrounded by another, outer conductor, thus sharing the same axis.

code   Set of symbols representing characters (e.g., ASCII code) or instructions in a computer program (a programmer writes source code, which must be translated into executable or machine code for the computer to use).

code names   Names that keep track of different variations within CPU models.

codec (compressor/decompressor)   Software that compresses or decompresses media streams.

color depth   Term to define a scanner's ability to produce color, hue, and shade.

COM port(s)   Serial communications ports available on a computer. COM*x* is used to designate a uniquely numbered COM port such as COM1, COM2, etc.

command   A request, typed from a terminal or embedded in a file, to perform an operation or to execute a particular program.

command prompt   Text prompt for entering commands.

command-line interface   User interface for an OS devoid of all graphical trappings.

CompactFlash (CF)   One of the older but still popular flash media formats. Its interface uses a simplified PC Card bus, so it also supports I/O devices.

compatibility modes   Feature of Windows to enable software written for previous versions of Windows to operate in newer operating systems.

compliance   Concept that members of an organization must abide by the rules of that organization. For a technician, this often revolves around what software can or cannot be installed on an organization's computer.

component failure   Occurs when a system device fails due to a manufacturing or some other type of defect.

Component Services   Programming tools in Windows for the sharing of data objects between programs.

compression   Process of squeezing data to eliminate redundancies, allowing files to use less space when stored or transmitted.

CompTIA A+ 220-901   The first half of the CompTIA A+ certification for computer technicians. The 901 exam focuses primarily on understanding terminology and technology, how to do fundamental tasks such as upgrading RAM, and basic network and mobile device support.

CompTIA A+ 220-902   The second half of the CompTIA A+ certification for computer technicians. The 902 exam focuses primarily on software, security, and troubleshooting.

CompTIA A+ certification   Industry-wide, vendor-neutral computer certification program that demonstrates competency as a computer technician.

CompTIA Network+ certification   Industry-wide, vendor-neutral certification for network technicians, covering network hardware, installation, and troubleshooting.

Computer   Default interface in Windows Vista and Windows 7 for Windows Explorer; displays hard drives and devices with removable storage.

Computer Management   Applet in Windows' Administrative Tools that contains several useful snap-ins, such as Device Manager and Disk Management.

computing process   Four parts of a computer's operation: input, processing, output, and storage.

Computing Technology Industry Association (CompTIA)   Nonprofit IT trade association that administers the CompTIA A+ and CompTIA Network+ exams, and many other vendor-neutral IT certification exams.

connectors   Small receptacles used to attach cables to a system. Common types of connectors include USB, PS/2, DB-25, RJ-45, HDMI, DVI, HD15, DisplayPort, and Thunderbolt.

consumables   Materials used up by printers, including paper, ink, ribbons, and toner cartridges.

container file   File containing two or more separate, compressed tracks, typically an audio track and a moving-picture track. Also known as a *wrapper*.

context menu   Small menu brought up by right-clicking on objects in Windows.

Control Panel   Collection of Windows applets, or small programs, that can be used to configure various pieces of hardware and software in a system.

controller card   Card adapter that connects devices, such as a drive, to the main computer bus/motherboard.

convergence   Measure of how sharply a single pixel appears on a CRT; a monitor with poor convergence produces images that are not sharply defined.

copy backup   Type of backup similar to a normal or full backup, in that all selected files on a system are backed up. This type of backup does not change the archive bit of the files being backed up.

copy command   Command in the command-line interface for making a copy of a file and pasting it in another location.

Core   Name used for the family of Intel CPUs that succeeded the Pentium 4, such as the Core i3, Core i5, and Core i7.

counter   Used to track data about a particular object when using the Performance Monitor.

cp   Copy command in Linux.

CPU (central processing unit)   "Brain" of the computer. Microprocessor that handles primary calculations for the computer. CPUs are known by names such as Core i5 and Phenom II.

CRC (cyclic redundancy check)   Very accurate mathematical method used to check for errors in long streams of transmitted data. Before data is sent, the main computer uses the data to calculate a CRC value from the data's contents. If the receiver calculates from the received data a different CRC value, the data was corrupted during transmission and is re-sent. Ethernet packets use the CRC algorithm in the FCS portion of the frame.

credit card reader   Device that can be attached to mobile phones and tablets to take credit card payments.

crimper   A specialized tool for connecting twisted pair wires to an RJ-45 connector. Also called a *crimping tool.*

CrossFire   Technology that combines the power of multiple AMD graphics cards in a system.

crossover cable   A standard UTP cable with one RJ-45 connector using the T568A standard and the other using the T568B standard. This reverses the signal between sending and receiving wires and thus simulates the connection to a switch.

CRT (cathode ray tube)   Tube of a monitor in which rays of electrons are beamed onto a phosphorescent screen to produce images. Also, a shorthand way to describe a monitor that uses CRT rather than LCD technology.

CSMA/CA (carrier sense multiple access/collision avoidance)   Networking scheme used by wireless devices to transmit data while avoiding data collisions, which wireless nodes have difficulty detecting.

CSMA/CD (carrier sense multiple access/collision detection)   Networking scheme used by Ethernet devices to transmit data and resend data after detection of data collisions.

cylinder   Single concentric track passing through all the platters in a hard disk drive. Imagine a hard disk drive as a series of metal cans, nested one inside another; a single can would represent a cylinder.

DAC (Discretionary Access Control)   Authorization method based on the idea that there is an owner of a resource who may at his or her discretion assign access to that resource. DAC is considered much more flexible than mandatory access control (MAC).

daily backup Backup of all files that have been changed on that day without changing the archive bits of those files. Also called *daily copy backup*.

daisy-chaining Method of connecting several devices along a bus and managing the signals for each device.

data classification System of organizing data according to its sensitivity. Common classifications include public, highly confidential, and top secret.

data roaming A feature of cellular data systems that enables the signal to jump from cell tower to cell tower and from your provider to another provider without obvious notice.

data storage Saving a permanent copy of your work so that you can come back to it later.

data structure Scheme that directs how an OS stores and retrieves data on and off a drive. Used interchangeably with the term file system. (*See also* file system.)

DB connectors D-shaped connectors used for a variety of connections in the PC and networking world. Can be male (with prongs) or female (with holes) and have a varying number of pins or sockets. Also called *D-sub*, *D-subminiature*, or *D-shell connectors*.

DB-9 A two-row DB connector (male) used to connect the computer's serial port to a serial-communication device such as a modem or a console port on a managed switch.

DB-15 connector A two- or three-row D-sub connector (female) used for 10Base5 networks, MIDI/joysticks, and analog video.

DB-25 connector D-sub connector (female), commonly referred to as a parallel port connector.

DC (direct current) Type of electricity in which the flow of electrons is in a complete circle in one direction.

dd Linux command for copying entire block volumes.

DDOS (distributed denial of service) An attack on a computer or network device in which multiple computers send data and requests to the device in an attempt to overwhelm it so that it cannot perform normal operations.

DDR SDRAM (double data rate SDRAM) Type of DRAM that makes two processes for every clock cycle. (*See also* DRAM.)

DDR2 SDRAM Type of SDRAM that sends 4 bits of data in every clock cycle. (*See also* DDR SDRAM.)

DDR3 SDRAM Type of SDRAM that transfers data at twice the rate of DDR2 SDRAM.

DDR4 SDRAM Type of SDRAM that offers higher density and lower voltages than DDR3, and can handle faster data transfer rates. Maximum theoretical capacity of DDR4 DIMMs is up to 512 GB.

DE (desktop environment) Name for the various user interfaces found in Linux distributions.

debug To detect, trace, and eliminate errors in computer programs.

decibels Unit of measurement typically associated with sound. The higher the number of decibels, the louder the sound.

dedicated server Machine that is not used for any client functions, only server functions.

default gateway In a TCP/IP network, the nearest router to a particular host. This router's IP address is part of the necessary TCP/IP configuration for communicating with multiple networks using IP.

definition file List of virus signatures that an antivirus program can recognize.

defragmentation (defrag) Procedure in which all the files on a hard disk drive are rewritten on disk so that all parts of each file reside in contiguous clusters. The result is an improvement in disk speed during retrieval operations.

degauss Procedure used to break up the electromagnetic fields that can build up on the cathode ray tube of a monitor; involves running a current through a wire loop. Most monitors feature a manual degaussing tool.

del (erase) Command in the command-line interface used to delete/ erase files.

desktop User's primary interface to the Windows operating system.

desktop replacement Portable computer that offers the same performance as a full-fledged desktop computer; these systems are normally very heavy to carry and often cost much more than the desktop systems they replace.

device driver Program used by the operating system to control communications between the computer and periphcrals.

Device Manager Utility that enables techs to examine and configure all the hardware and drivers in a Windows PC.

DFS (distributed file system) A storage environment where shared files are accessed from storage devices within multiple servers, clients, and peer hosts.

DHCP (Dynamic Host Configuration Protocol) Protocol that enables client hosts to request and receive TCP/IP settings automatically from an appropriately configured server.

differential backup Similar to an incremental backup. Backs up the files that have been changed since the last backup. This type of backup does not change the state of the archive bit.

digital camera Camera that simulates film technology electronically.

digital certificate Form in which a public key is sent from a web server to a web browser so that the browser can decrypt the data sent by the server.

Digital Living Network Alliance (DLNA) devices Dcvices that connect to a home network, discover each other, and share media. In theory, DLNA devices should work with minimal setup or fuss, even if sourced from different manufacturers.

digital zoom Software tool to enhance the optical zoom capabilities of a digital camera.

digitally signed driver A driver designed specifically to work with Windows that has been tested and certified by Microsoft to work stably with Windows.

digitizer The touchscreen overlay technology that converts finger and stylus contact into input data for the device to use.

DIMM (dual inline memory module)   32- or 64-bit type of DRAM packaging with the distinction that each side of each tab inserted into the system performs a separate function. DIMMs come in a variety of sizes, with 184-, 240-, and 288-pin being the most common on desktop computers.

DIN (Deutsches Institut für Normung)   Round connector shell with pins or holes that was standardized by the German national standards body. Largely obsolete, DIN and mini-DIN connectors have been used by keyboards, mice, video systems, and other peripherals attached to computers.

dipole antennas   Standard straight-wire antennas that provide the most omnidirectional function.

dir   Command used in the command-line interface to display the entire contents of the current working directory.

directory   Another name for a folder.

directory service   Centralized index that each PC accesses to locate resources in the domain.

DirectX   Set of APIs enabling programs to control multimedia, such as sound, video, and graphics. Used in Windows Vista and Windows 7 to draw the Aero desktop.

Disk Cleanup   Utility built into Windows that can help users clean up their hard drives by removing temporary Internet files, deleting unused program files, and more.

disk cloning   Taking a PC and making a duplicate of the hard drive, including all data, software, and configuration files, and transferring it to another PC. (*See* image installation.)

disk duplexing   Type of disk mirroring using two separate controllers rather than one; faster than traditional mirroring.

disk initialization   A process that places special information on every hard drive installed in a Windows system.

Disk Management   Snap-in available with the Microsoft Management Console that enables techs to configure the various disks installed in a system; available in the Computer Management Administrative Tool.

disk mirroring   Process by which data is written simultaneously to two or more disk drives. Read and write speed is decreased, but redundancy in case of catastrophe is increased.

disk quota   Application allowing network administrators to limit hard drive space usage.

disk striping   Process by which data is spread among multiple (at least two) drives. Increases speed for both reads and writes of data. Considered RAID level 0 because it does not provide fault tolerance.

disk striping with parity   Method for providing fault tolerance by writing data across multiple drives and then including an additional drive, called a parity drive, that stores information to rebuild the data contained on the other drives. Requires at least three physical disks: two for the data and a third for the parity drive. This provides data redundancy at RAID levels 5, 10, and 0+1 with different options.

disk thrashing   Hard drive that is constantly being accessed due to lack of available system memory. When system memory runs low, a Windows system will utilize hard disk space as "virtual" memory, thus causing an unusual amount of hard drive access.

diskpart   A fully functioning command-line partitioning tool.

display adapter   Handles all the communication between the CPU and the monitor. Also known as a *video card*.

Display applet   Tool in Windows XP and Windows 7 used to adjust display settings, including resolution, refresh rate, driver information, and color depth. (*See* Personalization applet for the comparable tool in Windows Vista.)

DisplayPort   Digital video connector used by Apple Mac desktop models and some PCs, notably from Dell. Designed by VESA as a royalty-free connector to replace VGA and DVI.

distended capacitors   Failed capacitors on a motherboard, which tend to bulge out at the top. This was especially a problem during the mid-2000s, when capacitor manufacturers released huge batches of bad capacitors.

distribution (distro)   A specific variant of Linux.

DLP (data loss prevention)   System or set of rules designed to stop leakage of sensitive information. Usually applied to Internet appliances to monitor outgoing network traffic.

DLP (digital light processing)   Display technology that reflects and directs light onto a display surface using micromechanically operated mirrors.

DLT (digital linear tape)   High-speed, magnetic tape storage technology used to archive and retrieve data from faster, online media such as hard disks.

DMA (direct memory access) modes   Technique that some PC hardware devices use to transfer data to and from the memory without using the CPU.

DMA controller   Resides between the RAM and the devices and handles DMA requests.

DMZ (demilitarized zone)   A lightly protected or unprotected subnet network positioned between an outer firewall and an organization's highly protected internal network. DMZs are used mainly to host public address servers (such as web servers).

DNS (domain name service)   TCP/IP name resolution system that translates a host name into an IP address.

DNS domain   Specific branch of the DNS name space. First-level DNS domains include .com, .gov, and .edu.

dock   A bar at the bottom of the Mac OS X desktop where application icons can be placed for easy access.

docking station   Device that provides a portable computer extra features such as a DVD drive or PC Card, in addition to legacy and modern ports. Similar to a port replicator. Also, a charging station for mobile devices.

document findings, actions, and outcomes   Recording each troubleshooting job: what the problem was, how it was fixed, and other helpful information. (Step 6 of 6 in the CompTIA troubleshooting theory.)

Documents folder   Windows folder for storing user-created files.

Dolby Digital   Technology for sound reductions and channeling methods used for digital audio.

domain Groupings of users, computers, or networks. In Microsoft networking, a domain is a group of computers and users that share a common account database and a common security policy. On the Internet, a domain is a group of computers that share a common element in their hierarchical name. Other types of domains exist—e.g., broadcast domain, etc.

domain-based network Network that eliminates the need for logging on to multiple servers by using domain controllers to hold the security database for all systems.

DoS (denial of service) An attack on a computer resource that prevents it from performing its normal operations, usually by overwhelming it with large numbers of requests in an effort to monopolize its resources.

DOS (Disk Operating System) First popular operating system available for PCs. A text-based, single-tasking operating system that was not completely replaced until the introduction of Windows 95.

dot-matrix printer Printer that creates each character from an array of dots. Pins striking a ribbon against the paper, one pin for each dot position, form the dots. May be a serial printer (printing one character at a time) or a line printer.

double-sided RAM RAM stick with RAM chips soldered to both sides of the stick. May only be used with motherboards designed to accept double-sided RAM. Very common.

dpi (dots per inch) Measure of printer resolution that counts the dots the device can produce per linear (horizontal) inch.

DPMS (display power-management signaling) Specification that can reduce monitor power consumption by 75 percent by reducing/eliminating video signals during idle periods.

DRAM (dynamic random access memory or dynamic RAM) Memory used to store data in most personal computers. DRAM stores each bit in a "cell" composed of a transistor and a capacitor. Because the capacitor in a DRAM cell can only hold a charge for a few milliseconds, DRAM must be continually refreshed, or rewritten, to retain its data.

drive letter A letter designating a specific drive or partition.

DriveLock   CMOS program enabling you to control the ATA security mode feature set. Also known as *drive lock*.

driver signing   Digital signature for drivers used by Windows to protect against potentially bad drivers.

DS3D (DirectSound3D)   Introduced with DirectX 3.0, a command set used to create positional audio, or sounds that appear to come from in front, in back, or to the side of a user. Merged with DirectSound into DirectAudio in DirectX 8. (*See also* DirectX.)

DSL (digital subscriber line)   High-speed Internet connection technology that uses a regular telephone line for connectivity. DSL comes in several varieties, including asynchronous (ADSL) and synchronous (SDSL), and many speeds. Typical home-user DSL connections are ADSL with faster download speeds than upload speeds.

D-subminiature   *See* DB connectors.

DTS (Digital Theatre Systems)   Technology for sound reductions and channeling methods, similar to Dolby Digital.

dual boot   Refers to a computer with two operating systems installed, enabling users to choose which operating system to load on boot. Can also refer to kicking a device a second time just in case the first time didn't work.

dual-channel architecture   Using two sticks of RAM (either RDRAM or DDR) to increase throughput.

dual-channel memory   Form of DDR, DDR2, and DDR3 memory access used by many motherboards that requires two identical sticks of DDR, DDR2, or DDR3 RAM.

dual-core   CPUs that have two execution units on the same physical chip but share caches and RAM.

dual-scan passive matrix   Manufacturing technique for increasing display updates by refreshing two lines at a time.

dual-voltage   Type of power supply that works with either 110- or 220-volt outlets.

dumpster diving   To go through someone's trash in search of information.

DUN (Dial-up Networking) Software used by Windows to govern the connection between the modem and the ISP.

duplexing Similar to mirroring in that data is written to and read from two physical drives, for fault tolerance. Separate controllers are used for each drive, both for additional fault tolerance and for additional speed. Considered RAID level 1. Also called *disk duplexing* or *drive duplexing*.

DVD (digital versatile disc) Optical disc format that provides for 4–17 GB of video or data storage.

DVD-ROM DVD equivalent of the standard CD-ROM.

DVD-RW/DVD+RW Incompatible rewritable DVD media formats.

DVD-Video DVD format used exclusively to store digital video; capable of storing over two hours of high-quality video on a single DVD.

DVI (Digital Visual Interface) Special video connector designed for digitalto-digital connections; most commonly seen on PC video cards and LCD monitors. Some versions also support analog signals with a special adapter.

dxdiag (DirectX Diagnostics Tool) Diagnostic tool for getting information about and testing a computer's DirectX version.

dye-sublimation printer Printer that uses a roll of heat-sensitive plastic film embedded with dyes, which are vaporized and then solidified onto specially coated paper to create a high quality image.

dynamic disks Special feature of Windows that enables users to span a single volume across two or more drives. Dynamic disks do not have partitions; they have volumes. Dynamic disks can be striped, mirrored, and striped or mirrored with parity.

ECC (error correction code) Special software, embedded on hard drives, that constantly scans the drives for bad sectors.

ECC RAM/DRAM (error correction code DRAM) RAM that uses special chips to detect and fix memory errors. Commonly used in high-end servers where data integrity is crucial.

effective permissions User's combined permissions granted by multiple groups.

EFI (Extensible Firmware Interface)   Firmware created by Intel and HP that replaced traditional 16-bit BIOS and added several new enhancements.

EFS (encrypting file system)   Storage organization and management service, such as NTFS, that has the capability of applying a cipher process to the stored data.

EIA/TIA   *See* TIA/EIA.

EIDE (Enhanced IDE)   Marketing concept of hard drive–maker Western Digital, encompassing four improvements for IDE drives, including drives larger than 528 MB, four devices, increase in drive throughput, and non–hard drive devices. (*See* ATAPI, PIO mode.)

electric potential   The voltage differential between any two objects, one of which is frequently ground or earth, resulting in a degree of attraction for the electrons to move from one of the objects to the other. A large difference between a person and a doorknob, for example, can lead to a shocking experience when the two touch. (*See* electrostatic discharge (ESD).)

electromagnetic interference (EMI)   Electrical interference from one device to another, resulting in poor performance of the device being interfered with. Examples: Static on your TV while running a blow dryer, or placing two monitors too close together and getting a "shaky" screen.

electrostatic discharge (ESD)   Uncontrolled rush of electrons from one object to another. A real menace to PCs, as it can cause permanent damage to semiconductors.

eliciting answers   Communication strategy designed to help techs understand a user's problems better. Works by listening to a user's description of a problem and then asking cogent questions.

e-mail (electronic mail)   Messages, usually text, sent from one person to another via computer. Can also be sent automatically to a group of addresses (mailing list).

emergency repair disk (ERD)   Saves critical boot files and partition information and is the main tool for fixing boot problems in older versions of Windows. Newer versions of Windows call this a system repair disc (Windows Vista/7) or recovery drive (Windows 8/8.1 and 10).

eMMC (embedded MMC)   A form of embedded flash memory widely seen in mobile devices.

emulator   Software or hardware that converts the commands to and from the host machine into an entirely different platform.

encryption   Making data unreadable by those who do not possess a key or password.

equipment rack   A metal structure used in equipment rooms to secure network hardware devices and patch panels. Most racks are 19 inches wide. Devices designed to fit in such a rack use a height measurement called *units*, or simply *U*.

erase lamp   Component inside laser printers that uses light to make the coating of the photosensitive drum conductive.

e-reader   Mobile electronic device used for reading e-books.

Error-checking   Windows graphical tool that scans and fixes hard drive problems. Often referred to by the name of the executable, chkdsk, or Check Disk. The Mac OS X equivalent is the Disk Utility, and Linux offers a command-line tool called fsck.

eSATA   Serial ATA-based connector for external hard drives and optical drives.

escalate   Process used when person assigned to repair a problem is not able to get the job done, such as sending the problem to someone with more expertise.

establish a plan of action and implement the solution   After establishing and testing a theory about a particular problem, techs solve the problem. (Step 4 of 6 in the CompTIA troubleshooting theory.)

establish a theory of probable cause   After identifying a problem, techs question the obvious to determine what might be the source of the problem. (Step 2 of 6 in the CompTIA troubleshooting theory.)

Ethernet   Name coined by Xerox for the first standard of network cabling and protocols. Based on a bus topology.

Ethic of Reciprocity   Golden Rule: Do unto others as you would have them do unto you.

EULA (End User License Agreement)   Agreement that accompanies a piece of software, to which the user must agree before using the software. Outlines the terms of use for the software and also lists any actions on the part of the user that violate the agreement.

event auditing   Feature of Event Viewer's Security section that creates an entry in the Security Log when certain events happen, such as a user logging on.

Event Viewer   Utility made available in Windows as an MMC snap-in that enables users to monitor various system events, including network bandwidth usage and CPU utilization.

expand   Command-line utility included with Windows that is used to access files within CAB files.

expansion bus   Set of wires going to the CPU, governed by the expansion bus crystal, directly connected to expansion slots of varying types (PCI, AGP, PCIe, etc.).

expansion bus crystal   Controls the speed of the expansion bus.

expansion slots   Connectors on a motherboard that enable users to add optional components to a system. (*See also* AGP, PCI, and PCIe.)

ExpressCard   The high-performance serial version of the PC Card that replaced PC Card slots on laptop PCs over the past decade. ExpressCard comes in two widths: 34 mm and 54 mm, called *ExpressCard/34* and *ExpressCard/54*.

extended partition   Type of nonbootable hard disk partition. May only have one extended partition per disk. Purpose is to divide a large disk into smaller partitions, each with a separate drive letter.

Extensible Authentication Protocol (EAP)   Authentication wrapper that EAP-compliant applications can use to accept one of many types of authentication. While EAP is a general-purpose authentication wrapper, its only substantial use is in wireless networks.

extension   Two, three, four, five, or more letters that follow a filename and identify the type of file. Common file extensions are .zip, .exe, .doc, .java, and .xhtml.

external data bus (EDB) Primary data highway of all computers. Everything in your computer is tied either directly or indirectly to the external data bus. (*See also* frontside bus *and* backside bus.)

face lock Technology that enables use of facial features to unlock a mobile device or personal computer.

Fast User Switching Account option that is useful when multiple users share a system; allows users to switch without logging off.

FAT (file allocation table) Hidden table that records how files on a hard disk are stored in distinct clusters; the only way DOS knows where to access files. Address of first cluster of a file is stored in the directory file. FAT entry for the first cluster is the address of the second cluster used to store that file. In the entry for the second cluster for that file is the address for the third cluster, and so on until the final cluster, which gets a special end-of-file code. There are two FATs, mirror images of each other, in case one is destroyed or damaged. Also refers to the 16-bit file allocation table when used by Windows 2000 and later NT-based operating systems.

FAT16 File allocation table that uses 16 bits to address and index clusters. Used as the primary hard drive format on DOS and early Windows 95 machines; currently used with smaller-capacity (2 GB or less) flash media devices.

FAT32 File allocation table that uses 32 bits to address and index clusters. Commonly used with USB flash-media drives and versions of Windows prior to XP.

FAT64 (exFAT) A Microsoft-proprietary file system that breaks the 4-GB filesize barrier, supporting files up to 16 exabytes (EB) and a theoretical partition limit of 64 zettabytes (ZB). Envisioned for use with flash media devices with a capacity exceeding 2 TB.

FCS (Frame Check Sequence) Portion of an Ethernet frame used for error checking, most commonly with the CRC algorithm.

fdisk Disk-partitioning utility used in DOS and Windows 9*x* systems.

fiber-optic cable High-speed cable for transmitting data, made of high-purity glass sealed within an opaque tube. Much faster than conventional copper wire such as coaxial cable.

file   Collection of any form of data that is stored beyond the time of execution of a single job. A file may contain program instructions or data, which may be numerical, textual, or graphical information.

file allocation unit   Another term for cluster. (*See also* cluster.)

file association   Windows term for the proper program to open a particular file; for example, the file association for opening or .mp3 files might be Winamp.

File Explorer   A tool in Windows 8/8.1/10 that enables users to browse files and folders.

file format   How information is encoded in a file. Two primary types are binary (pictures) and ASCII (text), but within those are many formats, such as BMP and GIF for pictures. Commonly represented by a suffix at the end of the filename; for example, .txt for a text file or .exe for an executable.

file server   Computer designated to store software, courseware, administrative tools, and other data on a LAN or WAN. It "serves" this information to other computers via the network when users enter their personal access codes.

file system   Scheme that directs how an OS stores and retrieves data on and off a drive; FAT32 and NTFS are both file systems. Used interchangeably with the term "data structure." (*See also* data structure.)

filename   Name assigned to a file when the file is first written on a disk. Every file on a disk within the same folder must have a unique name. Filenames can contain any character (including spaces), except the following: \ / : * ? " < > |

Finder   Mac OS X's file and folder browser.

fingerprint lock   Type of biometric device that enables a user to unlock a mobile device using a fingerprint.

firewall   Device that restricts traffic between a local network and the Internet.

FireWire (IEEE 1394)   Interconnection standard to send wide-band signals over a serialized, physically thin connector system. Serial bus developed by Apple and Texas Instruments; enables connection of 63 devices at speeds up to 800 Mbps.

firmware   Embedded programs or code stored on a ROM chip. Generally OS-independent, thus allowing devices to operate in a wide variety of circumstances without direct OS support. The system BIOS is firmware.

firmware upgrade   Process by which the BIOS of a motherboard can be updated to reflect patched bugs and added features. Performed, usually, through CMOS, though some motherboard manufacturers provide a Windows program for performing a firmware upgrade.

fitness monitor   Devices that encourage physical fitness by counting steps using accelerometers, registering heart rate through sensors, using GPS to track exercise, and offering vibration tools to remind the user to get moving. Fitness trackers fit into one of two type: fobs that clip to the body and more sophisticated fitness bands or watches.

Flash ROM   ROM technology that can be electrically reprogrammed while still in the PC. Overwhelmingly the most common storage medium of BIOS in computers today, as it can be upgraded without a need to open the computer on most systems.

flatbed scanner   Most popular form of consumer scanner; runs a bright light along the length of the tray to capture an image.

FlexATX   Motherboard form factor. Motherboards built in accordance with the FlexATX form factor are very small, much smaller than microATX motherboards.

Flip 3D   In the Aero desktop environment, a three-dimensional replacement for ALT-TAB. Accessed by pressing the WINDOWS KEY-TAB key combination.

floppy disk   Removable storage media that can hold between 720 KB and 1.44 MB of data.

floppy drive   System hardware that uses removable 3.5-inch disks as storage media.

flux reversal   Point at which a read/write head detects a change in magnetic polarity.

FM synthesis   Producing sound by electronic emulation of various instruments to more or less produce music and other sound effects.

form factor   Standard for the physical organization of motherboard components and motherboard size. Most common form factors are ATX, microATX, and Mini-ITX.

format   Command in the command-line interface used to format a storage device.

formatting   Magnetically mapping a disk to provide a structure for storing data; can be done to any type of disk, including a floppy disk, hard disk, or other type of removable disk.

FPU (floating point unit)   Formal term for math coprocessor (also called a numeric processor) circuitry inside a CPU. A math coprocessor calculates by using a floating point numerical system (which allows for decimals). Before the Intel 80486, FPUs were separate chips from the CPU.

fragmentation   Occurs when files and directories get jumbled on a fixed disk and are no longer contiguous. Can significantly slow down hard drive access times and can be repaired by using the defrag utility included with each version of Windows. (*See also* defragmentation.)

frame   A data unit transferred across a network. Frames consist of several parts, such as the sending and receiving MAC addresses, the data being sent, and the frame check sequence.

freeware   Software that is distributed for free, with no license fee.

frequency   Measure of a sound's tone, either high or low.

frontside bus   Wires that connect the CPU to the main system RAM. Generally running at speeds of 66–133 MHz. Distinct from the expansion bus and the backside bus, though it shares wires with the former.

front-view projector   Shoots the image out the front and counts on you to put a screen in front at the proper distance.

FRU (field replaceable unit)   Any part of a PC that is considered to be replaceable "in the field," i.e., a customer location. There is no official list of FRUs—it is usually a matter of policy by the repair center.

FTP (File Transfer Protocol)   Rules that enable two computers to talk to one another during a file transfer. Protocol used when you transfer a file from one computer to another across the Internet. FTP uses port numbers 20 and 21.

full-duplex Any device that can send and receive data simultaneously.

Full-Speed USB USB standard that runs at 12 Mbps. Also known as *USB 1.1.*

fully qualified domain name (FQDN) A complete, bottom-to-top label of a DNS host going from the specific host to the top-level domain that holds it and all of the intervening domain layers, each layer being separated by a dot. FQDNs are entered into browser bars and other utilities in formats like *mail .totalseminars.com.*

Function (fn) key Special key on many laptops that enables some keys to perform a third duty.

fuser assembly Mechanism in laser printers that uses two rollers to fuse toner to paper during the print process.

future-proofing Configuring a PC so that it will run programs (especially games) released in the coming years.

Gadgets Small tools, such as clocks or calendars, in Windows Vista and 7 that are placed on the Sidebar.

gain Ratio of increase of radio frequency output provided by an antenna, measured in decibels (dB).

gamepad An input device specifically designed for playing computer games. These usually consist of one or more thumbsticks, a directional pad, multiple face buttons, and two or more triggers.

GDI (graphical device interface) Component of Windows that utilizes the CPU rather than the printer to process a print job as a bitmapped image of each page.

general protection fault (GPF) Error code usually seen when separate active programs conflict on resources or data.

geometry Numbers representing three values: heads, cylinders, and sectors per track; defines where a hard drive stores data.

geotracking Feature in cellular phones that enables the cell phone companies and government agencies to use the ID or MAC address to pinpoint where a phone is at any given time.

giga   Prefix for the quantity 1,073,741,824 (2^{30}) or for 1 billion. One gigabyte would be 1,073,741,824 bytes, except with hard drive labeling, where it means 1 billion bytes. One gigahertz is 1 billion hertz.

glasses   Wearable computing device that enables a user to perform some computing functions via a pair of glasses.

Global Positioning System (GPS)   Technology that enables a mobile device to determine where you are on a map.

globally unique identifier (GUID) partition table (GPT)   Partitioning scheme that enables you to create more than four primary partitions without needing to use dynamic disks.

gpresult   Windows command for listing group policies applied to a user.

GPU (graphics processing unit)   Specialized processor that helps the CPU by taking over all of the 3-D rendering duties.

gpupdate   Windows command for making immediate group policy changes in an individual system.

grayscale depth   Number that defines how many shades of gray the scanner can save per dot.

grayware   Program that intrudes into a user's computer experience without damaging any systems or data.

grep   Linux command to search through text files or command outputs to find specific information or to filter out unneeded information.

group   Collection of user accounts that share the same access capabilities.

Group Policy   Means of easily controlling the settings of multiple network clients with policies such as setting minimum password length or preventing Registry edits.

GSM (Global System for Mobile Communications)   Wireless data standard for mobile devices.

guest account   Very limited built-in account type for Windows; a member of the Guest group.

GUI (graphical user interface) Interface that enables user to interact with computer graphically, by using a mouse or other pointing device to manipulate icons that represent programs or documents, instead of using only text as in early interfaces. Pronounced "gooey."

gyroscope Device that can detect the position of the tablet or phone in 3-D space.

HAL (hardware abstraction layer) Part of the Windows OS that separates system-specific device drivers from the rest of the operating system.

handshaking Procedure performed by modems, terminals, and computers to verify that communication has been correctly established.

hang Occurs when a computer or program stops responding to keyboard commands or other input; a computer or program in such a state is said to be 'hung.'

hang time Number of seconds a too-often-hung computer is airborne after you have thrown it out a second-story window.

hard drive Data-recording system using solid disks of magnetic material turning at high speeds to store and retrieve programs and data in a computer. Abbreviated HDD for *hard disk drive*.

hardware Physical computer equipment such as electrical, electronic, magnetic, and mechanical devices. Anything in the computer world that you can hold in your hand. A hard drive is hardware; Microsoft Word is not.

hardware protocol Defines many aspects of a network, from the packet type to the cabling and connectors used.

HBA (host bus adapter) Connects SATA devices to the expansion bus. Also known as the *SATA controller*.

HD (Hi-Definition) Multimedia transmission standard that defines high-resolution images and 5.1, 6.1, and 7.1 sound.

HDA (High Definition Audio) Intel-designed standard to support features such as true surround sound with many discrete speakers. Often referred to by its code name, Azalia.

HDD (hard disk drive) Data-recording system using solid disks of magnetic material turning at high speeds to store and retrieve programs and data in a computer.

HDMI (High Definition Multimedia Interface) Single multimedia connection that includes both high-definition video and audio. One of the best connections for outputting to television. Also contains copy protection features.

head actuator Mechanism for moving the arms inside a hard drive on which the read/write heads are mounted.

headphones Audio output device that sits on top of or in a user's ears.

heads Short for read/write heads used by hard drives to store data.

heat dope *See* thermal compound.

hex (hexadecimal) Base-16 numbering system using ten digits (0 through 9) and six letters (A through F). In the computer world, shorthand way to write binary numbers by substituting one hex digit for a four-digit binary number (e.g., hex 9 = binary 1001).

hibernation Power management setting in which all data from RAM is written to the hard drive before the system goes into Sleep mode. Upon waking up, all information is retrieved from the hard drive and returned to RAM.

hidden attribute File attribute that, when used, does not allow the dir command to show a file.

hierarchical directory tree Method by which Windows organizes files into a series of folders, called directories, under the root directory. (*See also* root directory.)

high gloss Laptop screen finish that offers sharper contrast, richer colors, and wider viewing angles than a matte finish, but is also much more reflective.

high-level formatting Format that sets up a file system on a drive.

high-voltage anode Component in a CRT monitor that has very high voltages of electricity flowing through it.

Hi-Speed USB USB standard that runs at 480 Mbps. Also referred to as *USB 2.0.*

home screen   The default "desktop" of a mobile device.

home server PC   A computer built to store files on a small office/home office (SOHO) network.

HomeGroup   A Windows 7 feature that connects a group of computers using a common password—no special user names required. Each computer can be a member of only one homegroup at a time. Homegroups enable simple sharing of documents and printers between computers.

honesty   Telling the truth—a very important thing for a tech to do.

horizontal cabling   Cabling that connects the equipment room to the work areas.

host   On a TCP/IP network, single device that has an IP address—any device (usually a computer) that can be the source or destination of a data packet. In the mainframe world, computer that is made available for use by multiple people simultaneously. Also, in virtualization, a computer running one or more virtual operating systems.

hostname   Windows command for displaying the name of a computer.

hotspot   Feature that enables a mobile device connected to a mobile data network to be used as a wireless access point (WAP) for other devices. Often these are stand-alone devices, though many cellular phones and data-connected tablets can be set up to act as hotspots.

hot-swappable   Any hardware that may be attached to or removed from a PC without interrupting the PC's normal processing.

HRR (horizontal refresh rate)   Amount of time it takes for a monitor to draw one horizontal line of pixels on a display.

HTML (Hypertext Markup Language)   ASCII-based, script-like language for creating hypertext documents such as those on the World Wide Web.

HTPC   A home theater PC designed to attach to a TV or projector for movie and TV viewing.

HTTP (Hypertext Transfer Protocol)   Extremely fast protocol used for network file transfers in the WWW environment. Uses port 80.

HTTPS (HTTP over Secure Sockets Layer)   Secure form of HTTP used commonly for Internet business transactions or any time when a secure connection is required. Uses port 443. (*See also* HTTP.)

hub   Electronic device that sits at the center of a star topology network, providing a common point for the connection of network devices. Hubs repeat all information out to all ports and have been replaced by switches, although the term "hub" is still commonly used.

hybrid   A network topology that combines features from multiple other topologies, such as the star-bus topology.

hyperthreading   CPU feature that enables a single pipeline to run more than one thread at once.

hypervisor   Software that enables a single computer to run multiple operating systems simultaneously.

IaaS (Infrastructure as a Service)   Cloud-hosted provider of virtualized servers and networks.

I/O (input/output)   General term for reading and writing data to a computer. "Input" includes data entered from a keyboard, identified by a pointing device (such as a mouse), or loaded from a disk. "Output" includes writing information to a disk, viewing it on a monitor, or printing it to a printer.

I/O addressing   Using the address bus to talk to system devices.

I/O advanced programmable interrupt controller (IOAPIC)   Typically located in the southbridge, acts as the traffic cop for interrupt requests to the CPU.

I/O base address   First value in an I/O address range.

ICH (I/O Controller Hub)   Official name for southbridge chip found in Intel's chipsets.

iCloud   Apple cloud-based storage. iCloud enables a user to back up all iPhone or iPad data, and makes that data accessible from anywhere. This includes any media purchased through iTunes and calendars, contacts, reminders, and so forth.

icon   Small image or graphic, most commonly found on a system's desktop, that launches a program when selected.

ICS (Internet Connection Sharing) Windows feature that enables a single network connection to be shared among several machines.

IDE (integrated drive electronics) PC specification for small- to medium-sized hard drives in which the controlling electronics for the drive are part of the drive itself, speeding up transfer rates and leaving only a simple adapter (or "paddle"). IDE only supported two drives per system of no more than 504 MB each, and has been completely supplanted by Enhanced IDE. EIDE supports four drives of over 8 GB each and more than doubles the transfer rate. The more common name for PATA drives. Also known as *intelligent drive electronics*. (*See* PATA.)

identify the problem To question the user and find out what has been changed recently or is no longer working properly. Step 1 of 6 in the CompTIA troubleshooting theory.

IEC-320 Connects the cable supplying AC power from a wall outlet into the power supply.

IEEE (Institute of Electronic and Electrical Engineers) Leading standards-setting group in the United States.

IEEE 1284 IEEE standard governing parallel communication.

IEEE 1394 IEEE standard governing FireWire communication. (*See also* FireWire.)

IEEE 1394a FireWire standard that runs at 400 Mbps.

IEEE 1394b FireWire standard that runs at 800 Mbps.

IEEE 802.11 Wireless Ethernet standard more commonly known as Wi-Fi.

ifconfig Linux command for finding out a computer's IP address information.

image deployment Operating system installation that uses a complete image of a hard drive as an installation media. Helpful when installing an operating system on a large number of identical PCs.

image file Bit-by-bit image of data to be burned on CD or DVD—from one file to an entire disc—stored as a single file on a hard drive. Particularly handy when copying from CD to CD or DVD to DVD.

IMAP4 (Internet Message Access Protocol version 4)   An alternative to POP3 that retrieves e-mail from an e-mail server, like POP3; IMAP uses TCP port 143.

IMC (integrated memory controller)   Memory controller circuitry built into the CPU that enables faster control over things like the large L3 cache shared among multiple cores.

IMEI (International Mobile Equipment Identity)   A 15-digit number used to uniquely identify a mobile device, typically a smartphone or other device that connects to a cellular network.

impact printer   Uses pins and inked ribbons to print text or images on a piece of paper.

impedance   Amount of resistance to an electrical signal on a wire. Relative measure of the amount of data a cable can handle.

IMSI (International Mobile Subscriber Identity)   A unique number that represents the actual user associated with a particular SIM card. The IMSI is usually available from the carrier, to ensure that stolen phones are not misused. The IMSI number can be used to unlock a phone as well.

incident report   Record of the details of an accident, including what happened and where it happened.

incremental backup   Backs up all files that have their archive bits turned on, meaning that they have been changed since the last backup. Turns the archive bits off after the files have been backed up.

Information Technology (IT)   Field of computers, their operation, and their maintenance.

infrastructure mode   Wireless networking mode that uses one or more WAPs to connect the wireless network nodes to a wired network segment.

inheritance   NTFS feature that passes on the same permissions in any subfolders/files resident in the original folder.

ink cartridge   Small container of ink for inkjet printers.

inkjet printer Uses liquid ink, sprayed through a series of tiny jets, to print text or images on a piece of paper.

installation disc Typically a CD-ROM or DVD that holds all the necessary device drivers.

instruction set All of the machine-language commands that a particular CPU is designed to understand.

integrity Always doing the right thing.

interface Means by which a user interacts with a piece of software.

Interrupt 13 (INT13) extensions Improved type of BIOS that accepts EIDE drives up to 137 GB.

interrupt/interruption Suspension of a process, such as the execution of a computer program, caused by an event external to the computer and performed in such a way that the process can be resumed. Events of this kind include sensors monitoring laboratory equipment or a user pressing an interrupt key.

inverter Device used to convert DC current into AC. Commonly used with CCFLs in laptops and flatbed scanners.

iOS The operating system of Apple mobile devices.

IP address Numeric address of a computer connected to the Internet. An IPv4 address is made up of four octets of 8-bit binary numbers translated into their shorthand numeric values. An IPv6 address is 128 bits long. The IP address can be broken down into a network ID and a host ID. Also called *Internet address.*

ipconfig Command-line utility for Windows servers and workstations that displays the current TCP/IP configuration of the machine. Similar to ifconfig.

IPS (in-plane switching) Display technology that replaces the older twisted nematic (TN) panels for more accurate colors and a wider viewing angle.

IPsec (Internet Protocol security) Microsoft's encryption method of choice for networks consisting of multiple networks linked by a private connection, providing transparent encryption between the server and the client.

IPv4 (Internet Protocol version 4)   Internet standard protocol that provides a common layer over dissimilar networks; used to move packets among host computers and through gateways if necessary. Part of the TCP/IP protocol suite. Uses the dotted-decimal format—$x.x.x.x$. Each x represents an 8-bit binary number, or 0-255. Here's an example: 192.168.4.1.

IPv6 (Internet Protocol version 6)   Protocol in which addresses consist of eight sets of four hexadecimal numbers, each number being a value between 0000 and FFFF, using a colon to separate the numbers. Here's an example: FEDC:BA98:7654:3210:080 0:200C:00CF:1234.

IrDA (Infrared Data Association) protocol   Protocol that enables communication through infrared devices, with speeds of up to 4 Mbps.

IRQ (interrupt request)   Signal from a hardware device, such as a modem or a mouse, indicating that it needs the CPU's attention. In PCs, IRQs are sent along specific IRQ channels associated with a particular device. IRQ conflicts were a common problem in the past when adding expansion boards, but the plug-and-play specification has removed this headache in most cases.

ISA (Industry Standard Architecture)   Design found in the original IBM PC for the slots that allowed additional hardware to be connected to the computer's motherboard. An 8-bit, 8.33-MHz expansion bus was designed by IBM for its AT computer and released to the public domain. An improved 16-bit bus was also released to the public domain. Replaced by PCI in the mid-1990s.

ISDN (integrated services digital network)   CCITT (Comité Consultatif Internationale de Télégraphie et Téléphonie) standard that defines a digital method for communications to replace the current analog telephone system. ISDN is superior to POTS telephone lines because it supports a transfer rate of up to 128 Kbps for sending information from computer to computer. It also allows data and voice to share a common phone line. DSL reduced demand for ISDN substantially. (*See also* POTS.)

ISO file   Complete copy (or image) of a storage media device, typically used for optical discs. ISO image files typically have a file extension of .iso.

ISO-9660   CD format to support PC file systems on CD media. Supplanted by the Joliet format and then the UDF format.

ISP (Internet service provider)   Company that provides access to the Internet, usually for money.

ITX   A family of motherboard form factors. Mini-ITX is the largest and the most popular of the ITX form factors but is still quite small.

iwconfig   Linux command for viewing and changing wireless settings.

jack (physical connection)   Part of a connector into which a plug is inserted. Also referred to as a *port*.

Joliet   Extension of the ISO 9660 format. Most popular CD format to support PC file systems on CD media. Joliet has been supplanted by UDF.

joule   Unit of energy describing (in this book) how much energy a surge suppressor can handle before it fails.

joystick   Peripheral often used while playing computer games; originally intended as a multipurpose input device.

Jump List   A Windows 7 menu that shows context-sensitive information about whatever is on the taskbar.

jumper   Pair of small pins that can be shorted with a shunt to configure many aspects of PCs. Often used in configurations that are rarely changed, such as master/slave settings on IDE drives.

Kerberos   Authentication encryption developed by MIT to enable multiple brands of servers to authenticate multiple brands of clients.

kernel   Core portion of program that resides in memory and performs the most essential operating system tasks.

keyboard   Input device. Three common types of keyboards exist: those that use a mini-DIN (PS/2) connection, those that use a USB connection, and those that use wireless technology.

Keychain   Mac OS X password management and storage service that saves passwords for computer and non-computer environments. Also, the *iCloud Keychain* adds synchronization among any OS X and iOS devices connected to the Internet for a user account.

Knowledge Base Large collection of documents and FAQs that is maintained by Microsoft. Found on Microsoft's website, the Knowledge Base is an excellent place to search for assistance on most operating system problems.

KVM (keyboard, video, mouse) switch Hardware device that enables multiple computers to be viewed and controlled by a single mouse, keyboard, and screen.

LAN (local area network) Group of computers connected via cabling, radio, or infrared that use this connectivity to share resources such as printers and mass storage.

laptop Traditional clamshell portable computing device with built-in LCD monitor, keyboard, and trackpad.

laser Single-wavelength, in-phase light source that is sometimes strapped to the head of sharks by bad guys. Note to henchmen: Lasers should never be used with sea bass, no matter how ill-tempered they might be.

laser printer Electro-photographic printer in which a laser is used as the light source.

Last Known Good Configuration Option on the Advanced Startup Options menu that enables your system to revert to a previous configuration to troubleshoot and repair any major system problems.

latency Amount of delay before a device may respond to a request; most commonly used in reference to RAM.

LBA (logical block addressing) Translation (algorithm) of IDE drives promoted by Western Digital as a standardized method for breaking the 504-MB limit in IDE drives. Subsequently universally adopted by the PC industry and standard on all EIDE drives.

LCD (liquid crystal display) Type of display commonly used on portable computers. LCDs have also replaced CRTs as the display of choice for desktop computer users. LCDs use liquid crystals and electricity to produce images on the screen.

LED (light-emitting diode) Solid-state device that vibrates at luminous frequencies when current is applied.

LED monitor LCD monitor that uses LEDs instead of CCFL tubes for backlighting, creating much higher contrast ratios and image quality.

Level 1 (L1) cache First RAM cache accessed by the CPU, which stores only the absolute most-accessed programming and data used by currently running threads. Always the smallest and fastest cache on the CPU.

Level 2 (L2) cache Second RAM cache accessed by the CPU. Much larger and often slower than the L1 cache, and accessed only if the requested program/data is not in the L1 cache.

Level 3 (L3) cache Third RAM cache accessed by the CPU. Much larger and slower than the L1 and L2 caches, and accessed only if the requested program/ data is not in the L2 cache.

Library Feature in Windows 7 and later that aggregates folders from multiple locations and places them in a single, easy-to-find spot in Windows Explorer or File Explorer. Default libraries in Windows include Documents, Music, Pictures, and Videos.

Lightning An eight-pin connector, proprietary to Apple, that can be inserted without regard to orientation. Used to connect mobile devices to a power or data source.

Lightweight Directory Access Protocol (LDAP) Protocol used by many operating systems and applications to access directories.

Li-Ion (Lithium-Ion) Battery commonly used in portable computing devices. Li-Ion batteries don't suffer from the memory effects of Nickel-Cadmium (Ni-Cd) batteries and provide much more power for a greater length of time.

line of sight An unobstructed view between two devices. Required for IR communications.

link light An LED on NICs, hubs, and switches that lights up to show good connection between the devices.

Linux Open-source UNIX-clone operating system.

liquid cooling A method of cooling a PC that works by running some liquid—usually water—through a metal block that sits on top of the CPU, absorbing heat. The liquid gets heated by the block, runs out of the block and into something that cools the liquid, and is then pumped through the block again.

Live DVD   The Windows installation media, which loads the Windows Preinstallation Environment (WinPE) directly from disc into memory and doesn't access or modify a hard drive or solid-state drive.

Local Security Policy   Windows tool used to set local security policies on an individual system.

local user account   List of user names and their associated passwords with access to a system, contained in an encrypted database.

Local Users and Groups   Tool enabling creation and changing of group memberships and accounts for users.

location data   Information provided by a mobile device's GPS; used for mapping functions as well as for location-aware services, such as finding nearby restaurants or receiving coupons for nearby shops.

log files   Files created in Windows to track the progress of certain processes.

logical drives   Sections of an extended partition on a hard drive that are formatted and (usually) assigned a drive letter, each of which is presented to the user as if it were a separate drive.

logon screen   First screen of the Windows interface, used to log on to the computer system.

LoJack   Security feature included in some BIOS/UEFI that enables a user to track the location of a stolen PC, install a key logger, or remotely shut down the stolen computer.

loopback plug   Device used during loopback tests to check the female connector on a NIC.

Low-Speed USB   USB standard that runs at 1.5 Mbps. Also called *USB 1.1*.

LPT port   Commonly referred to as a printer port; usually associated with a local parallel port.

LPX   First slimline form factor; replaced by NLX form factor.

ls Linux equivalent of the dir command, which displays the contents of a directory.

lumens Unit of measure for amount of brightness on a projector or other light source.

Mac (Also **Macintosh**.) Common name for Apple Computers' flagship operating system; runs on Intel-based hardware. CompTIA refers to the operating system as *Mac OS X*. Apple calls the current operating system *OS X*, dropping the Mac altogether.

MAC (media access control) address Unique 48-bit address assigned to each network card. IEEE assigns blocks of possible addresses to various NIC manufacturers to help ensure that the address is always unique. The Data Link layer of the OSI model uses MAC addresses to locate machines.

MAC address filtering Method of limiting wireless network access based on the physical, hard-wired address of the wireless NIC of a computing device.

machine language Binary instruction code that is understood by the CPU.

maintenance kits Set of commonly replaced printer components provided by many manufacturers.

MAM (mobile application management) Software enabling a company's IT department to manage mobile apps on employees' mobile devices.

mass storage Hard drives, optical discs, removable media drives, etc.

matte Laptop screen finish that offers a good balance between richness of colors and reflections, but washes out in bright light.

MBR (master boot record) Tiny bit of code that takes control of the boot process from the system BIOS.

MCC (memory controller chip) Chip that handles memory requests from the CPU. Although once a special chip, it has been integrated into the chipset or CPU on modern computers.

MCH (Memory Controller Hub) Intel-coined name for what is now commonly called the northbridge.

md (mkdir) Command in the command-line interface used to create directories.

MDM (mobile device management) A formalized structure that enables an organization to account for all the different types of devices used to process, store, transmit, and receive organizational data.

mega- Prefix that stands for the binary quantity 1,048,576 (2^{20}) or the decimal quantity of 1,000,000. One megabyte is 1,048,576 bytes. One megahertz, however, is a million hertz. Sometimes shortened to *Meg*, as in "a 286 has an address space of 16 Megs."

megapixel Term used typically in reference to digital cameras and their ability to capture data.

memory Device or medium for temporary storage of programs and data during program execution. Synonymous with storage, although it most frequently refers to the internal storage of a computer that can be directly addressed by operating instructions. A computer's temporary storage capacity is measured in kilobytes (KB), megabytes (MB), or gigabytes (GB) of RAM (random-access memory). Long-term data storage on hard drives and solid-state drives is also measured in megabytes, gigabytes, and terabytes.

memory addressing Taking memory address from system RAM and using it to address non-system RAM or ROM so the CPU can access it.

Memory Stick Sony's flash memory card format; rarely seen outside of Sony devices.

mesh topology Network topology where each computer has a dedicated line to every other computer, most often used in wireless networks.

Metro UI The original name for the Windows 8 user interface. Due to legal concerns, it was rebranded the "Modern UI."

MFT (master file table) Enhanced file allocation table used by NTFS. (*See also* FAT.)

Micro Secure Digital (MicroSD) The smallest form factor of the SD flash memory standard. Often used in mobile devices.

micro USB USB connector commonly found on Android phones.

microATX (µATX)   Variation of the ATX form factor, which uses the ATX power supply. MicroATX motherboards are generally smaller than their ATX counterparts but retain all the same functionality.

microBTX   Variation of the BTX form factor. MicroBTX motherboards are generally smaller than their BTX counterparts but retain all the same functionality.

microdrive   Tiny hard drives using the CompactFlash form factor. (*See also* CompactFlash (CF).)

microphone   An input device for recording audio.

microprocessor   "Brain" of a computer. Primary computer chip that determines relative speed and capabilities of the computer. Also called *CPU*.

Microsoft Certified IT Professional (MCITP)   An advanced IT certification specifically covering Microsoft products.

MIDI (musical instrument digital interface)   Interface between a computer and a device for simulating musical instruments. Rather than sending large sound samples, a computer can simply send "instructions" to the instrument describing pitch, tone, and duration of a sound. MIDI files are therefore very efficient. Because a MIDI file is made up of a set of instructions rather than a copy of the sound, modifying each component of the file is easy. Additionally, it is possible to program many channels, or "voices," of music to be played simultaneously, creating symphonic sound.

MIDI-enabled device   External device that enables you to input digital sound information in the MIDI format; for example, a MIDI keyboard (the piano kind).

migration   Moving users from one operating system or hard drive to another.

MIMO (multiple in/multiple out)   Feature of 802.11n devices that enables the simultaneous connection of up to four antennas, greatly increasing throughput. 802.11ac also uses MU-MIMO, which gives a WAP the capability to broadcast to multiple users simultaneously.

mini connector   One type of power connector from a PC power supply unit. Supplies 5 and 12 volts to peripherals. Also known as a *floppy connector*.

mini power connector   Connector used to provide power to floppy disk drives.

Mini Secure Digital (MiniSD)   The medium-sized form factor of the SD flash memory standard.

mini USB   Smaller USB connector often found on digital cameras.

mini-audio connector   Very popular, 1/8-inch-diameter connector used to transmit two audio signals; perfect for stereo sound.

mini-DIN   Small connection most commonly used for keyboards and mice. Many modern systems implement USB in place of mini-DIN connections. Also called *PS/2*.

Mini-ITX   The largest and the most popular of the three ITX form factors. At a miniscule 6.7 by 6.7 inches, Mini-ITX competes with microATX and proprietary small form factor (SFF) motherboards.

Mini-PCI   Specialized form of PCI designed for use in laptops.

Mini-PCIe   Specialized form of PCIe designed for use in laptops.

mirror set   A type of mirrored volume created with RAID 1. (*See also* mirroring.)

mirrored volume   Volume that is mirrored on another volume. (*See also* mirroring.)

mirroring   Reading and writing data at the same time to two drives for fault tolerance purposes. Considered RAID level 1. Also called *drive mirroring*.

Mission Control   A feature of Mac OS X that enables switching between open applications, windows, and more.

mkdir   *See* md.

MMC (Microsoft Management Console)   Means of managing a system, introduced by Microsoft with Windows 2000. The MMC enables an administrator to customize management tools by picking and choosing from a list of snap-ins. Available snap-ins include Device Manager, Users and Groups, and Computer Management.

MMX (multimedia extensions)   Specific CPU instructions that enable a CPU to handle many multimedia functions, such as digital signal processing. Introduced with the Pentium CPU, these instructions are used on all ×86 CPUs.

mode   Any single combination of resolution and color depth set for a system.

modem (modulator/demodulator)   Device that converts a digital bit stream into an analog signal (modulation) and converts incoming analog signals back into digital signals (demodulation). An analog communications channel is typically a telephone line, and analog signals are typically sounds.

module   Small circuit board that DRAM chips are attached to. Also known as a "stick."

Molex connector   Computer power connector used by optical drives, hard drives, and case fans. Keyed to prevent it from being inserted into a power port improperly.

monaural   Describes recording tracks from one source (microphone) as opposed to stereo, which uses two sources.

monitor   Screen that displays data from a PC. Can use either a cathode ray tube (CRT) or a liquid crystal display (LCD) to display images.

motherboard   Flat piece of circuit board that resides inside your computer case and has a number of connectors on it. Every device in a PC connects directly or indirectly to the motherboard, including CPU, RAM, hard drives, optical drives, keyboard, mouse, and video cards.

motherboard book   Valuable resource when installing a new motherboard. Normally lists all the specifications about a motherboard, including the type of memory and type of CPU usable with the motherboard.

mount point   Drive that functions like a folder mounted into another drive.

mouse   Input device that enables users to manipulate a cursor on the screen to select items.

move   Command in the command-line interface used to move a file from one location to another.

MP3   Short for MPEG Audio Layer 3, a type of compression used specifically for turning high-quality digital audio files into much smaller, yet similar-sounding, files.

MPA (Microsoft Product Activation)   Windows process to enable support of a Microsoft program by registering a unique code within the program with a Microsoft authorization server. Microsoft Product Activation prevents unauthorized use of Microsoft's software.

MPEG-2   Moving Pictures Experts Group standard of video and audio compression offering resolutions up to 1280 × 720 at 60 frames per second.

MPEG-4   Moving Pictures Experts Group standard of video and audio compression offering improved compression over MPEG-2.

MS-CHAP   Microsoft's variation of the Challenge Handshake Authentication Protocol that uses a slightly more advanced encryption protocol. Windows Vista uses MS-CHAP v2 (version 2), and does not support MS-CHAP v1 (version 1).

msconfig (System Configuration utility)   Executable file that runs the Windows System Configuration utility, which enables users to configure a system's boot files and critical system files. Often used for the name of the utility, as in "just run msconfig."

MSDS (material safety data sheet)   Standardized form that provides detailed information about potential environmental hazards and proper disposal methods associated with various computing components.

msinfo32   Provides information about hardware resources, components, and the software environment. Also known as *System Information*.

multi rail   A power supply configuration where the current is split into multiple pathways, each with a maximum capacity and its own Over Current Protection circuitry. CompTIA calls two-rail versions of this technology "dual rail."

multiboot installation   OS installation in which multiple operating systems are installed on a single machine.

multicore processing   Using two or more execution cores on one CPU die to divide up work independently of the OS.

multifactor authentication   Authentication schema requiring more than one unique authentication method. For example, a password and a fingerprint.

multimedia extensions (MMX)   Originally an Intel CPU enhancement designed for graphics-intensive applications (such as games). It was never embraced but eventually led to improvements in how CPUs handle graphics.

multimeter   Device used to measure voltage, amperage, and resistance.

multiple desktops   A GUI feature that enables a computer to have more than one desktop, each with its own icons and background. Mac OS X supports multiple Desktops with Spaces. Most Linux distros use multiple desktops, often called workspaces. Microsoft introduced the feature with Windows 10.

multisession drive   Recordable CD drive capable of burning multiple sessions onto a single recordable disc. A multisession drive also can close a CD-R so that no further tracks can be written to it.

multitasking   Process of running multiple programs or tasks on the same computer at the same time.

multi-touch   Input method on many smartphones and tablets that enables you to use multiple fingers to do all sorts of fun things, such as using two fingers to scroll or swipe to another screen or desktop.

music CD-R   CD using a special format for home recorders. Music CD-R makers pay a small royalty to avoid illegal music duplication.

mv   The move command in Linux and Mac OS X.

My Computer   An applet that enables users to access a complete listing of all fixed and removable drives contained within a system and to view/manage configuration properties of the computer. Also, an aspect of Windows Explorer.

Nano-ITX   A 4.7 inch by 4.7 inch variation of the ITX form factor.

NAT (Network Address Translation)   A means of translating a system's IP address into another IP address before sending it out to a larger network. NAT manifests itself by a NAT program that runs on a system or a router. A network using NAT provides the systems on the network with private IP addresses. The system running the NAT software has two interfaces: one connected to the network and the other connected to the larger network.

The NAT program takes packets from the client systems bound for the larger network and translates their internal private IP addresses to its own public IP address, enabling many systems to share a single IP address.

native resolution   Resolution on an LCD monitor that matches the physical pixels on the screen.

navigation pane   Windows 7's name for the Folders list in Windows Explorer.

net   Command in Windows that enables users to view a network without knowing the names of the other computers on that network.

NetBIOS (Network Basic Input/Output System)   Protocol that operates at the Session layer of the OSI seven-layer model. This protocol creates and manages connections based on the names of the computers involved.

NetBIOS Extended User Interface (NetBEUI)   The default networking protocol for early versions of Windows.

netbook   Small, low-power laptop used primarily for web browsing.

network   Collection of two or more computers interconnected by telephone lines, coaxial cables, satellite links, radio, and/or some other communication technique. Group of computers that are connected and that communicate with one another for a common purpose.

Network   Interface in Windows Vista and Windows 7 for Windows Explorer; displays networked computers and other devices, such as network printers.

network attached storage (NAS)   A device that attaches to a network for the sole purpose of storing and sharing files.

network connection   A method for connecting two or more computers together. (*See also* network.)

network ID   Logical number that identifies the network on which a device or machine exists. This number exists in TCP/IP and other network protocol suites.

network printer   Printer that connects directly to a network.

network protocol   Software that takes the incoming data received by the network card, keeps it organized, sends it to the application that needs it, and then takes outgoing data from the application and hands it to the NIC to be sent out over the network.

network technology   A practical application of a topology and other critical standards to provide a method to get data from one computer to another on a network. It defines many aspects of a network, from the topology, to the frame type, to the cabling and connectors used.

NFC (near field communication)   Mobile technology that enables short-range wireless communication between mobile devices. Now used for mobile payment technology such as Apple Pay and Google Wallet.

NIC (network interface card or controller)   Expansion card or motherboard interface that enables a PC to connect to a network via a network cable. A wireless NIC enables connection via radio waves rather than a physical cable.

Ni-Cd (Nickel-Cadmium)   Battery used in the first portable PCs. Heavy and inefficient, these batteries also suffered from a memory effect that could drastically shorten the overall life of the battery. (*See also* Ni-MH, Li-Ion.)

Ni-MH (Nickel-Metal Hydride)   Battery used in early portable PCs. Ni-MH batteries had fewer issues with the memory effect than Ni-Cd batteries. Ni-MH batteries in computing devices have been replaced by Lithium-Ion batteries. (*See also* Ni-Cd, Li-Ion.)

nit   Value used to measure the brightness of an LCD display. A typical LCD display has a brightness of between 100 and 400 nits.

NLQ (near-letter quality)   Designation for dot-matrix printers that use 24-pin printheads.

NLX   Second form factor for slimline systems. Replaced the earlier LPX form factor. (NLX apparently stands for nothing; it's just a cool grouping of letters.)

NMI (non-maskable interrupt)   Interrupt code sent to the processor that cannot be ignored. Typically manifested as a BSoD.

NNTP (Network News Transfer Protocol)   Protocol run by news servers that enable newsgroups.

non-system disk or disk error   Error that occurs during the boot process. Common causes for this error are leaving a nonbootable floppy disk, CD, USB stick, or other media in the system while the computer is booting.

nonvolatile memory Storage device that retains data even if power is removed; typically refers to a ROM or flash ROM chip, but also could be applied to hard drives, optical media, and other storage devices.

normal backup Full backup of every selected file on a system. Turns off the archive bit after the backup.

northbridge Chip that connects a CPU to memory, the PCI bus, Level 2 cache, and high-speed graphics. Communicates with the CPU through the frontside bus. Newer CPUs feature an integrated northbridge.

notebook *See* laptop.

notification area Contains icons representing background processes, the system clock, and volume control. Located by default at the right edge of the Windows taskbar. Many users call this area the system tray.

nslookup Command-line program in Windows used to determine exactly what information the DNS server is providing about a specific host name.

ntdetect.com One of the critical Windows NT/2000/XP startup files.

NTFS (New Technology File System) Robust and secure file system introduced by Microsoft with Windows NT. NTFS provides an amazing array of configuration options for user access and security. Users can be granted access to data on a file-by-file basis. NTFS enables object-level security, long filename support, compression, and encryption.

NTFS permissions Restrictions that determine the amount of access given to a particular user on a system using NTFS.

ntldr (NT Loader) Windows NT/2000/XP boot file. Launched by the MBR or MFT, ntldr looks at the boot.ini configuration file for any installed operating systems.

NVIDIA Corporation One of the foremost manufacturers of graphics cards and chipsets.

NVMe (Non-Volatile Memory Express) SSD technology that supports a communication connection between the operating system and the SSD directly through a PCIe bus lane, reducing latency and taking full advantage of the speeds of high-end SSDs. NVMe SSDs come in a couple of formats, such as an add-on expansion card and a 2.5-inch drive, like the SATA drives for portables. NVMe drives are a lot more expensive currently than other SSDs, but offer much higher speeds.

NX bit Technology that enables the CPU to protect certain sections of memory. This feature, coupled with implementation by the operating system, stops malicious attacks from getting to essential operating system files. Microsoft calls the feature Data Execution Prevention (DEP).

object System component that is given a set of characteristics and can be managed by the operating system as a single entity.

object access auditing Feature of Event Viewer's Security section that creates an entry in the Security Log when certain objects are accessed, such as a file or folder.

ODBC Data Source Administrator Programming tool for configuring the Open Database Connectivity (ODBC) coding standard. Data Source Administrator enables you to create and manage entries called Data Source Names (DSNs) that point OBDC to a database. DSNs are used by ODBC-aware applications to query ODBC to find their databases.

offline files Windows 7/8/8.1/10 feature that enables storing a local, duplicate copy of files and folders on a hard drive. When the laptop connects to a network, Windows automatically syncs those offline files with the files and folders on a file server or other PC.

ohm(s) Electronic measurement of a cable's impedance.

open source Software environment that is not controlled by a central creator or distributer.

OLED (organic light-emitting diode) Display technology where an organic compound provides the light for the screen, thus eliminating the need for a backlight or inverter.

OpenGL One of two popular APIs used today for video cards. Originally written for UNIX systems but now ported to Windows and Apple systems. (*See also* DirectX.)

optical disc/media Types of data discs (such as DVDs, CDs, BDs, etc.) that are read by a laser.

optical drive   Drive used to read/write to optical discs, such as CDs or DVDs.

optical mouse   Pointing device that uses light rather than electronic sensors to determine movement and direction the mouse is being moved.

optical resolution   Resolution a scanner can achieve mechanically. Most scanners use software to enhance this ability.

optical zoom   Mechanical ability of most cameras to "zoom" in as opposed to the digital ability.

option ROM   Alternative way of telling the system how to talk to a piece of hardware. Option ROM stores BIOS for the card in a chip on the card itself.

OS (operating system)   Series of programs and code that creates an interface so users can interact with a system's hardware; for example, Windows, Mac OS X, and Linux.

OS X   Current operating system on Apple Macintosh computers. Based on a UNIX core, early versions of OS X ran on Motorola-based hardware; current versions run on Intel-based hardware. The X is pronounced "ten" rather than "ex."

OSI seven-layer model   Architecture model based on the OSI protocol suite that defines and standardizes the flow of data between computers. The seven layers are

- **Layer 1, Physical layer**   Defines hardware connections and turns binary into physical pulses (electrical or light). Repeaters and hubs operate at the Physical layer.
- **Layer 2, Data Link layer**   Identifies devices on the Physical layer. MAC addresses are part of the Data Link layer. Bridges operate at the Data Link layer.
- **Layer 3, Network layer**   Moves packets between computers on different networks. Routers operate at the Network layer. IP and IPX operate at the Network layer.
- **Layer 4, Transport layer**   Breaks data down into manageable chunks. TCP, UDP, SPX, and NetBEUI operate at the Transport layer.
- **Layer 5, Session layer**   Manages connections between machines. NetBIOS and Sockets operate at the Session layer.

- **Layer 6, Presentation layer** Can also manage data encryption; hides the differences between various types of computer systems.
- **Layer 7, Application layer** Provides tools for programs to use to access the network (and the lower layers). HTTP, FTP, SMTP, and POP3 are all examples of protocols that operate at the Application layer.

overclocking To run a CPU or video processor faster than its rated speed.

P1 power connector Provides power to ATX motherboards; 20-pin with original ATX motherboards, 24-pin on current units.

P4 power connector Provides additional 12-volt power for the CPU to motherboards that support Pentium 4 and later processors.

P8 and P9 connectors Provide power to old, AT-style motherboards.

PaaS (Platform as a Service) Cloud-based virtual server(s). These virtualized platforms give programmers tools needed to deploy, administer, and maintain a web application.

packet Basic component of communication over a network. Group of bits of fixed maximum size and well-defined format that is switched and transmitted as a single entity through a network. Contains source and destination address, data, and control information.

page fault Minor memory-addressing error.

page file Portion of the hard drive set aside by Windows to act like RAM. Also known as *virtual memory* or *swap file*.

PAN (personal area network) Small wireless network created with Bluetooth technology and intended to link computers and other peripheral devices.

parallel execution When a multicore CPU processes more than one thread.

parallel port Connection for the synchronous, high-speed flow of data along parallel lines to a device, usually a printer.

Parental Controls Tool to enable monitoring and limiting of user activities; designed for parents to control the content their children can access.

parity Method of error detection where a small group of bits being transferred is compared to a single parity bit set to make the total bits odd or even. Receiving device reads the parity bit and determines if the data is valid, based on the oddness or evenness of the parity bit.

parity RAM Earliest form of error-detecting RAM; stored an extra bit (called the parity bit) to verify the data.

partition Section of the storage area of a hard disk. Created during initial preparation of the hard disk, before the disk is formatted.

partition boot table Sector of a partition that stores information important to its partition, such as the location of the OS boot files. Responsible for loading the OS on a partition.

partition table Table located in the boot sector of a hard drive that lists every partition on the disk that contains a valid operating system.

partitioning Electronically subdividing a physical hard drive into groups called partitions (or volumes).

passcode lock Mobile device security feature that requires you to type in a series of letters, numbers, or motion patterns to unlock the mobile device each time you press the power button.

passive matrix Technology for producing colors in LCD monitors by varying voltages across wire matrices to produce red, green, or blue dots.

passwd Linux command for changing a user's password.

password Key used to verify a user's identity on a secure computer or network.

Password Authentication Protocol (PAP) Oldest and most basic form of authentication. Also the least safe, because it sends all passwords in clear text.

password reset disk External storage media such as a floppy disk or USB flash drive with which users can recover a lost password without losing access to any encrypted, or password-protected, data. The password reset disk must be created proactively; if a user loses a password and did not already make a reset disk, it will be of no help to create one after the loss.

PATA (parallel ATA) Implementation that integrates the controller on the disk drive itself. (*See also* ATA, IDE, SATA.)

patch   Small piece of software released by a software manufacturer to correct a flaw or problem with a particular piece of software.

patch cables   Short (2 to 5 feet) UTP cables that connect patch panels to a switch or router.

patch panel   A panel containing a row of female connectors (ports) that terminate the horizontal cabling in the equipment room. Patch panels facilitate cabling organization and provide protection to horizontal cabling.

path   Route the operating system must follow to find an executable program stored in a subfolder.

PC Card   Credit card–sized adapter card that adds functionality in older laptops and other computer devices. PC Cards come in 16-bit and CardBus parallel format and ExpressCard serial format. (*See also* PCMCIA.)

PC tech   Someone with computer skills who works on computers.

PCI (Peripheral Component Interconnect)   Design architecture for the expansion bus on the computer motherboard that enables system components to be added to the computer. Local bus standard, meaning that devices added to a computer through this port will use the processor at the motherboard's full speed (up to 33 MHz) rather than at the slower 8-MHz speed of the regular bus. Moves data 32 or 64 bits at a time rather than the 8 or 16 bits the older ISA buses supported.

PCIe (PCI Express)   Serialized successor to PCI and AGP that uses the concept of individual data paths called lanes. May use any number of lanes, although a single lane (×1) and 16 lanes (×16) are the most common on motherboards.

PCIe 6/8-pin power connector   Connector on some power supplies for powering a dedicated graphics card.

PCI-X (PCI Extended)   Enhanced version of PCI, 64 bits wide. Typically seen in servers and high-end systems.

PCL (printer control language)   Printer control language created by Hewlett-Packard and used on a broad cross section of printers.

PCM (pulse code modulation)   Sound format developed in the 1960s to carry telephone calls over the first digital lines.

PCMCIA (Personal Computer Memory Card International Association)   Consortium of computer manufacturers who devised the PC Card standard for credit card–sized adapter cards that add functionality in older notebook computers and other computer devices. (*See also* PC Card.)

Pearson VUE   Company that administers the CompTIA A+ exams.

peer-to-peer network   Network in which each machine can act as both a client and a server.

pen-based computing   Input method used by many PDAs that combines handwriting recognition with modified mouse functions, usually in the form of a pen-like stylus.

Pentium   Name given to the fifth and later generations of Intel microprocessors; original had a 32-bit address bus, 64-bit external data bus, and dual pipelining. Also used for subsequent generations of Intel processors—the Pentium Pro, Pentium II, Pentium III, and Pentium 4. Currently used as a budget label for Intel CPUs.

Performance   Tab in Task Manager that tracks PC performance.

Performance Information and Tools   Applet that provides a relative feel for how your computer stacks up against other systems using the Windows Experience Index.

Performance Logs and Alerts   Snap-in enabling the creation of a written record of most everything that happens on the system.

Performance Monitor   Windows tool for observing a computer's performance.

Performance Options   Tool enabling users to configure CPU, RAM, and virtual memory settings.

peripheral   Any device that connects to the system unit.

permission propagation   Term to describe what happens to permissions on an object when you move or copy it.

persistence   Phosphors used in CRT screens continuing to glow after being struck by electrons, long enough for the human eye to register the glowing effect. Glowing too long makes the images smeary, and too little makes them flicker.

personal safety   Keeping yourself away from harm.

Personalization applet   Windows Vista applet with which users can change display settings such as resolution, refresh rate, color depth, and desktop features. The Windows 7 version focuses on managing themes, desktop icons, mouse pointers, and account pictures. (For other options, *see* Display.)

PGA (pin grid array)   Arrangement of a large number of pins extending from the bottom of the CPU package. There are many variations on PGA.

phablet   Portmanteau of "phone" and "tablet." Colloquial term for a large phone. (And yes, I had to look up "portmanteau" as well. Love my editors!)

Phillips-head screwdriver   Most important part of a PC tech's toolkit.

phishing   The act of trying to get people to give their usernames, passwords, or other security information by pretending to be someone else electronically.

Phoenix Technologies   Major producer of BIOS software for motherboards.

phosphor   Electro-fluorescent material that coats the inside face of a cathode ray tube (CRT). After being hit with an electron, it glows for a fraction of a second.

photosensitive drum   Aluminum cylinder coated with particles of photosensitive compounds. Used in a laser printer and often contained within the toner cartridge.

Pico-ITX   A 3.8- by 2.8-inch version of the ITX form factor.

pin 1   Designator used to ensure proper alignment of floppy drive and hard drive connectors.

pinch   Multi-touch gesture that enables you to make an image bigger or smaller.

ping (packet Internet groper)   Slang term for a small network message (ICMP ECHO) sent by a computer to check for the presence and aliveness of another. Used to verify the presence of another system. Also, the command used at a prompt to ping a computer.

pinned application   Windows method of attaching programs to the taskbar. A pinned application gets a permanent icon displayed on the taskbar.

pinwheel of death   Mac OS X indicator that is the equivalent of a Windows unresponsive application; in this case, a spinning rainbow wheel.

PIO (programmed I/O) mode   Series of speed standards created by the Small Form Factor Committee for the use of PIO by hard drives. Modes range from PIO mode 0 to PIO mode 4.

pipeline   Processing methodology where multiple calculations take place simultaneously by being broken into a series of steps. Often used in CPUs and video processors.

pixel (picture element)   In computer graphics, smallest element of a display space that can be independently assigned color or intensity.

PKI (public key infrastructure)   Authentication schema where public keys are exchanged between all parties using digital certificates, enabling secure communication over public networks.

Play Store   Storefront where Android users can purchase and download apps and digital media.

plug   Hardware connection with some sort of projection that connects to a port.

plug and play (PnP)   Combination of smart PCs, smart devices, and smart operating systems that automatically configure all necessary system resources and ports when you install a new peripheral device.

polygons   Multisided shapes used in 3-D rendering of objects. In computers, video cards draw large numbers of triangles and connect them to form polygons.

polymorph virus   Virus that attempts to change its signature to prevent detection by antivirus programs, usually by continually scrambling a bit of useless code.

POP3 (Post Office Protocol 3)   One of the two protocols that receive e-mail from SMTP servers. POP3 uses TCP port 110. While historically most e-mail clients used this protocol, the IMAP4 e-mail protocol is now more common.

pop-up   Irritating browser window that appears automatically when you visit a website.

port (networking) In networking, the number used to identify the requested service (such as SMTP or FTP) when connecting to a TCP/IP host. Examples: 80 (HTTP), 443, (HTTPS), 21 (FTP), 23 (Telnet), 25 (SMTP), 110 (POP3), 143 (IMAP), and 3389 (RDP).

port (physical connection) Part of a connector into which a plug is inserted. Physical ports are also referred to as jacks.

port forwarding Preventing the passage of any IP packets through any ports other than the ones prescribed by the system administrator.

port replicator Device that plugs into a USB port or other specialized port and offers common PC ports, such as serial, parallel, USB, network, and PS/2. Plugging a laptop into a port replicator can instantly connect the computer to nonportable components such as a printer, scanner, monitor, or full-sized keyboard. Port replicators are typically used at home or in the office with the nonportable equipment already connected.

port triggering Router function that enables a computer to open an incoming connection to one computer automatically based on a specific outgoing connection.

positional audio Range of commands for a sound card to place a sound anywhere in 3-D space.

POST (power-on self test) Basic diagnostic routine completed by a system at the beginning of the boot process to make sure a display adapter and the system's memory are installed; it then searches for an operating system. If it finds one, it hands over control of the machine to the OS.

POST card Device installed into a motherboard expansion slot that assists in troubleshooting boot problems by providing a two-digit code indicating the stop of the boot process where the problem is occurring.

PostScript Language defined by Adobe Systems, Inc., for describing how to create an image on a page. The description is independent of the resolution of the device that will actually create the image. It includes a technology for defining the shape of a font and creating a raster image at many different resolutions and sizes.

power conditioning Ensuring and adjusting incoming AC wall power to as close to standard as possible. Most UPS devices provide power conditioning.

power good wire   Used to wake up the CPU after the power supply has tested for proper voltage.

Power over Ethernet (PoE)   Technology that provides power and data transmission through a single network cable.

power options   Windows feature that enables better control over power use by customizing a balanced, power saver, or high-performance power plan.

power supply fan   Small fan located in a system power supply that draws warm air from inside the power supply and exhausts it to the outside.

power supply unit   Provides the electrical power for a PC. Converts standard AC power into various voltages of DC electricity in a PC.

Power Users group   After Administrator/Administrators, the second most powerful account and group type in Windows. Power users have differing capabilities in different versions of Windows.

PowerShell   *See* Windows PowerShell.

ppm (pages per minute)   Speed of a printer.

PPP (Point-to-Point Protocol)   Enables a computer to connect to the Internet through a dial-in connection and enjoy most of the benefits of a direct connection.

preboot execution environment (PXE)   Technology that enables a PC to boot without any local storage by retrieving an OS from a server over a network.

primary corona   Wire that is located near the photosensitive drum in a laser printer and is charged with extremely high voltage to form an electric field, enabling voltage to pass to the photosensitive drum, thus charging the photosensitive particles on the surface of the drum. Also called the *primary charge roller*.

primary partition   Partition on a Windows hard drive that can store a bootable operating system.

print resolution   Quality of a print image.

print spooler   Area of memory that queues up print jobs that the printer will handle sequentially.

printed circuit board (PCB) Copper etched onto a nonconductive material and then coated with some sort of epoxy for strength.

printer Output device that can print text or illustrations on paper. Microsoft uses the term to refer to the software that controls the physical print device.

printhead Case that holds the printwires in a dot-matrix printer.

printwires Grid of tiny pins in a dot-matrix printer that strike an inked printer ribbon to produce images on paper.

PRL (Preferred Roaming List) A list that is occasionally and automatically updated to a phone's firmware by the carrier so that the phone will be configured with a particular carrier's networks and frequencies, in a priority order, that it should search for when it can't locate its home carrier network.

Problem Reports and Solutions Control Panel applet in Windows Vista that lists all Windows Error Reporting issues (plus a few easy-to-check items like firewall and anti-malware status).

Processes Tab in Task Manager that lists all running processes on a system. Frequently a handy tool for ending buggy or unresponsive processes.

processing The second step of the computing process, where the CPU completes the tasks that the user's input has given it.

product key Code used during installation to verify legitimacy of the software.

profile A list of settings that a calibration device creates when calibrating monitors and printers.

program/programming Series of binary electronic commands sent to a CPU to get work done.

Programs and Features Windows Control Panel applet; enables uninstalling or changing program options and altering Windows features.

projector Device for projecting video images from PCs or other video sources, usually for audience presentations. Available in front- and rearview displays.

prompt A character or message provided by an operating system or program to indicate that it is ready to accept input.

proprietary Technology unique to a particular vendor.

proprietary crash screen A screen, differing between operating systems, that indicates an NMI.

protective cover A case or sleeve that protects a mobile device from physical damage.

protocol Agreement that governs the procedures used to exchange information between cooperating entities. Usually includes how much information is to be sent, how often it is to be sent, how to recover from transmission errors, and who is to receive the information.

proxy server Device that fetches Internet resources for a client without exposing that client directly to the Internet. Usually accepts requests for HTTP, FTP, POP3, and SMTP resources. Often caches, or stores, a copy of the requested resource for later use. Common security feature in the corporate world.

ps Linux command for listing all processes running on the computer.

Public folder Folder that all users can access and share with all other users on the system or network.

punchdown tool A specialized tool for connecting UTP wires to a punchdown block.

pwd Linux command that displays the user's current path.

quad-channel architecture Feature similar to dual-channel RAM, but requiring four sticks instead of two.

Quality of Service (QoS) Policies that control how much bandwidth a protocol, PC, user, VLAN, or IP address may use.

queue Area where objects wait their turn to be processed. Example: the print queue, where print jobs wait until it is their turn to be printed.

Quick Launch toolbar Enables a user to launch commonly used programs with a single click in Windows.

QVGA Video display mode of 320 × 240.

RAID (redundant array of independent [or inexpensive] disks) Method for creating a fault-tolerant storage system. RAID uses multiple hard drives in various configurations to offer differing levels of speed/data redundancy.

RAID 0 Uses byte-level striping and provides no fault tolerance.

RAID 1 Uses mirroring or duplexing for increased data redundancy.

RAID 5 Uses block-level and parity data striping. Requires three or more drives.

RAID 6 Disk striping with extra parity. Like RAID 5, but with more parity data. Requires five or more drives, but you can lose up to two drives at once and your data is still protected.

RAID 0+1 A RAID 0 configuration created by combining two RAID 1s. Provides both speed and redundancy, but requires at least four disks.

RAID 10 The opposite of RAID 0+1, two mirrored RAID 0 configurations. Also provides both speed and redundancy, and also requires four disks.

rails Separate DC voltage paths within an ATX power supply.

RAM (random access memory) Memory that can be accessed at random—that is, memory which you can write to or read from without touching the preceding address. This term is often used to mean a computer's main memory.

RAMDAC (random access memory digital-to-analog converter) Circuitry used on video cards that support analog monitors to convert the digital video data to analog.

Raspberry Pi Latest generation of ultra-small, ARM-based computer motherboards with support for many operating systems and peripherals.

raster image Pattern of dots representing what the final product should look like.

raster line Horizontal pattern of lines that forms an image on the monitor screen.

rd (rmdir) Command in the command-line interface used to remove directories.

read-only attribute   File attribute that does not allow a file to be altered or modified. Helpful when protecting system files that should not be edited.

ReadyBoost   Windows feature enabling the use of flash media as dedicated virtual memory.

rearview projector   Projector that shoots an image onto a screen from the rear. Rearview projectors are usually self-enclosed and very popular for TVs, but are virtually unheard of in the PC world.

reciprocity   *See* Ethic of Reciprocity.

Recovery Console   Command-line interface boot mode for Windows that is used to repair a Windows XP system suffering from massive OS corruption or other problems.

Recycle Bin   Location to which files are moved when they are deleted from a modern Windows system. To permanently remove files from a system, they must be emptied from the Recycle Bin.

Refresh your PC   Windows RE option in Windows 8 and later that rebuilds the OS, but preserves all user files and settings and any applications purchased from the Windows Store. Note well: Refresh deletes every other application on a system.

regedit.exe   Program used to edit the Windows Registry.

region code   Encoding that restricts you from playing DVD or Blu-ray Disc movies on a player that doesn't share the same region code.

register   Storage area inside the CPU used by the onboard logic to perform calculations. CPUs have many registers to perform different functions.

registered RAM   *See* buffered RAM.

registration   Usually optional process that identifies the legal owner/user of the product to the supplier.

Registry   Complex binary file used to store configuration data about a particular Windows system. To edit the Registry, users can use the applets found in the Control Panel or regedit.exe or regedt32.exe.

regsvr32 In contrast with regedit.exe, the regsvr32 command can modify the Registry in only one way, adding (or *registering*) dynamic link library (DLL) files as command components in the Registry.

Reliability and Performance Monitor Windows Vista's extended Performance applet.

remediation Repairing damage caused by a virus.

remnant Potentially recoverable data on a hard drive that remains despite formatting or deleting.

Remote Assistance Feature of Windows that enables users to give anyone control of his or her desktop over the Internet.

Remote Desktop Windows tool used to enable a local system to graphically access the desktop of a remote system.

Remote Desktop Protocol Protocol used for Microsoft's Remote Desktop tool. Uses port 3389.

remote network installation A common method of OS installation where the source files are placed in a shared directory on a network server. Then, whenever a tech needs to install a new OS, he or she can boot the computer, connect to the source location on the network, and start the installation from there.

removable media Any storage on a computer that can be easily removed. For example, optical discs, flash drives, or memory cards.

ren (rename) Command in the command-line interface used to rename files and folders.

Reset your PC Windows RE option in Windows 8 and later that nukes the system—deleting all apps, programs, user files, and user settings—and presents a fresh installation of Windows. Use Reset as the last resort when troubleshooting a PC. And back up data first, if possible.

resistance Difficulty in making electricity flow through a material, measured in ohms.

resistive touchscreen Type of touchscreen that responds to the pressure applied to the screen.

resistor   Any material or device that impedes the flow of electrons. Electronic resistors measure their resistance (impedance) in ohms. (*See* ohm(s).)

resolution   Measurement for monitors and printers expressed in horizontal and vertical dots or pixels. Higher resolutions provide sharper details and thus display better-looking images.

resources   Data and services of a PC.

respect   What all techs should treat their customers with.

response rate   Time it takes for all of the sub-pixels on the panel to go from pure black to pure white and back again.

restore point   System snapshot created by the System Restore utility that is used to restore a malfunctioning system. (*See also* System Restore.)

RET (resolution enhancement technology)   Technology that uses small dots to smooth out jagged edges that are typical of printers without RET, producing a higher-quality print job.

RFI (radio frequency interference)   Another form of electrical interference caused by radio wave–emitting devices, such as cell phones, wireless network cards, and microwave ovens.

RG-6   Coaxial cabling used for cable television. It has a 75-ohm impedance and uses an F-type connector.

RG-58   Coaxial cabling used for 10Base2 networks.

ring   Network topology where the computers form a circle and all data flows in one direction only.

RIP (raster image processor)   Component in a printer that translates the raster image into commands for the printer.

riser card   Special adapter card, usually inserted into a special slot on a motherboard, that changes the orientation of expansion cards relative to the motherboard. Riser cards are used extensively in slimline computers to keep total depth and height of the system to a minimum. Sometimes called a daughterboard.

RJ (registered jack) connector UTP cable connector, used for both telephone and network connections. RJ-11 is a connector for four-wire UTP; usually found in telephone connections. RJ-45 is a connector for eight-wire UTP; usually found in network connections.

RJ-11 *See* RJ (registered jack) connector.

RJ-45 *See* RJ (registered jack) connector.

rm Linux command for deleting files.

rmdir *See* rd (rmdir).

robocopy Powerful command-line utility for copying files and directories, even over a network.

ROM (read-only memory) Generic term for nonvolatile memory that can be read from but not written to. This means that code and data stored in ROM cannot be corrupted by accidental erasure. Additionally, ROM retains its data when power is removed, which makes it the perfect medium for storing BIOS data or information such as scientific constants.

root directory Directory that contains all other directories.

root keys Five main categories in the Windows Registry:
HKEY_CLASSES_ROOT
HKEY_CURRENT_USER
HKEY_USERS
HKEY_LOCAL_MACHINE
HKEY_CURRENT_CONFIG

router Device connecting separate networks; forwards a packet from one network to another based on the network address for the protocol being used. For example, an IP router looks only at the IP network number. Routers operate at Layer 3 (Network) of the OSI seven-layer model.

RS-232 Standard port recommended by the Electronics Industry Association (EIA) for serial devices.

run A single piece of installed horizontal cabling.

Run dialog box Command box in which users can enter the name of a particular program to run; an alternative to locating the icon in older versions of Windows. *Run* opens a program, folder, document, or website. Supplanted in Windows Vista and later with the Search box.

S.M.A.R.T. (Self-Monitoring, Analysis, and Reporting Technology) Monitoring system built into hard drives.

S/PDIF (Sony/Philips Digital Interface Format) Digital audio connector found on many sound cards. Users can connect their computers directly to a 5.1/7.1 speaker system or receiver. S/PDIF comes in both a coaxial and an optical version.

SaaS (Software as a Service) Cloud-based service to store, distribute, and update programs and applications. The SaaS model provides access to necessary applications wherever you have an Internet connection, often without having to carry data with you or regularly update software. At the enterprise level, the subscription model of many SaaS providers makes it easier to budget and keep hundreds or thousands of computers up to date.

Safe mode Important diagnostic boot mode for Windows that runs only very basic drivers and turns off virtual memory.

safety goggles Protective glasses that keep stuff out of your eyes.

sampling Capturing sound waves in electronic format.

SATA (serial ATA) Serialized version of the ATA standard that offers many advantages over PATA (parallel ATA) technology, including thinner cabling, keyed connectors, and lower power requirements.

SATA bridge Adapter that allows PATA devices to be connected to a SATA controller.

SATA Express (SATAe) The newest version of SATA that ties capable drives directly into the PCI Express bus on motherboards. Each lane of PCIe 3.0 is capable of handling up to 8 Gbps data throughput. A SATAe drive grabbing two lanes, therefore, could move a whopping 16 Gbps through the bus.

SATA power connector 15-pin, L-shaped connector used by SATA devices that support the hot-swappable feature.

satellites Two or more standard stereo speakers to be combined with a subwoofer for a speaker system (i.e., 2.1, 5.1, 7.1, etc.).

Scalable Link Interface (SLI) Technology for connecting two or more NVIDIA GPUs together in a system.

scan code Unique code corresponding to each key on the keyboard, sent from the keyboard controller to the CPU.

SCSI (small computer system interface) Powerful and flexible peripheral interface popularized on the Macintosh and used to connect hard drives, optical drives, tape drives, scanners, and other devices to PCs of all kinds. Normal SCSI enables up to seven devices to be connected through a single bus connection, whereas Wide SCSI can handle 15 devices attached to a single controller.

SCSI chain Series of SCSI devices working together through a host adapter.

SCSI ID Unique identifier used by SCSI devices. No two SCSI devices may have the same SCSI ID.

SD (Secure Digital) Very popular format for flash media cards; also supports I/O devices.

SDK (software development kit) Software that used to create custom applications or add features to existing applications on your mobile device.

SDRAM (synchronous DRAM) DRAM that is synchronous, or tied to the system clock. This type of RAM is used in all modern systems.

sector Segment of one of the concentric tracks encoded on the disk during a low-level format. A sector holds 512 bytes of data.

sector translation Translation of logical geometry into physical geometry by the onboard circuitry of a hard drive.

sectors per track (sectors/track) Combined with the number of cylinders and heads, defines the disk geometry.

secure boot UEFI feature that secures the boot process by requiring properly signed software. This includes boot software and software that supports specific, essential components.

segment The connection between a computer and a switch.

self-grounding   A less-than-ideal method for ridding yourself of static electricity by touching a metal object such as a computer case. Alternately, sending yourself to your own room as a form of punishment.

serial port   Common connector on older PC. Connects input devices (such as a mouse) or communications devices (such as a modem). Also referred to as a *COM port.*

server   Computer that shares its resources, such as printers and files, with other computers on a network. Example: network file system server that shares its disk space with a workstation that does not have a disk drive of its own.

service   A program that runs in the background of a PC but displays no icons anywhere. You can view a list of services in the Windows Task Manager. Also, a program stored in a ROM chip.

service pack   Collection of software patches released at one time by a software manufacturer.

Services   Tab in Windows Task Manager that lists all running services on a system.

set-top box   A device that adds "Smart TV" features, such as Internet streaming and show recording, to normal TVs.

Settings app   Windows 10 tool that combines a huge number of otherwise disparate utilities, apps, and tools traditionally spread out all over your computer into one fairly unified, handy Windows app.

setupapi.log   Log file that tracks the installation of all hardware on a system.

setuplog.txt   Log file that tracks the complete installation process, logging the success or failure of file copying, Registry updates, and reboots.

sfc (System File Checker)   Command-prompt program (sfc.exe) that scans, detects, and restores Windows system files, folders, and paths.

shadow mask   CRT screen that allows only the proper electron gun to light the proper phosphors.

Shared Documents   Windows premade folder that is accessible by all user accounts on the computer.

shared memory Means of reducing the amount of memory needed on a video card by borrowing from the regular system RAM, which reduces costs but also decreases performance.

share-level security Security system in which each resource has a password assigned to it; access to the resource is based on knowing the password.

shareware Program protected by copyright; holder allows (encourages!) you to make and distribute copies under the condition that those who adopt the software after preview pay a fee to the holder of the copyright. Derivative works are not allowed, although you may make an archival copy.

shunt Tiny connector of metal enclosed in plastic that creates an electrical connection between two posts of a jumper.

shutdown Windows and Linux command for shutting down the computer.

SID (security identifier) Unique identifier for every PC that most techs change when cloning.

sidebanding Second data bus for video cards; enables the video card to send more commands to the northbridge while receiving other commands at the same time.

Sidebar *See* Windows Sidebar.

signal-to-noise ratio Measure that describes the relative quality of an input port.

signature Code pattern of a known virus; used by antivirus software to detect viruses.

SIMM (single in-line memory module) DRAM packaging distinguished by having a number of small tabs that install into a special connector. Each side of each tab is the same signal. SIMMs come in two common sizes: 30-pin and 72-pin.

simple file sharing Allows users to share locally or across the network but gives no control over what others do with shared files.

simple volume Volume created when setting up dynamic disks. Acts like a primary partition on a dynamic disk.

single rail   Power supply configuration where all power is supplied along a single pathway.

single source   *See* closed source.

single-sided RAM   Has chips on only one side as opposed to double-sided RAM.

sleep timers   A feature that enables you to put the computer into Standby after a set period of time, or to turn off the monitor or hard drive after a time, thus creating your own custom power scheme.

slimline   Motherboard form factor used to create PCs that were very thin. NLX and LPX were two examples of this form factor.

slot covers   Metal plates that cover up unused expansion slots on the back of a PC. Useful in maintaining proper airflow through a computer case.

smart battery   Portable PC battery that tells the computer when it needs to be charged, conditioned, or replaced.

smart camera   A digital camera incorporating the interface and computational features of a mobile device.

smart card   Hardware authentication involving a credit card–sized card with circuitry that can be used to identify the bearer of that card.

smart TV   A television with network capabilities—both hardware and software—for use with streaming Internet video and audio.

smart watch   A watch incorporating features of and communicating with a mobile device.

SmartMedia   Format for flash media cards; no longer used with new devices.

smartphone   A cell phone enhanced to do things formerly reserved for fully grown computers, such as web browsing, document viewing, and media consumption.

S/MIME (Secure/Multipurpose Internet Mail Extensions)   Technology used to configure digital signature settings for e-mail, and contacts from a corporate address book, depending on how the corporate e-mail server is set up.

SMM (System Management Mode)   Special CPU mode that enables the CPU to reduce power consumption by selectively shutting down peripherals.

SMTP (Simple Mail Transport Protocol)   Main protocol used to send electronic mail on the Internet. Uses port 25.

snap-ins   Small utilities that can be used with the Microsoft Management Console.

snapshot   Virtualization feature that enables you to save an extra copy of the virtual machine as it is exactly at the moment the snapshot is taken.

SNMP (Simple Network Management Protocol)   A set of standards for communication with devices connected to a TCP/IP network. Examples of these devices include routers, hubs, and switches. Uses port 161.

social engineering   Using or manipulating people inside the networking environment to gain access to that network from the outside.

socket services   Device drivers that support the PC Card socket, enabling the system to detect when a PC Card has been inserted or removed, and providing the necessary I/O to the device.

SO-DIMM (small-outline DIMM)   Memory used in portable PCs because of its small size.

soft power   Characteristic of ATX motherboards, which can use software to turn the PC on and off. The physical manifestation of soft power is the power switch. Instead of the thick power cord used in AT systems, an ATX power switch is little more than a pair of small wires leading to the motherboard.

software   Single group of programs designed to do a particular job; always stored on mass storage devices.

solid core   A cable that uses a single solid (not hollow or stranded) wire to transmit signals.

solid ink printers   Printer that uses solid sticks of nontoxic "ink" that produce vibrant color documents with much less waste than color laser printers.

sound card   Expansion card that can produce audible tones when connected to a set of speakers.

southbridge   Part of a motherboard chipset; handles all the inputs and outputs to the many devices in the PC.

Spaces   Mac OS X feature enabling multiple desktops.

spam   Unsolicited e-mails from both legitimate businesses and scammers that account for a huge percentage of traffic on the Internet.

spanned volume   Volume that uses space on multiple dynamic disks.

SPD (serial presence detect)   Information stored on a RAM chip that describes the speed, capacity, and other aspects of the RAM chip.

speaker   Device that outputs sound by using magnetically driven diaphragm.

Spotify (spotify.com)   Internet streaming music site.

sprite   Bitmapped graphic, such as a BMP file, used by early 3-D games to create the 3-D world.

spyware   Software that runs in the background of a user's PC, sending information about browsing habits back to the company that installed it onto the system.

SRAM (static RAM)   RAM that uses a flip-flop circuit rather than the typical transistor/capacitor of DRAM to hold a bit of information. SRAM does not need to be refreshed and is faster than regular DRAM. Used primarily for cache.

SSD (solid-state drive)   Data storage device that uses flash memory to store data.

SSH (Secure Shell)   Terminal emulation program similar to Telnet, except that the entire connection is encrypted. Uses port 22.

SSID (service set identifier)   Parameter used to define a wireless network; otherwise known as the network name.

SSL (Secure Sockets Layer)   Security protocol used by a browser to connect to secure websites.

standard user account   User account in Windows that has limited access to a system. Accounts of this type cannot alter system files, cannot install new programs, and cannot edit some settings by using the Control Panel without supplying an administrator password.

standoffs   Small mechanical separators that screw into a computer case. A motherboard is then placed on top of the standoffs, and small screws are used to secure it to the standoffs.

star bus   A hybrid network topology where the computers all connect to a central bus—a switch—but otherwise take the form of a star topology.

star topology   Network topology where the computers on the network connect to a central wiring point, usually called a hub.

Start button   Button on the Windows taskbar that enables access to the Start menu.

Start menu   Menu that can be accessed by clicking the Start button on the Windows taskbar. Enables you to see all programs loaded on the system and to start them.

Start screen   Windows 10 version of the Start menu, which functions as a combination of the traditional Start menu and the Windows 8/8.1 Modern UI.

Startup Repair   A one-stop, do-it-all troubleshooting option that performs a number of boot repairs automatically.

static charge eliminator   Device used to remove a static charge.

static IP address   Manually set IP address that will not change.

stealth virus   Virus that uses various methods to hide from antivirus software.

stepper motor   One of two methods used to move actuator arms in a hard drive. (*See also* voice coil motor.)

stereo   Describes recording tracks from two sources (microphones) as opposed to monaural, which uses one source.

stick   Generic name for a single physical SIMM or DIMM.

Storage Spaces   In Windows 8 and later, a software RAID solution that enables users to group multiple drives into a single storage pool.

STP (shielded twisted pair)   Cabling for networks, composed of pairs of wires twisted around each other at specific intervals. Twists serve to reduce interference (also called crosstalk)—the more twists, the less interference. Cable has metallic shielding to protect the wires from external interference.

stranded core   A cable that uses a bundle of tiny wire filaments to transmit signals. Stranded core is not quite as good a conductor as solid core, but it will stand up to substantial handling without breaking.

stream loading   Process a program uses to constantly download updated information.

streaming media   Broadcast of data that is played on your computer and immediately discarded.

stripe set   Two or more drives in a group that are used for a striped volume.

striped volume   RAID 0 volumes. Data is spread across two drives for increased speed.

strong password   Password containing at least eight characters, including letters, numbers, and non-alphanumeric symbols.

structured cabling   TIA/EIA standards that define methods of organizing the cables in a network for ease of repair and replacement.

stylus   Pen-like input device used for pen-based computing.

su   Older Linux command for gaining root access.

subfolder   A folder located inside another folder.

subnet mask   Value used in TCP/IP settings to divide the IP address of a host into its component parts: network ID and host ID.

sub-pixels   Tiny liquid crystal molecules arranged in rows and columns between polarizing filters used in LCDs.

subwoofer   Powerful speaker capable of producing extremely low-frequency sounds.

sudo   Linux command for gaining root access.

Super I/O chip Chip specially designed to control low-speed, legacy devices such as the keyboard, mouse, and serial and parallel ports.

SuperSpeed USB A fast form of USB, with speeds up to 5 Gbps. Also called *USB 3.0.*

SuperSpeed+ USB Updated form of SuperSpeed USB providing speeds up to 10 Gbps. Also called *USB 3.1.*

surge suppressor Inexpensive device that protects your computer from voltage spikes.

SVGA (super video graphics array) Video display mode of 800×600.

swap file *See* page file.

swipe Gesture for mobile devices where you hold your finger on the screen and slide it across the screen, either right to left or top to bottom, depending on the type of application.

swipe lock Mobile device feature that uses a swipe gesture to unlock the mobile device.

switch Device that filters and forwards traffic based on some criteria. A bridge and a router are both examples of switches. In the command-line interface, a switch is a function that modifies the behavior of a command.

SXGA Video display mode of 1280×1024.

SXGA+ Video display mode of 1400×1050.

sync The process of keeping files on mobile devices up to date with the versions on desktop computers or over the Internet.

synchronize *See* sync.

syntax The proper way to write a command-line command so that it functions and does what it's supposed to do.

Sysprep (System Preparation Tool) Windows tool that makes cloning of systems easier by making it possible to undo portions of the installation.

system BIOS   Primary set of BIOS stored on an EPROM or flash ROM chip on the motherboard. Defines the BIOS for all the assumed hardware on the motherboard, such as keyboard controller, floppy drive, basic video, and RAM.

system bus speed   Speed at which the CPU and the rest of the PC operates; set by the system crystal.

system crystal   Crystal that provides the speed signals for the CPU and the rest of the system.

system disk   Any storage device with a bootable operating system.

system fan   Any fan controlled by the motherboard but not directly attached to the CPU.

System File Checker   *See* sfc.

System Monitor   Utility that can evaluate and monitor system resources, such as CPU usage and memory usage.

System Preferences   Mac OS X tool containing many administrative functions.

System Protection   Feature in Windows that enables you to restore any previous version of a file or folder.

system resources   In classic terms, the I/O addresses, IRQs, DMA channels, and memory addresses. Also refers to other computer essentials such as hard drive space, system RAM, and processor speed.

System Restore   Utility in Windows that enables you to return your PC to a recent working configuration when something goes wrong. System Restore enables you to select a restore point and then returns the computer's system settings to the way they were at that restore point—all without affecting your personal files or e-mail.

system ROM   ROM chip that stores the system BIOS.

system setup utility   *See* CMOS setup program.

System Tools   Menu containing tools such as System Information and Disk Defragmenter, accessed by selecting Start | Programs or All Programs | Accessories | System Tools.

system tray   Contains icons representing background processes and the system clock. Located by default at the right edge of the Windows taskbar. Accurately called the *notification area.*

system unit   Main component of the PC, in which the CPU, RAM, optical drive, and hard drive reside. All other devices—the keyboard, mouse, and monitor—connect to the system unit.

T568A   Wiring standard for Ethernet cable.

T568B   Wiring standard for Ethernet cable.

tablet   A mobile device consisting of a large touchscreen, enabling the user to browse the Web, view media, and even play games.

Tablet PC   Small portable computer distinguished by the use of a touchscreen with stylus and handwriting recognition as the primary modes of input.

tailgating   Form of infiltration and social engineering that involves following someone else through a door as if you belong in the building.

Take Ownership   Special permission allowing users to seize control of a file or folder and potentially prevent others from accessing the file/folder.

tap   Touchscreen gesture where you press a spot on the screen to start an app or interact with a running app.

Task Manager   Shows all running programs, including hidden ones, and is accessed by pressing CTRL-SHIFT-ESC. You can use the Task Manager to shut down an unresponsive application that refuses to close normally.

Task Scheduler   Windows utility enabling users to set tasks to run automatically at certain times.

taskbar   Contains the Start button, the notification area, the Quick Launch toolbar, and buttons for running applications. Located by default at the bottom of the desktop.

tasklist   A command-line version of the Task Manager.

TCP/IP (Transmission Control Protocol/Internet Protocol)   Communication protocols developed by the U.S. Department of Defense to enable dissimilar computers to share information over a network.

tech toolkit   Tools a PC tech should never be without, including a Phillips-head screwdriver, a pair of tweezers, a flat-head screwdriver, a hemostat, a Torx wrench, a parts retriever, and a nut driver or two.

telecommunications room   Area where all the cabling from individual computers in a network converges.

telephone scams   Social engineering attack in which the attacker makes a phone call to someone in an organization to gain information.

Telnet   Terminal emulation program for TCP/IP networks that allows one machine to control another as if the user were sitting in front of it. Uses port 23.

tera-   Prefix that usually stands for the binary number 1,099,511,627,776 (2^{40}). When used for mass storage, it's often shorthand for 1 trillion bytes.

terminal   Dumb device connected to a mainframe or computer network that acts as a point for entry or retrieval of information.

Terminal   A command-line interface tool available in Mac OS X and various Linux distros.

terminal emulation   Software that enables a computer to communicate with another computer or network as if the computer were a specific type of hardware terminal.

termination   Using terminating resistors to prevent packet reflection on a network cable.

terminator   Resistor that is plugged into the end of a bus cable to absorb the excess electrical signal, preventing it from bouncing back when it reaches the end of the wire. Terminators are used with coaxial cable and on the ends of SCSI chains. RG-58 coaxial cable requires resistors with a 50-ohm impedance. Also, a humanoid robot from the future designed by Skynet to destroy all human life. He'll be back.

test the theory   Attempt to resolve the issue by either confirming the theory and learning what needs to be done to fix the problem, or by not confirming the theory and forming a new one or escalating. (Step 3 of 6 in the CompTIA troubleshooting theory.)

tethering   The act of using a cellular-network-connected mobile device as a mobile hotspot.

texture   Small picture that is tiled over and over again on walls, floors, and other surfaces to create the 3-D world.

TFT (thin film transistor)   Type of LCD screen. (*See also* active matrix.)

theory of probable cause   One possible reason why something is not working; a guess.

thermal compound   Paste-like material with very high heat-transfer properties. Applied between the CPU and the cooling device, it ensures the best possible dispersal of heat from the CPU. Also called *heat dope* or *thermal paste*.

thermal printer   Printer that uses heated printheads to create high-quality images on special or plain paper.

thick client   CompTIA's name for a standard desktop computer. Runs desktop applications and meets recommended requirements for selected OS.

thin client   A system designed to handle only very basic applications with an absolute minimum amount of hardware required by the operating system. Meets minimum requirements for selected OS.

thread   Smallest logical division of a single program.

throttling   Power reduction/thermal control capability allowing CPUs to slow down during low activity or high heat build-up situations. Intel's version is known as SpeedStep, AMD's as PowerNow!.

throw   Size of the image a projector displays at a certain distance from the screen. Alternately, what you do with a computer that you just can't seem to get working.

Thunderbolt   An open standards connector interface that is primarily used to connect peripherals to devices, including mobile devices, if they have a corresponding port.

TIA/EIA (Telecommunications Industry Association/Electronic Industries Alliance)   Trade organization that provides standards for network cabling and other electronics.

tiers   Levels of Internet providers, ranging from the Tier 1 backbones to Tier 3 regional networks.

Tiles   The building blocks of Windows 8's Modern UI, as potentially "smart" app shortcuts, capable of displaying dynamic and changing information without even opening the app.

timbre   Qualities that differentiate the same note played on different instruments.

Time Machine   Mac OS X full backup tool that enables you to recover some or all files in the event of a crash; it also enables you to restore deleted files and recover previous versions of files.

TKIP (Temporal Key Integrity Protocol)   Deprecated encryption standard that provided a new encryption key for every sent packet.

TN (twisted nematic)   Older technology for LCD monitors. TN monitors produce a decent display for a modest price, but they have limited viewing angles and can't accurately reproduce all the color information sent by the video card.

tone generator   *See* toner.

tone probe   *See* toner.

toner   A fine powder made up of plastic particles bonded to iron particles, used to create the text and images on a laser printer. Also, generic term for two devices used together—a tone generator and a tone locator (probe)—to trace cables by sending an electrical signal along a wire at a particular frequency. The tone locator then emits a sound when it distinguishes that frequency.

toner cartridge   Object used to store the toner in a laser printer. (*See also* laser printer, toner.)

topology   The way computers connect to each other in a network.

touch interface   The primary user interface on modern mobile devices where keys are replaced with tactile interaction.

touchpad   Flat, touch-sensitive pad that serves as a pointing device for most laptops.

touchscreen   Monitor with a type of sensing device across its face that detects the location and duration of contact, usually by a finger or stylus.

tracert   Windows command-line utility used to follow the path a packet takes between two hosts. Called traceroute in Mac OS X and Linux.

traces   Small electrical connections embedded in a circuit board.

track   Area on a hard drive platter where data is stored. A group of tracks with the same diameter is called a cylinder.

trackball   Pointing device distinguished by a ball that is rolled with the fingers.

TrackPoint   IBM's pencil eraser–sized joystick used in place of a mouse on laptops.

transfer corona   Thin wire, usually protected by other thin wires, that applies a positive charge to the paper during the laser printing process, drawing the negatively charged toner particles off of the drum and onto the paper. Newer printers accomplish the same feat using a *transfer roller* that draws the toner onto the paper.

transfer rate   Rate of data transferred between two devices, especially over the expansion bus.

transistor-transistor logic (TTL)   A type of digital circuit found in early digital monitors.

transparency   Effect in the Aero desktop environment (Windows Vista/7) that makes the edges of windows transparent.

triad   Group of three phosphors—red, green, blue—in a CRT.

triple-channel architecture   A chipset feature similar to dual-channel RAM, but requiring three matched sticks instead of two.

Trojan horse   Program that does something other than what the user who runs the program thinks it will do. Used to disguise malicious code.

troubleshooting theory   Steps a technician uses to solve a problem. CompTIA A+ defines six steps: identify the problem; establish a theory of probable cause; test the theory to determine cause; establish a plan of action to resolve the problem and implement a solution; verify full system functionality and if applicable implement preventive measures; and document findings, actions, and outcomes.

Trusted Platform Module (TPM)   A hardware platform for the acceleration of cryptographic functions and the secure storage of associated information.

tunneling   Creating an encrypted link between two programs on two separate computers.

TV tuner   Typically an add-on device that allows users to watch television on a computer.

TWAIN (technology without an interesting name)   Programming interface that enables a graphics application, such as a desktop publishing program, to activate a scanner, frame grabber, or other image-capturing device.

U (Units)   The unique height measurement used with equipment racks; 1 U equals 1.75 inches.

UAC (User Account Control)   Windows feature that enables standard accounts to do common tasks and provides a permissions dialog box when standard and administrator accounts do certain things that could potentially harm the computer (such as attempt to install a program).

UART (universal asynchronous receiver/transmitter)   Device that turns parallel data into serial data and vice versa. The cornerstone of serial ports and modems.

UDF (universal data format)   Replaced the ISO-9660 formats, enabling any operating system and optical drive to read UDF formatted disks.

UEFI (Unified Extensible Firmware Interface)   Consortium of companies that established the UEFI standard that replaced the original EFI standard.

Ultra DMA   Hard drive technology that enables drives to use direct memory addressing. Ultra DMA mode 3 drives—called ATA/33—have data transfer speeds up to 33 MBps. Mode 4 and 5 drives—called ATA/66 and ATA/100, respectively—transfer data at up to 66 MBps for mode 4 and 100 MBps for mode 5. Mode 6 pushed the transfer rate to 133 MBps. Modes 4, 5, and 6 require an 80-wire cable and a compatible controller to achieve these data transfer rates.

Ultrabook Thin, powerful laptop powered by Intel processors and built according to the Intel design specification. Competes directly with the Apple Mac Air.

unattended installation A type of OS installation where special scripts perform all the OS setup duties without human intervention.

unauthorized access Anytime a person accesses resources in an unauthorized way. This access may or may not be malicious.

unbuffered RAM RAM without a buffer chip; in other words, normal, consumer-grade RAM.

UNC (Universal Naming Convention) Describes any shared resource in a network using the convention \\<server name>\<name of shared resource>.

Unicode 16-bit code that covers every character of the most common languages, plus several thousand symbols.

unsigned driver Driver that has not gone through the Windows Certification Program to ensure compatibility. The Windows Certification Program was formerly known as the Windows Hardware Quality Labs and the Microsoft Windows Logo Program.

UPC (Universal Product Code) Bar code used to track inventory.

update Individual fixes for Windows that come out fairly often, on the order of once a week or so.

Upgrade Advisor Examines your hardware and installed software (in the case of an upgrade) and provides a list of devices and software that are known to have issues with it. The Upgrade Advisor is available for download at www. microsoft.com for Windows Vista and Windows 7. Windows 8/8.1 offers the Upgrade Assistant for similar purpose. The Get Windows 10 app generates a compatibility report that functions similarly.

upgrade installation Installation of Windows on top of an earlier installed version, thus inheriting all previous hardware and software settings.

UPS (uninterruptible power supply)   Device that supplies continuous clean power to a computer system the whole time the computer is on. Protects against power outages and sags.

URL (uniform resource locator)   An address that defines the location of a resource on the Internet. URLs are used most often in conjunction with HTML and the World Wide Web.

USB (universal serial bus)   General-purpose serial interconnect for keyboards, printers, joysticks, and many other devices. Enables hot-swapping of devices.

USB host controller   Integrated circuit that is usually built into the chipset and controls every USB device that connects to it.

USB hub   Device that extends a single USB connection to two or more USB ports, almost always directly from one of the USB ports connected to the root hub.

USB root hub   Part of the host controller that makes the physical connection to the USB ports.

USB thumb drive   Flash memory device that uses the standard USB connection.

USB Type-C (connector)   Reversible USB type cable that supports USB SuperSpeed+ USB 3.1 with a top speed of 10 Gbps.

user account   Container that identifies a user to an application, operating system, or network, including name, password, user name, groups to which the user belongs, and other information based on the user and the OS being used. Usually defines the rights and roles a user plays on a system.

User Accounts applet   Applet in Control Panel that enables you to make changes to current accounts (local or global), and gives you access to the Settings charm (or app in Windows 10) when you opt to add a new account.

user interface   Visual representation of the computer on the monitor that makes sense to the people using the computer, through which the user can interact with the computer. This can be a graphical user interface (GUI) like Windows 7 or a command-line interface like the Windows PowerShell or the Recovery Console.

user profiles   Settings that correspond to a specific user account and may follow users regardless of the computers where they log on. These settings enable the user to have customized environment and security settings.

User's Files   Windows default location for content specific to each user account on a computer. It is divided into several folders such as Documents, Pictures, Music, and Video.

Users group   List of local users not allowed, among other things, to edit the Registry or access critical system files. They can create groups, but can only manage the groups they create.

USMT (User State Migration Tool)   Advanced application for file and settings transfer of multiple users.

Utilities   Mac OS X folder that contains tools for performing services on a Mac beyond what's included in System Preferences, including Activity Monitor and Terminal.

UTP (unshielded twisted pair)   Popular type of cabling for telephone and networks, composed of pairs of wires twisted around each other at specific intervals. The twists serve to reduce interference (also called crosstalk). The more twists, the less interference. Unlike its cousin, STP, UTP cable has no metallic shielding to protect the wires from external interference. 1000BaseT uses UTP, as do many other networking technologies. UTP is available in a variety of grades, called categories, as follows:

- **CAT 1 UTP**   Regular analog phone lines—not used for data communications.
- **CAT 2 UTP**   Supports speeds up to 4 Mbps.
- **CAT 3 UTP**   Supports speeds up to 16 Mbps.
- **CAT 4 UTP**   Supports speeds up to 20 Mbps.
- **CAT 5 UTP**   Supports speeds up to 100 Mbps.
- **CAT 5e UTP**   Supports speeds up to 1000 Mbps.
- **CAT 6 UTP**   Supports speeds up to 10 Gbps.
- **CAT 6a UTP**   Supports speeds up to 10 Gbps.
- **CAT 7 UTP**   Supports 10-Gbps networks at 100-meter segments; shielding for individual wire pairs reduces crosstalk and noise problems. CAT 7 is not a TIA/EIA standard.

V standards   Standards established by CCITT for modem manufacturers to follow (voluntarily) to ensure compatible speeds, compression, and error correction.

vendor specific   Stores that only sell products from one manufacturer, like the Apple store.

verify full system functionality   Making sure that a problem has been resolved and will not return. (Step 5 of 6 in the CompTIA troubleshooting theory.)

vertices   Used in the second generation of 3-D rendering; have a defined X, Y, and Z position in a 3-D world.

VESA (Video Electronics Standards Association)   Consortium of computer manufacturers that standardizes improvements to common IBM PC components. VESA is responsible for the Super VGA video standard and the VLB bus architecture.

VGA (video graphics array)   Standard for the video graphics adapter that was built into IBM's PS/2 computer. It supports 16 colors in a 640 × 480 pixel video display.

vi   Linux and Mac OS X command-line tool for editing text files.

video capture   Computer jargon for the recording of video information, such as TV shows or movies.

video card   Expansion card that works with the CPU to produce the images displayed on your computer's display.

video display   *See* monitor.

virtual assistant   Voice-activated technology that responds to user requests for information. Virtual assistants can be used to search the Internet, make reminders, do calculations, and launch apps.

virtual machine (VM)   A complete environment for a guest operating system to function as though that operating system were installed on its own computer.

virtual machine manager (VMM)   *See* hypervisor.

virtual memory   *See* page file.

virus   Program that can make a copy of itself without your necessarily being aware of it. Some viruses can destroy or damage files. The best protection is to back up files regularly.

virus definition or data file   Files that enable the virus protection software to recognize the viruses on your system and clean them. These files should be updated often. They are also called signature files, depending on the virus protection software in use.

virus shield   Passive monitoring of a computer's activity, checking for viruses only when certain events occur.

VIS (viewable image size)   Measurement of the viewable image that is displayed by a CRT rather than a measurement of the CRT itself.

VMM (virtual machine manager)   *See* hypervisor.

voice coil motor   One of two methods used to move actuator arms in a hard drive. (*See also* stepper motor.)

VoIP (Voice over Internet Protocol)   Collection of protocols that makes voice calls over a data network possible.

volatile   Memory that must have constant electricity to retain data. Alternatively, any programmer six hours before deadline after a nonstop, 48-hour coding session, running on nothing but caffeine and sugar.

volts (V)   Measurement of the pressure of the electrons passing through a wire, or voltage.

volume   Physical unit of a storage medium, such as tape reel or disk pack, that is capable of having data recorded on it and subsequently read. Also, a contiguous collection of cylinders or blocks on a disk that are treated as a separate unit.

volume boot sector   First sector of the first cylinder of each partition; stores information important to its partition, such as the location of the operating system boot files.

voucher   Means of getting a discount on the CompTIA A+ exams.

VPN (Virtual Private Network)   Encrypted connection over the Internet between a computer or remote network and a private network.

VRM (voltage regulator module)   Small card supplied with some CPUs to ensure that the CPU gets correct voltage. This type of card, which must be used with a motherboard specially designed to accept it, is not commonly seen today.

VRR (vertical refresh rate)   The amount of time it takes for a CRT to draw a complete screen. This value is measured in hertz, or cycles per second. Most modern CRTs have a VRR of 60 Hz or better.

wait state   Occurs when the CPU has to wait for RAM to provide code. Also known as *pipeline stall*.

WAP (wireless access point)   Device that centrally connects wireless network nodes.

wattage (watts or W)   Measurement of the amps and volts needed for a particular device to function.

wave table synthesis   Technique that supplanted FM synthesis, wherein recordings of actual instruments or other sounds are embedded in the sound card as WAV files. When a particular note from a particular instrument or voice is requested, the sound processor grabs the appropriate prerecorded WAV file from its memory and adjusts it to match the specific sound and timing requested.

Web browser   Program designed to retrieve, interpret, and display web pages.

Web server   A computer that stores and shares the files that make up websites.

webcam   PC camera most commonly used for Internet video.

Welcome screen   Logon screen for Windows. Enables users to select their particular user account by clicking on their user picture.

WEP (Wired Equivalent Privacy)   Wireless security protocol that uses a standard 40-bit encryption to scramble data packets. Does not provide complete end-to-end encryption and is vulnerable to attack.

Wi-Fi   Common name for the IEEE 802.11 wireless Ethernet standard.

Wi-Fi calling   Mobile device feature that enables users to make voice calls over a Wi-Fi network, rather than a cellular network.

Wi-Fi Protected Setup (WPS)   A standard included on many WAPs and clients to make secure connections easier to configure.

wide area network (WAN)   A widespread group of computers connected using long-distance technologies.

wildcard   Character used during a search to represent search criteria. For instance, searching for *.**docx** will return a list of all files with a .docx extension, regardless of the filename. The * is the wildcard in that search.

Windows 7   Version of Windows; comes in many different editions for home and office use, but does not have a Server edition.

Windows 7 Compatibility Center   Microsoft web page that lists the hardware and software that work with Windows 7.

Windows 8   Version of Windows noted for the Metro interface. Used for desktop and portable PCs and for mobile devices.

Windows Easy Transfer   Windows method of transferring files and settings to a new PC.

Windows Explorer   Windows utility that enables you to manipulate files and folders stored on the drives in your computer. Rebranded as File Explorer in Windows 8, 8.1, and 10.

Windows Hardware Certification Program   Microsoft's rigorous testing program for hardware manufacturers, which hardware devices must pass before their drivers can be digitally signed.

Windows logo key   Key on a keyboard bearing the Windows logo that traditionally brings up the Start menu, but is also used in some keyboard shortcuts.

Windows Memory Diagnostic   Tool found in Windows 7 and later that can automatically scan a computer's RAM when encountering a problem.

Windows PowerShell Command-line tool included with Windows. Offers a number of powerful scripting tools for automating changes both on local machines and over networks.

Windows Preinstallation Environment (WinPE) The installation program for Windows.

Windows Recovery Environment (WinRE) A special set of tools in the Windows setup that enables you to access troubleshooting and repair features.

Windows Sidebar User interface feature in Windows Vista that enables users to place various gadgets, such as clocks, calendars, and other utilities, on the right side of their desktop.

Windows Update Microsoft application used to keep Windows operating systems up to date with the latest patches or enhancements. (*See* Automatic Updates.)

Windows Vista Version of Windows; comes in many different editions for home and office use, but does not have a Server edition.

Windows XP Version of Windows that replaced both the entire Windows 9*x* line and Windows 2000; does not have a Server version. No longer supported by Microsoft.

Windows XP Mode A Windows XP virtual machine that ships with Professional, Enterprise, and Ultimate editions of Windows 7 to enable users to run programs that don't work on Windows 7.

Wired (wired.com) Hip Internet news site.

work area In a basic structured cabling network, often simply an office or cubicle that potentially contains a PC attached to the network.

workgroup A simple, decentralized network that Windows PCs are configured to use by default.

worm Very special form of virus. Unlike other viruses, a worm does not infect other files on the computer. Instead, it replicates by making copies of itself on other systems on a network by taking advantage of security weaknesses in networking protocols.

WPA (Wi-Fi Protected Access) Wireless security protocol that uses encryption key integrity-checking/TKIP and EAP and is designed to improve on WEP's weaknesses. Supplanted by WPA 2.

WPA 2 (Wi-Fi Protected Access 2) Wireless security protocol, also known as IEEE 802.11i. Uses the Advanced Encryption Standard (AES) and replaces WPA.

WQUXGA Video display mode of 2560 × 1600.

wrapper *See* container file.

WSXGA Video display mode of 1440 × 900.

WSXGA+ Video display mode of 1680 × 1050.

WUXGA Video display mode of 1920 × 1200.

WVGA Video display mode of 800 × 480.

WWW (World Wide Web) System of Internet servers that supports documents formatted in HTML and related protocols. Can be accessed by applications that use HTTP and HTTPS, such as web browsers.

www.comptia.org CompTIA's website.

WXGA Video display mode of 1280 × 800.

x64 Describes 64-bit operating systems and software.

x86 Describes 32-bit operating systems and software.

xcopy Command in the command-line interface used to copy multiple directories at once, which the copy command could not do.

xD (Extreme Digital) picture card Very small flash media card format.

Xeon Line of Intel CPUs designed for servers.

XGA (extended graphics array) Video display mode of 1024 × 768.

XPS (XML Paper Specification) print path   Printing subsystem in Windows. Has enhanced color management and good print layout fidelity.

XT bus   *See* PC bus.

ZIF (zero insertion force) socket   Socket for CPUs that enables insertion of a chip without the need to apply pressure. Intel promoted this socket with its overdrive upgrades. The chip drops effortlessly into the socket's holes, and a small lever locks it in.

Index

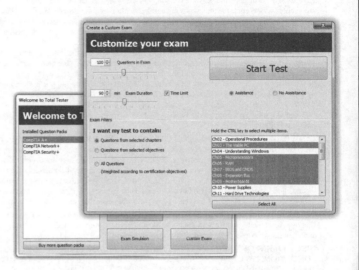